W9-DFM-104

CRITICAL SURVEY
OF
LONG FICTION

CRITICAL SURVEY
OF
LONG FICTION

English Language Series

Authors

A-Cald

1

Edited by
FRANK N. MAGILL

Academic Director
WALTON BEACHAM

SALEM PRESS
Englewood Cliffs, N.J.

LIBRARY OF CONGRESS CATALOG CARD NUMBER: 83-61341
Complete Set: ISBN 0-89356-359-5
Volume 1:   ISBN 0-89356-360-9

PRINTED IN THE UNITED STATES OF AMERICA

PREFACE

THE FICTIONAL NARRATIVE is today's most popular form of print entertainment. The medium springs from a noble tradition comprising oral and written poetic and dramatic expression—and even cues from forms of Oriental theater which combine dance and storytelling. Almost always based on conflicts or suspenseful situations designed to hold the reader's attention while the author expresses his own emotional responses to his creative impulse, the fictional narrative has often become a mirror of the cultural mores of the society that spawned it. *Critical Survey of Long Fiction*: English Language Series provides a means to examine or review a broad spectrum of the best examples of the form in the area defined in the title of the work. A foreign-language survey will follow, under the same title, as a continuation of the extant eight volumes.

Critical Survey of Long Fiction is the third entry in the Salem Press genre studies comprising extensive reviews of the works and influence of representative writers in the genre in question. The first such study covered short fiction (1981); the second, poetry (1982); the third is herewith; and the fourth, scheduled for release in 1984, will deal with drama. The current series provides individual critical assessments of 272 authors whose major works are in the field of the novel and the novella. Also included are twenty essays—some quite extensive—dealing with the history and development of the two forms, as well as with more than a dozen various classifications, such as the novel of manners, the Gothic novel, the realistic novel, and the like.

The format designed to elaborate each article is standardized and consists of seven sections in addition to the fundamental vital statistics of the target author. The titles and dates of release of the writer's long fiction are given first, followed by a brief note of the author's activity in other literary forms. The "Achievements" section attempts to summarize the subject's literary purposes and artistic influences, after which a literary biography explores the life experiences which may have influenced the author's creative process. The longest and most broadly critical commentary is found in the "Analysis" section, in which key works are examined and interpreted with the serious reader and student in mind. Then follows a compilation of the author's major publications other than long fiction, after which a limited bibliography will be found that concentrates on sources normally available in most American libraries. The front matter of Volume 8 shows the complete list of the twenty essays included, and the front matter of each of the other seven volumes gives the list of 272 authors whose articles appear therein. These authors were selected after exhaustive research and extensive consultations with a board of consultants.

One essay that deserves particular attention is that dealing with the novella, a 127-page discourse by Charles E. May, which covers the subject in considerable depth from Giovanni Boccaccio to modern times. Since the novella

v

comprises a substantial part of the genre referred to as "long fiction," May's essay deserves close attention by those concerned with the beginnings, the development, and the near-perfection of the form in the hands of Henry James, Joseph Conrad, Thomas Mann, and others.

The May essay is divided into chronological segments that follow the development of the novella, citing changes in form and content. After a short Introduction, the main article begins with "Boccaccio and the Renaissance," in which the author shows how *The Decameron* ushered in a new style that heralded the novella. In "Cervantes and the Renaissance Novella," May notes the changes that Cervantes introduced to refine Boccaccio's original novalla: Carvantes' stories were his own invention, not collected traditional tales, and their plots were more involved than the simple stories of his predecessor. This advance is not surprising considering the two and a half centuries that intervened between the creative impulses of the two writers.

Great strides continued in the shaping of the novella. The author explains in "German Novella Theory" that "with the comments of Schlegel and Goethe, the novella began to detach itself from the Boccaccio-Cervantes notion of the form and to develop a theory of its own." Thus the way was prepared for the development of the modern form exploited by Ernest Hemingway, William Faulkner, and countless others. In "Modern Novella: Criticism" and "Modern Novella: Generic Convention," the May article deals with this development in depth. May closes his articles with several pages of valuable citations covering both novella anthologies and novella criticism.

All of the essays herein have much to offer the student and the general reader interested in the development of long fiction from earliest times, but the stress here on the novella stems from the fact that the form is, unfortunately, much neglected today. Indeed, it is reported that many contemporary authors would like to write novellas but can find no favor with publishers, who cannot market the short works profitably; thus, the writer must turn to the novel or a collection of short stories to gain publication.

The first seven volumes of *Critical Survey of Long Fiction* are devoted to an overview of the long-fiction canon of each of the 272 authors represented in the set, with extended analyses of some major novels. In addition to their entertainment qualities, novels have long been a social force, especially with their cinema spin-offs, and many contributing scholars have stressed in their articles this aspect of the genre's purpose. Excerpts selected from *The Grapes of Wrath*, *For Whom the Bell Tolls*, the works of Britian's Angry Young Men, or the protest literature of the 1950's and 1960's in the United States, for example, have provided many ideas for public dialogues on various social issues. The successful novel, with its "slice of life" and realistic character development, creates for the reader a sense of engagement that stimulates an urge to join with the protagonist in changing the status quo. As a matter of fact, Charles Dickens with his novels probably exerted more social influence in his day than any other single agency.

The individual articles in this work speak for themselves, each contributing to the assigned purpose of providing a broad view of the body of literature known as English-language long fiction. Each author subject to study had his own vision of universal truth, and through his fiction translated his world to his readers. Our contributing staff members have attempted to interpret these visions faithfully.

Those who examine the articles in this set will find explications covering a great variety of literary talents. Jean-Paul Sartre's *Nausea* (frustration with an absurd and meaningless world) comes in for study as do Molly Bloom's interior-monologue technique and Virginia Woolf's stream-of-consciousness style. Mark Twain's frontier humor, Henry James's elegant style, and Ernest Hemingway's sparse-language methodology are also recognized. Lawrence Durrell's multiple point-of-view innovation is noted as are the remarkable mind and the instinctive talent of young Emily Brontë, a little-recognized phenomenon. The rapacity of Snopesism and the sense of world sadness in Benjy's view of Yoknapatawpha County existence are amply covered in Terry Heller's extensive article beginning on page 914.

Evocation of additional articles is perhaps better left to the individual, who will surely be able to find many personal favorites among the 272 outstanding authors represented in the Index at the end of Volume 8. Following the essays in the same volume appears "Terms and Techniques," a section defining eighty-six literary terms and expressions, a collection some may find useful as a refresher of specific meanings.

To all writers and staff members who had a part in the development of *Critical Survey of Long Fiction* I wish to offer my thanks. I am sure each of us shares the hope that this work will enhance your appreciation and enjoyment of the body of great literature examined herein.

FRANK N. MAGILL

CONTRIBUTORS

Writing Staff for Essays

John J. Conlon

Peter W. Graham

Clarence O. Johnson

Anna B. Katona

Fred B. McEwen

Michelle A. Massé

Charles E. May

Laurence W. Mazzeno

Sally Mitchell

William F. Nelson

Martha Nochimson

Louis H. Pratt

David Sadkin

Anne Waterman Sienkewicz

Robert Lance Snyder

Brian Stableford

Christopher J. Thaiss

Gary Topping

Writing Staff for Author Articles

Timothy Dow Adams

S. Krishnamoorthy Aithal

Andrew J. Angyal

Stanley Archer

Edwin T. Arnold III

Marilyn Arnold

Dean R. Baldwin

Jane L. Ball

Thomas Banks

Carol M. Barnum

Joseph F. Battaglia

Robert Becker

Kirk H. Beetz

Kate Begnal

Todd K. Bender

Frank Bergmann

Harold Branam

Anne Kelsch Breznau

Domenic Bruni

Mitzi M. Brunsdale

Hallman B. Bryant

C. F. Burgess

Karen Carmean

Leonard Casper

Edgar L. Chapman

Allan Chavkin

John R. Clark

Samuel Coale

John L. Cobbs

Steven E. Colburn

Michael E. Connaughton

Deborah Core

David Cowart

Carol I. Croxton

Ronald T. Curran

Diane D'Amico

Reed Way Dasenbrock

J. Madison Davis

Frank Day

Paul J. deGategno

Joan DelFattore

Lloyd N. Dendinger

A. A. DeVitis

Richard H. Dillman

Henry J. Donaghy

David C. Dougherty

Virginia A. Duck

David B. Eakin

Grace Eckley

Wilton Eckley

Bruce L. Edwards, Jr.

Richard A. Eichwald

Robert P. Ellis

Ann Willardson Engar

Howard Faulkner

John H. Ferres

Richard A. Fine

Kenneth Friedenreich

Ellen G. Friedman

Miriam Fuchs

Kristine Ottesen Garrigan

James R. Giles

Dennis Goldsberry

Peter W. Graham

John R. Griffin

James Grove

Stephen I. Gurney

Angela Hague

David Mike Hamilton

Robert D. Hamner

John P. Harrington

Robert Hauptman

William J. Heim

Terry Heller

Greig E. Henderson

Erwin Hester

Linda Howe

Mary Anne Hutchinson

Archibald E. Irwin

Joe Jackson

Abdul R. JanMohamed

Clarence O. Johnson

Judith L. Johnston

Feroza Jussawalla

Deborah Kaplan

Anna B. Katona

Richard Keenan

Steven G. Kellman

Catherine Kenney

Sue L. Kimball

James Reynolds Kinzey

John V. Knapp

Sarah B. Kovel

Lawrence F. Laban

Brooks Landon

Donald F. Larsson

Paul LaValley

Norman Lavers

Henry J. Lindborg

Robert Emmet Long

Michael Lowenstein

Philip A. Luther

James J. Lynch

Tim Lyons

James C. MacDonald

Fred B. McEwen

Dennis Q. McInerny

Bryant Mangum

Patricia Marks

Bruce K. Martin

Paul Marx

Charles E. May

Laurence W. Mazzeno

Joseph R. Millichap

Sally Mitchell

Robert A. Morace

Carole Moses

Lynn C. Munro

Earl Paulus Murphy

Stella A. Nesanovich

Martha Nochimson
Cóilín Owens
Donald Palumbo
Makarand Paranjape
David B. Parsell
William Peden
Robert C. Peterson
Alice Hall Petry
Janet Polansky
Honora Rankine-Galloway
K. Bhaskara Rao
Edward C. Reilly
Samuel J. Rogal
Carl E. Rollyson, Jr.
Joseph Rosenblum
Arthur M. Saltzman
Dale Salwak
John K. Saunders
Paul Schlueter
Lynne P. Shackelford
Walter Shear
Frank W. Shelton
Allen Shepherd
John C. Shields
Jack Shreve

Charles L. P. Silet
Linda Simon
Katherine Snipes
Sherry G. Southard
Sharon Spencer
Brian Stableford
William B. Stone
W. J. Stuckey
Mary Ellen Stumpf
Stan Sulkes
Eileen Tarcay
Christopher J. Thaiss
Linda F. Tunick
Jane Gentry Vance
Nancy Walker
Ronald G. Walker
John Michael Walsh
Ann Warren
Bernice Larson Webb
Judith Weise
Craig Werner
Roger E. Wiehe
Chester L. Wolford
Philip Woodard
Michele Wender Zak

LIST OF AUTHORS IN VOLUME 1

CRITICAL SURVEY
OF
LONG FICTION

CHINUA ACHEBE

Born: Ogidi, Nigeria; November 16, 1930

Principal long fiction
Things Fall Apart, 1958; *No Longer at Ease*, 1960; *Arrow of God*, 1964; *A Man of the People*, 1966.

Other literary forms
The twelve short stories of Chinua Achebe, written over a period of twenty years, were first published together in England by Heinemann under the title *Girls at War* (1972), though most of them had already appeared in various periodicals and in a Nigerian publication, *The Sacrificial Egg and Other Short Stories* (1962). Achebe's poems, most of them written during the Biafran crisis (1967-1970), came out soon after the war as *Beware, Soul Brother and Other Poems* (1971), and a year later in an enlarged edition. Doubleday & Company then published this Heinemann collection in America as *Christmas in Biafra and Other Poems* (1973). Achebe has gathered together various autobiographical, political, literary, and cultural essays under the intriguingly optimistic title, *Morning Yet on Creation Day* (1975), published by both Doubleday & Company and Heinemann. Finally, Achebe has also written two children's stories, *Chike and the River* (1966) and, jointly with John Iroaganachi, *How the Leopard Got His Claws* (1972).

Achievements
From the beginning of his literary career, with the publication of *Things Fall Apart*, Achebe recognized and accepted his role as that of spokesman for black Africa. The primary function of that role was to reinterpret the African past from an African's point of view. This he successfully does in *Things Fall Apart* and *Arrow of God*, which correct the imperialist myth of African primitivism and savagery by re-creating the Igbo culture of Eastern Nigeria, its daily routines, its rituals, its customs, and especially its people dealing with one another in a highly civilized fashion within a complex society. The reinterpretation necessitated, as well, a look at the invading culture: Achebe tilted the balance in the Africans' favor by depicting individuals in the British administration as prejudiced, imperceptive, unnecessarily bureaucratic, and emotionally impotent. Since his main subject was the African crisis, he did not go to great pains to explore the private lives of the British or to mollify the British public. He needed to show that white civilization and white people were not intrinsically superior, and to restore to the African a respect for his own culture and his own person. Achebe did not conceive his role as that of a mere propagandist, however, as any reader of the novels

would acknowledge. His interpretation paid due respect to Western civilization and seriously criticized aspects of his own. In spite of certain fictional shortcuts—which some critics regard as crucial flaws—Achebe's attempt was to arrive at an objective appraisal of the conflict between Africa and the West. In fact, the central focus of his two other novels—*No Longer at Ease* and *A Man of the People*—set in more contemporary times, is on the failure of Africans to meet challenges in the modern world. These novels are satirical attacks on contemporary Nigerian society.

Achebe's importance as a spokesman for and to his own people has drawn criticism from some Western readers who are more interested in the quality of a novel than in its social function. Achebe has had several angry words to say to such aesthetically minded critics. His defense is that literature is a human and humane endeavor, not primarily a formal one. Still, one can easily defend his novels on aesthetic grounds, even arguing, as Charles Larson has done, that Achebe is actually an innovative writer who has transformed the novel to suit the African setting. Certainly, the most remarkable thing that Achebe has done, especially in *Things Fall Apart* and *Arrow of God*, is to transform the English language itself into an African idiom. Bernth Lindfors and others have demonstrated the skill with which Achebe uses imagery, allusions, figures of speech, proverbs, sentence patterns, standard English, and various forms of substandard English to capture a particular historical moment as well as the African mentality, but just as important to unify the novels around major motifs and themes. Achebe has not written mere social documents or social manifestos, but creditable works of literature that can stand the test of critical analysis. Achebe's contribution to the African world goes far beyond these four novels, but they are his major literary achievement.

Biography

Chinua Achebe was born on November 16, 1930, in Ogidi, Eastern Nigeria. He gives some details about his family and his early life in an essay, "Named for Victoria, Queen of England" (1973, in *Morning Yet on Creation Day*). His parents, Isaiah and Janet Achebe, were both Christian, his father an evangelist and church teacher. His maternal grandfather, like Okonkwo in *Things Fall Apart*, was a wealthy and distinguished community leader. He was not Christian but exercised tolerance when Achebe was converted. Achebe was baptized Albert Chinualumogu after Queen Victoria's consort, but dropped the Albert while at his university, evidently as a reaction against the British and his Christian heritage. He explains, however, that he was never really torn between the two cultures. There was no agony such as one finds in African writers such as Cheikh Hamidou Kane. Achebe enjoyed the ritual of both religions. He did come to wonder if the apostates were not the Christians rather than the pagans, but he cites advantages brought in by Christianity: education, certain humane reforms, paid jobs. There seems to have been a pragmatic and tolerant strain in Achebe from the beginning.

For his secondary education, Achebe attended Government College, Umu-ahia (1944-1947), and he received his B.A. degree from University College, Ibadan, in 1953. During the next twelve years he worked for the Nigerian Broadcasting Corporation, first as producer in Lagos (1954-1958), then as controller in Enugu (1959-1961), and finally as Director of External Broadcasting in Lagos (1961-1966). In 1961, he married Christiana Chinwe Okoli. They have had two sons and two daughters. Also during these years Achebe wrote his four novels, beginning with his most famous, *Things Fall Apart* in 1958, and ending with *A Man of the People* in 1966. Achebe explains his novelistic career as the result of a revolution in his thinking during the nationalist movement after World War II. He decided that foreigners really could not tell the Nigerian story adequately. Joyce Cary's *Mister Johnson* (1939) was a prime example of this failure. Achebe regarded *Things Fall Apart* as an atonement for his apostasy, a ritual return to his homeland. As a consequence of his eight-year achievement as a novelist, Achebe was named chairman of the Society of Nigerian Authors and became a Member of Council at the University of Lagos. He also received the New Statesman Award for his third novel, *Arrow of God*. Among other honors were a Rockefeller Travel Fellowship to East and Central Africa (1960) and a UNESCO Travel Fellowship to the United States and Brazil (1963). It is clear that by 1966 Achebe was a distinguished member of the international literary community.

In 1967, however, his career was interrupted by the outbreak of the war in Biafra, Achebe's Igbo homeland in Eastern Nigeria. It came to be essentially a civil war. Achebe joined the Biafran Ministry of Information and played a diplomatic role in raising money for the Biafran cause. Bound as he was by emotional ties and personal commitment to his country's fate, Achebe had no time to write novels. All he could manage were short poems, which were published a year after the war was over (1971).

Achebe's career since the war has been taken up primarily by the academic world. In 1972, he was a Senior Research Fellow at the Institute of African Studies at the University of Nigeria in Nsukka. From 1972 to 1975, he was Professor at the University of Massachusetts at Amherst, and in 1975-1976 at the University of Connecticut. He then became Professor at the University of Nigeria, Nsukka. His major publications during that time were a collection of short stories, *Girls at War*, written over a period of years going back to his university days, and a collection of essays, *Morning Yet on Creation Day*, which give his views on a number of issues from the Biafran War to the problems of African literature in the Western world. It would seem that during the last ten years Achebe's work has been more in the critical rather than the creative mode.

His standing in the intellectual and literary world is perhaps the highest of any African writer. Numerous institutions, such as Dartmouth College and the Universities of Massachusetts, Sterling, and Southampton, have granted him honorary doctorates. He holds the impressive and influential position of Founding Editor of the African Writers Series, which, more than any other publisher, is responsible for the worldwide recognition of literary talent from the African continent.

Analysis

Chinua Achebe is probably the best-known and, at the same time, the most representative African novelist. He may very well have written the first African novel of real literary merit—such at least is the opinion of Charles Larson—and he deals with what one can call the classic issue that preoccupies his fellow novelists, the clash between the native cultures of black Africa and a white, European civilization. He avoids the emotionally charged subject of slavery and concentrates his attention on the political and cultural confrontation. His four novels offer, in a sense, a paradigm of it. He begins in *Things Fall Apart* with the first incursion of the British into the Igbo region of what is now Eastern Nigeria, and his subsequent novels trace (with some gaps) the spread of British influence into the 1950's, and beyond that into the post-independence period of the 1960's. The one period he slights, as he himself admits, is the generation between the old tribal life and the new Westernized Africa. He had difficulty imagining the psychological conflict of the man caught between two cultures. There is no example in Achebe of Cheikh Hamidou Kane's "ambiguous adventure." He does, however, share with Kane and with most other African novelists the idea that his function as a writer is a social one.

Achebe insists repeatedly on this social function in response to Western critics who tend to give priority to aesthetic values. He seems to suggest, in fact, that the communal responsibility and the communal tie are more fundamental than artistic merit for any writer, but certainly for the African writer and for himself personally at the present stage in African affairs. He describes himself specifically as a teacher. His purpose is to dispel the colonial myth of the primitive African and to establish a true image of the people and their culture. This message is intended, to some extent, for a Western audience, but especially for the Africans themselves, since they have come to believe the myth and have internalized the feeling of inferiority: Achebe's aim is to help them regain their self-respect, recognize the beauty of their own cultural past, and deal capably with the dilemmas of contemporary society. It is important, however, that Achebe is not fulfilling this role as an outsider. He returns to the traditional Igbo concept of the master craftsman and to the *Mbare* ceremony to explain the functional role of art in traditional society. He insists that creativity itself derives from a spiritual bond, the inspiration of a shared past and a shared destiny with a particular people: the alienated writer such as Ayi Kwei Armah cannot be in tune with himself and is therefore likely to be imitative rather than truly creative. It would appear, then, that Achebe values originality and freshness in the management of literary form, but considers them dependent on the sensitivity of the writer to his native setting.

Whereas Achebe's motivation in writing may be the restoration of pride in the African world, his theme, or rather the specific advice that he offers, albeit indirectly, is much more pragmatic. He does not advocate a return to the past or a rejection of Western culture. Like other African writers he decries the destructive consequences of colonial rule: alienation, frustration, and a loss of cohesiveness and a clear code of behavior. He recognizes as well, however, certain undesirable customs and superstitions in the old tribal ways that the foreign challenge exposed. His practical advice is to learn to cope with a changing world. He teaches the necessity of compromise: a loyalty to traditional wisdom and values, if not to tribal politics and outmoded customs, along with a suspicion of Western materialism but an openness to Western thought. He notes that in some cases the two cultures are not so far apart: Igbo republicanism goes even beyond the British-American concept of democracy, a view that the Ghanaian novelist, Armah, has developed as well. Unlike the Negritude writers of francophone Africa, Achebe, in his attempt to reinterpret the African past, does not paint an idyllic picture. He regrets the loss of mystery surrounding that past, but chooses knowledge, because he considers judgment, clarity of vision, and tolerance—virtues that he locates in his traditional society—to be the way out of the present confusion and corruption.

This key idea of tolerance pervades Achebe's work. One of his favorite stories (Yoruba, not Igbo) illustrates the danger in dogmatism. The god Echu, who represents fate or confusion, mischievously decides to provoke a quarrel between two farmers who live on either side of a road. He paints himself black on one side and white on the other, then walks up the road between the two farmers. The ensuing argument is whether the stranger is black or white. When he walks back down the road, each farmer tries to outdo the other in apologizing for his mistake. Achebe's most pervasive vehicle for this idea of tolerance, however, is in the concept of the *chi*, which is central to Igbo cosmology. Achebe interprets it as the ultimate expression of individualism, the basic worth and independence of every man. Politically it means the rejection of any authoritarian rule. Morally it means the responsibility of every man for his own fate. The *chi* is his other self, his spiritual identity responsible for his birth and his future. Thus, while one's *chi* defines his uniqueness, it also defines his limitations. As Achebe frequently notes in his novels, no one can defeat his own *chi*, and the acceptance of one's limitations is the beginning of tolerance.

It is the social purpose, this "message" of tolerance in Achebe's novels, that dictates the form. His plots tend to be analytic, static, or "situational," as Larson argues, rather than dynamic. Instead of narrative movement, there is juxtaposition of past and present, of the traditional and the modern. Achebe achieves balance through comparison and contrast. He uses exposition more than drama. His main characters tend to be representational. Their conflicts are the crucial ones of the society. The protagonists of the two traditional novels, *Things Fall Apart* and *Arrow of God*, are strong men who lack wisdom, practical sense, an ability to accept change, and a tolerance for opposing views. The protagonists of the more contemporary novels, *No Longer at Ease* and *A Man of the People*, are weak and vacillating. They accept change but are blinded by vanity and have no satisfactory code of conduct to resist the unreasonable pressures of traditional ties or the corruption and attractions of the new age. An even more predominant feature of the four novels is their style. Achebe makes the necessary compromise and writes in English, a foreign tongue, but manipulates it to capture the flavor of the native Igbo expression. He does this through idiom and figurative language, and through proverbs that reflect traditional Igbo wisdom, comment ironically on the inadequacies of the characters, and state the central theme.

Thus Achebe manages, through the authorial voice, to establish a steady control over every novel. To some extent one senses the voice in the proverbs. They represent the assessment of the elders in the tribe, yet the wisdom of the proverb is itself sometimes called into question, and the reader is invited to make the judgment. In general, it is Achebe's juxtaposing of character, incident, proverb, and tone that creates the total assessment. Against this background voice one measures the pride, vanity, or prejudice of the individuals who, caught in the stressful times of colonial or postcolonial Nigeria, fail to respond adequately. The voice does not judge or condemn; it describes. It reminds the Nigerian of the danger of self-deception. It also recognizes the danger of failing to communicate with others. Achebe keeps ever in mind the tale (found in numerous versions all over Africa) of mankind whose message to Chukwa (the Supreme Deity) requesting immortality is distorted by the messenger and thus fails in its purpose. The voice he adopts to avoid the distortion is one of self-knowledge, practical sense, pragmatism, and detachment, but also of faith, conviction, and humor. The voice is, in a sense, the message itself, moderating the confrontation between Africa and the West.

Significantly, Achebe takes the title of his first novel, *Things Fall Apart*, from W. B. Yeats's apocalyptic poem "The Second Coming," which prophesies the end of the present era and the entrance on the world's stage of another that is radically different. *Things Fall Apart* treats the early moments of that transition in an Igbo village. For those tribesmen the intrusion of the British is as revolutionary as the coming of a second Messiah, Yeats's terrible "rough beast." To some extent, Achebe creates a mythic village whose history stretches back to a legendary past. Chapters are devoted to the daily routines of the people, their family life, their customs, games, and rituals, their ancient wisdom, their social order, and legal practices. Achebe remains a realist, however, as he identifies also certain flaws in the customs and in the people. Superstition leads them to unnecessary cruelties. The protagonist, Okonkwo, reflects a basic conflict within the society. He is, on the one hand, a respected member of the society who has risen through hard work to a position of wealth and authority. He conscientiously accepts the responsibilities that the elders lay on him. At the same time, he is such an individualist that his behavior runs counter to the spirit of tribal wisdom. His shame over his father's weak character provokes him to be excessive in proving his own manhood. There is a defensiveness and uncertainty behind his outward assertiveness. It is true that the tribe has its mechanisms to reprimand and punish the Okonkwos for their errant behavior. Nevertheless, even before the British influence begins to disturb the region, the cohesiveness of the tribe is already in question.

One particular chink in Okonkwo's armor, which identifies a weakness also in the tribe as it faces the foreign threat, is his inflexibility, his inability to adapt or to accept human limitations. Since he, in his youth, overcame adversity (familial disadvantages, natural forces such as drought and excessive rains, challenges of strength as a wrestler) he comes to believe that he has the individual strength to resist all challenges to his personal ambition. He cannot accept the presence of forces beyond his control, including the forces of his own personal destiny. It is this and the other aspects of Okonkwo's character that Achebe develops in the first section of the novel against the background of the tribe to which he belongs. Part I ends with the symbolic act of Okonkwo's accidentally killing a young man during a funeral ceremony. Like death, the act is beyond his control and unexplainable, yet it is punishable. The elders exile him for seven years to the village of his mother's family. This separation from his village is itself symbolic, since in a way Okonkwo has never belonged to it. While he is away, the village changes. With the coming of the missionaries, traditional religious practices begin to lose their sanction, their absoluteness. In Part III, Okonkwo returns from exile but finds that his exile continues. Nothing is as it was. Open hostility exists between the new religion and the traditional one. The British government has begun to take over authority from the elders. The novel ends with Okonkwo's irrational killing of a messenger from the British District Officer and with his subsequent suicide. Okonkwo rightly assumes, it would seem, that no authority now exists to judge him: the old sanctions are dead, and he refuses to accept the new ones. He must be his own judge.

There is, however, if not a judge, a voice of reason and compassion, detached from the action but controlling its effects, that assures Okonkwo of a fair hearing. The voice is heard in the proverbs, warning Okonkwo not to challenge his own *chi* (his own spiritual identity and destiny), even though another proverb insists that if he says yes his *chi* will say yes too. It is heard in the decisions of the elders, the complaints of the wives, and the rebellion of Okonkwo's own son, Noye, who turns to Christianity in defiance against his father's unreasonableness. It is found in the tragic sense of life of Okonkwo's uncle, Uchendu, who advises this man in exile to bear his punishment stoically, for his sufferings are mild in comparison to those of many others. Achebe locates his voice in one particular character, Obierika, Okonkwo's closest friend and a man of thought rather than, like his friend, a man of action. In the important eighth chapter, Achebe measures his protagonist against this man of moderation, reflection, and humor, who can observe the white invader with tolerance, his own tribal laws with skepticism, and, at the end of the novel, his dead friend with respect and compassion, Achebe's voice can even be seen in the ironically insensitive judgment of the District Commissioner as the novel closes. As superficial and uninformed as that voice might be in itself, Achebe recognizes that the voice nevertheless exists, is therefore real, and must be acknowledged. The final view of Okonkwo and of the village that he both reflects and rejects is a composite of all these voices. It is the composite also of Okonkwo's own complex and unpredictable behavior, and of his fate which is the result of his own reckless acts and of forces that he does not comprehend. Amid the growing chaos one senses still the stable influence of the calm authorial voice, controlling and balancing everything.

From the early 1900's of *Things Fall Apart*, Achebe turns in his second novel, *No Longer at Ease*, to the mid-1950's just before independence. The protagonist, Obi Okonkwo, grandson of the tragic victim who lashed out against British insolence, resembles to some extent his grandfather in his inadequacy to deal with the pressures of his society, but has far different loyalties. The novel begins after things have already fallen apart; Nigeria is between societies. Obi no longer belongs to the old society. His father is the rebellious son of Okonkwo who left home for the Christian church and was educated in mission schools. Obi received a similar education and was selected by his community to study in England. This financial and personal obligation to Umuoria plagues Obi throughout the novel, for after his Western education he no longer shares the old customs and the old sense of loyalty. He considers himself an independent young man of the city, with a Western concept of government and administration. After his return from England he receives a civil service job and has visions of reforming the bureaucracy. The story is thus about the practical difficulties (it is not really a psychological study) of an ordinary individual separating himself cleanly from the past while adapting to the glitter and temptations of the new. Obi faces two particular problems. He has chosen to marry a woman, Clara, who belongs to a family considered taboo by the traditional community. He attempts to resist family and community pressure, but eventually succumbs. Meanwhile, Clara has become pregnant and must go through a costly and embarrassing abortion. Obi essentially abandons his responsibility toward her in his weak, halfhearted respect for his family's wishes. He likewise fails at his job, as he resists self-righteously various bribes until his financial situation and morals finally collapse. Unfortunately, he is as clumsy here as in his personal relations. He is arrested and sentenced to prison.

As in his first novel, Achebe's subject is the individual (and the society) inadequate to the changing times. His main concern is again a balanced appraisal of Nigerian society at a crucial stage in its recent history, because the greatest danger, as Achebe himself observes, is self-deception. He presents a careful selection of characters whose vanity, prejudice, or misplaced values allow them only a partial view of reality. Obi is, of course, the main example. He leaves his home village as a hero, is one of the few Nigerians to receive a foreign education, and, as a civil servant and proud possessor of a car, is a member of the elite. His vanity blinds him to such an extent that he cannot assess his proper relationship to his family, to Clara, or to his social role. His father, caught between his Christian faith and tribal customs, cannot allow Obi his independence. Mr. Green, Obi's British superior at the office, is trapped by stereotypical prejudices against Africans. There is no one individual such as Obierika within the novel to provide a reasonable interpretation of events.

One nevertheless feels the constant presence of Achebe as he balances these various voices against one another. Achebe also assures perspective by maintaining a detached tone through irony, wit, and humor. The narrator possesses the maturity and the wisdom that the characters lack. This novel also shows Achebe experimenting with structure as a means of expressing the authorial voice. The novel opens (like Leo Tolstoy's *The Death of Ivan Ilych*, 1886) with the final act, the trial and judgment of Obi for accepting a bribe. Achebe thus invites the reader to take a critical view of Obi from the very beginning. There is no question of getting romantically involved in his young life and career. This distancing continues in the first three chapters as Achebe juxtaposes present and past, scenes of reality and scenes of expectation. The real Lagos is juxtaposed directly against the idyllic one in Obi's mind. A picture of the later, strained relationship between Obi and Clara precedes the romantic scenes after they meet on board ship returning from England. Through this kind of plotting by juxtaposition, Achebe turns what might have been a melodramatic story of young love, abortion, betrayal, and corruption into a realistic commentary on Nigerian society in transition. In *Things Fall Apart* he rejects a paradisal view of the African past; in *No Longer at Ease* he warns against selfish, irresponsible, and naïve expectations in the present.

In his third novel, *Arrow of God*, Achebe returns to the past, taking up the era of British colonization a few years after the events of *Things Fall Apart*. The old society is still intact, but the Christian religion and the British administration are more firmly entrenched than before. Achebe again tries to re-create the former Igbo tribal existence, with an even more elaborate account of the daily life, the customs and rituals, and with the scattering throughout of native idioms and proverbs. The foreigners, too, receive more detailed attention, though even the two main personalities, Winterbottom and Clarke, hardly achieve more than stereotyped status. Rather than work them late into the story, this time Achebe runs the two opposing forces alongside each other almost from the very beginning, in order to emphasize the British presence. Now it is the political, not the religious, power that is in the foreground, suggesting historically the second stage of foreign conquest, but the Church also takes full advantage of local political and religious controversy to increase its control over the people. Achebe continues to be realistic in his treatment of traditional society. It is not an idyllic Eden corrupted by satanic foreign power. In spite of the attractive pictures of local customs, the six villages of Umuaro are divided and belligerent, and, in two instances at least, it is ironically the British government of the Christian Church that insures peace and continuity in the communal life. By this stage in the colonization, of course, it is difficult (and Achebe does not try) to untangle the causes of internal disorder among the Igbo.

Like Okonkwo, the protagonist in *Arrow of God* is representative of the social disorder. In him Achebe represents the confidence in traditional roles and beliefs challenged not only by the new British world view, but also by forces within. Personal pride, egotism, and intolerance sometimes obscure his obligation to the welfare of the community. Whereas Okonkwo is one among several wealthy members of the clan, Ezeulu occupies a key position as the priest of Ulu, chief god of the six villages. Thus the central cohesive force in the society is localized in this one man. In another way, too, Ezeulu differs from Okonkwo. Whereas Okonkwo stubbornly resists the new Western culture, Ezeulu makes such gestures of accommodation that his clan actually accuses him of being the white man's friend. Instead of disowning his son for adopting Christianity, he sends Oduche to the mission school to be his spy in the Western camp. Ezeulu's personality, however, is complex, as are his motives. Accommodation is his pragmatic way of preserving the tribe and his own power. When the opportunity arises for him to become the political representative of his tribe to the British government, he refuses out of a sense of loyalty to his local god. This complexity is, however, contradictory and confusing, thus reflecting again the transitional state of affairs during the early colonial period. Ezeulu does not always seem to know what his motives are as he jockeys for power with Winterbottom and with the priest Idemili of his own tribe. In trying to save the community he sets up himself and his god as the sole sources of wisdom. As priest—and thus considered half man and half spirit—he may, as Achebe seems to suggest, confuse his sacred role with his human vanity.

It is in the midst of this confusion that Achebe again questions the existence of absolutes and advises tolerance. The central concept of the *chi* reappears.

Does it say yes if man says yes? If so, man controls his own destiny. If not, he is severely limited. In any case, the concept itself suggests duality rather than absoluteness. Even Ezeulu, while challenging the new power, advises his son, Oduche, that one "must dance the dance prevalent in his time." Chapter 16, in which this statement appears, contains the key thematic passages. In it one of Ezeulu's wives tells her children a traditional tale about a people's relation with the spirit world. It turns upon the importance of character—the proper attitude one must have toward oneself and toward the gods. A boy accidentally leaves his flute in the field where he and his family had been farming. He persuades his parents to let him return to fetch it. An encounter with the spirits, during which he demonstrates his good manners, temperance, and reverence, leads to material reward. The envious senior wife in the family sends her son on a similar mission, but his rudeness and greed lead only to the visitation of evils on human society. The intended message is obvious, but the implied one, in the context of this novel, is that traditional values appear to be childhood fancies in the face of contemporary realities.

At the end of the chapter, Ezeulu puts those realities into focus. He describes himself as an arrow of god, whose very defense of religious forms threatens the survival of his religion, but he goes on to suggest the (for him) terrifying speculation that Oduche, his Christian son, and also Christianity and the white man himself, are arrows of god. At the end of his career, Ezeulu is opening his mind to a wide range of possibilities. This tolerance, however, is double-edged, for as Achebe seems to suggest, man must be not only receptive to unfamiliar conceptions, but also tough enough to "tolerate" the pain of ambiguity and alienation. Ezeulu is too old and too exhausted to endure that pain. The final blow is his son's death while performing a ritual dance. Ezeulu interprets it as a sign that Ulu has deserted him.

Indeed, the voice in *Arrow of God* is even more ambiguous than that in the first two novels. There is no Obierika to correct Ezeulu's aberrations. Akueke, his friend and adviser, is not a sure guide to the truth. Achebe works through dialogue even more than in *Things Fall Apart*, and the debates between these two men do not lead to a clear answer. Akueke cannot decipher the priest's motives or anticipate his actions. Ezeulu, as a strange compound of spirit and man, is to him "unknowable." Nor does Achebe make the task any easier for the reader. Ezeulu does not seem to understand his own motives. He considers himself under the spiritual influence of his god. His sudden, final decision not to seek a reconciliation with his people he imagines as the voice of Ulu. He thus sacrifices himself and his people (as well as the god himself) to the will of the god. Achebe remains silent on the issue of whether the voice is the god's or Ezeulu's. One can only speculate that since the tribe created the god in the first place (or so the legend went), it could also destroy him.

Like *No Longer at Ease*, Achebe's fourth novel, *A Man of the People*, seems rather lightweight in comparison with the two historical novels. It takes place not in Nigeria but in an imaginary African country, a few years after independence. Achebe seems to be playing with some of the popular situations in contemporary African literature, as though he were parodying them. The main character, Odili, has relationships with three different women: Elsie, a friend from the university who functions as a sort of mistress, but who remains a shadowy figure in the background; Jean, a white American with whom he has a brief sexual relationship; and Edna, a beautiful and innocent young woman with whom he "falls in love" in a rather conventional Western sense. There is also the typical estrangement of the university-educated son from his traditionally oriented father. Achebe contrives a somewhat romantic reconciliation during the last third of the novel. Finally, while all of Achebe's novels are essentially political, this one pits two candidates for public office against each other, with all the paraphernalia of personal grudges, dirty tricks, campaign rhetoric, and even a military coup at the end that ironically makes the election meaningless. (In fact, it was already meaningless because the incumbent, Nanga, had arranged that Odili's name not be officially registered.) Furthermore, the contest is a stock romantic confrontation between the idealism of youth and the corrupt opportunism of an older generation. While the story might at first glance appear to be a melodramatic rendering of the romantic world of love and politics, it so exaggerates situations that one must assume Achebe is writing rather in the comic mode.

Along with this choice of mode, Achebe also creates a more conventional plot line. The rising action deals with the first meeting after sixteen years between Odili, a grammar school teacher, and Nanga, the "man of the people," Odili's former teacher, local representative to Parliament, and Minister of Culture. In spite of his skepticism toward national politics, Odili succumbs to Nanga's charm and accepts an invitation to stay at his home in the city. The turning point comes when Odili's girl friend, Elsie, shamelessly spends the night with Nanga. Odili sees this as a betrayal by Elsie, even though he himself feels no special commitment to her. More important, Odili feels betrayed and humiliated by Nanga, who does not take such incidents with women at all seriously. His vanity touched by this rather trivial incident, Odili suddenly reactivates his conscience over political corruption and vows to seek revenge. The attack is twofold: to steal Edna, Nanga's young fiancée, who is to be his second wife, and to defeat Nanga in the next elections. Odili's motives are obviously suspect. The rest of the novel recounts his gradual initiation into love and politics. The revenge motive drops as the relationship with Edna becomes serious. The political campaign fails, and Odili ends up in the hospital after a pointless attempt to spy on one of Nanga's campaign rallies. Again, it is tempting to treat this as a conventional initiation story, except that Odili's experiences do not really cure him of his romantic notions of love and politics.

For the first time, Achebe elects to use the first-person point of view: Odili tells his own story. This may be the reason that the balancing of effects through juxtaposition of scenes and characters does not operate as in the earlier works. The tone is obviously affected as well: Odili is vain and pompous, blind to his own flaws while critical of others. Hence, Achebe has to manipulate a subjective narrative to express the objective authorial voice, as Mark Twain does in *The Adventures of Huckleberry Finn* (1884) or (to use an African example) Mongo Beti in *Le Pauvre Christ de Bomba* (1956, *The Poor Christ of Bomba*). The primary means is through Odili's own partial vision. Odili frequently makes criticisms of contemporary politics that appear to be just, and therefore do represent the judgment of Achebe as well. At the same time, Odili's affected tone invites criticism and provides Achebe with an occasion to satirize the self-deception of the young intellectuals whom Odili represents. Achebe also expresses himself through the plot, in which he parodies romantic perceptions of the contemporary world. In addition, he continues to include proverbs in the mouths of provincial characters as guides to moral evaluation.

Achebe emphasizes one proverb in particular to describe the political corruption in which Nanga participates. After a local merchant, Josiah, steals a blind beggar's stick to make his customers (according to a figurative twist of reasoning) blindly purchase whatever he sells, the public reacts indignantly with the proverb: "He has taken away enough for the owner to notice." Unlike Achebe's narrator in the first three novels, Odili cannot allow the proverb to do its own work. He must, as an academic, analyze it and proudly expand on its meaning. He had done this before when he became the "hero" of Jean's party as the resident expert on African behavior and African art. He may very well be correct about the political implications of the proverb, that the people (the owners of the country) are now being blatantly robbed by the politicians, but he fails to identify emotionally with the local situation. Nor is he objective enough to admit fully to himself his own immoral, hypocritical behavior, which he has maintained throughout the novel. He is an egotist, more enchanted with his own cleverness than concerned about the society he has pretended to serve. In like manner, at the close of the story Odili turns the real death of his political colleague, Max, into a romantic fantasy of the ideal sacrifice. Totally pessimistic about the reliability of the people, he returns once again to the proverb to illustrate their fickle behavior as the melodramatic villains: they always return the Josiahs to power. Achebe may to some extent share Odili's view of the public and the national leadership it chooses, but he is skeptical of the Odilis as well; and hence he positions the reader outside both the political structure and Odili as an observer of the society. Achebe, then, even in this first-person narrative did not abandon his authorial voice, nor the role of social spokesman that he had maintained in all his other novels.

Major publications other than long fiction

SHORT FICTION: *The Sacrificial Egg and Other Short Stories*, 1962; *Girls at War*, 1972.

POETRY: *Beware, Soul Brother and Other Poems*, 1971, 1972; *Christmas in Biafra and Other Poems*, 1973.

NONFICTION: *Morning Yet on Creation Day*, 1975.

CHILDREN'S LITERATURE: *Chike and the River*, 1966; *How the Leopard Got His Claws*, 1972 (with John Iroaganachi).

Bibliography

Carroll, David. *Chinua Achebe*, 1970.

Killam, G. E. *The Novels of Chinua Achebe*, 1969.

Larson, Charles. *The Emergence of African Fiction*, 1972.

Moore, Gerald. *Seven African Writers*, 1962.

Palmer, Eustace. *An Introduction to the African Novel*, 1972.

Ravenscroft, Arthur. *Chinua Achebe*, 1969.

Soyinka, Wole. *Myth, Literature and the African World*, 1976.

Thomas Banks

CONRAD AIKEN

Born: Savannah, Georgia; August 5, 1889
Died: Savannah, Georgia; August 17, 1973

Principal long fiction

Blue Voyage, 1927; *Great Circle*, 1933; *King Coffin*, 1935; *A Heart for the Gods of Mexico*, 1939; *Conversation: Or, Pilgrim's Progress*, 1940.

Other literary forms

Conrad Aiken was one of the most prolific of modern American writers, publishing more than forty separate volumes of poetry, novels, plays, short stories, and criticism. Aiken published five collections of stories, culminating in the *Collected Short Stories of Conrad Aiken* (1966). He is the author of *Mr. Arcularis* (1957), a play based on an adaptation by Diana Hamilton of his short story of the same title. His nonfictional writing includes introductions to *Two Wessex Tales by Thomas Hardy* (1919) and *Selected Poems of Emily Dickinson* (1924), as well as a lifetime of reviews, originally published in such leading journals as *The New Republic*, *Poetry*, *The Dial*, *The Nation*, and *The New Yorker*, and collected in *A Reviewer's ABC: Collected Criticism of Conrad Aiken from 1916 to the Present* (1958). An earlier critical work was *Skepticisms: Notes on Contemporary Poetry* (1919). His most famous nonfictional work, and one of his most lasting contributions to American literature, is his third-person autobiography *Ushant: An Essay* (1952). He published twenty-nine collections of poetry; the best of his early poems were collected in *Selected Poems* (1929), while the best of his total poetic output can be found in *Collected Poems* (1953, 1970). In addition, Aiken served as editor for numerous anthologies of poetry, including *A Comprehensive Anthology of American Poetry* (1929), and was a contributing editor of *The Dial* from 1917 to 1918. Finally, under the pseudonym Samuel Jeake, Jr., Aiken was a London correspondent for *The New Yorker* from 1934 to 1936.

Achievements

Aiken's literary reputation is based on his poetry, for which he received the Pulitzer Prize in 1930, the National Book Award in 1954, and the Bollingen Prize in 1956. Despite these major awards, his reputation seems fixed among the most major of minor poets, a position that virtually all of his critics agree is too low. Of his fiction, the short stories "Silent Snow, Secret Snow" and "Mr. Arcularis" are often anthologized and discussed, though few of his others are ever mentioned. His reputation as a novelist is even more tenuous; none of his novels is now in print, and few critical articles about them have been published. When his first novel, *Blue Voyage*, appeared, its initial reputation as an experimental novel and its personal revelations about Aiken's interior life brought the book some notoriety. Subsequent critical opinion, however, has treated *Blue Voyage* as an inferior version of James Joyce's *A Portrait of the Artist as a Young Man* (1916) or *Ulysses* (1922). *Great Circle*, Aiken's second novel, was praised by literary critics as a psychological case study and was admired by Sigmund Freud himself for its Freudian overtones. Aiken's last three novels received little praise or attention. *A Heart for the Gods of Mexico* was not even published in America until the collected edition of his novels appeared. Aiken himself considered *King Coffin* a failure; he admits in *Ushant* that his last novels were unsuccessful, and says that he does not mind his relative obscurity, but in a letter to his friend Malcolm Cowley, he wrote "Might I also suggest for your list of Neglected Books a novel by c. aiken called *Great Circle*, of which the royalty report, to hand this morning, chronicles a sale of 26 copies in its second half year?" Current critics, like Aiken's contemporaries, see the major value of his novels in their experimental nature, their Freudian images, and their amplification of the themes of Aiken's poetry.

Biography

Conrad Potter Aiken was born in Savannah, Georgia, on August 5, 1889. Both of his parents were New Englanders. His mother, Anna Potter Aiken, was the daughter of William James Potter, minister of the Unitarian First Congregational Society of New Bedford, Massachusetts, and a friend of Ralph Waldo Emerson. His father, William Ford Aiken, was a physician educated at Harvard. The central event of his childhood—and in fact of his whole life— took place in 1900 when, as an eleven-and-a-half year old boy, he discovered the dead bodies of his parents. Aiken's father had killed his mother with a revolver and then shot himself. This event remained forever embedded in his psyche. As Aiken writes in *Ushant*, "He had tiptoed into the dark room, where the two bodies lay motionless, and apart, and, finding them dead, found himself possessed of them forever."

Following this crucial event, Aiken's two brothers were separated from him, and he spent the remainder of his childhood living with a great-great aunt in New Bedford. He attended the Middlesex School in Concord and, in 1907, entered Harvard University during the same period as T. S. Eliot, John Reed, Walter Lippmann, E. E. Cummings, and Robert Benchley. At college, Aiken was president of the Harvard *Advocate*, a frequent contributor to the Harvard *Monthly*, and a leader among his classmates in literary discussions, but he also established a pattern which was to hold true throughout his life—he was always a loner, following neither particular schools of criticism nor prevailing literary styles. Placed on probation for poor class attendance as a senior, Aiken left Harvard in protest and spent half a year in Europe, thus establishing another constant pattern: for the remainder of his life he made frequent trips to Europe, living as often abroad as at home until World

War II, after which he lived in New England, primarily in Brewster, Massachusetts.

Following his return to Harvard, Aiken was graduated in 1912 and immediately began writing poems for his first collection, *Earth Triumphant and Other Tales in Verse* (1914). For the rest of his life, Aiken supported himself solely by his writing, except for a brief stint as an English tutor at Harvard in 1927. He married three times, divorcing his first wife, Jessie McDonald, after eighteen years of marriage and the rearing of three children; his second wife, Clarice Lorenz, he divorced after seven years. He remained married to his third wife, Mary Hoover, from 1937 until his death from a heart attack on August 17, 1973, in Savannah, Georgia, the city of his birth, to which he had returned to complete the great circle of his life.

For most of his career, Aiken simultaneously worked on his poetry, fiction, and criticism. From 1925 to 1935, he alternated short-story collections with novels. In 1939 and 1940, he published his last two novels, *A Heart for the Gods of Mexico* and *Conversation*, thereafter concentrating on poetry and criticism. During the 1920's and 1930's, Aiken was involved with such American expatriates as T. S. Eliot, Ezra Pound, and Malcolm Lowry, yet he was always deliberately apart from the center of artistic circles, choosing, for example, to live in London and Brewster rather than Paris and New York. The best source of information about Aiken's relation with other writers is *Ushant*, in which Eliot, Pound, and Lowry appear as the Tsetse, Rabbi Ben Ezra, and Hambo.

Analysis

The central event in Conrad Aiken's personal life—the murder-suicide of his parents—was also the central event of his artistic life, for all of his literary work is in some way aimed at coming to terms with the childhood tragedy. In *Ushant*, Aiken says of his parents that "he was irrevocably dedicated to a lifelong—if need be—search for an equivalent to it all, in terms of his own life, or work; and an equivalent that those two angelic people would have thought acceptable." The search for understanding of his personal tragedy motivated Aiken to try to understand the universal tragedy of modern man, what Joseph Warren Beach called "moral terror," the basic question of good and evil in the human heart that American writers have been struggling with since the advent of American letters. Aiken's search for a way to maintain equilibrium in the face of his contradictory love for his parents and his revulsion for their deaths lies outside of theological or conventional ethical questions; his search centered on his own consciousness, on himself. The major subject of each of his five novels is a search for self, an interior exploration— often expressed metaphorically as a circular journey. *Blue Voyage* and *Great Circle* focus on psychological understanding in which the protagonist attempts to get back to himself by a circular analysis of his past. *King Coffin* is a psychological horror story of a madman's decision to murder a complete stranger, a decision that eventually leads the protagonist around full circle until he kills himself. *A Heart for the Gods of Mexico* presents a literal journey—a train trip from Boston to Mexico—in which the narrator attempts to reconcile the beauty and strangeness of the changing landscape with the impending death of his woman companion. Finally, *Conversation* describes the circular arguments in a lover's quarrel which eventually runs its course, returning to its starting place.

In each novel, Aiken's chief character is trying to complete what in plane geometry is called a great circle of a sphere, a circle whose plane passes through the center of the sphere. For Aiken's protagonists, the circle is a descent into their pasts and the sphere is the shape of their lives. Because of this self-analysis, each novel is introspective and confessional. Taken together, the novels chart a series of points on Aiken's great circle, a graphic display of his search for understanding his own life. Each novel is based, in varying degrees, on autobiographical details from his life, and each is discussed in *Ushant*, where Aiken says "the artificer, in the very act of displaying himself in the new shape of the artifact, must remain wholly neutral to that part of himself which is his subject—which is to say, his all."

Aiken's attempt to get to the bottom of or to the other side of his parents' deaths led him on a series of physical voyages between America and Europe and on a series of literary voyages between poetry and fiction, which he called in his 1958 poem "The Crystal," "The westward pour of the worlds and the westward pour of the mind." In both his life and his art he speaks of a constant tension between two opposing forces: a desire for artistic expression, for bringing art to bear on the chaos of human existence which was in constant confrontation with what Frederick Hoffman calls "the shock of reality, which continually challenges the creative spirit and, in moments of terror or violence, may even severely dislocate it." Although the shortest distance between two points may be a straight line, when those points are located within these opposing spheres, then the shortest arc between the comfort of art and the moral terror of reality becomes the great circle that Aiken so thoroughly and so gracefully traced in his novels.

Writing in 1952 about his first novel *Blue Voyage* (which in *Ushant* he calls, half ironically, *Purple Passage*), Aiken said it was "a compromise in which the voice of Joyce had been too audible." This Joycean comparison refers to the hero of the novel, William Demarest, who has booked a second-class passage aboard a steamship enroute to England, ostensibly to search for his lost love Cynthia, but actually to search within himself for an explanation of his feelings about Cynthia and about himself as a writer. Demarest clearly resembles Aiken, both in autobiographical detail (when Demarest's parents die he is sent as a boy to live in New Bedford) and in critical reputation (Demarest names as his literary weakness the inability to present a "theme energetically and simply" instead of dressing it "in tissue upon tissue of proviso and aspect . . . from a hundred angles"). The novel is also Joycean in style, for when Demarest discovers that Cynthia is actually on board the ship, he returns to his stateroom and launches himself into a lengthy regression which Jay Martin in his *Conrad Aiken: A Life of His Art* (1962) calls a "preconscious monologue." This regression is filled with allusions to self-crucifixion, bizarre sexual dreams, fragments of popular songs, bits of English poetry, extended lists of numbers, noises, and a constant repetition of the capitalized word MISERY, all accompanied by the incessant throbbing of the ship's engines.

Jay Martin sees *Blue Voyage* as an attempt at combining the confessional and the aesthetic novel, and like *A Portrait of the Artist as a Young Man*, Aiken's first novel includes discussions of its hero's theories about art and literature with Aiken's Cranley/Lynch figure, a man named Silverstein, who acts as Demarest's psychoanalyst. *Blue Voyage* tries to go beyond Joyce's early work in terms of experimentation, for in the sixth chapter, Aiken presents a lyrical out-of-the-body experience in which the main characters of the novel perform a hallucinatory ritualistic parody of the Crucifixion which results in Cynthia's being metamorphosed into a Gothic stained-glass window. The book ends with a series of undelivered letters from Demarest to Cynthia which alternate between intense self-loathing and a passionate attempt to explain the letter writer to his lost love, to himself, and, by extension, to explain Aiken to his readers. As Demarest says in his second letter, "It is precisely the sort of thing I am always trying to do in my writing—to present my unhappy reader with a wide-ranged chaos—of actions and reactions, thoughts, memories and feelings—in the vain hope that at the end he will see that the whole thing represents only *one moment, one feeling, one person.*"

In his autobiography, Aiken's second novel, *Great Circle*, appears as *Dead Reckoning*, a punning title that encompasses the major themes of the novel: navigation along the great circle as a metaphor for exploration of the psyche of a man whose world, like the author's, turns over with the horrifying discovery of his parents' betrayal by sudden death. *Great Circle* opens with its protagonist, Andrew Cather, on board a train to Cambridge, where he will surprise his wife in the act of adultery, an act that was forewarned both by a friend and by signs the protagonist has refused to see. Andrew Cather, who is often called "One-eye Cather" because of an ambiguously explained injury to one eye, is not able to stop the marital infidelity he knows is coming, any more than the Cyclops in Homer's epic can avoid Odysseus' prophesied appearance.

Cather's discovery leads him to Aiken's familiar dilemma: how to maintain balance in the face of moral terror. Cather's initial response is to avoid the terror by avoiding consciousness of it, at first by maintaining a false air of melodrama about the situation and then by repeatedly drinking himself into a stupor. The combination of drunkenness and estrangement from his wife, whose adultery was consummated with Cather's best friend, causes him to fall into the lengthy reverie about his childhood which constitutes all of Chapter II, the most successfully sustained section in all of Aiken's prose fiction. This section is a sensually lyrical evocation of the summer in Cather's childhood in Duxbury, Massachusetts, during which he first felt the strangeness of his father's absence and his mother's attachment to his Uncle David. The chapter is Joycean in style and Faulknerian in content, full of lyrical passages that call up ocean and shore. Like Maisie from Henry James's *What Maisie Knew* (1897) or William Faulkner's Quentin Compson from *The Sound and the Fury* (1929), the young Andy Cather slowly comes to awareness about the sexuality of the adults who move around him. Reading a letter from his father to his mother, Andy Cather realizes imperfectly that his mother is having an affair with his uncle. The chapter ends with Andy's terrible discovery of the bodies of his mother and her lover, drowned during a storm. Speaking of this chapter, Jay Martin says, "Aiken intends it to be real, an exact and complete account of his experience insofar as it entered the consciousness of the boy."

The third chapter of *Great Circle* consists of a night-long amateur psychoanalysis session in which Cather speaks an exhaustive monologue in an attempt at talking through his marital problems in the present, the horror of his childhood discovery, and the interconnection between the two events. Realizing that he unconsciously associates the physical intimacies of marriage with the discovery of his mother, dead in his uncle's embrace, Cather makes an actual trip to Duxbury, thus confronting and completing the great circle voyage through his past and his psyche. Aiken's novel reflects Henry David Thoreau's argument at the conclusion of *Walden* (1854) that "Our voyaging is only great-circle sailing," for the horrible scene from his protagonist's childhood is, of course, suggestive of Aiken's own childhood tragedy. The image of circularity echoes throughout the novel, from the title to the description of Cather "hurrying from point to point on the earth's surface, describing his swift little arc" to the later statement that he is running "round in mad circles, like a beheaded hen." Later, Cather says to himself about the origin of his problems, "It is your own little worm-curve; the twist that is your own life; the small spiral of light that answers to the name of Andrew Cather." The entire second chapter is enclosed within outsized parentheses, suggestive of the great-circle, and in one of his childhood revelations, Cather remembers an old riddle—"Rats live on no evil star," a palindrome that "spells the same thing backward"—which reminds the reader that Andrew Cather's initials backward are Conrad Aiken's, and that Cather's attempt at rescuing his marriage through a series of therapeutic returns to his childhood is also Aiken's attempt at resolving his own problems by writing about them in novels.

Aiken's third novel, *King Coffin*, is the only one he leaves out of *Ushant*, probably because he considered it to be a major failure, unredeemable by subsequent analysis. Although most critics refer to *King Coffin* as a major failure, if they mention it at all, Aiken's best critic, Jay Martin, argues that the author meant *King Coffin* as a parody of a psychological novel, playing "lightly with a serious psychological subject while still retaining a real sense of its dignity and importance." The subject of the novel is an insane plan conceived half in jest by Jasper Ammen (a name suggestive of E. A. Robinson's *King Jasper*, 1936) to demonstrate his innate superiority by murdering an ordinary person chosen at random—a person Ammen comes to call "a specimen man" or "the anonymous one." The motive for the murder is the achievement of a perfectly pure relationship, in Ammen's simplification of Nietzschian/Emersonian ideas, between the superior man and the ordinary one. Initially, Ammen claims he has chosen his victim and is studying the dailiness of his life as background for a novel about "pure" murder, a novel he plans to call *King Coffin*.

As the actual novel progresses, Ammen begins to think of Jones, his intended victim, as "one-who-wants-to-be-killed." This short novel ends with Ammen's too-close identification with his victim; seeing that Jones's wife's newly born baby has died, Ammen decides that the perfect ending to his plan would be his own murder, thereby bringing the novel full circle: the random victim has unconsciously caused Ammen to kill himself. Although Jay Martin sees *King Coffin* as its protagonist's "attempt to recognize and resolve his own strangeness, to realize his ego completely by fully understanding its complexity," most critics have seen the book as a competent murder-mystery at best, clearly the least successful of Aiken's novels. Because Jasper Ammen is labeled a psychotic at the start of the novel, the rationalizations he uses for his bizarre plan never become compelling; they are neither the ravings of a madman nor the thoughts of a superior human. Instead they fall somewhere in between. *King Coffin* is considerably shorter than Aiken's previous novels and interesting mainly for its conception: Aiken creates a psychopathic killer who pretends to write the book that Aiken actually writes, just as the narrator of *Ushant*, a character Aiken calls only D., discusses his attempt at writing the very autobiography in which one reads his discussion.

Aiken's penultimate novel, *A Heart for the Gods of Mexico*, returns to the author's now-familiar themes. The story tells of a lengthy train trip from Boston to Mexico by day coach, taken by a woman who knows she is soon to die of heart failure; her fiancé, who is unaware of her condition; and her friend, who is half in love with her. Noni, the young woman who is soon to die, puzzles over her upcoming death in a manner that recalls *King Coffin*: "It seems so ridiculously random . . . it's *that* that's so puzzling." Unlike the psychopathic protaganist of that novel, however, the young woman is a sympathetic character. She and her friend are constantly struggling with such questions as whether the subterfuge is ethical, whether the trip is hastening her inevitable death, and whether the startling tropical beauty of Mexico should make them forget the impending death or revel in it.

Both critics and its author have described *A Heart for the Gods of Mexico* as a curious failure; the novel contains brilliant landscape scenes, strong and affecting portrayals of character, particular Noni's, and a passionate depiction of the traveler's meeting in Cuernavaca with Hambo, Aiken's name for Malcolm Lowry, the author of *Under the Volcano* (1947). Unlike *Blue Voyage* and *Great Circle*, however, this book lacks form. The trip is too long in getting started, and too much local color is presented along the way. *A Heart for the Gods of Mexico* is the shortest of Aiken's novels. The book offers no flashbacks, no self-analysis, no sense of any concentric structure except for the shape imposed on the novel by the narrative of the trip itself, Noni's "great-circle to Mexico" upon which she takes her "heart as an offering to the bloodstained altar of the plumed serpent."

Aiken's last novel, *Conversation*, records the bitterly circular quarrel of Timothy and Enid Kane, whose marital argument, like the one in *Great Circle*, is (on the surface, at least) about infidelity, this time on the part of the male. In some ways, the novel deals with feminism; Enid Kane wants to live in an urban environment while her husband, a painter, wants to live in the country on Cape Cod rather than remain in the city painting commissioned portraits. Timothy sees the journey to the country as a chance to get back in touch with his natural artistic creativity; his wife sees the move as "all that nonsense of yours about plain living and high thinking, about living the natural and honest life of our Pilgrim ancestors, and being independent—but it's no good for a woman." While Enid is wrong in thus belittling her husband's desire to paint freely, Timothy is also wrong in hiding the fact that the move is partly to get away from his in-town affair. The bucolic escape turns into a series of get-togethers with bohemian Greenwich Village artists and poets, such as Karl Roth, who represents the poet Maxwell Bodenheim. Enid Kane's reference to the Pilgrims suggests one of the connections between this portrait of the artist as a young married man, the novel's subtitle, and the excerpts from *A Journal of the Pilgrims at Plymouth* (1962) that head each chapter of the novel. Like the early visitors to Massachusetts, Timothy Kane wants to recapture a spirit of freedom so that he can overcome the sterility he has felt, both in his art and in his life, since the birth of his daughter. Although his daughter's birth represents the highest womanly creative act in his wife's mind, and although his daughter's freshly imaginative outlook on nature is exactly the kind of artistic rebirth Timothy is looking for, he comes to see during the course of the long, circuitous argument that his repressed anxieties about the physical details of his daughter's birth are the cause of his inability to hold a conversation with his wife. Like Andrew Cather, who is disgusted by the "filthy intimacies" of marriage, Timothy Kane finds the effect of childbirth, what his friend calls "that butcher-shop and meaty reality," to be "something for which love's young dream hadn't at all been prepared. A loss of belief."

The argument in *Conversation* continues along Aiken's familiar circular path, until, like a snake with its tail in its mouth, it comes back to where it began and resolves itself with the reunion of the Kanes and a decision to have a son; however, since no one can predict the sex of an unborn child before conception, it is clear that this resolution will likely lead the couple back onto another loop of their argument. In the middle of his last novel, Aiken presents a scene in which Kane is comparing his idea of marriage while still engaged with his vision after his child's birth. Using the metaphors of poetry and prose, Kane gives Conrad Aiken's final critical assessment of the relationship between his own work in the two genres: "The poetry had been too pure a poetry, its further implications (of all that the body, and passion, could exact, or time and diurnal intimacy dishevel and destroy) had been too little understood; and when the prose followed, it had inevitably seemed only too ingrainedly prosaic."

This assessment is accurate. Despite their relative merits, Aiken's five novels would probably not be read today were it not for the poetic reputation of their author. In his autobiography, Aiken says of his parents' deaths that "he was to discover, while at Harvard, that the staining sense of guilt and shame had been mysteriously exorcised, as no longer there," but clearly some degree of both guilt and shame must have remained throughout the author's life, despite the therapy gained from writing these five novels.

Major publications other than long fiction

SHORT FICTION: *Bring! Bring! and Other Stories*, 1925; *Costumes by Eros*, 1928; *Among the Lost People*, 1934; *Short Stories*, 1950; *Collected Short Stories*, 1960; *Collected Short Stories of Conrad Aiken*, 1966.

PLAYS: *Fear No More*, 1946; *Mr. Arcularis: A Play*, 1957.

POETRY: *Earth Triumphant and Other Tales in Verse*, 1914; *Turns and Movies and Other Tales in Verse*, 1916; *The Jig of Forslin*, 1916; *Nocturne of Remembered Spring and Other Poems*, 1917; *The Charnel Rose*, 1918; *Senlin: A Biography and Other Poems*, 1918; *The House of Dust*, 1920; *Punch: The Immortal Liar*, 1921; *Priapus and the Pool*, 1922; *The Pilgrimage of Festus*, 1923; *Prelude*, 1929; *Priapus and the Pool and Other Poems*, 1925; *Selected Poems*, 1929; *John Deth: A Metaphysical Legend, and Other Poems*, 1930; *Gehenna*, 1930; *The Coming Forth by Day of Osiris Jones*, 1931; *Preludes for Memmon*, 1931; *And in the Hanging Gardens*, 1933; *Landscape West of Eden*, 1934; *Time in the Rock: Preludes to Definition*, 1936; *And in the Human Heart*, 1940; *Brownstone Eclogues and Other Poems*, 1942; *The Soldier: A Poem by Conrad Aiken*, 1944; *The Kid*, 1947; *Skylight One: Fifteen Poems*, 1949; *The Divine Pilgrim*, 1949; *Collected Poems*, 1953, 1970; *A Letter from Li Po and Other Poems*, 1955; *The Fluteplayer*, 1956; *Sheepfold Hill: Fifteen Poems*, 1958; *Selected Poems*, 1961; *The Morning Song of Lord Zero*, 1963; *A Seizure of Limericks*, 1964; *Cats and Bats and Things with Wings: Poems*, 1965; *The Clerk's Journal*, 1971; *A Little Who's Zoo of Mild Animals*, 1977.

NONFICTION: *Skepticisms: Notes on Contemporary Poetry*, 1919; "Introduction," in *Two Wessex Tales by Thomas Hardy*, 1919; "Introduction," in *Selected Poems of Emily Dickinson*, 1924; *Ushant: An Essay*, 1952; *A Reviewer's ABC: Collected Criticism of Conrad Aiken from 1916 to the Present*, 1958.

ANTHOLOGIES: *A Comprehensive Anthology of American Poetry*, 1929; *Twentieth Century American Poetry*, 1944.

Bibliography

Denney, Reuel. *Conrad Aiken*, 1964.
Hoffman, Frederick J. *Conrad Aiken*, 1962.
Lawrence, Seymour, ed. *Wake XI*, 1952, Conrad Aiken number.
Martin, Jay. *Conrad Aiken: A Life of His Art*, 1962.

Timothy Dow Adams

WILLIAM HARRISON AINSWORTH

Born: Manchester, England; February 4, 1805
Died: Reigate, England; January 3, 1882

Principal long fiction
  Sir John Chiverton, 1826 (with John Partington Aston); *Rookwood*, 1834; *Crichton*, 1837; *Jack Sheppard*, 1839; *The Tower of London*, 1840; *Guy Fawkes*, 1841; *Old Saint Paul's*, 1841; *The Miser's Daughter*, 1842; *Windsor Castle*, 1843; *Saint James's*, 1844; *James the Second*, 1848; *The Lancashire Witches*, 1849; *The Star-Chamber*, 1854; *The Flitch of Bacon*, 1854; *The Spendthrift*, 1856; *Mervyn Clitheroe*, 1858; *Ovingdean Grange*, 1860; *The Constable of the Tower*, 1861; *The Lord Mayor of London*, 1862; *Cardinal Pole*, 1863; *John Law*, 1864; *The Spanish Match*, 1865; *Auriol*, 1865; *The Constable de Bourbon*, 1866; *Old Court*, 1867; *Myddleton Pomfret*, 1868; *The South-Sea Bubble*, 1868; *Hilary St. Ives*, 1869; *Tower Hill*, 1871; *Talbot Harland*, 1871; *Boscobel*, 1872; *The Manchester Rebels of the Fatal '45*, 1872 (originally published as *The Good Old Times*); *Merry England*, 1874; *The Goldsmith's Wife*, 1875; *Preston Fight*, 1875; *The Leaguer of Latham*, 1876; *Chetwynd Calverley*, 1876; *The Fall of Somerset*, 1877; *Beatrice Tyldesley*, 1878; *Beau Nash*, 1879; *Stanley Brereton*, 1881.

Other literary forms
  Most of William Harrison Ainsworth's work in forms other than the novel was limited to juvenilia. Before reaching nineteen, he had published dramas, poems, essays, tales, and translations in local Manchester periodicals. He also wrote several short books of verse and a brief political pamphlet before he became known as a novelist. Later, he contributed some reviews and verse to annuals and magazines. The songs and ballads scattered throughout his novels were collected for separate publication in 1855 and reprinted in 1872. Ainsworth's association with periodicals was long and significant. Most of his novels were first published as magazine serials. He edited *Bentley's Miscellany* (1839-1841 and 1854-1868), *Ainsworth's Magazine* (1842-1854), and the *New Monthly Magazine* (1846-1870).

Achievements
  Ainsworth has often been considered the heir of Sir Walter Scott. After writing two books that were criticized for glamorizing criminals, he produced dozens of solid historical novels that were entertaining, moral, and educational. Some featured real historical figures; others used invented characters who took part in significant events. Ainsworth's books had vivid scenes and exciting conflicts. They were filled with accurate detail about costume, food, ceremony, and architecture. Although *Windsor Castle* and *The Tower of Lon-*

don were novels, generations of tourists used them for guidebooks. Ainsworth covered the significant monarchs that were too recent to be in William Shakespeare's plays. Most ordinary people in the nineteenth century had their sense of English history largely from Scott, Shakespeare, and Ainsworth.

Ainsworth, however, contributed virtually nothing to the development of the novel; he merely did—and not nearly so well—what Scott had done before him. The literary novel was turning to realistic social and psychological examinations of contemporary life. Ainsworth's significance is as an author and editor of popular literature. His books refined and preserved elements of popular theater and Gothic fiction, adapting them to mid-century modes of publication. His novels are characterized by heightened confrontations and recurring climaxes; the techniques of suspended narration and the resources of serial construction; supernatural excitements, vivid tableaux, and memorable spectacles; a preference for romantic underdogs; and moral simplicity. Ainsworth made these touchstones of popular writing briefly respectable and then handed them down to the authors who catered to the much broader mass reading public of the late nineteenth century.

Biography

William Harrison Ainsworth was born February 4, 1805, to a prosperous family in Manchester. His father was a solicitor who had a substantial house on a good street, a suburban summer residence, and a fondness for collecting information about crime and criminals. Even before he could read, Ainsworth adored his father's stories of highwaymen and ghosts. Although he was brought up in a strict atmosphere of Whiggism and Nonconformity, Ainsworth also grew to love lost causes. From early youth he adopted Jacobite and Tory ideals.

When he was twelve, Ainsworth was sent to the Manchester Free Grammar School. He became passionately fond of the stage, and from the age of fifteen wrote and acted plays with schoolboy friends. One of them, *Giotto: Or, The Fatal Revenge*, included a dreadful storm, terrible and mysterious events, signs of the supernatural, and minute descriptions of scenery, buildings, and costumes.

In the next few years, Ainsworth published anonymous or pseudonymous pieces in a number of magazines, briefly edited a periodical of his own, and wrote to Charles Lamb for advice about two metrical tales and three short songs that he published in 1822 as *Poems* by Cheviot Ticheburn. Leaving school at seventeen, Ainsworth became an articled clerk; in 1824, when his father died, he went to London for further legal education. At the age of twenty-one he qualified as a solicitor. In 1826, however—almost as soon as he had finished preparing to practice law—he published the historical romance he had written with a fellow clerk in Manchester, married Anne Frances ("Fanny") Ebers, and took over the publishing and bookselling branches of his father-in-law's business.

Ainsworth hoped to conduct a gentlemanly trade that would publish good books which were not popular enough for other publishing houses, but he soon found the prospects were not what he had imagined; although he met many authors and produced some good works, his firm's biggest success was a cookbook. In 1829, after returning briefly to law, he became part of the circle formed by William Maginn to contribute to *Fraser's Magazine for Town and Country*—a circle that included Theodore Hook, Samuel Taylor Coleridge, Thomas Carlyle, and William Makepeace Thackeray and was therefore intimately linked to literary fashion. Ainsworth started begging friends for plots. Finally, inspired by Ann Radcliffe's Gothic fiction, he published *Rookwood* in April, 1834, a work that was an immediate success with both critics and public.

The next ten or twelve years were Ainsworth's best. His novels sold phenomenally. For much of the time he was producing two at once: *Guy Fawkes* ran in *Bentley's Miscellany* between January, 1840, and November, 1841, while at the same time *The Tower of London* came out in monthly parts in 1840, and *Old Saint Paul's* was serialized in the *Sunday Times* during 1841. Even while writing two novels at once, Ainsworth was a successful and conscientious editor. He succeeded Charles Dickens at the helm of *Bentley's Miscellany* in 1839 and then, in 1842, began *Ainsworth's Magazine*. He was also a social celebrity who gave elaborate dinners for friends, including virtually everyone active in literature during the 1840's.

By the decade's end, Ainsworth was rerunning his early novels in *Ainsworth's Magazine* and repeating scenes and characters in the new books he wrote. In 1853 he moved to Brighton. Although he continued to write constantly for almost thirty more years and although, as an editor, he still influenced the course of popular fiction, he was no longer—physically, creatively, or socially—at the heart of nineteenth century literature.

Almost nothing is known of Ainsworth as a private person. Neither of his wives shared his public life. Fanny, who bore him three daughters, separated from him three years before she died in 1838. Sarah Wells, who gave him another daughter in 1867, was married to Ainsworth secretly some time before they moved to Reigate in 1878. There he continued to write for whatever he could earn. His last novel was being serialized in a provincial newspaper when he died on January 3, 1882.

Analysis

Popular fiction requires, above all else, a work that holds the reader's interest. The best popular authors, furthermore, are generally those who believe and delight in the books they write. William Harrison Ainsworth began to publish just after Sir Walter Scott's death. There was as yet no clearly discernible indication of the direction fiction would take, but there was a vogue for stories about history and crime. These topics suited Ainsworth's personal taste—his early interest in his father's tales, his love of acting exciting roles, his fondness for Scott, Lord Byron, Christopher Marlowe, and for Gothic novelists such as M. G. Lewis and Ann Radcliffe. Before long, the vogue for such stories had passed. Its other practitioners, including Charles Dickens, moved on to different styles and themes, but Ainsworth remained in the groove he had carved. His method of composition bred a narrative technique that secured the reader's involvement but did not encourage analytical thought. His mind was attracted by snatches of legend, by the mood surrounding a place, by the intensely realized scenes without antecedents or consequences that often feature in daydreams. His books have very complicated stories but often lack a plot in the sense of shape, point, or consequence. His most successful works gain apparent unity because they are linked to a single place or use a well-known historical event as a frame. Ainsworth was not creative in the broad sense; he depended on research because it supplied a mass of details which helped disguise the fact that he lacked Scott's ability to create the texture and spirit of the past. The accurate details also gave Ainsworth's books respectability for a mass public that was becoming increasingly self-conscious; historical distance permitted both Ainsworth and his readers to be emotionally involved in scenes of horror, conflict, and danger.

Ainsworth's stories are far too complicated to summarize. At least three or four series of events move simultaneously; typically, one is historical, one uses fictional characters acting in historical events, and a third involves comic figures. Each individual story line is itself intricate. In any plot, at any moment, present action may be suspended by the entrance of a stranger who proceeds to recount the course of his life to date, and the stranger's narrative may itself be suspended for its own internal interruptions. The method is not, strictly speaking, dramatic, because the reader is likely to forget just what question is driving the story onward. The individual scenes, however, are vividly realized. Inevitably, at the end of an installment, one set of characters is left dangling, and a new set is taken up in the next. Ainsworth's creative use of the breaks imposed by the medium (in this case serialization) and his control of lighting effects and angles of vision anticipate the techniques of popular film and television.

Especially useful for creating effects, the topics of history and the supernatural were used by Ainsworth because they supplied cruelty, torture, flight, combat, and chills down the spine, tools for the *manipulation of emotions*. The supernatural elements that appear in almost all of Ainsworth's novels are used primarily for effect; Ainsworth neither explains the uncanny events nor does he (as serious Gothic novelists would) explore the mystery of evil. The supernatural, such as murders, storms, and riots, arouses emotional response; and the unreality of the supernatural may, like the distance of history, help rationalist readers from an industrialized world to release emotions that are no longer acceptable in daily life.

Ainsworth virtually always has at least one character who is disguised, who is using a false name, or who has mysterious, confused, obscure parentage. After two or three of Ainsworth's books, the reader learns that one can never be certain who people really are. The stories of concealed parentage and shifting identity allow readers in the most humdrum circumstances to step imaginatively into the shoes of a countess, a knight, or even royal offspring, secure in the expectation that anyone might turn out to be royalty in disguise. The device is a psychological strategy for Ainsworth, the bourgeois son of a Nonconformist family from a bleak industrial town who chose to become a Royalist, a Tory, and a Jacobite. It is also a paradigm for the escapism beloved by readers who found themselves increasingly interchangeable cogs in the nineteenth century's bureaucratic and commercial machines.

An immediate best-seller, *Rookwood* not only is typical Ainsworth but also might serve as a model to teach generations of adventure writers about constructing narrative books. The opening sentence reveals two people seated in a burial vault at midnight. The rest of the long first paragraph holds the reader's curiosity about these people in abeyance while it describes the architecture and effigies of the mausoleum in order to create an air of foreboding. The first chapter alternates passages of partial exposition with scenes of strong emotion; the second chapter is a chase built from a series of captures, struggles, and escapes. At the chapter's climax, Luke Rookwood—the protagonist—dives into a pool and does not emerge; the chapter ends, leaving him underwater. The next several chapters introduce other characters, new lines of action, and a great deal more historical exposition before telling the reader what happened to Luke.

Rookwood virtually catalogs the devices made popular by Gothic novelists thirty years earlier. In the opening chapter, Ainsworth introduces the inheritance theme and Luke's confused parentage, a death omen, croaking ravens, a Gypsy Queen, a preserved corpse with a significant ring on its finger, an evil Jesuit, a moving statue, a dead hand, and writing on the wall. The rest of the book supplies duels between relatives, a deathbed curse, a runaway bride, a portrait that changes expression, underground caverns, a supernatural summons, a miniature with an inscription that gives a clue to the past, a rediscovered marriage certificate, secret passageways, stormy nights, an interrupted burial, a purely incidental death by thunderbolt, corpses swaying from the gibbet, talismans, a deserted priory where gypsies dwell, a character who masquerades as a ghost, infallible prophecies in verse, love potions, a marriage in a subterranean shrine (formerly an anchorite's cell) with a corpse on the altar, disguises, a bride substituted for another in the dark, a heroine drugged into passivity, a battle between gypsies and highwaymen, and a faithless lover who dies from kissing a poisoned lock of hair. In the final scene, the villainess is shoved by a statue into a sarcophagus, where she perishes.

Like the typical Gothic romance, *Rookwood* has a Byronic hero of mixed good and evil (Luke), a persecuted maiden (Eleanor), and a romantic hero who gets the girl (Ranulph). Ranulph and Eleanor are uninteresting, and even Luke is not very successful; he arouses some sympathy at the outset because he is an underdog, but his transformation to villain is not explored fully enough to be convincing. To berate Ainsworth for lack of originality, however, is to miss the point. He used the traditional Gothic devices for the very reason that they were conventional; they had become a code, an emotional shorthand that triggered known responses. Ainsworth was thus able to control the reader's mood, orchestrate the emotional response, and build to repeated transports of excitement.

The most interesting character in *Rookwood* is Dick Turpin, the highwayman. He appears in an outstanding sequence that has little to do with the book's plot: after accidentally killing one of his friends, Turpin rides with a pistol in each hand and the reins between his teeth, barely ahead of pursuers, the entire distance from London to York. The action peaks every twenty miles or so when Turpin encounters characters from the main plot or exerts a superhuman effort to outfight or outrun the law.

Rookwood was almost totally unplanned; Ainsworth's visit to a gloomy mansion inspired him to attempt a deliberate imitation of Ann Radcliffe. He researched thieves' cant so he could include English highwaymen in place of Italian bandits; he interspersed dramatic songs, comic ballads, and gypsy dances as if he were writing a melodrama for the stage; and he decided how to solve the mysteries as he went along. The most telling indication of Ainsworth's relationship to his work is that he wrote the twenty-five thousand words of Turpin's ride to York in a day and a night of continuous work. He was so fully absorbed by the scene and its emotion that he continuously wrote until it was finished.

Setting remained an essential stimulus to Ainsworth's imagination. The architectural-historical books, of which *The Tower of London* is a good example, were largely responsible for his reputation as a novelist who supplied education along with the excitement. The single setting and the historical events should have helped Ainsworth focus the novel. The story that he chose, however, illuminates the artistic difficulties that grew from his ability to become wholly absorbed in his characters' emotions.

The Tower of London covers the struggle for the throne between the Protestant Lady Jane Grey and the Catholic Queen Mary. The book opens with a magnificent processional, described in exhaustive detail from contemporary sources. Within the frame of this processional, Ainsworth dangles passages of historical exposition, scenes from an assassination conspiracy, confrontations between as-yet-unidentified characters, a thunderstorm, a warning from an old crone, a moment of love at first sight, and other elements that establish emotional tone and provide the narrative hook. The handling of the historical plot line, however, shows how little the story element mattered to Ainsworth; he frequently reminds readers of the outcome already determined by history so that curiosity about the ending is not a prime motive for reading on.

The book is a good example of Ainsworth's visual imagination and the reciprocal influence of novel and stage. Ainsworth worked closely with his illustrator, George Cruikshank. After their previous collaboration on *Jack Sheppard*, they had seen that Cruikshank's illustrations were almost immediately turned into living tableaux for stage versions of the book. Before beginning each monthly part of *The Tower of London*, Ainsworth and Cruikshank visited the Tower together and decided on the exact setting. They examined the architectural detail, explored the possibilities for light and shadow and composing human forms, and decided what events would take place. Ainsworth apparently learned from the stage how to control the source of light. He conceals the identity of characters by showing them in profile against backlight; he blinds onlookers with sudden brightness; and, inevitably, he extinguishes candles or torches at crucial moments.

Ainsworth continued to manipulate feelings by using dungeons, secret passageways, and torture chambers; he describes—with full detail—a martyr burned at the stake and a prisoner gnawed by rats. The humor supplied in a running subplot about three giants and a dwarf is also largely visual. Ainsworth has trouble linking the characters from history with the fictional people acting out his typical story of concealed birth, attempted seduction, and true love. The historical scenes are sometimes well realized, in particular the scenes between Lady Jane and Lord Dudley that dramatize the conflict of patriotism and faith. Nevertheless, Ainsworth's emotional connection to the characters—which makes the scenes so powerful—virtually prevents him from shaping any opinion on the moral conflict. Although the book depicts a struggle in which Queen Mary is generally seen as the villain, he cannot despise her. At any given moment, his sympathy is entirely engaged by the character at the center of the scene he is writing. Thus, even with the Tower imposing unity, the book remains a collection of vivid fragments.

By the time of *Old Saint Paul's*, serious literary critics were beginning to dismiss Ainsworth and his novels. The best they could say was that his books were educational, but Richard H. Horne, in *A New Spirit of the Age* (1844), objected that even the history was nothing but "old dates, old names, old houses, and old clothes" and called *Old Saint Paul's* "generally dull, except when it is revolting." Part of the problem, for critics, was the simple fact that Ainsworth had become so popular. *Old Saint Paul's* was apparently the first novel serialized in an English newspaper. The *Sunday Times* paid Ainsworth one thousand pounds for first rights alone; after the book had run in weekly installments through 1841, he was able to sell it again in monthly parts, in three volumes, and in a steady stream of cheap, illustrated, and popular editions. It is still available in inexpensive form.

Artistically, the book is one of Ainsworth's most competent; a coherent invention integrates the history, the melodrama, and even the comedy. The story follows London grocer Stephen Bloundel and his family through the plague of 1665 and the fire of 1666. Most of the characters are fictional, although one historical person, the libertine Earl of Rochester, provides a unifying strand by pursuing the grocer's blue-eyed daughter Amabel from one end of the tale to the other. The story lines are adroitly interwoven (perhaps because Ainsworth was not tied to actual historical confrontations); the comic subplot involving a hypochondriac servant advances and comments on the main action while it supplies laughs. Memorable minor characters include the plundering nurse Judith Malmayns and the religious fanatic Solomon Eagle.

As always, Ainsworth is best at painting scenes. There are unforgettable pictures of London with green grass in the streets, of live burials and mass graves, of Saint Paul's filled with victims of plague, of King Charles II in a mad masque of death. In *Rookwood* (as in Gothic novels) the past simply provides distance and strangeness; it gives readers an excuse to enjoy vicariously passion, cruelty, and sheer excitement. *Old Saint Paul's* allows the same indulgence of feelings, but the novel's scenes of death and sexual passion have a legitimate relationship to the heightened sense of life and death implicit in the historical events.

The moral outlook of *Old Saint Paul's* suggests one reason why Ainsworth remained popular with middle-class and lower-middle-class readers long after the literary mainstream had left him behind. The grocer Stephen Bloundel is a rock of individualism and self-sufficiency; as a husband and a father he knows what is best for his family, rules with an iron hand, and preserves not only their lives but also (even in the face of fire) most of their goods. The protagonist—Bloundel's apprentice Leonard Holt—is intelligent, industrious, ambitious, loyal, and as successful as any Horatio Alger hero. His master makes him a partner; his suggestions about fighting the fire are so practical that King Charles gives him a title. Furthermore, his girl friend turns out to be an heiress in disguise and somehow, during the week of unrelieved fire-fighting, he manages to acquire new clothes suited to his improved station in life. Although Rochester and his crowd are seen as evil libertines through most of the book, Leonard has no ill-feeling toward them at the end. This paradoxical moral attitude—which despises the upper classes for idleness and sexuality yet rewards the industrious hero by giving him wealth and a title— is virtually universal in the cheap literature of mid-century.

The historical vein supplied boundaries and permissable exaggerations that gave free play to what Ainsworth could do well. He was much less successful when he attempted a partly autobiographical book in the manner of Dickens' *David Copperfield* (1849), his was entitled *Mervyn Clitheroe*; or, when he wrote sensation novels (including *Old Court, Myddleton Pomfret,* and *Hilary St. Ives*). The most popular form of the 1860's (and the direct ancestor of thrillers and detective stories), the sensation novel required tight plotting and a convincing contemporary milieu; Ainsworth's modern tales used his typical devices of misplaced inheritance, concealed identity, and inexplicable supernatural events, but the gaps tended to show when the actors wore modern dress.

If he was not particularly adept at writing sensation novels, however, Ainsworth was good at finding people who could. His middlebrow popular magazines effectively encouraged tight serial construction, the accumulation of incidents, and the interweaving of plots so that each installment could end in suspense. He discovered and encouraged two of the bestselling authors of the 1860's and 1870's, Ouida (Marie Louise de la Ramée) and Mrs. Henry Wood, whose famous *East Lynne* was written for *New Monthly Magazine* between 1859 and 1861 when Ainsworth was its editor. He reputedly read all submissions and wrote letters of advice to young authors. He also knew how to promote himself and was not above giving dinners to cultivate the influential librarian Charles Edward Mudie.

After the success of *Rookwood* in 1834, Ainsworth was a novelist everyone read. His first books were reviewed by leading journals; Ainsworth's *Jack Sheppard* sold more copies on first appearance than did Dickens' *Oliver Twist*, which came out at the same time. By the late 1860's, though, some of Ainsworth's novels were published only in penny magazines and sixpenny paperback editions. By the end of the century, he was generally considered boys' reading, a novelist to be classed with such writers as Frederick Marryat and G. A. Henty.

Ainsworth had not changed; the novel and the reading public had. The division between mass literature and serious literature grew wider as the number of literate consumers for popular fiction burgeoned. Eight of Ainsworth's novels ran as serials in *Bow Bells,* a penny-weekly magazine that featured household advice and needlework patterns; the romantic-historical-Gothic mode continued popular in *Bow Bells* and persisted as a women's escapist form into the twentieth century. At a Manchester testimonial in 1881, it was said that the Free Library had 250 volumes of Ainsworth's works in order to meet the demand by readers from the artisan class. The influence of his technique can be traced, finally, through the Jack Harkaway serials at the end of the century and on into the Hardy Boys books—which share with Ainsworth's best novels the spooky buildings, caves and underground passages, the effective use of lighting, the suspended narration, and the exclamation marks at the end of chapters.

Major publication other than long fiction
POETRY: *Ballads,* 1855.

Bibliography
Ellis, Stewart M. *William Harrison Ainsworth and His Friends*, 1911.
Elwin, Malcolm. *Victorian Wallflowers*, 1934.
Gribble, Francis. "Harrison Ainsworth," in *Fortnightly Review*. LXXVII, n.s. (March, 1905), pp. 533-542.
Horne, Richard H. *A New Spirit of the Age*, 1844.
Worth, George J. *William Harrison Ainsworth*, 1972.

Sally Mitchell

RICHARD ALDINGTON

Born: Portsmouth, England; July 8, 1892
Died: Sury-en-Vaux, France; July 27, 1962

Principal long fiction
Voyages to the Moon and the Sun, 1923 (translation); *Dangerous Acquaintances*, 1924 (translation); *Candide and Other Romances*, 1927 (translation); *The Great Betrayal*, 1928 (translation); *Death of a Hero*, 1929; *The Decameron of Giovanni Boccaccio*, 1930 (translation); *The Colonel's Daughter*, 1931; *All Men Are Enemies*, 1933; *Women Must Work*, 1934; *Very Heaven*, 1937; *Seven Against Reeves*, 1938; *Rejected Guest*, 1939; *Great French Romances*, 1946 (translation); *The Romance of Casanova*, 1946.

Other literary forms
Richard Aldington was one of the principal imagist poets. His imagist poems each render one impression of a scene, and most of them are short. "Whitechapel," which is frequently anthologized, evokes the sounds and sights of a particular section of London. His poems were collected in small volumes, including *Images* (1915) and *Images of War* (1919), among many others. The full range of his poetic skills can be seen in *The Complete Poems of Richard Aldington* (1948).

Aldington conceived masterfully ironic short stories. Set in England in the modern period, these stories frequently pit an individual idealist against a hypocritical society. *Roads to Glory* (1930) and *Soft Answers* (1932) contain the best of these contemporary sketches.

Aldington's translations of French, Italian, Greek, and Latin poems, fiction, and prose number more than twenty-eight volumes, including among others, poems by Folgore Da San Gemignano which Aldington entitled *The Garland of Months* (1917), Voltaire's *Candide and Other Romances* (1927), Julien Benda's *The Great Betrayal* (1928), and *The Decameron of Giovanni Boccaccio* (1930).

Aldington's literary reviews and critical studies demonstrate his scholarship, his genial wit, and his delight in the critical evaluation of contemporary and classical literature. His astounding capacity for work enabled him to produce hundreds of entertaining and informative essays of literary history and criticism. His introductions to the 1953 Penguin editions of D. H. Lawrence are valuable for their personal and critical insight. Aldington's collected short essays, most of them originally published as review essays in periodicals, include: *Literary Studies and Reviews* (1924), *French Studies and Reviews* (1926), and *Artifex: Sketches and Ideas* (1935).

His biographical and critical studies delighted and infuriated readers. Aldington wrote his first biography, *Voltaire* (1925), about the satirist who shared Aldington's skepticism. The next two biographies championed the work of a contemporary novelist, then under attack: *D. H. Lawrence: An Indiscretion* (1927) and *D. H. Lawrence: A Complete List of His Works, Together with a Critical Appreciation* (1935). *The Duke, Being an Account of the Life & Achievements of Arthur Wellesley, 1st Duke of Wellington* (1943) was Aldington's most popular historical biography; for this rollicking life story, Aldington won the James Tait Black Memorial Prize in 1947. The great majority of his critical biographies were published after Aldington ceased to write satirical fiction. Of interest to literary historians are his later studies of contemporary writers: *D. H. Lawrence: Portrait of a Genius But . . .* (1950), *Ezra Pound and T. S. Eliot, A Lecture* (1954), *A. E. Housman and W. B. Yeats, Two Lectures* (1955), and *Lawrence L'Imposteur: T. E. Lawrence, the Legend and the Man* (1954). The Prix de Gratitute Mistralienne was awarded to Aldington's *Introduction to Mistral* (1956).

Achievements

Aldington, judged on the basis of his contemporary influence as a poet, reviewer, and novelist, should be regarded as one of the major modernists; that his current reputation fails to match his achievements evidences the uncertainties of literary fame. His best-selling novel, *Death of a Hero*, despite its enormous popularity in the decade after its publication in English and its many translations, is out of print and will probably remain unavailable. Sparked by the publication of various collections of his letters, there has been a revival of interest in Aldington as a literary figure who knew other writers, but there has not been a comparable resurgence of scholarly interest in his work. His biographical studies of D. H. and T. E. Lawrence were widely read and almost as widely denounced when first published, because they presented brutally honest portraits of their subjects; in the context of current literary biographies, their critical attitude toward lionized literary greats seems measured, and perhaps even mild. Aldington's literary essays are models of clear, evaluative prose. His imagist poems, which were lauded by other poets and critics of poetry when first published, still seem fresh, though the Imagist movement ended more than fifty years ago. Aldington's long fiction appealed to a large reading public, who delighted in his satire, his wit, and his richly detailed portraits of contemporary culture.

Biography

Richard Aldington was born Edward Godfree Aldington in Portsmouth, England, on July 8, 1892. *Life for Life's Sake: A Book of Reminiscences* (1941), his genial autobiography, presents an amusing, cordial, and meticulously honest persona to his readers. That version of Aldington's personality is also celebrated in *Richard Aldington: An Intimate Portrait* (1965), sketches written by twenty-two people who knew him (including Roy Campbell, Lawrence Durrell, T. S. Eliot, Herbert Read, Alec Waugh, and Henry Williamson), and lovingly collected by Alister Kershaw and Frédéric-Jacques Temple. Those letters which have been published—*A Passionate Prodigality*, Aldington's letters to Alan Bird, 1949-1962 (1975) and *Literary Lifelines*, correspondence between Richard Aldington and Lawrence Durrell (1981)—reveal a witty, considerate, and self-deprecating egotist, who could, when angered by incompetence, hypocrisy, or prejudice, portray his target in a pitiless satire; he could also ridicule weaknesses in friends and in writers he greatly admired. The subjects were not always able to see the humor in his satirical sketches.

Contradicting the more generous interpretations of Aldington's character and behavior, there is the unflattering fictionalized portrait of Rafe in *Bid Me to Live* (1960), a novel by H. D. (Hilda Doolittle, Aldington's wife from 1913 to 1938, though their marriage dissolved during World War I). Until the forthcoming biography of Aldington by Charles Doyle is published, a completely accurate and detailed account of his life will be impossible; it is possible, however, to divide his long literary career into four broad phases: imagist poet from 1912 to 1919; literary essayist and translator from 1919 to 1928; novelist from 1928 to 1938; and critical biographer from 1939 to 1957.

From his childhood, Aldington recalled with pleasure long walks through the English country unspoiled by automobile traffic, his observations as an amateur naturalist and astronomer, and freely reading romances and British poetry in his father's large, general library. He also remembered, and satirized in his novels, the sentimentality, patriotic chauvinism, and narrow philistine manners of middle-class, Victorian citizens in the city of Dover. Like the hero of his novel, *Rejected Guest*, Aldington attended University College, London, and, like the hero of *Very Heaven*, he was forced to leave college by his father's financial failure. In 1911, Aldington began his professional career by reporting sporting events for a London newspaper and, in his spare time, writing poetry for publication. He was introduced to Ezra Pound and H. D. by Brigit Patmore, and he soon met Harold Monro, William Butler Yeats, May Sinclair, and Ford Madox Ford.

Aldington's first literary life, which ended in World War I, was given focus by his relationship with H. D. (they were married in October, 1913) and his involvement in the Imagist movement in poetry. Aldington credits H. D. with writing the first imagist poems, influenced by Greek forms, written in the free verse of the French symbolists. The imagists avoided the florid language of Georgian poetry by paring images to concrete, exact details and revising for concise, clear diction. In Aldington's view, H. D.'s aesthetic sense influenced his poetry, and also that of D. H. Lawrence and Amy Lowell. The point of Aldington's exaggeration, surely, is to remove Pound from the leadership of the imagists, and he insists that Pound merely named the group, arranged for the first publications in the Chicago magazine, *Poetry*, in 1912, and organized the first anthology, entitled *Des Imagistes*, in 1914. Critical of

Pound's despotic editorship, Aldington clearly preferred the democratic efficiency of Lowell, who organized and published three volumes entitled *Some Imagist Poets*, in 1915, 1916, and 1917. These three volumes included the work of Aldington, H. D., John Gould Fletcher, F. S. Flint, D. H. Lawrence, and Lowell. Aldington himself organized one more collection, *Imagist Anthology* (1930), but his imagist poetry, which was written simultaneously with that of H. D., belongs to his prewar world. The English periodical that became home for imagist poetry was *The Egoist*, formerly *The New Freewoman*, managed by Dora Marsden and Harriet Shaw Weaver, with Aldington as its literary editor from 1914 to 1916, sharing the post with H. D. once he entered the army.

Aldington's attitude toward fiction-writing and some of his style as a novelist were certainly influenced by Ford, whom Aldington served as a private secretary while Ford was composing *The Good Soldier* (1915), his novel about the collapse of an era, and *When Blood Is Their Argument* (1915), a propagandist attack on German culture. The psychologically unbalanced narrator, the convoluted time of the narrative, and the ranting tone of Aldington's *Death of a Hero* owe much to Ford's writing during the first year of the war. Aldington singles out Ford's war tetralogy, *Parade's End* (1924-1928), for praise, and it is useful to remember that Aldington wrote his own war book after Ford's had been published. Ford assumes an almost mythic place in Aldington's literary history, as one of the last Englishmen to believe in and support a republic of letters. For Aldington, the war destroyed that idealistic world, and the war itself forced a painful break in his life.

Feeling his duty but denying all moral aims of war, Aldington volunteered in 1916 and served until February of 1919, concluding his service as a captain in the army, and returning to England with lingering shell shock. His wartime experiences appear in deliberately phantasmagoric descriptions in *Death of a Hero*, and his postwar nightmares are described in *All Men Are Enemies*. During the war, he had begun an affair with Dorothy Yorke (their relationship continued until 1928) and separated from his wife. A fictionalized account of Aldington's choice between wife and lover may be found in George Winterbourne's complicated relations with Elizabeth and Fanny in *Death of a Hero*, but the physical appearance of the two women has been interchanged. Aldington's version of H. D.'s wartime life, her refusal of sexual relations with him, the birth of her daughter, Perdita (whose father's identity she concealed), her subsequent pneumonia, and her recovery under the care of Bryher (Winifred Ellerman), may be found fictionalized in *Women Must Work*.

The second phase in Aldington's literary career began when Ellerman persuaded her father, Sir John Ellerman, to use his influence to arrange a job for Aldington as a critic of French literature with *The Times Literary Supplement*. With that steady income, and the royalties from his poems and translations, Aldington and Yorke settled in a cottage in Berkshire formerly occupied by D. H. Lawrence. Aldington satirizes the stultifying social hierarchy and the narrow cultural life of provincial England after the war in *The Colonel's Daughter*. During this period, Aldington developed his new friendships with Herbert Read, who shared his experience in the war, and T. S. Eliot, whom he portrayed satirically in *Stepping Heavenward* (1931). In 1926, during the general strike, Aldington, like the hero of *All Men Are Enemies*, worked to bring out *The Times*, and he witnessed the violence between workers and police. He also strengthened his old friendship with D. H. Lawrence, as they discussed their growing alienation from their native land.

The beginning of the third phase in his literary life was in 1928: he began writing his first novel, he decided to leave England, and he broke off his affair with Dorothy Yorke to begin one with Brigit (Ethel Elizabeth) Patmore (their relationship lasted until 1938). By 1928, Aldington was receiving an adequate income in royalties from his accumulated publications, and he was able to move to Paris. There he met Hart Crane, Ernest Hemingway, James Joyce, and Thomas Wolfe, and became close friends with Jean Paulhan. He began writing *Death of a Hero* in Paulhan's resort house on Isle de Port-Cros. *Death of a Hero* was an enormously popular success, was published in numerous translations, and increased Aldington's financial security. During the decade of 1928 to 1938, he wrote seven novels satirizing British culture. His travels through Italy, Spain, and Portugal made him acutely aware of the changing political scene, and, in 1935, he relocated in the New World, as Lawrence had done earlier. After a short period in New York, he moved to a farm in Connecticut, where he remained during World War II.

In 1938, Aldington broke his relationship with Patmore, divorced H. D., and married Netta McCulloch, the ex-wife of Patmore's son. His new marriage produced a much beloved daughter, Catherine, who remained with her father after the marriage dissolved in 1950. From July, 1944, through April, 1946, Aldington worked in Los Angeles, writing movie scripts and completing *The Romance of Casanova*. At the end of that period, disenchanted with American culture, Aldington returned to France.

Aldington wrote no more novels, concentrating on critical biographies, including *Lawrence L'Imposteur* (1954), demythologizing Lawrence of Arabia, with disastrous consequences to his own reputation and sales. Aldington's carefully researched book demolished the heroic myth that T. E. Lawrence had created in *Seven Pillars of Wisdom* (1926), but the reading public chose to remain loyal to the romantic Lawrence of Arabia. That critical biography so damaged Aldington's credibility that his own novels declined in popularity and in critical acclaim. Aldington's satirical fiction became associated with his attack on Lawrence, and a myth of Aldington as the bitter, unbalanced, even envious writer overshadowed most subsequent evaluations of his work.

Financial difficulties resulting from the hostile response to his *Lawrence L'Imposteur* required Aldington to live a quiet life, in a cottage near Sury-en-Vaux. In his seventieth year, he accepted an invitation to visit the Soviet Union, where he was lionized for his sharp critiques of British culture (his equally biting satires of Communist fanatics were quietly ignored). Shortly after his return to France in 1962, Aldington died.

Analysis

Richard Aldington, one of the generation who were young adults in 1914, felt compelled to chronicle the impact of World War I on English culture and society, and all seven of his novels published between the wars explore some aspect of that obsession. Only the first of these novels describes the war itself, but all of them portray the social degeneration which Aldington connected with World War I. This fiction satirizes English class snobbery, moral hypocrisy, selfish commercialism, insensitivity to art, faddish adherence to publicized avant-garde figures, and a culpable ignorance of sexual feelings, which the Victorian generation repressed and the generation of 1914 indulged without restraint, with disastrous consequences.

Aldington's great war novel, *Death of a Hero*, though a popular success, was sharply criticized as a ranting, inartistic piece of writing. D. H. Lawrence, having read the manuscript, warned his friend, "if you publish this, you'll lose what reputation you have—you're plainly on your way to an insane asylum." Early reviewers found the novel's style "uncontrolled," "exasperatingly diffuse," and "puerile." Aldington let himself in for a flood of misguided critical response, because he disregarded the modernist preference for authorial impassivity. Eschewing the example of Gustave Flaubert and Joyce, Aldington found his models in Laurence Sterne and Ford Madox Ford. In *Death of a Hero*, as in Sterne's *The Life and Opinion of Tristram Shandy*, (1759-1767) and Ford's *The Good Soldier* (1915), readers find discursive narration, defense of feeling, confusion of author and narrator, temporal dislocation, polemical intrusion, and a tone shifting unexpectedly from angry indignation to ironic self-mockery.

Working through a monomaniacal narrator, Aldington nevertheless orders his madman's chaotic discourse by suggesting three formal analogies for the novel: a threnody, a tragedy, and a symphony. A threnody is a funeral lamentation which may be written as a choral ode or as a monody; Aldington chose the single-voiced monody, and the narrator's personality, disturbed by his war experience, distorts the story significantly, as a detailed analysis of Aldington's novel reveals. For example, the narrator begins speculating, "I sometimes think that George committed suicide in that last battle of the war," but by the time he narrates the death, the suicide is not a speculation, but a fact. By revealing the death of his hero at the beginning, the narrator rejects suspense; as in the performance of a Greek tragedy, the emotive and intellectual response of the audience is manipulated not by the facts of the case, but by the rendition. Although the narrator specifically mentions Aeschylus'

Oresteia (458 B.C.), the analogy to his tragic tale is by contrast. Both heroes are tormented by Furies, but Athena, goddess of war and wisdom, intervenes at Orestes' trial to give Apollo's logic triumph over the Furies' passion; in George's war, there is no logical resolution, and the desire for revenge creates a war of attrition—significantly George dies in the fourth and final year of World War I.

The symphonic form of the novel is emphasized in the tempo markings given to the four sections. The Prologue, dealing with the postwar world, is marked "allegretto," suggesting the spasmodic grasping for pleasures as a response to the suppressed guilt of the survivors in the 1920's. In Part II, "vivace" sets the pace of England's economic growth in the 1890's, which is connected with the fanatical patriotism of the Boer War, with an affected enthusiasm for culture, and with hypocritical attitudes toward sexuality. In Part III, "andante cantabile" marks the self-satisfied ease of the Georgian era, just before the war. The war itself is treated in Part IV, "adagio," a funeral march commemorating the death of George's generation. As in a symphony, there are several repeated and counterpointed motifs. "Bread and babies" is one of these motifs, linking economic growth and demands with increased population and ignorance about contraception. The "bread and babies" motif is heard in the narration of George's marriage and early career, in the sordid story of his parents' courtship and marriage, and, during the war, as one analysis of the forces making war inevitable. This motif is interwoven with others throughout the narrative, creating a complex pattern unlike the linear structure of a polemical speech. Neither an unedited memoir of a shell-shocked veteran nor a propagandistic tract, this novel is distinguished by its formal composition.

Aldington's deliberate use of sentiment, of repetition, of discontinuities in narrative time, of digressions, and of sudden shifts in mood reflect not only his narrator's postwar hysteria, but also his decision to address his readers' affective responses. Working in the tradition of Sterne and Ford, Aldington wrote a satiric novel that attempted to chronicle the transitional years from 1890 to 1918 in English cultural history.

Aldington's second novel, *The Colonel's Daughter,* demonstrates his control of a satiric narrative and his mastery of psychological and realistic detail, but the subject, Georgie Smithers, while sympathetically analyzed, is a caricature. A plain girl, Georgie fully shares the narrow cultural and moral perspective of her parents, unquestioning servants to the British Empire. Despite her service as a volunteer nurse, she has been untouched by the revolution in manners and morals introduced by war. She still wears her hair long, unbobbed, and her dress resembles a girl guide's uniform. A knowledgeable narrator presents Georgie's actions and some of her thoughts, offering occasional judgments; supplementing the narrator is a skeptical character, Purfleet, whose attitude toward Georgie shifts from amusement, to pity, to infatuation, to calculating irony. Naïvely, she reveals her desire to be married in her declaration, "I adore babies," and she would make any sincere man of her class a docile, faithful wife; unfortunately, there are few such relics left in her world. The one candidate who fortuitously appears, having been isolated from change by his position as civil servant in the colonies, treats her as a sister, and is easily seduced by a more fashionably amoral girl. Georgie reveals her compassionate nature and essential human goodness as she defends a working-class girl who becomes pregnant before she is married. Once Georgie overcomes her shock, she acts generously and intelligently to arrange a marriage, a job, and a home for the girl. As the reader contrasts her character with the mean-spirited people around her, Aldington's critique of English morality emerges. Under Purfleet's guidance, Georgie awakens to her own sexual desires, but she attracts no acceptable mate. After her father's death, Georgie finds herself fully conscious of being trapped in her poverty, in her duty to her mother, and in her solitude.

Appended to the novel is a short satiric and farcical epilogue, in which Bim and Bom, two Russians, attack the economic and social bases of English culture. In style and mood, this epilogue differs radically from the body of this sentimental, psychologically realistic novel, but Aldington's attack on hypocrisy, materialistic values, social injustice, and prudery remains the same.

All Men Are Enemies, Aldington's third novel, presents the odyssey of Anthony Clarendon from 1900 to 1927. Like Homer, Aldington begins his modern odyssey with a council of gods determining the fate of his hero. Athena, goddess of wisdom, gives the hero the gift of loving truth—clearly not the gift of devious Odysseus. Aphrodite places him under her erotic influence. Artemis, goddess of pain in childbirth, promises to stir up hatred for Clarendon. Ares promises him strength. The exiled goddess Isis, whom Aldington introduces to Zeus's council, dooms the hero to seek a lost beauty and an impossible perfection. Until the last pages of this novel, the curse of Isis prevails.

The first part of Clarendon's life includes his intellectual and emotional education, his first loves, and ends in 1914, as he parts from his perfect mate, Katha, an Austrian with whom he has enjoyed an ideal affair. The literary source of Katha's primal eroticism may be glimpsed in the D. H. Lawrentian name of her English aunt, Gudrun. The war separates these lovers, and the remaining three-fourths of the novel chronicles Clarendon's long, painful journey back to Katha.

Aldington skillfully describes the vivid nightmares and suicidal apathy of the war veteran, Clarendon, who condemns the meaningless frivolity and opportunism of postwar society. Clarendon's roots in prewar English culture have been destroyed, not only by his wartime experience of the blind hatred, nor by the deaths, but also by the pressures to conform: he observes, with profound regret, a friend encased by "a facetious social personality so long and carefully played up to that it had ended by destroying the real personality." He avoids that fate by leaving England, separating from his wife, and aimlessly traveling in Europe. By chance, a mutual acquaintance helps him relocate Katha, and they are reunited after a speedy automobile pursuit, a rough boat ride, and a tenderly hesitant courtship. As Odysseus is reconciled with Penelope, so Clarendon and Katha resume their idyllic love. The novel's conclusion celebrates the future happiness of these two battered survivors, their passion freely expressed. However improbable, the romantic denouement seems to fulfill Clarendon's wish that the postwar world not be as superficial as he had believed. Aldington's subsequent novels are less optimistic.

Women Must Work addresses the tragedy, as Aldington sees it, of the liberated career woman, who, despite her idealistic dreams, becomes selfish, unconsciously repeats the mistakes of her parents' generation, and, consequently, fails to enjoy her financial and social success. Etta Morison's culturally narrow childhood in a bourgeois family instills in her a desire to escape from restraint. Introduced to the woman suffrage movement by a friend named Vera, Etta plans her escape, learning the clerical skills by which she hopes to earn an independent living. Her strategy, advancement through education, has been a successful formula for heroes of the *Bildungsroman*, but, for a young woman, education opens fewer doors. Without her family's approval, Etta flees to London, finds a cheap room in a nearly respectable boardinghouse, and takes an underpaid job she hopes will lead to advancement; instead, it leads to near starvation and an improper proposal from her boss.

Unlike the unfortunate, fallen heroines of the naturalistic novel, Etta escapes the corrupting forces of her environment and moves into a better situation. She throws herself onto the mercy of a kind, wealthy woman devoted to woman suffrage and is hired as her personal secretary. As in a traditional romance, Etta falls in love with an attractive young nephew, but she scruples to take advantage of her position within her benefactor's house. The war separates the confessed lovers and then almost unites them, but Etta, after preparing for and promising her lover all the sexual joy she had previously denied him, again refuses, because her brother has been declared missing at the front. The young man, frustrated and uncomprehending, does not communicate with her again until the war's end, but then returns to attempt a reconciliation, only to find Etta pregnant by a wartime lover who has abandoned her. Unable to trust a man's fidelity, Etta rejects her soldier and turns to Vera, and the two women retreat into a pastoral cottage, where Etta's daughter is born. Their futile attempts to manage a farm reflect Aldington's own postwar experience and also demonstrates the impracticality of a pastoral retreat from the problems of the modern world. Casting off the faithful Vera, Etta rises again with the assistance of yet another woman, who launches her on a successful career in advertising—an occupation selected to symbolize the postwar commercial society. There is no moral triumph in her success once she returns to the city. Etta succeeds in advertising because she has learned to use people and to manipulate their desires to meet her own.

Etta's story resolves into a series of renunciations and frustrations which transform her personality, so that the idealistic young woman who longed to be independent becomes a hard, competitive, selfish, and tyrannical success in the business world. She has survived but at a cost that seems too great. Aldington's judgment is clear in his portrayal of Etta's unintentional alienation of her own rebellious, independent daughter. Despite herself, Etta repeats her parents' mistake by determining the life she wishes for her daughter, rather than allowing her daughter the liberty to choose for herself.

In its narrative, *Women Must Work* records the successive failure of several traditional fictional forms. The *Bildungsroman*, the naturalistic novel, the romance, the novel of the soil, and the urban success story all collapse as models for Etta's life. In Aldington's nightmare, the postwar degeneration of cultural and moral norms abandons both the novelist and the hero in a wilderness.

Aldington's fifth novel, *Very Heaven*, a nostalgic return to the outmoded *Künstlerroman*, portrays a sensitive, intelligent, individualist, Chris Heylin, as he encounters his society's hypocritical ethical codes, dullness, and huddling homogeneity. Forced to leave college by his incompetent father's financial failure, Chris confronts his mother's calculating plans for advancement through marriage. Although unable to prevent his sister's unwise union with a rich older man (who later infects her with venereal disease), he denounces her exchange of sex for money. Refusing a similarly advantageous marriage with an older, richer woman with whom he has enjoyed an affair, Chris makes his way alone in the city of London, living in a small, dirty apartment, toiling as an underpaid librarian and flunky to a condescending and conceited man with great wealth and a desire to flaunt it. His life brightens with the addition of a lover who has no sexual inhibitions, and who perfectly understands his problems. (Given the implicit determinism of Aldington's fictional world, the reader wonders what parents and upbringing produced this idyllic modern woman.)

After the hero has apparently attained happiness, in the prospect of a teaching job in a private school, a continuing love affair, and an extended European tour, he suffers a double disappointment, losing his promised job through rumors of his immoral affair and losing the sponsor of his European tour through arguments over religious and intellectual independence. The novel expires in Chris's lengthy meditation on his future, as he faces the sea and contemplates suicide. His meditation concludes with his refusal of despair, his renunciation of all formal codes, and his determination to try once more. The hero's final act, turning to walk toward the light of the town, deliberately recalls the end of D. H. Lawrence's *Sons and Lovers* (1913). This ending, inappropriate to the social reality depicted in Aldington's novel, seems unsuited to the practical character of Chris, whose idealism has been tempered by his contact with postwar materialism. Chris has been portrayed as a survivor, not a dreamer. This odd conclusion belongs to a novel written before World War I.

Seven Against Reeves offers a sympathetic, though comical portrait of a retired businessman beseiged by his ungrateful, socially ambitious family and by a series of leeches—gentry and artists—who want some of his earned money. Despite the punning allusion of its title, this novel does not resemble Aeschylus' tragedy *Seven Against Thebes* (467 B.C.). The picaresque adventures of Reeves, at home, in Venice, and on the Riviera, pit English generosity, shrewdness, and misplaced self-confidence against various exploiters, domestic and foreign. Reeves's gullibility and good intentions dimly reflect England's political history in the period between the wars, though Aldington's aim is less political than moral. The denouement, which is probably farcical, celebrates the authoritarian in Reeves as he asserts his own will over his wayward family; the parallel with the dictatorships briefly mentioned throughout this 1938 novel is unfortunate, for Aldington seems to be echoing or mocking a popularly sentimental conclusion. The father's strict authority over his family cannot be expected to solve their various, complicated problems, nor will his return to business restore moral order to English society.

Rejected Guest, which vividly portrays the life of the idle rich in the late 1930's, originates in the social disruption of World War I. Aldington consciously takes up one of the stereotyped stories, that of the illegitimate war baby, and uses it as a vehicle for exploring the postwar dislocation of values. Exposing the hypocrisy of assertions that, in this modern age, illegitimacy arouses no shameful prejudice, Aldington presents society's repeated rejection of David Norris. David's father was killed in the war; his mother abandoned him to his maternal grandparents to make a respectable marriage. Hurt by the ostracism of his home town and seeking to escape the poverty of his maternal family, David enrolled in University College, London, but lacked sufficient funds to complete his degree. Desperate, he applied to his wealthy paternal grandfather, who, moved by sentiment and remorse, and checked by shame, supplied a stipend large enough for David to live luxuriously, on the conditions that David live abroad and never claim kinship. Suddenly, with the values imposed by years of poverty, David finds himself living with a playboy guardian among the wealthy elite on the Riviera. He adapts, but, through his outsider's observations on the customs and morals of the international set, Aldington continues his satirical attack on postwar society.

Aldington's indictment of hypocrisy and selfishness seems, once again, to be mitigated by eros, as David falls helplessly in love with Diana, an independent and passionate young woman. Swimming, sailing, and making love in the blue Mediterranean, they plan a year-long sail through the tropics. When the Munich crisis threatens war, however, Diana's selfish instincts reassert their control, and she abandons him. David's wealthy grandfather dies without having provided for him in his will, and David is forced to accept a job as an office boy in London. The war baby finds no home among the people who produced him, for, as a living reminder of their failure in World War I, David disrupts their comfortable illusions. The political parallel in Aldington's ironic moral fable may be heard when David's playboy guardian advises him, "Kindly remember that I am only acting in your own interests," and David interrupts: "as the Nazi said when he robbed the Jew." The social elite of England and Europe, playing on the Riviera, choose to ignore their world's political affairs until war threatens to spoil their idleness. Aldington's critique of their selfish indifference is unambiguous.

Aldington's eighth and final novel, the historical fantasy, *The Romance of Casanova*, abandons the social and psychological problems of the twentieth century. A purely entertaining novel, *The Romance of Casanova* presents Giacomo Casanova as an elderly man wondering if he was ever loved for himself rather than for his reputation or his skill as a lover. Answering that doubt, Casanova narrates his affair with Henriette, the romance of his youth. He was captivated with her beauty even before learning her name, and he describes their lovemaking in passionate detail. Their affair was destroyed by his own infidelity and by his ambitious involvement in political intrigues. The novel was perhaps influenced by Aldington's measure of Hollywood's standards, clearly lower than his own as a novelist of the 1930's.

In her *Composition as Explanation* (1926), Gertrude Stein wrote that the most significant effect which World War I had had on literature was to force a contemporary self-consciousness. Her suggestion helps explain not only the themes but also the experimental forms of Aldington's long fiction. His contemporary self-consciousness demanded affective response to the war and its aftermath. He rejected Joyce's method in *Ulysses* (1922), which he found vulgar and incoherent, and embraced D. H. Lawrence's eroticism and cult of the personality. Though he denied that he was an interpreter of his age, he believed that an author's composition was shaped by the spirit of his time. Like Stein, he believed the attitude of the writer had changed as a result of the war; writers of his own age, he felt, were reacting against stagnation. His own fiction, reacting against the stagnation of old forms and the formlessness of modernist prose, provoked much hostile literary criticism yet won a following of appreciative readers. The uneven reputation of Aldington as a novelist validates Stein's paradoxical 1926 dictum: "The creator of a new composition in the arts is an outlaw until he is a classic."

Major publications other than long fiction
    SHORT FICTION: *At All Costs*, 1930; *Last Straws*, 1930; *Roads to Glory*, 1930; *Two Stories: Deserter and The Lads of the Village*, 1930; *A War Story*, 1930; *Stepping Heavenward*, 1931; *Soft Answers*, 1932.

PLAYS: *The Good-Humoured Ladies*, 1922 (translation); *French Comedies of the XVIIIth Century*, 1923 (translation); *Alcestis*, 1930 (translation); *A Life of a Lady*, 1936 (with Derek Patmore).

POETRY: *Images (1910-1915)*, 1915; *Latin Poems of the Renaissance*, 1915 (translation); *The Poems of Anyte of Tegea*, 1915 (translation); *The Garland of Months*, 1917 (translation); *Reverie: A Little Book of Poems for H. D.*, 1917; *The Love of Myrrhine and Konallis, and Other Prose Poems*, 1917; *Images of War*, 1919; *Images of Desire*, 1919; *Images*, 1919; *War and Love (1915-1918)*, 1919; *The Poems of Mealeager of Gadara*, 1920 (translation); *The Berkshire Kennet*, 1923; *Exile and Other Poems*, 1923; *A Fool i' the Forest*, 1924; *Fifty Romance Lyric Poems*, 1928 (translation); *Hark the Herald*, 1928; *Collected Poems*, 1929; *A Dream in the Luxembourg*, 1930; *The Eaten Heart*, 1929; *Movietones*, 1932; *The Poems of Richard Aldington*, 1934; *Life Quest*, 1935; *The Crystal World*, 1937; *The Complete Poems of Richard Aldington*, 1948.

NONFICTION: *Literary Studies and Reviews*, 1924; *Voltaire*, 1925; *French Studies and Reviews*, 1926; *D. H. Lawrence: An Indiscretion*, 1927; *Remy de Gourmont, Selections from All His Works*, 1929 (translation); *Artifex: Sketches and Ideas*, 1935; *D. H. Lawrence: A Complete List of His Works, Together with a Critical Association*, 1935; *W. Somerset Maugham: An Appreciation*, 1939; *Life for Life's Sake: A Book of Reminiscences*, 1941; *The Duke, Being an Account of the Life & Achievements of Arthur Wellesley, 1st Duke of Wellington*, 1943; *Jane Austen*, 1948; *Four English Portraits, 1801-1851*, 1948; *The Strange Life of Charles Waterton, 1782-1865*, 1949; *D. H. Lawrence: An Appreciation*, 1950; *D. H. Lawrence: Portrait of a Genius But . . .* , 1950; *Ezra Pound and T. S. Eliot, A Lecture*, 1954; *Lawrence L'Imposteur: T. E. Lawrence, the Legend and the Man*, 1954; *Pinorman: Personal Recollections of Norman Douglas, Pino Orioli, and Charles Prentice*, 1954; *A. E. Housman and W. B. Yeats, Two Lectures*, 1955; *Lawrence of Arabia: A Biographical Inquiry*, 1955; *Introduction to Mistral*, 1956; *Frauds*, 1957; *Portrait of a Rebel: The Life and Work of Robert Louis Stevenson*, 1957; *Richard Aldington: Selected Critical Writings, 1928-1960*, 1970 (Alister Kershaw, editor); *A Passionate Prodigality*, 1975 (Alan Bird, editor); *Literary Lifelines*, 1981 (Lawrence Durrell, editor).

MISCELLANEOUS: *Greek Songs in the Manner of Anacreon*, 1919 (translation); *A Book of 'Characters' from Theophrastus*, 1924 (translation).

Bibliography

Kershaw, Alister, and Frédéric-Jacques Temple, eds. *Richard Aldington: An Intimate Portrait*, 1965.

McGreevy, Thomas. *Richard Aldington, an Englishman*, 1931.

Smith, Richard E. *Richard Aldington*, 1977.

Judith L. Johnston

THOMAS BAILEY ALDRICH

Born: Portsmouth, New Hampshire; November 11, 1836
Died: Boston, Massachusetts; March 19, 1907

Principal long fiction

Daisy's Necklace and What Came of It, 1857; *The Story of a Bad Boy*, 1870; *Prudence Palfrey*, 1874; *The Queen of Sheba*, 1877; *The Stillwater Tragedy*, 1880; *The Second Son*, 1888.

Other literary forms

During his prolific literary career, Thomas Bailey Aldrich published short stories, poems, essays, and verse plays. Many of his letters are included in Ferris Greenslet's *The Life of Thomas Bailey Aldrich* (1908).

Achievements

Aldrich was one of America's best-known literary figures during the latter half of the nineteenth century. As a poet, he was already a popular success in 1855—at age nineteen. Ten years later, after having his more mature and less sentimental poetry praised by Henry Wadsworth Longfellow, Ralph Waldo Emerson, James Russell Lowell, and Oliver Wendell Holmes, he was considered worthy enough to be included in Ticknor & Fields's prestigious "Blue and Gold Series" of verse. He further enhanced his reputation when he turned to fiction in the late 1860's. *The Story of a Bad Boy* was enormously popular, and Aldrich's short stories soon were a consistent feature of *The Atlantic*. For the rest of his career, this magazine was his favorite place of publication, for its predominately genteel audience enjoyed his serialized novels and his clever, well-crafted short stories with surprise endings.

His stature as a major writer, strengthened during his successful tenure as editor of *The Atlantic*, was certainly apparent in 1884 when *The Critic*, a New York literary magazine, asked its readers to name the forty most important American writers. Aldrich finished seventh, outpolling Henry James, Mark Twain, Walt Whitman, and Bret Harte. Twenty years later his importance was again strikingly affirmed when he was one the first fifteen artists named to the National Academy of Arts and Sciences.

Aldrich's reputation, however, plummeted after his death. Critics such as H. L. Mencken, C. Hartley Grattan, and Vernon Louis Parrington denigrated his accomplishments, dismissing him as shallowly optimistic, blindly conservative, and uninteresting. They believed that he had nothing to say to the modern, post-World War I reader. Aldrich's stock has never recovered, and now he is primarily interesting to those who study the relationship between the genteel tradition and the growth of realism, particularly how his poetry possibly foreshadows the imagists; how his *The Story of a Bad Boy* breaks ground for Twain's "boys' books"; how his female characters reflect his age's literary treatment of women; and how *The Stillwater Tragedy* fits into the history of the American economic novel.

Biography

Thomas Bailey Aldrich was born in Portsmouth, New Hampshire, the sleepy seaport town he nostalgically re-created in much of his fiction—most notably in *The Story of a Bad Boy*, his autobiographical homage to adolescence. An only child, his early years were a bit unsettled because his father, in a restless search for business success, first moved the family to New York City in 1841 and then to New Orleans in 1846. In 1849, Aldrich's parents sent him back to Portsmouth for a better education, but his plans for entering Harvard suddenly ended when his father died of cholera. In 1852, because of his family's uncertain financial state, he had to accept a job as a clerk in his uncle's New York City counting house.

In 1855, after publishing his first book of poems (filled with echoes of John Keats, Alfred Tennyson, and Longfellow) and after having become well known with his sentimental and extremely popular "The Ballad of Baby Bell," Aldrich left his uncle's business. Having decided to be a man of letters, he spent the rest of the 1850's publishing more poetry, beginning his career as an editor by working for the *Home Journal* (1855-1859) and the *Saturday Press* (1859-1860), and writing his first novel, *Daisy's Necklace and What Became of It*— a confused, uninteresting attempt to burlesque the saccharine fiction of "the Feminine Fifties." At the same time, he was moving back and forth between two New York social-literary crowds: the genteel circle which included Bayard Taylor, E. C. Stedman, and Richard Stoddard, and the radical, bohemian circle which included Whitman.

Temperamentally uncomfortable with the rebellious, flamboyant bohemians, Aldrich in the 1860's inevitably found his intellectual home in the more conservative group. He felt, in fact, that the luckiest day of his life was when he moved to Boston in 1866 to be the editor of the periodical *Every Saturday*. Married by then, he settled into the fashionable life of Beacon Hill and became, as he once proudly noted, "Boston-plated." Deeply committed to this genteel society, Aldrich, unlike his friend William Dean Howells, never seriously questioned its values, and his art reflects this acceptance.

From 1868 to 1873, Aldrich turned from poetry and devoted himself to fiction, publishing *The Story of a Bad Boy* and his most famous short story, "Marjorie Daw." In 1874, after *Every Saturday* failed, he moved to Ponkapog (a village twelve miles from Boston) and spent six quiet, happy, and productive years writing poems, novels, and sketches. This idyll ended in 1881 when he replaced Howells as the editor of *The Atlantic*, a position Aldrich held until 1890. After this, he spent his remaining years writing, traveling overseas, and supervising the collecting of his works.

Analysis

Alexander Cowie, in *The Rise of the American Novel* (1948), called Thomas Bailey Aldrich an "Indian Summer writer." By this he meant that Aldrich's art represents a late and pleasantly light blooming of the genteel New England literary tradition. It is an easygoing, entertaining, and edifying art which attempts to break no new ground and usually does not disturb its readers.

Cowie's description is apt because it points to the conservatism and optimism resting at the heart of Aldrich's novels. Always ready to defend the traditional way, Aldrich reacts against the forces which threaten the established, secure order. Thus he nostalgically celebrates the idyllic, old-fashioned New England village while looking with disgust on the modern, industrialized towns and cities; he promotes the beauties of American capitalism while warning against the dangers of labor unions; he trusts the security of orthodox religious beliefs while shying away from the uncertainties of modern thought; and he affirms the ideal of the prudent, measured life while suspecting all types of erratic, impulsive behavior. In his fiction, then, tradition continually collides with the disruptive energy of change; and Aldrich usually depicts the triumph of orthodox values in such a struggle.

To make sure that his readers understand this conservative position, Aldirch clarifies and stresses it through his use of the narrative voice. Continually entering the novels, this voice always belongs to a cultured man who is a mirror image of Aldrich himself. In *Daisy's Necklace and What Came of It*, he is a well-read young writer grappling with a first novel filled with pastoral reveries, literary criticism (including an offhand attack of Walt Whitman), and editorials espousing various traditional beliefs. In *The Story of a Bad Boy*, he is this same young man grown a bit older. He now meditates on his lost youth and lingers over his birthplace, the ancient town of Rivermouth. Like Twain's St. Petersburg in *The Adventures of Tom Sawyer* (1876), this setting is enveloped in a romantic mist: its gigantic elms, its old houses, its crumbling wharves, and its memories of past glories evoke a time of past innocence for the narrator. This persona in Aldrich's next two novels, *Prudence Palfrey* and *The Queen of Sheba*, becomes an anonymous Victorian gentleman who is distanced from the Rivermouth setting, imperiously commenting on the struggles of young love, on the town's foibles, and on the dangers of rash behavior. Finally, in *The Stillwater Tragedy*, Aldrich uses this same gentleman to defend ardently the American businessman against the demands of the radical working man.

Aldrich's faith in the superiority of the genteel value system, a faith embodied in these narrators, helped him to maintain his conviction that art should be optimistic and instructive. He believed that art should never be morbid because it then had a subversive, unhealthy, and depressing effect on the audience. Also, it should avoid the low and vulgar areas of life, for such material inevitably undercuts the beauties of literature. Instead, the artist should work to maintain a hopeful, buoyant, noble tone as he creates wholesome, affirmative, radiant works. Then he will succeed in uplifting the reader. This view of art, which centers on his not upsetting or challenging his audience's existing value system, helps explain Aldrich's reservations about Whitman's and Emily Dickinson's poetry, as well as his antipathy toward the naturalism of Émile Zola. It also accounts for his urge to create happy endings within his novels and his usual unwillingness to stare too long at the darker sides of life. For example, *Prudence Palfrey*, *The Queen of Sheba*, and *The Stillwater Tragedy* end with the young lovers realizing their marriage plans after melodramatically overcoming various tensions and hardships. In each case, the narrative voice makes certain to assure the reader that the couples will live happily.

This is not to say that Aldrich never treats the more somber aspects of human existence. Most notably, in every novel, Aldrich creates orphaned, vulnerable protagonists who experience loneliness and alienation while missing the guidance of strong parental figures. Through them, Aldrich, who shared his culture's devotion to the family, tries to objectify the emotional trauma he felt when his father died. This darker side of his vision also appears when he examines—sometimes in a truncated way—the more irrational sides of human behavior: jealousy in *Prudence Palfrey*, madness in *The Queen of Sheba*, and uncontrollable rage in *The Stillwater Tragedy*. In the end, though, Aldrich usually avoids fully confronting this intriguing part of his fictional world. As a result, he is able to maintain the sunny climate of his novels— although the reader finds it difficult to forget or ignore the moments of danger and sadness haunting Aldrich's Indian Summer writing.

Early in 1869, *The Story of a Bad Boy* first appeared as a serial in the juvenile magazine *Our Young Folks*. Apparently Aldrich felt that it would primarily appeal to an adolescent audience; however, the novel's widespread popularity during the remainder of the nineteenth century indicates that it attracted the older reader, too. To a great extent, its general success stemmed from Aldrich's realistic treatment of his hero, Tom Bailey. He wanted the boy to be different from the saintly and unbelievable little "grown-ups" moralizing their way through the popular fiction of his time. This is why Aldrich calls Tom a "bad boy": it is his striking way of stressing that he will not create a pious stick figure. Rather his boy will be an amiable, impulsive flesh-and-blood human being who, like most healthy children, gets into a bit of trouble. Tom's badness, then, is not that of a subversive, delinquent child. Usually he respects adult authority, whether it emanates from his father, grandfather, or schoolteacher. He also frequently agrees with their criticisms of his occasionally wayward behavior. Thus Tom is Aldrich's realistic version of the genteel adolescent, and the boy's respectability explains why the novel has only the illusion of a conflict between Tom and his community.

This conception of Tom seems quite conventional now, but the boy's "badness" was a refreshing change for Aldrich's audience, who had grown tired of reading about perfect children. William Dean Howells, for example, in his review of the novel praised its resolution to show a boy's life as it is, not as it ought to be. In addition, As Walter Blair notes in *Mark Twain and Huck Finn* (1960), *The Story of a Bad Boy* might have spurred Twain's conception of *The Adventures of Tom Sawyer*. Although Twain was not much impressed when he first read Aldrich's novel in 1869, it probably helped him see the potential in writing a more realistic "boy's book." It also provided Twain with an example of the narrative strategy he would eventually employ, with variations, in his own novel: he saw how Aldrich generated a type of double perspective by having an adult narrator re-create an adolescent's vision of the world. This structure enables Aldrich to create a sense of tension as he moves the reader back and forth between the viewpoints of Tom Bailey the boy, who is spontaneous and sometimes adventurously foolish, and Tom Bailey the man, who is prudent and nostalgic.

When Aldrich locates the reader within the boy's perspective, he concentrates on dramatizing, rather than explaining, Tom's experiences. There are many of these moments, and they accumulate to give a strong sense of the everyday reality of childhood. They include Tom's boring Sundays in his grandfather's religious household, his trips to the woods and cliffs, his scuffles with other boys, his playacting, his winter exploits, and his elaborate pranks designed to upset temporarily the staid life of Rivermouth. These moments also include the novel's darker times. For example, in one of the most haunting scenes in Aldrich's fiction, Tom witnesses the death of his playmate Binny Wallace. The horrified Tom watches as the helpless boy, trapped on a runaway boat, drifts out to sea toward certain destruction. The boat gets ever smaller, the sea grows choppier, and then Binny disappears into the night which suddenly seems to sob with the cries of ghosts. Here, Aldrich lets Tom's consciousness tell the story and consequently the incident is alive in all its terror. Moreover, at other times, Aldrich objectifies his own sense of familial loss through Tom's perception (when the lonely boy yearns to be reunited with his parents and when he grieves over the death of his father); these episodes represent Aldrich's most personal examination of his bittersweet childhood.

Yet in all these episodes, no matter how deeply Aldrich immerses the reader within the boy's consciousness, one rarely forgets the adult point of view always hovering over Tom's story. Employed for many purposes, this voice speaks directly to both the adolescents and the adults in Aldrich's audience.

When the narrator speaks to the young, he becomes the friendly Victorian moralist drawing lessons from his own childhood and instructing them about the evils of smoking, the advantages of a boy learning how to box, the value of working hard, and the dangers in being impulsive. He is the voice of mature wisdom; and his prudence is often set in polite opposition to the values of

Tom Bailey the boy. This strategy, which allows Aldrich to critique as well as appreciate Tom's adventures, thus protects the novel from becoming a hymn to the anarchy of adolescence.

The narrator, however, becomes much more appealing (because he is not so smug or patronizing) when he speaks to adults. Intensely nostalgic, he luxuriates in remembering, with great detail, the Rivermouth of his youth. At the same time, his awareness of being caught in time occasionally makes him brood about death. He thinks about the fates of his boyhood chums who have already died. He also thinks about his dead father—confessing that he has never completely recovered from losing this sacred companion (here Aldrich directly states his feelings through the narrator). With these recollections and musings, Aldrich succeeds in creating a sharp, often poignant juxtaposition of childhood and adulthood. He touches upon the adult reader's desire to freeze time, so that cherished moments and people can be rescued from the always withering past. Most important, in catching this desire, he makes *The Story of a Bad Boy* more than a book only for boys.

Like *The Story of a Bad Boy*, Aldrich's *Prudence Palfrey* is a readable, episodic work set in Rivermouth and narrated by a persona closely aligned to Aldrich's conservative values. Yet it is not nearly as autobiographical as its predecessor, and Aldrich's decreasing reliance upon his personal experiences results in a weak plot. Having to create most of the story out of his imagination or from materials outside the realm of his immediate experience, Aldrich too often falls back on melodramatic strategies to further the plot. The hero John Dent loves Prudence Palfrey, a young woman having the qualities found in the stereotypical heroine of the popular genteel novel: she is earnest, pale, attractive, and, as her name indicates, prudent. The lovers are separated when Dent travels West to make his fortune, for without money, he cannot marry her. In a long section not well integrated into the novel, Aldrich describes John's Western experiences, as the young man makes a fortune, loses it to a villain, and then wanders in despair. In the meantime, the villain—who has an unnatural hatred for John—goes East, enters Rivermouth under the guise of being its new minister, and begins courting Prudence. Finally, in a thoroughly contrived denouement, complete with a secret will, striking coincidences, treacherous schemes, and sudden revelations, John returns home, unmasks the villain, suddenly becomes rich, and marries Prudence.

Such a plot hardly makes for great fiction. Still, in two ways, the work is important to an understanding of how Aldrich's aesthetic vision developed. First, it points to his changing conception of his genteel narrative voice, setting the direction for the magisterial persona of his next two novels, *The Queen of Sheba* and *The Stillwater Tragedy*. Less personal, less nostalgic, and less vulnerable than Tom Bailey in *The Story of a Bad Boy*, the anonymous narrator of *Prudence Palfrey* does not describe and relive his own childhood experiences. He is much more removed from the action which he oversees, and this distance allows him to assume a more objective stance toward Rivermouth. Thus while he obviously respects the town's backwoods tranquility and its preservation of traditional moral values, the narrator also can be quite critical of it. This tougher side of his perspective leads him to comment sarcastically on the pretensions of its wealthy inhabitants, to chide its gossiping, to laugh at its taste in architecture, and to note that it desperately needs new blood because it is in danger of becoming a sterile place.

Besides its employment of the narrative voice, *Prudence Palfrey* is interesting because, more than any of his other novels, it reflects Aldrich's devotion to the ideals of work, duty, discipline, and prudence. At times, it almost seems to be a casebook espousing the Victorian values affirmed by Thomas Carlyle in *Sartor Resartus* (1835); the major tensions in *Prudence Palfrey* invariably arise because its two most interesting characters, John Dent and his uncle Ralph Dent, fail to follow the model of the one-dimensional Prudence, who always behaves with restraint.

John Dent, for example, must curb his immoderate, often self-indulgent behavior before he can be worthy enough to marry Prudence. At the beginning of the novel, the narrator (who repeatedly celebrates the disciplined life) warns that John, whose father has just died, is in a perilous position. Because he is orphaned, he lacks the necessary guidance, and the narrator suggests that this loss of a loving but restraining hand makes John more susceptible to the specious attraction of the romantic quest. For John, this quest is linked to his desire to become suddenly rich in the gold fields: he dreams of a big nugget waiting for him and therefore rejects the Victorian ethic of working hard for long-term, more enduring rewards. Further, he rashly declares that he *will* come back rich or not come back at all.

Like all of Aldrich's undisciplined characters, John suffers. He becomes immersed in the outlaw society of the Western mining towns and yearns for the ordered Rivermouth. He becomes the victim of his dishonest partner. Finally, because of his lack of inner strength, he loses faith in himself after his reversals and sinks into self-pity. All this suffering, however, eventually purges him of his arrogance, light-mindedness, and impetuosity. The chastened John returns to Rivermouth—which he now values for its old-fashioned peace and integrity—and behaves like a conscientious young gentleman worthy of inheriting the money left to him by Parson Hawkins. (Even the Parson's will upholds the Victorian belief in work because it stipulates that John must try to become self-reliant before he can receive the money).

For the first half of *Prudence Palfrey*, Ralph Dent struggles, like his nephew, to control his emotions. Caught between his strong sense of duty as Prudence's surrogate father (the orphaned young woman is his ward) and his increasing sexual attraction toward her, the elder Dent frequently lets jealousy rule him. It leads him to instigate the dismissal of Parson Hawkins, whose friendship with Prudence seems to be standing between Dent and his ward. This action, along with his equally rash championing the new liberal minister without examining his background, causes Rivermouth to lose its conservative, safe old minister and to become victimized by the impostor. In addition, Dent's jealousy makes him react too violently to his nephew's desire to marry Prudence. As a result, instead of helping the confused young man, he spurs John's wild decision to go West.

At times, Dent is almost reminiscent of the evil stepfathers of melodrama, yet one finally sees him as a much more intriguing and sympathetic figure than these cardboard characters. As he confronts, with horror, the true nature of his attraction to Prudence and as he tries to overcome his passion, Dent becomes a complex portrait of a man frightening in his inability to control his feelings, pathetic in his love for the unsuspecting Prudence, and honorable in his efforts not to violate her trust in him. Thus he is potentially Aldrich's most tragic character. Aldrich abruptly defuses Dent's inner conflict before the halfway point of the novel, however, by having him suddenly conquer his passion. In the name of duty, Dent buries it for the rest of the novel—and the reader feels short-changed. It is not unbelievable that the uncle would eventually stifle his passion; but it *is* inconceivable, after the way he has struggled, that the decision should suddenly be so easy. Aldrich appears to have shied away from the full implications of this character, perhaps because he was afraid that Dent's dilemma was about to upset the comic intent of the novel.

The Stillwater Tragedy, Aldrich's contribution to the plethora of economic novels written in America during the last quarter of the nineteenth century, is his most ambitious attempt at long fiction. In his previous novels, he had not openly confronted social issues, although the pressures of the Gilded Age, the Industrial Revolution, and urban life are in the backgrounds of *The Story of a Bad Boy*, *Prudence Palfrey*, and *The Queen of Sheba*. Such issues, however, come to the forefront in *The Stillwater Tragedy*, as Aldrich leaves his usual Rivermouth setting to concentrate on the conflict between business and the rising labor unions in a small New England factory town. Most important, in depicting this struggle, Aldrich uses his fiction to express, as Walter Fuller Taylor explains in *The Economic Novel in America* (1942), a Right-Center, moderately conservative, middle-class economic vision. He attacks labor unions as disruptive forces endangering the American Dream while sympathizing with and often idealizing businessmen.

Aldrich tries to appear open-minded about the labor question, so he creates some "good" workers who are honest, simple, hard-working men. He also has his hero Richard Shackford acknowledge that workers, if unjustly treated, have a right to strike. Yet Aldrich finally fails in his attempt to be objective because he spends most of the novel depicting what he sees as the usual strike: an absurd, destructive act in which radical labor organizers, whom he calls ghouls, mislead the confused workers into betraying their fair-minded employers.

In building his conservative case, Aldrich overtly ties the passions motivating the labor union to one of the primary themes in his fiction: the dangers of any type of excessive human behavior. Therefore he argues, often through his narrator, who is an apologist for American business, that the labor unions' stubborn, irrational demands (especially their not permitting owners to hire apprentices to fill out the work force) ultimately hurt the workers by keeping the economic market unnaturally depressed. Aldrich also argues that most of the labor troubles are caused by foreign anarchists who enter America still nurturing their wild Old World angers. Finally, he explicitly portrays the "good" worker as the man who respects law and order, reasons out his position, and consequently obeys the commonsense policies of his farseeing employer. In contrast, the "bad" worker permits his emotions to rule him; this behavior is evidenced in the actions of the novel's two most important agitators—Torrini, a self-destructive, ungrateful drunkard who uses his eloquence to inflame the workers, and Durgin, a spiteful parasite who eventually commits murder.

To reinforce this theme, Aldrich goes so far as to show that Shackford's weakest moment in the novel is when the young man lowers himself to Torrini's level of behavior. Having always been cursed with a terrible temper, Aldrich's hero becomes outraged by the Italian's insubordination and gets involved in a physical confrontation with the worker. The workers, in response to this incident, admire Shackford for his use of force. Yet Aldrich makes sure that the reader takes a wider perspective, for he has Shackford's fiancée Margaret Slocum—another of Aldrich's perfectly prudent genteel heroines—rebuke her young man for not showing "the beauty of self control." Here, Margaret is certainly speaking for Aldrich, who has pitted two different value systems against each other in this episode to stress the moral superiority of the more sophisticated, affluent one. It is this superiority which makes Margaret's father so magnanimous toward his prodigal workers, causes Margaret to become an administering angel during the strike as she brings food to the workers' suffering families, and leads Shackford to forget Torrini's past abuses as he nurses the mortally injured worker. Obviously, Aldrich does everything he can to make the upper-class characters above criticism.

This obvious bias is one of the three major reasons the novel fails. In devoting so much of his energy to elevating the Slocums and Shackford, Aldrich never treats with any complexity the other side of the conflict. He rarely examines with sympathy or understanding the reasons why workers in the late 1870's felt the need to strike; and he never makes any of the workers more than one-dimensional—probably because he was too divorced from their lives to create a complex characterization.

The novel also fails because Aldrich cannot seem to decide whether he is writing a murder mystery, an antiunion polemic, or a conventional love story. As a result, the three story lines do not cohere into a whole, although they sometimes merge temporarily. Finally, *The Stillwater Tragedy* suffers because Aldrich's intrusive narrator tends to explain away the work's conflicts. After listening to his dogmatic and sometimes strident comments, the reader better understands why Howells frequently lamented Aldrich's reliance on this type of authorial voice. Howells felt that it undercut the fictional illusion and made his friend too often appear more like an essayist than a novelist. Even Aldrich at times felt that such intrusions could be a liability; for example, he criticized Henry James's *The American* (1877) for not being dramatic enough because of its omnipresent narrative voice. This criticism is strikingly ironic in the light of the fact that James eventually made the dramatic method the corner-stone of his fiction, while Aldrich never escaped his tendency to disrupt the dramatic flow of his narratives through editorializing.

Major publications other than long fiction

SHORT FICTION: *Out of His Head: A Romance*, 1862; *Marjorie Daw and Other People*, 1873; *Miss Mehetabel's Son*, 1877; *A Rivermouth Romance*, 1877; *A Midnight Fantasy, and the Little Violinist*, 1877; *From Ponkapog to Pesth*, 1883; *Two Bites at a Cherry*, 1894; *A Sea Turn and Other Matters*, 1902; *Ponkapog Papers*, 1903.

PLAY: *Judith of Bethulîa*, 1904.

POETRY: *The Bells: A Collection of Chimes*, 1855; *The Course of True Love Never Did Run Smooth*, 1858; *The Ballad of Babie Bell and Other Poems*, 1859; *Pampinea*, 1861; *Poems*, 1863; *The Poems of Thomas Bailey Aldrich*, 1865; *Cloth of Gold*, 1874; *Flower and Thorn*, 1877; *Baby Bell*, 1878; *Friar Jerome's Beautiful Book*, 1881; *XXXVI Lyrics and XII Sonnets*, 1881; *The Poems of Thomas Bailey Alrich*, 1882; *Mercedes and Later Lyrics*, 1884; *The Poems of Thomas Bailey Aldrich*, 1885; *Wyndham Towers*, 1890; *The Sisters' Tragedy, with Others Poems Lyrical and Dramatic*, 1891; *Unguarded Gates and Other Poems*, 1895; *Later Lyrics*, 1896; *Judith and Holofernes*, 1896; *The Poems of Thomas Bailey Aldrich*, 1897; *A Book of Songs and Sonnets Selected from the Poems of Thomas Bailey Aldrich*, 1906.

NONFICTION: *An Old Town by the Sea*, 1893.

MISCELLANEOUS: *Poems of Robert Herrick: A Selection from "Hesperides" and the "Noble Numbers,"* 1900 (edited).

Bibliography

Aldrich, Mrs. Thomas Bailey. *Crowding Memories*, 1920.

Cowie, Alexander. "Thomas Bailey Aldrich," in *The Rise of the American Novel*, 1948.

Greenslet, Ferris. *The Life of Thomas Bailey Aldrich*, 1908.

Howells, William Dean. "Mr. Aldrich's Fiction," in *The Atlantic*. XLVI (No-

vember, 1880), pp. 695-698.
Samuels, Charles E. *Thomas Bailey Aldrich*, 1965.

James Grove

KINGSLEY AMIS

Born: London, England; April 16, 1922

Principal long fiction
Lucky Jim, 1954; *That Uncertain Feeling*, 1955; *I Like It Here*, 1958; *Take a Girl Like You*, 1960; *One Fat Englishman*, 1963; *The Egyptologists*, 1965 (with Robert Conquest); *The Anti-Death League*, 1966; *Colonel Sun: A James Bond Adventure*, 1968 (as Robert Markham); *I Want It Now*, 1968; *The Green Man*, 1969; *Girl, 20*, 1971; *The Riverside Villas Murder*, 1973; *Ending Up*, 1975; *The Alteration*, 1976; *Jake's Thing*, 1978; *Russian Hide & Seek*, 1980.

Other literary forms
Kingsley Amis is best known as a novelist, but readers have turned often to his other writings for the insight they give into the man and his fiction. Many of the themes which are explored in depth in his novels are expressed indirectly in the peripheral works. He has published two collections of short stories, entitled *My Enemy's Enemy* (1962) and *Collected Stories* (1981). *Dear Illusion*, a novella, was published in 1972 in a limited edition of five hundred copies. His collections of poetry include: *Bright November* (1947), *A Frame of Mind* (1953), *A Case of Samples: Poems, 1946-1956* (1956), *The Evans Country* (1962), *A Look Round the Estate: Poems, 1957-1967* (1967), and *Collected Poems: 1944-1979* (1979). He edited *The New Oxford Book of Light Verse* (1978). Amis' criticism covers an extremely wide range; in addition to studies of figures as diverse as Jane Austen and Rudyard Kipling, he published one of the first significant critical books on science fiction, *New Maps of Hell: A Survey of Science Fiction* (1960), a work that has done much to encourage academic study of the genre and to win recognition for many gifted science-fiction writers. *Socialism and the Intellectuals* (1957), *The James Bond Dossier* (1965), *Lucky Jim's Politics* (1968), *On Drink* (1972), and four volumes of collected science fiction, edited with Robert Conquest and entitled *Spectrum: A Science Fiction Anthology* (1961, 1962, 1963, 1965) offer further evidence of the extraordinary range of his work.

Achievements
Almost from the beginning of his career, Amis has enjoyed the attention of numerous and influential commentators. Because his works have been filled with innovations, surprises, and variations in techniques and themes, it is not surprising that until recently critics and reviewers alike have found it difficult to make a definitive statement about his achievements. The range of his work is extraordinary: fiction, poetry, reviews, criticism, humor, science fiction, and biography. Of all of his writings, however, his achievement

depends most upon his novels.

Amis' early novels are considered by many critics to be "angry" novels of protest against the contemporary social, political, and economic scene in Britain. The themes include: resentment of a rigid class stratification; rejection of formal institutional ties and relationships; discouragement with the economic insecurity and low status of those without money; loathing of pretentiousness in any form; and disenchantment with the past. Because many of Amis' contemporaries, including John Wain, John Osborne, John Braine, and Alan Sillitoe, seemed to express similar concerns, and because many came from working or lower-middle-class backgrounds, went to Oxford or Cambridge, and taught for a time at a provincial university, journalists soon spoke of them as belonging to a literary movement. The "Angry Young Men," as their fictional heroes were called, were educated men who did not want to be gentlemen. Kenneth Allsop called them "a new, rootless, faithless, classless class" lacking in manners and morals; W. Somerset Maugham called them "mean, malicious and envious . . . scum," and warned that these men would some day rule England. Some critics even confused the characters with the writers themselves. Amis' Jim Dixon (in *Lucky Jim*) was appalled by the tediousness and falseness of academic life; therefore, Dixon was interpreted as a symbol of antiintellectualism. Dixon taught at a provincial university; therefore, he became a symbol of contempt for Cambridge and Oxford. Amis himself taught at a provincial university (Swansea); therefore, he and Dixon became one and the same in the minds of many critics. Like all literary generalizations, however, this one was soon inadequate. The most that can be said is that through Amis' early heroes there seemed to sound clearly those notes of disillusionment that were to become dominant in much of the literature of the 1950's.

Because it seems so artless, critics have also found Amis' fiction difficult to discuss. His straightforward plotting, gift for characterization, and ability to tell a good story, they say, are resistant to the modern techniques of literary criticism. Because Amis lacks the obscurity, complexity, and technical virtuosity of James Joyce or William Faulkner, these critics suggest that he is not to be valued as highly. In many of the early reviews, Amis is described as essentially a comic novelist, an entertainer, or an amiable satirist not unlike P. G. Wodehouse, the Marx Brothers, or Henry Fielding. Furthermore, his interest in mysteries, ghost stories, James Bond thrillers, and science fiction confirms for these critics the view that Amis is a writer lacking depth and serious intent.

Looking beyond the social commentary and entertainment found in Amis' work, other critics find a distinct relationship between Amis' novels and the "new sincerity" of the so-called Movement poets of the 1950's and later. These poets (including Amis himself, Philip Larkin, John Wain, and D. J. Enright, all of whom also wrote fiction) saw their work as an alternative to the symbolic and allusive poetry of T. S. Eliot and his followers. In a movement away from allusion, obscurity, and excesses of style, the Movement poets encouraged precision, lucidity, and craftsmanship. They concentrated on honesty of thought and feeling to emphasize what A. L. Rowse calls a "businesslike intention to communicate with the reader." Amis' deceptively simple novels have been written with the same criteria he imposed on his poetry; one cannot read Amis with a measure suitable only to Joyce or Faulkner. Rather, his intellectual and literary ancestors antedate the great modernist writers, and the resultant shape is that of a nineteenth century man of letters. His novels may be appreciated for their commonsense approach. He writes clearly. He avoids extremes or excessive stylistic experimentation. He is witty, satirical, and often didactic.

In looking back over Amis' career, recent critics have found a consistent moral judgment quite visible beneath the social commentary, entertainment, and traditional techniques that Amis employs. Beginning in a world filled with verbal jokes, masquerades, and incidents, Amis' view of life grew increasingly pessimistic until he arrived at a fearfully grim vision of a nightmare world filled with hostility, violence, sexual abuse, and self-destruction. Critics, therefore, view Amis most significantly as a moralist, concerned with the ethical life in difficult times. Amis' response to such conditions has been to use his great powers of observation and mimicry both to illuminate the changes in postwar British society and to suggest various ways of understanding and possibly coping with those changes. For all of these reasons, one can assert that Amis is on the verge of achieving a major reputation in contemporary English fiction, and, as is so often the case today, his is an achievement that does not depend upon any single work. It is rather the totality of his work with which readers should reckon.

Biography

Kingsley William Amis was born in London on April 16, 1922. His father, William Robert, was an office clerk with Coleman's Mustard and fully expected his only child to enter commerce. His son's intention, however, was to be a writer—a poet, really—though it was not until the publication of his rollicking and irreverent first novel, *Lucky Jim*, in 1954, that Amis achieved his goal. By Amis' own account, he had been writing since he was a child, but without notable success. To read his early poetry is an embarrassment for him, he has said, and his first novel, *The Legacy*, written while he attended St. John's College, Oxford (1941-1942, 1945-1947) and rejected by fourteen publishers, was later abandoned altogether because it was boring, unfunny, and loaded with affectation. He also considered the novel derivative: he felt that he was writing someone else's book while what he wanted to say needed a new story and a new style.

Several factors influenced Amis' development into a writer whose stories and style are unique and universally recognized. His comic proclivities were encouraged by his father—a man with "a talent for physical clowning and mimicry." Amis describes himself as "undersized, law-abiding, timid," a child able to make himself popular by charm or clowning, who found that at school he could achieve much by exploiting his inherited powers of mimicry. This was true not only at the City of London School (1934-1941)—where he specialized in the classics until he was sixteen, then switched to English—but also at Oxford, where he earned his B.A. (with honors) and M.A. degrees in English. His school friends have testified to Amis' capacity for making people laugh. Philip Larkin's description of their first meeting (1941), in the 1963 Introduction to his own novel, *Jill*, suggests that it was Amis' "genius for imaginative mimicry" which attracted him: "For the first time I felt myself in the presence of a talent greater than my own." John Wain has also recalled how, in the "literary group" to which both of them belonged, Amis was a "superb mimic" who relished differences of character and idiom.

This period of "intensive joke swapping," as Larkin called it, continued when Amis entered the army in 1942. He became an officer, served in the Royal Signals, and landed in Normandy in June, 1944. After service in France, Belgium, and West Germany, he was demobilized in October, 1945. He recalls how he and a friend wrote part of a novel based on "malicious caricatures" of fellow officers. This period also was to provide material for such stories as "My Enemy's Enemy," "Court of Inquiry" (based on a personal experience), and "I Spy Strangers," but its immediate effect was to open his eyes to the world, to all sorts of strange people and strange ways of behaving.

Amis' status as an only child also contributed to his development as a writer, for he found himself looking at an early age for "self-entertainment." He satisfied this need by reading adventure stories, science fiction, and boys' comics. During these years, too, Amis became interested in horror tales. He recalls seeing the Boris Karloff version of *Frankenstein* and *The Mummy* and the Fredric March version of *Dr. Jekyll and Mr. Hyde*. Since that time, Amis has been interested in what might be called the minor genres on grounds of wonder, excitement, and "a liking for the strange, the possibly horrific." Amis became aware that the detective story, various tales of horror or terror, and the science-fiction story provided vehicles for both social satire and investigation of human nature in a way not accessible to the mainstream novelist.

Along with his natural comic gifts and his interest in genre fiction, Amis' development was influenced by his early exposure to an English tradition which has resisted the modernist innovations so influential in America and on the Continent today. His dislike for experimental prose, for mystification, may be traced in part to the influence of one of his tutors at Oxford, the Anglo-Saxon scholar Gavin Bone, and to his readings of certain eighteenth century novelists whose ability to bring immense variety and plentitude to their work without reverting to obscurity or stylistic excess appealed to the young Amis.

Amis attributes his personal standards of morality both to his readings in Charles Dickens, Henry Fielding, and Samuel Richardson and to the training in standard Protestant virtues he received while growing up at home. Both of his parents were Baptists, but in protest against their own forceful religious indoctrination, their visits to church became less and less frequent as they grew older. Any reader of Amis works soon becomes aware that there is in his writings a clear repudiation of traditional Christian belief. Nevertheless, from his parents he received certain central moral convictions which crystallized a personal philosophy of life and art. Hard work, conscientiousness, obedience, loyalty, frugality, patience—these lessons and others were put forward and later found their way into his novels, all of which emphasize the necessity of good works and of trying to live a moral life in the natural—as opposed to the supernatural—world.

Analysis

Kingsley Amis' fiction is characterized by a recurring preoccupation with certain themes and concepts, with certain basic human experiences, attitudes, and perceptions. These persistent themes are treated with enormous variety, however, particularly in Amis' novels which draw on the conventions of genre fiction—the mystery, the spy thriller, the ghost story, and so on. Of the fourteen novels Amis has published, his development as a seriocomic novelist is especially apparent in *Lucky Jim, Take a Girl Like You, The Anti-Death League*, and *The Green Man*, his most substantial and complex works, each of which is representative of a specific stage in his career. All four of these novels are set in contemporary England. Drawing upon a variety of traditional techniques of good storytelling—good and bad characters, simple irony, straightforward plot structure, clear point of view—they restate, in a variety of ways, the traditional pattern of tragedy: a man, divided and complex, vulnerable both to the world and to himself, is forced to make choices that will determine his destiny. Built into this situation is the probability that he will bring down suffering on his head and injure others in the process.

In *Lucky Jim*, for example, Amis establishes a comic acceptance of many of life's injustices in the academic world. The novel is distinguished by clear-cut cases of right and wrong, a simple irony, and knockabout farce. Because he has neither the courage nor the economic security to protest openly, the hero lives a highly comic secret life of protest consisting of practical jokes and rude faces, all directed against the hypocrisy and pseudointellectualism of certain members of the British Establishment. While only hinted at in *Lucky Jim*, Amis' moral seriousness becomes increasingly evident beginning with *Take a Girl Like You*. Whereas in *Lucky Jim* the values are "hidden" beneath a comic narrative, gradually the comedy is submerged beneath a more serious treatment. Thus, *Take a Girl Like You* is a turning point for

Amis in a number of ways: the characterization is more complex, the moral problems are more intense, and the point of view is not limited to one central character. Distinguished also by a better balance between the comic and the serious, the novel is more pessimistic than its predecessors, less given to horseplay and high spirits.

In later novels such as *The Anti-Death League* and *The Green Man*, Amis continues to see life more darkly, shifting to an increasingly metaphysical, even theological concern. Contemporary England is viewed as a wasteland of the spirit, and his characters try vainly to cope with a precarious world filled with madness and hysteria, a world in which love and religion have become distorted and vulgarized. Threatened with death and ugly accidents by a malicious God, Amis' characters feel powerless to change, and in an attempt to regain control of their lives, act immorally. Amis' ultimate vision is one in which all of the traditional certainties—faith, love, loyalty, responsibility, decency—have lost their power to comfort and sustain. Man is left groping in the dark of a nightmare world.

In *Lucky Jim*, a bumbling, somewhat conscientious hero stumbles across the social and cultural landscape of contemporary British academic life, faces a number of crises of conscience, makes fun of the world and of himself, and eventually returns to the love of a sensible, realistic girl. This is the traditional comic course followed by Amis' first three novels, of which *Lucky Jim* is the outstanding example. Beneath the horseplay and high spirits, however, Amis rhetorically manipulates the reader's moral judgment so that he leaves the novel sympathetic to the hero's point of view. By triumphing over an unrewarding job, a pretentious family, and a predatory female colleague, Dixon becomes the first in a long line of Amis' heroes who stand for common sense and decency; for the belief that life is to be made happy now; for the notion that "nice things are nicer than nasty things."

To develop his moral concern, Amis divides his characters into two archetypal groups reminiscent of the fantasy tale: the generally praiseworthy figures, the ones who gain the greatest share of the reader's sympathy; and the "evil" characters, those who obstruct the good characters. Jim Dixon (the put-upon young man), Gore-Urquhart (his benefactor or savior), and Christine Callaghan (the decent girl to whom Dixon turns) are among the former, distinguished by genuineness, sincerity, and a lack of pretense. Among the latter are Professor Welch (Dixon's principal tormentor), his son, Bertrand (the defeated boaster), and the neurotic Margaret Peele (the thwarted "witch"), all of whom disguise their motives and present a false appearance.

One example should be enough to demonstrate Amis' technique—the introduction to the seedy, absentminded historian, Professor Welch. In the opening chapter, Amis establishes an ironic discrepancy between what Welch seems to be (a scholar discussing history) and what he is in reality (a "vaudeville character" lecturing on the differences between flute and recorder).

Although he tries to appear a cultured, sensitive intellecutal, all of the images point to a charlatan leading a boring, selfish life. His desk is "misleadingly littered." Once he is found standing, "surprisingly enough," in front of the college library's new-books shelf. Succeeding physical description undercuts his role-playing: he resembles "an old boxer," "an African savage," "a broken robot." What is more, his speech and gestures are mechanized by cliché and affectation. Professing to worship "integrated village-type community life" and to oppose anything mechanical, he is himself a virtual automaton, and becomes more completely so as the novel progresses. Although Amis does not term Welch a ridiculous phony, the inference is inescapable.

Central to the novel's theme is Dixon's secret life of protest. Although he hates the Welch family, for economic reasons he dares not rebel openly. Therefore, he resorts to a comic fantasy world to express rage or loathing toward certain imbecilities of the Welch set. His rude faces and clever pranks serve a therapeutic function—a means by which Dixon can safely release his exasperations. At other times, however, Dixon becomes more aggressive: he fantasizes stuffing Welch down the lavatory or beating him about the head and shoulders with a bottle until he reveals why he gave a French name to his son.

In Amis' later novels, when the heroes' moral problems become more intense, even life-threatening, such aggressive acts become more frequent and less controlled. In this early novel, however, what the reader remembers best are the comic moments. Dixon is less an angry young man than a funny, bumbling, confused individual for whom a joke makes life bearable. There are, of course, other ways in which to react to an unjust world. One can flail at it, as does John Osborne's Jimmy Porter (*Look Back in Anger*, 1957). One can try to escape from it, as will Patrick Standish in *Take a Girl Like You*, or, one can try to adapt to it. Like Charles Lumley's rebellion against middle-class values in John Wain's *Hurry On Down* (1953), Dixon's rebellion against the affectations of academia ends with an adjustment to the society and with a partial acceptance of its values. By remaining in the system, he can at least try to effect change.

Ostensibly another example of the familiar story of initiation, Amis' fourth novel, *Take a Girl Like You*, contains subtleties and ironies which set it apart from *Lucky Jim*. The characterization, the balance between the comic and the serious, and the emphasis on sexual behavior and the pursuit of pleasure blend to make this novel a significant step forward in Amis' development as a novelist.

The plot of this disturbing moral comedy is built around a variety of motifs: the travelogue and the innocent-abroad story, the theme of love-in-conflict-with-love, and the country-mouse story of an innocent girl visiting the big city for the first time. Jenny Bunn, from whose point of view more than half of the novel is narrated, is the conventional, innocent young woman who has not been touched by deep experience in worldly matters. Like Jim Dixon, she finds herself in an unfamiliar setting, confronting people who treat her as a stranger with strange ideas. Out of a simpleminded zeal for the virtues of love and marriage, she becomes the victim of a plausible, nasty man.

Jenny carries out several artistic functions in the story. She is chiefly prominent as the perceptive observer of events close to her. Again like Dixon, she is able to detect fraud and incongruities from a considerable distance. When Patrick Standish first appears, for example, she understands that his look at her means he is "getting ideas about her." Amis draws a considerable fund of humor from Jenny's assumed naïveté. His chief device is the old but appropriate one of naïve comment, innocently uttered but tipped with truth. Jenny, a young girl living in a restrictive environment and ostensibly deferential toward the attitudes and opinions of the adults who compose that environment, yet also guided by her own instinctive reactions, may be expected to misinterpret a great deal of what she observes and feels. The reader follows her as she is excited, puzzled, and disturbed by Patrick's money-mad and pleasure-mad world—a world without fixed rules of conduct. Many of the "sex scenes" between them are built upon verbal jokes, comic maneuvers, digressions and irrelevancies, all of which give life to the conventional narrative with which Amis is working.

Patrick Standish, from whose point of view a little less than half of the novel is narrated, is the antithesis of the good, moral, somewhat passive Jenny. Like the masterful, selfish Bertrand Welch, he is a womanizer and a conscious hypocrite who condemns himself with every word he utters. In spite of Patrick's intolerable behavior and almost crippling faults, Amis maintains some degree of sympathy for him by granting him more than a surface treatment. In the earlier novels, the villains are seen from a distance through the heroes' eyes. In *Take a Girl Like You*, however, an interior view of the villain's thoughts, frustrations, and fears allows the reader some measure of understanding. Many scenes are rhetorically designed to emphasize Patrick's isolation and helplessness. Fears of impotence, cancer, and death haunt him. He seeks escape from these fears by turning to sex, drink, and practical jokes, but this behavior leads only to further boredom, unsatisfied longing, and ill-health.

Also contributing to the somber tone of the novel are secondary characters such as Dick Thompson, Seaman Jackson, and Graham MacClintoch. Jackson equates marriage with "'legalised bloody prostitution.'" MacClintoch complains that, for the unattractive, there is no charity in sex. Jenny's ideals are further diminished when she attends a party with these men. The conversation anticipates the emotional barrenness of later novels, in which love is dead and in its place are found endless games. Characters speak of love, marriage, and virtue in the same tone as they would speak of a cricket game or a new set of teeth.

With *Take a Girl Like You*, Amis leaves behind the hilarity and high spirits on which his reputation was founded, in order to give expression to the note of hostility and cruelty hinted at in *Lucky Jim*. Drifting steadily from bewilderment to disillusionment, Jenny and Patrick signal the beginning of a new phase in Amis' moral vision. Life is more complex, more precarious, less jovial. The simple romantic fantasy solution at the end of *Lucky Jim* is not possible here.

The Anti-Death League represents for Amis yet another extension in philosophy and technique. The conventions of the spy-thriller provide the necessary framework for a story within which Amis presents, from multiple viewpoints, a world view that is more pessimistic than that of any of his previous novels. A preoccupation with fear and evil, an explicit religious frame of reference, and a juxtaposition of pain and laughter, cruelty and tenderness all go to create a sense of imminent calamity reminiscent of George Orwell's *Nineteen Eighty-Four* (1949). No longer does Amis' world allow carefree, uncomplicated figures of fun to move about, relying upon good luck and practical jokes to see them through their difficulties. Life has become an absurd game, and the players are suffering, often lonely and tragic individuals, caught in hopeless situations with little chance for winning the good life, free from anxieties, guilts, and doubts.

As the controlling image, the threat of death is introduced early in the novel in the form of an airplane shadow covering the principal characters. Related to this scene is an elaborate metaphor drawn from the language of pathology, astronomy, botany, and thermonuclear war. Part I of the three-part structure is entitled "The Edge of A Node"—referring to Operation Apollo, an elaborate project designed to destroy the Red Chinese with a horrible plague. As the narrative progresses, the characters are brought to the edge or dead center of the node.

Related to this preoccupation with death is the sexual unhappiness of the characters. Jim Dixon's romps with Margaret are farcical and at times rather sad. Patrick Standish's pursuit and conquest of Jenny Bunn are disgusting and somewhat tragic. In *The Anti-Death League*, the characters' pursuit of love and sex leads only to unhappiness and even danger. Two disastrous marriages and several unhappy affairs have brought Catherine Casement to the brink of madness. An unfaithful husband and a possessive lover have caused Luzy Hazell to avoid any emotional involvement whatsoever. A desire to get away from love impels Max Hunter, an alcoholic and unabashed homosexual, to join the army.

Along with the inversion of love, Amis dramatizes an inversion of religion. In place of a benevolent, supreme being, Amis has substituted a malevolent God whose malicious jokes lead to death and tragic accidents. In protest, Will Ayscue, the army chaplain, declares war on Christianity as the embodiment of the most vicious lies ever told. Max Hunter writes a poem against

God ("To a Baby Born Without Limbs"), organizes the Anti-Death League, and demolishes the local priory. James Churchill cites Max Hunter's alcoholism, the death of a courier, and Catherine's cancer as reasons for retreating from a world gone bad. While, in the preceding novels, laughter helps the heroes cope with specific injustices, in *The Anti-Death League*, laughter only intensifies the horror, the pain. Sometimes Amis shifts abruptly from laughter to pain to intensify the pain. A lighthearted moment with Hunter in the hospital is followed by a depressing scene between Catherine and Dr. Best. News of Catherine's cancer is juxtaposed with Dr. Best's highly comic hide-and-seek game.

Hysteria, depression, boredom: these are some of the moods in the army camp, bespeaking a malaise and a loss of hope from which neither sex nor religion nor drink offers any escape. Although the reader both condemns and laughs at the characters' foibles, he feels a personal involvement with them because he sees the suffering through the sufferers' eyes. Alone, trying to regain control of their lives, they act irresponsibly and immorally. Only Moti Naidu—like Gore-Urquhart, a moral voice in the novel—speaks truth in spite of the other characters' tragic mistakes. His recommendations that they aspire to common sense, fidelity, prudence, and rationality, however, go unheeded.

Although *The Green Man* offers the same preoccupation with God, death, and evil as *The Anti-Death League*, the novel is different from its predecessor in both feeling and technique. The work is, to begin with, a mixture of social satire, moral fable, comic tale, and ghost story. Evil appears in the figure of Dr. Thomas Underhill—a seventeenth century "wizard" who has raped young girls, created obscene visions, murdered his enemies, and now invades the twentieth century in pursuit of the narrator's thirteen-year-old daughter. God also enters in the person of "a young, well-dressed, sort of after shave lotion kind of man," neither omnipotent nor benevolent. For him, life is like a chess game whose rules he is tempted to break. A seduction, an orgy, an exorcism, and a monster are other features of this profoundly serious examination of dreaded death and all of its meaningless horror.

The novel is narrated retrospectively from the point of view of Maurice Allington. Like Patrick Standish and James Churchill, he spends most of his time escaping, or trying to escape, from himself—and for good reason. Death for him is a fearful mystery. Questions of ultimate justice and human destiny have been jarred loose of any religious or philosophical certainties. He suffers from "jactitations" (twitching of the limbs) as well as unpleasant and lengthy "hypnagogic hallucinations." What is more, problems with self extend to problems with his family and friends: he is unable to get along well with his wife or daughter, and his friends express doubts about his sanity. In fact, the only certainty Maurice has is that as he gets older, consciousness becomes more painful.

To dramatize Maurice's troubled mind, Amis also employs supernatural machinery as an integral part of the narrative. The windowpane through which Maurice sees Underhill becomes a metaphor for the great divide between the known, seen world of reality and the unknown, hence fearful world of the supernatural. Dr. Underhill, a doppelgänger, reflects Maurice's own true nature in his selfish, insensitive manipulation of women for sexual ends. Also, Underhill's appearances provide Maurice with an opportunity to ennoble himself. In his pursuit and eventual destruction of both Underhill and the green monster, Maurice gains self-knowledge—something few of Amis' characters ever experience. He realizes his own potential for wickedness, accepts the limitations of life, and comes to an appreciation of what death has to offer as an escape from earthbound existence. For the first time in his life, Maurice recognizes and responds to the loving competence of his daughter, who looks after him when his wife leaves.

On one level, this elaborately created story is a superbly entertaining, fantastic tale. On another level, it is a powerful and moving parable of the limitations and disappointments of the human condition. Unlike *Lucky Jim* and *Take a Girl Like You*, both of which are rooted in the real world and are guided by the laws of nature, *The Green Man*—and to some extent *The Anti-Death League*—employs fantastic and surreal elements. Ravens, specters, vague midnight terrors, all associated with guilt and despair, provide fitting emblems for Maurice's self-absorbed condition.

In retrospect, it is clear that Kinglsey Amis is a moralist as well as a humorist. The early novels exhibit a richly comic sense and a considerable penetration into character, particularly in its eccentric forms. With *Take a Girl Like You*, Amis begins to produce work of more serious design. He gives much deeper and more complex pictures of disturbing and distorted people, and a more sympathetic insight into the lot of his wasted or burnt-out characters. In all of his novels, he fulfills most effectively the novelist's basic task of telling a good story. In his best novels—*Lucky Jim, Take a Girl Like You, The Anti-Death League*, and *The Green Man*—Amis tries to understand the truth about different kinds of human suffering, and then passes it on to the reader without distortion, without sentimentality, without evasion, and without oversimplification. His work is based on a steadying common sense.

Major publications other than long fiction

SHORT FICTION: *My Enemy's Enemy*, 1962; *Dear Illusion*, 1972; *Collected Stories*, 1981.

POETRY: *Bright November*, 1947; *A Frame of Mind*, 1953; *A Case of Samples: Poems, 1946-1956*, 1956; *The Evans Country*, 1962; *A Look Round the Estate: Poems, 1957-1967*, 1967; *Collected Poems: 1944-1979*, 1979.

NONFICTION: *Socialism and the Intellectuals*, 1957; *New Maps of Hell: A Survey of Science Fiction*, 1960; *What Became of Jane Austen? and Other Questions*, 1970; *Tennyson*, 1973; *Kipling and His World*, 1975.

ANTHOLOGIES: *Spectrum: A Science Fiction Anthology*, 1961, 1962, 1963, 1965 (edited with Robert Conquest); *The New Oxford Book of Light Verse*, 1978 (edited).

MISCELLANEOUS: *The James Bond Dossier*, 1965; *Lucky Jim's Politics*, 1968; *On Drink*, 1972.

Bibliography

Barber, Michael. "The Art of Fiction—LIX: Kingsley Amis," in *Paris Review.* XVI (Winter, 1975), pp. 39-72.

Bergonzi, Bernard. *The Situation of the Novel*, 1970.

Bragg, Melvyn. "Kingsley Amis Looks Back," in *The Listener.* February 20, 1975, pp. 240-241.

Calpan, Ralph. *Contemporary British Novelists*, 1965.

Firchow, Peter. *The Writer's Place: Interviews on the Literary Situation in Contemporary Britain*, 1974.

Gardner, Philip. *Kingsley Amis*, 1981.

Gindin, James. *Postwar British Fiction: New Accents and Attitudes*, 1962.

Gohn, Jack B. *Kingsley Amis: A Checklist*, 1976.

Lodge, David. *Language of Fiction*, 1966.

O'Connor, William Van. *The New University Wits, and the End of Modernism*, 1963.

Rabinovitz, Rubin. *The Reaction Against Experiment in the English Novel, 1950-1960*, 1967.

Salwak, Dale. "An Interview with Kingsley Amis," in *Contemporary Literature.* XVI (Winter, 1975), pp. 1-18.

_____ . *Kingsley Amis: A Reference Guide*, 1978.

_____ . *Kingsley Amis: Writer as Moralist*, 1974.

_____ . *Literary Voices No. 2: Britain's Angry Young Men*, 1982.

Dale Salwak

SHERWOOD ANDERSON

Born: Camden, Ohio; September 13, 1876
Died: Colón, Panama Canal Zone; March 8, 1941

Principal long fiction
Windy McPherson's Son, 1916; *Marching Men*, 1917; *Winesburg, Ohio*, 1919; *Poor White*, 1920; *Many Marriages*, 1923; *Dark Laughter*, 1925; *Beyond Desire*, 1932; *Kit Brandon*, 1936.

Other literary forms
In addition to *Winesburg, Ohio*, which some critics regard as a collection of loosely related short stories, Sherwood Anderson produced three volumes of short stories: *The Triumph of the Egg* (1921); *Horses and Men* (1923); and *Death in the Woods and Other Stories* (1933). He published two books of prose-poems, *Mid-American Chants* (1918) and *A New Testament* (1927). *Plays: Winesburg and Others* was published in 1937. Anderson's autobiographical writings, among his most interesting prose works, include *A Story Teller's Story* (1924); *Tar: A Midwest Childhood* (1926), and the posthumously published *Sherwood Anderson's Memoirs* (1942). All three are such a mixture of fact and fiction that they are sometimes listed as fiction rather than autobiography. Anderson also brought out in book form several volumes of journalistic pieces, many of which had appeared originally in his newspapers: *Sherwood Anderson's Notebook* (1926); *Perhaps Women* (1931); *No Swank* (1934); *Puzzled America* (1935); and *Home Town* (1940). *The Modern Writer* (1925) is a collection of lectures.

Achievements
Anderson was not a greatly gifted novelist; in fact, it might be argued that he was not by nature a novelist at all. He was a brilliant and original writer of tales. His early reputation, which brought him the homage of writers such as James Joyce, Ford Madox Ford, Gertrude Stein, Ernest Hemingway, and F. Scott Fitzgerald, were the stories published in *Winesburg, Ohio*, *The Triumph of the Egg*, and *Horses and Men*. Anderson had published two novels before *Winesburg, Ohio* and was to publish five more afterward, but none of these achieved the critical success of his short pieces.

Anderson's difficulties with the novel are understandable when one sees that his great gift was for rendering moments of intense consciousness— "epiphanies," as James Joyce called them—for which the short story or the tale is the perfect vehicle. The novel form requires a more objective sense of a world outside the individual consciousness as well as the ability to move characters through change and development, and to deal to some extent with the effect of character on character. The best parts of Anderson's novels are those scenes in which he deals, as in the short stories, with a minor character trapped by his own eccentric nature in a hostile world.

Another serious limitation to Anderson's talent as a novelist was his inclination to preach, to see himself as a prophet and reformer and to make sweeping generalizations that are as embarrassing as they are inartistic. Even in *Poor White*, probably his best novel, his characters run to types and become, finally, representative figures in a social allegory. In his worst novels, the characters are caricatures whose absurdity is not perceived by their author. Anderson's style, which could at times work brilliantly, became excessively mannered, a kind of self-parody, which was a sure sign that he had lost his grip on the talent that had produced his best and earlier work.

Winesburg, Ohio is without doubt Anderson's great achievement. It is a collection of tales striving to become a novel; indeed, most critics regard it as a novel, a new form of the novel, which, though perhaps first suggested by Edgar Lee Master's *Spoon River Anthology* (1915), took on its own expressive form and became the model for later works such as Hemingway's *In Our Time* (1924) and William Faulkner's *The Unvanquished* (1938). A few of the Winesburg stories, such as "Godliness," are marred by a tendency to generalization, but on the whole they assume the coherence and solidity of such masterpieces as Mark Twain's *The Adventures of Huckleberry Finn* (1884) and Stephen Crane's *The Red Badge of Courage* (1895), which bristle with implications not only about the life of their times but also about the present. If Anderson had published only *Winesburg, Ohio*, he would be remembered and ranked as an important minor American novelist.

Biography

Sherwood Anderson was born September 13, 1876, in Camden, Ohio, to Irwin and Emma Anderson. When he was eight years old, his family moved to Clyde, Ohio, where Anderson spent his most impressionable years. In later life, Anderson remembered Clyde as an ideal place for a boy to grow up; it became a symbol of the lost innocence of an earlier America. Many of his best stories have a fictionalized Clyde as their setting, and his memory of it shaped his vision of the American past and became a measure of the inadequacies of the industrialized, increasingly mechanized America of city apartments and bloodless sophistication.

Anderson's family was poor. Irwin Anderson, a harness maker, was thrown out of work by industrialization and periods of economic instability. Thus he was forced to work at various odd jobs, such as house painter and paper hanger. Anderson's mother took in washing, while Sherwood and his brother did odd jobs to help support the family. In his autobiographical accounts of growing up, *A Story Teller's Story*, *Tar*, and *Memoirs*, Anderson expresses his humiliation at his impoverished childhood and his resentment toward his father for the inability to support his family. Anderson was particularly bitter about the hardship inflicted on his mother, to whom he was deeply attached. He held his father accountable for his mother's early death, and in *Windy McPherson's Son* one may see in the portrait of the father Anderson's view of his own father as a braggart and a fool whose drunkenness and irresponsibility caused the death of his wife. In time, Anderson's attitude toward his father softened; he came to see that his own gifts as a storyteller were derived from his father, who was a gifted yarn-spinner. Even more important in Anderson's development as a writer was the sympathy awakened in him by his father's failures. A braggart and a liar, Irwin Anderson nevertheless had romantic aspirations to shine in the eyes of the world; his pathetic attempts to amount to something made him grotesque by the standards of the world. An underlying tenderness for his father grew stronger as Sherwood Anderson grew older, enabling him to sympathize with those people in life who become the victim of the wrong kinds of dreams and aspirations. The portrayal of the narrator's father in "The Egg" is one example of Anderson's eventual compassion for such individuals.

Anderson's young manhood, however, was marked by a rejection of his father and a worship of progress and business success. He eagerly embraced the current version of the American dream as exemplified in the Horatio Alger stories: The poor boy who becomes rich. Anderson's own career followed that pattern with remarkable fidelity. He took on any odd job that would pay, whether it was selling papers or running errands, and earned himself the nickname "Jobby." After a brief stint in the army during the Spanish-American War and a year at the Wittenburg Academy completing his high school education, Anderson started in advertising in Chicago and moved up the financial ladder from one position to the next until he became the owner of a paint factory in Elyria, Ohio, the success of which depended upon his skill in writing advertising letters about his barn paint.

Anderson's personal life also developed in a traditional way. In 1904 he married a young woman from a middle-class family, had three children, and associated with the "best" people in Elyria. Around 1911, however, contradictory impulses at work in Anderson precipitated a breakdown. He worked hard at the paint factory and at night spent increasing amounts of time in an attic room writing fiction. The strain eventually took its toll, aided by the pressures of conflicting values: Anderson wanted business and financial success, yet, deep down, he believed in something very different. One day, without warning, he walked out of his paint factory and was later found wandering about the streets in Cleveland, dazed and unable to give his name and address. After a short stay in the hospital, Anderson returned to Elyria, closed out his affairs, and moved to Chicago.

Anderson later told the story of his departure from the paint factory and each time he told it, the details were different. Whatever the exact truth, the important fact appears to be that his breakdown was the result of serious strain between the kind of life he was leading and the kind of life something in him was urging him to live. Rex Burbank in *Sherwood Anderson* (1964) remarks that the breakdown was moral as well as psychological; it might also be called spiritual as well, for it had to do with feelings too vague to be attached to questions of right and wrong. Anderson, in his best work, was something of a mystic, a "Corn Belt mystic" one detractor called him, and his mystical sense was to be the principal source of his gift as a fiction-writer, as well as his chief liability as a novelist.

Anderson's life after he left the paint factory in Elyria was a mixture of successes and failures, wanderings from Chicago to New York, to New Orleans, and finally to Marion, Virginia, in 1927, where he built a house and became the publisher of two local newspapers. His first marriage had ended in divorce shortly after he moved to Chicago; he married three more times, his last to Eleanor Copenhaver, a Virginian. Anderson's financial status was always somewhat precarious. His reputation had been established early among Eastern intellectuals who were attracted to what they saw as Anderson's primitivism, a quality he learned to cultivate. Except for *Dark Laughter*, however, which was something of a best-seller, none of his books was very successful financially, and he was forced to lecture and to do journalistic writing. His most serious problem, though, was the waning of his creative powers and his inability after 1923 to equal any of his earlier successes. During his later years, before his final and happiest marriage, Anderson often was close to a breakdown, a state brought on by artistic and financial difficulties.

During his years in Virginia and under the influence of his fourth wife, Anderson increasingly became interested in social problems. He visited factories, wrote about labor strife, and lent his name to liberal causes. His deepest commitment, however, was not to politics but to his own somewhat vague ideal of brotherhood, which he continued to espouse. In 1941, while on a goodwill tour to South America for the State Department, he died of peritonitis.

Analysis

All novelists are to some extent autobiographical, but Sherwood Anderson is more so than most; indeed, all of Anderson's novels seem to arise out of the one great moment of his life, when he walked out of the paint factory and left behind the prosperous middle-class life of Elyria. In his imagination, his defection from material success took on great significance and became not only the common paradigm for his protagonists, but also the basis for his message to the modern world. Industrialization and mechanization, money-making, advertising, rising in the world, respectability—all of which Anderson himself had hankered after or had sought to encourage in others—became in his fiction the target of criticism. This is not to accuse him of insincerity, but only to point out the extent of his revulsion and the way in which he made his own personal experience into a mythological history of his region and even of the modern world. Anderson's heroes invariably renounce materialism and economic individualism and their attendant social and moral conventions and seek a more spiritual, more vital existence.

Anderson's first published novel, *Windy McPherson's Son*, though set in Caxton, Iowa, is clearly based on Anderson's boyhood in Clyde, Ohio, and his later years in Elyria and Chicago. Sam McPherson is a fictionalized version of "Jobby" Anderson, with his talent for money-making schemes; his father, like Anderson's own, is a braggart and liar who frequently disgraces his hardworking wife and ambitious son in front of the townspeople of Caxton. After his mother's death, Sam leaves Caxton and takes his talent for money-making to Chicago, where in effect he takes over management of an arms manufacturing plant. Sam becomes rich and marries the boss's daughter, but, instead of finding satisfaction in his wealth and position, he discovers that he is dissatisfied with business success and his childless marriage. He walks out of the business, abandons his wife, and wanders through the country attempting to find meaning in existence. After discovering that "American men and women have not learned to be clean and noble and natural, like their forests and their wide, clean plains," Sam returns to his wife Sue, bringing with him three children he has adopted. Out of some sense of responsibility, he allows himself to be led back into the darkened house from which he had fled, a curious and unsatisfactory "happy" ending.

Marching Men, Anderson's second novel, repeats the same basic pattern: success, revolt, search, revelation, elevation—but in a less convincing way. The setting is Coal Creek, a Pennsylvania mining town. The hero is Beaut McGregor, who rebels against the miners' passive acceptance of their squalid existence and escapes to Chicago, where he becomes rich. McGregor continues to despise the miners of Coal Creek until he returns for his mother's funeral; then, he has an awakening, a sudden illumination that gives him a spiritual insight that alters his existence. He sees the miners as men marching "up out of the smoke," and that insight and the marching metaphor become the inspiration for McGregor's transformation. Back in Chicago, he becomes the leader of a new movement called the "marching men," an organization as vague and diffuse as its aim: to find "the secret of order in the midst of disorder," in order that "the thresh of feet should come finally to sing a great song, carrying the message of a powerful brotherhood into the ears and brains of the marchers." A great march takes place in Chicago on Labor Day, and though the marching of the men makes its power felt when the day is over, it is clear that the movement, whatever its temporary success, has no future. The marchers disperse in roving gangs, and an "aristocratic" opponent of the movement muses on its success and failure, wondering whether in deliberately turning away from the success of business and embracing the ultimate failure of the marching men, Beaut McGregor did not achieve a higher form of success.

Though a failure as a novel, *Marching Men* is interesting as Anderson's attempt to give expression to his own kind of achievement and as a place to experiment with concepts successfully handled later in *Winesburg, Ohio*. Anderson had given up success in the business world for a precarious career as a writer; he saw himself as a prophet preaching ideals of brotherhood that had nothing to do with political movements or social programs, but that expressed a mystical yearning for order and unity. The metaphor of the marching men was intended to express this vague ideal. The quest for order and brotherhood was a theme to which Anderson was to return in his next novel, *Winesburg, Ohio*, where he found the form best suited to its expression. The format of *Marching Men*, with its lack of convincing motivation and realistic development, exposed the inadequacy of Anderson's marching metaphor for sustaining a full-length realistic novel.

Winesburg, Ohio is Anderson's masterpiece, a collection of interrelated stories which are less like chapters than like the sections of a long poem; within these pieces, however, there is what might be called a submerged novel, the story of George Willard's growth and maturation. Willard appears in many of the stories, sometimes as a main character, but often as an observer or listener to the tales of other characters. There is the story of Alice Hindeman, who refuses to elope with Ned Curry because she does not want to burden him and eventually runs naked out into the rain. There is also Wing Biddlebaum in "Hands" and Elmer Cowley of "Queer," who desperately try to be normal but only succeed in being queerer than ever. There is the Reverend Curtis Hartman, who spies through a chink in his study window the naked figure of Kate Swift and ends by having a spiritual insight: Christ manifest in the body of a naked woman. These minor characters raise an important critical question: What bearing have they on the submerged *Bildungsroman*?

In five stories, beginning with "Nobody Knows" and ending with "Sophistication" and including "The Thinker," "An Awakening," and "The Teacher," George Willard moves from a lustful relationship with Louise Trunion to a feeling of respectful communion with Helen White, discovering the ultimate reverence for life which Anderson describes as the only thing that makes life possible in the modern world. The discovery was one he himself had made in the early years of his newfound freedom in Chicago, following his escape from the paint factory. In "An Awakening," the pivotal story in the submerged novel, George is made to undergo a mystical experience in which he feels himself in tune with a powerful force swinging through the universe; at the same time, he feels that all of the men and women of his town are his brothers and sisters and wishes to call them out and take them by the hand, including, presumably, the so-called grotesques of the other stories.

The precise relationship of these other stories to those that constitute the growth and maturation of George Willard is a matter of continual critical conjecture, for *Winesburg, Ohio* is the kind of book that does not give up its meanings easily, partly because the kind of meaning the book has can only be suggested, but also because Anderson's way of suggesting is so indirect, at times even vatic. Anderson was possibly influenced by the French post-Impressionist painters such as Paul Cézanne and Paul Gauguin, whose works he had seen in Chicago; and his interest in rendering subjective states indirectly might well parallel theirs. Whether such influences were in fact exerted is arguable. What is clear, however, is that Anderson was by temperament an oral storyteller and that he depended upon tone, colloquial language, and folk psychology rather than the more formal structures of the novelist. In *Winesburg, Ohio* he was also a poet, working by suggestion and indirection, a method that produces intellectual and narrative gaps which the reader is obliged to cross under his own power.

One of the chief critical issues of *Winesburg, Ohio* is the nature of Anderson's characters. In an introductory story, "The Book of the Grotesque" (an early title for the novel), Anderson supplied a definition of a grotesque as one who took a single idea and attempted to live by it, but such a definition, while it can be applied to some characters such as Doctor Parcival of "The Philosopher," hardly fits others at all. In an introduction to the Viking edition of *Winesburg, Ohio* (1960), Malcolm Cowley suggested that the problem of the Winesburg characters was an inability to communicate with one another. Jarvis Thurston's article in *Accent* (1956), "Anderson and 'Winesburg': Mysticism and Craft," offers a more compelling view; the Winesburg characters, Thurston says, are all spiritual questers, and their often violent behavior is symptomatic, not of their inability to communicate, but of a blockage of the spiritual quest. Only George Willard succeeds in that quest, when he undergoes, in "An Awakening," a transcendent experience. Burbank, however, in *Sherwood Anderson*, emphasizes the difference between Willard and the other characters of *Winesburg, Ohio* in this way: they are all "arrested" in a state of loneliness and social isolation. George, on the other hand, because he has heard the stories of the grotesques and has absorbed their lives, has managed to break out of a meaningless existence into a meaningful one. Burbank calls George "an artist of life."

Whatever view one takes of Anderson's characters, it is clear that no simple explanation will suffice, especially not the old writer's, though some critics think of him as Anderson's spokesman. Indeed, the prospect of a single idea summarizing and explaining all of the characters seems ironic in the light of the old writer's assertion that such simplemindedness produces grotesques. *Winesburg, Ohio* has its own kind of unity, but it has its own kind of complexity as well. It is a book of contradictory impulses that stands conventional judgment on its head; at times it is funny and often at the same time profoundly sad. It is a book in praise of the emotions, but, at the same time, it is aware of the dangers of emotional excess.

Winesburg, Ohio was well received by reviewers and even had a moderate financial success. It also confirmed, in the minds of Eastern critics such as Van Wyck Brooks and Waldo Frank, Anderson's authentic American genius. He was seen as part of that native American tradition that came down through Abraham Lincoln, Walt Whitman, and Mark Twain, expressing the essential nature of American life, its strengths, its weaknesses, and its conflicts.

Winesburg, Ohio has not been without its detractors. From a certain point of view, the antics of a character such as Alice Hindeman dashing naked into the rain are ridiculous, and Anderson's style at times slips into the mode of the fancy writer of slick fiction; even his mysticism can be ridiculed if one sees it as Lionel Trilling does in *The Liberal Imagination* (1950) as a form picking a quarrel with respectable society. Despite its faults, however, *Winesburg, Ohio* still lives—vital, intriguing, moving. It remains a modern American classic, expressing in its eccentric way a certain quality of American life that is all but inexpressible.

Anderson's next novel was to be a more traditional sort of work with a hero and a heroine and a "happy" ending that included the requisite embrace, though the hero and the embrace were anything but popularly traditional. Hugh McVey, the protagonist of *Poor White*, is the son of a tramp, born on the muddy banks of the Mississippi and content to live there in a dreamy, sensual existence until taken up by a New England woman who does her best to civilize him. Hugh is tall and lanky, rather like Lincoln in appearance if more like Huck Finn in temperament. When Sarah Shepard, the New England woman, leaves Missouri, Hugh goes East to the town of Bidwell, Ohio, where he becomes the town's telegrapher, and then, out of boredom, begins inventing laborsaving machinery. Being naïve and something of a social outcast, Hugh is unaware of the changes his inventions make in Bidwell. He thinks he is making life easier for the laborers, but opportunists in the town get hold of Hugh's inventions; the factories they bring into being exploit both Hugh and the farm laborers, who, without work in the fields, have swarmed into the new factories, slaving long hours for low pay. Inadvertently, Hugh has succeeded in corrupting the lives of the very people he had set out to help.

Clearly, the story of McVey's "rise" from a dreamy loafer into a rich inventor and the changes that take place in Bidwell from a sleepy farm community into a bustling factory town are meant to tell the story of mid-America's transformation from a primitive, frontier society of hardworking, God-fearing people to an urban society that differentiates between the rich and the poor, the exploiters and the exploited, the slick new city types and the country-bred factory hands. It is meant to be a pathetic story. In welcoming industry and mechanization—and for the best of reasons—America has managed to stamp out and stifle the older, more primitive but vital life of the frontier. McVey's "love" affair is less clearly and convincingly done. He marries, is separated, and then reunited with the daughter of the rich farmer who exploits him. This part of the novel attempts to make a statement, presumably, about emotional life in the new industrial period, but it seems contrived and mechanical compared with the chapters dealing with McVey's rise.

Poor White, then, is not an entirely successful novel. There are too many flat statements and not enough scenes; the character of McVey—part Lincoln, part Huck Finn, part Henry Ford—seems at times too mechanical. Still, *Poor White* has its moments; it is an ambitious attempt to deal fictionally with the changes in American life which Anderson himself had experienced in his journey from poor boy to businessman to writer. It is by common assent his best novel after *Winesburg, Ohio*.

After *Poor White*, Anderson's career as a novelist seriously declined. He continued to write and to publish novels: *Many Marriages* in 1923, and in 1925, *Dark Laughter*, which became a best-seller. Both novels, however, betray what Anderson himself condemned in other writers: the tendency to oversimplify the psychological complexities of human nature. Both novels are anti-Puritan tracts, attacking sexual repression, which writers and popular critics of the day singled out as the source of so much modern unhappiness. In *Many Marriages*, John Webster, a washing-machine manufacturer who has found true sexual fulfillment with his secretary, decides to liberate his militantly virginal daughter by appearing naked before her and lecturing her and her mother on the need to free their sexual impulses. *Dark Laughter* retells the story of Anderson's escape from the paint factory by inventing an improbable hero who gives up his career as a journalist and goes back to the town in which he grew up. There he becomes the gardener and then the lover of the factory owner's wife, an experience meant to suggest the interrelation of physical and spiritual love.

Both *Many Marriages* and *Dark Laughter* suffer from Anderson's inability to think through the implications of his theme and to dramatize it effectively with developed characters and situations. The same limitations are reflected in his last two published novels, *Beyond Desire*, a novel about labor unions and strikes, which is badly confused and poorly written, and *Kit Brandon*, the story of a young woman who is the daughter-in-law of a bootlegger. The weaknesses of these last four novels show that Anderson's talent was not essentially novelistic. His real strengths lay in rendering an insight or an illumination and in bodying forth, often in a sudden and shocking way, an unexplained and unexplainable revelation: Wash Williams smashing his respectable mother-in-law with a chair, or the Reverend Curtis Hartman rushing out into the night to tell George Willard that he had seen Christ manifest in the body of a naked woman. Both of these scenes are from *Winesburg, Ohio*, a book that by its structure did not oblige Anderson to develop or explain his grotesque characters and their sudden and violent gestures. In *Many Marriages* and *Dark Laughter*, scenes of nakedness and sexual awakening are made ridiculous by Anderson's attempt to explain and develop what is better left evocative.

After his death in 1941, Anderson was praised by writers such as Thomas Wolfe and William Faulkner for the contribution he had made to their development and to the development of modern American fiction. Though he was limited and deeply flawed as a novelist, he ranks with Mark Twain, Stephen Crane, and Ernest Hemingway as an important influence in the development of American prose style, and he deserves to be remembered as the author of *Winesburg, Ohio* and a number of hauntingly evocative short stories.

Major publications other than long fiction
SHORT FICTION: *The Triumph of the Egg*, 1921; *Horses and Men*, 1923; *Death in the Woods and Other Stories*, 1933.
PLAY: *Plays: Winesburg and Others*, 1937.
POETRY: *Mid-American Chants*, 1918; *A New Testament*, 1927.
NONFICTION: *A Story Teller's Story*, 1924; *The Modern Writer*, 1925, *Tar: A Midwest Childhood*, 1926; *Sherwood Anderson's Notebook*, 1926; *Hello Towns!*, 1929; *Perhaps Women*, 1931; *No Swank*, 1934; *Puzzled America*, 1935; *Home Town*, 1940; *Sherwood Anderson's Memoirs*, 1942.

Bibliography
Burbank, Rex. *Sherwood Anderson*, 1964.
Howe, Irving. *Sherwood Anderson: A Biographical and Critical Study*, 1951.
Thurston, Jarvis A. "Anderson and *Winesburg*: Mysticism and Craft," in *Accent*. XVI (1956), pp. 107-128.
White, Ray Lewis, ed. *The Achievement of Sherwood Anderson: Essays in Criticism*, 1966.

W. J. Stuckey

AYI KWEI ARMAH

Born: Sekondi-Takoradi, Ghana; 1939

Principal long fiction

The Beautyful Ones Are Not Yet Born, 1968; *Fragments*, 1969; *Why Are We So Blest?*, 1972; *Two Thousand Seasons*, 1973; *The Healers*, 1978.

Other literary forms

Although Ayi Kwei Armah is primarily a novelist, he has written and published in other forms as well. Among his short stories, "Yaw Manu's Charm" has appeared in *The Atlantic* (1968) and "The Offal Kind" in *Harper's* (1969). His poem "Aftermath" is included in *Messages: Poems from Ghana* (1970). Armah has also worked as a translator for *Jeune Afrique* and the Algerian-based *Révolution Africaine*. His polemical essay, "African Socialism: Utopian or Scientific," appeared in *Présence Africaine* (1967).

Achievements

Though Armah has become Ghana's best-known writer on the international scene, he would probably prefer to measure his achievement by the reception of his African audience. He is vulnerable to suspicion and resentment both in Africa and abroad. Not only has he remained in exile from his own nation, choosing to live in other African countries, in Paris, and in the United States, but he has also attacked virulently the corruption and materialism of his country's elite and has absolutely condemned the white race (whether European or Arab) for its perverted mentality and for its past and present role in the destruction of African culture. There is an abrasive quality about Armah's early novels—their oppressive naturalism, their sadomasochistic sexuality, their melodramatic casting of blame—that demands more than mere tolerance on the part of his audience. These novels require the reader to go beyond the vehicle to the attitude and the argument that it reveals. A reasonably careful reading will get beyond this abrasiveness and may even dispel the suspicion and resentment, because Armah's real achievement lies in his making the novel not a simple outlet for his venom, but a functional instrument in the African cause. Armah is one of the few truly experimental African novelists. He takes a Western literary form and shapes it into a voice for the African in the modern world.

In his first novel, *The Beautyful Ones Are Not Yet Born*, he turns naturalism and romantic irony into a symbolic, existential statement. In the next two novels, he experiments with narration through multiple points of view. In all three cases, his purpose is to explore the isolation of the individual African in his transformed society. It is evident that Armah is searching for a voice.

In the last two novels the voice is that of the traditional historian and storyteller of the tribe. The Western concept of point of view merges with the oral tradition, and fictional realism merges with history, legend, and myth. Armah does not engage in experimentation for its own sake: technique and form are in the service of the larger human concern, the preservation of a culture and the fulfillment of his role within it.

Biography

Ayi Kwei Armah was born in 1939, in the seaport town of Sekondi-Takoradi in western Ghana. Unlike the unnamed protagonist of his first novel, Armah was able to attend mission schools and Achimota College, near the capital city of Accra, and he then received scholarships to continue his education in America. Like the "man" in *The Beautyful Ones Are Not Yet Born*, however, his early life was dramatically influenced by the effects of colonial rule. During World War II, the British sent Ghanaians to fight in Burma and on other battlefields; the postwar period was marked by economic crises, social unrest and strikes, the rise of political parties, and the achieving of independence.

Armah did not experience directly the events after independence. In 1959, he received a scholarship to attend Groton School in Massachusetts. He went on to Harvard, where he was graduated *summa cum laude* in Sociology. In 1963, he visited Algeria and worked as translator for the *Révolution Africaine*. He saw at firsthand what was happening in African countries after independence: a continuation of the old policies, of African subservience, and of poverty. The novel *Why Are We So Blest?* appears to be a distillation of Armah's experiences during these years.

During his brief return to Ghana in 1966, Armah attempted to apply his American education and his talents as a writer in various ways. He was a research fellow at the University, a journalist, a teacher of English, and a television scriptwriter. His second novel, *Fragments*, appears to be a spiritual biography of this frustrated attempt to adapt himself again to his society. In 1967, Armah was again in the United States, attending Columbia University on a writing fellowship, and then in Paris as editor-translator for the news magazine *Jeune Afrique*. In 1968, he taught at the University of Massachusetts and published his first novel, *The Beautyful Ones Are Not Yet Born*, which traces the Ghanaian experience from World War II to the overthrow of Kwame Nkrumah in 1966 but concentrates on the corruption in Ghanaian society around the time of the coup.

From 1968 to the present, Armah has devoted his energies primarily to writing and teaching. In 1972, he became a professor of creative writing and literature at the Teachers' College, Dar es Salaam, Tanzania, and later taught at the University of Lesotho. In the spring of 1979 he taught at the University of Wisconsin, and he is now teaching in Nigeria. His last three novels reflect this absence from his homeland. They concentrate less on the contemporary scene in Ghana, and more on international and intercultural relationships and on the historical and legendary situations in Ghana as representative of the African experience since the incursions of Arab and Western cultures.

Analysis

Ayi Kwei Armah's novels have provoked conflicting reactions. On the one hand, one can argue that Armah is essentially Western, not African. He is certainly not African in the manner of the Nigerian novelist Chinua Achebe. While Achebe's works are to some degree "social documents," Armah moves rapidly from social realism to a symbolic level, even within his first novel. His succeeding novels move away from external detail toward the inner life and the idealism of legend and myth. Achebe is a realist, Armah a romantic. Achebe maintains an objective stance in his analysis of the colonial and postcolonial eras in Nigeria. Armah's voice is strident and polemical. Whereas Achebe is likely to make the society itself as important a "character" as the individual protagonist, Armah, in his early works at least, focuses on the individual consciousness.

Armah's novels thus bear the obvious marks of contemporary European and American fiction. His protagonists are alienated anti-heroes who deserve sympathy and who are essentially correct in their moral attitudes, but who are ineffectual misfits. The society itself is clearly wrong but defeats the individual moral man through sheer force of numbers, viewing such protagonists as madmen or criminals. In fact, this society is the typical twentieth century wasteland, whether it is in Ghana, northern Africa, or the United States. Armah's Ghanaians resemble black Americans trying to be white in order to participate fully in the technological age. Finally, the protagonist within this society resembles, and often in fact is, the isolated artist—a typical Western figure, not at all African.

One can easily argue that if these are not incidental features, they are at least sketched into a larger picture that identifies Armah with an essentially African sensibility. Judging from his first five novels and not emphasizing simply the early works, one could conclude that Armah is an African writing for Africans. For him, the identity of the African artist is inseparable from the society that he serves. He would not want to be judged according to the Western criterion of art for its own sake, or by Western standards of what makes a satisfactory novel. He tries to make his novels functional within an African context. His primary stress is on the individual African sensibility isolated from his society. His novels are a search not so much for private redemption as for communal salvation, and in this respect he reflects an essentially African rather than Western mentality. He is a philosophical novelist: realism is in the service of, or sacrificed to, an idea. He is a social critic searching for a philosophical and historical framework. His protagonists are social failures but heroes in the cause of the greater Africa. His ultimate purpose is pan-African in scope, and his experimentation with technique and form, even though the source may be Western, is a search for the appropriate voice to further the end of common understanding.

Though the novels individually could not be called *Bildungsromans*, together they appear, in retrospect, to trace the individual protagonist from confusion and frustration to a sense of wholeness and communal belonging. The "man" in *The Beautyful Ones Are Not Yet Born* cannot be sure of his own identity or his moral values because he receives no reinforcement from his society, while Densu in the fifth novel, *The Healers*, rejects his immediate society and joins a small outcast community that understands the larger African tradition.

Armah has some interesting things to say sociologically as well. Like most contemporary African novelists, he deals with the traumatic experience of colonialism, the rapid change from traditional to modern society, the effects of the slave trade and of Western influence in general, the difficulties of adapting to the technological age, the political corruption immediately after independence, and the cultural vacuum. His novels move from the narrow confines of one Ghanaian city in *The Beautyful Ones Are Not Yet Born* to the larger international scene of America, Europe, and North Africa, in order to show at firsthand those forces that helped create the filth and artificiality surrounding his protagonist. In *Two Thousand Seasons* and *The Healers*, Armah leaves the 1960's to give a picture of African society in the distant and recent past. In general, he argues that foreign exploitation has perverted the traditional communal values, which are, if anything, superior to the ones that have replaced them. What seems to concern Armah particularly, however, are the psychological implications of this displacement. The protagonists of the second two novels are mentally disturbed and require professional therapy or convalescence. Juana of *Fragments* is a psychologist, and the outcast priests of *Two Thousand Seasons* and *The Healers* are practitioners of traditional therapies. The essential problem that Armah identifies is the impotence and extreme depression of the sensitive individual rejected by the westernized African society. In addition, Armah explores the nightmares and dreams of his frustrated protagonists, and in the last two novels seeks an answer to frustration through the revival of racial consciousness in myth and legend. The ultimate purpose of his novels is therapeutic.

If the central issue in Armah's novels is the relationship between the individual and his community, then *The Beautyful Ones Are Not Yet Born* is a depressing omen. The main character, the center of consciousness, has no name—not so much because he represents all men or even because he represents the man of integrity, though these are possible readings, but because he is anonymous. Society does not recognize his existence. He is an outcast because he attempts to hold on to moral values while the rest of society has succumbed to bribery, corruption, and materialism. This isolation is total.

Even his own family urges him to advance himself for their benefit within the corrupt system. The isolation, however, extends beyond family and community. Even in this first novel, Armah introduces the historical context. The "man" is trapped within the present. He has no sense of belonging to a Ghanaian or to an African tradition. He cannot identify the source of his integrity or of his moral judgment. Hence, he resides in a historical void which makes him question the very values that give him sustenance. Honesty seems unnatural, cruel, obstinate, even criminal and insane.

The story evolves at a specific time in the contemporary history of Ghana. Though Armah does not give dates, it is clear that the early episodes (Chapters 1-12) take place late in Kwame Nkrumah's reign, in the mid-1960's. The final three chapters deal with the hours just after Nkrumah's fall in February, 1966. The "man" is a controller for the railroad, a husband, and the father of two children. Armah describes in naturalistic detail a day in the man's life, his journey to and from work, the oppressiveness of the physical surroundings, the boring, insignificant responsibilities of his job, and the return home to an unsympathetic and accusing wife. The only dramatic event in these first chapters is the man's rejection of a bribe. To seek relief and reassurance, he pays a visit to his former teacher, who shares his moral awareness and can explain to some extent the origin of the present malaise, but who has withdrawn from society. The teacher has no family and hence no compelling responsibility. He refuses to participate in the corruption but also declines to fight it. All he can do for the man is understand his situation. He is, nevertheless, the first of a series of figures in the five novels who represent the wisdom of a way of life that Ghana no longer knows. Within this realistic and cynical first novel it is not surprising that the teacher lacks the confidence and the vision necessary to save the man or his society. In spite of this, Armah leaves no doubt as to the importance of the teacher and his philosophical appraisal of contemporary Ghana. He places the visit at the very center of the novel. From this point, the man must accept total isolation. He cannot lean on his elder and former guide: he must find his own solution.

The problem that faces the man in the final third of the novel involves him in the corruption of an old classmate who is a minister under Nkrumah. His wife and mother-in-law agree to participate in the illegal purchase of a fishing boat, which is primarily for the benefit of Minister Koomsan. When the man refuses complicity, he becomes even more of an outcast within the family. His wife constantly measures him against the successful Koomsan, who has surrounded himself with the things of modern civilization. The last three chapters, however, reverse the situation. Nkrumah falls. Koomsan, a pitifully frightened victim of the coup, comes to the man for aid. The two escape from the house just as the authorities arrive, and the man leads him to the fishing boat and to exile. The man himself swims back to shore and to his family. Though he has involved himself in the corruption he despises, the act of saving Koomsan must be seen as a heroic and humane gesture. The man's wife, at least, now recognizes his courage and his worth. The novel thus moves from almost total submergence in the repulsive details of daily life to a romantic but ironic act of heroism, whose ultimate significance is neverthless left ambiguous.

Armah is already suggesting the larger movement from realism to myth in the figurative and even symbolic dimension of the narrative. What first strikes the reader's attention, in fact overwhelms him, is the vivid and disgusting insistence on the filth, the excrement, and the vomit that one touches and breathes in the city. Yet this physical reality is at the same time the political and moral corruption that the society discharges as it continues to pursue and consume the "things" of Western technology. Koomsan's escape through the latrine is symbolically a wallowing in his own excrement. A second symbol special to this novel is the chichidodo bird, which despises excrement but subsists on the worms that the excrement nourishes: the man, as much as he may try to remain free of taint, is implicated in the social guilt. Finally, Armah uses a third image, the stream, that recurs in all four of the other novels. He seems to identify water in a traditional way as a purifying agent. During one of his walks, the man notices, in an otherwise muddy stream, a perfectly clear current which seems to have no source. He associates it with a gleam of light—his own moral awareness—a clarity of vision that he cannot trace to any source. He sets this clarity against the brightness of new things imported from the West, but it is not strong enough or permanent enough to give him hope. In spite of his heroism, his baptismal dip in the ocean, and his "rebirth," he still must recognize at the end that "the beautyful ones are not yet born."

In *Fragments*, Armah continues the exploration of the individual and his obligation to both family and community. The scene again takes place in the later 1960's, but the situations are considerably changed. Baako Onipa (the hero now has a name, which means "Only Person") is a "been-to," a member of the educated elite who has spent five years studying in the United States. In this respect, he resembles Armah himself, an American-educated intellectual who must have had similar difficulties readjusting to Ghanaian society. Like Armah, Baako is a writer searching for a role within his newly independent nation. No longer is the protagonist buried in lower-class poverty. His education gives him access to prominent men in the community and to the "things" of modern technology. He thus has the means to satisfy the expectations of his family, especially his mother. He resembles the man, however, in his inability to sacrifice his personal integrity in order to take advantage of his opportunities. In a sense, his situation is even more critical than that of the man. He is a highly sensitive artist. Whereas the man has perceived the "madness" of his obstinacy, Baako has already experienced insanity in America and is on the edge of it again throughout this novel, the title of which, *Fragments*, is thus particularly appropriate.

The story does not follow a clear chronological path, because Armah has chosen to present it through three centers of consciousness. The emphasis is thus not on the exterior world but, much more obviously than in *The Beautyful Ones Are Not Yet Born*, on the psychological responses to the world of the two main characters, Baako and Juana, a Puerto Rican psychologist who becomes Baako's confidante, and of Baako's grandmother, Naana, who represents the traditional wisdom of the people. The novel opens with Naana recalling Baako's ritual departure five years before and her anticipation of his cyclical return. Baako does return, unannounced however, to avoid the inevitable ritual ceremony. He dreads to face his family because he brings no gifts and because he knows that he will be unable to fulfill his mother's expectations. His mother expects what the man's wife expected in *The Beautyful Ones Are Not Yet Born*, money and the comforts of the modern age. Baako, in his rebellion against this imitation of Western values, goes to his former teacher, Ocran, for advice. Ocran has himself chosen to pursue his profession as an artist in solitude, because he sees no possibility for useful work within the contemporary Ghanaian society. Against Ocran's advice, the less experienced Baako has decided to make the attempt by turning his talents as novelist to a more public role as a television scriptwriter. He hopes to transform popular Ghanaian myths into scripts for television, and in general to raise the consciousness of the people by introducing them to the true traditions of Ghana. The authorities, preferring to use the television screen as an instrument of propaganda, reject this proposal as dangerous. Baako goes back to the privacy of the writing table and, thus isolated, gradually loses his mind. His family places him in an asylum, from which he is about to be rescued by Juana as the novel closes.

The threat of insanity, in fact, has plagued Baako from the very beginning. He goes to Juana for help early in the novel. She becomes his lover and, along with Ocran, his spiritual guide. The novel thus ends as does *The Beautyful Ones Are Not Yet Born*, ambiguously—but with a note of hope, and with the nucleus of a new community, two Ghanaians and the outsider, Juana, who represents not the evils of white society, but the sensitivities of a minority. Furthermore, Ocran seems to offer a temporary compromise between the two extremes that have driven Baako to insanity, a compromise that Armah develops in the later novels. Whereas society and family demand that Baako yield to their values, and Baako, while recognizing his inherent need for identity within the community, must maintain his integrity, Ocran proposes a kind of synthesis: Baako cannot expect to achieve his goal immediately. He must submit to a temporary isolation from the present society and work for the larger community of the future. Naana reinforces this view as her commentary closes the novel with a picture of contemporary Ghana in fragments. This novel thus has raised the argument to a more philosophical level than that of *The Beautyful Ones Are Not Yet Born* by using four different characters who reflect on the problem of the perceptive individual within a materialistic society.

In other ways, too, Armah moves away from the naturalism of his first novel. Even the naturalistic scenes, such as the killing of the "mad" dog, are obviously symbolic of something beyond themselves. Just as Juana observes a crowd of soldiers who close in on a dog that they only suspect to be mad, so she watches the community and the family judge and incarcerate Baako for his "insane" ideas. The novel also incorporates ritualistic and religious elements. Naana contrasts the unifying role of traditional ritual with the fragmentation of the present. The mother appeals to an itinerant, spiritualist preacher to aid her in praying for Baako's return. Baako and Juana discuss the similarities between Catholicism and animism, as opposed to the isolating force of Protestantism. Baako is concerned in particular with myth: he contrasts his overseas experience with the traditional hero's departure and triumphal return to save the community. He and Juana repeat the myth of Mame Water, who rises from the sea periodically to meet her lover and give him special powers, but at the same time leaves him with an excruciating sense of isolation. The water itself, like the stream from *The Beautyful Ones Are Not Yet Born*, flows into *Fragments*. Baako pictures himself swimming upstream against a cataract; water still seems to be a purifying force and the stream itself the natural flow of history.

In retrospect, *Why Are We So Blest?* appears to be a transition between Armah's first two novels and the mythical ones to follow. It continues the trend away from realistic description toward a study of multiple consciousness, a philosophical reflection, a larger international context, and an emphasis on personal relationships. The time of the novel, however, remains the same, the mid-to-late 1960's, as does the central premise: the individual isolated from his community and hence from his own identity. Again, Armah seems to be drawing from his own experience, this time as a student in an American university, and from the guilt feelings that inevitably arise in one who is given special treatment while his country suffers from the very hands that feed him. In a sense, the Ghanaian character, Modin, is Baako receiving the education that is so useless to him upon his return, though Armah has a far different fate for this avatar. The other major African character, Solo, shares with Modin a situation that Armah has not created in the first two novels. They both remain abroad, completely detached from their societies, Modin as a student and would-be revolutionary, Solo as a disillusioned revolutionary in exile. Solo, the dispassionate observer, finds in Modin a reincarnation (with variations) of his own past fascination with revolution and with a Western woman. This third major character is Aimée Reitsch, a white American coed of German ancestry, whose perverted fascination with Africa and with Modin precipitates his destruction.

The narrative in *Why Are We So Blest?* resembles that of *Fragments* in that it, too, has three centers of consciousness. The two principal actors in the drama, Modin and Aimée, have kept journals about their experiences, which Aimée leaves with Solo after Modin's death. Solo thus functions as editor, providing personal information and commentary and arranging the journal entries to reconstruct the story of their lives and his encounter with them in northern Africa. He opens the novel with an account of his own life before he met them and fills out this autobiography at intervals throughout the book. He is a reviewer of books eking out an existence in the fictional town of Laccryville (Algiers) and making occasional visits to the headquarters of a revolutionary organization which he once wished to join.

The story of Modin and Aimée, as Solo reconstructs it, goes back to Modin's days as a scholarship student in African Studies at Harvard. Immediately after arriving, he receives a warning from Naita, the black secretary of his sponsor, that he must not trust those who have brought him to America. They actually consider him their property. Modin eventually realizes that she is right about the white race in general being the black man's destroyer, but makes the mistake of considering Aimée an exception. He leaves for Africa with her to join the revolutionary organization in Laccryville. Its leaders are suspicious of Aimée and hence reject them both. Solo meets them and would like to do something to save Modin, but realizes that he is doomed. Modin and Aimée take off on a futile hitchhiking journey across the Sahara, only to be picked up by white male racists who sexually abuse them and leave Modin to die. Aimée returns to her middle-class life in America and Solo is left frustrated in his isolation. It would seem, however, that Solo as author has finally found his voice, and is fulfilling a useful function after all in this "book" that he is offering to the public. That is, Solo has discovered the role that Armah himself has chosen.

In this respect, *Why Are We So Blest?* looks forward to the positive and hopeful tone of the next two novels. What the "man" and Baako lacked, Solo has discovered. In other ways, too, this novel looks forward. The stream as a motif reappears, but it is no longer muddy as in *The Beautyful Ones Are Not Yet Born*, and the swimmer is no longer fighting against the current. Instead, Solo is observing its continuous flow and waiting for a place to enter and become a part of it. Madness, obsession, and psychological tension continue to be significant motifs, but while *Fragments* ends with Baako in an asylum, this novel opens with Solo's overcoming a bout of mental depression by committing himself to a month's convalescence in a hospital. His return to health accompanies a transformation in his view of society, the nature of revolution, and the role of militants. By this third novel, also, Armah has transformed the African female figure into a kind of soulmate. Naita possesses sexual purity, a natural grace, and a wisdom that could have been Modin's salvation. She attains an almost mythical dimension. The most significant symbol in the novel, in fact, is sexuality. Through it, Armah exposes the selfish aggressiveness of the white female and the cruel Fascism of the white male. The novel announces with violent acerbity a thesis that appears for the first time in Armah's fiction, the essential animosity between black and white. It bears the sure stamp of the Black Muslim movement that must have deeply affected him in America. The white race becomes identified as the destroyer, the enemy. The African has lost his identity because the white race has taken away the tradition and the community that gave him meaning.

In *Two Thousand Seasons*, Armah prophesies a more fruitful course. He makes a leap of faith in his narrative style and, more important, in his promise of an answer to the frustrated heroes of the first three novels. This novel has no hero, unless it be the community itself. No isolated personality is trapped within his own consciousness. The narrator, as character, is the ubiquitous member of every generation who knows the true history of the tribe. He is the "griot," the tribal historian, the wise man, the poet. He is a member of the select few whose task it is to maintain the spiritual coherence of the group. The story he tells is the group's chronicle. Thus Armah, as author, effaces himself by adopting the traditional and anonymous role of historian—a significantly symbolic act since Armah must recognize that he too finds his identity only if he merges with the community.

The chronicle begins a thousand years (two thousand seasons) ago, when the Akan tribe, probably intended to represent the black race, living in peace, harmony, and "reciprocity" on the edge of the desert, succumbs to the "predators" of the north, the Arab/Muslim civilization of North Africa. The narrator describes the destruction of the social order and the enslavement of the people. It is here that the community first loses its cohesiveness. A small nucleus of people, particularly women of the tribe, initiate and lead a revolt, and then a migration away from the desert toward the south. The eventual destination is present-day Ghana, but the people arrive only to find another threat from the sea. The Europeans have begun their exploitation of the continent. The last half of the novel concentrates on the disintegration of the tribe as the forces from without create division within. The narrator focuses on one particular period, when one generation of youths undergoing initiation escapes into the forest and organizes a resistance movement. A seer named Isanusi leads them and trains them in the "Way," the traditional values of the tribe. Their king, Koranche, subsequently persuades them to return, deceives them, and sells them into slavery. They are able to escape from the slave ship and make their way back to the forest retreat, bringing with them new recruits. These guerrilla warriors, the "beautiful ones," operate against the oppressive authorities who have betrayed the tribal traditions.

Armah has thus solved the essential problem facing the protagonists of the early novels. He has achieved the synthesis adumbrated by Ocran in *Fragments*. Though it may be impossible to join and serve the particular society in Ghana today, it is possible to participate spiritually in the larger society and in the genuine traditions of the people. This solution certainly explains the mythical and romantic mode of this novel in contrast to the naturalism or realism at the base of the first three. No longer caught within the contemporary world of the 1960's, the initiates of *Two Thousand Seasons* belong to an ancient tradition. A mythical pattern controls the novel. The tribe begins in Eden, falls from grace, and moves toward the cyclical return. It is this confidence in the future and in the total pattern of life that separates this novel from its predecessors. The racism of *Why Are We So Blest?* becomes a struggle for cultural identity on a panoramic scale. The whites, whether Muslim or Christian, are the enemy. Their culture is oppressive and destructive to blacks. They represent class divisions and hierarchical structures. The African "way" is reciprocity, equality, and a sharing of responsibility and power. Armah is obviously dealing in romantic terms. He is also trying to find his own *modus vivendi*: a justification of his "exile" and a role within the larger pattern of his nation's fate.

Armah calls *The Healers* a historical novel. It is, to be sure, based on particular events in the 1870's during the Second Asante War, and Armah's purpose—as in the previous novels, especially *Two Thousand Seasons*—is to offer an interpretation of Ghanaian (African) society and to reevaluate African history. His method, however, is not so much historical as romantic and mythical. The story is a mixture of fact and fiction, and the characters and events conform to an idea of the essential African mentality and the future of the African continent. It thus continues the optimistic chronicle of the previous novel. The storyteller is again the "anonymous" griot. The tale begins as an epic, *in medias res*. It proceeds immediately to narrate the initiation of nine Asante boys into manhood. Densu is obviously a young man of heroic proportions. He refuses to engage in the wrestling contest because the competition required violates the spirit of cooperation that he values. He nevertheless demonstrates his superior strength and grace in this and other games, while finally refusing to win to avoid being named the next chief in the tribe. He resists this temptation held out by Ababio, the evil adviser who remains Densu's nemesis throughout the novel. Densu's ambition is to join the spiritual ones, the "priests" or "healers" who live as outcasts in the forest and who preserve the values of the community which are being perverted by ambitious men such as Ababio. Before he can realize this goal, however, he must not only convince Damfo, the chief healer, and his spiritual guide, that he can truly sacrifice the things of common life, but also overcome Ababio's scheme to condemn him falsely for murder, and to engage in the war against the British as General Nkwanta's aid. The novel ends melodramatically with the betrayal and defeat of the Asante army, the last-minute acquittal of Densu at the murder trial, and the various African tribes dancing on the beach, ironically brought together by the invading British.

Armah thus suggests a future Pan-African unity. For the present, however—

if the events of the 1870's offer a paradigm for the contemporary situation—the solution to the sociological and psychological problems facing Ghanaians is much the same as that proposed in *Two Thousand Seasons*. The perceptive individual who works for a solution must not expect an immediate communal identity. Again, Armah clarifies the choices available through romantic simplification. In *Two Thousand Seasons*, the proponents of the Way face a challenge from the white predators and destroyers and from the zombies among their own people. In *The Healers*, the choice is between competition and manipulation on the one hand, and cooperation and inspiration on the other. Densu chooses to leave his tribe because he knows that the leaders and the people are not ready for the essential virtues of the true community. Instead, he is initiated by Damfo into the community of healers. Damfo, in his dealings with other people, never resorts to manipulation or even persuasion, but rather relies on spiritual understanding and respect. This is presented as the only way to establish a genuine community.

In this fifth novel, Armah seems to be consciously drawing in all the threads from his early works. The "beautyful ones," it would seem, are born, but they reside outside the society itself, preparing for the future. Unlike the "man," they fully accept the pain of nonconformity. The healer, Damfo, fulfills the tasks that frustrate the teacher, Ocran, Juana, Naana, and Solo. In his conversations with Densu, he employs a method of instruction that is both Socratic and therapeutic. The philosophical and psychological conflicts that plague the early heroes thus find their resolutions in the spiritual communication and intimate friendship between priest and initiate. Nightmares become dreams of self-discovery. Body, mind, and spirit achieve harmony in Densu. He sees the chaos of the present within the perspectives of history. He is also at home in the natural world. The stream that flows as a minor motif through the other novels is a significant part of the setting in *The Healers*. Densu wins the swimming contest not by competing but by becoming at one with the natural element. He later escapes arrest by holding on to roots at the bottom of the stream and breathing through a hollowed-out cane. Even later, he and Damfo master the stream in a long journey against the current. Finally, in this river of life Densu contemplates his own image and purpose. Clearly, Armah creates a hero in *The Healers* who has found his place in the stream of history, a hero who gives meaning to Armah's own chosen role in his community.

Major publications other than long fiction

SHORT FICTION: "Yaw Manu's Charm," in *The Atlantic*, 1968; "The Offal Kind," in *Harper's*, 1969.

POETRY: "Aftermath," in *Messages: Poems from Ghana*, 1970.

NONFICTION: "African Socialism: Utopian or Scientific," in *Présence Africaine*, 1967.

Bibliography

Achebe, Chinua. *Morning Yet on Creation Day*, 1975.
Fraser, Robert. *The Novels of Ayi Kwei Armah*, 1980.
Larson, Charles. *Modern African Stories: A Collection of Contemporary African Writing*, 1971.
Soyinka, Wole. *Myth, Literature and the African World*, 1976.

Thomas Banks

MARGARET ATWOOD

Born: Ottawa, Canada; November 18, 1939

Principal long fiction
The Edible Woman, 1969; *Surfacing*, 1972; *Lady Oracle*, 1976; *Life Before Man*, 1979; *Bodily Harm*, 1982.

Other literary forms
A skillful and prolific writer, Margaret Atwood has thus far published thirteen volumes of poetry. *Double Persephone* (1961), *The Animals in That Country* (1968), *The Journals of Susanna Moodie* (1970), *Procedures for Underground* (1970), *Power Politics* (1971), *You Are Happy* (1974), *Two-Headed Poems* (1978), and *Second Words* (1982) have enjoyed a wide and enthusiastic readership, especially in Canada. Five volumes have been published in small, limited editions: *The Circle Game* (1964), *Talismans for Children* (1965), *Kaleidoscopes Baroque: A Poem* (1965), *Speeches for Dr. Frankenstein* (1966), and *Expeditions* (1966). Included in the collections are two of Atwood's broadsides, *What Was in the Garden* and *Marsh, Hawk*. *Dreams of Animals*, another broadside printed from one of Atwood's original drawings, has been published in *Procedures for Underground*. Atwood has also written and illustrated books for children, *Up in the Tree* (1978) and *Anna's Pet* (1980). A volume of short stories, *Dancing Girls* (1977), and a book of criticism, *Survival: A Thematic Guide to Canadian Literature* (1972), further demonstrate Atwood's wide-ranging talent. Additionally, she has written articles and critical reviews too numerous to list. She also has contributed prose and poetry to literary journals such as *Acta Victoriana* and *Canadian Forum*. Atwood's drama, *Grace Marks*, though unpublished, has been produced on Canadian television as *The Servant Girl*.

Achievements
Early in her career, Atwood's work was recognized for its distinction. This is particularly true of her poetry, which has earned her numerous awards, including the E. J. Pratt Medal in 1961; the President's Medal from the University of Western Ontario in 1965; and the Governor-General's Award, Canada's highest literary honor, for *The Circle Game* in 1966. Atwood carried away first prize from the Canadian Centennial Commission Poetry Competition in 1967, and won a prize for poetry from the Union League Civic and Arts Foundation in 1969. Honorary doctorates have been conferred upon Atwood by Trent University and Queen's University. Additional literary prizes include the Bess Hokins Prize for poetry (1974); the City of Toronto Award (1977); the Canadian Bookseller's Association Award (1977); the St.

Lawrence Award for Fiction (1978); and the Radcliffe Medal (1980).

Biography

Margaret Atwood was born in Ottawa, Ontario, Canada, on November 18, 1939, the second of Carl Edmund and Margaret Killam Atwood's three children. At the age of six months, she was backpacked into the Quebec wilderness, where her father, an entomologist, pursued his special interests in bees, spruce budworms, and forest tent caterpillars. Throughout her childhood, Atwood's family spent several months of the year in the bush of Quebec and northern Ontario. She did not attend school full time until she was twelve.

Though often interrupted, Atwood's education seems to have been more than adequate. She was encouraged by her parents to read and write at an early age, and her creative efforts started at five, when she wrote stories, poems, and plays. Her serious composition, however, did not begin until she was sixteen.

In 1961, Atwood earned her B.A. in the English honors program from the University of Toronto, where she studied with poets Jay Macpherson and Margaret Avison. Her M.A. from Radcliffe followed in 1962. Continuing graduate work at Harvard in 1963, Atwood interrupted her studies before reentering the program for two more years in 1965. While she found graduate studies interesting, Atwood's energies were largely directed toward her creative efforts. To her, the Ph.D. program was chiefly a means of support while she wrote. Before writing her doctoral thesis, Atwood left Harvard.

Returning to Canada in 1967, Atwood accepted a position at Sir George Williams University in Montreal. By this time, her poetry was gaining recognition. With the publication of *The Edible Woman* and the sale of its film rights, Atwood was able to concentrate more fully on writing, though she taught at York University and was writer-in-residence at the University of Toronto. For Atwood, 1972 became a turning point in her life and career. At this time, her five-year marriage to an American writer came to an end, and with the publication of *Surfacing*, she was able to support herself through her creative efforts. Finally able to live off the proceeds of her writing, Atwood moved to a farm north of Toronto where she lives with novelist and friend, Graeme Gibson, and their daughter Jess, born in 1979.

Analysis

For Margaret Atwood, an unabashed Canadian, literature is a means to cultural and personal self-awareness. "To know ourselves," she writes in *Survival*, "we must know our own literature; to know ourselves accurately, we need to know it as part of literature as a whole." Thus, when she defines Canadian literary concerns, she relates her own as well, for Atwood's fiction grows out of this tradition. In her opinion, Canada's central reality is the act of survival: Canadian life and culture are decisively shaped by the demands of a harsh environment. Closely related, in Atwood's view, to this defining act of survival is the Canadian search for territorial identity—or, as Northrop Frye has put it, "Where is here?"

Atwood's heroines invariably discover themselves to be emotional refugees, strangers in a territory they can accurately label but one in which they are unable to feel at home. Not only are they alienated from their environment, but also they are alienated from language itself; for them, communication becomes a decoding process. To a great degree, their feelings of estrangement extend from a culture that, having reduced everything to products, threatens to consume them. Women are particularly singled out as products, items to be decorated and sold as commodities, though men are threatened as well. Indeed, Canadian identity as a whole is in danger of being engulfed by an acquisitive American culture, though Atwood's "Americans" symbolize exploitation and often turn out to be Canadian nationals.

Reflective of their time and place, Atwood's characters are appropriately ambivalent. Dead or dying traditions prevent their return to a past, a past most have rejected. Their present is ephemeral at best, and their future inconceivable. Emotionally maimed, her heroines plumb their conscious and unconscious impressions, searching for a return to feeling, a means of identification with the present.

Atwood often couches their struggle in terms of a journey, which serves as a controlling metaphor for inner explorations: the unnamed heroine of *Surfacing* returns to the wilderness of Quebec, Lesje Green of *Life Before Man* wanders through imagined Mesozoic jungles, Rennie Wilford of *Bodily Harm* flies to the insurgent islands of Ste. Agathe and St. Antoine. By setting contemporary culture in relief, these primitive sites define the difference between nature and culture and allow Atwood's heroines to gain new perspectives on their own realities. They can see people and places in relation to each other, not as isolated entities. Ultimately, however, this resolves little, for Atwood's novels end on a tenuous note. Although her heroines come to terms with themselves, they remain estranged.

Supporting her characters' ambivalence is Atwood's versatile narrative technique. Her astringent prose reflects their emotional numbness; its ironic restraint reveals their wariness. Frequent contradictions suggest not only the complexity of her characters but also the antagonistic times they must survive. By skillful juxtaposition of past and present through the use of flashbacks, Atwood evokes compelling fictional landscapes which ironically comment on the untenable state of modern men and women. Still, there remains some hope, for her characters survive with increased understanding of their world. Despite everything, life does go on.

The first of Atwood's novels to arouse critical praise and commentary, *Surfacing* explores new facets of the *Bildungsroman*. What might have been a conventional novel of self-discovery develops into a resonant search for self-recovery imbued with mythic overtones and made accessible through Atwood's skillful use of symbol and ritual. At the same time, Atwood undercuts the romantic literary conventions on which *Surfacing* is built by exposing the myth of ultimate self-realization as a plausible conclusion. To accept the heroine's final emergence as an end in itself is to misread this suggestively ironic novel.

The unnamed heroine of *Surfacing*, accompanied by her lover Joe and a married couple named David and Anna, returns to the Canadian wilderness where she was reared in hopes of locating her missing father. His sudden disappearance has recalled her from a city life marked by personal and professional failures which have left her emotionally anesthetized. While her external search goes forward, the heroine conducts a more important internal investigation to locate missing "gifts" from both parents. Through these, she hopes to rediscover her lost ability to feel. In order to succeed, however, she will need to expose the fiction of her life.

At the outset of her narrative, the heroine warns her readers that she has led a double life when she recalls Anna's question, "Do you have a twin?" She denies having one, for she apparently believes the elaborate fiction she has created, a story involving a spurious marriage, divorce, and abandonment of her child. As additional protection, the heroine has distanced herself from everyone. She refers to her family as "they," "as if they were somebody else's family." Her relationship with Joe is notable for its coolness, and she has only known Anna, described as her best friend, for two months.

By surrounding herself with friends whose occupation of making a film significantly entitled *Random Samples* reveals their rootlessness, the heroine seeks to escape the consequences of her actions. Indeed, she describes herself both as a commercial artist, indicating her sense of having sold out, and as an escape artist. Reluctantly approaching the past she sought to escape, the heroine feels as if she is in foreign territory.

That she feels alienated by the location of her past is not surprising, for she is an outsider in a number of telling ways: of English descent in French territory; a non-Catholic, indeed nonreligious person among the devout; a woman in a man's world. Her French is so halting that she could be mistaken for an American, representing yet another form of alienation, displacement by foreigners. Most of all, she is a stranger to herself. Rather than focusing on her self-alienation, she is consumed by the American usurpation of Canada, its wanton rape of virgin wilderness, in order to avoid a more personal loss of innocence.

Canada's victimization by Americans reflects the heroine's victimization by men. Having been subjected to the concept that "with a paper bag over their head they're all the same," the protagonist is perceived as either contemptible or threatening. Her artistic skills are denigrated by a culture in which no "important" artists have been women. Even her modest commercial success is treated as a personal assault by Joe, who has an "unvoiced claim to superior artistic skills." By telling herself that the wilderness can never recover from abuse, the protagonist denies her own recovery. Although she feels helpless at the beginning of the novel, she soon rediscovers her own capabilities, and as these are increasingly tested, she proves to be a powerful survivor. Thus, the wilderness, a self-reflection, provides the key to self-discovery.

Perhaps the most important lesson the heroine learns is that the wilderness is not innocent. Her encounter and response to a senselessly slaughtered heron evoke a sense of complicity, leading her to reflect on similar collusion in her brother's animal experiments when they were children. Finding her refuge in childhood innocence blocked, the heroine goes forward with her search. Once again, nature provides information, for in discovering her father's body trapped underwater, she finally recognizes her aborted child, her complicity in its death by yielding to her lover's demands. On a broader scale, she acknowledges death as a part of life and reclaims her participation in the life-process by conceiving a child by Joe.

In a ceremony evocative of primitive fertility rites, she seduces her lover. Then, assured of her pregnancy, she undergoes a systematic purgation in order to penetrate to the very core of reality. During this process, the protagonist discovers her parents' gifts—her father's sense of sight and her mother's gift of life. With body and mind reunited, she takes an oath in which she refuses to be a victim. Whole, she feels free to reenter her own time, no longer either victim or stranger.

Atwood's procedure for bringing her heroine to this state of consciousness is remarkable for its intricacy. Though she distrusts language, the protagonist proceeds to tell her story by describing what she sees. Since she has lost her ability to feel, much of this description seems to be objective—until the reader realizes just how unreliable her impressions can be. Contradictions abound, creating enormous uncertainty as intentional and unintentional irony collide, lies converge, and opinion stated as fact proves to be false. Given this burden of complexity, any simple conclusion to *Surfacing* is out of the question. Clearly, Atwood hints at a temporary union with Joe, but this is far from resolving the heroine's dilemma. Outer reality, after all, has not altered. Thus, Atwood's open-ended conclusion is both appropriate and plausible, for to resolve all difficulties would be to give in to the very romantic conventions which her fiction subverts.

Coming after the Gothic comedy of *Lady Oracle*, *Life Before Man* seems especially stark. Nevertheless, its similarity with all of Atwood's novels is apparent. A penetrating examination of contemporary relationships, it peels away protective layers of deceptions, stripping the main characters until their fallible selves are presented with relentless accuracy. Lesje Green and Elizabeth and Nate Schoenhof are adrift in a collapsing culture in which they struggle to survive. As she focuses on each character, Atwood reveals unrecognized facets of the others.

In this novel, wilderness and culture converge in the Royal Ontario Museum, where Lesje works as a paleontologist and Elizabeth works in public relations. There is little need for the bush country of Quebec, since culture is something of a jungle itself. Unlike the Mesozoic, however, the present anticipates its own extinction because of abundant evidence: pollution, separatist movements, political upheaval, lost traditions, disintegrating families. Man is in danger of drowning in his own waste. Whatever predictability life held in the past seems completely absent; even holidays are meaningless. Still, the novel is fascinated with the past, with the behavior of animals, both human and prehistoric, and with the perpetuation of memory, particularly as it records the history of families.

As in *Surfacing*, a violent death precipitates emotional withdrawal. Most affected is Elizabeth Schoenhof, whose lover Chris has blown off his head as a final gesture of defiance, the ultimate form of escape. His act destroys Elizabeth's sense of security, which resides both in her home and in her ability to manipulate or predict the actions of others. A supreme manipulator, Elizabeth attempts to make everyone act as reasonably as she. Not surprisingly, Elizabeth has at least two selves speaking different languages, genteel chic and street argot, and what passes for "civilized" behavior is merely an escape from honest confrontation with such basic human emotions as love, grief, rejection, and anger. In fact, all of the novel's characters prefer escape to self-realization, and while they pay lip service to social decorum, they quietly rebel.

Their rebellious emotions are reflected in the larger world, a political world aflame with separatist zeal. Rene Levesque, with whom Nate identifies, is gaining momentum for the separation of Quebec and the reestablishment of French as the major language, threatening to displace the English. Indeed, the world seems to be coming apart as international, national, and personal moves toward separation define this novel's movement. As a solution, however, separation fails to satisfy the characters' need to escape, for no matter how far they run, all carry the baggage of their past.

Elizabeth in particular has survived a loveless past, including abandonment by both parents, the painful death of her alcoholic mother, her sister's mental breakdown and drowning, and her Auntie Muriel's puritanical upbringing. All of this has turned Elizabeth into a determined survivor. Beneath her polished exterior is a street fighter from the slums, a primitive. Indeed, Elizabeth recognizes an important part of herself in Chris. Nate and Lesje share a different kind of past, where love created as much tension as affection. Lesje's Jewish and Ukrainian grandmothers treated her as disputed territory, speaking to her in languages she could not understand and driving her to seek refuge in her fantasy world of Lesjeland.

Feeling like a refugee in treacherous territory, each character attempts to build a new, stable world, notwithstanding the continual impingement of the old, messy one. Nate, having forsaken his mother's futile idealistic causes to save the world, falls in love with Lesje, whom he envisions as an exotic subtropical island free from rules. For a time, Elizabeth inhabits a clean expanse of space somewhere between her bed and the ceiling, and Lesje explores prehistoric terrain, wishing for a return to innocence. When these fantasies diminish in power, the characters find substitutes, challenging the reader to reexamine the novel's possibilities.

Despite its bleak tone, its grimy picture of a deteriorating culture, its feeling of estrangement and futility, its rejection of simplistic resolutions, *Life Before Man* is not without hope. Each character emerges at the end of this novel with something he or she has desired. Nate has Lesje, now pregnant with his child—a child who, in turn confirms Lesje's commitment to life by displacing her preoccupation with death. Having exorcised the evil spirits of her past, Elizabeth experiences a return of direct emotion.

There is, however, a distinct possibility that the apparent resolution is as ambivalent as that of *Surfacing*. What appears to be a completely objective third-person point of view, presiding over chapters neatly cataloged by name and date, sometimes shifts to first-person, an unreliable first-person at that. Through her revolving characters, their identification with one another, and their multiple role-reversals, Atwood creates contradictory, problematic, and deceptive human characters who defy neat categorization. Taken separately, Nate, Elizabeth, and Lesje can easily be misinterpreted; taken as a whole, they assume an even more complex meaning, reflecting not only their own biased viewpoints but also the reader's. Atwood's ability to capture such shifting realities of character and place is one of her chief artistic distinctions.

Rather like the narrator of *Surfacing*, Rennie Wilford in *Bodily Harm* has abandoned her past, the stifling world of Griswold, Ontario, to achieve modest success as a free-lance journalist. To Rennie, Griswold represents values of duty, self-sacrifice, and decency found comic by contemporary standards. It is a place where women are narrowly confined to assigned roles which make them little better than servants. Rennie much prefers city life, with its emphasis on mobility and trends such as slave-girl bracelets and pornographic art. In fact, Rennie has become an expert on just such trends, so adept that she can either describe or fabricate one with equal facility. Having learned to look only at surfaces, Rennie has difficulty accepting the reality of her cancerous breast, which *looks* so healthy.

Her cancer serves as the controlling metaphor in the novel, spreading from diseased personal relationships to a political eruption on St. Antoine. Indeed, the world seems shot through with moral cancer. The symptoms are manifest: honesty is a liability, friends are "contacts," lovers are rapists, pharmacists are drug pushers, and no one wants to hear about issues. What should be healthy forms of human commerce have gone out of control, mirroring the rioting cells in Rennie's breast. When confronted by yet another manifestation of this malaise, a would-be murderer who leaves a coil of rope on her bed, Rennie finds a fast escape route by landing a magazine assignment on St. Antoine.

Her hopes of being a tourist, exempt from participation and responsibility, are short-lived as she is drawn into a political intrigue more life-threatening than her cancer. Before reaching St. Antoine, she learns of its coming election, ignoring Dr. Minnow's allusions to political corruption and makeshift operations. What puzzles her most about their conversation is his reference to the "sweet Canadians." Is he being ironic or not, she wonders. Her superficial observations of island life reveal little, though plenty of evidence points to a violent eruption. Rennie seems more concerned about avoiding sunburn and arrest for drug possession than she is about the abundant poverty and casual violence. Her blindness allows her to become a gun-runner, duped by Lora Lucas, a resilient survivor of many injurious experiences, and Paul, the local connection for drugs and guns, who initiates Rennie into genuine, albeit unwilling, massive involvement.

As a physical link to life, Paul's sexual attention is important to Rennie, who appreciates the value of his touch. His hands call forth the "missing" hands of her grandmother, her doctor's hands, and Lora's bitten hands, hands which deny or offer help. Paul's "aid" to the warring political factions, like Canada's donation of canned hams and Rennie's assistance, is highly questionable, and the results are the reverse of what was planned. Trying to escape from his botched plan, Rennie is brought to confront her own guilt.

Again, Atwood uses flight as a route to self-discovery and deprivation as a source of spiritual nourishment. In Rennie's case, however, these are externally imposed. In her underground cell, with only Lora as company, Rennie ultimately sees and understands the violent disease consuming the world, a disease growing out of a human need to express superiority in a variety of ways and at great spiritual expense. Rennie becomes "afraid of men because men are frightening." Equally important, she understands that there is no difference between *here* and *there*. Finally, she knows that she is not exempt: "Nobody is exempt from anything."

If she survives this ordeal, Rennie plans to change her life, becoming a reporter who will tell what truly happened. Once again, though, Atwood leaves this resolution open to questions. Rennie is often mistaken about what she sees and frequently misinterprets events. Her entire story may well be a prison journal, an account of how she arrived there. When projecting her emergence from prison, she uses the future tense. For Atwood's purposes, this is of relative unimportance, since Rennie has been restored in a way she never anticipated. In the end, stroking Lora's battered hand, Rennie finally embodies the best of Griswold with a clear vision of what lies beneath the surface of human reality.

Atwood's own vision is as informed and humane as that of any comtemporary novelist. Challenging her readers to form their own judgments, she combines the complexity of the best modern fiction into the moral rigor of the great nineteenth century novelists. Atwood's resonant symbols, her ironic reversals, and her suggestive economy set narrative standards few other novelists can meet, and her example challenges readers and writers alike to confront the most difficult and important issues of the contemporary world.

Major publications other than long fiction

SHORT FICTION: *Dancing Girls*, 1977; *True Stories*, 1982.

POETRY: *Double Persephone*, 1961; *The Circle Game*, 1964; *Talismans for Children*, 1965; *Kaleidoscopes Baroque: A Poem*, 1965; *Speeches for Dr. Frankenstein*, 1966; *Expeditions*, 1966; *The Animals in That Country*, 1968; *The Journals of Susanna Moodie*, 1970; *Procedures for Underground*, 1970; *Power Politics*, 1971; *You Are Happy*, 1974; *Selected Poems*, 1976; *Two-Headed Poems*, 1978; *Second Words*, 1982.

NONFICTION: *Survival: A Thematic Guide to Canadian Literature*, 1972.

CHILDREN'S LITERATURE: *Up in the Tree*, 1978; *Anna's Pet*, 1980.

Bibliography

Christ, Carol P. *Diving Deep and Surfacing: Women Writers on Spiritual Quest*, 1980.

Davidson, Arnold E., and Cathy N. Davidson, eds. *The Art of Margaret Atwood: Essays in Criticism*, 1981.

Karen Carmean

LOUIS AUCHINCLOSS

Born: New York, New York; September 17, 1917

Principal long fiction

The Indifferent Children, 1947; *Sybil*, 1952; *A Law for the Lion*, 1953; *The Great World and Timothy Colt*, 1956; *Venus in Sparta*, 1958; *Pursuit of the Prodigal*, 1959; *The House of Five Talents*, 1960; *Portrait in Brownstone*, 1962; *The Rector of Justin*, 1964; *The Embezzler*, 1966; *A World of Profit*, 1969; *I Come as a Thief*, 1972; *The Winthrop Covenant*, 1976; *The Dark Lady*, 1977; *The Country Cousin*, 1978; *The House of the Prophet*, 1980; *The Cat and the King*, 1981; *Watchfires*, 1982.

Other literary forms

A lawyer by profession, Louis Auchincloss is known for short fiction and critical essays as well as for his novels; among his strongest collections of short fiction are *The Romantic Egoists* (1954), *Powers of Attorney* (1963), and *Tales of Manhattan* (1967), each of which presents stories linked by narration, characters, or theme in such a way as to resemble a novel. To date, Auchincloss' best-known critical works are those dealing with his most prominent American literary ancestors: *Edith Wharton* (1961), *Reflections of a Jacobite* (1961, on Henry James), and *Reading Henry James* (1975). Among his other volumes of collected essays are *A Writer's Capital, Life, Law and Letters* (1974) and *Persons of Consequence: Queen Victoria and Her Circle* (1979).

Achievements

During the 1950's, Auchincloss emerged as a strong social satirist and novelist of manners, rivaling in his best work the accomplishments of John Phillips Marquand and John O'Hara. Unlike those writers, however, Auchincloss was clearly an "insider" by birth and breeding, belonging without reservation to the social class and power structure that he so convincingly portrayed. Some thirty years later, despite recent ventures into the domain of the historical novel, Auchincloss stands nearly alone as an American novelist of manners, unrivaled in his analysis of social and political power.

Freely acknowledging his debt to Henry James and Edith Wharton as well as to Marcel Proust and the Duc de Saint-Simon, Auchincloss continues to transform the stuff of success into high art, providing his readers with convincing glimpses behind the scenes of society and politics where top-level decisions are often made for the most personal and trivial of reasons. As a rule, his featured characters are credible and well developed, if often unsympathetic; Auchincloss' apparent aim is to describe what he has seen, even at the risk of alienating readers who care so little about his characters as not to wonder what will become of them. At the same time, Auchincloss' characteristic mode of expression leaves him open to accusations that he is an "elitist" writer, featuring characters who are almost without exception white, Anglo-Saxon, and Protestant. Such accusations, however, do little to undermine the basic premise that emerges from the body of Auchincloss' work: for good or for ill, the people of whom he writes are those whose decisions and behavior have determined the shape of the American body politic.

Biography

Louis Stanton Auchincloss was born September 17, 1917, in New York City, where he has spent his entire life except for his years of education and military service. A graduate of the prestigious Groton School, he entered Yale University in 1935 with plans to become a writer, only to withdraw several months short of graduation in 1939 after his initial efforts at publication had been rejected. Deciding instead to pursue a career in law, he received his LL.B. degree from the University of Virginia in 1941 and worked briefly for the firm of Sullivan and Cromwell in New York City before joining the Navy, from which he emerged in 1945 with the rank of lieutenant.

Returning to Sullivan and Cromwell after World War II, Auchincloss again tried his hand at creative writing, this time with demonstrable success. In 1951, he withdrew from the practice of law and devoted himself to writing full time, only to decide after some three years that law and literature were indeed compatible, even symbiotic, and that the writer's life excluding all other pursuits was a bore. In 1954, he returned to the practice of law with the Manhattan firm of Hawkins, Delafield, and Wood, of which he has been a partner since 1958. The previous year, he had married the former Adele Lawrence, to whom he has since dedicated several of his publications.

Analysis

For a writer with a full-time professional career, Louis Auchincloss has been astoundingly prolific, producing nearly one book of fiction or nonfiction each year since the age of thirty. Like that of many highly prolific writers, the quality of his work is decidedly uneven. At his best, however, Auchincloss meets and surpasses the standard set by J. P. Marquand and John O'Hara for twentieth century American social satire, displaying a resonant erudition that somehow eluded the two older writers even in their brightest moments. Even in the best of his novels, the results of Auchincloss' erudition are sometimes too conspicuous for the reader's comfort, but they can easily be overlooked in favor of the authenticity displayed by characters portrayed in convincing situations.

To date, Auchincloss' reputation as a major writer rests primarily on novels written during the 1960's, a time somewhat past the vogue of social satire in the United States but coinciding neatly with the author's full maturity: the worst of his mistakes were behind him, and he had not yet experienced the temptation to repeat himself. *Pursuit of the Prodigal*, published in 1959, shows Auchincloss approaching the height of his powers, yet not quite free of his earlier mode as he portrays the tribulations of a "maverick" lawyer who is uncomfortable with the conventions into which he was born. Set in the immediate postwar years, *Pursuit of a Prodigal*, despite the distinct insider's voice, shows a clear indebtedness to Marquand's *Point of No Return*, published a decade earlier. The following year, however, Auchincloss broke new and enviable ground with *The House of Five Talents*, ostensibly the memoirs, composed in 1948, of the septuagenarian Miss Gussie Millinder, heiress and survivor of an impressive nineteenth century New York fortune. The author's demonstrated skill at characterization and narration served clear notice of his new, mature promise, soon to be fulfilled with *Portrait in Brownstone*, *The Rector of Justin*, and *The Embezzler*, any one of which would suffice to confirm Auchincloss' reputation as the successor to O'Hara and Marquand as a master observer of American society and a superior stylist.

It is hardly surprising that Auchincloss has achieved his greatest success with books narrated by the characters themselves, frequently by two or more characters in successive sections of one novel. Although his early novels and certain of his short stories bear witness to his control of third-person narration, Auchincloss is doubtless at his best when assuming the voice and persona of a featured character, striking a thoroughly convincing tone of vocabulary, style, and reflection. At times, his narrators are authentically unreliable without, however, approaching the virtuoso performances sought and achieved by Marquand in such works as *The Late George Apley* (1937) or *H. M. Pulham, Esq.* (1941). Unlike Marquand, Auchincloss seeks less to ridicule his characters than to represent them true to life, allowing the reader to draw his or her own conclusions. It is to Auchincloss' credit that he can credibly assume such diverse personae as those of Miss Gussie Millinder and the three main characters of *The Embezzler*, as well as the slightly fussy schoolmaster who narrates *The Rector of Justin*.

Given the fact that Auchincloss has chosen to serve as a chronicler of his generation and those immediately preceding, it stands to reason that a number of his featured characters are drawn rather closely upon recognizable models—perhaps too closely in *The House of the Prophet*, rather less so in *The Embezzler* and *The Rector of Justin*. Such a practice has both its benefits and its pitfalls. At his best, Auchincloss meets and surpasses the aims of the finest historical fiction, showing rounded characters where the record presents only flatness. On other occasions, however, his presentation is so sparse as to require the reader's knowledge of the facts behind the fiction. This is not to say, however, that any of Auchincloss' novels are simple *romans à clef*; in each case, Auchincloss is careful to discover and point a message that goes far deeper than a simple recitation of documented facts.

Together with the highest-minded of his characters, Auchincloss exhibits and values a strong sense of moral and ethical responsibility; unlike certain of his predecessors and erstwhile competitors in the genre, he never indulges in sensationalism or exposé for its own sake. Even when scandal invades the lives of his characters, as often it must, there is no perceptible intent to scandalize or titillate the reader. Indeed, given the Proustian atmosphere that reigns in many of Auchincloss' novels, the reader often waits in vain for the comic catharsis, however slow to build, with which Marcel Proust frequently rewards his readers' patience. Still, it must be noted that Auchincloss presents all but the meanest of his characters with considerable indulgence, providing a human warmth that is totally lacking in the work of such satirists as Sinclair Lewis and often absent in the more bitter works of O'Hara and Marquand.

A New Yorker by proclivity as well as by birth, Auchincloss remains, above all, a New York novelist; his characters, like their author, spend most of their time in the metropolis, leaving it only for such traditional watering-places as Newport and Bar Harbor, or for higher civic duty in Washington, D.C. The author's sense of place serves to illustrate and to explain the dominant role traditionally played by New Yorkers in the shaping of American society.

In the first work of his "mature" period, *The House of Five Talents*, Auchincloss undertakes a personal record of upper-level Manhattan society through the still-perceptive eyes of one Augusta Millinder, age seventy-five, whose immigrant grandfather, Julius Millinder, founded one of the less conspicuous but more durable of the major New York fortunes. The Millinders had, by the time of Augusta's birth in 1873, established a position of quiet dominance, based upon diversified investments. The world in which Augusta and her more attractive elder sister Cora grew to maturity was thus one of easy movement and understated privilege, pursued frequently aboard yachts and in private railroad cars. As a memoirist, Augusta remains securely inside the closed world that she describes, yet she is privileged to have a gift for shrewd observation.

As the second and less attractive of two daughters, "Gussie" Millinder learned at an early age to view male admiration with a jaundiced eye. Indeed, the only man to whom she ever became engaged had proposed several years earlier to her vacuous sister Cora, who subsequently married a French prince. Although it seems likely that Lancey Bell, a rising young architect, has proposed to Gussie in good faith, she remains so skeptical that she breaks the engagement, having developed such inner resources that she no longer believes marriage to be necessary or desirable. In fact, the marriages in and around Gussie's family do little to encourage her faith in that institution. Soon after ending her engagement, Gussie becomes a reluctant participant in the dismantling of her own parents' marriage and household. Her father, aged sixty, has become enamored of a former actress half his age and wishes to marry her, supported in his folly by Gussie's older brother Willie and sister-in-law Julia.

Although the divorce and remarriage eventually take place as planned, Gussie has discovered in the meantime her own increasingly formidable talent for high-minded meddling. She has also begun to explore the extent of a freedom uniquely available to rich and well-read spinsters. Although dissuaded from attending college in her youth, she has taken enough courses at Columbia during her early adulthood to qualify her for part-time teaching in a private school. Later, around the age of forty, she becomes deeply involved in volunteer work. By 1948, when she at last addresses herself to her memoirs, she has led a life both independent and fulfilling, but not without its disappointments.

Appropriately, Gussie's greatest disappointments have less to do with spinsterhood than with her various relatives, many of whom seem to have a singular talent for ruining their lives, at least when measured by Gussie's demanding but forgiving standards. Gussie's personal favorite appears to have been her nephew Lydig, a versatile and talented former army flight instructor who tries his hand at various pursuits successfully but without commitment, only to seek fulfillment in a life of adventure. Having taken up mountain-climbing, he dies in an avalanche around the age of thirty, a year before the stock market crash of 1929.

The changes wrought by the Depression and its consequences upon the Millinders are recorded with a sympathetic but dispassionate eye by Gussie, whose own personal fortune is sufficiently great to sustain major loss without requiring more than minimal changes in her privileged life-style. Among the few things she is obliged to forfeit is her private railroad car, while the chauffeured limousine remains. To the others, Gussie remains a rock of stability in a river of change, able to avert disaster with a well-placed loan (or gift) and a bit of timely meddling. At seventy-five, however, she admits that her interventions have not always been the right ones, much as they may have seemed so at the time. Several marriages remain broken beyond all possible repair and certain of her cousins face congressional investigation for their leftist sympathies.

Self-aware, yet not too much so for credibility, Gussie Millinder remains one of Auchincloss' most engaging narrators and one of his most satisfying creations, combining in her large and slightly outrageous person the best qualities of observer and participant in the action that she records.

Auchincloss' next novel, *Portrait in Brownstone*, attempts a broader picture of New York society. While fulfilling much of the promise held forth by *The House of Five Talents*, it falls short of its predecessor in tightness of construction, in part because of a multiplicity of narrative voices and viewpoints. Each chapter is presented from the viewpoint of a particular character, and while certain characters speak for themselves, others do not, presumably because their self-awareness is so limited as to require the author's third-person intervention.

The principal character of *Portrait in Brownstone*, although never a viewpoint character, is one Derrick Hartley, a minister's son from New England whose Harvard education and contacts facilitate his rapid rise within the presumably closed world of New York high finance. In the hands of O'Hara or Marquand, such a character as Derrick would emerge as a perceptive outsider with just a hint of the romantic hero; Auchincloss, however, presents Derrick as a thoroughgoing professional and opportunist, quick to impose his own stamp upon the closed world that almost did not allow him within its confines. He is also quick to enjoy and exploit the attentions of two female cousins, nieces of the employer whom he will eventually replace.

Set principally in the period during and surrounding World War I, *Portrait in Brownstone* underlines the contrast between "old money" and well-bred industry. Derrick, although polished and considerably less of an arriviste than certain of Auchincloss' later protagonists, has a talent for making money that renders him conspicuous among the Denison descendants, for whom the presence of money has obviated the need for making it.

After a brief and disastrous infatuation with the treacherous and ultimately unhappy Geraldine, Derrick returns his attentions to the younger, somewhat plainer cousin, Ida Trask, who had been his first love. Although disabused of her earlier illusions, Ida agrees to marry Derrick and soon bears him two children, a daughter and then a son. Ida, as a main viewpoint character, narrates much of the novel's action, developing considerably as a character in proportion to a growing awareness of her own innate strengths; for Ida is a survivor, a resourceful, intelligent woman who, born in a later time, might well have rivaled her own husband's success. In any case, she is the only woman in the novel who could possibly handle the strains of marriage to a hard-driving businessman such as Derrick, whose strongest attentions and affections are reserved for his work. Like Gussie Millinder, Ida has developed character and intelligence in the absence of great beauty. Unlike Gussie, however, she is willing and able to function competently within the demands of marriage and parenthood. Because of her intelligence and understanding, her marriage to Derrick survives a number of shocks, including their daughter's marital problems and a late-blooming affair between Derrick and Geraldine.

Minor character that she may be, it is Ida's cousin Geraldine whose life and eventual suicide polarize the action of the novel. Although it is Ida who should resent Geraldine and not the other way around, Geraldine continues to envy Ida's relatively stable marriage and often genuine happiness. As Ida observes, "She remained to the end the little girl who had come down with a bright face and bright flowing hair to find in her Christmas stocking a switch and a book of sermons while mine was crammed with packages that I dared not open." Childless despite several marriages, resentful of Derrick's mechanical approach to lovemaking during their brief affair, Geraldine begins drinking heavily to dull the pain of bright promise unfulfilled.

Among the other characters portrayed in some detail are the Hartleys' two children, born shortly before World War I. Dorcas, who has inherited her father's temperament but little of his discipline, seeks a career of her own in publishing that is cut short by her marriage to a rebellious young editor who accepts the Hartleys' largesse while professing to scorn its source. Eventually, Dorcas enters into a second marriage with one Mark Jesmond, an associate of Derrick who, during an earlier career as a lawyer, had handled the details of her divorce from the editor. Dorcas at last finds fulfillment of sorts in assisting Mark in efforts to "depose" her father from headship of his firm, much as Derrick himself had done years earlier to Ida's uncle Linnaeus Tremain. Dorcas' brother Hugo, meanwhile, is beginning to enter adulthood at the age of thirty-five, thanks mainly to his mother's direct intervention in the choice of his wife and career: Ida, it seems, has begun to assert herself as a matriarch.

Although marred by loose construction and a multiplicity of viewpoints, *Portrait in Brownstone* is notable for the keenness of its observation and the presentation of several memorable scenes. In any case, Auchincloss' readers did not have long to wait before the publication of *The Rector of Justin*, considered by several critics to be the finest of his novels.

Despite the fact that it shares with *Portrait in Brownstone* the potential pitfalls of loose construction and multiple viewpoints, *The Rector of Justin* is considerably more successful both as novel and as document. Auchincloss manages to broaden the appeal of the novel through his choice of subject matter, focusing upon the concept and execution of the American preparatory school. In analyzing the life and career of one Francis Prescott, founder of "Justin Martyr, an Episcopal boys' boarding school thirty miles west of Boston," Auchincloss provides through various viewpoint characters a thoughtful examination, both historical and philosophical, of a powerful American institution.

The main narrator of *The Rector of Justin* is Brian Aspinwall, whose arrival at Justin coincides with the outbreak of World War II in Europe. Brian has recently returned to the United States after several years of study at Oxford, where doctors have diagnosed a heart murmur that renders him unfit for service in the British Army. Unsure as yet of his vocation to become an Episcopal priest, Brian welcomes the prospect of teaching at Justin as an opportunity to test his suitability for the priesthood as well as for teaching, another possibility. Drawn gradually deeper into the affairs of the school and its founder-headmaster, Brian records his observations and experiences in a journal that forms the backbone of the book. Later, as the idea of recording the school's history begins to take form in his mind, he includes the testimony—both oral and written—of Dr. Prescott's family, friends, and former students. The result is thus more unified and better organized than *Portrait in Brownstone*, despite the old-maidish Brian's obvious limitations both as narrator and as observer.

By the time of Brian's arrival, Francis Prescott is nearly eighty years of age and long overdue for retirement; as both founder and headmaster, however, he is such an institution that no one has given serious thought to replacing him. Brian vacillates between admiration and harsh criticism for the old man and his "muscular Christianity." To Brian's incredulity, the aging Prescott remains unfailingly democratic in pronouncements both public and private, seemingly unaware of the fact that he and his school have helped to perpetuate an American class system that Prescott personally deplores. This basic irony continues to animate the novel, providing as it does the subject matter for Brian's continuing research.

Early in the novel, Brian learns that Prescott, as a young man, took pains to examine at close range the British public-school system preparatory to founding a boarding school of his own; at no point does Prescott or anyone near him appear to have considered the difference between British aristocracy and American democracy. In fact, many of the questions raised in Brian's mind are left hanging, at least for the reader, calling attention to the anomalous role of private education in America. Prescott, for his part, continues to deny the existence of an American ruling class even when faced with evidence to the contrary from his own alumni rolls.

Brian's continuing research gradually uncovers a wealth of conflicting evidence concerning Prescott's accomplishment. It is clear in any case that the realization of Prescott's lifelong dream has been achieved only at great personal cost. Brian finds the darker side of Justin's history in both a document penned by the long-dead son of the school's charter trustee, on whose behalf Prescott's efforts failed miserably, and in the spoken recollections of Prescott's youngest daughter, ironically named Cordelia. When Brian meets her, Cordelia is in her middle forties, an unreconstructed Greenwich Village bohemian with nymphomaniacal tendencies that, on one occasion, send Brian fleeing for his life. Prescott, it seems, did much to ruin not only her early first marriage but also a later liaison with a mortally wounded veteran of World War I. Cordelia ascribes much of her unhappiness to the fact that both men, as "old boys" of Justin Martyr, perceived a higher obligation to her father than to herself.

Ending with Prescott's death in retirement at age eighty-six, *The Rector of Justin* concludes much as it began, undecided as to the ultimate value of Prescott's achievement. Brian, however, has made a decision; now a fully ordained priest, he continues as a member of the faculty at Justin Martyr.

Together with *The House of Five Talents*, *The Rector of Justin* stands as one of Auchincloss' more impressive accomplishments; in few of his other novels are the interdependent questions of privilege and responsibility discussed with such thoughtfulness or candor. If the book has a major weakness it is that the characters, especially Prescott himself, are often stretched so flat as to strain the reader's belief; even then, it is possible to accept flatness in the case of a character who adamantly refuses to admit life's ambiguities.

Published some two years after *The Rector of Justin*, *The Embezzler* builds on the author's known strengths to provide a strong social satire in the tradition of O'Hara and Marquand, yet transcends the accomplishments of both authors with its spareness and authority. Recalling in its essentials one of the subplots in *The House of Five Talents*, wherein Gussie Millinder reluctantly covers the defalcations of a distant relative threatened with exposure, *The Embezzler* credibly re-creates the heyday of high finance in America before, during, and after the crash of 1929.

The title character and initial narrator of *The Embezzler* is Guy Prime, writing in 1960 to set straight the record of his notoriety some twenty-five years earlier. His antagonist and eventual successor as narrator is Reginald (Rex) Geer, an erstwhile friend and associate since college days. The gathering tension between the two men, reflected in the conflict between their recollections of the same events, provides the novel with its major human interest. "Yes," reflects Guy Prime in the early pages of the novel,

> . . . they would all cut me dead in the street today, my old friends. Rex Geer, who might be a haberdasher in Vermont but for our Harvard friendship, would turn away his stony countenance and splash me with the wheels of his Rolls-Royce. Alphonse de Grasse, his partner, and one of my old golf foursome, might furtively nod as he hurried by, but only if he was sure that Rex's glassy eye was not upon him.

Throughout the novel, it is up to the reader to weigh conflicting testimony and to form his or her own considered judgments.

Grandson of a former Episcopal bishop of New York, Guy Prime has grown up less rich than other of Auchincloss' main characters. His breeding and Harvard education, however, qualify him to function competently at the upper reaches of Manhattan's financial establishment. His classmate Rex Geer, like Derrick Hartley the son of a rural New England parson, is perhaps even better suited than Guy to the "art" of making money. Rex is not, however, a social climber; to interpret him as such, as a number of the characters do, is to oversimplify a personality of multiple and often conflicting motivations. Guy, for his part, is hardly less complex, an essentially humane man whose interactions with his fellow mortals are inevitably compounded by a flair for the dramatic and a tendency toward hero-worship.

From the start, the friendship of Guy Prime and Rex Geer is complicated by their interlocking relationships with women whom neither man quite understands. The first of these is Guy's wealthy cousin Alix Prime, a doll-like heiress with whom Rex falls suddenly and disastrously in love, quite to his own consternation. Although ambitious and industrious, Rex is immune to the blandishments of inherited wealth and quite undone by the common opinion that he covets Alix for her money. The second woman is Guy's wife Angelica, reared mainly in Europe by her expatriate mother. An affair in middle life between Rex and Angelica permanently alters the lives of all three characters, serving at least in part as Guy's justification for his ventures into thievery. To Guy's way of thinking, the affair between his wife and his best friend suffices to suspend his belief in permanent values; the fact remains, however, that Guy has already begun to borrow large sums of money from Rex to cover high-risk stock market activities. With the increase of risk, Guy "simply" begins to pledge the value of securities that have been left in trust with his firm.

Later testimony supplied by Rex (and by Angelica herself in a short concluding chapter) casts serious doubt upon some of the assertions made by Guy in the brief memoir that has been discovered following his death in 1962. Even so, there are few hard-and-fast answers to the questions that remain in the reader's mind. Auchincloss does not make any serious attempt to justify the plainly unethical conduct of his principal character; what he seeks, rather, is a credible re-creation of a significant moment in recent American history, leading immediately to the extensive financial reforms implemented by the administration of Franklin D. Roosevelt. To a far greater degree than in his earlier novels, Auchincloss presents characters caught and portrayed in all their understandably human ambiguity. Despite its limited scope and relative brevity, *The Embezzler* may well be the tightest and finest of Auchincloss' novels to date.

A prophet, according to Scripture, is not without honor save in his own house. In *The House of the Prophet*, Auchincloss, drawing from that proverb, has fashioned the most noteworthy of his recent novels. Felix Leitner, a respected attorney, widely read pundit, and adviser to presidents, emerges diminished from the examination of his life undertaken by Roger Cutter, an erstwhlie assistant and aspiring biographer. A variety of lesser narrative voices, including those of Leitner's two former wives, do their best to show the private truth behind the public image.

As in many of his later efforts, Auchincloss in *The House of the Prophet* returns with diminished success to a number of conventions and devices that have served him well in the past: the basic format of the novel, including the fussy, would-be "historian," owes much to *The Rector of Justin*, while Leitner, speaking occasionally in his own voice, recalls both Rex Geer and Guy Prime of *The Embezzler*. Although the action and characters are both credible and engrossing, *The House of the Prophet* gives the disturbing impression of a novel that one has already read, in which only the names and certain of the circumstances have been changed. Unfortunately, the elements that have helped to shape Auchincloss' strongest novels do not lend themselves readily to formula.

In its weakest moments, *The House of the Prophet* borders upon self-parody. Roger Cutter, the "main" narrator whose memories and intentions form the backbone of the novel, often comes across as Brian Aspinwall in caricature: rendered impotent for life by a diabetic crisis sustained in early adulthood, Roger is (even more obviously than the old-maidish Brian) cast in the role of house eunuch, free to observe and record the master's movements while remaining immune to any possible entanglement with the numerous female characters. Only in its documentary interest and its plausible interpretations of recent American history does *The House of the Prophet* bear serious comparison with the strongest of the author's earlier novels.

Viewed purely as a "political" novel, *The House of the Prophet* is a creditable example of the genre, showing that Auchincloss, when he chooses, can examine politics with the same shrewd powers of observation that he customarily applies to business and the law. As Leitner the pundit grows increasingly conservative with the onset of old age, his changing opinions are attributed less to the ossification of his mind than to the necessary tension between the "prophet" and his changing times. Toward the end of his life, for example, Leitner prepares a brilliant but outrageous column suggesting that America, through the forced resignation of Richard Nixon, "is engaging in one of the most ancient of tribal rituals: the burial of the fisher king." Roger Cutter, appalled by the likely consequences should such opinions be allowed to appear in print under Leitner's respected byline, acts quickly and effectively to have the column suppressed. Leitner's intelligence, however touched by senility, remains as keen and sensitive as ever; he has simply outlived his own time.

To date, Auchincloss' two subsequent novels have dealt with historical subjects, the Duc de Saint-Simon (*The Cat and The King*) and the American Civil War (*Watchfires*). In his sixty-fifth year, he remains active as a novelist, with an enviable and largely secure reputation. His later novels, however, reveal a tendency toward repetition that threatens to undermine, even in retrospect, the reputation justly earned by his best work.

Major publications other than long fiction
SHORT FICTION: *The Romantic Egotists*, 1954; *Powers of Attorney*, 1963; *Tales of Manhattan*, 1967; *Second Chance*, 1970; *The Partners*, 1974.
NONFICTION: *Edith Wharton*, 1961; *Reflections of a Jacobite*, 1961; *Edith Wharton: A Woman of Her Time*, 1971; *A Writer's Capital, Life, Law and Letters*, 1974; *Reading Henry James*, 1975; *Persons of Consequence: Queen Victoria and Her Circle*, 1979.

Bibliography
Adams, J. Donald. *Speaking of Books and Life*, 1965.
Hicks, Granville. *Literary Horizons: A Quarter Century of American Fiction*, 1970.

Milne, W. Gordon. *The Sense of Society: A History of the American Novel of Manners*, 1977.
Spender, Stephen. *Great Ideas Today*, 1965.
Tuttleton, James W. *The Novel of Manners in America*, 1972.

David B. Parsell

JANE AUSTEN

Born: Steventon, England; December 16, 1775
Died: Winchester, England; July 18, 1817

Principal long fiction

Sense and Sensibility, 1811; *Pride and Prejudice*, 1813; *Mansfield Park*, 1814; *Emma*, 1815; *Northanger Abbey*, 1818; *Persuasion*, 1818.

Other literary forms

In addition to her six novels, Jane Austen was the author of various short juvenile pieces, most of them literary burlesques mocking the conventions of the eighteenth century novel. Her other works are *Lady Susan*, a story told in letters and written c. 1805; *The Watsons*, a fragment of a novel written about the same time (both appended by J. E. Austen-Leigh to his 1871 *Memoir of Jane Austen*); and *Sanditon*, another fragmentary novel begun in 1817 and first published in 1925. All these pieces appear in *Minor Works* (Vol. VI of the *Oxford Illustrated Jane Austen*, 1954, R. W. Chapman, editor). Jane Austen's surviving letters have also been edited and published by Chapman.

Achievements

Austen, who published her novels anonymously, was not a writer famous in her time, nor did she wish to be. From the first, though, her novels written in and largely for her own family circle, gained the notice and esteem of a wider audience. Among her early admirers were the Prince Regent and the foremost novelist of the day, Sir Walter Scott, who deprecated his own aptitude for the "big Bow-Wow" and praised her as possessing a "talent for describing the involvements and feelings and characters of ordinary life which is to me the most wonderful I ever met with." Since the days of Scott's somewhat prescient praise, her reputation has steadily grown. The critical consensus now places Jane Austen in what F. R. Leavis has termed the "Great Tradition" of the English novel. Her talent was the first to forge, from the eighteenth century novel of external incident and internal sensibility, an art form that fully and faithfully presented a vision of real life in a particular segment of the real world. Austen's particular excellences—the elegant economy of her prose, the strength and delicacy of her judgment and moral discrimination, the subtlety of her wit, the imaginative vividness of her character drawing—have been emulated but not surpassed by subsequent writers.

Biography

Jane Austen's life contained little in the way of outward event. Born in 1775, she was the seventh of eight children. Her father, the Reverend George Austen, was a scholarly clergyman, the rector of Steventon in rural Hampshire. Mrs. Austen shared her husband's intelligence and intellectual interests, and the home they provided for their children was a happy and comfortable one, replete with the pleasures of country life, genteel society, perpetual reading, and lively discussion of ideas serious and frivolous. Jane Austen, who never married, was devoted throughout her life to her brothers and their families, but her closest relationship was with her older sister Cassandra, who likewise remained unmarried and whom Austen relied upon as her chief critic, cherished as a confidante, and admired as the ideal of feminine virtue.

On the rector's retirement in 1801, Austen moved with her parents and Cassandra to Bath. After the Reverend George Austen's death in 1804, the women continued to live for some time in that city. In 1806, the Austens moved to Southampton, where they shared a house with Captain Francis Austen, Jane's older brother, and his wife. In 1808, Edward Austen (who subsequently adopted the surname Knight from the relations whose two estates he inherited) provided his mother and sisters with a permanent residence, Chawton Cottage, in the Hampshire village of the same name. At this house, Austen was to revise her manuscripts that became *Sense and Sensibility*, *Pride and Prejudice*, and *Northanger Abbey* and to write *Mansfield Park*, *Emma*, and *Persuasion*. In 1817, it became evident that she was ill with a serious complaint whose symptoms seem to have been those of Addison's disease. To be near medical help, she and Cassandra moved to lodgings in Winchester in May, 1817. Austen died there less than two months later.

Analysis

Jane Austen's novels—her "bits of ivory," as she modestly and perhaps half playfully termed them—are unrivaled for their success in combining two sorts of excellence that all too seldom coexist. Meticulously conscious of her artistry (as, for example, is Henry James) Austen is also unremittingly attentive to the realities of ordinary human existence (as is, among others, Anthony Trollope). From the first, her works unite subtlety and common sense, good humor and acute moral judgment, charm and conciseness, deftly marshaled incident and carefully rounded character.

Austen's detractors have spoken of her as a "limited" novelist, one who, writing in an age of great men and important events, portrays small towns and petty concerns, who knows (or reveals) nothing of masculine occupations and ideas, and who reduces the range of feminine thought and deed to matrimonial scheming and social pleasantry. Though one merit of the first-rate novelist is the way his or her talent transmutes all it touches and thereby creates a distinctive and consistent world, it is true that the settings, characters, events, and ideas of Austen's novels are more than usually homogeneous. Her tales, like her own life, are set in country villages and at rural seats, from which the denizens venture forth to watering places or travel to London. True, her characters tend to be members of her own order, that prosperous and courteous segment of the middle class called the gentry. Unlike her novel-writing peers, Austen introduced few aristocrats into the pages of her novels, and the lower ranks, though glimpsed from time to time, are never brought forward. The happenings of her novels would not have been newsworthy in her day. She depicts society at leisure rather than on the march, and in portraying pleasures her literary preference is modest: architectural improvement involves the remodeling of a parsonage rather than the construction of Carlton House Terrace and Regent's Park; a ball is a gathering of country neighbors dancing to a harpsichord, not a crush at Almack's or the Duchess of Richmond's glittering fête on the eve of Waterloo.

These limitations are the self-drawn boundaries of a strong mind rather than the innate restrictions of a weak or parochial one. Austen was in a position to know a broad band of social classes, from the local lord of the manor to the retired laborer subsisting on the charity of the parish. Some aspects of life that she did not herself experience she could learn about firsthand without leaving the family circle. Her brothers could tell her of the university, the navy in the age of Nelson, or the world of finance and fashion in Regency London. Her cousin (and later sister-in-law) Eliza, who had lost her first husband, the Comte de Feuillide, to the guillotine, could tell her of Paris during the last days of the old regime. In focusing on the manners and morals of rural middle-class English life, particularly on the ordering dance of matrimony that gives shape to society and situation to young ladies, Austen emphasizes rather than evades reality. The microcosm she depicts is convincing because she understands, though seldom explicit assesses, its connections to the larger order. Her characters have clear social positions but are not just social types; the genius of such comic creations as Mrs. Bennet, Mr. Woodhouse, and Miss Bates is that each is a sparkling refinement on a quality or set of qualities existing at all times and on all levels. A proof of Austen's power (no one questions her polish) is that she succeeds in making whole communities live in the reader's imagination with little recourse to the stock device of the mere novelist of manners: descriptive detail. If a sparely drawn likeness is to convince, every line must count. The artist must understand what is omitted as well as what is supplied.

The six novels that constitute the Austen canon did not evolve in a straightforward way. Austen was, memoirs relate, as mistrustful of her judgment as she was rapid in her composition. In the case of *Pride and Prejudice*, for example, readers can be grateful that when the Reverend George Austen's letter offering the book's first incarnation, *First Impressions* (1797), to a publisher met with a negative reply, she was content to put the book aside for more than a decade. *Sense and Sensibility* was likewise a revision of a much earlier work. If Austen was notably nonchalant about the process of getting her literary progeny into print, one publisher with whom she had dealings was yet more dilatory. In 1803, Austen had completed *Northanger Abbey* (then entitled *Susan*) and through her brother Henry's agency had sold it to Crosby and Sons for ten pounds. Having acquired the manuscript, the publisher did not think fit to make use of it, and in December, 1816, Henry Austen repurchased the novel. He made known the author's identity, so family tradition has it, only after closing the deal. For these various reasons the chronology of Austen's novels can be set in different ways. Here, they will be discussed in order of their dates of publication.

Sense and Sensibility, Austen's first published novel, evolved from *Elinor and Marianne*, an epistolary work completed between 1795 and 1797. The novel is generally considered her weakest, largely because, as Walton Litz convincingly argues, it strives but fails to resolve "that struggle between inherited form and fresh experience which so often marks the transitional works of a great artist." The "inherited form" of which Litz speaks is the eighteenth century antithetical pattern suggested in the novel's title. According to this formula, opposing qualities of temperament or mind are presented in characters (generally female, often sisters) who despite their great differences are sincerely attached to one another.

In *Sense and Sensibility*, the antithetical characters are Elinor and Marianne Dashwood, the respective embodiments of cool, collected sense and prodigal, exquisite sensibility. In the company of their mother and younger sister, these lovely young ladies have, on the death of their father and the succession to his estate of their half-brother, retired in very modest circumstances to a small house in Devonshire. There the imprudent Marianne meets and melts for Willoughby, a fashionable gentleman as charming as he is unscrupulous. Having engaged the rash girl's affections, Willoughby proceeds to trifle with them by bolting for London. When chance once again brings the Dashwood sisters into Willoughby's circle, his manner toward Marianne is greatly altered. On hearing of his engagement to an heiress, the representative of sensibility swoons, weeps, and exhibits her grief to the utmost.

Meanwhile, the reasonable Elinor has been equally unlucky in love, though she bears her disappointment quite differently. Before the family's move to Devonshire, Elinor had met and come to cherish fond feelings for her sister-in-law's brother Edward Ferrars, a rather tame fellow (at least in comparison with Willoughby) who returns her regard—but with a measure of unease. It soon becomes known that Ferrars' reluctance to press his suit with Elinor stems from an early and injudicious secret engagement he had contracted with shrewd, base Lucy Steele. Elinor high-mindedly conceals her knowledge of the engagement and her feelings on the matter. Mrs. Ferrars, however, is a lady of less impressive self-control; she furiously disinherits her elder son in favor of his younger brother, whom Lucy then proceeds to ensnare. Thus Edward, free and provided with a small church living that will suffice to support a sensible sort of wife, can marry Elinor. Marianne—perhaps because she has finally exhausted her fancies and discovered her latent reason, perhaps because her creator is determined to punish the sensibility that throughout the novel has been so much more attractive than Elinor's prudence—is also provided with a husband: the rich Colonel Brandon, who has long loved her but whom, on account of his flannel waistcoats and his advanced age of five-and-thirty, she has heretofore reckoned beyond the pale.

The great flaw of *Sense and Sensibility* is that the polarities presented in the persons of Elinor and Marianne are too genuinely antithetical to be plausible or dynamic portraits of human beings. Elinor has strong feelings, securely managed though they may be, and Marianne has some rational powers to supplement her overactive imagination and emotions, but the young ladies do not often show themselves to be more than mere embodiments of sense and sensibility. In her second published novel, *Pride and Prejudice*, Austen makes defter use of two sisters whose values are the same but whose minds and hearts function differently. This book, a complete revision of *First Impressions*, the youthful effort that had, in 1797, been offered to and summarily rejected by the publisher Cadell, is, as numerous critics have observed, a paragon of "classic" literature in which the conventions and traditions of the eighteenth century novel come to full flowering yet are freshened and transformed by Austen's distinctive genius.

The title *Pride and Prejudice*, with its balanced alliterative abstractions, might suggest a second experiment in schematic psychology, and indeed the book does show some resemblances to *Sense and Sensibility*. Here again, as has been suggested, the reader encounters a pair of sisters, the elder (Jane Bennet) serene, the younger (Elizabeth) volatile. Unlike the Dashwoods, however, these ladies both demonstrate deep feelings and perceptive minds. The qualities alluded to in the title refer not to a contrast between sisters but to double defects shared by Elizabeth and Fitzwilliam Darcy, a wealthy and well-born young man she meets when his easygoing friend Charles Bingley leases Netherfield, the estate next to the Bennets' Longbourn. If so rich and vital a comic masterpiece could be reduced to a formula, it might be appropriate to say that the main thread of *Pride and Prejudice* involves the twin correction of these faults. As Darcy learns to moderate his tradition-based view of society and to recognize individual excellence (such as Elizabeth's, Jane's, and their Aunt and Uncle Gardiners') in ranks below his own, Elizabeth becomes less dogmatic in her judgments, and in particular more aware of the real merits of Darcy, whom she initially dismisses as a haughty, unfeeling aristocrat.

The growing accord of Elizabeth and Darcy is one of the most perfectly satisfying courtships in English literature. Their persons, minds, tastes, and even phrases convince the reader that they are two people truly made for each other; their union confers fitness on the world around them. Lionel Trilling has observed that, because of this principal match, *Pride and Prejudice* "permits us to conceive of morality as style." Elizabeth and Darcy's slow-growing love may be *Pride and Prejudice*'s ideal alliance, but it is far from being the only one, and a host of finely drawn characters surround the heroine and hero. In Jane Bennet and Charles Bingley, whose early mutual attraction is temporarily suspended by Darcy and the Bingley sisters (who deplore, not without some cause, the vulgarity of the amiable Jane's family), Austen presents a less sparkling but eminently pleasing and well-matched pair. William Collins, the half pompous, half obsequious, totally asinine cousin who, because of an entail, will inherit Longbourn and displace the Bennet females after Mr. Bennet's demise, aspires to marry Elizabeth, but, when rejected, gains the hand of her plain and practical friend Charlotte Lucas. Aware of her suitor's absurdities, Charlotte is nevertheless alive to the advantages of the situation he can offer. Her calculated decision to marry gives a graver ring to the irony of the novel's famous opening sentence: "It is a truth universally acknowledged, that a single man in possession of a good fortune, must be in want of a wife." The last of the matches made in *Pride and Prejudice* is yet more precariously based. A lively, charming, and amoral young officer, George Wickham, son of the former steward of Pemberley, Darcy's estate, and source of many of Elizabeth's prejudices against that scrupulous gentleman, first fascinates Elizabeth, then elopes with her youngest sister, mindless, frivolous Lydia. Only through Darcy's personal and financial intervention is Wickham persuaded to marry the ill-bred girl, who never properly understands her disgrace—a folly she shares with her mother. Mrs. Bennet, a woman deficient in good humor and good sense, is—along with her cynical, capricious husband, the ponderous Collins, and the tyrannical Lady Catherine De Bourgh—one of the great comic creations of literature. Most of these characters could have seemed odious if sketched by another pen, but so brilliant is the sunny intelligence playing over the world of *Pride and Prejudice* that even fools are golden.

  Mansfield Park, begun in 1811 and finished in 1813, is the first of Austen's novels to be a complete product of her maturity. The longest, most didactic, least ironic of her books, it is the one critics generally have most trouble reconciling with their prevailing ideas of the author. Although *Mansfield Park* was composed more or less at one stretch, its conception coincided with the final revisions of *Pride and Prejudice*. Indeed, the critics who offer the most satisfying studies of *Mansfield Park* tend to see it not as a piece of authorial bad faith or self-suppression, a temporary anomaly, but as what Walton Litz calls a "counter-truth" to its immediate predecessor.

  Pleased with and proud of *Pride and Prejudice*, Austen nevertheless recorded her impression of its being "rather too light, and bright, and sparkling"—in need of shade. That darkness she found wanting is supplied in *Mansfield Park*, which offers, as Trilling observes in his well-known essay on the novel, the antithesis to *Pride and Prejudice*'s generous, humorous, spirited social vision. *Mansfield Park*, Trilling argues, condemns rather than forgives:

"its praise is not for social freedom but for social stasis. It takes full notice of spiritedness, vivacity, celerity, and lightness, only to reject them as having nothing to do with virtue and happiness, as being, indeed, deterrents to the good life."

Most of the action of *Mansfield Park* is set within the little world comprising the estate of that name, a country place resembling in large measure Godmersham, Edward Austen Knight's estate in Kent; but for her heroine and some interludes in which she figures, Austen dips into a milieu she has not previously frequented in her novels—the socially and financially precarious lower fringe of the middle class. Fanny Price, a frail, serious, modest girl, is one of nine children belonging to and inadequately supported by a feckless officer of marines and his lazy, self-centered wife. Mrs. Price's meddling sister, the widowed Mrs. Norris, arranges for Fanny to be reared in "poor relation" status at Mansfield Park, the seat of kindly but crusty Sir Thomas Bertram and his languid lady, the third of the sisters. At first awed by the splendor of her surroundings, the gruffness of the baronet, and the elegance, vigor, and high spirits of the young Bertrams—Tom, Edmund, Maria, and Julia—Fanny eventually wins a valued place in the household. During Sir Thomas' absence to visit his property in Antigua, evidence of Fanny's moral fineness, and the various degrees in which her cousins fall short of her excellence, is presented through a device that proves to be one of Austen's most brilliant triumphs of plotting. Visiting the rectory at Mansfield are the younger brother and sister of the rector's wife, Henry and Mary Crawford, witty, worldly, and wealthy. At Mary's proposal, amateur theatricals are introduced to Mansfield Park, and in the process of this diversion the moral pollution of London's Great World begins to corrupt the bracing country air.

Just how the staging of a play—even though it be *Lovers' Vows*, a sloppy piece of romantic bathos, adultery rendered sympathetic—can be morally reprehensible is a bit unclear for most twentieth century readers, especially those who realize that the Austens themselves reveled in theatricals at home. The problem as Austen here presents it lies in the possible consequences of role-playing: coming to feel the emotions and attitudes one presents on the stage or, worse yet, expressing rather than suppressing genuine but socially unacceptable feelings in the guise of mere acting. In the course of the theatricals, where Fanny, who will not act, is relegated to the role of spectator and moral chorus, Maria Bertram, engaged to a bovine local heir, vies with her sister in striving to fascinate Henry Crawford, who in turn is all too ready to charm them. Mary Crawford, though it is "her way" to find eldest sons most agreeable, has the good taste to be attracted to Edmund, the second son, who plans to enter the Church. Mary's vivacity, as evidenced by the theatricals, easily wins his heart.

Time passes and poor Fanny, who since childhood has adored her cousin Edmund, unintentionally interests Henry Crawford. Determined to gain the affections of this rare young woman who is indifferent to his charms, Crawford ends by succumbing to hers. He proposes. Fanny's unworldly refusal provokes the anger of her uncle. Then, while Fanny, still in disgrace with the baronet, is away from Mansfield Park and visiting her family at Portsmouth, the debacle of which *Lovers' Vows* was a harbinger comes about. The *homme fatal* Henry, at a loss for a woman to make love to, trains his charms on his old flirt Maria, now Mrs. Rushworth. She runs away with him; her sister, not to be outdone in bad behavior, elopes with an unsatisfactory suitor. Mary Crawford's moral coarseness becomes evident in her casual dismissal of these catastrophes. Edmund, now a clergyman, finds solace, then love, with the cousin whose sterling character shines brightly for him now that Mary's glitter has tarnished. Fanny gains all she could hope for in at last attaining the heart and hand of her clerical kinsman.

Austen's next novel, *Emma*, might be thought of as harmonizing the two voices heard in *Pride and Prejudice* and *Mansfield Park*. For this book, Austen claimed to be creating "a heroine whom no one but myself will much like," an "imaginist" whose circumstances and qualities of mind make her the self-crowned queen of her country neighborhood. Austen was not entirely serious or accurate: Emma certainly has her partisans. Even those readers who do not like her tend to find her fascinating, for she is a spirited, imaginative, healthy young woman who, like Mary Crawford, has potential to do considerable harm to the fabric of society but on whom, like Elizabeth Bennet, her creator generously bestows life's greatest blessing: union with a man whose virtues, talents, and assets are the best complement for her own.

Emma's eventual marriage to Mr. Knightley of Donwell Abbey is the ultimate expression of one of Austen's key assumptions, that marriage is a young woman's supreme act of self-definition. Unlike any other Austen heroine, Emma has no pressing need to marry. As the opening sentence of the book implies, Emma's situation makes her acceptance or rejection of a suitor an act of unencumbered will: "Emma Woodhouse, handsome, clever, and rich, with a comfortable home and happy disposition, seemed to unite some of the best blessings of existence; and had lived nearly twenty-one years in the world with very little to distress or vex her."

Free though circumstance allows her to be, Emma has not been encouraged by her lot in life to acquire the discipline and self-knowledge that, augmenting her innate intelligence and taste, would help her to choose wisely. Brought up by a doting valetudinarian of a father and a perceptive but permissive governess, Emma has been encouraged to think too highly of herself. Far from vain about her beauty, Emma has—as Mr. Knightley, the only person who ventures to criticize her, observes—complete yet unfounded faith in her ability to judge people's characters and arrange their lives. The course of *Emma* is Miss Woodhouse's education in judgment, a process achieved through repeated mistakes and humiliations.

As the novel opens, the young mistress of Hartfield is at loose ends. Her beloved governess has just married Mr. Weston, of the neighboring property, Randalls. To fill the newly made gap in her life, Emma takes notice of Harriet Smith, a pretty, dim "natural daughter of somebody," and a parlor-boarder at the local school. Determined to settle her protégée into the sort of life she deems suitable, Emma detaches Harriet from Robert Martin, a young farmer who has proposed to her, and embarks upon a campaign to conquer for Harriet the heart of Mr. Elton, Highbury's unmarried clergyman. Elton's attentiveness and excessive flattery convince Emma of her plan's success but at the same time show the reader what Emma is aghast to learn at the end of Book I: that Elton scorns the nobody and has designs upon the heiress herself.

With the arrival of three new personages in Highbury, Book II widens Emma's opportunities for misconception. The first newcomer is Jane Fairfax, an elegant and accomplished connection of the Bates family and a girl whose prospective fate, the "governess trade," shows how unreliable the situations of well-bred young ladies without fortunes or husbands tend to be. Next to arrive is the suave Mr. Frank Churchill, Mr. Weston's grown son, who has been adopted by wealthy relations of his mother and who has been long remiss in paying a visit to Highbury. Finally, Mr. Elton brings home a bride, the former Augusta Hawkins of Bristol, a pretentious and impertinent creature possessed of an independent fortune, a well-married sister, and a boundless fund of self-congratulation. Emma mistakenly flatters herself that the dashing Frank Churchill is in love with her, and then settles on him as a husband for Harriet; she suspects the reserved Miss Fairfax, whose cultivation she rightly perceives as a reproach to her own untrained talents, of a clandestine relationship with a married man. She despises Mrs. Elton, as would any person of sense, but fails to see that the vulgar woman's offensiveness is an exaggerated version of her own officiousness and snobbery.

Thus, the potential consequences of Emma's misplaced faith in her judgment intensify, and the evidence of her fallibility mounts. Thoroughly embarrassed to learn that Frank Churchill, to whom she has retailed all her hypotheses regarding Jane Fairfax, has long been secretly engaged to that woman, Emma suffers the death-blow to her smug self-esteem when Harriet announces that the gentleman whose feelings she hopes to have aroused is not, as Emma supposes, Churchill but the squire of Donwell. Emma's moment of truth is devastating and complete, its importance marked by one of Jane Austen's rare uses of figurative language: "It darted through her, with the speed of an arrow, that Mr. Knightley must marry no one but herself!" Perhaps the greatest evidence of Emma's being a favorite of fortune is that Mr. Knightley feels the same as she does on this matter. Chastened by her series of bad judgments, paired with a gentleman who for years has loved and respected her enough to correct her and whom she can love and respect in turn, Emma participates in the minuet of marriage with which Austen concludes the book, the other couples so united being Miss Fairfax and Mr. Churchill and Harriet Smith (ductile enough to form four attachments in a year) and Robert Martin (stalwart enough to persist in his original feeling).

Emma Woodhouse's gradual education, which parallels the reader's growing awareness of what a menace to the social order her circumstances, abilities, and weaknesses combine to make her, is one of Austen's finest pieces of plotting. The depiction of character is likewise superb. Among a gallery of memorable and distinctive characters are Mr. Woodhouse; Miss Bates, the stream-of-consciousness talker who inadvertently provokes Emma's famous rudeness on Box Hill; and the wonderfully detestable Mrs. Elton, with her self-contradictions and her fractured Italian, her endless allusions to Selina, Mr. Suckling, Maple Grove, and the *barouche landau*. Life at Hartfield, Donwell, and Highbury is portrayed with complexity and economy. Every word, expression, opinion, and activity—whether sketching a portrait, selecting a dancing partner, or planning a strawberry-picking party—becomes a gesture of self-revelation. *Emma* demonstrates how, in Austen's hands, the novel of manners can become a statement of moral philosophy.

Northanger Abbey was published in a four-volume unit with *Persuasion* in 1818, after Austen's death, but the manuscript had been completed much earlier, in 1803. Austen wrote a preface for *Northanger Abbey* but did not do the sort of revising that had transformed *Elinor and Marianne* and *First Impressions* into *Sense and Sensibility* and *Pride and Prejudice*. The published form of *Northanger Abbey* can therefore be seen as the earliest of the six novels. It is also, with the possible exception of *Sense and Sensibility*, the most "literary." *Northanger Abbey*, like some of Austen's juvenile burlesques, confronts the conventions of the Gothic novel or tale of terror. The incidents of her novel have been shown to parallel, with ironic difference, the principal lines of Gothic romance, particularly as practiced by Ann Radcliffe, whose most famous works, *The Romance of the Forest* (1791) and *The Mysteries of Udolpho* (1794), had appeared several years before Jane Austen had begun work on her burlesque.

Like *Emma*, *Northanger Abbey* is centrally concerned with tracing the growth of a young woman's mind and the cultivation of her judgment. In this less sophisticated work, however, the author accomplishes her goal through a rather schematic contrast. As an enthusiastic reader of tales of terror, Catherine Morland has Gothic expectations of life despite a background most unsuitable for a heroine. Like the Gothic heroines she admires, Catherine commences adventuring early in the novel. She is not, however, shipped to Venice or Dalmatia, but taken to Bath for a six-week stay. Her hosts are serenely amiable English folk, her pastimes the ordinary round of spa pleasures; the young man whose acquaintance she makes, Henry Tilney, is a witty clergyman rather than a misanthropic monk or dissolute rake. Toward this delightful, if far from Gothic, young man, Catherine's feelings are early inclined. In turn, he, his sister, and even his father, the haughty, imperious General Tilney, are favorably disposed toward her. With the highest expectations, Catherine sets out to accompany them to their seat, the Abbey of the novel's title (which, like that of *Persuasion*, was selected not by the author but by Henry Austen, who handled the posthumous publication).

At Northanger, Catherine's education in the difference between literature and life continues. Despite its monastic origins, the Abbey proves a comfortable and well-maintained dwelling. When Catherine, like one of Radcliffe's protagonists, finds a mysterious document in a chest and spends a restless night wondering what lurid tale it might chronicle, she is again disappointed: "If the evidence of her sight might be trusted she held a washing-bill in her hand." Although Catherine's experience does not confirm the truth of Radcliffe's sensational horrors, it does not prove the world a straightforward, safe, cozy place. Catherine has already seen something of falseness and selfish vulgarity in the persons of Isabella Thorpe and her brother John, acquaintances formed at Bath. At Northanger, she learns that, though the General may not be the wife-murderer she has fancied him, he is quite as cruel as she could imagine. On learning that Catherine is not the great heiress he has mistakenly supposed her to be, the furious general packs her off in disgrace and discomfort in a public coach.

With this proof that the world of fact can prove as treacherous as that of fiction, Catherine returns sadder and wiser to the bosom of her family. She has not long to droop, though, for Henry Tilney, on hearing of his father's bad behavior, hurries after her and makes Catherine the proposal which he has long felt inclined to offer and which his father has until recently promoted. The approval of Catherine's parents is immediate, and the General is not overlong in coming to countenance the match. "To begin perfect happiness at the respective ages of twenty-six and eighteen is to do pretty well," observes the facetious narrator, striking a literary pose even in the novel's last sentence, "and . . . I leave it to be settled by whomsoever it may concern, whether the tendency of this work be altogether to recommend parental tyranny, or reward filial disobedience."

Persuasion, many readers believe, signals Austen's literary move out of the eighteenth century and into the nineteenth. This novel, quite different from those that preceded it, draws not upon the tradition of the novelists of the 1790's but on that of the lionized poets of the new century's second decade, Sir Walter Scott and Lord Byron. For the first time, Austen clearly seems the child of her time, susceptible to the charms of natural rather than improved landscapes, fields and sea cliffs rather than gardens and shrubberies. The wistful, melancholy beauty of autumn that pervades the book is likewise romantic. The gaiety, vitality, and sparkling wit of *Pride and Prejudice* and *Emma* are muted. The stable social order represented by the great estate in

Mansfield Park has become fluid in *Persuasion*: here the principal country house, Kellynch Hall, must be let because the indigenous family cannot afford to inhabit it.

Most important, *Persuasion*'s heroine is unique in Jane Austen's gallery. Anne Elliott, uprooted from her ancestral home, spiritually isolated from her selfish and small-minded father and sisters, separated from the man she loves by a long-standing estrangement, is every bit as "alienated" as such later nineteenth century heroines as Esther Summerson, Jane Eyre, and Becky Sharp. Anne's story is very much the product of Austen's middle age. At twenty-seven, she is the only Austen heroine to be past her first youth. Furthermore, she is in no need of education. Her one great mistake—overriding the impulse of her heart and yielding to the persuasion of her friend Lady Russell in rejecting the proposal of Frederick Wentworth, a sanguine young naval officer with his fortune still to make and his character to prove— is some eight years in the past, and she clearly recognizes it for the error it was.

Persuasion, many readers believe, signals Austen's literary move out of the eighteenth century and into the nineteenth. This novel, quite different from those that preceded it, draws not upon the tradition of the novelists of the 1790's but on that of the lionized poets of the new century's second decade, Sir Walter Scott and Lord Byron. For the first time, Austen clearly seems the child of her time, susceptible to the charms of natural rather than improved landscapes, fields and sea cliffs rather than gardens and shrubberies. The wistful, melancholy beauty of autumn that pervades the book is likewise romantic. The gaiety, vitality, and sparkling wit of *Pride and Prejudice* and *Emma* are muted. The stable social order represented by the great estate in *Mansfield Park* has become fluid in *Persuasion*: here the principal country house, Kellynch Hall, must be let because the indigenous family cannot afford to inhabit it.

Most important, *Persuasion*'s heroine is unique in Jane Austen's gallery. Anne Elliott, uprooted from her ancestral home, spiritually isolated from her selfish and small-minded father and sisters, separated from the man she loves by a long-standing estrangement, is every bit as "alienated" as such later nineteenth century heroines as Esther Summerson, Jane Eyre, and Becky Sharp. Anne's story is very much the product of Austen's middle age. At twenty-seven, she is the only Austen heroine to be past her first youth. Furthermore, she is in no need of education. Her one great mistake—overriding the impulse of her heart and yielding to the persuasion of her friend Lady Russell in rejecting the proposal of Frederick Wentworth, a sanguine young naval officer with his fortune still to make and his character to prove— is some eight years in the past, and she clearly recognizes it for the error it was.

Persuasion is the story of how Anne and Frederick (now the eminent Captain) Wentworth rekindle the embers of their love. Chance throws them together when the vain, foolish Sir Walter Elliott, obliged to economize or rent his estate, resolves to move his household to Bath, where he can cut a fine figure at less cost, and leases Kellynch to Admiral and Mrs. Croft, who turn out to be the brother-in-law and sister of Captain Wentworth. Initially cool to his former love—or rather, able to see the diminution of her beauty because he is unable to forgive her rejection—the Captain flirts with the Musgrove girls; they are sisters to the husband of Anne's younger sister Mary and blooming belles with the youth and vigor Anne lacks. The old appreciation of Anne's merits, her clear insight, kindness, highmindedness, and modesty, soon reasserts itself, but not before fate and the Captain's impetuosity have all but forced another engagement upon him. Being "jumped down" from the Cobb at Lyme Regis, Louisa Musgrove misses his arms and falls unconscious on the pavement. Obliged by honor to declare himself hers if she should wish it, Wentworth is finally spared this self-sacrifice when the susceptible young lady and the sensitive Captain Benwick fall in love. Having discovered the intensity of his devotion to Anne by being on the point of having to abjure it, Wentworth hurries to Bath, there to declare his attachment in what is surely the most powerful engagement scene in the Austen canon.

Though the story of *Persuasion* belongs to Anne Elliott and Frederick Wentworth, Austen's skill at evoking characters is everywhere noticeable. As Elizabeth Jenkins observes, all of the supporting characters present different facets of the love theme. The heartless marital calculations of Mr. Elliott, Elizabeth Elliott, and Mrs. Clay, the domestic comforts of the senior Musgroves and the Crofts, and the half fractious, half amiable ménage of Charles and Mary Musgrove all permit the reader more clearly to discern how rare and true is the love Anne Elliott and her captain have come so close to losing. The mature, deeply grateful commitment they are able to make to each other is, if not the most charming, surely the most profound in the Austen world.

Major publications other than long fiction
SHORT FICTION: *Minor Works*, 1954 (Vol. VI of the *Oxford Illustrated Jane Austen*, R. W. Chapman, editor).
NONFICTION: *Jane Austen's Letters*, 1952 (R. W. Chapman, editor).

Bibliography
Austen-Leigh, J. E. *Memoir of Jane Austen*, 1926.
Chapman, R. W. *Jane Austen: A Critical Bibliography*, 1955.
Duckworth, Alistair. *The Improvement of the Estate*, 1972.
Jenkins, Elizabeth. *Jane Austen*, 1952.
Litz, A. Walton. *Jane Austen: A Study of Her Artistic Development*, 1965.
Trilling, Lionel. "*Mansfield Park*," in *The Opposing Self*, 1959.

Peter W. Graham

JAMES BALDWIN

Born: New York, New York; August 2, 1924

Principal long fiction
Go Tell It on the Mountain, 1953; *Giovanni's Room*, 1956; *Another Country*, 1962; *Tell Me How Long the Train's Been Gone*, 1968; *If Beale Street Could Talk*, 1974; *Just Above My Head*, 1979.

Other literary forms
Before he published his first novel, James Baldwin had established a reputation as a talented essayist and reviewer. Many of his early pieces, later collected in *Notes of a Native Son* (1955) and *Nobody Knows My Name: More Notes of a Native Son* (1961), have become classics; his essays on Richard Wright, especially "Everybody's Protest Novel" (1949) and "Many Thousands Gone" (1951), occupy a central position in the development of "universalist" Afro-American thought during the 1950's. Culminating in *The Fire Next Time* (1963), an extended meditation on the relationship of race, religion, and the individual experience in America, Baldwin's early prose demands a reexamination and redefinition of received social and cultural premises. His more recent nonfiction books, *No Name in the Street* (1971) and *The Devil Finds Work* (1976), reflect a more militant political stance and have been received less favorably than Baldwin's universalist statements. Nevertheless, along with essays such as the prize-winning "Atlanta: The Evidence of Things Unseen" (*Playboy*, 1981), they demonstrate Baldwin's continuing eloquence and insight. Less formal and intricate, though in some cases more explicit, reflections of Baldwin's beliefs can be found in *A Rap on Race* (1971), an extended discussion with Margaret Mead, and *A Dialogue* (1975), a conversation with Nikki Giovanni.

Baldwin has also written children's fiction (*Little Man, Little Man*, 1975), the text for a photographic essay (*Nothing Personal*, 1964, with Richard Avedon), an unfilmed scenario (*One Day, When I Was Lost: A Scenario Based on The Autobiography of Malcolm X*, 1972), drama, and short stories. Most critics prefer Baldwin's first play, *The Amen Corner* (written mid-1950's, published 1965), to *Blues for Mister Charlie* (1964), despite the latter's four-month Broadway run. Although he has published little short fiction since the collection *Going to Meet the Man* (1965), Baldwin is an acknowledged master of the novella form. "Sonny's Blues" (1957), the story of the relationship of a jazz musician to his "respectable" narrator-brother, anticipates many of the themes of Baldwin's later novels and is widely recognized as one of the great American novellas.

Achievements

Baldwin's public role as a major Afro-American racial spokesman of the 1950's and 1960's, guarantees his place in American cultural history. Though not undeserved, this reputation more frequently obscures than clarifies the nature of his literary achievement, which involves his relationship to Afro-American culture, existential philosophy, and the moral tradition of the world novel. To be sure, Baldwin's progression from an individualistic, universalist stance through active involvement with the integrationist Civil Rights movement to an increasing sympathy with militant Pan-Africanist thought parallels the general development of Afro-American thought between the early 1950's and the mid-1970's. Indeed, his novels frequently mirror both Baldwin's personal philosophy and its social context. Some, most notably *Another Country*, attained a high degree of public visibility when published, leading to a widely accepted vision of Baldwin as a topical writer. To consider Baldwin primarily as a racial spokesman, however, imposes a stereotype which distorts many of his most penetrating insights and underestimates his status as a literary craftsman.

More accurate, though ultimately as limited, is the view of Baldwin primarily as an exemplar of the Afro-American presence in the "mainstream" of the American tradition. Grouped with Ralph Ellison as a major "post-Wright" black novelist, Baldwin represents, in this view, the generation which rejected "protest literature" in favor of "universal" themes. Strangely at odds with the view of Baldwin as racial spokesman, this view emphasizes the craftsmanship of Baldwin's early novels and his treatment of "mainstream" themes such as religious hypocrisy, father-son tensions, and sexual identity. Ironically, many younger Afro-American novelists accept this general view of Baldwin's accomplishment, viewing his mastery of Jamesian techniques and his involvement with Continental literary culture as an indication of alienation from his racial identity. Recasting Eldridge Cleaver's political attack on Baldwin in aesthetic terms, the Afro-American writer Ishmael Reed dismisses Baldwin as a great "white" novelist. A grain of truth lies in Reed's assertion; Baldwin rarely creates new forms. Rather, he infuses a variety of Euro-American forms, derived from Wright and William Faulkner as well as from Henry James, with the rhythms and imagery of the Afro-American oral tradition.

Like the folk preacher whose voice he frequently assumes in secular contexts, Baldwin combines moral insight with an uncompromising sense of the concrete realities of his community, whether defined in terms of family, lovers, race, or nation. This indicates the deepest level of Baldwin's literary achievement; whatever his immediate political focus or fictional form, he possesses an insight into moral psychology shared by only a handful of novelists. Inasmuch as the specific circumstances of this psychology involve American racial relations, this insight aligns Baldwin with Wright, Faulkner, Mark Twain, and

Harriet Beecher Stowe. Inasmuch as his insight involves the symbolic alienation of the individual, it places him with American romantics such as Nathaniel Hawthorne and European existentialists such as Albert Camus. Since his insight recognizes the complex pressure exerted by social mechanisms on individual consciousness, it reveals affinities with James Joyce, George Eliot, and Ellison. As a writer combining elements of all of these traditions with the voice of the anonymous Afro-American preacher, Baldwin cannot be reduced to accommodate the terms of any one of them. Refusing to lie about the reality of pain, he provides realistic images of the moral life possible in an inhospitable world that encompasses the streets of Harlem and the submerged recesses of the mind.

Biography

James Baldwin once dismissed his childhood as "the usual bleak fantasy." Nevertheless, the major concerns of his fiction consistently reflect the social context of his family life in Harlem during the Depression. The dominant figure of Baldwin's childhood was clearly that of his stepfather, David Baldwin, who worked as a manual laborer and preached in a storefront church. Clearly the model for Gabriel Grimes in *Go Tell It on the Mountain*, David Baldwin had moved from New Orleans to New York City, where he married Baldwin's mother, Emma Berdis. The oldest of what was to be a group of nine children in the household, James assumed a great deal of the responsibility for the care of his half-brothers and sisters. Insulated somewhat from the brutality of Harlem street life by his domestic duties, Baldwin, as he describes in *The Fire Next Time*, sought refuge in the Church. Undergoing a conversion experience, similar to that of John in *Go Tell It on the Mountain*, at age fourteen in 1938, Baldwin preached as a youth minister for the next several years. At the same time, he began to read, immersing himself in works such as *Uncle Tom's Cabin* (1852) and the novels of Charles Dickens. Both at his Harlem junior high school, where the Afro-American poet Countée Cullen was one of his teachers, and at his predominantly white Bronx high school, Baldwin contributed to student literary publications. The combination of family tension, economic hardship, and religious vocation provides the focus of much of Baldwin's greatest writing, most notably *Go Tell It on the Mountain*, *The Fire Next Time*, and *Just Above My Head*.

If Baldwin's experience during the 1930's provided his material, his life from 1942 to 1948 shaped his characteristic approach to that material. After he was graduated from high school in 1942, Baldwin worked for a year as a manual laborer in New Jersey, an experience which increased both his understanding of his stepfather and his insight into America's economic and racial systems. Moving to Greenwich Village in 1943, Baldwin worked during the day and wrote at night for the next five years; his first national reviews and essays appeared in 1946. The major event of the Village years, however, was

Baldwin's meeting with Richard Wright in the winter between 1944 and 1945. Wright's interest helped Baldwin secure first a Eugene F. Saxton Memorial Award and then a Rosenwald Fellowship, enabling him to move to Paris in 1948.

After his arrival in France, Baldwin experienced more of the poverty which had shaped his childhood. Simultaneously, he developed a larger perspective on the psychocultural context conditioning his experience, feeling at once a greater sense of freedom and a larger sense of the global structure of racism, particularly as reflected in the French treatment of North Africans. In addition, he formed many of the personal and literary friendships which contributed to his later public prominence. Baldwin's well-publicized literary feud with Wright, who viewed the younger writer's criticism of *Native Son* (1940) as a form of personal betrayal, helped establish Baldwin as a major presence in Afro-American letters. Although Baldwin's first novel, *Go Tell It on the Mountain*, was well-received critically, it was not so financially successful that he could devote his full time to creative writing. As a result, Baldwin continued to travel widely, frequently on journalistic assignments, while writing *Giovanni's Room*, which is set in France and involves no black characters.

Returning to the United States as a journalist covering the Civil Rights movement, Baldwin made his first trip to the American South in 1957. The essays and reports describing that physical and psychological journey propelled Baldwin to the position of public prominence which he maintained for more than a decade. During the height of the movement, Baldwin lectured widely and was present at major events such as the March on Washington and the voter registration drive in Selma, Alabama. In addition, he met with most of the major Afro-American activists of the period, including Martin Luther King, Elijah Muhammad, James Meredith, and Medgar Evers. Attorney General Robert Kennedy requested that Baldwin bring together the most influential voices in the black community, and, even though the resulting meeting accomplished little, the request testifies to Baldwin's image as a focal point of Afro-American opinion. In addition to this political activity, Baldwin formed personal and literary relationships—frequently tempestuous ones—with numerous white writers, including William Styron and Norman Mailer. A surge in literary popularity, reflected in the presence of *Another Country* and *The Fire Next Time* on the best-seller lists throughout most of 1962 and 1963, accompanied Baldwin's political success and freed him from financial insecurity for the first time. He traveled extensively throughout the decade, and his visits to Puerto Rico and Africa were to have a major influence on his subsequent political thought.

Partly because of Baldwin's involvement with prominent whites and partly because of the sympathy for homosexuals evinced in his writing, several black militants, most notably Eldridge Cleaver, attacked Baldwin's position as "black spokesman" beginning in the late 1960's. As a result, nationalist spokesmen such as Amiri Baraka and Bobby Seale gradually eclipsed Baldwin in the public literary and political spotlights. Nevertheless, Baldwin, himself sympathetic to many of the militant positions, has continued his involvement with public issues, such as the fate of the Wilmington, North Carolina, prisoners which he addressed in an open letter to Jimmy Carter shortly after Carter's election to the presidency. More recently, Baldwin has returned to the South to assess the changes of the last three decades and to examine the meaning of events such as the Atlanta child murders. Although he has never married and lives much of the time in France and Turkey, Baldwin places a high value on family contacts; he has dedicated much of his writing to nephews and nieces and maintains strong ties with his brothers and sisters.

Analysis

Uncompromising in his demand for personal and social integrity, James Baldwin has from the beginning of his career charged the individual with full responsibility for his or her moral identity. Both in his early individualistic novels and his later political fiction, he insists on the inadequacy of received definitions as the basis for self-knowledge or social action. Echoing the existentialist principle "existence precedes essence," he intimates the underlying consistency of his vision in the introductory essay in *Notes of a Native Son*: "I think all theories are suspect, that the finest principles may have to be modified, or may even be pulverized by the demands of life, and that one must find, therefore, one's own moral center and move through the world hoping that this center will guide one aright." This insistence on the moral center and movement in the world cautions against associating Baldwin with the atheistic or solipsistic currents of existential thought. Never denying the possibility of transcendent moral power—which he frequently images as the power of love—he simply insists that human conceptions must remain flexible enough to allow for the honest perception of experience. Fully recognizing the reality of existential pain and despair, Baldwin invokes honesty and self-acceptance as the necessary supports for the love capable of generating individual communication and at least the groundwork for political action.

Baldwin's social vision, reflecting his experience in a racist culture, acknowledges the forces militating against self-knowledge and moral responsibility. Each of his novels portrays a series of evasive and simplifying definitions built into religious, economic, and educational institutions. These definitions, which emphasize the separation of self and other, control the immediate contexts of individual experience. As a result, they frequently seem to constitute "human nature," to embody the inevitable limits of experience. While sympathizing with the difficulty of separating the self from context without simultaneously denying experience, Baldwin insists that acquiescing to the definitions inevitably results in self-hatred and social immorality. The individual incapable of accepting his or her existential complexity flees to the illusion of certainty provided by the institutions which assume responsibility for directing moral decisions. This cycle of institutional pressure encouraging existential evasion insuring further institutional corruption recurs in each of Baldwin's novels. On both personal and social levels, the drive to deny the reality of the other—racial, sexual, or economic—generates nothing save destruction. Derived from the streets of Harlem rather than from Scripture, Baldwin's response echoes Christ's admonition to "love thy neighbor as thyself." The derivation is vital; in Baldwin's novels, those who extract the message from the Bible rather than from their lives frequently aggravate the pain which makes evading reality seem attractive.

The immediate focus of Baldwin's attention has gradually shifted from consciousness to context, creating the illusion of a change in his basic concerns. While he has always worked in the realistic tradition of the novel, his choice of specific forms parallels this shift in thematic focus, though again his most recent work indicates an underlying unity in his fiction. His first novel, *Go Tell It on the Mountain*, employs a tightly focused Jamesian form to explore the developing awareness of the adolescent protagonist John Grimes, who is not yet aware of the evasive definitions conditioning his experience. After a second Jamesian novel, *Giovanni's Room*, Baldwin adapted the relatively unstructured Dreiserian mode in *Another Country* and *Tell Me How Long the Train's Been Gone*. Characters such as Rufus Scott and Vivaldo Moore in *Another Country* continue to struggle for individual awareness, but Baldwin's new narrative stance emphasizes the impact of the limiting definitions on a wide range of particular social circumstances. Attempting to balance the presentation of consciousness and context, Baldwin's most recent novels, *If Beale Street Could Talk* and *Just Above My Head*, synthesize the earlier technical approaches. Returning to the immediate focus on the individual consciousness in these first-person narratives, Baldwin creates protagonists capable of articulating their own social perceptions. Consciousness and context merge as Baldwin's narrators share their insights and, more important, their processes with their fellow sufferers.

These insights implicitly endorse William Blake's vision of morality as a movement from innocence through experience to a higher innocence. Beginning with an unaware innocence, individuals inevitably enter the deadening and murderous world of experience, the world of the limiting definitions. Those who attempt to deny the world and remain children perish alongside those who cynically submit to the cruelty of the context for imagined personal benefit. Only those who plunge into experience, recognize its cruelty, and resolve to forge an aware innocence can hope to survive morally. Specifically, Baldwin urges families to pass on a sense of the higher innocence to their children by refusing to simplify the truth of experience. This painful honesty makes possible the commitment to love despite the inevitability of pain and isolation. It provides the only hope, however desperate, for individual or social rejuvenation. To a large extent, Baldwin's career develops in accord with the Blakean pattern. John Grimes begins his passage from innocence to experience in *Go Tell It on the Mountain*; Rufus Scott and Vivaldo Moore, among others, struggle to survive experience in *Another Country*, which intimates the need for the higher innocence. Baldwin's recent novels portray the entire process, focusing on the attempt first to find and then to pass on the higher innocence. *Just Above My Head*, with its middle-aged narrator and his teenaged children, clearly represents a more highly developed and realistic stage of the vision than *If Beale Street Could Talk*, with its teenaged mother-narrator and her newborn infant.

Go Tell It on the Mountain centers on the religious conversion and family relationships of John Grimes, whose experience parallels that of Baldwin during his youth. Although he believes himself to be the natural son of Gabriel Grimes, a preacher who, like Baldwin's stepfather, moved to New York after growing up in the South, John is actually the son of Gabriel's wife Elizabeth and her lover, Richard, who committed suicide prior to John's birth. Growing up under the influence of his hypocritical and tyrannical stepfather, John alternately attempts to please and transcend him. Gabriel expends most of his emotional energy on his openly rebellious son Roy, whose immersion in the violent life of the Harlem streets contrasts sharply with John's involvement with the "Temple of the Fire Baptized," the storefront church where his conversion takes place. To the extent that Baldwin organizes *Go Tell It on the Mountain* around John's attempt to come to terms with these pressures, the novel appears to have a highly individualistic focus.

The overall structure of the novel, however, dictates that John's experience be viewed in a larger context. Of the three major sections of *Go Tell It on the Mountain*, the first, "The Seventh Day," and the third, "The Threshing Floor," focus directly on John. The long middle section, "The Prayers of the Saints," a Faulknerian exploration of history, traces the origins of John's struggle to the experience of his elders, devoting individual chapters to Elizabeth, Gabriel, and Gabriel's sister Florence. Together the prayers portray the Great Migration of blacks from South to North, from rural to urban settings. Far from bringing true freedom, the movement results in a new indirect type of oppression. As Elizabeth recognizes: "There was not, after all, a great difference between the world of the North and that of the South which she had fled; there was only this difference: the North promised more. And this similarity: what it promised it did not give, and what it gave, at length and grudgingly with one hand, it took back with the other." Even in his most individualistic phase, then, Baldwin is aware of the power of institutional pressures. The origins of John's particular struggle against the limiting definitions go back to their impact on both Elizabeth and Gabriel.

Elizabeth's relationship with John's true father, at least in its early stages, appears to offer hope for at least a limited freedom from external definition.

Highly intelligent and self-aware, Richard struggles to transcend the limitations imposed on black aspiration through a rigorous program of self-education, which he shares with Elizabeth. Despite his intelligence and determination, however, Richard maintains a naïve innocence concerning the possibility of self-definition in a society based on racist assumptions. Only when arrested on suspicion of a robbery he had nothing to do with does he recognize that his context defines him simply as another "nigger." Unable to reconcile this imposed definition with his drive for social transcendence, he despairs and commits suicide. This act, in turn, destroys Elizabeth's chance for obtaining a greater degree of freedom. She is not, however, simply a victim. Fearing that Richard will be unable to cope with the responsibility of a family, she fails to tell him of her pregnancy. Far from protecting him, this evasion contributes to his destruction by allowing Richard to view his situation as purely personal. Elizabeth's own choice, conditioned by the social refusal to confront reality, combines with the racist legal system to circumscribe her possibilities. Forced to care for her infant son, she marries Gabriel, thus establishing the basic terms for John's subsequent struggle.

Seen in relation to John in "The Seventh Day," Gabriel appears to be one of the most despicable hypocrites in American literature. Seen in relation to his own history in "The Prayers of the Saints," however, he appears victimized by the institutional context of his youth. In turn, he victimizes his family by attempting to force them into narrowly defined roles. The roots of Gabriel's character lie in the "temple-street" dichotomy of his Southern childhood. Encouraged by his religious mother to deny his sensuality, Gabriel undergoes a conversion experience and immerses himself in the role of preacher. As a result, he enters into a loveless asexual marriage with his mother's friend Deborah, herself a victim of the racist psychology—enforced by blacks and whites—which condemns *her* after she has been brutally raped by a group of whites. Eventually, Gabriel's repressed street self breaks out and he fathers a son by the sensual Esther. Again attempting to deny his sensuality, Gabriel refuses to acknowledge this son, Royal. Like John's half-brother Roy, the first Royal immerses himself in the street life which Gabriel denies; he dies in a Chicago barroom brawl. Gabriel fears that Roy will share Royal's fate, but his attempt to crush his second son's street self merely strengthens the resulting rebellion. Faced with the guilt of Royal's death and the sense of impending doom concerning Roy, Gabriel retreats into a solipsism which makes a mockery of his Christian vocation. Far from providing a context for moral responsibility, the Church—both in the South and in the North—simply replaces the original innocence of religious fervor with a cynical vision of religion as a source of the power needed to destroy the innocence of others.

Against this backdrop, John's conversion raises a basic question which will recur in slightly different circumstances in each of Baldwin's novels: Can an individual hope to break the cycle of evasion which has shaped his personal and social context? In John's case, the problem takes on added dimensions, since he remains ignorant of many of the events shaping his life, including those involving his own birth. By framing the prayers with John's conversion, Baldwin stresses the connection between past and present, but the connection can be perceived as either oppressive or liberating. The complex irony of "The Threshing Floor" section allows informed readings of John's conversion as either a surrender to evasion or as a movement toward existential responsibility. Focusing primarily on John's internal experience as he lies transfixed on the church floor, "The Threshing Floor" revolves around a dialogue between an "ironic voice" which challenges John to return to the street and the part of John which seeks traditional salvation. Throughout John's vision, the narrative voice shifts point of view in accord with John's developing perception. As John accepts the perceptions implied by his vision, the ironic voice shifts its attention to yet deeper levels of ambiguity. To the extent that John resolves these ambiguities by embracing the Temple, his experience seems to increase the risk that he will follow Gabriel's destructive example.

Several image patterns, however, indicate that John may be moving nearer to a recognition of his actual complexity. Chief among these are those involving the curse of Ham, the rejection of the father, and the acceptance of apparent opposites. From the beginning of the vision, the ironic voice ridicules John for accepting the curse of Ham, which condemns him both as son and as "nigger." Manipulating John's sense of guilt for having indulged his street self by masturbating, the ironic voice insists that John's very existence "proves" Gabriel's own sexual weakness. If Gabriel condemns John, he condemns himself in the process. As a result, John comes to view himself as the "devil's son" and repudiates his subservience before his "father." Without this essentially negative, and ultimately socially derived, definition of himself, John finds himself in an existential void where "there was no speech or language, and there was no love."

Forced to reconstruct his identity, John progresses from this sense of isolation to a vision of the dispossessed with whom he shares his agony and his humanity. John's vision of the multitude whose collective voice merges with his own suggests suffering as the essential human experience, one obliterating both the safety and the isolation of imposed definitions. Significantly, this vision leads John to Jesus the Son rather than God the Father, marking an implicit rejection of Gabriel's Old Testament vengeance in favor of the New Testament commitment to an all-encompassing love. The son metamorphosizes from symbol of limitation to symbol of liberation. Near the end of his vision, John explicitly rejects the separation of opposites—street and temple, white and black—encouraged by his social context: "The light and the darkness had kissed each other, and were married now, forever, in the life and the vision of John's soul." Returning to his immediate environment from the depths of his mind, John responds not to the call of Gabriel but to that of

Elisha, a slightly older member of the congregation with whom he has previously engaged in a sexually suggestive wrestling match reminiscent of that in D. H. Lawrence's *Women in Love* (1920). John's salvation, then, may bring him closer to an acceptance of his own sensuality, to a definition of himself encompassing both temple and street. Baldwin ends the novel with the emergence of the newly "saved" John onto the streets of Harlem. His fate hinges on his ability to move ahead to the higher innocence suggested by his vision of the dispossessed rather than submitting to the experiences which have destroyed and deformed the majority of the saints.

Another Country, Baldwin's greatest popular success, analyzes the effects of this deforming pressure on a wide range of characters, black and white, male and female, homosexual and heterosexual. To accommodate these diverse consciousnesses, Baldwin employs the sprawling form usually associated with political rather than psychological fiction, emphasizing the diverse forms of innocence and experience in American society. The three major sections of *Another Country*, "Easy Rider," "Any Day Now," and "Toward Bethlehem," progress generally from despair to renewed hope, but no single consciousness or plot line provides a frame similar to that of *Go Tell It on the Mountain*. Rather, the novel's structural coherence derives from the moral concerns present in each of the various plots.

Casting a Melvillean shadow over the novel is the black jazz musician Rufus Scott, who is destroyed by an agonizing affair with Leona, a white Southerner recently arrived in New York at the time she meets him. Unable to forge the innocence necessary for love in a context which repudiates the relationship at every turn, Rufus destroys Leona psychologically. After a period of physical and psychological destitution, he kills himself by jumping off a bridge. His sister Ida, an aspiring singer, and his friend Vivaldo Moore, an aspiring white writer, meet during the last days of Rufus' life and fall in love as they console each other over his death. Struggling to overcome the racial and sexual definitions which destroyed Rufus, they seek a higher innocence capable of countering Ida's sense of the world as a "whorehouse." In contrast to Ida and Vivaldo's struggle, the relationship of white actor Eric Jones and his French lover Yves seems Edenic. Although Baldwin portrays Eric's internal struggle for a firm sense of his sexual identity, their shared innocence at times seems to exist almost entirely outside the context of the pressures that destroyed Rufus. The final major characters, Richard and Cass Silenski, represent the cost of the "American dream." After Richard "makes it" as a popular novelist, their personal relationship decays, precipitating Cass's affair with Eric. Their tentative reunion after Richard discovers the affair makes it clear that material success provides no shortcut to moral responsibility.

Baldwin examines each character and relationship in the context of the institutional pressures discouraging individual responsibility. His portrait of Rufus, the major accomplishment of *Another Country*, testifies to a moral insight and a raw artistic power resembling that of Wright and Émile Zola. Forgoing the formal control and emotional restraint of his earlier novels, Baldwin opens *Another Country* with the image of Rufus who "had fallen so low, that he scarcely had the energy to be angry." Both an exceptional case and a representative figure, Rufus embodies the seething anger and hopeless isolation rendering Baldwin's United States a landscape of nightmare. Seeing his own situation as unbearable, Rufus meditates on the fate of a city tormented by an agony like his own: "He remembered to what excesses, into what traps and nightmares, his loneliness had driven him; and he wondered where such a violent emptiness might drive an entire city." Forcing the reader to recognize the social implications of Rufus' situation, Baldwin emphasizes that his specific situation originates in his own moral failure with Leona. Where Gabriel Grimes remained insulated from his immorality by arrogance and pride, Rufus feels the full extent of his self-enforced damnation. Ironically and belatedly, his destitution clarifies his sense of the extent of his past acceptance of the social definitions which destroy him.

Wandering the streets of Manhattan, Rufus feels himself beyond human contact. Desperately in need of love, he believes his past actions render him unfit for even minimal compassion. His abuse of Leona, who as a white woman represents both the "other" and the source of the most obvious social definitions circumscribing his life as a black male, accounts for his original estrangement from family and friends, who find his viciousness uncharacteristic. All, including Rufus, fail to understand soon enough that his abuse of Leona represents both a rebellion against and an acceptance of the role dictated by racial and sexual definitions. Separated from the psychological source of his art—jazz inevitably rejects the substructure of Euro-American definitions of reality—Rufus falls ever further into a paranoia which receives ample reenforcement from the racist context. Largely by his own choice, he withdraws almost entirely from both his black and white acquaintances. Once on the street following Leona's breakdown, he begins to recognize not only his immediate but also his long-term acceptance of destructive definitions. Thinking back on a brief homosexual affair with Eric to which he submitted out of pity rather than love, Rufus regrets having treated his friend with contempt. Having rejected the other in Eric and Leona, Rufus realizes he has rejected a part of himself. He consigns himself to the ranks of the damned, casting himself beyond human love with his plunge off the bridge.

While not absolving Rufus of responsibility for his actions, Baldwin treats him with profound sympathy, in part because of his honesty and in part because of the enormous power of the social institutions which define him as the other. Throughout *Another Country*, Baldwin emphasizes that white heterosexual males possess the power of definition, although their power destroys them as surely as it does their victims. Television producer Steve Ellis, a moral cripple embodying the basic values of the American economic system, nearly destroys Ida and Vivaldo's relationship by encouraging Ida to accept a cynical definition of herself as a sexual commodity. Vivaldo, too, participates in the cynicism when he visits the Harlem prostitutes, indirectly perpetuating the definitions which reduce blacks to sexual objects, and thus implicating himself in Rufus' death. In fact, every major character with the exception of Eric bears partial responsibility for Rufus' destruction, since each at times accepts the definitions generating the cycle of rejection and denial. The constituting irony, however, stems from the fact that only those most actively struggling for moral integrity recognize their culpability. Vivaldo, who attempts to reach out to Rufus earlier on the night of his suicide, feels more guilt than Richard, who simply dismisses Rufus as a common "nigger" after his mistreatment of Leona.

This unflinching portrayal of moral failure, especially on the part of well-meaning liberals, provides the thematic center of *Another Country*. Baldwin concludes the novel with the image of Yves's reunion with Eric, who is apparently on the verge of professional success with a starring role in a film of a Fyodor Dostoevski novel. This combination of personal and financial success seems more an assertion of naïve hope than a compelling part of the surrounding fictional world. The majority of the narrative lines imply the impossibility of simple dissociation from institutional pressure. Ultimately, the intensity of Rufus' pain and the intricacy of Ida and Vivaldo's struggle overshadow Eric and Yves's questionable innocence. As Ida tells Vivaldo, "Our being together doesn't change the world." The attempt to overcome the cynicism of this perception leads to a recognition that meaningful love demands total acceptance. Ida's later question, "how can you say you loved Rufus when there was so much about him you didn't want to know?" could easily provide the epitaph for the entire society in *Another Country*.

In *Just Above My Head*, Baldwin creates a narrator, Hall Montana, capable of articulating the psychological subtleties of *Go Tell It on the Mountain*, the social insights of *Another Country*, and the political anger of *Tell Me How Long the Train's Been Gone*. Like other observer-participants in American literature, such as Nick Carraway in *The Great Gatsby* (1925) and Jack Burden in *All the King's Men* (1946), Hall tells both his own story and that of a more publically prominent figure, in this case his brother Arthur, a gospel singer who dies two years prior to the start of the novel. Significantly, *Just Above My Head* also reconsiders Baldwin's own artistic history, echoing countless motifs from his earlier writings. Though not precisely a self-reflexive text, *Just Above My Head* takes on added richness when juxtaposed with Baldwin's treatment of religious concerns in *Go Tell It on the Mountain*; the homosexuality theme in *Giovanni's Room*; the relationship between brothers and the musical setting in "Sonny's Blues"; racial politics in *Blues for Mister Charlie* and *Tell Me How Long the Train's Been Gone*; the Nation of Islam in *The Fire Next Time* and *No Name in the Street*; and, most important, the intermingled family love and world politics in *If Beale Street Could Talk*. Baldwin's reconsideration of his own history, which is at once private like Hall's and public like Arthur's, emphasizes the necessity of a continual reexamination of the nature of both self and context in order to reach the higher innocence.

Similarly, Hall's resolve to understand the social and existential meaning of Arthur's experience originates in his desire to answer honestly his children's questions concerning their uncle. Refusing to protect their original innocence—an attempt he knows would fail—Hall seeks both to free himself from the despair of experience and to discover a mature innocence he can pass on to the younger generation. Tracing the roots of Arthur's despair to pressures originating in numerous limiting definitions and failures of courage, Hall summarizes his, and Baldwin's social insight:

> The attempt, more the necessity, to excavate a history, to find out the truth about oneself! is motivated by the need to have the power to force others to recognize your presence, your right to be here. The disputed passage will remain disputed so long as you do not have the authority of the right-of-way. . . . Power clears the passage, swiftly: but the paradox, here, is that power, rooted in history, is also, the mockery and the repudiation of history. The power to define the other seals one's definition of oneself.

Recognizing that the only hope for meaningful moral freedom lies in repudiating the power of definition, Hall concludes: "Our history is each other. That is our only guide. One thing is absolutely certain: one can repudiate, or despise, no one's history without repudiating and despising one's own."

Although Baldwin recognizes the extent to which the definitions and repudiations remain entrenched in institutional structures, his portrayal of Hall's courage and honesty offers at least some hope for moral integrity as a base for social action. If an individual such as Hall can counteract the pressures militating against personal responsibility, he or she may be able to exert a positive influence on relatively small social groups such as families and churches, which in turn may affect the larger social context. Nevertheless, Baldwin refuses to encourage simplistic optimism. Rather than focusing narrowly on Hall's individual process, he emphasizes the aspects of the context which render that success atypical. Although Hall begins with his immediate context, his excavation involves the Korean War, the Civil Rights movement, the rise of Malcolm X, and the role of advertising in American culture. Hall's relation with his family and close friends provides a Jamesian frame for the Dreiserian events of the novel, somewhat as John's conversion frames the historical "Prayers of the Saints" in *Go Tell It on the Mountain. Just Above My Head*, however, leaves no ambiguity concerning the individual's ability to free himself or herself from history. Only a conscious decision to accept the pain and guilt of the past promises any real hope for love, for the higher innocence. Similarly, Baldwin reiterates that, while the desire for safety is understandable, all safety is illusion. Pain inevitably returns, and, while the support of friends and lovers may help, only a self-image based on existential acceptance rather than repudiation makes survival possible.

Arthur's death, occupying a thematic and emotional position similar to Rufus' in *Another Country*, provides the point of departure for Hall's excavation. A gifted gospel singer as a teenager, Arthur rises to stardom as the "emperor of soul." Despite his success, however, he never frees himself from doubts concerning his own identity or feels secure with the experience of love. Even though his parents offer him a firm base of love and acceptance, Arthur feels a deep sense of emotional isolation even as a child, a sense reenforced by his observations of life in Harlem and, later, in the South. Though he accepts his own homosexuality with relatively little anxiety, his society refuses the freedom necessary for the development of a truly satisfying emotional life. The Edenic innocence of Eric and Yves clearly fails to provide a sufficient response to the institutional context of *Just Above My Head*.

Arthur's childhood experiences provide clear warnings against the attempt to maintain innocence through simplistic self-definition. Julia Miller, like John in *Go Tell It on the Mountain*, undergoes a salvation experience and embarks on a career as a child evangelist. Encouraged by her parents, friends of the Montanas who rely on their daughter for economic support, she assumes a sanctimonious attitude which she uses to manipulate her elders. Arthur's parents deplore the indulgence of Julia, unambiguously rejecting that idea that her religious vocation lifts her beyond the "naughty" street side of her personality. Ultimately, and in great pain, Julia confronts this truth. After her mother's death, she discovers that her father Joel views her primarily as an economic and sexual object. His desire to exploit her earning potential even when she says she has lost her vocation reflects his underlying contempt for the spirit. This contempt leads to an incestuous rape which destroys Julia's remaining innocence and drives her to a life as a prostitute in New Orleans. Eventually, Julia recovers from this brutalization, but her example provides a clear warning to Arthur against confusing his vocation as a gospel singer with a trancendence of human fallibility.

The experiences of the members of Arthur's first gospel group, the Trumpets of Zion, reveal how institutions infringe even on those not actively committed to simplifying definitions. At one extreme, the social definitions establish a context which accepts and encourages murder—symbolic and real—of the other. Peanut, a member of the Trumpets and later Arthur's companion on the road, vanishes into the Alabama night following a civil rights rally, presumably murdered by whites seeking to enforce the definition of blacks as niggers. Equally devastating though less direct is the operation of the context on Red, another member of the Trumpets, who turns to drugs in an attempt to relieve the pain of the Harlem streets. Even Hall finds himself an unwilling accomplice to the imposition of social definitions when he is drafted and sent to Korea. Powerless to alter the institutional structure, Hall recognizes, and tells Arthur, that the American military spreads not freedom but repudiation in the third world. Hall's subsequent employment by an advertising agency involves him in another aspect of the same oppressive system. Viewed as an anomaly by his employers, as an atypical high-class nigger, Hall nevertheless participates in the creation of images designed to simplify reality for economic gain which will be used to strengthen the oppressive system. The juxtaposition of Julia's false innocence with the destructive experiences of Peanut, Red, and Hall protects Arthur against the urge to dismiss any aspect of his awareness. A large part of his power as a singer derives from his recognition of the reality of both street and temple, expressed in his ability to communicate sexual pain in gospel songs and spiritual aspiration in the blues.

Arthur, then, appears ideally prepared for the responsible exercise of existential freedom. His failure even to survive underscores the destructive power of the corrupt institutional context. The roots of Arthur's doom lie in his homosexual relationship with Crunch, the final member of the Trumpets. Highly desirable physically, Crunch feels locked into a definition of himself as a sexual object prior to his involvement with Arthur. In its early stages, Arthur and Crunch's love, like that of Yves and Eric in *Another Country*, seems an idyllic retreat, a spot of innocence in the chaos of experience. The retreat, however, proves temporary, in part because Crunch cannot free himself from the urge for self-simplification and in part because of the continuing presence of the outside world. Uneasy with his sexual identity, Crunch becomes involved with Julia when he discovers the extent of her father's abuse. Arthur recognizes that Crunch is not abandoning him by reacting to Julia's pain and accepts the relationship. Granted sufficient time for adjustment, Arthur and Crunch seem capable of confronting their experience and forging a higher innocence as the basis for a lasting love. The time does not exist. Crunch is drafted and sent to Korea. Separated from Arthur's reassurance and tormented by self-doubt, Crunch never fully accepts his sexuality. After his return to Harlem, he and Arthur gradually lose contact.

The repeated losses—of Peanut, Red, Crunch—create a sense of isolation which Arthur never overcomes. The expectation of loss periodically overpowers his determination to communicate, the determination which makes him a great singer. Even during periods of real joy, with his French lover Guy in Paris or with Julia's brother Jimmy, who is both his pianist and his lover, Arthur suffers acute emotional pain. Attempting to survive by rededicating himself to communication, to his artistic excavation of history, Arthur drives himself past the limits of physical and psychological endurance. He dies in the basement bathroom of a London pub after a lover's quarrel, clearly only temporary, with Jimmy. By concluding Arthur's life with an image of isolation, Baldwin emphasizes the power of the limiting definitions to destroy even the most existentially courageous individual.

Arthur's death, however, marks not only a conclusion but also the beginning of Hall's quest for the higher innocence, which he, along with his wife Ruth, Julia, and Jimmy, can pass on to the younger generation. This higher innocence involves both individual and social elements, ultimately demanding the mutual support of individuals willing to pursue excavation of their own histories. This support expresses itself in the call and response dynamic, a basic element of Afro-American oral culture which Arthur employs in his interaction with audiences while singing. As Baldwin re-creates the traditional form, the interaction begins with the call of a leader who expresses his own emotional experience through the vehicle of a traditional song which provides a communal context for the emotion. If the community recognizes and shares the experience evoked by the call, it responds with another traditional phrase which provides the sense of understanding and acceptance that enables the leader to go on. Implicitly the process enables both individual and community to define themselves in opposition to dominant social forces. If the experience of isolation is shared, it is no longer the same type of isolation which brought Rufus to his death. In *Just Above My Head*, the call and response rests on a rigorous excavation requiring individual silence, courage, and honesty expressed through social presence, acceptance, and love. Expressed in the interactions between Arthur and his audiences, between Hall and his children, between Baldwin and his readers, this call and response provides a realistic image of the higher innocence possible in opposition to the murderous social definitions.

As in John's vision in *Go Tell It on the Mountain* and Rufus's self-examination in *Another Country*, the process begins in silence, which throughout Baldwin's novels offers the potential for either alienation or communication. The alienating silence coincides thematically with institutional noise—mechanical, social, political. The majority of Americans, Baldwin insists, prefer distracting and ultimately meaningless sounds to the silence which allows self-recognition. Only individuals sharing Arthur's willingness to remove himself from the noise can hope to hear their own voices and transform the silence into music. Every moment of true communication in *Just Above My Head* begins in a moment of silence which effectively rejects the clamor of imposed definitions. The courage needed for the acceptance of silence prepares the way for the honest excavation of history which must precede any meaningful social interaction. The excavation remains a burden, however, without that interaction. No purely individual effort can alter the overwhelming sense of isolation imposed by social definitions. The individual stage of the process merely heightens the need for acceptance, presence, and love. Arthur sounds the call amid the noise; he cannot provide the response. Perhaps, Baldwin indicates, no one, not even Jimmy, can provide a response capable of soothing the feeling of isolation emanating from early experiences. Nevertheless, the attempt is vital. Julia recognizes both the necessity and the limitation of presence when she tells Hall of her relationship with Jimmy: "I don't know enough to change him, or to save him. But I know enough to be there. I *must* be there."

If presence—being there—is to provide even momentary relief, it must be accompanied by the honest acceptance underlying love. Refusing to limit his acceptance, Hall answers his son Tony's questions concerning Arthur's sexuality with complete honesty. Understanding fully that his acceptance of Arthur entails an acceptance of the similar complexity in himself and in Tony, Hall surrenders his voice to Jimmy's, imaginatively participating in a love which repudiates social definition, which rises up out of the silence beyond the noise. Implicitly, Hall offers both Tony and his daughter Odessa the assurance of presence, of acceptance, of love. They need not fear rejection if they have the courage to accept their full humanity. The assurance cannot guarantee freedom, or even survival. It can, and does, intimate the form of mature innocence in the world described by the composite voice of Baldwin, Jimmy, and Hall, a world that "doesn't have any morality. Look at the world. What the world calls morality is nothing but the dream of safety. That's how the world gets to be so fucking moral. The only way to know that you are safe is to see somebody else in danger—otherwise you can't be sure you're safe."

Against this vicious safety, a safety which necessitates limiting definitions imposed on others, Baldwin proposes a responsibility based on risk. Only by responding to the call sounding from Arthur, from Jimmy and Hall, from Baldwin, can people find freedom. The call, ultimately, emanates not only from the individual but also from the community to which he or she calls. It provides a focus for repudiation of the crushing definitions. Hall, using Jimmy's voice, describes the call: "The man who tells the story isn't *making up* a story. He's listening to us, and can only give back, to us, what he hears: from us." The responsibility lies with everyone.

Major publications other than long fiction

SHORT FICTION: *Going to Meet the Man*, 1965.

PLAYS: *Blues for Mister Charlie*, 1964; *The Amen Corner*, 1965; *One Day, When I Was Lost: A Scenario Based on The Autobiography of Malcolm X*, 1972.

NONFICTION: *Notes of a Native Son*, 1955; *Nobody Knows My Name: More Notes of a Native Son*, 1961; *The Fire Next Time*, 1963; *Nothing Personal*, 1964 (with Richard Avedon); *No Name in the Street*, 1971; *A Rap on Race*, 1971 (with Margaret Mead); *A Dialogue*, 1975 (with Nikki Giovanni); *The Devil Finds Work*, 1976.

CHILDREN'S LITERATURE: *Little Man, Little Man*, 1975.

Bibliography
Bone, Robert. *The Negro Novel in America*, 1965.

Cruse, Harold. *The Crisis of the Negro Intellectual*, 1967.
Eckman, Fern Marja. *The Furious Passage of James Baldwin*, 1966.
Gayle, Addison, Jr. *The Way of the New World*, 1975.
Kinnamon, Kenneth. *James Baldwin: A Collection of Critical Essays*, 1974.
O'Daniel, Therman B. *James Baldwin: A Critical Evaluation*, 1977.

Craig Werner

J. G. BALLARD

Born: Shanghai, China; November 15, 1930

Principal long fiction

The Wind from Nowhere, 1962; *The Drowned World*, 1962; *The Drought*, 1964 (later published as *The Burning World*); *The Crystal World*, 1966; *Crash*, 1973; *Concrete Island*, 1974; *High Rise*, 1975; *The Unlimited Dream Company*, 1979; *Hello America*, 1981.

Other literary forms

J. G. Ballard has been a prolific short-story writer; there are approximately twenty collections of his stories, though some are recombinations of stories in earlier collections, and the American and British collections constitute two series in which the same stories are combined in different ways. He has written occasional essays on imaginative fiction, and also on surrealist painting—he contributed an introduction to a collection of work by Salvador Dali. The best of his short fiction is to be found in two retrospective collections: *Chronopolis and Other Stories* (1971) and *The Best Short Stories of J. G. Ballard* (1978).

Achievements

Ballard is one of a handful of writers who, after establishing early reputations as science-fiction writers, subsequently achieved a kind of "transcendence" of their genre origins to be accepted by a wider public. This shift partly represented a trend in his work—the novels of his middle period were not science fiction—but he has sustained his high reputation through a recent return to more extravagantly fantastic themes. For a time in the early 1960's, Ballard seemed to constitute a one-man avant-garde in British science fiction, and his influence was considerable enough for him to become established as the leading figure in the movement which came to be associated with the magazine *New Worlds* under the editorship of Michael Moorcock. His interest in science-fiction themes was always of a special kind; he is essentially a literary surrealist who finds the near future a convenient imaginative space. His primary concern is the effect of environment—both "natural" and manmade—upon the psyche, and he has therefore found it appropriate to write about gross environmental changes and about the decay and dereliction of the artificial environment; these interests distance him markedly from other modern science-fiction writers and have helped him to become a writer *sui generis*.

Biography

James Graham Ballard was born and reared in Shanghai, China, where his father—originally an industrial chemist—was involved in the management of the Far East branch of a firm of textile manufacturers. The Sino-Japanese war had begun, and Shanghai was effectively a war zone by the time Ballard was seven years old; all of his early life was affected by the ever-nearness of war. After Japan's entry into World War II and her invasion of Shanghai, Ballard was interned in a prisoner-of-war camp. This was in the summer of 1942, when he was eleven; he was there for more than three years.

Ballard has said that his experience of the internment camp was "not unpleasant"—it was simply a fact of life which, as a child, he accepted. Children were not mistreated by the guards, and the adults made sure that the children were adequately fed even at their own expense. He has observed that his parents must have found the regime extremely harsh. Although his family was among the fortunate few who avoided malaria, his sister nearly died of a form of dysentery.

After his release, Ballard went to England in 1946. His family stayed in the Far East for a while, and his father did not return until 1950, when he was driven out of China by the Communist victory. Ballard has recalled that after spending his early years in "Americanized" Shanghai, England seemed very strange and foreign. He went to Leys' School in Cambridge for a while, then went to King's College, Cambridge, to study medicine. His ultimate aim at this time was to become a psychiatrist. At Cambridge he began writing, initially intending to maintain the activity as a hobby while he was qualifying. In fact, though, he dropped out of his course after two years and subsequently went to London University to read English. The university seems to have found him unsuitable for such a course, and he left after his first year.

He then embarked upon a series of short-term jobs, including working for an advertising agency and selling encyclopedias. Eventually, to end this aimless drifting, he enlisted in the Royal Air Force and was sent for training to Moosejaw, Saskatchewan, Canada. He was not suited to the air force either, but while in Canada he began reading magazine science fiction, and while waiting for his discharge back in England he wrote his first science-fiction story, "Passport to Eternity" (it was not published for some years). Shortly after this, in 1955, he married and worked in public libraries in order to support his family.

In 1956, Ballard began submitting short stories to Ted Carnell, editor of the British magazines *New Worlds* and *Science Fantasy*. Carnell was not only enthusiastic about Ballard's work but also helped him to obtain a new job working on a trade journal. Eventually, Ballard became assistant editor of *Chemistry and Industry*, a job which he held for four years. He moved in 1960 to the small Thames-side town of Shepperton, where he still lives. By this time he had three children and was struggling to find time to devote to his writing. During a two-week annual holiday he managed to write *The Wind from Nowhere*, whose publication in America represented something of a breakthrough for him—the same publisher began to issue a series of short-story collections, and the income from these books allowed him to become a full-time writer. His wife died in 1964, at which time his youngest child was only five years old, and his career as a writer has since been combined with the exacting pressures of being a single parent. In consequence, he has led since 1964 a relatively uneventful life, although his literary career has remained strong.

Analysis

J. G. Ballard's first seven novels can be easily sorted into two groups. The first four are novels of worldwide disaster, while the next three are stories of cruelty and alienation set in the concrete wilderness of contemporary urban society. All nine of his novels are, however, linked by a concern with the disintegration of civilization on a global or local scale.

Ballard's early disaster stories follow a well-established tradition in British imaginative fiction. British science-fiction writers from H. G. Wells to John Wyndham always seem to have been fascinated by the notion of the fragility and vulnerability of man's empire, and have produced many careful and clinical descriptions of its fall. The earlier works in this tradition are didactic tales, insisting on the vanity of human wishes and reveling in the idea that when the crunch comes, only the tough will survive. Ballard, in contrast, is quite unconcerned with drawing morals—his disaster stories are not at all social Darwinist parables. His main concern is with the psychological read-justments which the characters are forced to make when faced with the disintegration of their world: he sees the problem of catastrophic change largely in terms of adaptation.

In *The Wind from Nowhere*, which is considerably inferior to the three other disaster novels, a slowly accelerating wind plucks the man-made world apart. No one can stand firm against this active rebellion of nature—neither the American armed forces nor the immensely rich industrialist Hardoon, who seeks to secrete himself within a gigantic concrete pyramid, which the wind eventually topples into an abyss. *The Wind from Nowhere* has a whole series of protagonists and shows the catastrophe from several viewpoints. This was one of the well-tried methods of retailing disaster stories, but it was unsuited to Ballard's particular ambitions, and in the other novels of this early quartet he employed single protagonists as focal points—almost as measuring devices to analyze in depth the significance of parallel physical and psychological changes.

In *The Drowned World*, Earth's surface temperature has risen and is still gradually rising. Water released by the melting of the ice caps has inundated much of the land, and dense tropical jungle has spread rapidly through what were once the temperate zones, rendering them all but uninhabitable. Ballard suggests that the world is undergoing a kind of retrogression to the environment of the Triassic period. The novel's protagonist is Robert Kerans, a biologist monitoring the changes from a research station in partly submerged London.

The psychological effects of the transfiguration first manifest themselves as dreams in which Kerans sees "himself" (no longer human) wandering a primitive world dominated by a huge, fierce sun. These dreams, he concludes, are a kind of memory retained within the cellular heritage of mankind, now called forth again by the appropriate stimulus. Their promise is that they will free the nervous system from the domination of the recently evolved brain, whose appropriate environment is gone, and restore the harmony of primeval proto-consciousness and archaic environment. Kerans watches other people trying to adapt in their various ways to the circumstances in which they find themselves, but sees the essential meaninglessness of their strategies. He accepts the pull of destiny and treks south, submitting to the psychic metamorphosis that strips away his humanity until he becomes "a second Adam searching for the forgotten paradises of the reborn sun."

The Drowned World was sufficiently original and sophisticated to be incomprehensible to most of the aficionados of genre science fiction, who did not understand what Ballard was about or why. A minority, however, recognized its significance and its import; its reputation is now firmly established as one of the major works of its period.

In *The Drought*, the pattern of physical change is reversed; Earth becomes a vast desert because a pollutant molecular film has formed on the surface of the world's oceans, inhibiting evaporation. The landscape is gradually transformed, the concrete city-deserts becoming surrounded by seas of hot sand instead of arable land, while the seashore retreats to expose new deserts of crystalline salt. The soil dies and civilization shrivels, fires reducing forests and buildings alike to white ash. Ransom, the protagonist, is one of the last stubborn few who are reluctant to join the exodus to the retreating sea. From his houseboat he watches the river dwindle away, draining the dregs of the social and natural order. He lives surrounded by relics of an extinguished past, bereft of purpose and no longer capable of emotional response.

Eventually, Ransom and his surviving neighbors are driven to seek refuge in the "dune limbo" of the new seashore and take their places in a new social order dominated by the need to extract fresh water from the reluctant sea. Here, he finds, people are simply marking time and fighting a hopeless rearguard action. In the final section of the story, he goes inland again to see what has become of the city and its last few inhabitants. They, mad and monstrous, have found a new way of life, hideous but somehow appropriate to the universal aridity—which is an aridity of the soul as well as of the land.

In *The Crystal World*, certain areas of the Earth's surface are subjected to a strange process of crystallization as some mysterious substance is precipitated out of the ether. This is a more localized and less destructive catastrophe than those in *The Drowned World* and *The Drought*, but the implication is that it will continue until the world is consumed. The initially affected area is in Africa, where the novel is set. The central character is Dr. Sanders, the assistant director of a leper colony, who is at first horrified when he finds his mistress and some of his patients joyfully accepting the process of cystallization within the flesh of their own bodies. Eventually, of course, he comes to realize that no other destiny is appropriate to the new circumstances. What is happening is that time and space are somehow being reduced, so that they are supersaturated with matter. Enclaves from which time itself has "evaporated" are therefore being formed—fragments of eternity where living things, though they cannot continue to live, also cannot die, but undergo instead a complete existential transubstantiation. Here, metaphors developed in *The Drought* are literalized with the aid of a wonderfully gaudy invention.

The transformation of the world in *The Crystal World* is a kind of beautification, and it is much easier for the reader to sympathize with Sanders' acceptance of its dictates than with Kerans' capitulation to the demands of his dreams. For this reason, the novel has been more popular within the science-fiction community than either of its predecessors. It is, however, largely a recapitulation of the same theme, which does not really gain from its association with the lush romanticism that occasionally surfaces in Ballard's work—most noticeably in the short stories set in the imaginary American west-coast artists' colony Vermilion Sands, a beach resort populated by decadent eccentrics and the flotsam of bygone star-cults who surround themselves with florid artificial environments.

Seven years elapsed between publication of *The Crystal World* and the appearance of *Crash*. Although Ballard published numerous retrospective collections in the interim, his one major project was a collection of what he called "condensed novels"—a series of verbal collages featuring surreal combinations of images encapsulating what Ballard saw as the contemporary zeitgeist. In the world portrayed in these collages, there is a great deal of violence and perverted sexual arousal. Ubiquitous Ballardian images recur regularly: dead birds, junked space hardware, derelict buildings. Mixed in with these are secular icons: the suicide of Marilyn Monroe, the assassin's victim John F. Kennedy, and other personalities whose fates could be seen as symbolic of the era in decline.

The theme of *Crash* is already well developed in the condensed novels (collected in the United Kingdom under the title *The Atrocity Exhibition* and in the United States under the title *Love and Napalm: Export USA*). Cars, within the novel, are seen as symbols of power, speed and sexualilty—a commonplace psychoanalytic observation, to which Ballard adds the surprising further representation of the car crash as a kind of orgasm. The protagonist of the novel, who is called Ballard, finds his first car crash, despite all the pain and attendant anxiety, to be an initiation into a new way of being, whereby he is forced to reformulate his social relationships and his sense of purpose. Ballard apparently decided to write the book while considering the reactions of members of the public to an exhibition of crashed cars which he held at the New Arts Laboratory in London.

Although it is mundane by comparison with his previous novels—it is certainly not science fiction—*Crash* is by no means a realistic novel. Its subject matter is trauma and the private fantasization of alarming but ordinary events. The hero, at one point, does bear witness to a transformation of the world, but it is a purely subjective one while he is under the influence of a hallucinogen. He sees the landscapes of the city transformed, woven into a new metaphysics by the attribution of a new context of significance derived from his perverted fascination with cars and expressway architecture.

The two novels which followed *Crash* retain and extrapolate many of its themes. *Concrete Island* and *High Rise* are both robinsonades whose characters become Crusoes in the very heart of modern civilization, cast away within sight and earshot of the metropolitan hordes but no less isolated for their proximity. In *Concrete Island*, a man is trapped on a traffic island in the middle of a complex freeway intersection, unable to reach the side of the road because the stream of cars is never-ending. Like Crusoe, he sets out to make the best of his situation, using whatever resources—material and social—he finds at hand. He adapts so well, in the end, that he refuses the opportunity to leave when it finally arrives.

The high-rise apartment block which gives *High Rise* its title is intended to be a haven for the well-to-do middle class, a comfortable microcosm to which they can escape from the stressful outside world of work and anxiety. It is, perhaps, *too* well insulated from the world at large; it becomes a private empire where freedom from stress gives birth to a violent anarchy and a decay into savagery. If *Concrete Island* is spiritually akin to Daniel Defoe's *Robinson Crusoe* (1719), then *High Rise* is akin to William Golding's *Lord of the Flies*, (1954), though it is all the more shocking in translocating the decline into barbarism of Golding's novel from a remote island to suburbia, and in attributing the decline to adults who are well aware of what is happening rather than to children whose innocence provides a ready excuse. As always, Ballard's interest is in the psychological readjustments made by his chief characters, and the way in which the whole process proves to be ultimately cathartic.

A major theme in the condensed novels, which extends into the three novels of the second group, is what Ballard refers to as the "death of affect"— a sterilization of the emotions and attendant moral anesthesia, which he considers to be a significant contemporary trend induced by contemporary life-styles. The greatest positive achievement of the characters in these novels is a special kind of ataraxia—a calm of mind rather different from the one Plato held up as an ideal, which allows one to live alongside all manner of horrors without being unusually moved to fear or pity.

Another gap, though not such a long one, separates *High Rise* from *The Unlimited Dream Company*, a messianic fantasy of the redemption of Shepperton from suburban mundanity. Its protagonist, Blake, crashes a stolen aircraft into the Thames River at Shepperton. Though his dead body remains trapped in the cockpit, he finds himself miraculously preserved on the bank. At first he cannot accept his true state, but several unsuccessful attempts to leave the town and a series of visions combine to convince him that he has a specially privileged role to play: he must teach the people to fly, so that they can transcend their earthly existence to achieve a mystical union with the vegetable and mineral worlds, dissolving themselves into eternity as the chief characters did in *The Crystal World*. Though the name of the central character is significant, the book also appears to be closely allied with the paintings of another artist: the eccentric Stanley Spencer, who lived in another Thames-side town (Cookham) and delighted in locating within its mundane urban scenery images of biblical and transcendental significance.

It is slightly surprising to find Ballard writing a novel of redemption after having written so many in which the possibility and desirability of salvation were so comprehensively ruled out in favor of a determined insistence that *adaptation* is the one true way. Although Ballard has always insisted that the ending of *The Drowned World* is a happy one, most readers insist on seeing the book in downbeat terms, and find his later works (with the possible exception of *The Crystal World*) progressively more depressing. There is a sense, though, in which *The Unlimited Dream Company* is also a novel of adaptation which simply reverses the pattern of the earlier works. Here, it is not Blake who must adapt to changes in the external world, but Shepperton which must adapt to *him*—and he, too, must adapt to his own godlike status. Blake is himself the "catastrophe" which visits Shepperton, the absolute at large within it whose immanence cannot be ignored or resisted. If the novel seems to the reader to be upbeat rather than downbeat, this is mainly the consequence of a crucial change of viewpoint—and had the reader been willing to accept such a change he might well have found *The Drowned World* equally uplifting.

If *The Unlimited Dream Company* does not represent such a dramatic change of pattern as first appearances suggest, *Hello America* is certainly, for Ballard, a break with his own tradition. There is not very much in the novel which seems new, in thematic terms, although it recalls his short stories much more than his previous novels, but there is nevertheless a sense in which it represents a radical departure. The plot concerns the "rediscovery" in the twenty-second century of a largely abandoned America by an oddly assorted expedition from Europe. What they find are the shattered relics of a whole series of American mythologies. The central character, Wayne, dreams of resurrecting America and its dream, restoring the mythology of technological optimism and glamorous consumerism to operational status. He cannot do so, of course, but there is a consistent note of ironic nostalgia in his hopeless ambition. What is remarkable about the book is that it is a confection, an offhand entertainment to be enjoyed but not taken seriously. From Ballard the novelist, this is totally unexpected.

Actually, Ballard has frequently shown himself to be a witty writer—a master of the ironic aside—but his wit has been allowed to dominate only in some of his shorter pieces. In the novels, his wit—though present—has been subdued, and sometimes even hidden, in the early novels by various hypothetical exotica and in the later ones by the coldly serious tone and the morally shocking representations. No one contemplating this oeuvre could have anticipated that Ballard was likely to produce a book of fun in which he would come close to satirizing and caricaturing some of his own concerns.

This change of direction is possibly a purely temporary matter—a kind of brief holiday from more serious concerns. On the other hand, it may be indicative of an actual change of temperament on Ballard's part. Certainly, in the early 1980's he seems to be showing signs of being more prolific than he was at any time in the 1970's; a collection of mostly new stories will be released in the near future. A Ballard redeemed from his previous preoccupations, ready to confront the world anew, holds interesting possibilities.

In one of his earliest essays on science fiction—a "guest editorial" which he contributed to *New Worlds* in 1962—Ballard committed the heresy of declaring that H. G. Wells was "a disastrous influence on the subsequent course of science fiction." He suggested that it was time to throw overboard the vocabulary of ideas to which science-fiction writers and readers had become accustomed, and with them its customary narrative forms and conventional plots. It was time, he said, to turn to the exploration of inner space rather than outer space, and to realize that "the only truly alien planet is Earth." He offered his opinion that Salvador Dali might be the most pertinent source of inspiration for modern writers of science fiction. The rhetorical flourishes which fill this essay caution readers against taking it all *too* seriously, but in the main this is the prospectus which Ballard has been trying to follow. He has practiced what he preached, shaking off the legacy of H. G. Wells, dedicating himself to the exploration of inner space and the development of new metaphysical (particularly metapsychological) systems, and steering well clear of the old plots and narrative formulas. In so doing, he made himself one of the most original writers of his generation; no doubt he still has important work to do.

Major publications other than long fiction

SHORT FICTION: *The Voices of Time*, 1962; *Billenium*, 1962; *Passport to Eternity*, 1963; *The Terminal Beach*, 1964; *The Impossible Man*, 1966; *Love and Napalm: Export U.S.A.*, 1969 (originally published as *The Atrocity*

Exhibition); *Vermilion Sands*, 1971; *Chronopolis and Other Stories*, 1971; *The Best Short Stories of J. G. Ballard*, 1978.

Bibliography

Goddard, James, and David Pringle, eds. *J. G. Ballard: The First Twenty Years*, 1976.

Pringle, David. *Earth Is the Alien Planet: J. G. Ballard's Four-Dimensional Nightmare*, 1979.

Stableford, Brian. "J. G. Ballard," in *Science Fiction Writers*, 1982. Edited by E. F. Bleiler.

                                                                    Brian Stableford

JOHN BARTH

Born: Cambridge, Maryland; May 27, 1930

Principal long fiction

The Floating Opera, 1956; *The End of the Road*, 1958; *The Sot-Weed Factor*, 1960; *Giles Goat-Boy: Or, The Revised New Syllabus*, 1966; *Chimera*, 1972; *Letters: A Novel*, 1979; *Sabbatical*, 1982.

Other literary forms

While John Barth's novels have ensured his eminence among contemporary American writers, his short fictions have been no less influential or controversial. In addition to five novels and one tripartite novel, he has published one collection of shorter works: *Lost in the Funhouse* (1968), the technical involutions of which plumb the nature of narrative itself and disrupt conventional relationships between teller and tale. Barth has also written two essays of particular significance. In "The Literature of Exhaustion," he discusses those writers whose suspicion that certain forms of literature have become obsolete is incorporated both thematically and technically in the fictions they produce. He highlights the successes of Jorge Luis Borges, Vladimir Nabokov and Samuel Beckett in the face of apparent artistic impasse; they acknowledge and push beyond the boundaries staked out by their literary predecessors and employ a potentially stifling sense of "ultimacy" in the creation of new work, so that their forms become metaphors for their aesthetic concerns. "The Literature of Replenishment" seeks to correct any misreading of the former essay as a complaint that contemporary writers have little left to accomplish save the parody of conventions which they arrived upon too late to benefit from themselves. Barth's method is to define and legitimize postmodernism by placing its most interesting practitioners—he singles out Italo Calvino and Gabriel García Márquez for praise—in a direct line of succession which may be traced through the great modernists of the first half of the twentieth century back to Laurence Sterne and Miguel de Cervantes.

Achievements

Perhaps Barth's method is a mark of a growing receptivity among readers and critics to formally venturesome fiction; perhaps it is merely a result of the writer's inevitable passage from unexpected new voice to mature artist. Whatever the case, Barth is one avant-gardist who has infiltrated the literary establishment with relative ease, with no perceptible compromise. He remains America's foremost existential novelist, but his approach to the rather somber question of the arbitrariness of moral values and the absence of intrinsic meaning has always been richly overlaid with humor that is at times intricate and esoteric and often expansive and full of delight in its own verbal virtuosity. He has shown a career-long obsession with mythology, with how classical tales may be reconstituted in and provide resonance for contemporary fiction, and with how the novel may continue to respond to the age-old and seemingly insatiable need for the coherent pleasures of narrative.

Barth still has his detractors, whose accusations typically focus on his tendency to overwork his jokes (a condemnation which often attends *Giles Goat-Boy*) or to surrender to vulgar effects (as in his revisionist history of John Smith's encounter with Pocahontas in *The Sot-Weed Factor*). Nevertheless, few would dispute Barth's stature as the most widely appreciated postmodernist, a designation which he embraces despite its connotation of self-absorption and unreadability.

Biography

The quintessential university writer-in-residence, John Barth must take special satisfaction in having witnessed the solid entrenchment of his work in literary anthologies and undergraduate survey courses. He was born John Simmons Barth on May 27, 1930, in Cambridge, Maryland, the contemporary and historical environs of which have provided the setting for much of his writing. He attended Cambridge High School, after which he accommodated his passion for jazz and the drums with a brief stay at the Juilliard School of Music. His unspectacular showing there led him to enroll at The Johns Hopkins University, a move made possible when he won a scholarship he forgot he had applied for. He achieved the highest grade average in the College of Arts and Sciences upon receiving the B.A. in 1951.

To pay off tuition debts and support his wife (Harriet Anne Strickland, whom he had married in 1950), Barth took a job in the Classics Library, where he first became absorbed in the Oriental tale-cycles which would later inform the style and content of his own fiction. During this period came his first publications in student literary magazines, including one story, "Lilith and the Lion," whose appearance in *The Hopkins Review* when Barth was twenty may rightly be considered his first professional work. His master's project was *The Shirt of Nessus*, a novel based on a love triangle including a father and son and populated by rapists, murderers, bootleggers, and lunatics; Barth confesses it a miscarriage, and he says it now rests in the Dorchester marshes on Chesapeake Bay.

Having received his M.A. in the spring of 1952, he began studying for a Ph.D. in the aesthetics of literature while tutoring and teaching freshman composition courses, until the cost of supporting both his family (his third child was born in January, 1954) and his education compelled him to teach full time. He took a position at Pennsylvania State University in 1953; his experience with freshman composition there would eventually find its way into *The End of the Road*. (He did not earn his doctorate until 1969, from the University of Maryland.) While at Penn State, Barth began a series of one hundred stories, in the bawdy manner of Giovanni Boccaccio's *The Decameron* (1348-1353), detailing the history of Dorchester County. He abandoned the project within a year, but fifty of the proposed hundred stories were completed; a handful were published separately and others later were incorporated into *The Sot-Weed Factor*.

Barth advanced from instructor to associate professor at Penn State, where he taught until 1965, and it was during this twelve-year period that he established his reputation. In the fall of 1954, Barth found a photograph of an old showboat; borrowing something of the conversational style of Laurence Sterne's *Tristram Shandy* (1759-1767) and some plot devices from *Don Casmurro* (1900), by the Brazilian novelist Joachim María Machado de Assis, he began *The Floating Opera* in January, 1955. It was completed in three months, but several publishers rejected it, and Appleton-Century-Crofts demanded many revisions before publishing it in 1956. By the fall of 1955, however, Barth was already at work on *The End of the Road*. Like *The Floating Opera*, with which it is often associated as a philosophical companion-piece, it was finished in three months and was ultimately published by Doubleday in 1958.

The Floating Opera was nominated for a National Book Award, which it failed to win; neither the book nor its successor sold well. Barth was denied a Guggenheim grant in 1958, but his school's research fund did manage $250 to send him to Maryland to gather information for his next project. He had expected *The Sot-Weed Factor* to be another three-month venture, but that mammoth refurbishing of the eighteenth century picaresque turned out to be nearly three years in the writing. That novel, too, met with relative public indifference, but it later became his first major critical success when it was released in paperback in 1964.

Giles Goat-Boy was begun in 1960, and it would be six years from inception to publication. In 1965, Barth left Penn State for a full professorship at the State University of New York in Buffalo. *Giles Goat-Boy* introduced Barth to the best-seller lists in 1966, but he was already at work on *Lost in the Funhouse*, a brain-teasing, technically probing collection of multimedia pieces which came out in 1968, for which Barth received his second unsuccessful nomination for a National Book Award.

His next book did earn that elusive honor, however; *Chimera*, Barth's most direct confrontation of ancient narrative in the form of three metafictions, won the National Book Award in 1973. In that same year, Barth changed locale once more, accepting a post at his alma mater, Johns Hopkins. It was not until 1979 that his next book, *Letters*, was published. Instead of creating a new form, Barth decided, as he had done in *The Sot-Weed Factor*, to resuscitate a traditional one: in this case, the epistolary novel. *Letters* plumbs the author's personal literary history as well, for its principal correspondents are characters from Barth's earlier novels.

Whether the familiar hybrid of writer-teacher nourishes or diminishes creativity will not be decided on the basis of one man's example, but Barth has found the academic atmosphere to be not only hospitable to his talents but also generous as an occasion and setting for his fiction: two of his novels are set specifically in college communities, and the theme of education—be it in a school, under the auspices of a spiritual adviser, or in the shifting, multifarious outside world of affairs—has been repeatedly highlighted in Barth's work. Barth currently lives with his second wife, Shelley Rosenberg (whom he married in 1970), dividing his time between Maryland, where he conducts creative writing seminars, and New York, where he keeps a summer home and does much of his writing.

Analysis

The literary historian and the literary technician meet in the novels and attitudes of John Barth. His eagerness to affirm the artificiality of the art he creates enables him to strip-mine the whole range of narrative that precedes his career for usable personalities and devices; similarly, by beginning with the premise of literature as a self-evident sham, he greatly enlarges the field of possibility within his own fictions, so that outrageous plot contrivances, protean characters (or characters who are essentially banners emblazoned with ruling philosophies), and verbal acrobatics all become acceptable. Barth's general solution for handling the fracture between art and reality is not to heal it, but rather to heighten his readers' awareness of it. This is why, despite his penchant for intellectual confrontation and long interludes of debate in his novels, Barth most often looks to humor—jokes and pranks, parody, and stylistic trickery—to make the philosophy palatable.

Barth meticulously reconstructs the fabric and feel of allegory (*Giles Goat-Boy*) or of the *Künstlerroman* (*The Sot-Weed Factor*), then minimizes the appropriateness of such patterns in the contemporary world by vigorously mocking them. He takes on formidable intellectual questions—the impossibility of knowing external reality, the unavailability of intrinsic values, the fragility of the self in an incurably relativistic universe—but chooses to do so in, to borrow one of his own most durable metaphors, a funhouse atmosphere. In fact, in Barth's fiction, abstract discussion is consistently revealed as a dubious alternative to passionate participation in life. Given the ambiguous state of the self, exposure to the world could be fatal if not for the strategy of fashioning and choosing from among a variety of masks which afford the beleaguered self a sense of definition and a schedule of valid responses to whatever situations the world presents. The willful choosing of masks is Barth's main theme; it suggests that the alternative to despair in the face of universal chaos and indifference is the responsibility to exercise one's freedom, much as an artist exercises his creative faculties in writing and editing tales that satisfy him. In this sense, Barth's heroes are artists of the self, who view the elasticity of character as a challenge to their mythmaking abilities, and who treat their private lives as fictions which are amenable to infinite revision.

"Good heavens," complains Todd Andrews in *The Floating Opera*, "how does one write a novel! I mean, how can anybody stick to the story, if he's at all sensitive to the significance of things?" The doubts and false starts which frustrate the progress of this protagonist's Inquiry—a hodgepodge of papers contained in peach baskets in his hotel room, for which, life being on so tenuous a lease from eternity, he pays rent on a daily basis—reflect those which would potentially stymie Barth himself, were he not to make them part of his subject. Like his narrator/alter ego in *The Floating Opera*, Barth contends with the problem of making art out of nihilism. In Andrews' hands, that problem takes the shape of a book-long (and, he confesses, lifelong) obsession with how, and whether, to live. There is little of traditional suspense to propel the narrative; after all, this is an examination of a decision *not* to commit suicide, so that Andrews' private undertaking of Hamlet's well-known question has led him to accept life, at least provisionally and despite its absence of intrinsic values.

The quality of life is described by the title of the novel and symbolized by the barge show—part vaudeville, part minstrel show—which flashes in and out of view as it moves along the river. No other image in literature so effectively captures the idea of Heraclitean flux: the "performance" is never the same for any two spectators, nor can one resume watching it at the same place in the show as when it last passed by. Furthermore, the nature of this floating phenomenon is operatic: sentimental, bizarre, wildly melodramatic, and often simply laughable. The players are amateurish, and they are best appreciated by an unrefined audience who are not bothered by the gaps in their understanding or by the unevenness of the performance. Andrews entertains the notion of building a showboat that has a perpetual play going on, and the novel itself is the alternative result; like the floating extravaganza, it is "chock-full of curiosities" and considers every possible taste: games, violence, flights of fancy and philosophy, legal and sexual intrigue, war and death, artwork and excrement. The implication here, as emphasized by T. Wallace Whittaker's rendition of William Shakespeare (one of the more delicate turns on the bill, to please the ladies), is that not only are all people players on a stage, but also they are apparently purposeless, scriptless players at that.

There is something of the floating opera in the stylistic range of the novel as well. Todd Andrews is a monologist in the comic, voluble tradition of Tristram Shandy. In fact, both men write autobiographical inquiries into the strangeness of the human condition which digress and associate so frequently that they are destined to become life works; both are artists racing to create against death, although Andrews is as likely to be felled by rational suicide as by his heart murmur; and both combine intellectual pursuits with technical "entertainments" (which include, in Barth's novel, repeated paragraphs, a double column of narrative "options," and a reproduction of the handbill announcing the schedule of events in "Adam's Original and Unparalleled Ocean-Going Floating Opera").

Motivation sets these two narrators apart, however, for if Tristram is compelled by life's delights, Andrews is alienated by its absurdity. Andrews is engaged in a search for purpose; his life hangs in the balance. His Inquiry began as an attempt to come to terms with his father's suicide in 1930, an event too complex to chalk up to an escape from debts incurred after the stock-market crash. It then absorbed a letter to his father which, with the obsessive diligence of Franz Kafka in a similar enterprise, Andrews had begun in 1920 and continued to redraft even after his father's death. The Inquiry continued to blossom until, by the time the novel opens in 1954, it is autobiography, journal, and religious/philosophical treatise all in one, and it floats by at the moment of focus on the decision (made on one of two days in June, 1937), after a failed effort, not to commit suicide. (Todd Andrews admonishes the reader not to confuse his name with its meaning of "death" in German; his name, which misspells the German word, is more aptly read as "almost death.")

Given the kinds of experience he relates, his final acceptance of life is rather surprising. His father's suicide is but one of a series of incidents which suggest that life may not be worth the salvaging effort. Sexuality, for example, is represented by his wonder at the ridiculousness of the act when, at age seventeen, he spies himself in a mirror in the midst of intercourse, and later, when his five-year affair with Jane Mack is revealed to have been directed by her husband, Harrison. Andrews' most profound confrontation with his own self, during World War I, reveals him to be "a shocked, drooling animal in a mudhole." When an enemy soldier stumbles upon him, they share their terror, then silent communion and friendship . . . and then Andrews stabs him to death. All actions are equally pointless; all commitments are arbitrary; all attempts to solve human incomprehension are laughable.

From rake to saint to cynic, Andrews endures without much joy as an expert lawyer, although he does admit to a certain detached interest in the law's arbitrary intricacies, epitomized in the search for the legitimate will among the seventeen left to posterity by Harrison Mack, Sr., which, when found, decides the fate of more than one hundred pickle jars brimming with his excrement. Andrews is actually comfortable enough living in the Dorset Hotel among a collection of society's aged castoffs, until a casual reference by his mistress to his clubbed hands initiates a kind of Sartrean nausea at the utter physical fact of himself; his growing detestation of that mortal coil, coupled with an absolute conviction that all value is artificially imposed, leads him to the brink of suicide, in the form of a scheme to blow up the opera boat (which, in the restored 1967 edition of the novel, would include hundreds of spectators, the Macks and Jeannine, their—or possibly Andrews'—daughter among them).

What stays him is the revelation that, if all values are arbitrary, suicide is not less arbitrary; furthermore, even arbitrary values may offer a way to live. This uneasy treaty with a relativistic universe is Andrews' provisional conclusion to the Inquiry, for the suicide does not come off. Some accident—a psychological shudder, an instinct beyond the intellect's dominion, or a spasm of sentimental concern for the little girl who had suffered a sudden convulsion—disrupts the plan, so the novel's philosophical journey concludes in the anticlimax promised by the narrator at the outset. If Barth frustrates some readers by forsaking the questions he has so fastidiously prepared them for, they must understand that the willingness to handle the sublime and the ridiculous alike with a shrug of good humor is part of the point: in the end, even nihilism is shown to be yet one more posture, one more mask.

In his next novel, *The End of the Road*, Barth's speculations on the nature and necessity of masks becomes more formulaic, although with somewhat bleaker results for his hero. Jake Horner—the name is borrowed from William Wycherly's sly seducer in *The Country Wife* (1673)—suffers from "cosmopsis," a disease of hyperconsciousness: the awareness that one choice is no more inherently valid or attractive than another. When a nameless black doctor materializes near a bench at Pennsylvania Station, he discovers Jake as hopelessly rooted to the spot as the statuette Jake keeps of the tortured Laocoön. The doctor recognizes his paralysis and initiates a program of therapy which forces his patient into action. He explains that no matter how arbitrary the system of "choosing" which he advocates may appear, "Choosing is existence: to the extent that you don't choose, you don't exist." All of Jake's subsequent activities—the plot of the novel—represent his execution of the doctor's precepts.

At the outset, Jake's quest is meticulously prescribed *for* him. He is advised to begin with simple, disciplined choices between well-defined alternatives; should he happen to get "stuck" again beyond his mentor's reach, he is to choose artificially according to Sinistrality, Antecedence, and Alphabetical Priority. He is made to worship the hard facts of an almanac and to travel in straight lines to scheduled locations; because it is a monument to fixity, he is to devote himself to teaching of prescriptive grammar at Wicomico State Teachers College. In short, Jake is to undergo Mythotherapy: the regular assignment of roles to the befuddled ego in order to facilitate participation in the world.

Once Jake's quest is complicated by relationships which overextend the narrative "masks" behind which he operates, that neatly contrived therapy proves insufficient. Joe and Rennie Morgan, characters evolved from Harrison and Jane Mack in *The Floating Opera*, confuse his roles: Joe is a strident god whose rational self-control and mechanical theorizing make him his wife's mentor and Jake's intimidator; Rennie's sexuality and mixture of admiration and helplessness toward her husband are provocative, but she involves Jake in a script he cannot handle. His "road" grows tortuous and overwhelming, as his strictly plotted career is diverted into adulterous liaisons and philo-sophical tournaments, deceit and death. The profundity of his relapse into irresponsibility is much greater this time, however, for he is not the only one victimized by it. By failing to control his roles at critical times, he becomes the instrument of Rennie's death: Rennie will not lie to ensure a safe oper-ation, and Jake's frantic role-playing in order to secure an abortion ends in a grisly death at the hands of Jake's doctor. The reality of Rennie's bleeding on the table is one which, unlike his callous affair with the lonely Peggy Rankin, Jake cannot manipulate or evade; it is the end of the road for him as a free agent in the world. Because he apparently requires further training in order to function successfully, he escapes with the doctor to a new site of the Remobilization Farm.

Of course, Jake's intellectual adversary fares little better under the pressure of real events. Joe Morgan personifies Todd Andrews' supposition that an arbitrary value could be transformed into the "subjective equivalent of an absolute" which might then provide the coherent way of life so crucial to a man who deifies the intellect. Both Jake and Joe begin from the premise of relativism, which explains their mutual attraction, but while Jake tends to succumb to "weatherlessness" (a numbness incurred by the randomness of events and the loss of an essential I), Joe is smug about the rational system he and his wife abide by. That self-assurance sanctions Rennie's being exposed to Jake's influence and provokes Jake to undermine him. When Joe is revealed as something less than pure mind and standards (Jake and Rennie spy him through a window masturbating, grunting, picking his nose), the god loses his authenticity, and the affair merely emphasizes Joe's fall from eminence. Rennie does bring her guilt to Joe, but he returns her to Jake to reenact the betrayal until she can account for it rationally; in the same way, he refuses to face up to the fact of her death, which was indirectly engineered by his experimental obsession, and proves himself to be far more comfortable in handling abstract ideas than in facing up to the welter of uncertainties beyond his field of expertise.

The road's end serves as a final blessing to Jake; the conclusion of the novel is not the completion of a quest but a relief from it. Since the turbulence of the world of affairs has proved unmanageable, he capitulates and numbly offers his "weatherless" self up to the auspices of the doctor, the price for performing Rennie's abortion. Jake retreats into submission after a disastrous initiation into the world.

In his next two novels, Barth grants his philosophical preoccupations the panoramic expansiveness and formal openness of a Henry Fielding or François Rabelais, as if seeking epic dimension for what might well be considered in his first novels to be merely the idiosyncracies of constipated personalities.

The Sot-Weed Factor features a riotously inventive plot and a cast of characters including poets and prostitutes, lords and brigands, landowners and Indians, merchants and thieves, but the triumph of the novel is in its authentic language and texture: for some eight hundred pages, Barth's novel impersonates one of those sprawling eighteenth century picaresque English novels, complete with protracted authorial intrusions, outrageous coincidences, dizzying turns of plot, and a relish for lewd humor.

Barth borrows a satirical poem on colonial America by Ebenezer Cooke (1708) for the foundation of his novel and resuscitates Cooke himself to be his hero. Barth's Eben Cooke is a timid, awkward fellow, who, unlike Andrews and Horner, maintains a steadfast virginity—sexual, social, and political—in a world teeming with sin and subterfuge. His steadfast adherence to a chosen mask—that of poet laureate of Maryland—with its requisite responsibilities keeps him on course. Until he happens upon that identity, Eben is overwhelmed by "the beauty of the possible," so much so that he cannot choose among careers; a broad education shared with his twin sister, Anna, at the hands of the ubiquitous Henry Burlingame, serves to increase his wonder rather than to specify a direction, so that the reader discovers him as a young man who haunts the London taverns, somewhat ill at ease among more raucous peers. He cannot muster an identity reliable enough to survive the pressure of alternatives.

What could have become a lifelong "cosmopsic" stagnation is interrupted by an encounter with a whore, Joan Toast; instead of having sex, Eben chooses to defend his innocence, for he sees in it a symbolic manifestation of his ultimate role. He exalts the deliciously earthy Joan into a bodiless goddess of verse; it is this indifference to reality that will enable him to survive, if not to transcend, the subversive and often grotesque facts of the New World, and the astounding contrasts between the poet's rhapsodizing and the world's stubborn brutishness provide much of the novel's ironic humor.

That confrontation with the New World is set into motion by Eben's father, who, when advised of his son's failure to lead a useful life in London, commands him to set off for his tobacco (sot-weed) estate in Maryland. Armed with a sense of his true calling, Eben wins from Lord Baltimore an agreement to write the "Marylandiad," a verse epic glorifying the province he knows nothing about, and is granted the laureateship in writing. The balance of *The Sot-Weed Factor* is a prolonged trial of Eben's confidence: his initiation into political intrigue and worldly corruption lays siege to his high-flown illusions about mankind. The people he meets are rapacious victimizers, ravaged victims, or crass simpletons, and Eben's promised land, his Malden estate, turns out to be an opium den and brothel. One illusion after another is stripped away, until the poet's tribute to Maryland is metamorphosed into the bitter satire on the deformities of America and Americans found in the poem by the historical Cooke.

Eben would not survive the conspiracies and uglinesses of reality were it not for the tutelage and example of Henry Burlingame. Whereas Eben labors to maintain one role—his "true" self—after years of aimlessness, Burlingame accepts and celebrates a series of roles, for he argues that, in a world of "plots, cabals, murthers, and machinations," an elastic personality will prove most useful. Therefore, he ducks in and out of the novel unpredictably, assuming a variety of guises (including that of John Coode, Baltimore's devilish enemy, Lord Baltimore himself, and even Eben Cooke) as the situation demands. Eben's discussions with his mentor, although they do not cause him to forsake his belief in the essential truth of man's perfectibility and of his own career, do instruct him in how to dissemble when necessary, as exemplified during the voyage to America, when an exchange of roles with his servant, Bertram, proves expedient. In a sense, *The Sot-Weed Factor* boils down to the contrast and the tentative accommodations made between the ideal and the real, or between innocence and experience, as represented by the virgin-poet, who is linked to a past (his father) and to a future (his commission), and by the orphaned jack-of-all-trades, who embraces adventures and lovers with equal vivacity.

The Sot-Weed Factor insists on no conclusive resolution between these attitudes; as is Barth's custom throughout his fiction, the struggles between theoretical absolutes must end in compromise. If Eben's first problem is to rouse himself out of languor, his second is to realize the inadequacy of a single, unalterable role. Accordingly, Eben repudiates his sexual abstinence in order to wed the diseased, opium-addicted Joan Toast—his ruined Beatrice, who has followed him secretly to America—and so accepts a contract between the ideal and the actual. Similarly, Burlingame can only win and impregnate his beloved Anna after he completes his search for his family roots, which is to say, after he locates a stable identity. The novel ends in good comic fashion: lovers are finally united; plot confusions are sorted out. Significantly, however, Barth adds twists to these conventions, thereby tempering the comic resolution: Joan dies in childbirth, and Burlingame disappears without trace. Barth replicates the eighteenth century picaresque novel only to parody it; he seduces the reader into traditional expectations only to undermine them.

For many readers, the most satisfying passages in *The Sot-Weed Factor* are not the philosophical or the literary exercises but rather the bawdy set pieces, the comic inventories and the imaginative diaries; nor should any discussion of this novel neglect to mention the war of name-calling between whores, or the "revisionist" rendition of Captain Smith's sexual assault on the otherwise impregnable Pocahontas. Barth has written of his enjoyment of Tobias Smollett's *Roderick Random* (1748) for its "nonsignificant surfaces," and in such glittering surfaces lie the charm of *The Sot-Weed Factor* as well. Fiction invades history and finds in its incongruities and intricacies of plot, character, and motivation a compatible form. Of all the deceptions perpetrated in the novel, perhaps none is so insidious as that of American history itself—the ultimate ruse of civilization, an imperfect concealment of savagery and self-ishness. To remain innocent of the nature of history is irresponsible; Eben Cooke's practiced detachment, as implied by his virginity, is morally unacceptable. This lesson enables him to mature both artistically and ethically, and to dedicate himself to the world of which he claims to be poet laureate.

Following immediately upon his satire of the historical past is Barth's satire of the future—a computer narrative. The novel-long analogy ruling *Giles Goat-Boy* transforms the universe into a university; this Newest Testament portrays a world divided (between East and West Campus) and waiting for the Grand Tutor, the Savior of the academic system, to protect Studentdom from the satanic Dean o' Flunks.

Barth provides Giles, an amalgam of multicultural messiah-heroes, as the updated instrument of human destiny. Giles (Grand Tutorial Ideal, Laboratory Eugenical Specimen) is the child of the prodigious WESCAC computer and a virgin. Raised as a goat (Billy Bocksfuss) by an apostate scientist-mentor, Max Spielman, he eventually leaves the herd to join humanity as a preacher of the Revised New Syllabus on the West Campus of New Tammany College. The novel traces his attempts to verify and institute his claim to be Grand Tutor. Such a task entails a loss of innocence comparable in kind (although far more extensive in its implications for humanity) to those undertaken by his predecessors in Barth's canon; in *Giles Goat-Boy*, the initiation into complexity assumes a mythical overlay, as the hero passes from his exotic birth to his revelation of purpose in the womb of WESCAC (in whose mechanical interior he and Anastasia, a student who serves as Female Principle, come together); to a series of "assignments" through which he must prove his worth; to his role as lawgiver and deposer of the false prophet, Harold Bray; and finally, to his sacrificial death for the sake of mankind.

Giles's career invokes Lord Raglan's systematic program for the stages of the hero's life, and yet the reader is irresistibly drawn to make correlations between the novel's allegorical personalities and events, and counterparts in journalistic reality. East and West Campus are barely fictional versions of Russia and the United States, with the H-bomb, in the form of WESCAC, the source of their power struggle. John F. Kennedy, Nikita Khruschev, Joseph McCarthy, Albert Einstein, and other contemporary world figures populate the novel, as do such ancient luminaries as Moses, Socrates, and Christ Himself (Enos Enoch, accompanied by Twelve Trustees). These textures give *Giles Goat-Boy* the authority of sociopolitical history, but as is the case in *The Sot-Weed Factor*, Barth's penchant for discovering his own artifice casts a thick shadow of unreliability over the proceedings. For example, the reader must share in the doubts over Giles's legitimacy, both filial and messianic: not only do many people fail to accept his Grand Tutorhood (he predicts betrayal by the masses, who will drive him out on a rusty bicycle to his death on Founder's Hill), but also he himself is never completely certain that his words have not been programmed into him by WESCAC. The document itself—the pages before the reader—brought to "J. B." by Giles's son, is framed by disclaimers, editorial commentaries, footnotes, and postscripts, so that, finally, the "true text" is indistinguishable from the apocrypha. Moreover, Barth's liberal infusion of verse, puns, allusions, and stylistic entertainments strains the heroic conventions which he has assembled from a great variety of literary and mythic sources. In short, the quality of revelation as espoused by Gilesianism is consistently affected by the doubt and self-effacement implied in the structure of the narrative.

Despite Barth's typical supply of structural equivocations, *Giles Goat-Boy* is his most ambitious attempt to recognize correspondences between factual and fictional accounts, between politics and mythology, between public and personal history. If the hero's quest leads him into a world of complexity, there is at least, by virtue of these correspondences, the promise of insight. Under Burlingame's direction in *The Sot-Weed Factor*, the reader learns that the human personality, correctly apprehended, is a compendium of various, even contradictory, selves; in *Giles Goat-Boy*, this lesson is applied to the whole history of human learning and progress. Only when Giles accepts the all-encompassing nature of truth—PASS ALL and FAIL ALL are inextricably connected, not separable opposites but parts of a mystical oneness—does he mature into effectiveness. His passage through experience will include failure, but failure will guarantee growth, itself evidence of passage. Giles is a condenser in whom worldly paradoxes and dichotomies—knowledge and instinct, asceticism and responsibility, Spielman and Eirkopf, West and East Campus, and all other mutually resistive characters and systems of thought—manage a kind of synthesis. Keeping in mind that Giles's story originates from a fundamental willingness to accept his humanity over his "goathood," one comes to appreciate that, although the novel is a satirical fantasy, it is inspired by the same receptivity to experience and the same optimistic energy in the face of desperate circumstances that are exalted by the tradition of quest literature.

The image of Giles and Anastasia united in WESCAC is the philosophical center of the novel; at this climactic moment, flesh is integrated with spirit, animal with human, and scientific hardware with "meaty tubes," all in the service of the improvement of the race. The gospel of *Giles Goat-Boy* is that the very impulse to enter the labyrinth is an affirmation, however unlikely the hero's chances against the beasts and devils (such as Stoker, the gloomy custodian of the power station) who reside within. Giles's victory is a transcendence of categories, a faith in the unity of the universe, and that revelation is enough to overcome the lack of appreciation by the undergraduates. No obstacle or imposture of the dozens which antagonize the hero obscures the meeting of goat-boy with computer; the circuitry of myth remains intact, even in this age of broken atoms.

"When my mythoplastic razors were sharply honed, it was unparalleled sport to lay about with them, to have at reality." So proclaimed Jake Horner in *The End of the Road* while praising articulation as his nearest equivalent to a personal absolute. The narrative impulse is the principal source of faith for Barth's array of protagonists, insofar as faith is possible in an undeniably relativistic environment. In *Letters*, he allows those characters a fuller opportunity to engage in an authorial perspective. *Letters* solidifies Barth's associations with Modernists such as James Joyce and Samuel Beckett; here Barth takes license not only with established literary forms—specifically, the epistolary novel—but also with his private literary past, as he nonchalantly pays visits and respects to old fictional personalities. Because *Letters*, by its very form, intensifies one's awareness of the novel as a fabricated document (and, for that matter, of characters as collections of sentences), it is Barth's most transparently metafictional work; as the novel's subtitle unabashedly declares, this is "an old time epistolary novel by seven fictitious drolls and dreamers each of which imagines himself actual." *Letters* breaks down into seven parts, one for each letter of the title, and covers seven months of letter-writing. Place the first letter of each of the eighty-eight epistles in *Letters* on a calendar so that it corresponds with its date of composition, and the title of the novel will appear; like *Ulysses* (1922), *Letters* testifies to the diligence, if not to the overindulgence, of the craftsman.

Among these letter-writers are a group recycled from previous works as well as two figures, Germaine Pitt (Lady Amherst) and the Author, newly created for this book. In spite of Barth's assertions to the contrary, an appreciation of these characters is rather heavily dependent on a familiarity with their pre-*Letters* biographies: Todd Andrews emerges from *The Floating Opera* as an elderly lawyer who writes to his dead father and is drawn to incest while enjoying one last cruise on Chesapeake Bay; Jacob Horner remains at the Remobilization Farm to which he had resigned himself at the conclusion of *The End of the Road*, and where his latest Information Therapy demands that he write to himself in an elaborate reconstitution of the past; Ambrose Mensch, the now-mature artist out of "Lost in the Funhouse," directs his correspondences to the anonymous "Yours Truly" whose message he found in a bottle years earlier, and constructs his life, including an affair with Germaine Pitt, in accordance with Lord Raglan's prescription for the hero. The reader also meets descendants of previous creations: Andrew Burlingame Cook VI busily attempts to shape the nation's destiny in a Second American Revolution, and Jerome Bonaparte Bray, a mad rival to Barth himself who may be a gigantic insect, seeks to program a computer-assisted novel, *Numbers*, to compete with the authority of the one that treated him so shabbily.

The third level of writers in *Letters* includes the two who have no prior existence in Barth's works: Germaine Pitt, a colorful widow who had been the friend of Joyce, H. G. Wells, Aldous Huxley, and other literary notables, anxiously campaigns as Acting Provost to ensure the prestige of her college against the administrative dilutions and hucksterism of one John Schott; the Author enters the novel as Pitt's own alternative candidate for an honorary doctorate (which Schott proposes to give to the dubious activist, State Laureate A. B. Cook VI), and he writes to everyone else in the vicinity of *Letters*.

The most consistent theme tying the letters and authors together is the conflict between restriction and freedom. The setting is the volatile America of the 1960's, when sexual, moral, political, and even academic norms underwent the most serious reevaluation in American history. Obviously, Barth's creative history is the most evident aspect of this theme, and the repetitions and echoes among his novels and within *Letters* seduce the reader into joining his search for pattern in the flux of human affairs. The ambiguous nature of history itself has also been one of his most durable themes—one recalls a chapter in *The Sot-Weed Factor* which examined the question of whether history is "a Progress, a Drama, a Retrogression, a Cycle, an Undulation, a Vortex, a Right- or Left-Handed Spiral, a Mere Continuum, or What Have You"—and the suggestion here is that any sort of orthodoxy can be revealed, especially in times of social crisis, as fictional. Student protests against the Establishment are replicated in the antagonism between characters and an established text; the societal disruptions in the novel disrupt and contaminate the narrative.

In contrast to Samuel Richardson's definitive use of the epistolary form, *Letters* is populated by characters who are more than vaguely aware of their unreality, and therefore of the need to bargain with Barth for personal status and support. When the Author intrudes as a character, no convention is above suspicion; although he describes himself as turning away from the "fabulous irreal" toward "a détente with the realistic tradition," if this novel is the result, it is a severely qualified détente, indeed. Perhaps the structural "confusion" of the novel explains the smugness of Reg Prinz, an avant-garde filmmaker who wants to create a version of all of Barth's books in a medium which he feels to be superior and more up-to-date. What had been a playful interest in the relationships between creative media in *Lost in the Funhouse* has escalated in *Letters* into a battle for aesthetic dominance between the word-hating Prinz and the word-mongering Barth. (That Prinz is a prisoner of the novel, of course, enables Barth to sway the outcome of this battle, at least temporarily.)

Letters, like history itself, concludes in blood and ambiguity; one suspects that Barth means to undergo a catharsis of the books and characters that have obsessed him and that continue to infiltrate his creative consciousness. It is testimony to Barth's ability to elicit admiration for his craft that the reader does not leave *Letters*—or, for that matter, most of his fictions—with a sense of defeat. The keynote of his literary career is exuberance; if nihilism and existential gloom have been his thematic preoccupations, their potentially numbing effects are undercut by Barth's cleverness, his stylistic ingenuity, and his campaign for the rewards of narrative.

Barth's *Sabbatical* continues to bend philosophy into escapade. Subtitled "A Romance," *Sabbatical* is rather a postmodernization of romance: all the well-established Barthian formal intrigues, ruminative digressions, plot coincidences (the married pair of main characters, in the same vein as *The Sot-Weed Factor*, are both twins), and other examples of literary self-consciousness complicate the vacation cruise of Fenwick Scott Key Turner, a former CIA agent and a contemporary novelist, and his wife, Susan, herself an established academic and critic. The nine-month sea journey—a frequent theme for Barth—leads to the birth of the novel itself, in whose plot the narrating "parents" seek clues to some conspiratorial Agency "plot" against them. (Fenwick has written an exposé that makes his "life as voyage" a perilous journey indeed—even when on sabbatical.) So the creative couple prepare, nurture, take pride in, and exhaustively analyze their verbal offspring, while the real world blows into their story from the shore in another dizzying mixture of fact and fiction.

Yet, as readers have come to expect from Barth, the imagination is exalted above and beyond its moorings in the "real world," all the while calling attention to its own altitude. As Frenwick declares to his loving coauthor: "I won't have our story be unadulterated realism. Reality is wonderful; reality is dreadful; reality is what it is." And the intensity, the scope, ant the truth of reality are more appropriately the province of experimental technique.

Barth has consistently affirmed a kind of faith in the saving graces of the fiction whose very tradition he has so vigorously transformed. It is Barth's privilege to be able to objectify and transcend the philosophical predicaments of his characters in those imaginative enviroments where arbitrariness gives way to intricacy, and frustration to delight.

Major publication other than long fiction
SHORT FICTION: *Lost in the Funhouse*, 1968.

Bibliography
Morrell, David. *John Barth: An Introduction*, 1976.
Scholes, Robert. *The Fabulators*, 1967.
Stark, John O. *The Literature of Exhaustion*, 1974.
Tanner, Tony. *City of Words: American Fiction, 1950-1970*, 1971.
Tharpe, Jac. *John Barth: The Comic Sublimity of Paradox*, 1977.
Weixlmann, Joseph N. *John Barth: An Annotated Bibliography*, 1975.

Arthur M. Saltzman

DONALD BARTHELME

Born: Philadelphia, Pennsylvania; April 7, 1931

Principal long fiction
Snow White, 1967; *The Dead Father*, 1975

Other literary forms
Donald Barthelme's reputation rests on his achievement as a short-story writer. He once commented that Vladimir Nabokov's "fat books always seem to be leaning on [his] little thin ones." "I am always working on a novel," Barthelme once told an interviewer, "But they always seem to fall apart in my hands." In the same discussion, he mentioned that four of his stories ("Perpetua," "Critique de la Vie Quotidienne," "Henrietta and Alexandra," and "Flying to America") were once parts of a novel that failed. Perhaps Robert Scholes identifies one of the central reasons why Barthelme has written primarily short fiction when he comments that "Metafiction . . . tends toward brevity because it attempts, among other things, to assault or transcend the laws of fiction—an understanding which can only be achieved within fictional form." It may be reasonable to suspect that such an assault too long sustained tends to divide and dissipate the reader's attention. Any prolonged attack tends to create a sympathy for the victim, and tradition—in this case, realism—usually has the home-court advantage in struggles of this nature.

Achievements
Barthelme is a much-imitated postmodern writer of metafictions, parafictions, and fabulations, a leading figure in the school which includes John Barth, John Hawkes, Richard Brautigan, Robert Coover, Thomas Pynchon, William H. Gass, Jerzy Kosinski, Kurt Vonnegut, Ishmael Reed, and Ronald Sukenick. Asked in an interview to name works in which he perceives new directions in fiction, Barthelme mentioned John Ashbery's *Three Poems* (1972), Jurgen Becker's *Ränder* (1968), Peter Handke's *Offending the Audience, and Self-Accusation*, (1971), and Oswald Wiener's *The Improvement of Central Europe: A Novel* (1969). In the same interview, he also listed his favorite writers: François Rabelais, Arthur Rimbaud, Heinrich von Kleist, Franz Kafka, Gertrude Stein, Flann O'Brien, Samuel Beckett, Gass, Walker Percy, Gabriel García Márquez, Barth, Pynchon, Kenneth Koch, Ashbery, and Grace Paley.

Barthelme has spent a year in Denmark (1965), received a Guggenheim Fellowship (1966), won the National Institute of Arts Award (1972) for *Sadness* and the National Book Award for *The Slightly Irregular Fire Engine: Or, The Hithering Dithering Djinn* (1972), a children's story.

Biography

Born in Philadelphia, Donald Barthelme, the eldest of five children, grew up in Texas with his sister and three brothers. His father, Donald, earned his degree in architecture and his mother a degree in English at the University of Pennsylvania. When he returned to his home state, Barthelme's father established his own architectural firm and in 1946 became a professor of architectural design at the University of Houston, where he had a long and distinguished career. Barthelme recalls his father's concern with what was then avant-garde architecture and frequent visits by artists and architects. No doubt his mother, Helen Bechtold Barthelme, had a good deal to do with the ample supply of books around the house, which ran from Norse mythology to adventure stories such as those of Rafael Sabatini. John Dos Passos was part of the family library, and Barthelme added T. S. Eliot and James Joyce. He has said that an anthology of modern French poetry given him by his father influenced his development as a writer, much as his father's concern with modernism did.

Barthelme was reared a Roman Catholic (from which he long ago lapsed into a vague existentialism) and attended diocesan schools. Somewhat tall, bearded, and bespectaled (gold-rimmed glasses), Barthelme is shy and orderly. He lives in a modern leather-and-chrome, Ingres-and-Lindner Greenwich Village apartment with an attached private forest. Despite his frequent appearances in *The New Yorker* and his chic living quarters, however, Barthelme still holds title to his Texas background, wears cowboy boots, and, like Kurt Vonnegut, another architect's son, sees himself as the heir of a normal, middle-class childhood in Houston.

Barthelme began writing, publishing, and editing in secondary school and continued to do so at the University of Houston, where he studied journalism off and on between 1949 and 1957. (During this time, he studied as often as he could with Maurice Nathanson, a philosophy professor later at Yale.) While an undergraduate, he worked as a reporter for the *Houston Post*, edited the university newspaper, the *Cougar*, and the yearbook. Some of his early work reflects his later use of parody and satire in general. In 1953, Barthelme was drafted into the Army and served in Louisiana, Japan, and Korea, where he arrived on the day the truce was signed. He edited an army newspaper and returned after his tour of duty ended to the staff of the *Houston Post*. At the same time, he joined the public relations department of the University of Houston, where he wrote speeches for the president and edited the *Forum*, a literary magazine which he founded, and *Acta Diurna*, the faculty newsletter.

His work on the *Forum* in 1956 led not only to his publishing Joseph Lyons, Roger Callois, Gregory Bateson, Leslie Fiedler, Hugh Kenner, Alain Robbe-Grillet, and Jean-Paul Sartre, but also to a period of intense reading in various academic disciplines. During this time, he skimmed numerous learned periodicals (among them, the *Journal of Philosophy and Phenomenological*

Research and the *Journal of Philosophy*, where he discovered essays by Walker Percy and William H. Gass.

When the counterculture was forming ranks in the early 1960's, Barthelme was advancing his career in public relations, editing, reporting, and, at the age of thirty, serving as director of the Contemporary Arts Museum of Houston. He moved to New York in 1962 and became managing editor of *Location*, an art and literary review conceived by Tom Hess and Harold Rosenberg. Only two issues were published in the next two years: they featured such writers as Marshall McLuhan, Ashbery, Koch, and Gass. Barthelme admired a number of *The New Yorker* writers, and he joined the magazine as a regular beginning in 1963 and 1964, when he published ten pieces. In the early 1980's, Barthelme still appears regularly in *The New Yorker*. Barthelme has taught at the State University of New York at Buffalo, Boston University, and the City College of New York, and now lives on West 11th Street in New York City with his Danish wife, Birgit.

Analysis

Both of Donald Barthelme's novels, *Snow White* and *The Dead Father*, extend and magnify the stylistic techniques and the philosophy of postmodern fiction. They are characterized by incongruities, discontinuities, and jarring new perspectives. In both works, Barthelme deconstructs cultural myths: in *Snow White*, romantic love, and in *The Dead Father*, the Oedipus complex. Further, Barthelme attacks such notions of plot, character, structure, climax, and denouement. In fact, linguistic and cultural coherence in general as well as the two literary genres parodied in the novels—the romance and the quest novel—are relentlessly satirized.

The principle of collage distinguishes nearly all of Barthelme's work. He employs it in such a way as to create a series of discontinuities: images, levels of discourse, narrative styles, time-frames, and characterizations frequently work against one another. Explaining his idea of the function of collage, he has said that "the point of collage is that unlike things are stuck together to make, in the best case, a new reality. This new reality . . . may be or imply a comment on the other reality from which it came, and may also be much else."

Barthelme creatively transforms the doubt which such a technique creates in a way that transcends existential dread; he moves beyond the feeling of absurdity. His irony is as creative as it is destructive, making his readers laugh as he mocks the fragile authority of rigid conventions—conventions which support a false sense of security. Liberation and wit temper the destructive edge of his parody. "We all doubt authority," he has said, "We're not sure we understand it. We doubt our competence to understand it." In his fiction—and particularly in his two novels—Barthelme deconstructs conventional authority in an effort to provoke the reader to imagine what might replace and possibly transcend it.

Snow White is a metafiction, a loosely structured series of deadpan comedic moments which defy plot, characterization, point of view, linear time, and realism in general. The book proceeds in the self-indulgent style of a Woody Allen film: reflexive, episodic, incongruous. Hilarious in its parody of linguistic and social conventions, it is a Swiftian modest proposal to deconstruct the mythopoeic impulse embodied in the Grimm-Disney fairy tale of Snow White and the Seven Dwarfs.

Barthelme's text satirizes the "horsewife" end state which frequently awaits the fruition of romantic love—that odd mix of the domestic with the demoniac—and the insidious way in which culture insures that gender becomes destiny. This so-called theme, however, is more a *leitmotiv* in a book which parodies the very form in which it operates. Barthelme's novels do not have a clear teleology; they defy the Aristotelian impulse toward design and resolution, refusing to construct meaning for the reader. *Snow White* makes fun of making fun of making meaning. It calls attention to the spectacle of itself, to itself as an activity, at the same time that it parodies the pseudo-realistic novel which neatly resolves conflicts over the meaning and purpose of life. The common themes that Hogo de Bergerac (the villain-cynic of *Snow White*) knows full well—"The death of the heart . . . the terror of aloneness, and the rot of propinquity, and the absence of grace"—are present in *Snow White*, but they are in no way clearly developed or resolved. They are simply there.

The development of this fragmented parody is far more complex than any critical summary can indicate. In *Snow White*, Barthelme consistently shatters the narrative flow with scenes of the President of the United States worrying about the characters, lists of college courses, and Chinese foods that sound like baby talk, summary statements from literary and psychological texts, passages on the limitations of language which is in many ways the major focus in the novel, and language "clips" from popular universes of discourse. *Snow White* is a collage rather than a straightforward parodistic story set in modern times. The tale of Snow White and her dwarfs moves through this fragmented parody like a serious digression that never reaches closure. Her seven suitors were born in various national parks and are, she says, "the equivalent of about two *real men*, as we know from the films and from our childhood when there were giants on the earth."

Snow White herself does not amount to much more than her six beauty spots which constitute her full-length, fill-in-the-blanks portrait on the initial page. Dan, one of the seven dwarfs, sees her as basically the bath towels she uses to dry herself: "We can easily dispense with the slippery and untrustworthy and expensive effluvia that is Snow White, and cleave instead to the towel." It is finally nearly impossible to separate the satire on language in *Snow White* from its sustained—if discontinuous—parody of the imprisoning nature of romantic love viewed as a cultural pattern. Keeping his readers constantly at bay, Barthelme makes it impossible for them to be sure of his intention. In his distrust of language, Barthelme creates in the reader an equal suspicion of the potential meaning inherent in the activities it can describe.

Reality, in general, is problematical in this extended and disjointed metafiction which has no conclusion. Laughing at the myth of Snow White (and mixing it with the one of Rapunzel), Barthelme depicts Snow White's prince as fleeing the pressure of his role and hiding out in a monastery. When he finally returns, he sets up an elaborate spy network outside her building. Eventually, he drinks the poison meant for Snow White—a vodka Gibson on the rocks—and dies in convulsions and green foam. As Snow White says, "'he is *pure frog*. So I am disappointed. Either I have overestimated Paul, or I have overestimated history.'"

Whatever Snow White has done, it never becomes enough to escape the text of the myth which imprisons her. She continues to cast chrysanthemums on Paul's grave, and the modern "dwarfs" continue to wash buildings and stir the huge vats of Chinese baby food, seeking equanimity as happy bourgeoisie. The Snow White myth of romantic love has been ridiculed in this displacement of the forest to the city and the transformation of dwarfs and their raven-haired charge to a *ménage à huit*: all seven live together and have communal sex with "Snow White" in the shower. These incongruous transpositions lead the reader to the last page of the novel, which lists possible endings from which to choose: "The Failure of Snow White's Arse." "Revirgination of Snow White." "Apotheosis of Snow White." "Snow White Rises into the Sky."

Barthelme's satire does not offer anything to replace what his irony atomizes, but neither the dominant tone of mockery nor the irresolution of conflict is a sign of despair, cynicism, or bitterness. Barthelme's deadpan humor—like Woody Allen's—creates a space between the audience and antiquated mythologies. Rather than bearing the audience, as realism so easily can, back into the past, *Snow White* clears a sufficient space between the readers and the texts by which they, like the main character, live their lives. There is breathing room in which to consider new directions. Why the audience stays bound in a static and unfulfilling relation to its own dwarfed notions of reality is perhaps explained best by Snow White's comment to her own seven disappointments: "'It must be laid, I suppose, to a failure of the imagination. I have not been able to imagine anything better.'"

The story line of *The Dead Father*, Barthelme's second novel, is relatively straightforward—a rarity in his fiction. It details the deceitful quest of a wooden-legged Dead Father, who is dead only "in a sense." His is a gigantic "corpse" 3,200 cubits long and attached to a cable hauled by nineteen men to his grave. In time, he is forced to surrender to his son Thomas all of the symbols of his power—passport, keys, buckle, sword. Four principal non-characters—Thomas, Julie, Emma, and Edmund—agonize over the existential questions posed by this ordeal and by fathers in general. Much of their humor mocks the goatish desires of the Dead Father for the sexual favors with which they torment him in open acts of carnal self-indulgence.

Freudians, parodied in *Snow White*, recover some face in *The Dead Father*. The mother, a shadowy figure who trails the action throughout, is never bedded by her son. Yet neither her final send-off to the grocery store nor the sexuality of the Dead Father's children quite domesticates the Oedipal myth.

In *The Dead Father*, Barthelme plies the same forms of linguistic distrust which informed *Snow White*. The uncharacteristic clarity of the narrative line, however, would seem to suggest that the authority of his subject fractures the ironic distance Barthelme usually puts between himself, his readers, and his subject. The more sexually and verbally playful, the more irreverently ironic and bizarre this parodistic quest fantasy becomes, the more sympathy it tends to generate for the father who is being degraded and stripped of his authority. The father is never quite exorcised, and, even in a fiction with most of its ribs showing, he manages to achieve a certain wholeness.

His virility is grossly parodied in the sexual quest for the golden fleece—a pubic hair from Julie, a ruse to lure the Dead Father to his prepared gravesite. The length to which Barthelme goes to trivialize his virility, ultimately has power to coopt the autonomy and independence, the very identity of his children, only confirms the vitality of the myth the Dead Father represents. ("He is like a bubble you do not wish to burst.") His dimensions are mythic, and his dismemberment and death cannot help but recall that of Osiris and the latent possibility of reassembly, regeneration, and immortality. The Dead Father is a mythic hero-god and Oedipal Father, a symbol of authority and divinity associated with the building and binding forces—with Eros itself—which create and maintain culture. In Barthelme's ironic deconstruction, he is more revitalized than he is destroyed.

The Dead Father reads like a demoniac dream, with alternating currents of dread and mockery, clarity and babel, affirmation and destruction. Frequent interludes of disconnected discourse scramble dialogue with undisguised epistemological distrust. Yet these never succeed in distancing the reader from the authority of the father and the myth of Oedipus in the manner in which *Snow White* deflates the myth of romantic love. Barthelme himself acknowledges the greater power of this myth of patriarchy as the Dead Father is very much alive throughout. "Often," the reader is told, "[the] memory is more potent than the living presence of a father." Even as he is stripped of his symbols of authority, emasculated (his leg is hacked off), and pitched in his huge grave to be bulldozed from consciousness, the Dead Father lingers as the most powerful presence in the book.

In the end, *The Dead Father* is a story about the funeral journey of a "dead" father who, the reader eventually learns, will never really die. It is satiric, reflexive metafiction with an ending that is not a true ending and a beginning that is not a genuine beginning. The book's essentially false plot (Everything exists and happens "in a sense") relates the story of a death that can never be, except in the fantasy kingdom of the Wends: the land of the Oedipal wish fulfilled; a kind of Magic Kingdom where "each Wend impregnates his own mother and then fathers himself." *The Dead Father* is a metasatirical smirk at all literary efforts to bury the myth of Oedipus. Once again, the limitations of language are exposed.

In both *Snow White* and *The Dead Father*, Barthelme weaves the fraying edges of culture myth into satiric knots. His debts to S. J. Perelman, James Thurber, Woody Allen, *The New Yorker* cartoons, and the tone of chic *Angst* in general locate him in the coolly cosmopolitan vein of Western satire and squarely in the tradition of Jonathan Swift. Along with Jorge Luis Borges, Samuel Beckett, Alain Robbe-Grillet, Gertrude Stein, Eugéne Ionesco, Nathalie Sarraute, William Burroughs, Thomas Pynchon, Vladimir Nabokov, and John Barth, he shares a reflexive impulse toward metafiction, a tradition with roots reaching as far back as Laurence Sterne's *Tristram Shandy* (1759-1767).

For those who prefer "to use the hand-rail of plot when they step off into the dark stairs of fiction," Barthelme will always appear to celebrate, in the words of Pearl Kazin Bell, "unreason and decay." He will be seen as challenging revered cultural mythologies—as he does in both novels in different ways—and other forms of coherence that make a prison-house for the imagination out of the linguistic rubble of tradition. If, however, Barthelme is an iceman in a tradition of cold black humor, readers must remember that ice not only splits the structures it invades; but it also melts, leaving space for the imagination to create new patterns, and for healing.

Still, Barthelme's audience will always be more cosmopolitan than that of his contemporary, Kurt Vonnegut, whose middle-class nostalgia and short stories give him an audience as broad as his vein of traditional humanism. Barthelme is a stylistic heckler, an acid comic, a "cool" writer. In challenging the adequacy of language to hold meanings, he attracts a select audience: one able to enjoy the threatening energy behind a crackling wit that plays devilishly with the very nature of meaning. Perhaps, like Snow White's prince, it must be an audience able to enjoy, without expiring, a little poison with its vodka Gibson on the rocks.

Major publications other than long fiction
    SHORT FICTION: *Come Back, Dr. Caligari*, 1964; *Unspeakable Practices, Unnatural Acts*, 1968; *City Life*, 1970; *Sadness*, 1972; *Guilty Pleasures*, 1974; *Amateurs*, 1976; *Great Days*, 1979; *Sixty Stories*, 1981.
    CHILDREN'S LITERATURE: *The Slightly Irregular Fire Engine: Or, The Hithering, Dithering Djinn*, 1971.

Bibliography

Baker, John F. "PW Interviews: Donald Barthelme," in *Publisher's Weekly*. November 11, 1974, pp. 6-7.

Bellamy, Joe David. *The New Fiction: Interviews with Innovative American Writers*, 1974.

Davis, Robert Con. "Postmodern Paternity: Donald Barthelme's *The Dead Father*," in *Delta*. May 8, 1979, pp. 127-140.

Dickstein, Morris. "Fiction Hot and Kool: Dilemmas of the Experimental Writer," in *TriQuarterly*. XXXIII (Spring, 1975), pp. 257-277.

Gass, William H. *Fiction and the Figures of Life*, 1971.

Gilman, Richard. *The Confusion of Realms*, 1969.

――――――. "Donald Barthelme," in *Partisan Review*. XXXIX (Summer, 1972), pp. 382-396.

Gordon, Lois. *Donald Barthelme*, 1981.

Hassan, Ihab. *Paracriticisms*, 1975.

Hicks, Jack. *In The Singer's Temple*, 1981.

Klinkowitz, Jerome. *A Comprehensive Bibliography and Annotated Secondary Checklist*, 1977.

――――――. *Literary Disruptions: The Making of a Post-Contemporary Fiction*, 1975.

Leitch, Thomas M. "Donald Barthelme and the End of the End." in *Modern Fiction Studies*. XXVIII (Spring, 1982), pp. 129-143.

Leland, John. "Remarks Re-Marked: Barthelme, What Curios of Signs!," in *Boundary 2*. V (1977), pp. 795-811.

Longleigh, Peter. "Donald Barthelme's *Snow White*," in *Critique*. XI (1969), pp. 30-34.

Malory, Barbara. "Barthelme's *The Dead Father*" in *Linguistics in Literature*. II (1977), pp. 44-111.

McCaffery, Larry. "Barthelme's *Snow White*: The Aesthetics of Trash," in *Critique*. XVI (1975), pp. 19-32.

Schickel, Richard. "Freaked Out on Barthelme," in *The New York Times Magazine*. August 16, 1970, pp. 14-15, 42.

Schmitz, Neil. "Donald Barthelme and the Emergence of Modern Satire," in *Minnesota Review*. I (Fall, 1971), pp. 109-118.

Ronald T. Curran

H. E. BATES

Born: Rushden, England; May 16, 1905
Died: Little Chart, England; January 29, 1974

Principal long fiction

The Two Sisters, 1926; *Catherine Foster*, 1929; *Charlotte's Row*, 1931; *The Fallow Land*, 1932; *The Poacher*, 1935; *A House of Women*, 1936; *Spella Ho*, 1938; *Fair Stood the Wind for France*, 1944; *The Cruise of the Breadwinner*, 1946; *The Purple Plain*, 1947; *The Jacaranda Tree*, 1949; *The Scarlet Sword*, 1950; *Love for Lydia*, 1952; *The Feast of July*, 1954; *The Nature of Love: Three Short Novels*, 1954; *The Sleepless Moon*, 1956; *Death of a Huntsman: Four Short Novels*, 1957; *The Darling Buds of May*, 1958; *A Breath of French Air*, 1959; *An Aspidistra in Babylon: Four Novellas*, 1960; *When the Green Woods Laugh*, 1960; *The Day of the Tortoise*, 1961; *A Crown of Wild Myrtle*, 1962; *The Golden Oriole: Five Novellas*, 1962; *Oh! To Be in England*, 1963; *A Moment in Time*, 1964; *The Distant Horns of Summer*, 1967; *A Little of What You Fancy*, 1970; *The Triple Echo*, 1970.

Other literary forms

H. E. Bates published approximately four hundred short stories in magazines, newspapers, special editions, and collections; in fact, he is probably better known as a short-story writer than as a novelist. Many of his more successful efforts were long stories, and so it is natural that he eventually turned to the novella as a favorite medium. Works in this form were published most often in collections, occasionally as independent works, as with *The Cruise of the Breadwinner* (1946) and *The Triple Echo* (1970). His first published work was a one-act play, *The Last Bread* (1926), and throughout his career he aspired to write for the stage, though with little success. *The Day of Glory* had a short run in 1945. A major portion of Bates's nonfiction works consist of essays on nature and country life. In this form, he excelled, bringing to his subject a deep knowledge and understanding based on a lifetime of country living. In addition, he produced three volumes of children's books, a memoir of his mentor Edward Garnett, and a highly regarded though unscholarly study entitled *The Modern Short Story: A Critical Survey* (1941). His autobiography is in three volumes: *The Vanished World* (1969); *The Blossoming World* (1971); and *The World in Ripeness* (1972).

Achievements

From the publication of *The Two Sisters* in 1926 until the outbreak of World War II, Bates was known principally to literati in Britain and America as an accomplished writer of stories and novels about rural England. In spite of good reviews in the highbrow and popular press and the enthusiastic recommendation of such critics and colleagues as David Garnett, Geoffrey West, Richard Church, Edward O'Brien, and Graham Greene, Bates's books sold moderately at best—not more than a few thousand copies each. The one exception to this general neglect came in 1938 with *Spella Ho*, which was well received in England and serialized in condensed form in *The Atlantic*. When war broke out, Bates was recruited for the RAF and given a commission unique in literary and military history: to write short stories about the air war and the men who fought it. The result was two best-sellers, *The Greatest People in the World* (1942) and *How Sleep the Brave* (1943); paperbound copies sold in the hundred of thousands. Following these, and coincident with a change of publishers, Bates produced a string of best-selling novels about the war: *Fair Stood the Wind for France*, *The Purple Plain*, *The Jacaranda Tree*, and *The Scarlet Sword*. To many critics of the time, it appeared that Bates had capitulated to popular taste, but shortly afterward he published his finest novel, *Love for Lydia*. During the 1950's, Bates's reputation assured substantial fees for his magazine stories, but his artistic reputation was more enhanced in this period by the novellas, a number of which recaptured rural life in prewar England. Versatility, however, was his new trademark, as the fiction embraced an ever-widening variety of characters, moods, and settings. In 1958, Bates returned to the ranks of the best-sellers with *The Darling Buds of May*, a farce about the uninhibited Larkin family and modern country life. Four additional Larkin novels followed and were equally successful commercially, but artistically inferior. At the time of his death, Bates had slipped into obscurity once again, yet popular interest remains high, stimulated in part by televised versions of *Love for Lydia*, *Fair Stood the Wind for France*, *A Moment in Time*, and several stories and novellas. Films have been made of *The Purple Plain*, *The Darling Buds of May*, *The Triple Echo*, and "Dulcima." The full measure of Bates's achievement is only beginning to be appreciated.

Biography

Herbert Ernest Bates was born on May 16, 1905, in Rushden, Northamptonshire, England's center of shoe and boot manufacture. His father, employed in the boot factories since boyhood, vowed that his children would never follow the same career; accordingly, H. E., Stanley, and Edna were reared in strict Methodist respectability and educated at local schools. In his early years Bates reacted strongly against the red brick ugliness of his home town, preferring country life with his maternal grandfather, George Lucas. Lucas was by far the most significant influence on Bates's life and fiction, instilling in him a passion for nature and a lifelong interest in rural affairs. A bright student, Bates won a scholarship to nearby Kettering Grammar School, where he performed indifferently until meeting Edmund Kirby, an English master lately returned from World War I. Inspired and encouraged by Kirby, Bates resolved to become a writer, and though he could have attended university, chose not to, electing instead to try newspaper writing and then clerking in a warehouse. There in his spare time he wrote a sprawling novel which Kirby advised him to burn. Undeterred, he tried a second, *The Two Sisters*, which traveled to ten publishers before being read by Jonathan Cape's great discoverer of new talent, Edward Garnett. Garnett recognized, where others had not, the sensitivity, feeling for character, and the gift for nature writing which are the hallmarks of all Bates's fiction.

Having no university connections and never comfortable in London, Bates stayed in Rushden and continued his literary apprenticeship under Garnett and Kirby. Even before this, he had discovered in the Continental masters, especially Anton Chekhov, Ivan Turgenev, Leo Tolstoy, and Guy de Maupassant, the models for his own short fiction. Other influences were Stephen Crane, Ernest Hemingway, Thomas Hardy, and W. H. Hudson. Reading constantly and writing regularly, Bates remained in Rushden until his marriage in 1931. Virtually all the stories and novels of this period are set in and around Rushden and neighboring Higham Ferrers, and much of this work is autobiographical.

In 1931, Bates married Marjorie (Madge) Cox, and the couple made their home in a former barn in Little Chart, Kent, where they remained until Bates's death. Madge has been called "the perfect wife" for Bates: "She made his writing possible by creating an island of stability and calm in which he could work." The move to Kent made no immediate impact on Bates's fiction, as he continued to write stories and novels set in Northamptonshire. By the outbreak of the war, he had exhausted his store of midlands material, but induction into the RAF gave him a whole new set of experiences and widened the scope of his fiction. The stories written for the RAF were first published under the pseudonym "Flying Officer X," but when their authorship became public, Bates's name became a household word. *Fair Stood the Wind for France* was inspired by snippets overheard in barracks and pubs about airmen downed over France. The three war novels which followed in quick succession derived from postings to Burma and India. Royalties from these books made the Bates family (by now grown to six with the birth of two girls and two boys) financially secure for the first time. Of nearly equal importance was an operation in 1947 that relieved Bates of a lifetime of acute intestinal pain.

Financial security and good health may have contributed to a burst of creativity, for *Love for Lydia* and a fine collection of stories, *Colonel Julian*, quickly followed. Inspiration for *Love for Lydia* came from Bates's early Northamptonshire experiences, but the stories show an expanded awareness of contemporary matters. In 1956, however, *The Sleepless Moon* was greeted with such savagery from reviewers that Bates vowed never to write another novel. Unlike Hardy, Bates broke his vow, but with the exception of *The Distant Horns of Summer*, he avoided serious long fiction, concentrating instead on humor (the Larkin novels) and popular materials. For aesthetic outlets, he turned to the short story and the novella. During the last two decades of his life, Bates remained a very private man. Never given to literary cliques nor arty socializing, he lived quietly in Little Chart, traveling extensively to France and Italy, but otherwise indulging his passion for gardening and family life, writing daily from early morning until noon. In 1966, he suffered a severe heart attack, followed by pneumonia, but recovered sufficiently to return to writing. His last works of importance are the three-volume autobiography and *The Triple Echo*, a novella. He died in 1974 in a Canterbury hospital of causes never revealed.

Analysis

H. E. Bates's primary concern as a writer was for the individual and the forces that threaten his or her happiness or fulfillment. He is not, however, a political, social, moral, or philosophical theorist; ideas as such play almost no part in Bates's fiction. Most of his protagonists are "ordinary" people— farmers, laborers, waitresses, housewives, children, pensioners, and young men of no particular education or accomplishments. Curiously, he approaches his material from two very different, almost contradictory, points of view. Many of the stories and a few of the lesser novels are essentially Romantic in outlook, glorifying nature, promoting individual achievement and freedom, assuming the essential goodness of people. On the other hand, many stories, novellas, and virtually all of the most successful novels are naturalistic in their portrayal of individuals at the mercy of forces they cannot understand or control, of nature as indifferent or even hostile, or of life itself as an almost Darwinian struggle. These two viewpoints coexist from the very beginning and contribute to Bates's great versatility. At the same time, the style is always clear and straightforward, uncomplicated by the experimental techniques of modern writing, the story line remaining strong and simple. These features of style and plot, together with the generally rural settings of his fiction, make Bates appear somewhat anachronistic among contemporaries whose themes and techniques are more "modern." Although Bates broke no new ground for fiction, he kept vigorous the historical trends of Continental and American story-writing, while in the novel he continued along lines suggested by Joseph Conrad and Thomas Hardy.

The most ambitious of Bates's early novels, *The Poacher*, is essentially a Bates family history in which the central figure, Luke Bishop, is modeled after Grandfather Lucas, while Bates and his father are seen in Eddie Vine and his father, Walter. Luke Bishop is born about 1860 to a shiftless, poaching, shoemaker father whose ways he follows until the father is killed by a gamekeeper and Luke marries. Like Grandfather Lucas, he takes a small farm on poor soil and wrests from it a living growing produce, grain, pigs, and chickens. Meanwhile, industry moves to Nenweald (Rushden), ending the freewheeling days of the cottage shoemakers, and brings with it the railroad, shops, and a new social tone of middle-class respectability. Bishop's wife, who becomes a school mistress, embodies these new values, while Bishop clings to the old, imparting them to Eddie. At sixty, Luke is convicted of poaching and jailed. After serving his jail sentence, Luke returns to Nenweald only to realize that he no longer belongs there or anywhere; his world has vanished in the steam of factories and railroad engines and in the smoke of World War I.

The Poacher is a powerful and moving personal history which seeks neither glamour nor pity for its central character but takes an unflinching look at the changes in England's farms and small towns between 1880 and 1920. Bates is at his best in the taut, swift scenes of poaching and in re-creating the inner life of his unimaginative, uncouth, and bewildered protagonist. Essentially passive, Bishop is unable to cope with the changes that swirl about him; he is a product of the nineteenth century, ignored by "progress" and changes in mores. Through Bishop, Bates engages the reader's sympathy for those trampled by such progress, but because the novel's point of view is restricted, Bishop's story is not fully integrated into its setting. At times the novel seems claustrophobic, at the edges of the reality it attempts to re-create. As social commentary it is less effective than as personal history; nevertheless, Luke Bishop is a vivid human presence, representing a vigorous but now departed way of life.

In the dramatic opening scene of *Spella Ho*, Bates's most successful prewar novel, Bruno Shadbolt watches his mother die of cold and consumption in an unheated hovel standing in the shadow of Spella Ho, a mansion of fifty-three chimneys. Throughout, the ugly, illiterate, determined, amoral Shadbolt and the aristocratic mansion are the poles between which the action moves. The story traces Shadbolt's slow and uneven rise from carter to wealthy industrialist. Along the way, he is aided by four women who change him in various ways—educating him, teaching him manners, altering his tastes—but who paradoxically leave untouched his essential nature, his monomaniacal drive to overcome poverty and anonymity. In his pursuit of wealth and self-fulfillment, Shadbolt represents nineteenth century industrialists at their worst, but Bates's novel is not a one-sided attack on Victorian greed and materialism. By raising himself, Shadbolt brings prosperity and change to Nenweald (Rushden), providing jobs, goods, housing, transportation, and services to people who eagerly desire them. If Shadbolt's factories exploit workers and despoil the countryside, they also transform the standard of living. In taking this evenhanded approach, Bates is not so much interested in being fair to England's captains of industry as he is in exploring a final crushing irony: that Shadbolt's legacy will be judged in the end as a monstrosity of ugliness and filth, while nothing of his personal triumph or his finer side will remain. Even Spella Ho, which he buys and restores, testifies not to his achievement but to that of refined aristocrats.

In addition to Shadbolt, there is a convincing cast of minor characters, individually rendered in detail. Once again, however, Bates fails to place his characters and action in a convincing context; for a novel concerned with social change, *Spella Ho* is curiously weak in period details. Between its opening in 1873 and its close in 1931, the novel changes little in scenery. The factories, gasworks, bus lines, and houses which Shadbolt builds are said to transform Nenweald utterly, but these changes are merely glimpsed. Once again, therefore, Bates provides a character study of great passion and interest, a fascinating grotesque utterly authentic in personality. In addition, there are vivid and arresting portraits of late Victorian individuals and types, but the characters move through a vague world on which their impact is somehow strangely slight.

For more than a decade after *Spella Ho*, Bates's novels occupied themselves with materials related to World War II. When Bates returned to his older material, therefore, it was with new eyes and understanding, fortified by advances in technique. *Love for Lydia* is unquestionably Bates's finest novel. On one level it parallels F. Scott Fitzgerald's *The Great Gatsby* (1925) as a hymn to the jazz age as lived in the small towns of England. The main characters are young people: Lydia Aspen, heir to a considerable fortune and aristocratic heritage; Richardson, young Bates thinly disguised; Tom and Nancy Holland, son and daughter of solid English farmers; Blackie Johnson, a mechanic and taxi driver; and Alec Sanderson, a small-town playboy of great charm but weak character. Lydia has been reared by her father, unusually sheltered and alone; when he dies, she moves to Evensford (Rushden, once again) to live with her aunts, who encourage her to gain experience of life. She and Richardson fall in love. There is a great deal of essentially innocent dancing and drinking, but Lydia's beauty is fatal: Sanderson, believing that Lydia has rejected him, accidentally drowns while drunk; Tom becomes her new love, only to die by accident or suicide of a shotgun blast. Richardson leaves to work in London, and for two years Lydia stumbles through a cloud of alcohol and dissipation. When Richardson returns, she is recovering in a sanatorium. Eventually they are reconciled.

The self-absorbed 1920's, with its burst of promiscuity and hedonism, is the perfect setting for this exploration of the valuable and permanent qualities desired in human relationships. Love of self, love of life, and romantic love compete, capsizing friendships, shattering values, upsetting traditional social arrangements until some balance can be restored. Self-absorbtion turns Lydia into a kind of Circe, destroying those who love her, and the quiet, uncertain Richardson into a morose, sarcastic loner. Healing comes when these two learn to give of themselves, as when Lydia can accept Blackie's friendship and Richardson finally puts aside his wounded pride to offer Lydia the affection she needs. Unlike the naturalistic novels of the 1930's, *Love for Lydia* is dominated by the interrelationships of its characters. Events are controlled not by unseen forces but by the emotions of the characters, who are responsible for their actions and yet are victims of their own weaknesses and strengths. People in this novel are also fully a part of the world around them: Evensford breathes with its own life of dirty alleys and greasy shops, while, as always in Bates's fiction, the countryside throbs with life. In an unusual reversal, winter is the time of rebirth—the season when Lydia first joins the world and the season in which, three years later, she and Richardson are reunited. Thus, Bates deals not so much with the malaise of the age as with personal choices and the tendency of people to allow the worst in themselves to rule the better.

The Distant Horns of Summer deals with a rather different theme—the nature of "reality." The novel centers on a young girl, Gilly, only seventeen, who has been hired by the parents of five-year-old James to look after the boy for the summer. James, like many children, lives most happily in a make-believe world in which his two friends are Mr. Pimm and Mr. Monday, two elderly men who in James's imagination treat him as a grown-up. Gilly takes the job in part to escape a man with whom she had fallen in love while working in a shop, only to fall in love with a tourist calling himself Ainsworth. He betrays her, of course, and when she tries to locate him, she finds that he, in a sense, does not exist, since she calls him by his assumed name. At the same time, James wanders off and loses himself literally and figuratively in his own world. When Gilly reports him missing, the police concern themselves more with the imaginary Pimm and Monday than with the real boy; a Miss Philpot, slightly dotty and never entirely sober, constructs her own version of events and concludes that Gilly is a nymphomaniac. Even when James is found, the confusions are unresolved.

Bates's exploration of reality has none of the philosophical seriousness of Samuel Beckett's novels; as always, it is with the particular individuals and experiences that he is concerned. Thus, much of the novel is told through the eyes of young James, whose childish confusions about what is "true" and what is not are entirely natural; but James, like children generally, knows quite well what is make-believe and what is not. Thus, he resents Ainsworth's unconvincing attempts to talk about Mr. Pimm and Mr. Monday, just as he is deeply hurt when he discovers that the camera Ainsworth lends him has no film. His pain at this discovery is as real as Gilly's upon learning that Ainsworth is an impostor whose affection for her is merely a pose. "Things are not as they seem" is not an abstract proposition but a concrete issue leading to betrayal and pain. Gilly, James, and Ainsworth are convincingly drawn, and even the minor figures are sharply etched and lifelike. As always, the style is bright and clear, the descriptive passages full of sharp detail, the dialogue natural and idomatic. Like the Kentish summer in which it is set, the novel radiates a mellow ripeness and melancholy which could be mistaken for romantic lassitude were it not that Bates infuses everything with intense vitality.

No discussion of Bates's fiction can afford to ignore his mastery of the short-novel form. With the short-story writer's gift of sketching character swiftly yet fully, and his ability to portray rural settings, Bates creates a number of memorable pieces focusing primarily on character. The earliest of these is *Seven Tales and Alexander* (1929), a romantic, idyllic re-creation of the days when young Bates and Grandfather Lucas would pick fruit to sell at the market. Closer to the novella form per se is *The Cruise of the Bread-winner*, a chilling study of bravery and coming to manhood during World War II. In the 1950's, Bates turned increasingly to this form, publishing two collections. From one of these comes "Dulcima," a curious story of sexual exploitation, centering on Dulcima, a heavy-legged, ungainly woman who attaches herself to a lonely old farmer, cheats him of his money, and taunts him with references to a boyfriend who does not exist. The vain and miserly farmer who thus allows himself to be deluded participates in his own destruction. *An Aspidistra in Babylon*, the title story of a collection published in 1960, reverses the plot of "Dulcima," portraying the seduction of a young girl by a dashing soldier. Told through the girl's eyes, the story centers on trust— hers for the soldier, the soldier's aunt's for her. She is both betrayer and betrayed, stealing from the old woman to finance an elopement with the soldier, who spends the money on another woman. The most unusual of Bates's novellas is among his last—*The Triple Echo*. Set during World War II, it features a young wife whose husband has been captured by the Japanese and a young soldier who eventually goes AWOL. The wife has been turned by farm drudgery into a man, dressing and acting like one. The soldier, to avoid detection by the military police, disguises himself as her sister. Sex roles reverse with the complexity of a Shakespearean comedy, but the story does more than explore androgeny, for beneath it runs an antiwar strain, a suggestion that such unnatural role reversals are part of the ruin of war.

The enduring qualities of Bates's fiction have little to do with the themes he explores, for he is not a modern "problem" writer. Rather, his fiction commands attention because of its style, its treatment of nature, and its explorations of individual character. Bates writes in the purest English, with a sparkling clarity and sure sense of rhythm. Except in the earliest works, his stories and novels are presented vividly, pictorially, directly; there is always an immediacy and sensuousness about his work. He has been compared favorably and accurately with the Impressionist painters, whose works he collected. Most especially, when he writes of nature, whether a bright summer day, a dreary wintry rain, or a brilliant early spring afternoon, his prose quivers with life and brilliant images. Occasionally, he tends toward lushness, but restraint, understatement, and quick, sure strokes are his characteristic virtues. His characters are similarly drawn: They spring from the page whole and solid. Seldom are they sophisticated or intellectual; more often they are inarticulate, emotional, bewildered. Even in the novels, characters seldom develop or reveal complex layers of themselves; rather, they struggle as best they can with what emotional and intellectual equipment they have. Perhaps for this reason, Bates is not an intellectual's writer; his tendency is to look past the beauties of style and the flashes of insight for something that is not there. What is present, however, is fiction of high quality, waiting to receive the attention it deserves.

Major publications other than long fiction

SHORT FICTION: *Day's End and Other Stories*, 1928; *Seven Tales and Alexander*, 1929; *The Black Boxer*, 1932; *The Woman Who Had Imagination*, 1934; *Cut and Come Again*, 1935; *Something Short and Sweet*, 1937; *The Flying Goat*, 1939; *My Uncle Silas*, 1939; *The Beauty of the Dead*, 1940; *The Greatest People in the World*, 1942; *How Sleep the Brave*, 1943; *The Bride Comes to Evensford and Other Tales*, 1949; *Dear Life*, 1949; *Colonel Julian*, 1951; *The Daffodil Sky*, 1955; *Sugar for the Horse*, 1957; *The Watercress Girl*, 1960; *Now Sleeps the Crimson Petal*, 1961; *The Fabulous Mrs. V.*, 1964; *The Wedding Party*, 1965; *The Wild Cherry Tree*, 1968; *The Four Beauties*, 1968; *The Yellow Meads of Asphodel*, 1976.

PLAY: *The Last Bread*, 1926.

NONFICTION: *Through the Woods*, 1936; *Down the River*, 1937; *The Modern Short Story: A Critical Survey*, 1941; *In the Heart of the Country*, 1942; *Country Life*, 1943; *O More Than Happy Countryman*, 1943; *Edward Garnett*, 1950; *The Country of White Clover*, 1952; *The Face of England*, 1952; *The Vanished World*, 1969; *The Blossoming World*, 1971; *The World in Ripeness*, 1972.

Bibliography

Alderson, Frederick. "Bates Country: A Memoir of H. E. Bates (1905-1974)," in *London Magazine*. IXX (July, 1979), pp. 31-42.
Cavaliero, Glen. *The Rural Tradition in the English Novel 1900-1939*, 1977.
Garnett, David. *Great Friends: Portraits of Seventeen Writers*, 1980.

Dean R. Baldwin

ANN BEATTIE

Born: Washington, D.C.; September 8, 1947

Principal long fiction
Chilly Scenes of Winter, 1976; *Falling in Place*, 1980.

Other literary forms
Besides her two novels, Ann Beattie has published three volumes of short stories: *Distortions* (1976), *Secrets and Surprises* (1976), and *The Burning House* (1982). She considers herself primarily a short-story writer rather than a novelist and is a frequent contributor of short fiction to *The New Yorker*, where many of her collected stories first appeared. In 1980, Beattie wrote a dramatization of her short story "Weekend" for the Public Broadcasting Service, her only attempt at scriptwriting to date.

Achievements
In the spring of 1980, shortly after *Falling in Place* appeared, the American Academy and Institute of Arts and Letters awarded Beattie four thousand dollars for her work. Earlier, in 1978, she had received a Guggenheim fellowship. These two awards characterize the recognition, especially from the literary establishment, which Beattie has acquired almost from the beginning of her career. Margaret Atwood, Mary Lee Settle, John Updike, and Richard Yates have all praised her work. Several critics have compared her fiction with that of Updike and John Cheever, whose fictional suburban worlds her second novel explores. Although a few reviewers have found Beattie's subjects and characters lacking in emotion and depth, her style too flat, many others have cited her as the much needed spokesman for the "Woodstock generation"—those young adults who attended college in the idealistic 1960's, hoped for a new social and political order, but found themselves lost in the spiritless and narcissistic 1970's. As Whitney Balliett commented in *The New Yorker*, Beattie is "*the* chronicler of the white, Eastern, middle-class rock generation." For this reason, she has been compared with J. D. Salinger, one of her literary idols, and Kurt Vonnegut. Both, like Beattie, served as voices for their respective generations. Beattie's fiction has consistently appeared in highly selective, prestigious magazines. Besides being published in *The New Yorker*, her work has appeared in *The Atlantic Monthly*, *Fiction Magazine*, the *New England Review*, the *Transatlantic Review*, and the *Virginia Quarterly Review*, to name a few. In October, 1979, United Artists Studios released a film version of *Chilly Scenes of Winter*, entitled *Head over Heels*, but it had a restricted run in New York, Los Angeles, and only eight other cities and closed after doing poorly at the box office. Beattie's largest audience remains the readers

of *The New Yorker*, where her stories regularly appear.

Biography

Ann Beattie was born September 8, 1947, in Washington, D.C., to James A. and Charlotte Crosby Beattie. She grew up and was educated in Washington, attending American University in the late 1960's. Like the characters in her two novels, she was a student during the turbulent and rebellious 1960's. Although she resents the counterculture stereotype some reviewers have applied to her characters, Beattie admitted in an interview for *The New York Times Book Review*, that her characters are "essentially" her own "age, and so they were a certain age in the 60's and had certain common experiences and tend to listen to the same kind of music and get stoned and wear the same kind of clothes." In her first novel, in fact, she clearly portrays the effect of the end of the 1960's on these characters. She has also confessed that for herself and for her friends the end of this decade of hope and activism was something terrible and disheartening.

After receiving her B.A. in 1969 from American University, Beattie moved to Connecticut, where she did graduate work in English. She received an M.A. from the University of Connecticut in 1970, then did further graduate study from 1970 to 1972. As she acknowledged in *The New York Times Book Review* interview, she entered a Ph.D. program without any set goal—a lack of direction common to her fictional characters—and largely "because a personnel agency told her she couldn't get a job without cutting her nails," something she refused to do.

In 1972, Beattie married David Gates, a psychiatrist. She was also busy writing. Early stories appeared in *The Atlantic* in 1973 and in *The New Yorker* in 1974, and others have continued to appear regularly in national publications since the mid-1970's. Significantly, Beattie's husband is also a musician, and music for the novelist, as for the characters in her books and her entire generation, plays an important role in providing both mood and theme for a large range of thoughts and activities.

During the 1970's, Beattie continued to publish steadily. From 1975 to 1977, she was visiting writer and lecturer at the University of Virginia in Charlottesville; from 1977 to 1978, she was Briggs-Copeland Lecturer in English at Harvard University. In 1978, she received a Guggenheim fellowship, largely as a result of her first novel and her first collection of short stories, both of which appeared in 1976. Beattie, her husband, and her dog—the couple have no children—currently reside in West Redding, Connecticut, the suburban Connecticut setting of her second novel and many of her short stories. found in *The New Yorker*.

Analysis

Discussing her fiction with Bob Miner for *The Village Voice* in 1976, Ann

Beattie commented: "My stories are a lot about chaos . . . and many of the simple flat statements that I bring together are usually non sequiturs or bordering on non sequiturs—which reinforces the chaos." Later, in 1980, after *Falling in Place* appeared, Beattie reiterated this theme of disorder in her fiction while mentioning the personal function her art serves: "My writing is obviously some attempt to grapple with . . . alienation," she has told Joyce Maynard, "while at the same time not giving answers, because I don't think there are answers to give." For Beattie, life is absurd; random events just "fall into place" accidentally. Most people hold meaningless, boring jobs and are caught in frustrating, stagnant relationships. To compensate, some go crazy; others drink too much or use drugs—or all three. The world is useless, life hopeless. What matters is commitment to friends, but even this is difficult because human behavior is inconsistent and ambiguous. Such a bleak vision informs both of Beattie's novels as well as her short stories, placing her work clearly within the current of the most pessimistic twentieth century literature.

The distinctive features of Beattie's fiction, however, are not her themes. Alienation and nihilism are not unique in modern literature. Rather, Beattie's major contributions are her characterizations and her subjects. Her male characters are sensitively drawn creations in whom, as John Updike points out, the novelist "succeeds in showing love from the male point of view" in all of its dimensions of "nostalgia, daydream, and sentimental longing." The adolescents in *Falling in Place* and the vagabonds from the 1960's who populate both novels are convincing, detailed figures—at times humorous, at times tragic. Beattie's novels and stories also paint a particularly vivid yet devastating portrait of the contemporary age: the "lost" generation of the 1970's, the love children of the 1960's grown-up in a hopelessly commercial, narcissistic world where marital and familial relations are psychically destructive and often physically violent. Through the characters of Horton, Nina, and Spangle in *Falling in Place*, but especially Charles and Sam in *Chilly Scenes of Winter*, Beattie captures the confusion, lack of motivation, and despair that the end of the 1960's brought to many people. Through Charles' mother and stepfather, and the Knapps and their acquaintances in *Falling in Place*, she captures the violence and disintegration of contemporary family life.

With her straightforward, flat style, Beattie mirrors the "sad and aimless lives" she seeks to chronicle. She writes in simple declarative sentences, usually in the present tense, and always with an intensely accurate eye for realistic, often banal detail. The reader knows what and when Beattie's characters eat, when and how they shower and shave, when thy make love, even when they urinate. The result is deadpan humor and irony, and, perhaps above all, the experience for the reader of the profound tedium and pointlessness of the characters' lives. In the tradition of neorealistic literature, moreover, Beattie avoids any judgment of her characters.

Although Beattie has told Joyce Maynard that she tries to read "nothing [written] before 1960" if she can help it, her fiction directly acknowledges several earlier literary influences. Her nihilism and style derive from Ernest Hemingway and Albert Camus, both cited by John Knapp in *Falling in Place*, while "the literary patron saint" of *Chilly Scenes of Winter*, as both John Updike and Blanche Gelfant have suggested, is clearly J. D. Salinger. "Not only does Miss Beattie in a kitchen-cabinet inventory echo the epic bathroom-cabinet inventory in *Zooey*," Updike points out; "she invokes the master's works specifically" by naming a character J. D. and by having Charles quote Holden Caulfield. She also alludes to several scenes in both *Catcher in the Rye* (1951) and *Nine Stories* (1953) and borrows at least one theme from Salinger, as well as a close brother-sister relationship. Beattie's view of the 1970's, the aftermath of the 1960's and their effect on her characters, however, derives from her own experiences.

In *Chilly Scenes of Winter*, Beattie has told Bob Miner, she was "going out" of her "way . . . to say something about the 60's having passed. . . ." She continued: "Most of the people I know are let-down—they feel cheated—and these are the people I am writing about." As a result, the novel becomes what Blanche Gelfant has called a "dirge . . . to the termination of the decade. . . ." Like a dirge, *Chilly Scenes of Winter* is slow-paced, somber, and virtually plotless. Death is its principal theme. Its hero, Charles—Beattie never gives him a last name, perhaps as a gesture toward universalizing his grief—is obsessively in love with a married woman and hopelessly burdened with a suicidal mother, an insecure stepfather, and a boring government job. He does little other than complain to his sister Susan, a child of the 1970's who does not fully understand his loss; go to work, where he fills out far too few pointless government reports; drink with his friend Sam; and grieve for himself, his lost love, and the past era. With Sam, he represents the lost idealism of the 1960's, and he openly mourns the dead of the period: not the political martyrs Gelfant names, Martin Luther King, Jr., and John and Robert Kennedy, but the meaningful rock figures for the Woodstock generation, Janis Joplin and Jim Morrison. To add to this grief, Charles dwells on other failing rock stars: Elvis Presley, who is over forty and sluggish, and Bob Dylan, now a family man with children. Worse, a salesclerk with whom Sam works reports that Rod Stewart is dead, leaving Charles and Sam to ponder whether the rumor is true and whether Stewart's death really matters to anyone other than themselves. They also wonder whether people in 1975 even know who Janis Joplin was.

While such grief over rock stars may seem pointless and silly—Charles and Sam are objects of satire as well as sympathy—Beattie implies that for a whole generation of people who marched and made love ("not war") to music—who thought, as Charles does in the novel, "that songs are always appropriate"—the literal and figurative deaths of these "heros" symbolize the death of the idealism that energized the 1960's. With this loss, motivation and commitment were also lost. "Everybody's so pathetic," Sam comments at one point. "Is it just the end of the sixties?"

"It" is more than just the end of the 1960's. Death and disorder of many kinds haunt *Chilly Scenes of Winter*. Set symbolically in the dead period of the year, the winter of 1974-1975, the novel portrays the disintegration of life in America for many people and in many forms. Charles's mother is hospitalized for a suicide attempt, while his stepfather, Pete, must deal with a debilitating marriage, his failure to communicate with his stepchildren, neither of whom likes him, and the fact that it is too late for him to have children of his own. There is also an economic recession in the country, and many people are unemployed. Sam, a Phi Beta Kappa college graduate, is unable to get a decent job or raise money to attend law school. A men's clothing salesman, he, like others, is eventually laid off. An old lover of Charles, Pam Smith, returns from California after a violent love affair with another woman. Pam has become a radical lesbian-feminist, though she is still confused enough to sleep with Sam and preaches what is all too clear from the novel: "Marriage is *dying*." Charles fantasizes alternately about Laura, the woman he loves who has herself returned to a shaky marriage, and about his own death. Thoughts of Amy Vanderbilt's apparent suicide—she fell from a window— also haunt him. Even Sam's dog has died. The winter is bitterly cold, influenza widespread. Life is chilly, relationships uncertain. What seems to matter is the long-standing friendship of Charles and Sam and their helping each other when times are hard. Charles tends Sam when the latter has the flu, and he offers Sam a place to live when he loses his job. Sam, in turn, cheers the morose Charles and listens to his obsessive talk of Laura. Sam is even willing to drive Charles past Laura's house at night just so he can see the light in the kitchen window. The two are so tolerant that they willingly rescue Pam Smith when she calls from the New Jersey Turnpike in the middle of a snowy evening.

For all its vivid details, *Chilly Scenes of Winter* is only partly successful. Its portrait of the paranoid, obsessive Charles is convincing, and Beattie is successful in her first attempt to sustain character and situation in the extended narrative form. The book is also humorous despite its gloomy themes. Banal details—the condition of Sam's toothbrush, Charles's and Sam's pointless, self-pitying conversations, including one about the fate of Hydrox cookies— related in what Updike called Beattie's "resolutely unmetaphorical style" lead to an ironic juxtaposition of the ludicrous and the serious. The problem is that such details eventually become meaningless and boring. Also, as Anatole Broyard suggested in a review of Beattie's *Secrets and Surprises*, the trouble with an "interest in uncommitted lives," such as those Beattie depicts in her first novel, is that "they do not build. They don't accumulate dimensions." Details, largely non sequiturs, repeat and accumulate, but Charles's life really goes nowhere and means nothing. Without an ideological base, commitment to friends alone does not fill the need for meaning. Even the end, Beattie herself admitted, is not positive. Together in the final scene, in an apparently happy ending to the love story in the novel, Charles and Laura are nevertheless "mismatched enough that the rest of their life clearly isn't going to be easy." He focuses on her sexuality while she is worrying about her future.

Beattie's realistic, telegraphic style in *Chilly Scenes of Winter* clearly resembles Camus' and Hemingway's, as do her themes, but Charles lacks the sensuality and rage of Camus' Meursault, the honor and courage of Hemingway's heroes. Charles is simply a nice guy, at times a bit maudlin and self-centered. Also, though Beattie is in debt to Salinger, evoking his "world" through direct references and borrowing his theme of "the world's betrayal of the innocent," her first novel, as Blanche Gelfant points out, lacks the balance of "sentimentality and slickness which Salinger maintained." In *Chilly Scenes of Winter*, "sentimentality . . . prevails."

Where *Chilly Scenes of Winter* focused on the obsessive love of Charles for Laura and the subject of youth in mourning for an era and the music that accompanied it, *Falling in Place*, as many critics have noted, invades Cheever and Updike country, suburban Connecticut and New York, to study the violence and decay of family life. Both novels are chilling, realistic indictments of contemporary American life, but *Falling in Place* is a far more ambitious and more successful work.

The principal events of the novel take place during the summer of 1979 when Skylab is expected to fall to Earth. Where characters in *Chilly Scenes of Winter* had to deal with bitter cold and snow, here they are oppressed by sweltering heat and fear of the sky literally falling. Life is just as absurd, however, and besides Skylab and the myth of Icarus, alluded to in the first chapter, the title refers to the haphazard, inexplicable way life progresses and events "just fall into place." It is also a hint at the novel's episodic, shifting structure. Where *Chilly Scenes of Winter* employed a limited, third-person point of view, focusing solely on Charles's depressive thinking, *Falling in Place* alternates among a number of major characters, with at least five serving as centers of consciousness. As in her earlier novel, Beattie uses a simple, unmetaphorical style and is successful in matching that style to her vision of life. *Falling in Place* is also successful in creating a strong sense of a multiplicity of fragmented lives carried on in an urban setting, a sense of the number of people touched directly by what for some are merely newspaper headlines.

The characters in the novel are also more interesting and poignantly drawn than those in *Chilly Scenes of Winter*, and they cover a broader range: there are adolescents as well as middle-aged men, drug-using young adults and suburban housewives. Moreover, as Richard Locke pointed out when discussing the novel for *The New York Times Book Review*, "these characters are not just sketched in." They are complete personalities "we learn and come to feel a lot about. . . ." The Knapp family epitomizes the dissolution of family life in contemporary America without becoming stereotypical. John Knapp, for example, is a sensitive man, an advertising agency employee besieged with middle-age boredom, troubled children, and a frustrating marriage. He is having an affair with Nina, one of Beattie's displaced young adults, a college-educated Lord and Taylor salesclerk who frequently gets stoned on marijuana. Unable to ask his wife for a divorce, John is, like most of Beattie's characters, essentially passive. Instead of taking direct action to change the depressing course of his life, he lets a supposedly short-term move to Rye, New York, from New Haven, his home—a move initally to help his ailing mother—turn into a means of lasting separation from his wife. At the same time, John is nostalgic for the early years of his marriage and aware of the fragility of life. His insecurity surfaces in his incessant telephone calls to Nina, a neurotic means of trying to achieve connectedness via a technological device.

Besides her successful portrait of John Knapp, Beattie also captures the meaningless, difficult lives of John's wife Louise, her friends, and the Knapps' children. Louise and her friends spend their days housekeeping, playing tennis, drinking, and coping with lethargic children. Bitter and sarcastic, Louise is cut off from John yet financially dependent upon him. She is at once unable and unwilling to understand his humor when he makes a sexual joke as a way of reaching out to her. Mary and John Joel, John and Louise's children, suffer from the adolescent disease of nonchalance—a pretense to cover any genuine concern about life they may actually feel. Mary is foul-mouthed and malicious toward her brother, and she spends her summer fantasizing about a rock star, Peter Frampton, playing with makeup with her friend Angela, and trying not to seem to care about passing her summer-school English course. John Joel is troubled, overweight, and constantly fighting with his sister. Most of his summer is spent in a tree outside the family home. His only friend is Parker, a near psychotic boy who gives John Joel a gun and challenges him to shoot Mary. John Joel does, in a pointless, gratuitous act of violence which perfectly expresses the malaise from which all of Beattie's characters suffer.

Violence and disorder of this type are everywhere in *Falling in Place*. Cynthia, Mary's English teacher, hates her job teaching idle, rich teenagers who play practical jokes on her—once replacing her lunch with a dead squirrel. Peter Spangle, her lover and Nina's former boyfriend, has nightmares of nuclear holocaust. A crazy magician from California visiting his mother in New Haven follows Cynthia, silently courting her by strewing flowers outside her apartment door. Watergate is a reality, Skylab is falling, and New York is experiencing odd-even gas rationing. Besieged by the inexplicable, Beattie's characters are unable to express what they feel and think and are troubled about. Idealism is dead—the flame at John Kennedy's grave goes out all the time, Louise points out. Even romance—the one "genuinely magical" moment in a world that is "tiresome, pointless"—is futile. The magician, a symbol of this romance, can do only minor tricks; he can change nothing in reality; he cannot undo mistakes.

Falling in Place succeeds in showing the lives of Americans afflicted by a lack of direction and values, by confusion and despair, and by inexplicable violence. Beattie's realistic portrait of contemporary American life and her characterization of the people affected by such news events as Skylab and Watergate make her fiction valuable, despite its weaknesses—its "flat" style, episodic plots, and overbearing pessimism. *Falling in Place* also marks an improvement in Beattie's skill in handling the novel form, though whether she will write another novel is difficult to predict. She has told several interviewers that she feels inept in the form and cannot "envision ever writing another one."

Major publications other than long fiction
SHORT FICTION: *Distortions*, 1976; *Secrets and Surprises*, 1979.

Bibliography

Balliett, Whitney. "Books: *Falling in Place*," in *The New Yorker*. LVI (June 9, 1980), pp. 148-154.

Gelfant, Blanche H. "Ann Beattie's Magic State, or the End of the Sixties," in *New England Review*. I (1979), pp. 374-384.

Locke, Richard. "Keeping Cool," in *The New York Times Book Review*. LXXXV (May 11, 1980), pp. 1, 38-39.

Maynard, Joyce. "Visiting Ann Beattie," in *The New York Times Book Review*. LXXXV (May 11, 1980), pp. 1, 39-41.

Miner, Bob. "Ann Beattie: 'I Write Best When I'm Sick,'" in *The Village Voice*. August 9, 1976, pp. 33-34.

Updike, John. "Review of *Chilly Scenes of Winter*," in *The New Yorker*. LII (November 29, 1976), pp. 164-166.

                                                              Stella A. Nesanovich

STEPHEN BECKER

Born: Mt. Vernon, New York; March 31, 1927

Principal long fiction

The Season of the Stranger, 1951; *Shanghai Incident*, 1955; *Juice*, 1959; *A Covenant with Death*, 1965; *The Outcasts*, 1967; *When the War Is Over*, 1969; *Dog Tags*, 1973; *The Chinese Bandit*, 1975; *The Last Mandarin*, 1979; *The Blue-Eyed Shan*, 1982.

Other literary forms

In addition to his novels, Stephen Becker has written screenplays, magazine articles, reviews, and short stories such as "To Know the Country," in *Harper's* (August, 1951), and "A Baptism of Some Importance," in *Story* (1954). His interest in history has prompted him to write social commentary and biography: *Comic Art in America: A Social History of the Funnies, the Political Cartoons, Magazine Humor, Sporting Cartoons, and Animated Cartoons* (1959), and *Marshall Field III: A Biography* (1964).

Becker is also a distinguished translator whose credits include Romain Gary's *The Colors of the Day* (1953), Pierre-Dominique Gaisseau's *The Sacred Forest* (1954), Louis Carl and Joseph Petit's *Mountains in the Desert* (1954), André Dhotel's *Faraway* (1957), René Puissesseau's *Someone Will Die Tonight in the Caribbean* (1959), André Schwartz-Bart's *The Last of the Just* (1960), Elie Wiesel's *The Town Beyond the Wall* (1964), André Malraux's *The Conquerors* (1976), Louis-Philippe's *Diary of My Travels in America* (1978), and Agustin Gomez-Arcos' *Ana No* (1980).

Becker's novel *A Covenant with Death* was adapted for the screen and filmed by Warner Bros. in 1967.

Achievements

In his novels, Becker has managed to combine entertainment with a serious treatment of thematic concerns. His novels contain plots which engross the reader's attention, keeping him interested until the very last page. For this reason, Becker has appealed primarily to a popular audience, and his work has not been noticed much by academic audiences. This is unfortunate, since his style is, as Stephen Geller of *The New York Times Book Review* says, "fluid and graceful," his language "acutely and effectively imagistic," and his thematic concerns comparable to those of Joseph Conrad and Gabriel García Márquez.

Biography

Stephen David Becker was born in Mt. Vernon, New York, on March 31,

1927. His father was David Becker, a pharmacist, and his mother was Lillian Kevitz Becker. He attended Harvard University beginning in 1943, served in the United States Marine Corps in 1945, and then returned to Harvard, receiving his B.A. in 1947.

In 1947, Becker was awarded a Paul Harris Fellowship; he went to China and pursued graduate studies at Yenching University while teaching at Tsing Hua University, in Peking, from 1947 to 1948. On December 24, 1947, he married Mary Elizabeth Freeburg. He continued his education in Paris, where he lived for four years.

Becker's first novel, *The Season of the Stranger*, which is set in China, appeared in 1951 and was favorably received by reviewers. From 1951 to 1952, he was a teaching fellow in history at Brandeis University. In 1953, he published his first translation, Romain Gary's *The Colors of the Day*; since then, he has published a number of well-received translations, including André Schwartz-Bart's *The Last of the Just*.

In 1954, Becker was awarded a Guggenheim Fellowship in creative writing, and in 1955, his second novel, *Shanghai Incident*, was published. From 1955 to 1956, Becker worked as an editor for Western Printing Company in New York. In 1959, his third novel, *Juice*, appeared; this was followed by *Comic Art in America* in 1960, and by *Marshall Field III* in 1964. In 1965, *A Covenant with Death* was published, and in 1967 Becker published his fifth novel, *The Outcasts*. During the summer of that year, Becker served as a visiting Professor of English at the University of Alaska.

In 1970, Becker's novel *When the War Is Over* was published. This novel, about a boy executed as a Confederate guerilla long after the end of the Civil War, closely examines the moral and social motivations for war. It was perceived by many of its readers to be an antiwar statement and thereby became quite popular on college campuses during the early 1970's. In 1971, Becker taught literature at Bennington College. In 1973, his next novel, *Dog Tags*, about the Korean War, appeared but did not achieve the same degree of popularity as *When the War Is Over*. In 1975, Becker published the first of a series of novels dealing with postwar Southeast Asia, *The Chinese Bandit*. This was followed in 1979 by *The Last Mandarin* and in 1982 by *The Blue-Eyed Shan*.

Becker has also written screenplays, short stories, reviews, magazine articles, and newspaper columns. He has lectured in China, France, Alaska, and Mexico, and has lived in New York, Massachusetts, Alaska, China, France, and the Guiana. In 1979, Becker moved to the British Virgin Islands, where he now lives with his wife and three children.

Analysis

All of Stephen Becker's novels have entertaining, engrossing plots; often there are unexpected twists, ironies, and complications; always there is suspense. Although Becker takes great care in shaping his plots, it is clear that they are merely the framework which he uses to explore his recurring themes.

In *The Season of the Stranger*, Li-ling, one of the major characters, says that "heroism is the other side of cowardice, as love is of hate, and as love and hate grow together so may we worship cowardly heroes." Becker's protagonists are always "cowardly heroes"—that is, they are not the larger-than-life, superhuman heroes of comics or cartoons. Instead, they are ordinary, fallible human beings whose intentions are mostly good, but whose actions are often misguided. Greenwood, in *The Blue-Eyed Shan*, attempts to save an archaeological treasure; instead, his actions bring war to a peacful people. In *The Outcasts*, Morrison's bridge, of which he is so proud, leads directly to the destruction of a whole village's way of life. Often, the protagonist's actions appear heroic, while their motivations are cowardly, or perhaps their actions are heroic but are perceived as cowardly. Benny, in *Dog Tags*, is separated from his unit in Germany, endangers himself to save the life of a concentration camp survivor, and is shot. When he wakes up in the hospital, he is accused by the army of desertion. Frequently, the actions of the protagonist, despite his other failings, are truly heroic, sometimes in a spectacular way, as in *The Last Mandarin*, when Burnham rescues himself and his friends from gangsters, or sometimes in a quieter, more subtle manner, as in *The Outcasts*, when Morrison is rude to an American tourist.

Becker's approach to thematic issues, as well, is to explicate their complexities: he presents two ideas which are diametrically opposed, but as the novel progresses, it becomes clear that the two opposites not only coexist, but also are sometimes inseparable, even indistinguishable, and that they are not by any means unchanging. Good and evil, right and wrong, order and chaos, innocence and ignorance, truth and falsehood, life and death—all become harder to define, harder to separate. Burnham's enemy in *The Last Mandarin* becomes his friend; Benny, the healer in *Dog Tags*, feels most alive when he is about to kill a man; Judge Lewis, in *A Covenant with Death*, comes to doubt that the law is capable of providing justice. As Morrison in *The Outcasts* learns, "Heroes pick their noses and villains are kind to old women, and the dashing soldier of fortune has crab lice. Your beautiful carrion crows are only vultures after all, and their real beauty is the way they save us from drowning in carrion."

One thing which all of Becker's protagonists have in common, no matter what their circumstances, is that they find themselves in conflict with rules, institutions, or mechanisms of social order which are accepted as right and just without question by nearly everyone around them. In *Dog Tags*, Benny questions the right of the army to criticize any action taken by a P.O.W., whether it appears treasonous or not. Later, he rebels against the complacent injustice of the medical establishment in his town. In *The Outcasts*, Morrison wonders whether it is justifiable to destroy beauty and innocence in the name of a progress which will provide the starving with food and shelter.

There is more at stake for Becker's protagonists, however, than simply questions or doubts: each of the characters finds that if he acquiesces, he will become a part of that which he cannot accept. Morrison cannot allow the army to cross the bridge without objection because then he will be in league with the destroyers. Burnham, in *The Last Mandarin*, cannot bring back Kanamori and his treasures, or he will be a party to the corruption of the government. Each of the protagonists finds some way to defy the institution or mechanism which threatens to absorb him, and therefore to maintain or regain his integrity as an individual in an environment which makes anonymity and conformity the norm.

Becker's first novel, *The Season of the Stranger*, was published in 1951, three years after his return from Peking, and is set in China during the Communist Revolution. It is the story of Andrew Girard, an American who is a professor at a university in Peking. Like all of Becker's protagonists, he is a "cowardly hero," but is perhaps less cowardly and more admirable than most of Becker's heroes. He has come to China because he loves what he knows of it, but his ideas about who and what the Chinese are are being challenged, not only by the political situation in which he finds himself, but also by his relationship with Li-ling, the daughter of Hsieh Ming-p'u, one of the most powerful and corrupt men in China. Girard finds himself on the side of the students, who back the Communists, because he agrees with many of their ideas in principle. His commitment is primarily an intellectual one at first, but as the Communists move closer to the city, the violence escalates, and as Girard sees his friends die for their beliefs, his commitment deepens, and so do his conflicts. He loves Chinese culture, but it is built on traditions which are often corrupt, restrictive, and unjust. He believes that human nature, setting aside differences of custom and tradition, is the same everywhere, and that no differences are irreconcilable, but daily he is confronted with what appear to be irreconcilable differences. He believes that right and wrong are separate and easily defined, but he is forced to see good in people he regards as evil, and evil in his friends and in himself, and to admit that good comes from evil actions and that good intentions can cause great suffering.

His relationship with Li-ling also creates conflicts for him, and for Li-ling. They are products of diametrically opposed cultures. Li-ling has been reared to be a traditional Chinese daughter and wife, and she values the old ways, often even as she rejects them, in a way which Girard cannot understand. In addition, Li-ling perceives and accepts differences between them, the existence of which Girard would prefer to deny. One of these differences arises from his nationality: Girard is happy in China, for the first time he says, but Li-ling believes he is unconsciously using his students, his friends, their political conflict, and his relationship with her as pieces in a game which he can give up at any time to go home. He thinks that his friendship with the students and his love for her give him the right to consider himself Chinese, but the difference between them is obvious: he is an American, and that fact alone gives him a power that none of the Chinese has, a superiority which he enjoys and which he uses carelessly and relies too much upon to keep him safe. She believes that he is playing at being Chinese, that he enjoys belonging to China because his differences there give him a notoriety and authority he could not have elsewhere.

Girard is stung by her statements; he denies that he enjoys using his power as an American to manipulate others. It is true, however, that he is too complacent, assuming that his American citizenship guarantees his security. It does bring him safety in government quarters, but it also brings him danger from Hsieh Ming-p'u, who would rather see his daughter dead than "polluted" by foreign blood,

Li-ling recognizes the danger her father poses to Girard, but Girard refuses to believe in it. He has won Li-ling, the Communists have won the city, and to him the war is over. He refuses to relinquish his belief in the basic goodness of human nature, and to believe that anyone could do harm merely for the sake of causing pain. It is this belief that makes him at once heroic and foolish: foolish because it makes him naïve, unaware of his danger until it is too late. It also makes him heroic, however, because it allows him to view himself and others with respect, and to retain his integrity as an individual in the face of the Chinese assumption that all foreigners are alike, and in the face of the temptation to succumb to Hsieh Ming-p'u's brand of selfishness and complacency; and because it gives him enough faith and optimism to want to keep trying to make life better for the people he loves, in spite of the hardships, the dangers, and the uncertainty.

Becker's fourth novel, *A Covenant with Death*, is considered to be one of his best. Like his third novel, *Juice*, it concerns itself with the law, and with the interaction between fallible, inconstant human beings and fixed, impersonal institutions. The novel's protagonist, Ben Lewis, is a twenty-nine year-old man who is a judge merely because his father was a friend of the governor. His duties as a judge have been fairly routine until now, when he is faced with his first capital case. The defendant is Bryan Talbot. Accused of killing his wife, convicted and sentenced to be hanged by another judge, Talbot had become hysterical on the day appointed for his execution and, while asserting his innocence, killed the hangman in full view of several witnesses, one of them Lewis himself. His execution was postponed, and in the interval, it was discovered that he was indeed innocent of the murder of his wife. The handling of his case then falls to Lewis, who goes through the formality of declaring him innocent of the death of his wife and releasing him. He is immediately rearrested for the murder of the hangman, and, as he waives his right to trial by jury and pleads innocent, claiming that he acted in self-defense, it becomes

Lewis' duty to rule on his innocence or guilt.

This decision becomes the turning point in Lewis' life. Because there are no legal precedents on which he can rely, he must make the decision entirely on his own: he must, in a sense, make the law, according to his own system of values. He must, therefore, for the first time in his life, decide what his values are. In making this decision, he will decide not only Bryan Talbot's fate but also his own.

In his confrontation with himself, he must resolve several conflicts. The most important of these is the temptation to become complacent, to take the easy way out, to cease to question and explore. Only in retrospect does he realize that his relationship with Rosemary failed, in part, because of his willingness to accept what she was on the surface, and his reluctance to probe, to ask uncomfortable questions, and to know her as she was, rather than as he preferred to see her. He also realizes that his fear of having to rule on the Talbot case is really a fear of responsibility. He has been a competent, if young, judge, but he has not really felt any sense of commitment to his profession. The decisions he has had to make in the past have been minor, and he has only had to follow the rules in order to pass judgment. He has been playing at the law, but his decision requires more of him. He can no longer sink back into his robes and remain a merely impersonal organ of an institution. The decision requires that he take his profession seriously, that he relinquish the anonymity of the institution and assert his own beliefs as an individual, and that he take the responsibility for his beliefs, whatever the consequences.

Lewis makes a trip laden with symbolic overtones into the desert, where he can think in peace. When he returns, he has made his choice, not only about Talbot, but also about himself and his life. He has discovered that to be human is everything, and to be human is to be an individual, to retain one's integrity, and to live as fully as possible, never ceasing to question and explore. In the decision he writes for the court, he reminds himself and those at the trial that the law was made by human beings in order to ensure survival, and that as the population grew so did the number of laws, until now the law is an institution with a life of its own. It is, moreover, an institution which sometimes loses touch with its original aim, survival, and which therefore fosters impersonal, anonymous, and inhuman justice. As Lewis reminds them, what is just is not always what is right. By the end of the novel, Lewis has come to an understanding of himself and of those he loves. He has come of age, both as a judge and as an individual.

It is easy to see why Becker's sixth novel, *When the War Is Over*, was popular with many college students in the early 1970's: it is a vivid and unforgettable document of the horror and senselessness of war. Based on actual events, it is the story of Marius Catto, a lieutenant in the Union Army, and Thomas Martin, a young Confederate soldier who shoots Catto and is captured just before the end of the Civil War. Since he is not wearing a confederate uniform (there were no supplies left for him), he is considered a guerrilla, and is therefore court-martialed by the army and sentenced to death. Despite the protest of Catto and other officers, he is to be shot; Catto is ordered to head the firing squad. What makes all of this even more senseless is that, by the time Martin's execution is carried out, the war has been long over.

Like Girard and Lewis, Catto is another of Becker's "cowardly heroes." He is basically a decent person but fears death and women; he is imperfect enough to admit that killing is somehow satisfying, but moral enough to worry about his feelings of satisfaction. The conflict between individual and institution is sharper and clearer here than in any of Becker's previous novels. Even before Martin comes on the scene, Catto is tired of the army, of the restrictions, the pompous officers, the incompetent soldiers. It is the only life he knows, though, and he is committed to it. He has been promoted to lieutenant, later to captain, and is proud of his achievements and happy in his privileges. He is not always as quick to obey orders as his superior officers would like him to be, because he is loyal to his men and rebellious in their behalf. General Hooker, particularly, goes out of his way to try to round off Catto's rough edges.

Hooker is a man who is devoted to the army—to the institution—and no individual can be allowed to damage the army in any way. He plays strictly by the rules and is obsessed with discipline, because he believes that any breach of discipline which goes unpunished sets a dangerous precedent and undermines the safety of everyone. He is not an evil man, or even an unsympathetic one; in fact, after imposing a brutal punishment on Haller, one of the men in Catto's unit, he goes to see him in the hospital. Ultimately, to Hooker, however, the individual is unimportant, except in relationship to the army.

This is Hooker's reason for ordering Thomas Martin shot, even though the war is over and it will serve no practical purpose. Catto, however, knows Martin and likes him. He even feels like a father to him at times. To Catto, Thomas Martin is not a symbol: he is a human being, a young boy with a life which is being unjustly and arbitrarily taken away. Catto sees his men as individuals first, soldiers second. That is also how he sees himself, although he does not realize it until just before the execution. Hooker orders that Catto command the firing squad; he knows how much this will disturb Catto, but hopes to force him to see that the army must come before his own feelings and beliefs. In fact, just the opposite happens: forced to choose, Catto chooses himself. He refuses the order and is placed under arrest.

Sitting in his room, Catto has plenty of time to think about the course of action he has chosen. In the end, he decides to carry out his orders after all, and command Martin's firing squad. Most of his men believe that he has been intimidated by the threat of court-martial and has backed down. Jacob, Martin's friend, believes Catto to be a coward, and refuses to speak to him; but Catto is not a coward. He has taken on this task for several reasons. He wants to spare Lieutenant Silliman, an innocent and idealistic man, the pain of disillusionment that he has felt. He has also chosen to do it in order to keep the shooting from being merely a ritual performed by an impersonal and uncaring institution. He cannot keep Thomas Martin from dying, but he can make sure that he is killed with compassion. Most important, however, Catto has chosen to do it because in making this choice, he is, as he puts it, "fashioning his own destiny." Until now, he has made no real choice of his own; the army has made all of his decisions for him and has therefore borne the responsibility for all of his actions as well. Refusing Hooker's order to shoot Martin was the first real choice Catto ever had to make, and he comes to see that it was the wrong choice. It was wrong of him to refuse because he refused not out of moral courage, but moral cowardice: he refused not because killing is wrong, but because it was too hard for him to kill his friend. In choosing to carry out the order, then, he is choosing to perform an act from which he has already been released; therefore, commanding Martin's death is his own action, as much as the army's, and it is one for which he chooses to take the responsibility. It is his first step toward taking control of his own life instead of giving control of it always into other hands.

Becker causes the death of Thomas Martin to seem even more unjust by his depiction of the boy. Martin is about sixteen, from a backwoods Southern family, and his actions derive from the same motivation as those of all the men in Catto's unit: loyalty. He is always cheerful, always willing to help, and never complains. He has complete trust in General Willich, who promises him his sentence will not be carried out, so that when it is, it is not only an injustice but a betrayal as well. Martin also serves as a balm for Hooker's wounded pride: Lincoln once stopped him from shooting a boy who had fallen asleep on duty, and Hooker has never stopped resenting that curb on his power. He believes it has thwarted his career, and in his mind, the death of Martin will help him to balance the scales.

Becker also heightens the sense of the injustice of Martin's death by surrounding the boy with symbols which carry Christian overtones. When Catto first sees him, for example, he appears, by an illusion of light to be carrying a staff and to be surrounded by multicolored halos. Later, Catto notices an innocence in Martin which arises less from inexperience than from fundamental goodness. In addition, Martin at one point suffers from appendicitis, referred to several times as "side pleurisy," and requires an appendectomy. Another point made several times is that Martin is the last Confederate to be shot; never in the novel are any references made to other Confederates who have been executed. Martin's death seems isolated, then, from any others, and is spoken of several times as a sacrifice. So, although there is no point-by-point analogy made between Martin and Christ, the images connected with Martin tend to confer on him a significance over and above that of an ordinary boy.

Although the novel's protagonist is Catto, and the events and changes in Catto are the primary focus of the novel, it seems clear that Becker, more than in any of his other novels, was using this book to make a statement. Throughout his career, he has combined fiction and history; his novels provide insight into both the nature of human beings and the atmosphere surrounding historical events. All of his previous novels, however, had smoothly merged the fiction and the history. In this book, Becker deliberately separated the two in an Epilogue in which he stated which of his characters were drawn from history and which were created from his imagination. In doing so, he made it impossible for the reader to take the book as mere entertainment. Instead, the reader is forced to realize that, although the account is fictionalized, the event, the execution of Thoman Martin, with all of its injustice, actually happened.

The Last Mandarin is more a pure adventure story than were any of Becker's previous novels. It has all of the elements of a traditional potboiler: a rebellious, hardboiled detective who was thrown out of the army by General Douglas MacArthur himself; an abundance of villains; a beautiful woman; a treasure; plot twists and surprises; shootouts; even car chases. It is by far the most entertaining of Becker's books, but, like all of his previous novels, it is not simply entertainment.

Jack Burnham more closely resembles a traditional adventure-story hero than any of Becker's other protagonists. He is sent by the United States Government into China to retrieve a war criminal, Kanamori Shoichi. It is 1949, and Peking is about to fall to the Communist Army. Burnham has agreed to hunt for Kanamori, despite his aversion to the army, because he and his family had been victims of Kanamori's sadism during the war, and Burnham wants his chance to take revenge. Like a traditional hero, he has old and loyal friends on the fringes of the underworld who serve as sources of information; he has special skills which enable him to do his job; he has a sense of humor and a wisecrack for every situation; he is intelligent enough to draw the right conclusions from the clues he digs up, and ingenious enough to do and say the right things in order to get out of tight spots; and during the course of his search, he acquires loyal friends who rescue him from seemingly hopeless situations, and falls in love with a woman whom he rescues from seemingly hopeless situations. Burnham's character has more depth, however, than that of the true potboiler hero.

When Burnham begins his search, he is filled with hate for Kanamori; he wants Kanamori to pay with his life for the crimes he committed. The man he finds, however, is no longer the warrior Kanamori. He is crippled in mind and body by the tortures of his enemies and his overwhelming horror and guilt at his own actions. Sometimes, he does not even remember his own name. He has been living for three years as an old mute woman in the Beggars' Hospital; his job is trundling the dead babies to the cemetery for burial. Seeing him, Burnham can no longer hate him. He is filled with pity for him, realizing that the suffering he has imposed upon himself is far greater than any punishment the army could design. Looking back, Burnham finds that Kanamori's crimes seem remote, and he realizes that there would be no sense in hanging him now. He forgives Kanamori and leaves him. Later, Kanamori helps him to rescue Hao-lan, the woman he loves, and they become friends.

Becker's treatment of the thematic issues in *The Last Mandarin* is similar to that of other novels and is accomplished primarily by allowing the reader to observe the development of the protagonist. By the time Burnham leaves China, for example, he is no longer so certain of the distinction between good and evil: they are coming to resemble each other, he says, "like all old couples." Like Becker's other protagonist, Burnham finds himself confronted by a conflict between individuality and impersonality. The Burnham who arrives in Peking at the opening of the novel is a man who is acting on behalf of an institution and searching for a war criminal who, to him, symbolizes evil. It is easy for him to see people one-dimensionally, in terms of their use to him in his quest. His love for Hao-lan, however, forces him to see beyond the war criminal to the human being who has suffered so deeply. In *The Last Mandarin*, Burnham discovers, as do all of Becker's protagonists, that horror and suffering and injustice are fundamental and will always exist and can only be redeemed by love. He also discovers that doing the thing which he believes to be right, rather than the thing which appears to others to be right, is the only way to retain integrity, individuality, and his humanity.

Major publications other than long fiction

NONFICTION: *Comic Art in America: A Social History of the Funnies, the Political Cartoons, Magazine Humor, Sporting Cartoons, and Animated Cartoons*, 1959; *Marshall Field III: A Biography*, 1964.

MISCELLANEOUS: *The Colors of the Day*, 1953 (translation); *The Sacred Forest*, 1954 (translation); *Mountains in the Desert*, 1954 (translation); *Faraway*, 1957 (translation); *Someone Will Die Tonight in the Caribbean*, 1959 (translation); *The Last of the Just*, 1960 (translation); *The Town Beyond the Wall*, 1964 (translation); *The Conquerors*, 1976 (translation); *Diary of My Travels in America*, 1978 (translation); *Ana No*, 1980 (translation).

Bibliography

Evory, Ann, ed. *Contemporary Authors*, 1982 (New Revised Series).
Vinson, James, ed. *Contemporary Novelists*, 1972.

Ann Warren

SAMUEL BECKETT

Born: Foxrock, Ireland; April 13, 1906

Principal long fiction

Murphy, 1938; *Molloy*, 1951; *Malone meurt*, 1951 (*Malone Dies*); *L'Innommable*, 1953 (*The Unnamable*); *Watt*, 1953; *Comment c'est*, 1961, (*How It Is*); *Mercier et Camier*, 1970 (*Mercier and Camier*, 1974); *Le Dépeupleur*, 1971 (*The Lost Ones*, 1972); *Company*, 1980; *Mal vu mal dit*, 1981 (*Ill Seen Ill Said*).

Other literary forms

Samuel Beckett has worked in every literary genre since his first publication, an essay, appeared in 1929. He is a painstaking and increasingly astringent writer, yet the Grove Press American edition of his *Collected Works* had grown to twenty-four volumes by 1981, and Beckett is known to have withheld from publication a large number of manuscripts. His first book, published in 1931, was the critical study *Proust*, and during the next fifteen years, Beckett published a number of essays and book reviews that have yet to be collected in book form. After struggling with an unpublished play titled *Eleuthéria* in the late 1940's, he began publication of the series of plays that are as important as his novels to his present literary reputation. These include, notably, *En attendant Godot* (1952, *Waiting for Godot*), *Fin de partie* (1957; *Endgame*, 1958), *Krapp's Last Tape* (1958), *Happy Days* (1961), and many short pieces for the stage, including mimes. In addition to these works for the stage, he has written scripts for television, such as *Eh Joe* (1967), scripts for radio, such as *All That Fall* (1957), and one film script, titled *Film* (1967). Most, but not all, of his many short stories are gathered in various collections, including: *More Pricks Than Kicks* (1934), *Nouvelles et textes pour rien* (1955, *Stories and Texts for Nothing*, 1967), *No's Knife: Collected Shorter Prose 1947-1966* (1967), *First Love and Other Shorts* (1974), and *Pour finir encore et autres foirades* (1976, *Fizzles*). Beckett's poetry, most of it written early in his career for periodical publication, has been made available in *Poems in English* (1961) and *Collected Poems in English and French* (1977). Many of the various collections of his short pieces mix works of different literary genres, and Richard Seaver has edited a general sampling of Beckett works of all sorts in an anthology entitled *I Can't Go On, I'll Go On: A Selection from Samuel Beckett's Work* (1976).

Achievements

Beckett did not begin to write his most important works until he was forty years of age, and he had to wait some time beyond that for widespread recognition of his literary achievements. Since he received the Nobel Prize for literature in 1969, however, he has retained a solid reputation as one of the most important and demanding authors of plays and novels in the twentieth century.

In the 1930's, when he began to write, Beckett seemed destined for the sort of footnote fame that has overtaken most of his English and Irish literary companions in that decade. His work appeared to be highly derivative of the avant-garde coterie associated with *Transition* magazine and especially of the novels of James Joyce, who as an elder Irish expatriate in Paris befriended and encouraged the young Beckett. By the time that he was forty years old and trying to salvage a literary career disrupted by World War II, Beckett's anonymity was such that his own French translation of his first novel *Murphy* had sold exactly six copies by the time he presented the same skeptical Paris publisher with another manuscript.

Nevertheless, it was at that time—the late 1940's—that Beckett blossomed as a writer. He withdrew into a voluntary solitude he himself refers to as "the siege in the room," began to compose his works in French rather than in English, and shed many of the mannerisms of his earlier work. The immediate result was the trilogy of novels that constitutes his most important achievement in prose fiction: *Molloy, Malone Dies*, and *The Unnamable*. This period also produced *Waiting for Godot*, and it was this play that first brought Beckett fame. *Waiting for Godot*, considered a formative influence on the "theater of the absurd," stimulated the first serious critical treatments of Beckett's work. Although Beckett is known to attach more personal importance to his novels than to his plays, it was not until the 1960's that critics went beyond his plays and began to bring his prose works under close scrutiny. Then, as now, most criticism of Beckett's fiction focused on the trilogy and the austere prose fiction in French that followed it.

In the years since then, Beckett's novels have risen in critical estimation from essentially eccentric if interesting experiments to exemplars of self-referential "postmodern" fiction commonly cited by literary theorists. Disagreements about the nature of particular works and skepticism about the bulk of commentary generated by very brief prose fragments have also inevitably accompanied this rather sudden enshrinement of a difficult and extremely idiosyncratic body of work. At present, however, even the most antagonistic analyses of Beckett's novels grant them a position of importance and influence in the development of prose fiction since World War II, and they also accept Samuel Beckett's stature as one of the most important novelists since his friend and Irish compatriot James Joyce.

Biography

Samuel Barclay Beckett was born in Foxrock, a modestly affluent suburb of Dublin, Ireland. He gives Good Friday, April 13, 1906, as his birthdate, but some convincing contrary evidence suggests that this particular day may have been chosen more for its significance than its accuracy. His parents, William and Mary (May) Jones Roe, belonged to the Protestant middle-class known as Anglo-Irish in Ireland. Beckett's childhood, in contrast to the unpleasant imagery of many of his novels, was a relatively cheery one of genteel entertainment at the family home, Cooldrinagh, private education at Portora Royal School in County Fermanagh, and greater success on the cricket green than in the classroom.

Beckett matriculated to Trinity College, Dublin, in 1923, and there he developed his first literary interests. He completed a curriculum in Romance languages at Trinity, and this led to an appointment as lecturer at the École Normale Superieure in Paris after graduation in 1927. In Paris, Beckett began to associate with the bohemian intellectual circles of French, English, and American writers for which the city was then famous. Beckett returned to Dublin for a brief time in 1930 for graduate work and a teaching position at Trinity, but within a few months, he returned to the Continent for travel throughout Germany and France and an extended reunion with his friends in Paris, including James Joyce. His first works of fiction, the stories in *More Pricks Than Kicks* (1934) and the novel *Murphy* (1938), are set in Dublin and its environs, but their intellectual preoccupations and bohemian antag- onism toward middle-class complacency derive more from the environment of Paris than that of Ireland.

At the outbreak of World War II, Beckett was a permanent resident of Paris. As an Irish citizen, he could have returned home, but instead, he took refuge from the German occupation of Paris in the French countryside. There, he assisted the Resistance and began to write the novel *Watt* (1953), which marks a movement toward the style of his major fiction in its strangely dis- located senses of time and place. After the war, Beckett was decorated with the Croix de Guerre for his assistance to the French underground, and this award is generally cited as evidence of an essential humanism underlying the frequently misanthropic tenor of his novels. All evidence suggests, however, that the experience of the war increased Beckett's antagonism toward social affiliations and his skepticism about humanistic values.

Beckett returned to Paris after the war, and from 1946 to 1950, he retired into that "siege in the room," his most fertile period in a long literary career. By the time *Waiting for Godot* established his reputation, he had already developed the reclusive life-style he has maintained ever since, despite per- sistent media attention. He was married to longtime companion Suzanne Deschevaux-Dumesnil in secrecy in London in 1961, and he refused to attend the award ceremony for his Nobel Prize in Literature in 1969. Since then, Beckett has divided his time between Paris and the country village of Marne, while producing a slow but steady stream of intricately conceived and com- posed short prose fictions and dramatic pieces.

Analysis

It is a matter of some pleasure to Samuel Beckett that his work resists explication. His most important novels and plays are artfully constructed contemplations on their own form rather than commentaries on the familiar world of causal relationships and social contingencies. His most important novels abandon progressive narrative for the more difficult and subtle suggestiveness of haunting images, deliberate enigmas, and complexly ironic epigrams.

Although Beckett's work resists criticism, the author has issued critical statements and congenially submitted to interviews with critics. He manages to transform both sorts of critical occasions into intellectual performances as provocative, and occasionally as humorous, as his fiction. Two particular comments by Beckett, out of many stimulating ones, may serve as instructive introductions to the body of his prose works. In his first published book, *Proust*, Beckett wrote that artistic creation is essentially an excavatory process, comparable to an attempt to reach an ideal, impossibly miniscule, core of an onion. Beckett's novels relentlessly pursue this sort of process, stripping away layers of assumptions about the self and the world, peeling away conventional modes of thought to reach a pure essence of existence free of the inevitably distorting effects of intellect, logical structure, and analytical order. This image of the onion is a rich one because it communicates the sense in Beckett's work that this excavatory process is unending, that disposal of each mode of thought reveals yet another, even more resistant habit of mind. Beckett himself often speaks of his novels as a series, and it is this progressive penetration through one form of thought to another that marks the stages in the series.

Thirty years after *Proust*, Beckett submitted to an unusually provocative interview with Tom Driver that was published in Columbia University Forum in the summer of 1961. In this interview, he dwelled specifically on form. After contrasting the orderly form of most art to the intransigently chaotic nature of existence, he said: "The Form and the chaos remain separate. The latter is not reduced to the former. . . . to find a form that accommodates the mess, that is the task of the artist now." Beckett's novels reveal three stages in this attempt to discover a literary form that will accommodate the chaotic nature of existence. In the first stage, represented by *Murphy* and *Watt*, the process is a destructive one of ridiculing literary convention by parody and satire to suggest an as yet undiscovered alternative form of expression. In the second stage, represented by the trilogy, the attempt to give voice to that alternative takes the form of the disordered and at times deliberately incoherent monologues of individual narrators. In the third stage, represented by *How It Is* and the subsequent short prose pieces, the process takes the form of presenting metaphorical worlds that accommodate their own chaos.

This last stage, especially, is marked by the unpleasant emphasis on miserable degradation and the recurring private images that have given Beckett an undeserved reputation for misanthropy and deliberate obscurity. These charges are effectively rebutted by his own stated sense of "the task of the artist now." Beckett's works do not provide relaxing reading experiences. They are designed to disorient, to dislocate, and to thwart intellectual complacency. The formidable difficulties they present to the reader, however, are essential records of the intellectual ambience of advanced mid-twentieth century thought.

Beckett's earliest fiction, the stories in *More Pricks Than Kicks*, described the passive resistance to social conformity and death under anesthesia of a protagonist named Belacqua (an allusion to Dante). Beckett's first novel, *Murphy*, presents the same resistance and senseless death in the story of Murphy, given the most common surname in Ireland. Murphy is the first of numerous Beckett protagonists who seek to relinquish all ties to their environment and their compulsion to make sense of it. The centerpiece of *Murphy* is an analysis of the discrete zones of his mind in the sixth chapter. The third and last of these zones is a darkness of selflessness in which mind itself is obviated. It is this zone beyond consciousness that most Beckett protagonists seek; it is their failure to reach it that creates the tension in most of Beckett's fiction.

Murphy is surrounded by representatives of two frames of reference that prevent his withdrawal from the world. The first is nationality, represented here by character-types such as the drunken Irish poet Austin Ticklepenny and monuments to national ideals such as the statue of Cuchulain in the Dublin General Post Office. The second frame of reference is erudition, represented here by a plethora of arcane references to astronomy, astrology, philosophy, and mathematics. Assaulted by these adjuncts of identity, Murphy remains unable to disengage himself fully from the world, to withdraw completely into the third zone of his mind.

The problem that Beckett confronts in *Murphy* is central to all of his novels: to define consciousness in a novel without the usual novelistic apparatus of recognizable environment, nationality, and psychology. The novel only approaches such a definition in the chapter on Murphy's mind and in the image of an eerily withdrawn character named Mr. Endon. Elsewhere, Beckett is able to suggest an alternative only by destructive means: by heaping scorn on things Irish, by deflating intellectual pretensions, and by parodying novelistic conventions. These forms of ridicule make *Murphy* Beckett's most humorous and accessible novel. The same reliance on ridicule, however, ensures that *Murphy* remains derivative of the very forms of thought and literature it intends to challenge.

Although it was not published until 1953, after *Molloy* and *Malone Dies*, *Watt* was written a decade earlier and properly belongs among Beckett's early novels. It is a transitional work, written in English, in which one can observe intimations of the central concerns of the trilogy of novels written in French.

Like Murphy, Watt is an alienated vagabond seeking succor from the complexities of existence. In the opening and closing sections of this four-part novel, Watt's world is a recognizably Irish one populated with middle-class characters with small social pretensions. In the central two sections, however, Watt works as a servant on the surreal country estate of a Mr. Knott. *Watt* most resembles Beckett's later fiction in these central sections. In them, Watt ineffectually attempts to master simpler and simpler problems without the benefit of reliable contingencies of cause and effect or even the assurance of a reliable system of language. The structure of the novel is ultimately dislocated by the gradual revelation that the four parts are not in fact presented in chronological order and that they have been narrated by a character named Sam rather than by an omniscient narrator. Sam's account proves unreliable in particulars, thus completing the process by which the novel undermines any illusion of certainty concerning the interaction of the characters Watt ("What?") and Knott ("Not!").

Watt, like *Murphy*, relies on satire of literary precedents and disruption of novelistic conventions. There are allusions in the novel to the work of W. B. Yeats and James Joyce and to the poet Æ (George William Russell), to cite only the Irish precedents. The great disruption of novelistic conventions is effected by "Addenda" of unincorporated material at the end of the text and by pedantic annotations throughout the novel. Nevertheless, *Watt* does look forward to *Molloy* in its central sections, dominated by episodic problems such as the removal of Knott's slops and the attempt of the wretched Lynch family to have the ages of its living members total exactly one thousand. The full emergence of this sort of episodic narrative in Beckett's fiction, however, seems to have required the focus of attention on language itself (rather than on literary conventions) that was one important effect of his decision to begin to compose novels in French rather than English.

Mercier and Camier, although published in 1970, was written in French in 1946, soon after Beckett returned to Paris at the end of the war. Like *Watt*, it is best placed among Beckett's works by date of composition rather than publication. Written at the outset of the "siege in the room" that produced Beckett's major novels, it illuminates the process by which the style of the trilogy emerged from concentration on elements of composition rather than on the social concerns that dominate most conventional novels.

Mercier and Camier is an account of an aimless journey by two decrepit characters out of and back into a city that resembles Dublin. A witness-narrator announces his presence in the opening sentence, but remains otherwise inconspicuous. The descriptions of the two characters' generally enigmatic encounters with others, however, is periodically interrupted by subtly disported tabular synopses that call attention to the arbitrary features of the narrator's accounts. The novel is thus a shrewdly self-conscious narrative performance, with the emphasis falling on the telling rather than on the meaning of the tale.

The belated publication of *Mercier and Camier* was a welcome event because it represents what must have seemed to Beckett an unsatisfactory attempt to open the novel form to accommodate the "mess" he finds dominant in the world. His composition of the novel in French produced a spare prose style and calculated use of language that would prove essential to his later fiction. Like *Watt*, however, the novel retained a peripheral witness-narrator; this may have been one of the sources of Beckett's dissatisfaction with the novel, for immediately after it, he shifted to the monologue essential to the trilogy that followed.

Beckett's major accomplishment in prose fiction is the trilogy of novels begun with *Molloy*, written in French in 1947 and 1948. All three are narrative monologues, all seek to explain origins, and all expose various forms of self-knowledge as delusions. Thus, they approach that ideal core of the onion in their quest for explanations, and they assert the governing "mess" of incoherence, which continues to resist artificial if comforting intellectual fabrications.

In structure, *Molloy*, translated into English by Beckett in collaboration with Patrick Bowles, is the most complex work in the trilogy. The first part of the novel is the narrative of the derelict Molloy, who discovers himself in his mother's room and attempts unsuccessfully to reconstruct his arrival there. The second part is the narrative of the Catholic and bourgeois detective Jacques Moran, who has been commissioned by an authority named Youdi to write a report on Molloy. As Moran's report proceeds, he gradually begins to resemble Molloy. His narrative ends with the composition of the sentence with which it began, now exposed as pure falsehood.

Molloy and Moran are counterparts whose narratives expose the alternative fallacies, respectively, of inward and outward ways of organizing experience. Molloy's self-involved preoccupations, such as his chronic flatulence, function as counterparts of Moran's more social preoccupations, such as Catholic liturgy and his profession. Both are left in unresolved confrontation with the likelihood that the ways they have attempted to make sense of their origins and present circumstances are pure sham. The special brillance of *Molloy* is the manner in which this confrontation is brought about by the terms of each narrator's monologue. The prose style of the novel is dominated by hilarious deflations of momentary pretensions, ironic undercutting of reassuring truisms, and criticism of its own assertions. It is in this manner that *Molloy* manages to admit the "mess" Beckett seeks to accommodate in the novel form: its compelling and humorous narratives effectively expose the limits rather than the fruits of self-knowledge.

Malone Dies is the purest of the narrative performances of Beckett's storytellers. In it, a bedridden man awaits death in his room and tells stories to pass the time. His environment is limited to the room, the view from a window, and a meager inventory of possessions he periodically recounts with incon-sistent results. Beyond these, he is limited to the world of his stories about a boy named Sapo, an old man named MacMann, an employee in an insane asylum named Lemuel, and others. All are apparently fictions based on dif-ferent periods in Malone's own life. At the end of the novel, his narrative simply degenerates and ends inconclusively in brief phrases that may suggest death itself or simply the end of his willingness to pursue the stories further.

It is essential to the novel that Malone criticize his own stories, revise them, abandon them, and rehearse them once again. His predicament is that he knows the stories to be false in many respects, but he has no alternative approach to the truth of his own origins. Like Beckett, Malone is a compulsive composer of fictions who is perpetually dissatisfied with them. As a result, *Malone Dies* is one of the most completely self-critical and self-involved novels in the twentieth century stream of metafictions, or novels about the nature of the novel. It demonstrates, with bitter humor and relentless self-exami-nation, the limits of fiction, the pleasure of fiction, and the lack of an accept-able substitute for fiction.

In *The Unnamable*, Beckett pursues the preoccupations of *Molloy* and *Malone Dies* to an extreme that puts formidable difficulties before even the most devoted reader of the modern novel. In *Molloy*, the focus was on two long narrative accounts; in *Malone Dies*, it narrowed to concentrate on briefer stories; and in *The Unnamable*, it shrinks further to probe the limits of lan-guage itself, of words and names. As the title suggests, these smaller units of literary discourse prove to be just as false and unreliable as those longer literary units had in Beckett's previous two novels. In *The Unnamable*, there is no character in the ordinary sense of the term. Instead, there are only bursts of language, at first organized into paragraphs, then only into contin-uous sentences, and finally into pages of a single sentence broken only by commas.

The premise of the novel is that a paralyzed and apparently androgynous creature suspended in a jar outside a Paris restaurant speaks of himself and versions of himself labeled with temporary names such as Mahood and Worm. As he speaks, however, he is diverted from the content of his speech by disgust with its elements, its words. The names of Murphy, Molloy, and Malone are all evoked with complete disgust at the complacent acceptance of language inherent in the creation of such literary characters. *The Unnam-able* thus attempts to challenge assumptions of literary discourse by diverting attention from plot and character to phrase and word. It is tortuous reading because it calls into question the means by which any reading process proceeds.

The preoccupation with speaking in the novel leads naturally to a corollary preoccupation with silence, and *The Unnamable* ends with a paradoxical assertion of the equal impossibility of either ending or continuing. At this point, Beckett had exhausted the means by which he attempted to admit the "mess" into the form of the novels in his trilogy. He managed to proceed, to extend the series of his novels, by exploring the richness of metaphorical and generally horrific environments like that of the unnamable one suspended, weeping, in his jar.

Beckett's critics commonly refer to the series of prose fictions begun with *How It Is* as "post-trilogy prose." The term is useful because it draws a distinction between the methods of Beckett's works as well as their chronology. Even in the midst of the incoherence of *The Unnamable*, there were references to the familiar world, such as the fact that the narrator was located in Paris. In *How It Is* and the works that have followed, however, the environment is an entirely metaphorical and distinctly surreal one. Without reference to a familiar world, these works are governed by an interior system of recurrent images and memories. *How It Is* marks the beginning of this most recent stage in the series of Beckett's works, and so its French title *Comment c'est* is an appropriate phonetic pun meaning both "how it is" and *commencer*, or "to begin."

In *How It Is*, the speaker, named Bom, is a creature crawling in darkness through endless mire, dragging with him a sack of canned provisions, and torturing and being tortured by other creatures with their indispensable can openers. His narrative takes the form of brief, unpunctuated fragments separated by spaces on the page. Each fragment is of a length that can be spoken aloud, as they ideally should be, and the style may be in part a product of Beckett's experience in the production of plays. There is a second character named Pim, against whom the narrator tends to define his own status. The novel, which many prefer to term a prose poem, is thus broken into three parts: before Pim, with Pim, and after Pim.

The Bom and Pim interaction is an excruciating account of misery in a nether world of darkness and slime. It is related entirely in retrospect, however, and the changing relationships of domination and subordination are less important than the manner in which the language of the fragments creates its own system of repetitions and alterations of phrases. *How It Is* dramatizes, in fact, how it *was* for Bom, and in place of clear references to the familiar world, it offers a verbal model for the mechanics of memory. This remains a consistent, if extraordinarily complex, extension of Beckett's attempt to accommodate the "mess" of chaos in the novel form. Its extremely calculated prose creates a sense of the consistent, but inexplicable and ultimately uninformative, impingement of the past on the present.

The Lost Ones is a representative example of Beckett's prose fiction immediately following *How It Is*. He composed many brief prose pieces in this period, abandoned most of them, and resurrected them for publication at the urging of enthusiastic friends. Most are published in collections of his short works. *The Lost Ones*, however, is a more sustained narrative performance (sixty-three pages in the American edition). It was abandoned in an incomplete form in 1966 but retrieved and supplemented with an effective conclusion in 1970. It has also gained greater attention than most of Beckett's works from this period because of an innovative stage adaptation by the Mabou Mines Company in New York City in 1973.

The Lost Ones is unique among Beckett's works because it focuses on a group rather than an individual. In fifteen unnumbered passages of prose, it describes the workings of a huge cylinder populated by male and female figures who maneuver throughout its various areas by means of ladders. The prose style is remarkably understated in comparison to the painful, if metaphorical, imagery of *How It Is*, and the primary action is the continual reorganization of this closed set of persons according to an entropic process of diminishing energies. Mathematical computation, a motif in many of Beckett's novels, is a primary feature in *The Lost Ones*. As language had in so many of Beckett's earlier novels, numerical calculations prove an inadequate means of organizing experience in this work, and the crucial final paragraph added in 1970 is a fatalistic exposure of the worthlessness of these computations as indications of the past, present, or future of this surreal environment. As in many of Beckett's later prose pieces, the metaphorical environment created by the prose is open to many interpretive referents. The text is subtly allusive—the French title, for example, evokes Lamartine—and the viability of literature as an effective indication of past, present, or future is among the possible subjects of this spare and immensely suggestive text.

Excepting *The Lost Ones* and other aborted works, nearly twenty years elapsed between the writing of *How It Is* and the next of Beckett's prose fictions to approach the novel in form if not in length. *Company* ended this relative silence, during which Beckett produced a variety of works in other genres. Like *How It Is* and the intervening works, *Company* presents a generally metaphorical environment and a consistent emphasis on the workings of memory. Unlike Beckett's other recent works, however, it was composed in English and apparently generated out of contemplation of distinctly autobiographical images.

Company is a narrative by a figure immobilized on his back in darkness. Despite this surreal premise, it dwells on images of a familiar, suggestively Irish environment marked by features such as Connolly's store and the Ballyogan Road. It thus combines the astringency of Beckett's "post-trilogy prose" with the references to an identifiable world common in the trilogy. It is, however, far from a regression from experimental form or an abandonment of the attempt to accommodate the "mess" in a novel. Instead, it represents the fruit of Beckett's years of careful manipulation of a spare prose style in his second language. Like *How It Is*, *Company* concentrates on the inexplicable workings of memory. Unlike *How It Is*, the novel does so in a passive and restrained mixture of nostalgic and ironic images free of the vulgar and painful hostility of that earlier novel. In less flamboyant ways than Beckett's earlier works, *Company* also manages to underscore its own nature as an artificial, literary construction. Its governing metaphor of "company" manages to encompass both the memories surrounding the narrator and the meeting of author and reader of a literary text.

Beckett's most recent prose fiction, *Ill Seen Ill Said*, is a series of paragraphs consisting primarily of sentence fragments. They describe a woman and her attempt to capture the details of her environment. The devotion to detail is such that vocabulary, rather than image, tends to capture attention, frequently because of intentional neologisms, interior rhymes, and sporadic echoes. It is more an evocation of a mood than a plotted novel, one that reveals the author, having rid himself of complacent use of language in earlier works, as a prose stylist with marked affinities to a poet. *Ill Seen Ill Said*, despite the disparagement of voice in its title, marks the emergence in Beckett's works of a devotion to pure sensation unmodulated by systems of logic or desire. It is in this respect that *Ill Seen Ill Said* is a necessary and inevitable extension of "the task of the artist now" addressed in a long series of novels. Rather than suggesting an alternative literary expression by destructive irony or subverting complacency by incoherent monologue, it attempts to present consciousness free of artificial order in a distinctly lyrical form of prose fiction.

In an early essay on the Irish poet Denis Devlin published in *Transition* in 1938, Beckett offered this dictum: "Art has always been this—pure interrogation, rhetorical question less the rhetoric." Like so many of his statements on other writers, this has a special relevance to Beckett's own literary career. Over a period of a half century, he has produced fictions that relentlessly question assumptions of intellectual and literary order. He has done so with a single-minded devotion to what he takes to be "the task of the artist now" and so compiled an oeuvre that is unique in the twentieth century in its concentration on a central purpose and in its literary expression of the great philosophical preoccupations of its time. Beckett's work has been discussed by critics in reference to other innovative thinkers of the century as disparate as Albert Einstein, Sigmund Freud, and Jean-Paul Sartre. In addition to fueling the literary debates of his time, his work may be said to have created, in part, contemporary literary theories such as structuralism and deconstruction. Despite their formidable difficulties, then, Beckett's novels have an indisputable importance to anyone seriously interested in the intellectual climate of the twentieth century.

Major publications other than long fiction

SHORT FICTION: *More Pricks Than Kicks*, 1934; *Nouvelles et textes pour rien*, 1955; (*Stories and Texts for Nothing*, 1967); *No's Knife: Collected Shorter Prose 1947-1966*, 1967; *First Love and Other Shorts*, 1974; *Pour finir encore et autres foirades*, 1976 (*Fizzles*).

PLAYS: *En attendant Godot*, 1952 (*Waiting for Godot*); *Fin de partie*, 1957

(*Endgame*, 1958); *All That Fall*, 1957 (radio play); *Krapp's Last Tape*, 1958; *Embers*, 1959 (radio script); *Happy Days*, 1961; *Words and Music*, 1962 (radio play); *Cascando*, 1963; *Play*, 1964; *Eh Joe*, 1967 (television script); *Come and Go*, 1967; *Sans*, 1969; *Not I*, 1974; *Ends and Odds*, 1976; *Rockaby and Other Short Pieces*, 1981.

POETRY: *Whoroscope*, 1930; *Echoes Bones and Other Precipitates*, 1935; *Poems in English*, 1961; *Zone*, 1972 (translation); *Collected Poems in English and French*, 1977.

NONFICTION: *Proust*, 1931.

ANTHOLOGIES: *An Anthology of Mexican Poetry*, 1958; *I Can't Go On, I'll Go On: A Selection from Samuel Beckett's Work*, 1976 (Richard Seaver, editor).

Bibliography

Bair, Deirdre. *Samuel Beckett: A Biography*, 1978.

Cohn, Ruby, ed. *Samuel Beckett: The Comic Gamut*, 1962.

Esslin, Martin, ed. *Samuel Beckett: A Collection of Critical Essays*, 1965.

Fletcher, John. *The Novels of Samuel Beckett*, 1970.

Mercier, Vivian. *Beckett/Beckett*, 1977.

Pilling, John. *Samuel Beckett*, 1976.

Robinson, Michael. *The Long Sonata of the Dead: A Study of Samuel Beckett*, 1969.

Worth, Katherine, ed. *Beckett the Shape Changer*, 1975.

John P. Harrington

APHRA BEHN

Born: Wye, England; July (?), 1640
Died: London, England; April 16, 1689

Principal long fiction

The Unhappy Mistake, 1687, 1697; *The Dumb Virgin*, 1687; *The Lucky Mistake*, 1688; *Agnes de Castro*, 1688; *The Fair Jilt*, 1688; *Oroonoko: Or, The History of the Royal Slave*, 1688; *The History of the Nun: Or, The Fair Vow-Breaker*, 1689; *The Nun*, 1697; *The Wandering Beauty*, 1698.

Other literary forms

As a truly professional writer, perhaps the first British female to have written for profit, Aphra Behn moved easily through the various literary genres and forms. Her plays include *The Forced Marriage: Or, The Jealous Bridegroom* (1670); *The Amorous Prince* (1671); *The Dutch Lover* (1673); *The Town Fop* (1676); *Abdelazar* (1677); *The Debauchee* (1677); *The Rover: Or, The Banished Cavalier*, I, II (1677, 1681); *Sir Patent Fancy* (1678); *The Roundheads: Or, The Good Old Cause* (1681); *The City Heiress: Or, Sir Timothy Treat-All* (1682); *The False Count* (1682); *The Lucky Chance* (1686); *The Emperor of the Moon* (1687); *Widow Ranter* (1690); and *The Younger Brother* (1696).

Although she enjoyed only mild success as a poet, her verse was probably no better or worse than that of a large number of second-rank versifiers of the Restoration. Behn's best poetry can be found in the song "Love in fantastic triumph sate" (1677), from her tragedy of *Abdelazar*, and in a metrical "Paraphrase on Oenone to Paris" for Jacob Tonson's volume of Ovid's *Epistles* (1680). The remainder of her verse includes a long, amorous allegory, *A Voyage to the Isle of Love* (1684); an adaptation of Bernard de Fontenelle's epic which she entitled *A Discovery of New Worlds* (1688); and two occasional pieces: A Pindarick on the Death of Charles II (1685) and "A Congratulatory Poem to Her Most Sacred Majesty" (1688).

Achievements

Behn's achievement as a novelist should be measured principally in terms of the modest gains made by that form in England during the seventeenth century. Prior to *Oroonoko*, the English novel lingered in the shadows of the theater. Thus, the small reading public contented itself with works such as John Lyly's *Euphues, the Anatomy of Wit* (1579), Sir Philip Sidney's *Arcadia* (1590), Thomas Lodge's *Rosalynde* (1590), Thomas Nashe's *The Unfortunate Traveler: Or, The Life of Jack Wilton* (1594), and Thomas Deloney's *Jack of Newbury* (1597)—all long, episodic stories, sprinkled with overly dramatic characterization and improbable plot structures. In *Oroonoko*, however, Behn advanced the novel to the point where her more skilled successors in the eighteenth century could begin to shape it into an independent, recognizable form.

Behn possessed the natural gifts of the storyteller, and her narrative art can easily stand beside that of her male contemporaries. A frankly commercial writer, she simply had no time, in pursuit of pleasure and the pen, to find a place in her narratives for intellectual substance. Nevertheless, she told a story as few others could, and the force of her own personality contributed both reality and a sense of immediacy to the still inchoate form of seventeenth century British fiction.

Biography

The details of Aphra Behn's birth are not known. The parish register of the Sts. Gregory and Martin Church, Wye, contains an entry stating that Ayfara Amis, daughter of John and Amy Amis, was baptized on July 10, 1640. Apparently, John Johnson, related to Lord Francis Willoughby of Parham, adopted the girl, although no one seems to know exactly when. Ayfara Amis accompanied her stepparents on a journey to Surinam (later Dutch Guiana) in 1658, Willoughby having appointed Johnson to serve as deputy governor of his extensive holdings there. Unfortunately, the new deputy died on the voyage; his widow and children proceeded to Surinam and took up residence at St. John's, one of Lord Willoughby's plantations. Exactly how long they remained is not clear, but certainly the details surrounding the time spent at St. John's form the background for *Oroonoko*.

Recent biographers have established the summer of 1663 as the most probable date of Behn's return to England. At any rate, by 1665 Behn was again in London and married to a wealthy merchant of Dutch extraction, who may well have had connections in, or at least around, the court of Charles II. In 1665 came the Great Plague and the death of Behn's husband; the latter proved the more disastrous for her, specifically because (again for unknown reasons) the Dutch merchant left nothing of substance for her—nothing, that is, except his court connections. Charles II, in the midst of the first of his wars against Holland, hired Aphra Behn as a secret government agent to spy upon the Dutch, for which purpose she proceeded to Antwerp. There she contacted another British agent, William Scott, from whom she obtained various pieces of military information, which she forwarded to London. Although she received little credit for her work, and even less money, Behn did conceive of the pseudonym Astrea, the name under which she published most of her poetry. The entire adventure into espionage proved a dismal failure for her; she even had to borrow money and pawn her valuables to pay her debts and obtain passage back to England. Once home, early in 1667, she found no relief from her desperate financial situation. Her debtors threatened prison, and the government refused any payment for her services. Prison followed, although the time and the exact length of her term remain unknown. Behn's most recent biographers speculate that she was aided in her release by John Hale (d. 1692)—a lawyer of Gray's Inn, wit, intellectual, a known homosexual, the principal subject of and reason for Behn's sonnets, and the man with whom she carried on a long romance. When she did gain her release, she determined to dedicate the rest of her life to writing and to pleasure, to trust to her own devices rather than to rely upon others who could not be trusted.

Behn launched her career as a dramatist in late December, 1670, at the new Duke's Theatre in Little Lincoln's Inn Fields, London. Her tragicomedy *The Forced Marriage* ran for six nights and included in the cast the nineteen-year-old Thomas Otway (1652-1685), the playwright-to-be only recently arrived from Oxford. Because of the length of the run, Behn, as was the practice, received the entire profit from the third performance, which meant that she could begin to function as an independent artist. She followed her first effort in the spring of 1671 with a comedy, *The Amorous Prince*, again at the Duke's; another comedy, *The Dutch Lover*, came to Drury Lane in February, 1673, and by the time of her anonymous comedy *The Rover*, in 1677, her reputation was secure. She mixed easily with the literati of her day, such as Thomas Killigrew, Edward Ravenscroft, the Earl of Rochester, Edmund Waller, and the poet laureate John Dryden, who published her rough translations from Ovid in 1683. With her reputation came offers for witty prologues and epi-logues for others' plays, as well as what she wanted more than anything—money. A confrontation with the Earl of Shaftesbury and the newly emerged Whigs during the religious-political controversies of 1678, when she offended Charles II's opponents in a satirical prologue to an anonymous play, *Romulus and Hersilia*, brought her once again to the edge of financial hardship, as she was forced to abandon drama for the next five years.

Fortunately, Behn could fall back upon her abilities as a writer of popular fiction and occasional verse, although those forms were not as profitable as the London stage. Her series *Love Letters Between a Nobleman and His Sister* (1683-1687) and *Poems upon Several Occasions* (1684) were well received, but the meager financial returns from such projects could not keep pace with her personal expenses. When she did return to the state in 1686 with her comedy *The Lucky Chance*, she met with only moderate success and some public abuse. *The Emperor of the Moon*, produced the following season, fared somewhat better, although by then the London audience had lost its stomach for a female playwright—and a Tory, at that. She continued to write fiction and verse, but sickness and the death of her friend Edmund Waller, both in October, 1688, discouraged her. Five days after the coronation of William III and Mary, on April 16, 1689, Behn died. She had risen high enough to merit burial in Westminster Abbey; John Hoyle provided the fitting epitaph: "Here lies proof that wit can never be/Defense enough against mortality."

Analysis

More than a half-century ago, Vita Sackville-West, in trying to estimate Aphra Behn's contribution to English fiction, asked "what has she left behind her that is of any real value?" Sackville-West bemoaned Behn's failure in her fiction to reflect fully London life, London characters, London scenes; attention to exotic themes, settings, and characters merely debased and wasted her narrative gifts. Such a judgment, while plausible, fails to consider Behn's fiction in its historical and biographical context. Her tales abound with German princes, Spanish princesses, Portuguese kings, French counts, West-Indian slaves, and various orders of bishops, priests, and nuns, yet, Behn's *real* world was itself highly artificial, even fantastic: the intrigue of the Stuart court, the ribaldry of the London stage, the gossip of the drawing room, the masquerade, and the card parlor. Behn, in her *real* world, took in the same scenes as did John Dryden, Samuel Pepys, and the Earl of Rochester. Thus, to assert that her fiction neglects her actual experience in favor of fantastic and faraway window dressing may be too hasty a conclusion.

In *Castro*, Behn lets loose various powers of love, with the result that her heroines' passions affect the fortunes of their lovers. Thus, Miranda (*The Fair Jilt*) reflects the raving, hypocritical enchantress whose very beauty drives her lovers mad; Ardelia (*The Nun*) plays the capricious lover, whose passion carries her through a series of men, as well as a nunnery; and Agnes de Castro presents a slight variation from the preceding, in that the titled character is a product of circumstance: she is loved by the husband of her mistress.

Another primary theme in Behn's work is the often discussed noble savage that has traditionally been assigned to *Oroonoko*, as has the subordinate issue of antislavery in that same novel. In 1975, Professor George Guffey suggested a withdrawal from the feminist-biographical positions (those from which the noble savage/antislavery ideals spring) and a movement toward "a hitherto unperceived level of political allusion." Guffey did not label *Oroonoko* a political allegory but did suggest that readers should look more closely at events in England between 1678 and 1688. Guffey maintains that the novelist deplores not the slavery of a black, noble savage but the bondage of a *royal prince*—again a reference to the political climate of the times. The interesting aspect of Guffey's analysis is that his approach lends substance to Behn's principal novel and to her overall reputation as a literary artist, and it parries the complaint that she failed to echo the sound and the sense of her own age.

In 1678, Sir Roger L'Estrange (1616-1704) published *Five Love Letters from a Nun to a Cavalier*, a translation of some fictional correspondence by the minor French writer Guilleraques. Behn used the work as a model for at least three of her prose pieces—*Love Letters Between a Nobleman and His Sister*, *The History of the Nun*, and *The Nun*. For the latter two, the novelist took advantage, at least on the surface, of the current religious and political controversies and set forth the usual claims to truth.

There may be some validity to the claim that *The History of the Nun* exists as one of the earliest examinations by a novelist into the psychology of crime and guilt. The events, at the outset, proceed reasonably enough but become less believable, and, by the novel's conclusion, the events appear to be exceedingly unreal. Despite this difficulty, the novel does have some value. Behn demonstrates her ability to develop thoroughly the key aspects of the weaknesses and the resultant sufferings of the heroine, Isabella. Behn immediately exposes the concept that "Mother Church" can take care of a girl's problems, can easily eradicate the desires of the world from her heart and mind, can readily transform a passionate maiden into a true, devoted sister of the faith. In addition, despite her wickedness, Isabella is still very much a human being worthy of the reader's understanding. At every step, the girl pays something for what she does; with each violation against the Church and each crime of passion, she falls deeper into the darkness of her own guilt. What she does, and how, is certainly contrived; how she reacts to her misdeeds reflects accurately the guilty conscience of a believable human being.

The second "Nun" novel, not published until 1697, certainly leads the reader through a more complicated plot entanglement than the 1688 story, but it contains none of the virtue exhibited in the earlier work. The interesting aspect of *The Nun*'s plot is that Behn kills the heroine, Ardelia, first; only afterward do the principal rivals, Don Sebastian and Don Henriques, kill each other in a fight. The interest, however, is only fleeting, for those events do not occur until the end of the novel. All that remains of the bloody situation is Elvira, Don Sebastian's unfaithful sister. After weeping and calling for help, she is seized with a violent fever (in the final paragraph) and dies within twenty-four hours. Certainly, Behn's ingenuity in this piece demands some recognition, if for no other reason than her adeptness, according to James Sutherland, at "moving the pieces around the board."

Because of the relative sanity of its plot, in contrast to the two previous tragedies, *Agnes de Castro* comes close to what Behn's feminist supporters expect of her. In other words, in this piece, pure evil or a series of tragic events cannot be blamed entirely on love or upon reckless female passion. Although Don Pedro genuinely loves his wife's maid-of-honor, Agnes, she, out of loyalty to her mistress, refuses to yield to his passion. Such action encourages the other characters to exhibit equal degrees of virtue. Constantia, Don Pedro's wife, seems to understand that the power of Agnes' charms, although innocent enough, is no match for her husband's frailty of heart over reason. Thus, she resents neither her husband nor her maid; in fact, she is willing to tolerate the presence of Agnes to keep her husband happy.

The novel, however, does not exist as a monument to reason. Something must always arise, either in politics or romance, to disrupt reasonable people's attempts at harmony. In the novel, a vengeful woman lies to Constantia and plants the rumor in her mind that Agnes and Don Pedro are plotting against her. Such a report breaks Constantia's trust in her husband and her maid, and the honest lady dies of a broken heart. The novel, however, remains believable for Behn simply emphasizes the frailty of honor and trust in a world dominated by intrigue and pure hatred. Given the political and religious climates of the decade, the setting and the plot of *Agnes de Castro* are indeed flimsy facades for the court and coffeehouse of seventeenth century London.

Although in *The Fair Jilt*, Behn continued to develop the conflict between love and reason, the novel has attracted critical attention because of its allusions to the writer's own experiences. Again, she lays claim to authenticity by maintaining that she witnessed parts of the events and heard the rest from sources close to the action and the characters. In addition, the events occur in Antwerp, the very city to which the novelist had been assigned for the performance of her spying activities for Charles II's ministers.

From the outset of the novel, Behn establishes the wickedness of Miranda, who uses her beauty to enchant the unsuspecting and even tempts the weak into commiting murder. Obviously, had Behn allowed her major character to succeed in her evil ways, nothing would have been gained from the novel. What results is the triumph of the hero's innate goodness; as weak as he is, he has endured. His loyalty and devotion have outlasted and, to a certain extent, conquered Miranda's wickedness.

Behn's literary reputation today rests almost totally upon a single work, *Oroonoko*. The novel succeeds as her most realistic work principally because she recounts the specifics of Surinam with considerable detail and force. Behn installs her hero amid the splendor of a tropical setting, a Natural Man, a pure savage untouched by the vices of Christian Europe, unaware of the white man's inherent baseness and falsehood.

In lashing out at the weaknesses of her society, Behn does not forget about one of her major concerns—love. Thus, Oroonoko loves the beautiful Imoinda, a child of his own race, but the prince's grandfather demands her for his own harem. Afterward, the monarch sells the girl into slavery, and she finds herself in Surinam—where Oroonoko is brought following his kidnaping. The prince embarks upon a term of virtuous and powerful adventures in the name of freedom for himself and Imoinda, but his captors deceive him. Thereupon, he leads a slave revolt, only to be captured by the white scoundrels and tortured. Rather than see Imoinda suffer dishonor at the hands of the ruthless white planters and government officers, Oroonoko manages to kill her himself. At the end, he calmly smokes his pipe—a habit learned from the Europeans—as his captors dismember his body and toss the pieces into the fire.

The final judgment upon Behn's fiction may still remain to be formulated. Presently, evaluations of her work tend to extremes. Some critics assert that her novels, even *Oroonoko*, had no significant influence on the development of the English novel, while others argue that her limited attempts at realism may well have influenced Daniel Defoe, Samuel Richardson, Henry Fielding, and others to begin to mold the ostensibly factual narrative into the novel as the twentieth century recognizes it. From Behn came the background against which fictional plots could go forward and fictional characters could function. Her problem, which her successors managed to surmount, was the inability (or refusal) to make her characters and events as real as their fictional environment. That fault (if it was a fault) lay with the tendencies and the demands of the age, not with the writer. Indeed, it is hardly a failure for a dramatist and a novelist to have given to her audience exactly what they wanted. To have done less would have meant an even quicker exit from fame and an even more obscure niche in the literary history of her time.

Major publications other than long fiction

FICTION: *Love Letters Between a Nobleman and His Sister*, 1683-1687.

PLAYS: *The Forced Marriage: Or, The Jealous Bridegroom*, 1670; *The Amorous Prince*, 1671; *The Dutch Lover*, 1673; *The Town Fop*, 1676; *The Debauchee*, 1677; *The Rover: Or, The Banished Cavalier*, I, II, 1677, 1681; *Abdelazar*, 1677; *Sir Patent Fancy*, 1678; *The Young King*, 1679; *The Roundheads: Or, The Good Old Cause*, 1681; *The City Heiress: Or, Sir Timothy Treat-All*, 1682; *The False Count*, 1682; *The Lucky Chance*, 1686; *The Emperor of the Moon*, 1687; *Widow Ranter*, 1690; *The Younger Brother*, 1696.

POETRY: *Poems upon Several Occasions, with a Voyage to the Island of Love*, 1684; *Miscellany: Being a Collection of Poems by Several Hands*, 1685; *La Montre: Or, The Lover's Watch*, 1686 (prose and verse); *The Case for the Watch*, 1686 (prose and verse); *Lycidas: Or, The Lover in Fashion*, 1688 (prose and verse); *A Discovery of New Worlds*, 1688 (adaptation); *The Lady's Looking-Glass, to Dress Herself By: Or, The Art of Charming*, 1697 (prose and verse).

Bibliography

Bernbaum, Ernest. *Mrs. Behn's Biography a Fiction*, 1913.

Duffy, Maureen. *The Passionate Shepherdess: Aphra Behn, 1640-1689*, 1977.

Guffey, George, and Andrew Wright. *Two English Novelists: Aphra Behn and Anthony Trollope*, 1974.

Link, Frederick M. *Aphra Behn*, 1968.

O'Donnell, Mary Ann. *Experiments in the Prose Fiction of Aphra Behn*, 1981.

Sackville-West, Vita. *Aphra Behn: The Incomparable Astrea*, 1927.

Woodcock, George. *The Incomparable Aphra*, 1948.

Samuel J. Rogal

SAUL BELLOW

Born: Lachine, Canada; June 10, 1915

Principal long fiction

Dangling Man, 1944; *The Victim,* 1947; *The Adventures of Augie March,* 1953; *Seize the Day,* 1956; *Henderson the Rain King,* 1959; *Herzog,* 1964; *Mr. Sammler's Planet,* 1970; *Humboldt's Gift,* 1975; *The Dean's December,* 1982.

Other literary forms

In addition to his nine novels, Saul Bellow has published short stories, plays, and a variety of nonfiction. His stories have appeared in *The New Yorker, Commentary, Partisan Review, Hudson Review, Esquire,* and other periodicals, and his short-story collection *Mosby's Memoirs and Other Stories* was published in 1968. His full-length play *The Last Analysis* was produced for a short run on Broadway in 1964 and published the following year, while three one-act plays, *Orange Soufflé, A Wen,* and *Out from Under,* were staged in 1966 in America and Europe. Another one-act play, *The Wrecker,* was published, though not staged, in 1954. Throughout his career, Bellow has written numerous articles on a variety of topics. In 1976, he published an account of his trip to Israel, *To Jerusalem and Back: A Personal Account.*

Achievements

Often described as America's best living novelist, Bellow has enjoyed enormous critical praise and a wide readership as well. His popularity is, perhaps, surprising, because his novels do not contain the usual ingredients one expects to find in best-selling fiction—suspense, heroic figures, and graphic sex and violence. In fact, his novels are difficult ones that wrestle with perplexing questions, sometimes drawing from esoteric sources such as the anthroposophy of Rudolf Steiner and the psychology of Wilhelm Reich. One of America's most erudite novelists, Bellow often alludes to the work of philosophers, psychologists, poets, anthropologists, and other writers in his fiction. He has stated that the modern movelist should not be afraid to introduce complex ideas into his work. He finds nothing admirable about the anti-intellectualism of many modern writers and believes that most of them have failed to confront the important moral and philosophical problems of the modern age. Opposed to the glib pessimism and the "complaint" of the dominant tradition of modern literature, Bellow has struggled for affirmation at a time when such a possibility is seen by many writers as merely an object of ridicule.

In contrast to many American writers who produced their best work when they were young and then wrote mediocre or poor fiction as they grew older,

Bellow has consistently published work of the highest quality. Moreover, his fiction reveals an immense versatility; he has not selected one style and merely repeated it. In his work, one finds highly structured Flaubertian form as well as picaresque narrative, naturalistic realism as well as romance.

Bellow is a master of narrative voice and perspective, a great comic writer (perhaps the best in America since Mark Twain), and a fine craftsman whose remarkable control of the language allows him to move easily from the highly formal to the colloquial. Most important, he writes novels that illuminate the dark areas of the psyche and that possess immense emotional power. Bellow has complained that many contemporary authors and critics are obsessed with symbolism and hidden meanings. A literary work becomes an abstraction for them, and they contrive to evade the emotional power inherent in literature. Bellow's novels do not suffer from abstraction; they deal concretely with passion, death, love, and other fundamental concerns: he is able to evoke the whole range of human emotions in his readers.

Biography

Saul Bellow was born in Lachine, Quebec, Canada, on June 10, 1915, the youngest of four children. Two years before, his parents, Abraham and Liza (Gordon) Bellow, had immigrated to Canada from St. Petersburg, Russia. The family lived in a very poor section of Montreal, where Bellow learned Yiddish, Hebrew, French, and English. When he was nine, the family moved to Chicago.

In 1933, he entered the University of Chicago but two years later transferred to Northwestern University, where he received a bachelor's degree. In 1937, he entered the University of Wisconsin at Madison to study anthropology but left school in December to marry and to become a writer. He was employed briefly with the Works Progress Administration Writers' Project and then led a bohemian life, supporting himself with teaching and odd jobs. During World War II, he served in the merchant marine and published his first novel, *Dangling Man*.

After publishing his second novel, *The Victim*, he was awarded a Guggenheim Fellowship in 1948, which enabled him to travel to Europe and work on *The Adventures of Augie March*. This third novel won the National Book Award for Fiction in 1953 and established Bellow as one of America's most promising novelists.

After his return from Europe in 1950, he spent a large part of the next decade in New York City and Dutchess County, New York, teaching and writing before moving back to Chicago to publish *Herzog*. While *Seize the Day* and *Henderson the Rain King* did not receive the critical attention they deserved, *Herzog* was an enormous critical and financial success, even becoming a best-seller for a period of time.

The next two novels, *Mr. Sammler's Planet* and *Humboldt's Gift*, helped increase his reputation but also created some controversy. *Mr. Sammler's Planet* was critical of the excesses of the late 1960's, and some complained that Bellow had become a reactionary. Although Bellow opposed the Vietnam War, he found it difficult to identify with the "counterculture." *Humboldt's Gift* disturbed some critics, who complained that Bellow's interest in the ideas of Rudolf Steiner indicated that he was becoming an escapist; it was a mistaken assumption. An ardent supporter of Israel, Bellow traveled to that country in 1975 and published an account of his journey, *To Jerusalem and Back*. In 1976 he was awarded the Nobel Prize for Literature.

Bellow has been married four times and has three sons by his first three wives. At present, he lives in Chicago, where he prefers to shun the publicity that other writers cultivate. His ninth novel, *The Dean's December*, was published early in 1982.

Analysis

Saul Bellow's mature fiction can be considered as a conscious challenge to modernism, the dominant literary tradition of the age. For Bellow, modernism is a "victim literature" because it depicts an alienated individual who is conquered by his environment. According to him, this "wasteland" tradition originated in the middle of the nineteenth century with the birth of French realism and culminates in the work of Samuel Beckett and other nihilistic contemporary writers. This victim literature reveals a horror of life and considers humanist values useless in a bleak, irrational world. Modernism assumes that the notion of the individual self which underlies the great tradition of the novel is an outmoded concept, and that modern civilization is doomed.

Bellow has never accepted the idea that mankind has reached its terminal point, but his first two novels owe a large debt to the wasteland modernism that he would explicitly reject in the late 1940's. *Dangling Man* is an existentialist diary that owes much to Fyodor Dostoevski's *Notes from the Underground* (1864). The demoralized protagonist Joseph is left "dangling" as he waits to be drafted during World War II. A moral casualty of war, he has no sense of purpose and feels weary of a life that seems boring, trivial, and cruel. Excessively self-conscious and critical of those around him, he spends most of his time alone, writing in his journal. He can no longer continue his past work, writing biographical essays on philosophers of the Enlightenment. Although he is alienated, he does realize that he should not make a doctrine out of this feeling. The conclusion of the novel reveals Joseph's ultimate failure to transcend his "victimization"; he is drafted and greets his imminent regimentation enthusiastically.

Bellow's next novel, *The Victim*, also depicts a passive protagonist who is unable to overcome his victimization. As Bellow has admitted, the novel is partially modeled on Dostoevski's *The Eternal Husband* (1870) and uses the technique of the *Doppelgänger* as Dostoevski did in *The Double* (1846). Bellow's novel presents the psychological struggle between Asa Leventhal, a Jew, and Kirby Allbee, his Gentile "double." A derelict without a job, Allbee suggests that Leventhal is responsible for his grim fate. Leventhal ponders the problem of his guilt and responsibility and tries to rid himself of his persecuting double. Despite his efforts to assert himself, he is still "dangling" at the end of the book—still a victim of forces that, he believes, are beyond his control.

After his second novel, Bellow became disenchanted with the depressive temperament and the excessive emphasis on form of modernist literature. His first two novels had been written according to "repressive" Flaubertian formal standards; they were melancholy, rigidly structured, restrained in language, and detached and objective in tone. Rebelling against these constricting standards, Bellow threw off the yoke of modernism when he began to write his third novel. The theme, style, and tone of *The Adventures of Augie March* are very different from his earlier novels, for here one finds an open-ended picaresque narrative with flamboyant language and an exuberant hero who seeks to affirm life and the possibility of freedom. While the environment has a profound influence upon Joseph and Asa Leventhal, Augie refuses to allow it to determine his fate. During the course of many adventures, a multitude of Machiavellians seek to impose their versions of reality upon the good-natured Augie, but he escapes from them, refusing to commit himself.

With his third novel, then, Bellow deliberately rejected the modernist outlook and aesthetic. The problem was to find an alternative to modernism without resorting to glib optimism. It seems that he found an alternative in two older literary traditions—in nineteenth century English humanism and in a comedy that he considers typically Jewish. Unlike the modernists, who denigrate the concept of the individual, Bellow believes in the potential of the self and its powerful imagination that can redeem ordinary existence and affirm the value of freedom, love, joy, and hope.

While comedy in Bellow is a complex matter, its primary function seems to be to undercut the dejection that threatens his heroes. The comic allows Bellow's protagonists to cope with the grim facts of existence; it enables them to avoid despair and gain a balanced view of their problematical situation. Comedy, the spirit of reason, allows them to laugh away their irrational anxieties. Often Bellow seems to encourage his worst anxieties in order to bring them out into the open so that he can dispose of them by comic ridicule.

If *The Adventures of Augie March* presents Bellow's alternative to a "literature of victimization," his subsequent novels can be regarded as probing, exploratory studies in spiritual survival in a hostile environment.

Seize the Day is a much more somber novel than *The Adventures of Augie March*. Bellow felt that his liberation from Flaubertian formalism had gone too far, and that he must use more restraint in his fourth novel. He realized that Augie was too effusive and too naïve. The protagonist of *Seize the Day* is similar to the protagonists of the first two novels, but while Tommy Wilhelm is a "victim," Bellow's attitude toward him is different from his attitude toward Joseph and Asa Leventhal. In his fourth novel, Bellow sought to show the spiritual rebirth of such a "victim."

The short novel, divided into seven parts, presents the day of reckoning in the life of a forty-four-year-old ex-salesman of children's furniture whose past consists of a series of blunders. Living in the Hotel Gloriana (which is also the residence of his wealthy father, Dr. Adler), Wilhelm feels that he is in a desperate situation. He is unemployed and unable to obtain money from his unsympathetic father. He gives his last seven hundred dollars to be invested for him by the mysterious psychologist Dr. Tamkin, a man who has become not only his surrogate father and financial adviser but also his instructor in spiritual and philosophical matters. Furthermore, Wilhelm's wife, Margaret, from whom he is separated, is harassing him for money. Depressed and confused by the memories of his failures in the past and absorbed by his problems in the present, Wilhelm needs love and compassion. Dr. Adler, Dr. Tamkin, and Margaret all fail him.

Seize the Day is a harsh indictment of a money-obsessed society, where a father is unable to love a son who is unsuccessful. Tamkin's speech on the two souls, no doubt the most important passage in the novel, helps clarify Bellow's social criticism. The psychologist argues that there is a war between man's "pretender soul," his social self, and his "real soul." When the pretender soul parasitically dominates its host, as is common in modern society, one becomes murderous. If one is true to the real soul, however, and casts off the false pretender soul, one can learn to love and "seize the day."

Bellow shows that all of the characters in the novel are products of an exploitative, materialistic society—all are dominated by their pretender souls. Dr. Adler has fought his way up the economic ladder to success. Revered by the residents of the Hotel Gloriana, he is full of self-love. He desires to spend his remaining years in peace and refuses to acknowledge his paternal obligation to his desperate son. Wilhelm's appeals for money are actually pleas for some sign of paternal concern. He provokes his father, trying to disturb the polite barrier of aloofness that the old man has constructed to prevent any kind of real communication between father and son. While Wilhelm is a difficult son for a father to cherish, Dr. Adler is a cold-hearted man who has no real affection for his son, or for anyone else except for himself. When, at the end of the novel, Wilhelm begs him for some kind of sympathy, the hard-boiled Adler brutally rejects him, revealing his hatred for his "soft" son.

Dr. Adler's failure as a father results in Wilhelm's turning to the strange psychologist Dr. Tamkin. Down on his luck, Tamkin is a confidence man hoping to make easy money. He is another one of Bellow's eccentric fast talkers, full of fantastic stories and philosophical and psychological insights.

Wilhelm is attracted to him not only because he is a father figure who promises to save him from his dire financial crisis but also because he is one man in a cynical society who speaks of spiritual matters. The direct result of Tamkin's advice is the loss of Wilhelm's money, but while the doctor is a phony whose flamboyant personality enables him to dupe the naïve ex-salesman, he does indirectly allow Wilhelm to obtain a kind of salvation.

Wilhelm is the only character in the novel who is able to forsake his pretender soul. He is a product of society as the other characters are, but he is different from them in his instinctive distaste for the inveterate cynicism at the heart of society. Accepting society's definition of success, he considers himself a failure. He suffers immensely and constantly ponders his life and his errors in the past. Yet while he can at times degenerate into a buffoon indulging in self-pity and hostility, he is also attracted to the idealism that Tamkin occasionally expounds.

A significant moment occurs near the end of the novel when Wilhelm suddenly feels a sense of brotherhood with his fellow travelers in the New York subway. For once he has transcended his self-absorption, though he is immediately skeptical of this intuitive moment. At the very end of the novel, there is another heightened moment in which he does make the breakthrough foreshadowed in the subway scene. Having lost all of his money, he pursues into a funeral home a man who resembles Tamkin. Suddenly he finds himself confronting a corpse, and he begins to weep uncontrollably. His weeping is not merely out of self-pity, as some have suggested, but for mankind. Understanding that death and suffering are an inextricable part of the human condition, he feels humility and is able to overcome his excessive self-absorption. He is finally able to cast off his pretender soul. The work concludes with a powerful affirmation and suggests an alternative to the spiritual death of a materialistic, predatory society.

Bellow's next novel, *Henderson the Rain King* is the first fully realized work of his maturity. It is Bellow's first novel of which one can say that no other writer could have conceived it, much less written it. Although it has some characteristics of the picaresque, the fable, and the realistic novel, *Henderson the Rain King* assumes the most widely used form for longer works during the English romantic era—the quest-romance. The tone of the novel is somewhat different from that typically heard in the quest-romance, however; it is exuberant and comic, and the book is full of wit, parody, farce, and ironic juxtapositions.

The novel might be seen as Bellow's version of Joseph Conrad's *Heart of Darkness* (1902). Like Conrad's Marlow, Eugene Henderson recalls his journey into the heart of Africa and his bizarre adventures there, which culminate in his meeting with a Kurtz-like instructor who has a profound influence upon him. While Kurtz reveals to Marlow man's potential for degradation, Dahfu conveys to Henderson man's promise of nobility. With its allusions to William

Wordsworth, Samuel Taylor Coleridge, Percy Bysshe Shelley, and William Blake, the novel affirms the possibility of the individual's regeneration by the power of the human imagination; it is a trenchant rejection of Conrad's pessimism.

The novel can be divided into three basic parts: Chapters 1-4 depict Henderson's alienation; Chapters 5-9 present his journey to the African tribe of the Arnewi; Chapters 10-22 portray his journey to the African tribe of the Wariri and his spiritual regeneration.

The first section presents Henderson's discursive recollections of his life before he set out for Africa, in which he attempts to reveal the reasons for the journey. While these chapters provide a plethora of information about him, he is never able to articulate the reasons for his "quest," as he calls it. Bellow is suggesting in this section that there are no clear-cut reasons for the African journey. Henderson leaves his wife and family for the African wilderness because of his dissatisfaction with his meaningless existence. A millionaire with tremendous energy but no scope for it, Henderson has spent most of his life suffering or making others suffer. Middle-aged, anxious about his mortality, and unable to satisfy the strident inner voice of "I want, I want," he leaves for Africa, hoping to burst "the spirit's sleep," as he phrases it, echoing Shelley's *The Revolt of Islam* (1818).

With his loyal guide Romilayu, he first visits the Arnewi tribe. These people are "children of light" who represent a healthy existence; they are gentle, peaceful, and innocent. Queen Willatale, who rules the tribe, informs Henderson that man wants to live—"grun-tu-molani." It is an important message for Henderson, but he soon demonstrates that he is unable to follow Willatale's wisdom. Desiring to help the tribe, whose water supply has been infested by frogs, he decides to kill the creatures. His bomb is too powerful and destroys the cistern as well as the frogs. Henderson has violated the code of the Arnewi, who abhor violence and have love for all living creatuers.

After Henderson leaves the Arnewi, he visits the Wariri, "the children of darkness," who are violent and hostile, reminiscent of the predatory society of Bellow's earlier novels. He does meet one extraordinary individual, however, and establishes a friendship with him. King Dahfu is a noble man who completes Henderson's education begun with the Arnewi. He perceptively observes that Henderson's basic problem is his avoidance of death: he is an "avoider." Dahfu helps him by persuading him to go down into a lion's den to overcome his anxiety over mortality. Dahfu believes, too, that Henderson can absorb the qualities of the lion and slough off his porcine characteristics.

Dahfu is another one of Bellow's eccentric teachers who speaks both wisdom and nonsense. His greatest importance for Henderson is that he embodies the nobility of man, who can by the power of his imagination achieve spiritual regeneration. At the end of the novel, Henderson finally bursts the spirit's sleep and leaves Africa for America. He has a sense of purpose and can love others. He plans to become a physician and will return home to his wife.

Herzog is Bellow's best and most difficult novel to date. It is a retrospective meditation by a middle-aged professor who seeks to understand the reasons for his disastrous past. A complex discursive work, pervaded by sardonic humor, it defies traditional labeling but owes a debt to the novel of ideas, the psychological novel, the epistolary novel, and the romantic meditative lyric. *Herzog* is a meditative work in which the protagonist compulsively remembers and evaluates his past, striving to avoid complete mental breakdown. There are reminiscences within reminiscences, and the story of Moses Herzog's life is related in fragments. Bellow's method enables the reader to see how Herzog's imagination recollects and assembles the fragments of the past into a meaningful pattern.

Distraught over his recent divorce from his second wife, Madeleine, Herzog has become obsessed with writing letters to everyone connected with that event as well as to important thinkers, living and dead, who concern him. He associates his domestic crisis with the cultural crisis of Western civilization, and therefore he ponders the ethics of Friedrich Nietzsche as well as those of his psychiatrist Dr. Edvig. His letter-writing is both a symptom of his psychological disintegration and an attempt to meditate upon and make sense of suffering and death.

At his home in the Berkshires, Herzog recalls and meditates upon the events of his recent past; the five-day period of time that he recalls reveals the severity of his psychological deterioration. His mistress Ramona believes that a cure for his nervous state can be found in her Lawrentian sexual passion, but he considers her "ideology" to be mere hedonism; impulsively, he decides to flee from her to Martha's Vineyard, where he has friends. After arriving there, the unstable professor leaves almost immediately and returns to New York. The next evening he has dinner with Ramona and spends the night with her, waking in the middle of the night to write another letter. The following morning he visits a courtroom while waiting for a meeting with his lawyer to discuss a lawsuit against Madeleine. Hearing a brutal child-abuse and murder case causes the distraught professor to associate Madeleine and her lover with the brutal child-murderers; he flies to Chicago to murder them. As he spies upon them, he realizes his assumption is absurd and abandons his plan. The next morning he takes his young daughter Junie for an outing but has a car accident and is arrested by the police for carrying a gun. He confronts an angry Madeleine at the police station and manages to control his own temper. Later, he is released and returns to his run-down home in the Berkshires, and the novel ends where it began.

Interspersed within these recollections of the immediate past are memories of the more distant past. By piecing these together, one learns the sad story of Herzog's domestic life. Feeling a vague dissatisfaction, the successful professor divorced his first wife Daisy, a sensible Midwestern woman, and began affairs with a good-natured Japanese woman, Sono, and the beautiful, bad-tempered Madeleine. After marrying Madeleine, Herzog purchased a house in the Berkshires, where he intended to complete his important book on the Romantics. Soon they returned to Chicago, however, where both saw a psychiatrist, and Madeleine suddenly announced that she wanted a divorce. The shocked Herzog traveled to Europe to recuperate, only to return to Chicago to learn that Madeleine had been having an affair with his best friend and confidant the whole time their marriage had been deteriorating.

Herzog's grim past—his disastrous marriages and the other sad events of his life that he also recalls—becomes emblematic of the pernicious influence of cultural nihilism. Herzog is devoted to basic humanist values but wonders if he must, as the ubiquitous "reality-instructors" insist, become another mass man devoted to a brutal "realism" in the Hobbesian jungle of modern society. His antipathy for the wastelanders' cynicism is strong, but he knows his past idealism has been too naïve. Repeatedly, the "reality instructors" strive to teach ("punish") Herzog with lessons of the "real"—and the "real" is always brutal and cruel. Sandor Himmelstein, Herzog's lawyer and friend, proudly announces that all people are "whores." It is an accurate description not only of Himmelstein but also of his fellow reality instructors. Their cynical view is pervasive in modern society, in which people play roles, sell themselves, and seduce and exploit others for their own selfish ends.

The turning point of the novel is Herzog's revelation in the courtroom episode. Intellectually, he has always known about evil and suffering, but emotionally he has remained innocent. His hearing of the case in which a mother mistreats and murders her son while her lover apathetically watches is too much for him to bear; here is a monstrous evil that cannot be subsumed by any intellectual scheme. In a devastating moment the professor is forced to realize that his idealism is foolish.

At the end of the novel, Herzog has achieved a new consciousness. He recognizes that he has been selfish and excessively absorbed in intellectual abstractions. A prisoner of his private intellectual life, he has cut himself off from ordinary humanity and everyday existence. He sees that his naïve idealism and the wastelanders' cruel "realism" are both escapist and therefore unacceptable attitudes; they allow the individual to evade reality by wearing masks of naïve idealism or self-serving cynicism. The exhausted Herzog decides to abandon his compulsive letter-writing and to stop pondering his past. The threat of madness has passed, and he is on the road to recovery.

Mr. Sammler's Planet is a meditative novel of sardonic humor and caustic wit. The "action" of the novel centers upon the protagonist's recollection of a brief period of time in the recent past, though there are recollections of a more distant past, too. Once again the mental state of the protagonist is Bellow's main concern. Like Herzog, Artur Sammler has abandoned a scholarly project because he finds rational explanations dissatisfying; they are unable to justify suffering and death. The septuagenarian Sammler is yet another of Bellow's survivors, a lonely humanist in a society populated by brutal "realists."

This seventh novel, however, is not merely a repetition of Bellow's previous works. Sammler is detached and basically unemotional, yet he reveals a mystical bent largely absent in Bellow's other protaganists. He is drawn to the works of Meister Eckhart and other thirteenth century German mystics. While he does not literally believe in their ideas, he finds reading their works soothing. His religious inclination is a recent phenomenon.

Sammler had been reared in a wealthy, secular Jewish family in Krakow. As an adult, he became a haughty, cosmopolitan intellectual, useless to everyone, as he readily admits. On a visit to Poland in 1939, when the Germans suddenly attacked, he, his wife, and others were captured and ordered to dig their own graves as the Nazis waited to murder them. Although his wife was killed in the mass execution, miraculously he escaped by crawling out of his own grave. After the war ended, Sammler and his daughter Shula were rescued from a displaced persons camp by a kind nephew, Dr. Elya Gruner, who became their patron.

The experience of the Holocaust destroyed what little religious inclination Sammler possessed, but in his old age he has become concerned with his spiritual state. Unfortunately, it is difficult to pursue spiritual interests in a materialistic society hostile to them. The basic conflict in the novel is between Sammler's need to ponder the basic questions of existence—a need accentuated by the dying of the noble Gruner—and the distractions of contemporary society. In the primary action of the novel, Sammler's main intention is to visit the dying Gruner, who finds Sammler a source of great comfort. Several "accidents" distract Sammler from his goal, and on the day of his nephew's death, he arrives too late.

The "accidents" which encumber Sammler reveal clearly the "degraded clowning" of contemporary society. Sammler is threatened by a black pickpocket who corners the old man and then exposes himself. In the middle of a lecture he is shouted down by a radical student who says that Sammler is sexually defective. His daughter Shula steals a manuscript from an Indian scholar, and Sammler must waste precious time to recover it. Even Gruner's self-centered children, who have little compassion for their dying father, distract Sammler by their thoughtless actions.

Opposed to Gruner, who is part of the "old system" which esteems the family, the expression of emotion, and the traditional humanist values, is the contemporary generation, a kind of "circus" characterized by role-playing, hedonism, amorality, self-centeredness, and atrophy of feeling. Despite its flaws, Bellow sympathizes with the "old system." The novel concludes after Sammler, despite the objections of the hospital staff, goes into the postmortem room and says a prayer for Gruner's soul.

As in Bellow's previous novels, the tension and the humor of *Humboldt's Gift* have their origin in the protagonist's attempt to free himself from the distractions of contemporary society and pursue the needs of his soul. The protagonist Charlie Citrine strives to define for himself the function of the artist in contemporary America. He tries to come to terms with the failure and premature death of his one-time mentor, Von Humboldt Fleisher, who had the potential to be America's greatest modern poet but achieved very little. Charlie wonders if the romantic poet can survive in a materialistic society; he wonders, too, if he can overcome his fear of the grave and exercise his imagination. A writer who has squandered his talent, Charlie has intimations of terror of the grave and intimations of immortality. He spends much time reading the Anthroposophical works of Rudolf Steiner, although he is skeptical of some of Steiner's more esoteric teachings, he is sympathetic to the spiritual world view of anthroposophy, even finding the notion of reincarnation quite persuasive.

The primary nemesis of Charlie's spiritual life is Ronald Cantabile, a small-time criminal. Renata, Charlie's voluptuous mistress, Denise, his ex-wife, and Pierre Thaxter, a confidence man, are also major distractions. When Charlie, on the advice of a friend, refuses to pay Cantabile the money he owes him from a poker game, the criminal harasses him. In fact, the proud, psychopathic Cantabile refuses to leave Charlie alone even after he agrees to pay him the money. He continually humiliates Charlie and even tries to involve him in a plot to murder the troublesome Denise.

Denise, Renata, and Thaxter also distract Charlie from pondering the fate of Humboldt and meditating upon fundamental metaphysical questions. Hoping Charlie will return to her, Denise refuses to settle her support suit and continues to demand more money. When Charlie is forced to put up a two-hundred-thousand-dollar bond, he is financially ruined, and the loss of his money results in the loss of the voluptuous Renata, who decides to marry a wealthy undertaker. A third disillusioning experience involves Thaxter, who has apparently conned Charlie. Charlie had invested a small fortune in a new journal, *The Ark*, which was supposed to restore the authority of art and culture in the United States. Thaxter, the editor of *The Ark*, never puts out the first issue and has, it appears, stolen the money. His confidence game symbolizes America's lack of respect for art and culture, impractical subjects in a practical, technological society.

Charlie does, however, overcome these "distractions," Humboldt's posthumously delivered letter, accompanied by an original film sketch (his "gift") and a scenario that the two had written at Princeton years before, provide the genesis for Charlie's salvation. The original film idea and the scenario of their Princeton years enable Charlie to attain financial security, but more important, Humboldt's letter provides the impetus for Charlie's decision at the end of the novel to repudiate his past empty life and to pursue the life of the imagination. Humboldt's ideas, bolstered by the poetry of Blake, Wordsworth, and John Keats, enable Charlie to avoid the fate of the self-destructive artist. He decides to live in Europe and meditate upon the fundamental questions—in short, to take up a different kind of life.

When, at the end of the novel, Charlie gives Humboldt and the poet's mother a proper burial, Bellow suggests that Charlie's imagination is ready to exert itself and wake him from his self-centered boredom and death-in-life. The final scene of the novel promises Charlie's spiritual regeneration.

Bellow's most recent novel, *The Dean's December*, is "a tale of two cities," Chicago and Bucharest, in which the protagonist, a dean at an unnamed college in Chicago, ponders private and public problems. Albert Corde experiences at firsthand the rigid penitentiary society of the Communist East as well as the anarchic society of the non-Communist West, which seems on the verge of disintegration. The novel is a protest against the dehumanization of the individual. The East has enslaved its population, while the West has "written off" its doomed "Underclass." Like *Humboldt's Gift*, this novel can be seen as a kind of retrospective crisis meditation in which the protagonist attempts to come to terms with an immensely complex and threatening "multiverse," as Augie March calls it.

The complicated plot defies a succinct summary, but one can outline the basic situation. The dean and his wife Minna arrive in Rumania to visit her dying mother. Corde tries to help his despairing wife, who is unable to reconcile herself to the grim reality of her mother's death. He also ponders the controversy that he has provoked in Chicago. The dean has published two articles in *Harper's* in which he comments upon the political and social problems of the city. The articles outrage the powerful members of Chicago society, and the administration of his college disapproves of the controversy that the dean has provoked. Moreover, Corde creates another controversy when he pressures the police to solve the murder of a white graduate student, Rickie Lester. A sensational trial, a media "circus," is the result of the dean's search for justice.

While more than any other novel of Bellow, *The Dean's December* is concerned with contemporary public issues, especially the vile conditions of the inner city, it is also concerned with the spiritual state of the individual. In fact, Bellow suggests that there is a connection between the spiritual malady of the individual and the spiritual anarchy of society. The novel is a protest against not only man's lack of political freedom but also his spiritual enslavement that is the result of his inability to see clearly and to experience reality. Corde implies that this inability to experience reality is largely a product of "seeing" the world with a kind of reductive journalism completely lacking in imagination. Disgusted with contemporary journalism which provides only substitutes for reality, Corde intends to incorporate "poetry" into writing. The novel suggests that in Corde's kind of poetic vision there is hope for the spiritual rebirth of the individual and society.

Major publications other than long fiction
SHORT FICTION: *Mosby's Memoirs and Other Stories*, 1968.
PLAYS: *The Wrecker*, 1954; *The Last Analysis*, 1965; *Orange Soufflé*, 1965; *A Wen*, 1965.
NONFICTION: *The Future of the Moon*, 1970; *To Jerusalem and Back: A Personal Account*, 1976.
ANTHOLOGY: *Great Jewish Short Stories*, 1963.

Bibliography
Chavkin, Allan. "Bellow's Alternative to the Wasteland: Romantic Theme and Form in *Herzog*," in *Studies in the Novel*. XI (Fall, 1979), pp. 326-337.
Clayton, John J. *Saul Bellow: In Defense of Man*, 1968.
Cohen, Sarah B. *Saul Bellow's Enigmatic Laughter*, 1974.
Dutton, Robert T. *Saul Bellow*, 1982.
Goldman, Leila, ed. *The Saul Bellow Journal*, 1982.
Malin, Irving. *Saul Bellow's Fiction*, 1967.
Nault, Marianne. *Saul Bellow: His Works and His Critics, an Annotated International Bibliography*, 1977.
Noreen, Robert. *Saul Bellow: A Reference Guide*, 1978.
Opdahl, Keith. *The Novels of Saul Bellow: An Introduction*, 1967.
Porter, M. Gilbert. *Whence the Power? The Artistry and Humanity of Saul Bellow*, 1974.
Rodrigues, Eusebio L. *Quest for the Human: An Exploration of Saul Bellow's Fiction*, 1981.
Rovit, Earl. *Saul Bellow: A Collection of Critical Essays*, 1975.
Scheer-Schazler, Brigitte. *Saul Bellow*, 1972.
Tanner, Tony. *Saul Bellow*, 1965.
Trachtenberg, Stanley. *Critical Essays on Saul Bellow*, 1979.

Allan Chavkin

ARNOLD BENNETT

Born: Hanley, England; May 27, 1867
Died: London, England; March 27, 1931

Principal long fiction

A Man from the North, 1898; *Anna of the Five Towns*, 1902; *The Grand Babylon Hotel*, 1902; (published in the United States as *T. Racksole and Daughter*); *The Gates of Wrath*, 1903; *Leonora*, 1903; *A Great Man*, 1904; *Teresa of Watling Street*, 1904; *Sacred and Profane Love*, 1905; (published in the United States as *The Book of Carlotta*); *Hugo*, 1906; *Whom God Hath Joined*, 1906; *The Sinews of War*, 1907 (with Eden Phillpotts, published in the United States as *Doubloons*); *The Ghost*, 1907; *The City of Pleasure*, 1907; *The Statue*, 1908 (with Eden Phillpotts); *Buried Alive*, 1908; *The Old Wives' Tale*, 1908; *The Glimpse*, 1909; *Helen with the High Hand*, 1910; *Clayhanger*, 1910; *The Card*, 1911 (published in the United States as *Denry the Audacious*); *Hilda Lessways*, 1911; *The Regent*, 1913 (published in the United States as *The Old Adam*); *The Price of Love*, 1914; *These Twain*, 1915; *The Lion's Share*, 1916; *The Pretty Lady*, 1918; *The Roll-Call*, 1918; *Lilian*, 1922; *Mr. Prohack*, 1922; *Riceyman Steps*, 1923; *Elsie and the Child*, 1924; *Lord Raingo*, 1926; *The Strange Vanguard*, 1928 (published in the United States as *The Vanguard* in 1927); *Accident*, 1929; *Piccadilly*, 1929; *Imperial Palace*, 1930; *Venus Rising from the Sea*, 1932.

Other literary forms

Besides fifteen major novels, Arnold Bennett published thirty-three other novels generally considered potboilers by his critics. Some of them Bennett himself regarded as serious works; others he variously called "fantasias," "frolics," "melodramas," or "adventures." His total published work exceeds eighty volumes, including eight collections of short stories, sixteen plays, six collections of essays, eight volumes of literary criticism, three volumes of letters, six travelogues, and volumes of autobiography, journals, and reviews, as well as miscellaneous short articles, introductions, pamphlets, "pocket philosophies," and a few poems. Much of his journal has never been published. Bennett collaborated in the production of five films and operas, three of which were adapted from his plays and novels. Four of his plays and novels were adapted for film by other screenwriters, and two of his novels were adapted for the stage.

Achievements

Bennett's early novels played an important role in the transition from the Victorian to the modern novel. A somewhat younger contemporary of Thomas Hardy, Henry James, and Joseph Conrad, he helped to displace the "loose, baggy" Victorian novel and to develop the realistic movement in England. With fine detail he portrayed the industrial Five Towns, his fictional version of the six towns of pottery manufacturing in Staffordshire County. His early career was strongly influenced by the aestheticism in form and language found in works by Gustave Flaubert, Guy de Maupassant, and Ivan Turgenev, and he admired the naturalism of Honoré de Balzac, Emile Zola, and the Goncourts. Later, however, he rejected what he called the "crudities and . . . morsels of available misery" of naturalism, and, while retaining an interest in form and beauty, he came to feel that aesthetics alone is an empty literary goal and that the novelist must combine "divine compassion," believability, and the creation of character with the "artistic shapely presentation of truth" and the discovery of "beauty, which is always hidden." With these aims in mind, he chose as the subject of his best works that which is beautiful and remarkable about the lives of unremarkable, middle-class people. Although his novels rarely sold well enough to earn his living, his best novels were highly regarded by critics and fellow authors. He carried on a correspondence of mutual encouragement and criticism with Conrad and H. G. Wells; some of these letters have been published. Conrad, a master of style, wrote: "I am . . . fascinated by your expression, by the ease of your realization, the force and delicacy of your phrases." Despite their acclaim for Bennett's best work, however, even his admirers regretted his propensity to write potboilers for money.

Because of the volume of his work, Bennett is remembered today as a novelist, but in his lifetime his income derived from his equally prodigious output of plays and journalism; his "pocket philosophies" and critical reviews also won him an enormous public prestige. During the 1920's he was virtually the arbiter of literary taste, a reviewer who could make or break a book's sales or a newcomer's career. He was among the first to praise the literary merits of such controversial newcomers as D. H. Lawrence, T. S. Eliot, William Faulkner, Virginia Woolf, and James Joyce. Bennett regarded himself less as a novelist than as a professional writer who should be able to, and did, undertake any genre with competence and craftsmanship. (The exception was poetry; he never wrote poetry to meet his own standards.) His reputation suffered in the latter part of his career for those very qualities, which too often fell short of genius and inspiration. He did reach the level of greatness occasionally, however, and his literary reputation is firmly established with the inclusion of *The Old Wives' Tale* in most lists of the great English novels.

Biography

Enoch Arnold Bennett was born on May 27, 1867, in Shelton, Staffordshire County, England, near the six towns that constitute the Potteries region in cental England, the scene of much of Bennett's early work. His father, Enoch Bennett, was successively a potter, a draper, a pawnbroker, and eventually, through hard work and study, a solicitor. Bennett attended the local schools, where he passed the examination for Cambridge University. He did not attend college, however, because his autocratic father kept him at home as clerk in the solicitor's office.

As a means of escape from the grime and provincialism of the Potteries district, Bennett began writing for the *Staffordshire Sentinel* and studying shorthand. The latter skill enabled him to become a clerk with a London law firm in 1888. In London, he set about seriously to learn to write. He moved to Chelsea in 1891 to live with the Frederick Marriott family, in whose household he was introduced to the larger world of the arts. His first work published in London was a prizewinning parody for a competition in *Tit-Bits* in 1893; this work was followed by a short story in *The Yellow Book* and, in 1898, his first novel, *A Man from the North*. He became the assistant editor and later the editor of the magazine *Woman*, writing reviews pseudonymously as "Barbara," a gossip and advice column as "Marjorie," and short stories as "Sal Volatile." It is generally thought that this experience provided a good background for female characterization. As he became better known as a journalist, Bennett began writing reviews for *The Academy* and giving private lessons in journalism. His journalistic income allowed him in 1900 to establish a home at Trinity Hall Farm, Hockliffe, in Bedfordshire. To Hockliffe he brought his family after his father had been disabled by the softening of the brain which eventually killed him. Bennett wrote prodigiously there, producing not only his admired *Anna of the Five Towns* but also popular potboilers and journalism, including the anonymous "Savoir-Faire Papers" and "Novelist's Log-Book" series for *T. P.'s Weekly*. This production financed some long-desired travel and a move to Paris in 1903.

Bennett lived in France for eight years, some of the busiest and happiest of his life. Shortly after his arrival, he observed a fat, fussy woman who inspired the thought that "she has been young and slim once," a thought that lingered in his mind for five years and inspired his masterwork, *The Old Wives' Tale*. Meanwhile, he continued writing for newspapers and magazines, including the first of his series "Books and Persons," written under the nom de plume "Jacob Tonson" for *The New Age*. Between 1903 and 1907 he also wrote ten novels. In 1907, he married Marguerite Soulié, an aspiring actress who had worked as his part-time secretary. From the beginning of the marriage, it was evident that the two were incompatible, but she did provide him with an atmosphere conducive to his undertaking the novel which had germinated for so long and which he felt beforehand would be a masterpiece. He determined that *The Old Wives' Tale* should "do one better than" Guy de Maupassant's *Une Vie* (1883), and his careful crafting of the book was recognized by critics, who immediately acclaimed it as a modern classic. Before moving back to England in 1913, he wrote six more novels, three of which are among his best: *Clayhanger*, *The Card*, and *Hilda Lessways*. In

1911, he traveled in the United States, where his books were selling well and were highly respected. After the tour, he moved to the country estate Comarques at Thorpe-le-Soken, Essex, where he had access to the harbor for a yacht, his means of gaining what relaxation he could.

The yacht was important to Bennett, because he had suffered since youth from a variety of ailments, mostly resulting from his high-strung temperament. He had a serious stammer or speech paralysis, which exhausted him in speaking; compulsive personal habits; and a liver ailment and chronic enteritis which restricted his diet and caused great discomfort when he ate incautiously. As he grew older, he suffered increasingly from excruciating neuralgia, headaches, and insomnia, almost without relief near the end of his life. Except for the yacht, his recreation was to write; he probably wrote his light works as a relief from the tension of the serious novels, yet he demanded good style from himself even for them. His craftsmanship was conscious and intense, and his drive to produce great quantity while still maintaining quality undoubtedly sapped his strength both physically and psychologically, and contributed to his death at the age of sixty-four.

Bennett's physical maladies were probably exacerbated by World War I and the collapse of his marriage. Although he continued his usual pace of writing during the war—five more novels between 1914 and 1919—much of his energy was spent in patriotic activities ranging from entertaining soldiers to front-line journalism. From May 9, 1918, until the end of the war, he served as volunteer director of British propaganda in France. He refused knighthood for his services. After the war, he tried to restore his depleted finances by writing plays, which had been more remunerative than novels, but the later ones were unsuccessful. In 1921, he and Marguerite separated. He gave her a settlement so generous that for the rest of his life he was under pressure to publish and sell his writing. Contemporary critics believed that these years of low-novel production marked the end of his creativity.

Bennett surprised his critics, however, with *Riceyman Steps*, which was critically acclaimed and was awarded the James Tait Black Novel prize, Bennett's only literary award. This was followed by *Lord Raingo* and *Imperial Palace*, as well as six less distinguished novels and one unfinished at his death. This creative resurgence may have resulted in part from his relationship with Dorothy Cheston, who bore his only child, Virginia, in 1926. His journalistic career had never waned, and in the 1920's he continued his "Books and Persons" series in the *Evening Standard*, with a prestige that influenced the reading public and allowed him to promote the careers of many young authors. Bennett's health was steadily deteriorating, however, and in 1931 he died in his Chiltern Court flat from typhoid fever.

Analysis

As a self-designated professional author, Arnold Bennett not only wrote an extraordinary quantity in a great variety of genres but also created a broad range of themes and characters. A common approach or theme is difficult to detect in a corpus of forty-eight novels which include fantasy, realism, romance, naturalism, satire, symbolism, comedy, tragedy, melodrama, Freudian psychology, allegory, economics, regionalism, cosmopolitanism, politics, medicine, and war. Nevertheless, in spite of this diversity, Bennett is generally esteemed for his realistic novels, which are considered his serious work. In most, if not all, of these fifteen novels, certain related themes recur, rising from his youthful experiences of growing up in Burslem under the domination of his father. His desire to escape the intellectual, aesthetic, and spiritual stultification of his Burslem environment led to a cluster of themes related to escape: rebellion against the ties of the home conflicting with love for one's roots; aspiration versus complacence and philistinism; fear of failure to escape and fear of failure after escape; and the problem of coping with success if it comes. Another cluster of themes relates to his conflict with his father and the shock of his father's debilitating illness and death: the generation gap, emotional repression by dominating parents, the cyclical influence of parents on their children, a soul parent who vies in influence with the natural parent, degeneration and illness, the pathos of decrepitude in old age, awe at the purpose or purposelessness of life.

A Man from the North, Bennett's first novel, includes the themes of aspiration, emotional repression, the soul parent, illness and death, and failure after escape. It is the story of Richard Larch, an aspiring writer from the Potteries, who goes to London to experience the greater intellectual and moral freedom of a cosmopolis. There he meets his soul father, Mr. Aked, a journalist and failed novelist who introduces Larch to the drama—the "tragedy"—of ordinary lives. Aked, however, is an unsuccessful guide; he dies. Larch is also unable to succeed; he eventually marries a woman he does not love and settles down to the sort of life Aked had described. It is the story of what Bennett himself might have been if he had not succeeded after leaving Burslem.

Anna of the Five Towns, on the other hand, is the story of the failure to escape. Anna is repressed by her overbearing and miserly father; under the influence of her soul mother, Mrs. Sutton, she learns to aspire to a few amenities, such as new clothes for her wedding, but these aspirations come too late to change her life significantly. Accepting the values of the community rather than escaping them, she marries Henry Mynors, her more prosperous suitor, rather than Willie Price, the man she loves in her own way. While the themes of these books are similar, they differ in that Anna stays and copes with her environment with some success. She does not escape Bursley (Bennett's fictional name for Burslem), but she escapes her father's control and improves her perceptions of beauty and human relationships to some degree. The books also differ in that *A Man from the North* presents an unrelentingly grim memory of Burslem. Later, however, Bennett read George Moore's *A Mummer's Wife* (1885), and its section on Burslem showed him that "beauty, which is always hidden," could be found in the lives of its people and in art expressing those lives. Thus, Bennett returned to the locale for *Anna of the Five Towns*, and although the portrayal is still grim, Anna's life has tragic beauty. Anna rebels against the ties of home, but she also has some love for her roots there, in the person of Willie Price.

Between *Anna of the Five Towns* and *The Old Wives' Tale*, Bennett wrote eleven minor novels, some of which were serious and some not, but all taught him something that contributed to the greatness of *The Old Wives' Tale*. Several of them were light comedies, and in writing these Bennett developed the assured comic touch which marks even his serious novels. Three of them were Five Towns novels about female characters from various segments of Bursley society; in these he developed those skills in characterizing women which were so admired in his finest novels. These skills were honed in France, where Bennett learned a great deal about the literary presentation of sex. During these years, Bennett said, he learned more about life than he had ever known before.

When Bennett was ready to write his masterpiece, *The Old Wives' Tale*, he had reached full artistic maturity and was at the height of his literary power. He had published one critically acclaimed novel and several others that had allowed him to improve his characterization, especially of women, to temper his realism with humor, and to perfect his themes in various plots. His dislike of Burslem's grime and provincialism had been balanced by compassion for its inhabitants and awareness of what beauty and aspiration could be found there. His personal involvement in the town had been modified by experience in London and Paris, so that he could be objective about the sources of his material. This balance of technique and emotion is reflected in the structure of *The Old Wives' Tale*. The novel counterpoints the lives of two sisters, Constance and Sophia Baines, the first of whom stays in Bursley while the second leaves but later returns. Their stories parallel not only each other but also those of preceding and succeeding generations. In fact, the first section of the book is subtitled "Mrs. Baines" (the mother).

In section one, *The Old Wives' Tale* takes up in mid-career one generation's old wife, with a husband so ill that the wife is running his draper's business and rearing two young daughters. As the girls grow up, Mrs. Baines finds them increasingly hard to handle. During a town festival in which an elephant has to be executed for killing a spectator, Mr. Baines dies. Shortly afterward, Sophia elopes with Gerald Scales, a traveling salesman, and Constance marries Samuel Povey, the former shop assistant, whom Mrs. Baines considers "beneath" her. When Samuel and Constance take over the business, introducing progressive marketing methods. Mrs. Baines retires to live with her elder sister, and dies there. The story of Mrs. Baines, then, is the end of the life of a woman who "was young and slim once," although she is not depicted so and that part of her life is understood only by later comparison with the stories of her daughters.

The cycle of Mrs. Baines continues with Constance, who represents the person who stays in Bursley, held by the roots of the past. As Mrs. Baines's successor, Constance marries a husband whose aspiration is to improve, not to leave, Bursley, and they run the business with a combination of youthful progressiveness and family tradition. Constance and Samuel have a son, Cyril. After a scandal in which Samuel's cousin is executed for murdering his alcoholic wife, Samuel dies. Constance continues the business for a while, unresponsive to further progressive business practices, and spoils her son until he becomes hard for her to manage. She is finally forced to retire from business by changes in the business structure of Bursley, and Cyril escapes from her and Bursley to London to study art. As a result, Constance comes to depend emotionally on Cyril's cousin, Dick.

Sophia, the rebel against Bursley, finds a soul mother in the school teacher, who introduces her to a world of wider intellectual aspiration. In her eagerness to experience more than Bursley offers, however, she elopes with a salesman, who represents sophistication and romance to her. They go to France, where they squander their money and slip into mutual disillusionment and recrimination. After observing the public execution of the murderer of a courtesan, Sophia becomes ill and is abandoned by Gerald. She eventually acquires a boarding house in Paris, where she supports several dependents and survives the siege of Paris through single-minded hoarding and hard work. She becomes a reclusive fixture on her street, much like Constance on her square in Bursley. When she becomes ill and the business becomes hard for her to manage, she sells it and returns to Bursley to grow old and die.

Each daughter's life recapitulates Mrs. Baines's in certain respects. Each marries, loses a husband, succors children or other dependents, runs a business, gradually loses control over her life (the change marked in each case by a symbolic execution), loses health and strength, and retires to die as a burdensome old woman like the one Bennett saw in the Paris restaurant. Further, although they are not women, the two Povey young men, Cyril and his cousin Dick, recapitulate the early years of Sophia and Constance: Cyril, the rebel who leaves Bursley but does not succeed; and Dick, the stay-at-home progressive idealist. At the end, Dick is engaged to marry a slim, young counterpart to Constance, who will no doubt carry on the cycle. The thematic repetitions are not so obvious as they appear here, of course; the variations of individual character allow the reader a sense of more difference than similarity.

The variations also mark a further step in Bennett's use of his themes. Constance and Sophia are not so warped by Bursley as was Anna in *Anna of the Five Towns*; in fact, Sophia, who escapes, is warped more than Constance, who stays. Both have strength derived from their roots, and while neither can be said to escape or to achieve happiness or grace in living, both transcend Bursley more successfully than other townspeople. The theme of their decrepitude in old age is a separate one, also used in other novels, but not related to the escape and success themes. The Baineses are grouped in other Five Towns stories with those who succeed on Bursley's terms. Beginning in 1906 in *Whom God Hath Joined*, in the collection of short stories *The Matador of the Five Towns* (1912), and in *The Old Wives' Tale*, there is a growing emphasis upon those members of Burslem society who have some education, culture, and sophistication. Perhaps Bennett had been reassured by his personal success that his childhood in Burslem could be accepted.

Whether it is true that Bennett had come to accept his past, it is certainly true that his next serious book, *Clayhanger*, was his most nearly autobiographical. After the completion of the trilogy of which *Clayhanger* was the first volume, Bennett turned from the Five Towns to London as the setting for his novels. The Clayhanger trilogy is the story of a man who at first is defeated in his desire to escape Bursley. Having been defeated, however, he learns from his soul father to rise above Bursley's philistinism. Over the years, he breaks one after another of his bonds to Bursley until he has succeeded in escaping intellectually, and eventually, he completely abandons the Five Towns.

Much of this story occurs in the third volume of the trilogy, *These Twain*. *Clayhanger* itself is the story of the generational conflict between Edwin Clayhanger and his father Darius. The conflict is similar to the one between Anna and her father in *Anna of the Five Towns* and between Sophia and Mrs. Baines in *The Old Wives' Tale*, but in *Clayhanger* it is much more intense and more acutely observed. Edwin is sensitively introduced in the first two chapters; he has within him "a flame . . . like an altar-fire," a passion "to exhaust himself in doing his best." He is rebelling against his father, whose highest aspiration for his son is to have him take over his printing business. The advancement of the theme in *Clayhanger* over its treatment in the earlier novels is that the generational conflict is presented sympathetically on both sides. In Chapters Three and Four, Darius is portrayed as sensitively as Edwin has been previously. In an intensely moving chapter, his childhood of promise, stifled at seven years by poverty and abusive child labor, is described. Because Darius as a "man of nine" was unable to "keep the family," they were sent to the poorhouse. They were rescued from this degradation by Darius' Sunday school teacher (his soul father), who had recognized Darius' promise and who got Darius a decent job as a printer's devil. This background of deprivation and emotional sterility prevents Darius from expressing his softer emotions, such as his love for Edwin; his total dedication to the business which he built and by which he supports his family is thoroughly empathetic to the reader. It is no wonder that he can conceive nothing nobler for Edwin than to carry on this decent business. Because Darius can never discuss these traumatic childhood experiences, Edwin never understands him any more than he understands Edwin.

In his desire to hold onto his son and keep him in the family business, Darius simply ignores and overrides Edwin's inchoate talent for architecture. Later, he uses Edwin's financial dependence to squelch his desire to marry Hilda Lessways, whom Edwin has met through the architect Osmond Orgreave. Although Edwin resents his father's domination, he cannot openly rebel; he feels inadequate before his father's dominance, and he looks forward to the day when he will have his vengeance. This day comes when Darius becomes ill with softening of the brain, the same ailment that killed Bennett's own father. The progression of the illness and Edwin's emotions of triumph, irritation, and compassion are exquisitely detailed. Even after Darius' death, however, Edwin is not free from his father's presence, for he becomes increasingly like his father, learning to take pride in the business and to tyrannize over his sisters and Hilda, with whom he is reconciled at the end of the book. *Clayhanger* thus concludes with the apparent defeat of aspiration by the cycle of parental influence.

The hope of eventual success has been raised, however, by the death of Darius, that primary symbol of Bursley repression, and the return of Hilda, the symbol of aspiration. In *Hilda Lessways*, the second book of the trilogy, Bennett picks up her parallel story of generational conflict with her mother and cultural conflict with Turnhill, another of the Five Towns. Hilda's story is far less compelling than Edwin's, though, and adds little to the plot development. More important, its structure repeats what Bennett did successfully in *The Old Wives' Tale*: it contrasts two efforts to cope with Bursley, which provide for a double perspective on the problem, and then brings them together for the denouement made possible by that combined perspective. The double perspective also allows Bennett to maintain his characteristic objectivity and touch of humor. *These Twain* presents the marriage of Edwin and Hilda. Through a series of adjustments and small victories, the two are able to achieve a social success in the Five Towns which allows them to wean themselves emotionally from the Potteries and leave forever. The *Clayhanger* trilogy thus deals with escape and success, rather than some aspect of failure as in the earlier novels.

These Twain was the last Five Towns novel. In changing his fictional settings from Bursley to London or the Continent, Bennett also extended his themes from success or failure in escaping poverty and provincialism to success or failure in handling the accomplished escape. Perhaps that is another reason, besides the ones usually offered, for Bennett's long period of low productivity and substandard potboilers from 1915 to 1922. Between *Anna of the Five Towns* and *The Old Wives' Tale*, one should remember, there had been a similar period of low-quality work during which Bennett perfected skills that made the Five Towns novels great. Similarly, in his postwar characters Audrey Moze, George Cannon, G. J. Hoape, Lilian Share, and Mr. Prohack, Bennett experimented with stories of people who must cope with financial or social responsibilities for which they may have been poorly prepared. Also in these stories he experimented more boldly with varieties of sexual relationships: in *The Lion's Share*, implied lesbianism; in *The Pretty Lady*, prostitution; in *Lilian*, a mistress. Furthermore, although these next qualities do not show up clearly in the low-quality work of this period, the use of symbols and psychological insight must have been developing in Bennett's mind. These qualities emerge rather suddenly and very effectively in the novels beginning with *Riceyman Steps*. They may account for some of the high acclaim which that novel received after the period of reorientation, but the adapted themes were perfected by 1923, as well.

The themes in *Riceyman Steps* are variations on those of the Five Towns novels, not departures which might seem necessary to a metropolitan setting. The decayed and grimy industrial area of Clerkenwell is in many respects Bursley resituated in London. Henry Earlforward, the miser, represents Bursley's industrial materialism. Henry, like Edwin Clayhanger, has succeeded in that environment; he has a well-respected bookstore that offers him financial self-sufficiency. Unlike Edwin, however, Henry's complacent rootedness to Clerkenwell progressively cuts him off from grace, beauty, then love, and finally even life. His wife, Violet, also has financial security, but because she fears the loss of her success, she has become almost as miserly as he. Both are described as sensual; Henry's rich red lips are mentioned several times, and Violet, formerly a widow, wears red flowers in her hat. Money, however, is the chief object of their eroticism. Henry's miserliness is his passion, and he gives Violet her own safe as a wedding gift. Violet becomes "liquid with acquiescence" after seeing the hoarded disorder of his house, and she urges him to bed after he has shown her the gold coins in his private safe. The passion for money soon overrides the related passion of human love. Henry especially, and Violet in acquiescence, lock doors more tightly about themselves to protect their treasures until each is figuratively shut into a private, iron-walled safe. Starving emotionally and intellectually in their isolation, they finally starve themselves physically as well, rather than spend money for adequate food. Here, aspiration gone awry, the fear of failure and the inability to cope with success become literally debilitating diseases. Violet dies of a tumor and malnutrition and Henry of cancer. After death, they are scarcely missed, the ultimate symbols of the stultification which Bennett's characters strive with varying success to escape.

After *Riceyman Steps*, the next few novels—*Lord Raingo*, *Accident*, and *Imperial Palace*—continue the themes of coping with success, and the protagonists are given increasing ability to handle it. Much as Clayhanger finally overcomes the problems of escape, Evelyn Orcham in *Imperial Palace* is the culminating figure in the second cluster of themes. Ironically, Bennett died shortly after he had resolved the problems underlying the themes of his serious novels.

All of Bennett's serious works are firmly rooted in the realistic tradition (although he used more symbolism than has generally been recognized), and he excelled in the presentation of detail that makes his themes and characters credible. In the late years of his career, he was criticized by Virginia Woolf for portraying people's surroundings, rather than the people themselves, and forcing his readers to do his imagining for him, even though he believed that character creating was one of the three most important functions of a novel. Woolf's criticism was sound enough to seriously damage Bennett's standing as a major novelist, and it has been the keystone of critical opinion ever since. Yet, a sense of environmental impact has always been accepted as an important means of characterization in realistic literature. Woolf's criticism says as much about changing styles in literature as it does about the merits of Bennett's fiction. More important, it was a criticism aimed at Bennett's total canon, since his potboilers had not yet died of their natural ailments when Woolf wrote. Sophia and Constance Baines, Edwin and Darius Clayhanger, and Henry Earlforward are finely articulated, memorable characters. It is, after all, for his best work that any artist is remembered. Bennett's sense of place, characters, and universality of themes combine to make his finest novels memorable; *The Old Wives' Tale* is sufficient to secure Bennett's stature as one of the outstanding novelists of his era.

Major publications other than long fiction
SHORT FICTION: *The Loot of Cities*, 1905; *Tales of the Five Towns*, 1905; *The Grim Smile of the Five Towns*, 1907; *The Matador of the Five Towns*, 1912; *The Woman Who Stole Everything*, 1927; *Selected Tales*, 1928; *The Night Visitor*, 1931.

PLAYS: *Polite Farces*, 1900; *Cupid and Commonsense*, 1908; *What the Public Wants*, 1909; *The Honeymoon: A Comedy in Three Acts*, 1911; *Milestones: A Play in Three Acts*, 1912 (with Edward Knoblock); *The Great Adventure: A Play of Fantasia in Four Sets*, 1913; *The Title*, 1918; *Judith*, 1919; *Sacred and Profane Love*, 1919; *Body and Soul*, 1922; *The Love Match*, 1922; *Don Juan*, 1923; *London Life*, 1924 (with Edward Knoblock); *Mr. Prohack*, 1927 (with Edward Knoblock); *The Return Journey*, 1928 (produced); *Flora*, 1933 (in *Five Three-Act Plays*).

NONFICTION: *Journalism for Women*, 1898; *Fame and Fiction*, 1901; *The Truth About an Author*, 1903; *How to Become an Author*, 1903; *Things That Interested Me*, 1906; *Things Which Have Interested Me*, 1907, 1908; *Books and Persons: Being Comments on a Past Epoch*, 1908-1911; *Literary Tastes*, 1909; *Those United States*, 1912 (published in the United States as *Your United States*); *Paris Nights*, 1913; *From the Log of the Velsa*, 1914; *The Author's*

Craft, 1914; *Over There*, 1915; *Things That Have Interested Me*, 1921, 1923, 1926; *Selected Essays*, 1926; *Mediterranean Scenes*, 1928; *The Savour of Life*, 1928; *The Journals of Arnold Bennett*, 1929, 1930, 1932-1933.

Bibliography

Hall, James. *Arnold Bennett: Primitivism and Taste*, 1959.
Hepburn, James G. *The Art of Arnold Bennett*, 1963.
Lucas, John. *Arnold Bennett: A Study of His Fiction*, 1974.
Pound, Reginald. *Arnold Bennett: A Biography*, 1971.
Swinnerton, Frank A. *Arnold Bennett*, 1950.
Wain, John. *Arnold Bennett*, 1967.
Young, Kenneth. *Arnold Bennett*, 1976.

Carol I. Croxton

THOMAS BERGER

Born: Cincinnati, Ohio; July 20, 1924

Principal long fiction

Crazy in Berlin, 1958; *Reinhart in Love*, 1962; *Little Big Man*, 1964; *Killing Time*, 1967; *Vital Parts*, 1970; *Regiment of Women*, 1973; *Sneaky People*, 1975; *Who Is Teddy Villanova?*, 1977; *Arthur Rex*, 1978; *Neighbors*, 1980; *Reinhart's Women*, 1981.

Other literary forms

Thomas Berger has published numerous articles, reviews, and short stories in magazines such as the *Saturday Evening Post, Esquire, Harper's,* and *Playboy.* He has written three plays, all unpublished, but one of which, *Other People*, was staged in 1970 at the Berkshire Theatre Festival in Massachusetts.

Achievements

For more than twenty years, Berger has been one of America's most productive, most respected, and most challenging literary figures. His eleven novels, including the highly acclaimed *Little Big Man* and critically and popularly successful works such as *Who Is Teddy Villanova?* and *Neighbors*, seem sure to earn for him a lasting place in American letters. His Reinhart series (four volumes to date) is one of the most unique and significant accomplishments of postwar American literature, forming as it does both a sociological epic and an index to the changing face of the American novel over the last twenty-five years. Acknowledged as a masterful prose stylist, Berger writes novels that are aggressively intelligent without being ostentatiously "difficult," works that are often hilariously funny without losing their serious bite.

In 1970, Richard Schickel correctly identified Berger as "one of the most radical sensibilities now writing in America," and bemoaned the fact that Berger had not received the recognition he deserved. More than a decade later, Thomas R. Edwards intensified this complaint with the charge that the failure to read and discuss Berger's work was no less than "a national disgrace." Edwards, however, was writing on the front page of *The New York Times Book Review* and his praise for *Neighbors* was flanked by an interview with Berger, conducted by Schickel. In short, the recognition and acclaim that so long eluded Berger's writing seem to be catching up with his career, and a growing number of doctoral dissertations and scholarly articles indicates that his work is being studied as well as applauded. Reviewing *Neighbors* for the *Chicago Tribune*, Frederick Busch may have best summed up Berger's stature as a novelist when he said: "This is a novel by Thomas Berger, and everything he writes should be read and considered."

Biography

Thomas Louis Berger was born in Cincinnati, Ohio, on July 20, 1924, and grew up in the nearby suburban community of Lockland. Disenchanted after a short bout with college, Berger enlisted in the Army, serving from 1943 to 1946, his experiences giving him some of the background for his first novel, *Crazy in Berlin*.

After the war, he returned to college, receiving his B.A. at the University of Cincinnati in 1948. He continued his studies as a graduate student in English at Columbia (1950-1951), where he completed course work for an M.A., and he began a thesis on George Orwell, never completing it. Instead, Berger turned his attention to the writers workshop at the New School for Social Research. In that workshop, under the aegis of Charles Glicksberg, Berger began to write short stories. "I produced one story a week for three months, most of them melancholy in tone, maudlin in spirit, and simple of mind," he recounts, "Hemingway then being my model." Berger dismisses his short fiction, explaining "the marathon is my event, and not the hundred-yard dash." Despite this assessment, Berger's short fiction has appeared in magazines ranging from the *Saturday Evening Post*, to *Harper's*, *Esquire*, *Playboy*, and *North American Review*.

From 1948 through 1951, Berger supported his writing by working as a librarian at the Rand School of Social Science. Between 1951 and 1952, he was a staff member of *The New York Times Index*, and the following year he was a copy editor for *Popular Science Monthly*. Until 1964 and the publication of his third novel, *Little Big Man*, Berger had to supplement the income from his fiction with free-lance editing. From 1971 to 1973, Berger wrote a characteristically idiosyncratic film column for *Esquire*, managing to discuss almost everything *but* major motion pictures of the day.

Since 1950, Berger has been married to Jeanne Redpath, an artist he met at the New School. He has moved about, living among other places in London and on an island in Maine. He now lives outside of New York and is currently a visiting writing teacher at Yale.

Analysis

The dust-jacket blurb written by Thomas Berger for *Who Is Teddy Villanova?* reviews the general scheme of his career, pointing out that each of his novels "celebrates another classic genre of fiction: the western [*Little Big Man*], the childhood memoir [*Sneaky People*], the anatomical romance [*Regiment of Women*], the true-crime documentary [*Killing Time*], and the Reinhart books [*Crazy in Berlin*, *Reinhart in Love*, and *Vital Parts*] together form a sociological epic." *Who Is Teddy Villanova?* extended this pattern to the classic American hard-boiled detective story, *Arthur Rex* extended it to Arthurian romance, *Neighbors* traces its lineage most directly to Franz Kafka, and *Reinhart's Women* continues the Reinhart series. The mistaken notion that these "celebrations" of classic novel forms are really parodies has dogged Berger's career, but unlike parody, his novels start from rather than aim toward literary traditions; he achieves a testing and broadening of possibilities rather than a burlesquing of limitations. If anything, his celebrations serve as kinds of *deparodisations*, twisting genres already self-conscious to the point of parody in ways that radically defamiliarize them.

Most critics have failed to consider that Berger's manipulations of novel forms are ultimately self-exploring and reflexive literary experiments. He tries to make of each novel an "independent existence," an alternative verbal reality he hopes the reader will approach "without the luggage of received ideas, *a priori* assumptions, sociopolitical axes to grind, or feeble moralities in search of support." This verbal world both owes its existence to a number of traditional and arbitrary literary conventions of representation and seeks to remind the reader that the working of those conventions is of interest and significance in itself—not only as a means to the representation of reality.

Failing to appreciate the independent existence of Berger's fictional worlds, reviewers have misread *Little Big Man* as an indictment of American abuse of Indians, *Regiment of Women* as a polemic for or against the women's movement, *Neighbors* as a critique of suburban life, and so on. Such a topical approach to these novels ignores the possibility that Berger's real theme is language, and that underlying the manically different surfaces of his novels is a constant preoccupation with the ways in which problems of human existence stem from the confusion of language with reality. Again and again, Berger's novels find new ways to suggest that the structures and institutions that order and give meaning to existence are much less important than the ways in which one talks about them, and that the ways one talks about those organizing beliefs inevitably have been designed by someone to influence and/or manipulate someone else's perception and judgment. His ex-wife spells this out for Reinhart when she chides: "It ought to begin to occur to you that life is just a collection of stories from all points of self-interest."

Accordingly, the lives of Berger's characters are affected more by words than by actions. Victimized by definitions that exclude or threaten them, by rhetoric that makes them lose sight of physical facts, and by language designed more to preclude than to encourage clear thinking, his characters are enslaved by language. For this reason, the plot of a Berger novel typically chronicles the efforts of the protagonist to free himself from someone else's verbal version of reality. In this way, Jack Crabb in *Little Big Man* bounces back and forth not only between white and plains Indian cultures, but also between competing codes of conduct designed to legitimize all manner of cruelty. Berger shows how Jack's greatest problems are actually matters of definition, as he inevitably finds himself defined as white when the situation is controlled by Indians and as Indian when the situation is controlled by whites. All of Berger's novels explore the processes of victimization, as each Berger protagonist struggles, whether consciously or unconsciously, to free himself from the inexorable tendency to think of himself as a victim of outrages and impositions, both humorously small and tragically large.

While Berger refuses to subscribe to any single codified philosophy, whether romantic, existential, or absurd, his characters do live in worlds that seem to operate largely on Nietzschean principles. As Frederick Turner has observed, Berger's moral stance is consistently "beyond sentimentality, beyond classic American liberalism," concerning itself with fundamentals rather than with surfaces. Like Friedrich Nietzsche, Berger assumes that "there are higher problems than the problems of pleasure and pain and sympathy," though few of his characters would subscribe to this view—their pleasure, their pain, and their sympathy being of paramount importance to them.

Those characters are a string of outrageously impossible but compellingly plausible individuals who seem, in Berger's words, to be "persistent liars" and "monsters of one persuasion or another." Berger is uniformly fond of these "monsters," and his characters can never be branded as "good" or "evil," since all are as appealing in their often bizarre excesses as they are sadly humorous in their deficiencies. Most important, all of Berger's characters *do their best.* They may trick, abuse, and betray one another, but in a world where understanding seems full of drawbacks and the irresponsible consistently victimize those who feel obligations, they are finally no more nor less than normal. In the courtroom of his novels, Berger refuses to become either judge or advocate, choosing instead to establish a dialectic of wildly opposing viewpoints. He explains that his job is to maintain these characters in equilibrium, a concern of "art and not politics or sociology."

No analysis of Berger's novels would be complete without mentioning the delights of his prose style. Berger is one of a handful of American writers, contemporary or otherwise, for whom the sentence is an event in itself. His style challenges the reader with precise but often elaborate or serpentine sentences, reflecting his conviction that "the sentence is the cell beyond which the life of the book cannot be traced, a novel being a structure of such cells: most must be vital or the body is dead." What sentence vitality means to Berger can be seen in the way he elaborates the commonplace metaphor of the "ham-fisted" punch in *Who Is Teddy Villanova?*:

> He had struck me on the forehead, that helmet of protective bone, an impractical stroke even for such stout fingers as his, had he not turned his hand on edge and presented to my skull the resilient karate blade that swells out between the base of the smallest digit and the wrist: in his case, the size and consistency of the fleshy side of a loin of pork.

This marvelous punch knocks out Russell Wren, Berger's private-eye narrator, who comes to with the equally meticulous and mannered realization: "My loafers were in a position just ahead of his coal-barge brogans, a yard from where I slumped; meanwhile, my feet, twisted on their edges and crushed under the crease between thigh and buttock, were only stockinged: he had knocked me out of my shoes!" Leonard Michaels described this style as "one of the great pleasures of the book . . . educated, complicated, graceful, silly, destructive in spirit," and his comment applies to all of Berger's novels. Noting that he looks for himself through the English language, Berger states that for him language is "a morality and a politics and a religion."

In Berger's first novel, *Crazy in Berlin*, the twenty-one-year-old Carlo Reinhart, a United States Army medic in occupied Berlin, struggles to reconcile the conflicting claims of Nazism, Judaism, Communism, and Americanism, and his own German heritage—all overshadowed by the more fundamental concepts of friendship, victimization, and survival. This first of the Reinhart novels also features the points of view of a manic series of contradictory characters, including an American intelligence officer who is an idealistic Communist, a Russian officer who wants to become a capitalist, and a cynical ex-Nazi now working as a Russian agent.

In the second Reinhart novel, *Reinhart in Love*, Berger's bumbling protagonist is discharged from the army, in which he had been happy, and returns to civilian life, which he finds singularly disastrous. His comic misadventures are guided by Claude Humbold, a wonderfully devious real-estate agent/con man for whom Reinhart reluctantly works, by the enterprising and calculating Genevieve Raven, whom he is tricked into marrying, and by Splendor Mainwaring, his black friend whose special talent is getting Reinhart into impossible situations.

Had Berger never written anything but *Little Big Man*, he would have earned a respected place in American literary history. This story of Jack Crabb's life in both the Cheyenne and white cultures of the historical as well as the dime-novel Old West has been called variously "the best novel about the West," "a Barthian western," and "a seminal event in what must now seem the most significant cultural and litarary trend of the last decade—the attempt on many fronts to develop structures, styles, ways of thinking that are beyond any version of ethnocentrism." The story has been transcribed ostensibly from the tape-recorded reminiscences of "the late Jack Crabb— frontiersman, Indian scout, gunfighter, buffalo hunter, adopted Cheyenne— in his final days upon this earth." That Jack's final days come 111 years after his first, and that he also claims to have been the sole white survivor of the Battle of the Little Bighorn, raises obvious questions about the truth of his account. Furthermore, Jack's narrative comes to the reader through the patently unreliable editorship of "Ralph Fielding Snell," a fatuous, gullible, self-professed "man of letters" who also happens to mention that he has suffered three or four nervous breakdowns in the past few years. Against these reflexive, metafictional devices, Berger balances the disarming realism of Jack Crabb's narration, its tone resonating with the wondering honesty and credibility of Huck Finn.

Frederick Turner has noted that part of the real power of this narration is derived from Jack's coming "to understand both myth and history as radically human constructs." What Turner means by "radically human constructs" can be understood from the way in which *Little Big Man* combines very different rhetorics or "codes" for talking about the Old West. Indeed, Jack's narrative consists of excerpts from and imitations of actual histories of the West, auto-biographies, dime novels, Indian studies, and other codes that are mixed together in unpredictable combinations. This jumbling of codes and voca-bularies (for example, Jack may mingle the crassest of frontier expressions with terms such as "colloquy," "circumferentially," "hitherto," or "tumult") exposes the perceptual biases of the "official" codes which have been devel-oped for talking about the Old West—whether by Zane Grey, Francis Park-man, or L. A. Hoebel (an expert on Cheyenne culture). Jack begins to realize that even when his situation seems to be defined by bullets or arrows, the real conflict lies in the clash between the often antithetical ways in which he must think of himself, whether he is to define himself and act according to Cheyenne terms, cavalry terms, capitalist terms, journalistic terms, and so on.

Accordingly, the panorama of Jack's adventures, ranging from his adoption by the Cheyenne to his gunfight with Wild Bill Hickok to his being the only white survivor of Custer's Last Stand, is shadowed by the panorama of his changing narrative styles: not only does Berger pack every classic Western theme into the novel, but he also fills it with subtly varied "codes" that make it—like all of his novels—at least in part an exploration of the workings of language. The genius of this novel is that its metafictional devices are so well woven into the fabric of Jack's fascinating story that they have eluded all but a handful of readers, reviewers, and scholars. By any standards, *Little Big Man* is a masterpiece, one of the most delightful novels ever written.

Killing Time is a kind of reflexive, even self-destructive murder mystery. Based in part on accounts by Frederic Wertham in *The Show of Violence* (1949) and Quentin Reynolds in *Courtroom* (1950) of an actual sensational murder case in 1937, *Killing Time* tells the story of Joseph Detweiler, "an awfully nice guy" who is also a psychopathic murderer. The novel opens with the discovery that someone has murdered three people in an apartment. The plot seems to be developing into a routine murder mystery or police proce-dural as the investigative machinery goes into action, but the murderer, Joe Detweiler, turns himself in even before police suspicions about him crystallize. The balance of the novel, therefore, focuses on Detweiler's conversations with the police and his lawyer. Berger's book declines, however, to become a courtroom drama and proceeds instead through a variety of conventions from the detective story and the psychological thriller, to the courtroom drama and other well-codified genres.

Although Joe is a multiple murderer and is quite mad, all other personalities in *Killing Time* lack character in comparison. Joe is the criminal, but he alone among the policemen, lawyers, and judges truly believes in law and justice. His philosphy is bizarre, but Joe manages to change the perspectives of all those who know him. What really separates Joe from those around him is his profound mistrust of language. He sees actions as truth, while language is just "talking about talk."

To a significant extent, Berger is "talking about talk" in *Killing Time*, just as he is exploring the nature of language and the nature of fiction, for this is a supremely reflexive novel. The book is full of fictions within its larger fictional frame; all of the characters apart from Joe are cast as conscious and unconscious makers of fiction. For example, Joe's lawyer derives his greatest satisfaction from "a favorable verdict returned by a jury who knew it had been hoaxed," and he explains to Joe that in the courtroom, "reality is what the jury believes." By presenting character after character whose verbal deceptions and artistry are obviously analogous to the techniques of the novelist (one character even becomes a novelist), and by putting his characters in situations analogous to that of the reader of a novel, Berger reminds his reader that the novel is just as much a hoax as any of those created by its characters. As Berger most bluntly states in the front of the book: "A novel is a construction of language and otherwise a lie."

Vital Parts, the third Reinhart novel, picks up the adventures of its protagonist in the 1960's, as the forty-four-year-old Reinhart rapidly adds to the list of windmills with which he has unsuccessfully tilted. Bob Sweet, a flashy boyhood acquaintance, replaces Claude Humbold as his business mentor, luring him into his most dubious venture to date: a cryonics foundation for freezing the dead. His tough-minded wife, Genevieve, and his surly hippie son, Blaine, both despise him, while Winona, his fat, unhappy, sweetly innocent daughter worships him. Caught in a cultural crossfire, Reinhart threatens to succumb to the pressures and perversities of modern life.

Berger's next novel, *Regiment of Women*, managed to offend reviewers and readers on both sides of the women's movement. A dystopian novel set in America in the year 2047, the book presents a society in which traditional male and female roles have been completely reversed. Not only do women control the corporate, artistic, legal, and military machinery of this society, but also they sexually dominate it, strapping dildos over their pants to assault men. In such an inverted society, to be "manly" is to wear dresses and makeup, to hold only powerless jobs, to have silicone breast implants, and to be emotionally incapable of rational thought or significant action. To be "effeminate" is to bind breasts, to wear false beards, to dress in pants and suits, to be rough, physical, aggressive, and to have a reduced life expectancy caused by stress.

Berger's protagonist in this future world is a twenty-nine-year-old insecurity riddled male secretary named Georgie Cornell. An unlikely sequence of events lands him first in prison, arrested for wearing women's clothing (slacks, shirt, tie, and coat) and incorrectly suspected of being a men's liberation agent. Driven to discover accidentally that he is stronger than his female captors, Georgie escapes and is promptly appropriated as an agent/hero by the men's liberation underground. For the rest of the novel, Georgie struggles to discover his "natural" identity, a process which forces him to cast off received idea after received idea, discarding sexual generalizations to forge a particular definition of self. He is joined in this "rebellion" by a woman FBI agent so demented that she wants only to be "masculine"—to wear dresses and makeup, to be gentle and sensitive.

Despite its topical focus, *Regiment of Women* is fundamentally concerned not with sexual roles but with the more basic problem of the hypostatizing power of language. From start to finish, the novel reminds the reader that Georgie's reality has been almost completely gloved by language, and in so doing, also calls attention both to the way language operates in the reader's reality and to the ways in which a novelist manipulates language to create an independent "reality." At the bottom of this concern with language and rhetoric lies Berger's belief that victimization in any realm starts as a linguistic phenomenon in which the generalizations and attendant rhetoric of some self-interest part company with the particulars of immediate experience. Accordingly, *Regiment of Women* is a book much more concerned with the discovery of true individuality and freedom and with the workings of language than with sexual politics.

Berger's seventh novel, *Sneaky People*, is easily his most gentle (although much of its action concerns plans for a murder). *Sneaky People* reveals Berger's ear for the American vernacular as it chronicles the coming of age of a young boy, Ralph Sandifer, in a dreamy small-town world where nothing is as bucolic as it seems. Ralph's father owns a used-car lot and plans to have one of his employees murder Ralph's mother. The drab, mousey-seeming mother secretly writes and sells pornography of the must lurid sort. Indeed, this is a book which seems to say that it is "sneaky" acts which best reveal character, and it is a book that is itself something of a sneaky act, and continues Berger's obsession with the nature of language.

Berger has described *Sneaky People* as "my tribute to the American language of 1939—to be philologically precise, that of the lower-middle class in the eastern Middle West, on which I am an authority as on nothing else." The characters in this novel speak the vital, unleveled, pre-television American vernacular of the 1930's, and the prose style of *Sneaky People* is in a sense the real subject of the book, reflecting Berger's belief that "the possibilities for wit—and thus for life—decline with the homogenization of language."

Berger's mastery of and play with prose style reaches its most exuberant high in *Who Is Teddy Villanova?* which invokes the conventions of the hard-boiled detective novel but also defies almost all of the expectations that attend those conventions. *Who Is Teddy Villanova?* gives evidence of Berger's great respect for the masters of this genre—Dashiell Hammett, Raymond Chandler, and Ross Macdonald—but it also adds a number of outlandish twists, most prominent among them being a first-person narrator who introduces himself with "Call me Russell Wren," and who tells his story "in a rococo style reminiscent by turns of Thomas DeQuincey, Thomas Babington Macaulay, and Sir Thomas Malory." Wren is an ex-instructor of English more concerned with finding readers for the play he is writing than with finding out why a series of thugs and policemen brutalize him either in search of or in the name of a mysterious Teddy Villanova, about whom Wren knows absolutely nothing. The novel follows Wren through one misadventure after another as he pursues the elusive Villanova with Ahab's passion and some curiously "fishy" metaphors (a huge thug slips thorugh a doorway "as deftly as a perch fins among subaqueous rocks").

In truth, Wren does confuse his own small-fish situation with that of Herman Melville's great quest, and his confusion is symptomatic of a more profound problem: when faced with experience, Wren always tries to organize it in terms of the fictional worlds of literary and television private eyes. Like Ralph Fielding Snell in *Little Big Man*, another preposterous "man of letters," Wren perpetually falls victim to his own linguistic hypostatizations as he persistently confuses the literary life of fictional detectives with his own situation. A detective who questions him observes: "I suspect you are living the legend of the private eye, which I confess I had always believed mythical." Wren's narrative style is governed by his immersion in the literary myth of the private eye and his prose style is governed by his pseudointellectual background, producing such wonderfully incongruous lines as: "This wench is my ward . . . Toy with her fine foot if you like, but eschew her quivering thigh and the demesnes that there adjacent lie." The result is humorously self-conscious, almost forcing the reader to step back from the action of the novel and consider its implications for the act of reading and for language use itself.

Its dust jacket announces that *Arthur Rex* is "Thomas Berger's salute to the Age of Chivalry from his own enmired situation in the Time of the Cad," and this novel has been prominently praised as "the Arthur story for our times." Berger brings to the Arthur legend both a profound respect for its mythic power and a modern perspective on the nature of its myth, as can be seen in a comment by Sir Gawaine, when, late in his life, he is asked if he does not long for the old days of action. Gawaine answers no, explaining:

> I am happy to have had them in my proper time, but of a life of adventure it can be said that there is no abiding satisfaction, for when one adventure is done, a knight liveth in expectation of another, and if the next come not soon enough he falleth in love, in the

sort of love that is an adventure, for what he seeketh be the adventure and not the lovingness. And methinks this sequence is finally infantile, and beyond a certain age one can no longer be interested in games.

Berger's version of the Arthur legend in no way diminishes the glory of Arthur's attempt or the measure of his achievement, and it equally honors the stylistic achievement of Sir Thomas Malory's telling of the legend. Berger does devote greater attention to the cause of Arthur's final tragedy, which centers in his account, on the erosion of the innocent belief that life can be governed by the simple principle of opposing good to evil. Complexity finally overwhelms Arthur: to Launcelot, he sadly admits that "evil doing hath got more subtle, perhaps even to the point at which it cannot properly be encountered with the sword." What Arthur does not realize is that strict adherence to a rigid code of conduct may create more problems than it solves, threaten order more than ensure it. Only too late do Arthur and some of his wiser knights begin to understand that the Code of Chivalry, like any inflexible system of abstract principles, comes into conflict with itself if pursued too blindly. In Berger's hands, Arthur's most anguishing discovery is not that he has been betrayed by his queen and his most trusted knight, but that his philosophy has been shallow, because "to the profound vision there is no virtue and no vice, and what is justice to one, is injustice to another."

Arthur recognizes the flaw in his great dream, but Berger makes it clear that Arthur's legend is not to be judged by the success or failure of that dream. The Lady of the Lake assures the dying Arthur that he could not have done better in his life than he did, and the ghost of Sir Gawaine offers to his king the Round Table's poignant epitaph: "We sought no easy victories, nor won any. And perhaps for that we will be remembered."

Earl Keese, Berger's protagonist in *Neighbors*, is a quiet, resonable, forty-nine-year-old suburbanite who tells people that his home sits "at the end of the road," because that phrase sounds less "dispiriting" than "dead end." In fact, his life has long since reached its apparent dead end, and it takes the arrival of mysterious and maddening new neighbors, Harry and Ramona, to confront Keese with a sequence of situations so outrageous that he can no longer maintain the hoax of his previously complacent life. Not only do Harry and Ramona (zany versions of Nietzsche's "free spirits") fail to observe the social amenities, but also they seem committed to deliberate provocation, pushing him to see how far he will go to avoid humiliation.

Their visits increasingly seem like motiveless assaults as their comings and goings produce a series of off-balance events that gradually strip Keese of his easy social assumptions and habitual responses. As his bizarrely embarrassing experiences increasingly blur the line between comedy and nightmare, his relations with all those around him begin to undergo subtle changes. He realizes that his life has grown so stale that Harry's and Ramona's aggravations may actually offer him a salvation of sorts—the chance to take control of and give style to his life. As Keese finally admits to Harry, "Every time I see you as a criminal, by another light you look like a kind of benefactor."

Madcap physical changes punctuate Berger's plot—entrances, exits, fights, a damaged car, a destroyed house—but for all its action, *Neighbors* might best be described as a series of functions of language: puns, platitudes, theories, definitions, excuses, accusations, rationalizations, promises, questions, threats—all acts performed with words. Keese knows better than to trust completely what he sees (he suffers from "outlandish illusions"), but he uncritically does believe his ears, consistently confusing rhetoric with reality, mistaking verbal maps for the territory of experience. In fact, *Neighbors* may offer the most verbal world Berger has created; like *Little Big Man*, it is a book in which language becomes the only operating reality. Vocabularies from law and ethics intertwine throughout the novel, and Berger does not fail to exploit the incongruities of the two lexicons. Terms having to do with guilt, justice, punishment, revenge, motive, confession, blame, crime, and accusation appear on virtually every page, resonating at once with the rhetoric of the courtroom and with that of Franz Kafka's *The Trial* (1925). Keese's "guilt" is not unlike that of Kafka's Joesph K., and the slapstick humor of this book records a deadly serious philosophical trial.

In *Reinhart's Women*, the now fifty-four-year-old Reinhart finally discovers something he can do well: cooking. The novel finds Reinhart ten years after his divorce from Genevieve, living with and supported by his daughter, Winona, now a beautiful and successful fashion model. His son, Blaine, last seen as a surly radical in *Vital Parts*, now is a surly, snobbish, and successful stockbroker, unchanged in his disdain for his father. Having finally admitted that he is hopeless as a businessman, Reinhart has withdrawn from the world and contents himself with managing his daughter's household and with cooking "in a spirit of scientific inquiry." Actually, cooking has become for him an aesthetic philosophy, and for the first time in his life he does not "feel as if he were either charlatan or buffoon." "Food," Reinhart notes, "is kinder than people."

Long completely at the mercy of unmerciful women, particularly his mother and his ex-wife, Reinhart can now even take in stride the news that his daughter is having a lesbian affair with a successful older businesswoman. Age has taught him that "the best defense against any moral outrage is patience: wait a moment and something will change: the outrage, he who committed it, or, most often, oneself."

Winona's lover (a female version of the con men who have always directed Reinhart's forays into business) contrives to lure Reinhart back into the world, first as a supermarket product-demonstrator, then as a guest "chef" for a spot appearance on a local television show, and the novel closes with the strong prospect of his own show: "Chef Carlo Cooks." His apparent successes, however, are not confined to the kitchen, as Reinhart escapes the gentle and loving tyranny of his daughter, emerges unscathed from an encounter with his ex-wife, and begins a promising relationship with a young woman who seems in many ways a female version of himself—intelligent, considerate, awkward. In fact, Reinhart begins to gather around him a small band of kindred souls, hoping to buy and run a quaint small-town café. Once again, the lure of business proves irresistible for Reinhart, and once again the prospect of disaster cannot be discounted, but this time the odds seem more in Reinhart's favor. Jonathan Baumbach has summed up this most recent of the Reinhart books as "Berger's most graceful and modest book, a paean to kindness and artistry, a work of quiet dazzle."

Berger's first novel, *Crazy in Berlin*, started Reinhart, "a stumbling American Odysseus," on what Berger has termed "his long career of indestructibility." The subsequent novels in the series—*Reinhart in Love*, *Vital Parts*, and *Reinhart's Women*—follow Reinhart as he grows older and, ultimately, wiser. Said by one critic to be "a clowning knight errant, pure of heart—that is, a custodian of our conscience and of our incongruities," Reinhart is an incurable idealist who really has no faith in idealism. Complexity, Reinhart's essence, is also his nemesis: he can always see both sides to every argument, feel responsibility for any injustice, and though he realizes that "true freedom is found only by being consistent with oneself," he has a very hard time figuring out how to do this, particularly in the novels before *Reinhart's Women*. Essentially, Reinhart seeks a consistent rationale for his unimpressive, awkward, but indomitable individuality. Combining the features of "a big bland baseball bat" with those of "an avatar of Job the beloved of a sadistic God," Reinhart can never shake the suspicion that he does not fit anywhere, but is nevertheless responsible for the general confusion that surrounds and usually engulfs him.

Reinhart is as ill-suited for despair, however, as he is for success. Although reminded by a successful aquaintance that he is "redundant in the logistics of life," he can never really be disillusioned, even though his dreams steadily fall prey to the practical opportunism of those around him. No match for a mother who can tell him, "if I ever thought you had truck with Filth, I'd slip you strychnine," or a shrewish wife whose advice to him is "if you're going to be an ass-kisser, then you ought to at least kiss the asses of winners," Reinhart can recognize the distinction between his secular search for a Holy Grail and the social meliorism that passes for idealism. Like all of Berger's characters, Reinhart never gives up: an indomitable toughness underlies his numerous weaknesses, and whatever the situation, he always muddles through, scarred but undaunted.

Reinhart may be Berger's greatest creation, and the Reinhart series spans Berger's career, a monument at once to its manic diversity and to its underlying unity. Both the vitality and the vision of the Reinhart books offer ample evidence that Berger is one of America's most original and most gifted novelists.

Bibliography

Landon, Brooks. "The Radical Americanist," in *The Nation*. CCV, no. 5 (August 20, 1977), pp. 151-153.

_____ . "Thomas Berger," in *Dictionary of Literary Biography Yearbook: 1980*, 1981. Edited by Karen L. Rood, Jean W. Ross, and Richard Ziegfeld.

Schickel, Richard. "Bitter Comedy," in *Commentary*. L (July, 1970), p. 76.

_____ . "Interviewing Thomas Berger," in *The New York Times Book Review*. LXXXV (April 6, 1980), p. 1.

Trachtenberg, Stanley. "Berger and Barth: The Comedy of 'Decomposition,'" in *Comic Relief*, 1978. Edited by Sarah B. Cohen.

Turner, Frederick. "Melville and Thomas Berger: The Novelist as Cultural Anthropologist," in *Centennial Review*. XIII (Winter, 1969), pp. 102-121.

_____ . "The Second Decade of *Little Big Man*," in *The Nation*. CCV, no. 5 (August 20, 1977), pp. 149-151.

Brooks Landon

ELIZABETH BOWEN

Born: Dublin, Ireland; June 7, 1899
Died: London, England; February 22, 1973

Principal long fiction

The Hotel, 1927; *The Last September*, 1929; *Friends and Relations*, 1931; *To the North*, 1932; *The House in Paris*, 1936; *The Death of the Heart*, 1938; *The Heat of the Day*, 1949; *A World of Love*, 1955; *The Little Girls*, 1964; *Eva Trout*, 1968.

Other literary forms

The first seven of Elizabeth Bowen's novels were republished by Jonathan Cape in Cape Collected Editions between the years 1948 and 1954, when Cape also republished four of her short-story collections: *Joining Charles* (1929), *The Cat Jumps and Other Stories* (1934), *Look at All Those Roses* (1941), and *The Demon Lover* (1945). The other books of short stories are *Encounters* (1923), *Ann Lee's and Other Stories* (1926), *Stories by Elizabeth Bowen* (1959), and *A Day in the Dark and Other Stories* (1965). *The Demon Lover* was published in New York under the title *Ivy Gripped the Steps* (1946) and, as the original title indicates, has supernatural content which scarcely appears in the novels. Bowen's nonfiction consists of *Bowen's Court* (1942), a description of her family residence in Ireland; *Seven Winters* (1942), an autobiography; *English Novelists* (1946), a literary history; *Collected Impressions* (1950), essays; *The Shelbourne* (1951), a work about the hotel in Dublin; *A Time in Rome* (1960), travel essays; and *Afterthought* (1962), broadcasts and reviews. A play, coauthored with John Perry and entitled *Castle Anna* was performed in London in March, 1948, but remains unpublished.

Achievements

Considered a great lady by those who knew her, Bowen draws an appreciative audience from readers who understand English gentility—the calculated gesture and the controlled response. Bowen's support has come from intellectuals who recognize the values of the novel of manners and who liken her work to that of Jane Austen and Henry James. Her contemporaries and colleagues included members of the Bloomsbury Group and of Oxford University, where the classical scholar C. M. Bowra was a close friend. Many readers know Bowen best through her novel *The Death of the Heart* and her short stories, especially "The Demon Lover," "Joining Charles," and "Look at All Those Roses," which are frequently anthologized in college texts. Bowen was made a Commander of the British Empire in 1948, and was awarded the honorary Doctor of Letters degree at Trinity College, Dublin, in 1949, and at Oxford University in 1957. She was made a Companion of

Literature in 1965.

Biography

Although born in Ireland, Elizabeth Dorothea Cole Bowen came from a pro-British family who received land in County Cork as an award for fighting with Oliver Cromwell in 1649. The family built Bowen's Court in 1776—what the Irish call a "big house"—as a Protestant stronghold against the mainly Catholic Irish and lived there as part of the Anglo-Irish ascendancy. Bowen was educated in England and spent some summers at Bowen's Court. Not until after the Irish Rising in 1916 did she come to realize the causes of the Irish struggle for independence; and in writing *Bowen's Court*, she admitted that her family "got their position and drew their power from a situation that shows an inherent wrong."

Her barrister father, when he was nineteen, had disobeyed forewarnings and carried home smallpox, which killed his mother and rendered his father mad. Preoccupied with the desire for a son, the attempt to have one nearly killed his wife in 1904, and burdened with the debts of Bowen's Court, he suffered severe mental breakdowns in 1905 and 1906 and again in 1928. He was the cause of Elizabeth's removal to England where, as an Irish outcast, her defense was to become excessively British. Living in a series of locations with her mother, she was kept uninformed of family circumstances; and, as an adult, her novels provided for her an outlet for her sense of guilt, the result of feeling responsible for the unexplained events around her. Her lack of roots was intensified with the death of her mother in 1912.

Bowen studied art, traveled in Europe, and worked as an air-raid warden in London during World War II. In 1923, she married Alan Charles Cameron, who was employed in the school system near Oxford, and they lived there for twelve years. She inherited Bowen's Court in 1928 when her father died; and in 1952, she and her husband returned there to live. Bowen's husband, however, died that year. She sold the home in 1960 and returned to Oxford.

Bowen's career as novelist spanned years of drastic change, 1927 to 1969, and, except for *The Last September*, she wrote about the present; her war experiences are reflected in the short-story collection *The Demon Lover* and in the novel *The Heat of the Day*. After 1935, she also wrote reviews and articles for *The New Statesman* and other publications, the Ministry of Information during World War II, *The Tatler* (in the 1940's), and helped edit the *London Magazine* in the late 1950's. Afflicted with a slight stammer, Bowen lectured infrequently but effectively; two of her B.B.C. broadcasts, "left as they were spoken," may be read in *Afterthought*. After a visit to Ireland in 1973, she died in London, leaving an unfinished autobiographical work, "Pictures and Conversations," which was intended to be published the next year.

Analysis

Elizabeth Bowen had a special talent for writing the conversations of children around the age of nine, as she does in *The House in Paris*. Somewhat corresponding to her personal experience, her novels often present a homeless child, orphaned and shunted from one residence to another, or a child with one parent who dies and leaves the adolescent in the power of outwardly concerned but mainly selfish adults. Frequently, management by others prolongs the protagonist's state of innocence into the twenties, when the woman must begin to assert herself and learn to manage her own affairs. (At age twenty-four, for example, Eva Trout does not know how to boil water for tea.) On the other side of the relationship, the controlling adult is often a perfectly mannered woman of guile, wealthy enough to be idle and to fill the idleness with discreet exercise of power over others. The typical Bowen characters, then, are the child, the unwanted adolescent, the woman in her twenties in a prolonged state of adolescence, and the "terrible woman" of society. Young people, educated haphazardly but expensively, are culturally mature but aimless. Genteel adults, on the other hand, administer their own selfish standards of what constitutes an impertinence in another person; these judgments disguise Bowen's subtle criticism of the correct English.

Typical Bowen themes follow as "loss of innocence," "acceptance of the past," or "expanding consciousness." The pain and helplessness attendant upon these themes and the disguise of plentiful money make them unusual. Although she writes about the privileged class, three of her four common character types do not feel privileged. To handle her themes, Bowen frequently orders time and space by dividing the novels into three parts, with one part set ten years in the past and with a juxtaposition of at least two locations. The ten-year lapse provides a measure of the maturity gained, and the second location, by contrast, jars the consciousness into revaluation of the earlier experience.

The fact that the Bowen women often have nothing to do is very obvious in *The Hotel*, set in Bordighera on the Italian Riviera, but, of greater interest, it is, like Ireland, another place of British occupancy. Guests' activities are confined to walking, talking, taking tea, and playing tennis. Mrs. Kerr is the managing wealthy woman who feeds on the attentions of her protégé, Sydney Warren, and then abandons Sydney when her son arrives. At age twenty-two, Sydney, for lack of better purpose, studies for a doctorate at home in England. Back in Italy, she gets engaged to a clergyman as a means of achieving an identity and popularity; but her better sense forces reconsideration, and she cancels the engagement and asserts her independence.

The Last September, set in 1920 when the hated British soldiers (the Black and Tans) were stationed in Ireland to quell rebellion, shows Sir Richard and Lady Myra Naylor entertaining with tennis parties at their big house. Like Elizabeth Bowen, who wrote in *Afterthought* that this novel was "nearest my heart," Lois Farquar is a summer visitor, aged nineteen, orphaned, and asking herself what she should do. An older woman tells her that her art lacks talent.

Almost engaged to a British soldier, Gerald Lesworth, she might have a career in marriage; but Lady Naylor, in the role of graceful-terrible woman, destroys the engagement in a brilliant heart-to-heart talk, in which she points out that he has no prospects.

As September closes the social season, Gerald Lesworth is killed in ambush; and as Lois—much more aware now and less innocent—prepares to depart for France, her home Danielstown is burned down, which signals her separation from the protected past.

After *Friends and Relations*, Bowen entered the most fruitful part of her career. Her next four novels are generally considered to be her best work. *To the North* has rather obvious symbolism in a protagonist named Emmeline Summers whose lack of feeling makes her "icy." She runs a successful travel agency with the motto "Travel Dangerously" (altering "Live Dangerously" and "Travel Safe"); the motto reflects both her ability to understand intellectually the feelings of others through their experience and her orphan state in homelessness. Emmeline tries to compensate for her weaknesses by imposing dramatic opposites: without a home of her own, she overvalues her home with her widowed sister-in-law, Cecilia Summers; frequently called an angel, she has a fatal attraction to the devil-like character Markie Linkwater. When Cecilia plans to remarry (breaking up the home), when Markie (bored with Emmeline) returns to his former mistress, and when Emmeline's travel business begins to fail rapidly because of her preoccupation with Markie, she smashes her car while driving Markie north; "traveling dangerously" at high speeds, she becomes the angel of death.

The cold of the North suggested by the novel's title also touches other characters. Lady Waters, who offers Emmeline weekends on her estate as a kind of second home, feeds mercilessly on the unhappiness of failed loves and gossip. Lady Waters tells Cecilia to speak to Emmeline about her affair with Markie and thereby initiates the fateful dinner party, which leads to the accident. Pauline, the niece of Cecilia's fiancé, is the orphaned-adolescent character on the verge of becoming aware of and embarrassed by sex. Bowen describes Emmeline as the "stepchild of her uneasy century," a century in which planes and trains have damaged the stability and book knowledge of sexual research (indicated by the reading of Havelock Ellis), thereby freeing relationships but failing to engage the heart. The travel and the lack of warmth make the title a metaphor for the new century's existence. With her tenuous hold on home, love, and career, Emmeline commits suicide.

The House in Paris is set in three locations, which reflect different aspects of the protagonist, Karen Michaelis: England, the land of perfect society; Ireland, the land of awareness; France, the land of passion and the dark past. Parts I and III take place in a single day in Paris; Part II occurs ten years earlier, during four months when Karen was age twenty-three. The evils of the house in Paris become apparent in the flashback and can be appreciated only through recognition of the terrible woman who runs it, Mme. Fisher, and the rootlessness of the foreign students who stay there. Among other students, Mme. Fisher has had in her power Karen and her friend Naomi Fisher (Mme. Fisher's daughter), and the young Max Ebhart, a Jew with no background. Ten years later, when Max wants to break his engagement with Naomi to marry another, Mme. Fisher interferes, and he commits suicide.

The book begins and ends in a train station in Paris. In Part I, Leopold— age nine and the illegitimate child of Karen and Max Ebhart—and Henrietta—age eleven and the granddaughter of a friend of Mme. Fisher—arrive on separate trains: Henrietta from England in the process of being shuttled to another relative, and Leopold from his adoptive parents in Italy to await a first acquaintance with his real mother. Leopold and Henrietta Mountjoy, meeting in the house in Paris, become symbolic of the possibility that, with Mme. Fisher bedridden for ten years (since the suicide) and now dying, the future will be free of the mistakes of the past. Mme. Fisher, in an interview with Leopold, tells him that the possibility of finding himself "like a young tree inside a tomb is to discover the power to crack the tomb and grow up to any height," something Max had failed to do.

Dark, egotistic, self-centered, and passionate like his father, Leopold constructs imaginatively a role for his unknown mother to play and then breaks into uncontrollable weeping when a telegram arrives canceling her visit. The mature and implacable Henrietta, orphaned like Leopold but accustomed to the vicissitudes of adult life, shows him how to crack out of the tomb of childhood. In Part III, quite unexpectedly, Ray Forrestier, who had given up diplomacy and taken up business to marry Karen in spite of her illegitimate child, urges a reunion with Leopold, takes matters into his own hands, and brings Leopold to Karen.

The three part structure of Bowen's novels is most fully realized in *The Death of the Heart*; the parts are labeled "The World," "The Flesh," and "The Devil," which follow the seasons of winter, spring, and summer. The world of Windsor Terrace, the Quaynes' residence in London, is advanced and sterile. Portia enters into this world at age fifteen, an orphan and stepsister to the present Thomas Quayne. Thomas' wife Anna, who has miscarried twice and is childless, secretly reads Portia's diary and is indignant at the construction Portia puts on the household events. Portia sees much "dissimulation" at Windsor Terrace, where doing the "right" thing does not mean making a moral choice. As one of Bowen's radical innocents who has spent her youth in hotels and temporary locations, Portia says no one in this house knows why she was born. She has only one friend in this, her first home: the head-servant Matchett who gives Portia some religious training. Of the three male friends who wait upon Anna—St. Quentin Martin, Eddie, and Major Brutt—Portia fastens on the affections of Eddie.

Spring, in Part II, brings a much-needed vacation for the Quaynes. Thomas and Anna sail for Capri, and Portia goes to stay with Anna's former governess at Seale-on-Sea. At the governess' home, dubbed Waikiki, Portia is nearly drowned in sensuality—the sights, smells, sounds, feelings—of a vulgar and mannerless household. Portia invites Eddie to spend a weekend with her at Seale-on-Sea, which further educates her in the ways of the flesh.

Portia's more open nature, on her return to London in Part III, is immediately apparent to Matchett, who says she had been "too quiet." The Devil's works are represented both obviously and subtly in this section, and they take many identities. St. Quentin, Anna, Eddie, even the unloving atmosphere of Windsor Terrace make up the Devil's advocacy. St. Quentin, a novelist, tells Portia that Anna has been reading her diary, a disloyalty and an invasion of privacy with which, after some contemplation, Portia decides she cannot live. Herein lies the death of her teenage heart, what Bowen calls a betrayal of her innocence, or a "mysterious landscape" that has perished.

Summer at Windsor Terrace brings maturity to Portia, as well as others: Anna must confront her own culpability, even her jealousy of Portia; St. Quentin, his betrayal of Anna's reading of the diary; Thomas, his neglect of his father and his father's memory; and even Matchett takes a terrified ride in the unfamiliar cab, setting out in the night to an unknown location to pick up Portia. They all share in the summer's maturation that Portia has brought to fruition.

William Shakespeare's Portia preferred mercy to justice, paralleling the Portia in this novel. Bowen's Portia observes everything with a "political seriousness." The scaffolding of this novel supports much allusion, metaphor, and drama—all artfully structured. The world, the flesh, and the Devil as medieval threats to saintliness are reinterpreted in this context; they become the locations of the heart that has been thrust outside Eden and comprise a necessary trinity, not of holiness but of wholeness. This novel earns critics' accord as Bowen's best.

Ranked by many critics as a close second to *The Death of the Heart*, in *The Heat of the Day*, Bowen uses the war to purge the wasteland conditions that existed before and during the years from 1940 through 1945. Middle-class Robert Kelway has returned from Dunkirk (1940) with a limp that comes and goes according to the state of his emotions. At the individual level, it reflects the psychological crippling of his youth; at the national level, it is the culmination of the condition expressed by the person who says "Dunkirk was waiting there in us."

Upper-class Stella Rodney has retreated from the privileges of her past into a rented apartment and a war job. Having grown impassive with the century, divorced with a son (Roderick) in the army, she has taken Robert as her lover. She has become so impassive, in fact, that in 1942, a sinister and mysterious government spy named Harrison tells her that Robert has been passing information to the enemy, and she says and does nothing.

Critics have commented frequently on this novel's analogies to *Hamlet* (1600-1601), an obvious example being Holme Dene (Dane home), Robert Kelway's country home. Psychologically weak, Robert is ruled by his destructive mother, who also had stifled his father and planted the seeds of Robert's defection from English ways. While Stella visits Holme Dene and learns to understand Robert, her son visits a cousin who tells him that Stella did not divorce her husband, as was commonly thought, but rather was divorced by him while he was having an affair, although he died soon after the divorce. Roderick, however, has managed to survive Stella's homelessness with a positive and manly outlook and, when he inherits an estate in Ireland, finds that it will give him the foundation for a future.

In *Eva Trout*, the various autobiographical elements of Bowen's work come to life: Bowen's stammer in Eva's reticence, the tragic deaths of both parents, the transience and sporadic education, the delayed adolescence, the settings of hotels and train stations. Eva Trout lives with a former teacher, Iseult Arbles, and her husband Eric while she waits for an inheritance. She turns twenty-four and receives the inheritance, which enables her to leave their home, where the marriage is unstable, to buy a home filled with used furniture. She also escapes the clutches of Constantine, her guardian who had been her father's male lover.

Eva discovers that a woman with money is suddenly pursued by "admirers," and Eric visits her in her new home. Eva subsequently lets Iseult think that Eric has fathered her child, whom she adopts in America. After eight years in American cities, where Eva seeks help for the deaf-mute child Jeremy, Eva and Jeremy return to England. From England, they flee to Paris where a doctor and his wife begin successful training of Jeremy. Back in England, Eva attempts the next phase of reaching security and a normal life. She seeks a husband and persuades the son of Iseult's vicar to stage a wedding departure with her at Victoria Station. All her acquaintances are on hand to see the couple off, but Jeremy—brought from Paris for the occasion—playfully points a gun (he thought a toy) at Eva and shoots her. In the midst of revelry, on the eve of her happiness, Eva drops dead beside the train.

Eva Trout makes a poignant and haunting last heroine for the Bowen sequence and a final bitter statement on the elusiveness of security and happiness.

Major publications other than long fiction
SHORT FICTION: *Encounters*, 1923; *Ann Lee's and Other Stories*, 1926; *Joining Charles*, 1929; *The Cat Jumps and Other Stories*, 1934; *Look at All Those Roses*, 1941; *The Demon Lover*, 1945 (published in the United States as *Ivy Gripped the Steps*, 1946); *Stories by Elizabeth Bowen*, 1959; *A Day in the Dark and Other Stories*, 1965.
NONFICTION: *Bowen's Court*, 1942; *Seven Winters*, 1942; *English Novelists*,

1946; *Collected Impressions*, 1950; *The Shelbourne: A Center of Dublin Life for More Than a Century*, 1951; *A Time in Rome*, 1960; *Afterthought: Pieces About Writing*, 1962.

Bibliography

Austin, Alan E. *Elizabeth Bowen*, 1971.
Heath, William. *Elizabeth Bowen: An Introduction to Her Novels*, 1961.
Kenney, Edwin J. *Elizabeth Bowen*, 1974.

Grace Eckley

KAY BOYLE

Born: St. Paul, Minnesota; February 19, 1903

Principal long fiction

Plagued by the Nightingale, 1931; *Year Before Last*, 1932; *Gentlemen, I Address You Privately*, 1933; *My Next Bride*, 1934; *Death of a Man*, 1936; *Monday Night*, 1938; *Primer for Combat*, 1942; *Avalanche*, 1943; *A Frenchman Must Die*, 1946; *1939*, 1948; *His Human Majesty*, 1949; *The Seagull on the Step*, 1955; *Three Short Novels*, 1958; *Generation Without Farewell*, 1960; *The Underground Woman*, 1975.

Other literary forms

Although she has published some fifteen novels, Kay Boyle's principal recognition has been for her shorter works. First published in the small magazines of the 1920's, her stories were collected in *Wedding Day and Other Stories* (1930) and *First Lover and Other Stories* (1933). The 1930's, declared her vintage period by critics, brought an O. Henry Prize for the title story of *The White Horses of Vienna and Other Stories* (1936), followed in 1941 by another for "Defeat," a story on the French collapse which also appeared in *Primer for Combat*. Published widely in *Harper's*, *The New Yorker*, *Saturday Evening Post*, and *The Atlantic*, and collected in *Thirty Stories* (1946), Boyle won the praise of contemporaries as the "best story teller now living" and the "economical housewife of the short story technique." Active as an editor and critic on small magazines such as *Contempo* and on progressive political journals, she also translated such European writers as Joseph Delteil, Raymond Radiguet, and Marie-Louise Soupault. Two volumes of short stories, *The Smoking Mountain: Stories of Postwar Germany* (1951) and *Nothing Ever Breaks Except the Heart* (1966), reflect wartime and postwar Europe. Collected recently in *Fifty Stories* (1980), Boyle's short fiction continues to appear in American periodicals.

Her poetry, also first published in small magazines, was collected in *A Glad Day* (1938) and *Collected Poems* (1962). *American Citizen Naturalized in Leadville, Colorado* (1944), based upon the experience of an Austrian refugee in the United States military, is dedicated to Carson McCullers, "whose husband is also overseas," and *Testament for My Students and Other Poems* (1970) concerns "that desperate year, 1968."

As a European correspondent after World War II, Boyle wrote nonfiction prose of both journalistic and literary distinction, including her reportage of the war crimes trial of Heinrich Babb for *The New Yorker* and her essays on civil rights and the military establishment. Two memoirs, her edition of *The Autobiography of Emanuel Carnevali* (1967) and her chapters in Robert

McAlmon's *Being Geniuses Together, 1920-1930* (1968), capture the literary underground of that period, while Boyle's most recent essays, collected in *The Long Walk at San Francisco State and Other Essays* (1970), reflect the antiwar movement of the 1960's. She has also published three illustrated children's novels, *The Youngest Camel* (1939), and the Pinky novels.

Achievements

Perhaps more consistently and tenaciously than any other twentieth century American writer, Boyle has sought to unite the personal and political, the past and present, the feminine and the masculine. Recognized in both the literary and the popular realms, her rich oeuvre unites the American and the European experience of twentieth century history.

Helpful though it may be as an outline, the conventional division of Boyle's achievement into an aesthetic period before 1939 and a polemical period after may obscure Boyle's constant focus upon the dialectic between subject and object. In the exploration of personal experience, her intense imaginative reconstruction posits the integration of conflicting aspects of the self, the struggle between self-abnegation and self-assertion, and the liberation of the individual from repressive aspects of personal or family relationships. Usually presented as a union of archetypally masculine and feminine characteristics in an individual or in a couple, often a pair of same-sex friends, Boyle's image of the completed self is one of growth beyond confining roles.

In her exploration of the self as a political creature, Boyle asserts the life-affirming potential of the individual and the community against destructive authoritarian or absolutist constructs, whether within the family or in the larger society. In her intense evocation of personal awakening to political morality, Boyle's synthesis reaches beyond the narrowly ideological to affirm the human search for tenderness in a landscape which, although distorted by repression, gives hope for regeneration. Like Thomas Mann, Ignazio Silone, and Andre Malraux, Boyle seeks to integrate the individual psyche into the larger social milieu, to make the self meaningful in history, exercising that responsibility which Mann called for when he said that had the German intellectual community remained accountable, Nazism would have been prevented.

Using modernist techniques to refute contemporary nihilism, Boyle restores perspective to the confrontation between the individual sensibility and a complex, often hidden, social reality. Her decision to address a broad audience upon political as well as personal themes, sometimes seen as a "betrayal" of her talent, might more fully be understood as a commitment to the exercise of moral responsibility through literature. Exploring the need to unite discordant psychic and political elements and to assert the life-affirming, Boyle provides in her work a model of balanced wholeness in the larger as well as the smaller world.

Biography

The cross between Kay Boyle's Midwestern roots and cosmopolitan experience produced the distinctive flavor of her work. Although born into an upper-class St. Paul family, Boyle spent her early years not in the Midwest but in the eastern United States, France, Austria, and Switzerland, and especially in the mountains, which become a symbol of human transcendence in her work. The active and involved nature of her childhood is expressed in her love of horses, riding, and skiing, and its aesthetic and creative aspect in the family custom of gathering sketches and stories into marbled covers for gift books. Katherine Evans Boyle, the "shining light" to whom Boyle dedicated her first works, provided an image of strength and purpose, introducing her daughter to the most avant-garde of European art and literature, as well as the most progressive of American populist politics. Her grandfather, Jesse Peyton Boyle, a dynamic, charismatic St. Paul businessman whom Boyle later called a "charming reactionary," was a model of the aggressive, compelling patriarch, in contrast to the more vulnerable and intuitive male figure typified by her father, Howard Peyton Boyle.

The next years saw Boyle return to the Midwest and then to the Greenwich Village literary and political circles which would provide her with friends and supporters. A series of financial reversals brought the family to Cincinnati, where Howard Boyle became established in the retail automotive business. After a brief stay at Shipley, Boyle studied violin at the Cincinnati Conservatory and architecture at Ohio Mechanics Institute, later calling hers "no education at all," saying that she had never been "properly through the eighth grade," and had instead pursued writing on her own, a training she advocated later for her students as well. Less than twenty years old, Boyle moved to New York, attended a few classes at Columbia, worked as a secretary, and met Greenwich Village literati of a progressive bent. In the space of her short stay, she worked for *Broom*, a journal of European and American experimentalism, and became acquainted with Harriet Monroe's *Poetry* magazine; with Lola Ridge, whose Gaelic ancestry she shared; and with William Carlos Williams, who became her friend and mentor. Described as a shy, timid ingenue, Boyle appears in Williams' memoirs attending Fourteenth Street parties with John Reed, Louise Bryant, Jean Toomer, Kenneth Burke, and Hart Crane.

The 1920's were another expatriate decade for Boyle. In 1921, she married Richard Brault, a French student whom she had met in Ohio, and she returned with him to his family's provincial seat. Williams recalls meeting a lonely and isolated Boyle in the vicinity of Le Havre, in which atmosphere her first two novels take place. When the marriage deteriorated and ended a few years later, Boyle remained in Paris and the Riviera, playing a central role in the literary underground of American exiles and the European avant-garde. Centered around the publication of small magazines, these groups brought Boyle together with Ernest Walsh, the effervescent poet, critic, and editor of *This Quarter*, the lover and compatriot whose death from lung injuries incurred as a pilot is recounted in *Year Before Last*.

The aesthetic of Boyle's group, represented by *Transition* magazine and Eugene Jolas, was eclectic, drawing on the work of Ernest Hemingway, James Joyce, Gertrude Stein, Ezra Pound, William Carlos Williams, and Carl Sandburg. Experimental, antirational, and antirealist, this loosely knit group ascribed to an informal creed known as Orphism, set down in the 1929 manifesto "the Revolution of the Word," signed by Boyle, Laurence Vail, Hart Crane, and others interested in representing a primarily interior reality in a rhythmic, "hallucinatory" style cognizant of current psychological and anthropological lore and inimical to standard realism and the genteel tradition. It was in this milieu that Boyle developed the lyrical subjectivism reflected in her early poems and stories, a quality she found in D. H. Lawrence and Arthur Rimbaud, Walt Whitman and Edgar Allan Poe, Stein and Joyce.

Following Walsh's death and the birth of her first child, Sharon, Boyle, out of money and dispirited, joined a communal art colony led by Raymond Duncan, Isadora's brother, whose personal charisma and exploitative idealism are reflected in a number of novelistic relationships in which one will is subsumed in another. Rescued from this amalgam of Jean Jacques Rousseau, Leo Tolstoy, and pseudoanarchistic principles by Caresse and Harry Crosby, whose unconventional sun religion and Black Sun Press were underground institutions, Boyle spent her next years in the French and British settings, which are reflected in the novels of the period. In 1931, she married the scholar and poet Laurence Vail, and in the following years bore three more daughters, Apple-Joan, Kathe, and Clover.

Emerging aboveground in the late 1930's with a Simon and Schuster contract, Boyle published a major short-story collection, *The White Horses of Vienna*, which introduced the Lippizanner horses that became an important symbol in later works. Three highly praised short novels and two longer ones followed, including her own favorite, *Monday Night*, and she received a Guggenheim Fellowship to pursue the metaphor of aviation for human history. Before the fall of France in 1939, she wrote about the collapse of Europe's democracies before Fascism. The war novels of that period are usually set in small French villages where an expatriated woman becomes involved in the political choices of various men, usually Austrians made nationless by the Anschluss. As the setting of her fiction moved from the interior to the external world, Boyle's style became more popular, often a journalistic diary, and more suited to the wider audiences of the *Saturday Evening Post* and the *Ladies Home Companion*. This development, decried by some critics, damaged her standing in literary circles in a way that it did not for an author such as Katherine Anne Porter, Boyle's friend, who kept her hackwork clearly separate from her artistic life. The conflict between resistance and collaboration addressed in her novels surfaced in Boyle's private life as well when Vail, whose sentiments are possibly expressed by several characters in *Primer for Combat*, disapproved of her efforts to secure visas for Jewish refugees, citing the "historical necessity" of Fascism. Following their divorce, Boyle married Baron Joseph Von Franckenstein, an Austrian refugee whose experiences are reflected in *American Citizen Naturalized in Leadville, Colorado* (1944), in *His Human Majesty*, and in the general situation of Austrian anti-Fascists in the continental novels of the war period.

After the fall of France, the popular novels *Avalanche* and *A Frenchman Must Die* brought the resistance experience to American audiences. Perhaps because of an establishment bias against best sellers, against explicitly political intent, or, in some cases, against the notion of a woman writing about war and the "masculine side of the male character," as one critic stated, and surely because of their superficial and rather formulaic character, these novels received negative reviews from Diana Trilling, Edmund Wilson, and *The New Yorker*. Despite this criticism, Boyle continued to address the question of individual political choice in short novels such as *Decision*, set in post-Civil War Spain, and in *Sea Gull on the Step*, which points out the growing inappropriateness of American occupation policy. After the war, Boyle's work became even more journalistic in her role as a European correspondent, chiefly in occupied Germany, where Von Franckenstein directed Amerika Dienst, an International Information Agency service, and Boyle reported on the war crimes trial of Heinrich Babb. She also commented upon European moral and political conditions in her short stories of the period, developing as she did so a vision of German and European history that she would use in later novels and in a planned nonfiction project. Like Thomas Mann, Ignazio Silone, and other anti-Fascist intellectuals, Boyle addressed the vulnerabilities which continued to expose western democracies to the totalitarian threat explored by Erich Fromm, Hannah Arendt, and many others.

Returning in 1953 to an America caught up in the events of McCarthyism, Boyle lost her job with *The New Yorker*, while Von Franckenstein, a war hero captured and tortured in Nazi Germany during his career with the OSS and an able civil servant, was removed from his state department post for his "questionable" loyalty in associating with Boyle, who was deemed a security risk. After frequent testimony by both before Internal Security committees, Von Franckenstein was reinstated in 1957. In 1958, the first American edition of *Three Short Novels*, including *The Crazy Hunter*, *The Bridegroom's Body*, and *Decision*, appeared, followed by *Generation Without Farewell*, Boyle's most ambitious postwar novel.

Following Von Franckenstein's death from cancer in 1963, Boyle continued her political commitment and her writing during the anti-Vietnam War movement, a cause in which her earlier analysis of French colonialism and European Fascism made her especially active. Supporting civil disobedience to military recruitment and induction and to weapons research and manufacture, she organized protest groups and petitions and traveled with one such group to Cambodia, where they brought the war there to media attention. The Christmas Eve of 1967, which Boyle spent in jail for her part in a sit-in at an Oakland induction center, is drawn upon in her most recent novel, *The Underground Woman*. As a teacher of creative writing at San Francisco State, she courted dismissal to join the student protest. Having received the San Francisco Art Commission's Award of Honor in 1978, Boyle retired from teaching in 1980, the year in which *Fifty Stories* appeared. In 1982, *Three Short Novels* was reissued with an introduction by the Canadian writer Margaret Atwood.

Analysis

From *Plagued by the Nightingale*, published in the early 1930's, to *The Underground Woman* in the 1970's, Kay Boyle's novels explore a complex dialectic between the personal and the political. Within the individual psyche and the social world as well there is a conflict between the human will to liberation and the authoritarian will to dominance. Not autobiographical in the usual sense, most of Boyle's early novels are imaginative reconsiderations of episodes which, although recognizable in outline in her personal life, are universalized into paradigms of human experience. Her first novel, *Plagued by the Nightingale*, which Hart Crane admired, introduced an expatriate American bride to her husband's family in their decaying French provincial seat. A crippling congenital disease afflicting all the family males, an emblem of general social decay, prevents the young husband, Nicole, from asserting independence, and requires the family to be always on the lookout to perpetuate itself. Bridget, the young wife, and Luc, a family friend whose energy and vivacity have earmarked him for marriage to one of Nicole's three sisters, are alternately drawn into and repelled by the patriarchal family's power to protect and engulf. By making the birth of an heir the condition upon which the young couple's inheritance depends, Nicole's father threatens to bring them entirely within the control of the patriarchal family. Freeing both herself and Nicole from the grasp of this decaying culture, Bridget chooses to bear a child not by Nicole, whose tainted genes would continue the cycle, but by Luc, a vigorous outsider whose health and vitality promise liberation and autonomy. Although ostensibly a narrative of personal life, this first novel becomes political in its exploration of the relationship between the self and the family, the will to immerse oneself in the group or to aspire to self-determination. The decaying and yet compelling power of the patriarchal family becomes a metaphor for Western culture itself in its paralyzing traditionalism and sacrifice of the individual to authority.

Continuing this exploration of personal experience in search of security and selfhood, *Year Before Last* recounts Hannah's final year with her lover Martin, a poet and editor terminally ill with a lung disease. In the conflict

276

Critical Survey of Long Fiction

between Martin's former lover Eve, who is his partner in the publication of the small magazine that is truly the group's creative life, and Hannah, self-sacrifice and self-assertion in pursuit of love and art are polarized. Eve, "strong and solitary" yet unfulfilled, and Hannah, vulnerable, nurturing, yet unaffirmed, both seek realization through Martin. ("What are we but two empty women turning to him and sucking him dry for a taste of life?"), only to find it in themselves as they join in his care. They are complementary aspects of the self united to assert the primacy of love and art. In this resolution of two opposing sets of personal qualities, here presented as a bond between two women in support of a positive male, the self is empowered in the larger world of artistic creation.

This resolving dyad of two women appears in slightly different guise in *My Next Bride*, the final novel of this early self-exploratory group. Victoria, left emotionally and materially destitute, joins an art colony whose tunic-wearing, dancing anarchists are led by a charismatic, idealistic, but ultimately exploitive male, Sorrel, the reverse of the vital, creative male seen in Martin. Searching for security and idealism, Victoria falls instead into complete self-abnegation in a series of underworld trials, including prostitution and abortion, which represent total abandonment of selfhood and self-determination. She finally returns to herself with the support of two friends, one of whom becomes her lesbian lover and symbolizes the union of the submissive and the assertive, the passive and the active that appears in Boyle as an emblem of the healed psyche. Boyle's treatment of homosexual themes, especially her use of the homosexual couple as an image of the completed self, is remarkable for its freedom from negative stereotypes.

In *Gentlemen, I Address You Privately*, Boyle breaks free from the reconstruction of her own experience to enter a totally imaginative landscape with a mythic quality never so markedly present before, a quality which comes to dominate the best of her later work. Here, the dyad is of two men, one a cleric cut off from experience in the contemplative heights of art and religion, the other a sailor plunged entirely into atavistic life at sea. Deserting cell and ship alike, they enter the human world, descending from Mont St. Michel (like all Boyle's mountains, a symbol of the transcendent and the ideal) to the muck of a squatter's hut, where they hide out as farmhands. In the common-law marriage of Quespelle, a brutal peasant who delights chiefly in killing rabbits, and Leonie, a madonnalike yet buddingly fertile female akin to William Faulkner's Lena Grove, the destructive and nurturing forces of the real world appear. This sharply polarized image of the human family, brutal masculinity and submissive femininity, proves too dualistic for reproduction and growth. A more positive figure of the male is posited in Munday, the gentle, intuitive aesthete who acts in defense of the old dog Quespelle intends to shoot, the bedraggled horse, the rabbits, and finally Leonie. Quespelle leaves for the city, Munday is left with Leonie. The two have a "new taste for life," transformed by the love which "binds the two . . . together, hand and foot, and then sends (them) out, away from any other comfort"; Adam and Eve emerge from paradise to establish the human community in this Faulknerian affirmation of the self in opposition to both authoritarian families and absolute ideas.

This liberation is again apparent in the better-known short novels, *Crazy Hunter* and *The Bridegroom's Body*, set in a Lawrentian English countryside where life must break free of repressive families and social structures. In *Crazy Hunter*, Nan must assert herself against the control of her mother, Mrs. Lombe, so she purchases a gelding against her mother's wishes but is disappointed when the horse suddenly goes blind. In condemning the horse to be shot, Mrs. Lombe becomes the authoritarian hunter whose presence is strong in Boyle's novel, her destructive power threatening both her husband Candy and Nan, who must assume her mother's strength without her repressiveness. Nan, in teaching the horse to jump at risk to her life, and Candy, putting his body between the veterinarian's pistol and the horse's flying hooves, establish the father's legitimate power and the daughter's liberation from the mother's control in defense of vital yet vulnerable life. The horse, which becomes for Boyle a symbol of this life-force, retains its conventional identification with passion and strength while taking on more complex qualities of aspiration, idealism, and vulnerable beauty. Usually regarded as a primarily masculine symbol, the horse in Boyle is strongly associated with the gentle, intuitive male, or with the female, and particularly with emerging female sexuality.

In *The Bridegroom's Body*, the repressive domination associated with the mother and confined to the immediate family in *Crazy Hunter* becomes patriarchal in its extension to the entire community in the country estate of the Glouries. A remote, rainy, brooding, and yet potentially fertile land, the estate is dominated by predatory hunters led by Lord Glourie, an insensitive, uncommunicative sportsman, an upper-class Quespelle, whose chief interests are hunting and drinking with other hunters. This predatory patriarchy is mirrored in the natural world by Old Hitches, chief of the swans, whose dominance is threatened by the Bridegroom, a young swan who has set up his nest in defiance of the patriarch and in assertion of a more gentle and intuitive male potency. Lady Glourie, an energetic, forceful woman in her tweeds and sturdy shoes, struggles to maintain life in an atmosphere completely lacking in spiritual and emotional fulfillment by caring for the sick sheep, the swan-master's pregnant wife, and the Bridegroom himself. An isolated figure made illegitimate and ineffective by the hunters, she longs for a female friend, hopes which rise only to be dashed when Miss Cafferty, the nurse called to care for the pregnant woman, proves not a comradely version of Lady Glourie, but rather her total opposite—young, conventionally attractive in her bright green dress, and seemingly vulnerable to male approval.

Miss Cafferty eventually vindicates herself, however, imploring Lady Glourie to "see her own beauty," her strength against the "butchers, murderers— men stalking every corner of the ground by day and night." This plea leaves Lady Glourie with the "chill" which Boyle expresses as the promise of regeneration, of union between the two versions of female strength which have as yet "no record, no sign, no history marked on them."

Recognizing the destructive power of authoritarian personal and political ideologies in a more overtly public way, the psychological detective story *Monday Night* places the search of two American exiles, Wilt and Bernie, against a collapsing moral order in prewar Europe. They pursue the case of Monsieur Sylvestre, a chemist whose testimony holds such sway in the courts that he alone has convicted a series of young men of murder in several mysterious deaths by claiming to find traces of poisonous substances in the victims' "viscera." The Americans learn that Sylvestre himself has been the murderer; this "misanthropy too savage to be repudiated" is motivated by the fact that the young men, like the Bridegroom, affirm some kind of spontaneous and generous emotional life with their families, a life Sylvestre himself has repudiated by rejecting his lover and their young son and follows by expunging himself from his world. Against the backdrop of a brisk arms business carried on with both sides in the Spanish Civil War and instances of French chauvinism and contempt for foreign nationals and their own people in a series of fixed bicycle races, one French spokesman pleads for moral action against destructive totalitarianism ("It is you who could stop it if you, your country really cared"), for "everlasting and violent freedom" against the dead authoritarianism represented by Sylvestre. Expressing the terror of vulnerable humanity, Wilt, awakened to a moral apprehension, questions, "Is it possible that a madman whose passion it has been to toy with human life and with the honor and liberty of countless victims was put in a position of highest authority?"

This individual moral awakening to larger choice underlies all the "war" novels of the 1940's. In an acclaimed short novel, *Decision*, a detached journalist is awakened to the modern hell of Fascist Spain through her chance encounter with two young men, republicans under surveillance, executed for their part in a Madrid prison hunger strike. The human capacity for resistance, expressed by a republican flamenco singer with the phrase "you get up on stage and bellow your heart out," is found in an even more life-affirming form in women, whose "power of the weak," to use Elizabeth Janeway's term, means:

We, as women, have learned and forgotten more than they have ever set down in books . . . we are sustained in our weakness by something they never even heard a whisper of . . . by a consecration to the very acts of hope, tenderness, love, whatever the name may be, which no man [that is, no fascist] has any share in.

In an awakening not narrowly political but moral in Hannah Arendt's sense, the narrator believes "at that instant . . . in each individual death, and the look of the sky as it must have been to them then, at the last trembling moment of defiance."

This apprehension of personal and political commitment exists in all the longer war novels. Set usually in mountain villages in the Savoy or the Tirol, where the ambiguity of the national identity makes choice necessary, these novels posit some encounter between an American woman exile and one or more men, often Austrian skiers, whose stateless position requires choice of a personal nationality. This interplay occurs in the context of the village and the larger nation, where alternating mendacity and heroism, resistance and collaboration, illustrates the consequences of such choices. In the short novel *1939*, Ferdl Eder's attempts to join the French army, frustrated by chauvinistic discrimination against foreigners, leaves him with no recourse but to accept the hated German passport; he leaves his American lover, who has herself abandoned a secure marriage to assert her choice.

Primer for Combat, the most involved of this group, expresses the need for what Phyl, the American woman, calls "participation . . . in the disaster. In humanity's disaster." Against a tapestry of characters in a French village during the first days of the occupation, in an introspective diary format, Boyle, in a manner reminiscent of Ignazio Silone and André Malraux, posits a complex relationship between Fascism, colonialism, classism, and democracy and self-determination as they are internalized in personal commitment. Phyl is awakened from the moral torpor of her fascination with the Austrian Wolfgang, whose opportunistic collaboration she comes to recognize by contrast with Sepp Von Horneck, another Austrian, who, refusing to exchange liberation for reconstruction, escapes to join the Gaullist forces. Ultimately, Phyl's choice is not between men but between models of human action, acquiescence, or self-assertion. "I have found my own people," she says; "I have found my own side, and I shall not betray them." Fascism is located not within the political but within the personal realm, "not a national indication but an internal one." *Primer for Combat*, the best of the war novels, synthesizes the contradiction between the personal and the political.

In two novels addressing the postwar period of occupation, *Seagull on the Step* and *Generation Without Farewell*, Boyle's vision of the dialectic between the personal and the political becomes more fully a clash between the human and the totalitarian impulses in the heart and in history. In *Generation Without Farewell*, like *His Human Majesty* a study of the human response to authoritarianism, hunters stalk their prey in an occupied German village. Both Germans and Americans, led by the American Colonel Roberts, the universal authoritarian, hunt a wild boar believed hidden in the seemingly primeval forest surrounding the village. An expression of the people's will to survive and affirm the positive aspects of their nationality against the dead hand of their Nazi past, the boar is identified by an American observer, Seth Honerkamp, with an anti-Fascist spirit and the great composers of the past. Jaeger, an anti-Nazi German searching for his roots in a past not distorted by Fascism, sees in the hunt his people's historic tendency to create an "other" whose extermination becomes an obsession, destroying human liberty and ultimately the very source of the culture. The will to liberty breaks free, however, when Robert's wife Katherine and daughter Millie, both expressions of the reproductive and nurturing power contained in the Demeter-Persephone myth so pervasive in Boyle, join Jaeger and Christop Horn. Horn is Millie's lover, whose identification with the Lippizanner horses in his care connects him with the most fertile and, at the same time, the most transcendent elements of the national spirit they represent. This identification is shared by Millie, whose pregnancy by Horn parallels the mare's pregnancy in a particularly female vision of the survival and continuity of the culture itself. Although the repressive qualities of both German and American authority unite in the hunt for the boar, an attempt to ship the horses to Brooklyn, and an epidemic of polio—the essentially American disease which fatally strikes Horn despite Jaeger and Honerkamp's efforts to secure an iron lung—Katherine joins Millie to protect the coming child, leaving a revitalized Jaeger and Honerkamp to continue their pursuit for the life-affirming aspects of both German and American culture.

The myth of the sorrowing mother in search of her daughter appears again in Boyle's last novel, *The Underground Woman*. Against the background of the American antiwar movement, Athena Gregory's psychic restoration is connected to a vision of human transcendence expressed in a community of women. Athena, a university classics teacher, her husband lost to cancer and her daughter to a satanic cult, finds herself jailed during a sit-in at an induction center. Through a process of bonding not only with the other war protesters but also with the black, Hispanic, and poor white women there, she finds personal and political transformation in an intense female friendship with Calliope, another older woman whose intuitive, emotional nature balances Athena's own rational analytical one. She also forms a friendship with a young woman musician, who replaces Athena's daughter Melanie, irrevocably lost to a cult serving Pete the Redeemer, an exploitative, charismatic leader who demands complete surrender of the will. Released from jail and from her mourning, Athena asserts her new self in a symbolic defense of all daughters when she successfully resists Pete's attempt to commandeer her home. In this affirmative vision of female power, Athena resolves the conflict between her two selves, the respectable, above-ground Athena sprung from Zeus's head and heir to his rationality, and the more emotional, intuitive "underground woman," as she joins Calliope to save the deer from the hunters and the Hispanic prostitute's children from the state. In this last novel, Kay Boyle's vision of personal and political self-affirmation advances the dialectic between subjective experience and objective reality which has marked it from the beginning.

Major publications other than long fiction

SHORT FICTION: *Short Stories*, 1929; *Wedding Day and Other Stories*, 1930; *First Lover and Other Stories*, 1933; *The White Horses of Vienna and Other Stories*, 1936; *The Crazy Hunter*, 1940; *Thirty Stories*, 1946; *The Smoking Mountain: Stories of Postwar Germany*, 1951; *Nothing Ever Breaks Except the Heart*, 1966; *Fifty Stories*, 1980.

POETRY: *A Glad Day*, 1938; *American Citizen Naturalized in Leadville, Colorado*, 1944; *Collected Poems*, 1962; *Testament for My Students and Other Poems*, 1970.

NONFICTION: *365 Days*, 1936 (edited with others); *Breaking the Silence: Why a Mother Tells Her Son About the Nazi Era*, 1962; *The Autobiography of Emanuel Carnevali*, 1967; *Being Geniuses Together, 1920-1930*, 1968 (with Robert McAlmon); *The Long Walk at San Francisco State and Other Essays*, 1970; *Enough of Dying! An Anthology of Peace Writings*, 1972.

CHILDREN'S LITERATURE: *The Youngest Camel*, 1939, 1959; *Pinky, the Cat Who Liked to Sleep*, 1966; *Pinky in Persia*, 1968.

Bibliography

Carpenter, Richard C. "Kay Boyle," in *College English*. XV (November, 1953).

——————. "Kay Boyle: The Figure in the Carpet," in *Critique*. VII (Winter, 1964-1965).

Gado, Frank. *Kay Boyle: From the Aesthetics of Exile to the Polemics of Return*, 1968.

Moore, Harry T. *The Age of the Modern and Other Essays*, 1971.

Janet Polansky

JOHN BRAINE

Born: Bradford, England; April 13, 1922

Principal long fiction

Room at the Top, 1957; *The Vodi*, 1959 (also known as *From the Hand of the Hunter*, 1960); *Life at the Top*, 1962; *The Jealous God*, 1965; *The Crying Game*, 1968; *Stay with Me Till Morning*, 1970 (also known as *The View from Tower Hill*); *The Queen of a Distant Country*, 1972; *The Pious Agent*, 1975; *Waiting for Sheila*, 1976; *Finger of Fire*, 1977; *One and Last Love*, 1981.

Other literary forms

Although John Braine is first and foremost a novelist, he has also received recognition for his contributions as a television reporter for *The Spectator*, as a film critic for *The Daily Express*, and as a book reviewer for *The People*. His only stage drama, *The Desert in the Mirror* (1951), was unsuccessful, but he has won national awards for two television adaptations of his novels: *Man at the Top* (1970, 1972) and *Waiting for Sheila* (1976). The seriousness of Braine's concern with the general problems facing the novelist is clear in his two most significant nonfiction works: *Writing a Novel* (1974) and *J. B. Priestly* (1978). In the former, he establishes guidelines for the aspiring novelist and shows how a professional writer who cannot afford to make wrong decisions "manufactures books according both to British and American readers." In the latter, Braine celebrates the life and career of a man to whom he has felt closer than "any other living writer."

Achievements

Braine's reputation is that of a frank, serious, tough-minded novelist writing from an Irish-Catholic, lower-middle-class background. His experiences in urban, industrialized Bradford, in the rural area of West Riding, and in the upper-middle-class environment of surburban London also figure prominently in his novels. Through all of his novels runs the theme of the stature of the self. He depicts real characters who have allowed their jobs, social position, material ambitions, class membership, purely physical tendencies, and social and cultural ideals to subvert their essential sensitive and loving selves. His novels belong thematically to a tradition of realistic fiction (associated particularly with England) that tries to find a public significance in personal experience.

Braine's often vitriolic criticism of English society and the frequently harsh reality of his novels have had a marked influence on contemporary British fiction. This influence began in 1957 when his first novel, *Room at the Top*, became an instant success and brought him international recognition.

Together with Kingsley Amis, Alan Sillitoe, John Osborne, John Wain, and other contemporaries, Braine ushered in with this novel a new generation of writers whose concerns led commentators to identify them as "Angry Young Men"—an epithet suggesting writers of social protest or critics of man's plight in the modern world. Their works shared a commonality of theme and style: a realistic portrayal of working-class or lower-middle-class life in England, a preference for provincial backgrounds, an anti-hero who directs his protests against the class structure and the welfare state, and an unadorned use of everyday language. Through his hero, Joe Lampton, Braine made a conspicuous contribution to that gallery of "angries": driven by ambition, envy, and greed, Joe possesses no admiration or liking for the class into which he is gate-crashing. He wants its advantages and privileges but not its conventions. Had *Room at the Top* appeared before Amis' *Lucky Jim* (1958), or Osborne's *Look Back in Anger* (1957), Braine's name might be better-known today than that of his contemporaries. Praised for its vitality, honesty, and realism, and criticized for its sentimentality and weak construction, Braine's first novel had the mixture of strengths and weaknesses characteristic of this new generation of writers.

Although *Room at the Top* was one of the most discussed—and probably one of the most praised—novels of 1957, some critics were less than enthusiastic about the promise of this new writer, and they surfaced to review his next two novels. Neither his sequel, *Life at the Top*, nor the intervening novel, *The Vodi*, enjoyed the same popularity and prestige. In considering the former, some critics felt that Braine was merely capitalizing on the success of his first novel; in the words of the reviewer for the *Saturday Review*, *Life at the Top* was "disappointingly close, both in theme and in treatment, to the serials that appear in slick magazines." As for the latter, a number of critics felt that Braine's skillful storytelling and compassionate insights into human suffering failed to compensate for such technical defects as disparity of tone, obscure details, uneven pace, and lack of climactic power. The reviewer for *The Times Literary Supplement* wrote that the book succeeded "not where it [tried] to be new but where it [did again] what was well done in *Room at the Top*."

Admirers of Braine's work were delighted to find that his succeeding novels were not imitations of anything he had written before. Many saw *The Jealous God* as an important turning point in his career. His control of characters, refined style, exploration of a religious theme, and command of point of view and focus dispelled fears that he was a one-novel writer. *The Crying Game*, on the other hand, was praised as an exposé of the decadent urban life but was criticized for weak conflicts and insufficient distance between author and hero. Others found the writing to be hasty and its characters unpleasant. On this disappointing novel with virtually no story, Anthony Burgess commented, "the hedonism is too often self-conscious, . . . and the narrative style gives off the stale apple smell of old popular magazines."

Since then, Braine has written six more novels, all of which have met with varying critical success. As an analysis of marital discord, *Stay with Me Till Morning* was deemed repetitious and ambiguous, perplexing many critics. Just as unclear, perhaps, was *The Queen of a Distant Country*. Some critics found the conversations about writers and the writer's world to be authentic, while other commentators held that this was an extremely pompous and self-indulgent book about Braine himself. His next two novels—*The Pious Agent* and *Finger of Fire*—were judged to be routinely competent exercises in the spy genre; some felt that they were saved only by Braine's characterization and smooth, sophisticated style. *Waiting for Sheila*, on the other hand, was seen as a working model for Braine's own novelistic methods. It was praised for its plotting, characterization, and celebration of sex, but reviewers regretted that Braine had not allowed himself to be carried away in a longer, in-depth study of decadent London. Most recently, *One and Last Love* was called by the London *Sunday Times* "a rhapsody" and "deliberately provoking." Reviewers felt that Braine's narrative power and his ability to evoke people and places, past memories and present experience, remain as vivid as ever in this most "autobiographical" novel of all.

As Braine's latest novel shows, he is a writer who is still capable of surprises. Among postwar British novelists, he is distinguished by his stubborn integrity and by his craftsmanship.

Biography

John Gerard Braine was born April 13, 1922, in the Nonconformist city of Bradford, Yorkshire. His parents, Fred and Katherine, were lower-middle-class Catholics and therefore part of a distinguishable minority. His father was a works superintendent for the Bradford Corporation, his mother a librarian whose Irish-Catholic family came, along with a colony of Irish, to Yorkshire during the potato famine of the 1840's. Much like the attitude of the headmaster's wife toward her students in Cyril Connolly's *Enemies of Promise*, (1939), Braine's mother expected great things of her son; she "supercharged" him, to use Connolly's words, and he responded both as a student and later as a professional writer.

Braine's formal education, while it lasted, was "very good." From 1927 to 1933 he attented the state-run Thackley Boarding School, where, along with his exposure to Charles Dickens and Thomas Babington Macaulay, he found the predominantly Protestant, working-class atmosphere an asset to an aspiring writer: "One is pitchforked into the only tenable position for a writer; on the outside, looking in." After passing his examinations with honors, he was graduated in 1933 to St. Bede's Grammar School, Heaton, and for the first time was made aware of "a split between the social world of home and school." At Thackley, Braine had been "a mildly mixed-up little boy"; at St. Bede's, he found himself "wildly at variance with the whole world" as he knew it. His recurring nightmare is that he is back at St. Bede's and aware of improperly done homework, wasting time, allowing people to get ahead of him, guilt, and above all, physical pain. Although he left school at sixteen without graduating, five years later he received his school certificate by correspondence courses. Braine has no regrets about either school, however, for the experiences gave him what he needed: the essentials of English grammar and lessons about the world in which he lived, "which meant knowing about what had happened in the past."

For the next two years, Braine drifted in typical success-story pattern from one dull job to another—as an assistant in a furniture shop, a secondhand bookshop, and a pharmaceutical laboratory, as well as a "progress chaser" in a piston ring factory. In 1940, he became a librarian at the Bingley, Yorkshire Public Library and—with time out as a telegrapher in the Royal Navy (1940-1943), a free-lance writer in London (1951-1953), a patient suffering from a recurrence of tuberculosis (between 1952 and 1954), and a student at library school—worked as a librarian until 1957. In that year, success of *Room at the Top* finally made it possible for him to quit his job and devote all his time to writing. He was then undeniably confirmed in his vocation as a writer.

Although Braine says he cannot remember ever wanting to be anything but a writer, his struggle toward that goal had little of the heady directness that characterizes Joe Lampton's shortcut to the top. The writer in him first broke loose in 1951, when he left behind the security of a home, job, and family tradition in business to pursue the vocation of a free-lance writer in London. He knew he was a writer, though to prove it he had published only one story, a few poems and articles (the latter in the *Tribune* and *New Statesman*), and had written an unperformed play, *The Desert in the Mirror*. Although he was attracted by a desire for independence, the excitement of the "big city," London, and the illusion of bohemia; the most important reason for this change was the feeling that he had about Bingley in particular and the North in general, "the feeling that there was something to be said." Only by leaving the North could he see it clearly enough to write about it. "It was like stepping away from an oil painting: when one's too near, one can see only a collection of smudges."

The confidence to begin what later became *Room at the Top* (originally entitled *Born Favourite*) came when literary agent, David Higham, read Braine's profile of his Irish grandmother in *New Statesman*. Paul Scott, then in charge of fiction at Higham's, told Braine he should write a novel, that the novel was his "true medium." In September, Turnstile Press offered him an advance subject to a synopsis and a sample chapter; not until 1953, however—after Turnstile's rejection, his mother's death, treatment for tuberculosis, and four more rejections—was the novel accepted for publication. Looking back on this period in his life, Braine feels that the sacrifices he made were necessary ones: "What gave my novel edge and urgency was my consciousness of what I had sacrificed in order to write it." In the foundations of *Room at the Top* are buried his despair on first arriving in London, his tears after the failure of *Desert in the Mirror*, and the agony when Turnstile rejected the novel. "There had to be suffering, there had to be failure, there had to be total commitment." Indeed, this commitment continued as Braine went on to write ten more novels in the following twenty-five years. In each of the novels, the reader finds a preoccupation with what Braine is most familiar: Northern England, Catholicism, and the relationships between men and women.

Analysis

"What I care about the most," John Braine wrote in the 1960's, "is telling the truth about human beings and the world they live in. . . . And every word I write is a celebration of my love for the created world and everyone and everything within it." In *Room at the Top*, *The Jealous God*, and *Waiting for Sheila*, Braine demonstrates the kind of truth-telling he describes, a truth-telling distinguished by exact observations, honesty of vision, and a clear and workmanlike style. Typically, his heroes are harried by a desire for personal affirmation, a desire they can seldom articulate or suppress. Worldly success, sensual gratification, money especially, are the only ends they know or can name, but none of these slakes their restlessness. Braine's heroes grapple desperately for money, they lacerate themselves climbing to success, yet they remain sullen and bewildered, always hopeful for some unexpected sign by which to release their bitter craving for a state of grace or, at least, illumination. In the midst of humanity's inevitable corruption and consequent need for redemption, Braine implies a vision much like that of J. B. Priestley's: "a vision of a just society, a civilized and harmonious whole, a society in which there would be no alienation."

Braine's assault on British life begins with *Room at the Top*, a familiar "rags-to-riches" story about an individual who has glimpses of life beyond the reach of his environment, his struggle to achieve, his success after the sacrifice of his own soul. To this pattern, Braine has added another theme: any society is corrupt which demands the sacrifice of integrity as the price of success. Thus, Joe Lampton, as narrator, represents in the modern British novel a new species: the predatory, northern, working-class hero with long-range ambitions to achieve lusty affluence.

A significant departure for Braine is evident in his fourth novel, *The Jealous God*, in which he draws on his experiences as a Catholic to trace the influence of the Church upon the personal life of a deeply religious yet sensual man. Unlike Joe Lampton, whose ambitions were material, Vincent Dungarvan's ambitions are spiritual. Superimposed on this material is a study of an overpowering mother-son relationship, all of which gives new life to what E. M. Forster called "the undeveloped heart."

Waiting for Sheila, on the other hand, looks at an aspect of sex that is a major theme in other Braine novels as well: what it means to be a man. With its tragic implications, vivid class-consciousness, and powerful portrayal of upper-middle-class life in a London suburb, *Waiting for Sheila* typifies the realistic impulse behind all of Braine's writing as he catches the wave of a permissive society.

About *Room at the Top*, Kenneth Allsop quotes Braine as saying: "In the Welfare State the young man on the make has to be a bit tougher and learn how to fiddle more cleverly. My job in writing about Joe Lampton was to look at him clearly." Like all of his novels, this one is rich in class overtones. Braine's working-class hero comes to a large provincial town from a slummy outpost of depression, demanding more than a minimum of material comforts and a chance to sneer at the pretension of the bourgeoisie. Lampton demands the best—"an Aston-Martin, 3-guinea linen shirts, a girl with a Riviera suntan"—and gets it by marrying the rich man's daughter. His triumph over his upbringing and his natural instincts is, however, a sour one; the price of his success is the abandonment of his true love-relationship with an older woman and her subsequent suicide, a catastrophe for which his arrival at the top proves no compensation.

Braine's Yorkshire heritage is a strong presence in the novel. The speech, landscape, and people of his home county reflect a conscious provincialism in much of his work. Here Bradford shows up as the archetypal industrial city which "more than any other in England is dominated by a success ethos." Warley, like Bradford, is a drab, soot-covered city where human life is secondary to trade, where there is little culture, and where there are the very rich and the very poor.

The novel also invites comparisons with the works of Horatio Alger. Like the typical Alger hero, Joe Lampton achieves his ambition not by hard work or even by ruthlessness, but by being lucky enough to attract the attention of a rich man. Whereas the Alger hero does this by saving the rich man's daughter from some menace, Lampton does it by impregnating the rich man's daughter, a girl he does not love. Moreover, whereas Alger leaves the reader with the assurance that his hero is going to live happily ever after, at the end of *Room at the Top*, the reader knows very well that Lampton is bound to lead a miserable life. Powerful in scheme, plot, and, narrative thrust, *Room at the Top* is a moral fable about ambition which very much epitomizes its age.

Essentially a variation on the eternal triangle, Braine's fourth novel, *The Jealous God*, dramatizes the conflict between an unmarried Catholic (Vincent Dungarvan), a divorced Protestant with whom he has an affair (Laura Heycliff), and the teachings of his Church. This time, Braine portrays the everyday working-class life of the Irish in a smoke-gray milltown in the North of England. Unlike *Room at the Top*, *The Jealous God* never visits the modern industrial world of Warley with its struggles for economic and social success.

Here, Braine's concerns are spiritual, not material.

Like Joe Lampton, the hero is still an outsider, but this time he is a Catholic history teacher who finds himself torn between his vocation and the novelty of sex. Also unlike Lampton, he is, at thirty, still a virgin, a nonsmoker, and almost a teetotaler. Although his ardently Catholic mother hopes he will go into the Church to make up for his father's failure, Dungarvan is sidetracked by his first affair, with Laura Heycliff, a pretty librarian, and then by his sister-in-law, Maureen, who seduces him. Unlike Lampton, for whom sex was as simple and desirable as money, Dungarvan has a complicated conception of the ideal relationship between the sexes. Unlike Lampton, too, he is not a character type: neither conformist nor rebel, he is himself—confused, full of conflicts, hard to get along with, but himself.

A mixture of romantic novel, egocentric narrative, fantasy, and explicit sexual document, Braine's ninth novel, *Waiting for Sheila*, once again dissects the trappings of success as modern society has come to view it. Jim Seathwaite, a Northerner, is a familiar hero to readers of *Room at the Top*. He moved to a southern Surrey suburb, became successful as general manager of Droylsden's department store, and married Sheila, the chairman's former secretary. The usual Braine touch of price tags places Seathwaite in the "made it" grade: they own a five-bedroom, two-bath home with all of the modern conveniences, including a professionally landscaped garden. Beneath this veneer, however, the reader comes to learn of an inadequate man scarred by a wartime childhood during which his mother was unfaithful to his father, who died the day he discovered her infidelity. Braine's innovative use of the theme of the unfaithful wife (rather than the more common theme of the unfaithful husband) is but one of several departures in this novel.

The novel is deceptively simple in style and structure. For example, throughout the book Braine observes the unities: the reader does not leave Seathwaite's home; the action occurs within a few hours. Braine tells the story in the first person, in a stream-of-consciousness narrative—another departure for him—from the point of view of a thirty-year-old neurotic who has a conscience. He is sitting in solitude and drinking himself stupid while recalling his childhood, his adolescence, and his early manhood in one long, Freudian confession. Almost like a patient on a psychiatrist's couch, he hints, then finally reveals the truth: his wife is also unfaithful, and he feels as helpless as did his father. The reader learns that he finds in the lascivious Sheila the earth-mother and bitch-lover he sensed first, at seven, in his mother—a self-indulgent beauty who drove his working-class father to drink and a muddy grave. Thus, another theme in the work is the nuances and compromises of marriage—a general theme with which Braine is concerned in all of his books.

If he has never been short of detractors, Braine has had his defenders, too. Over the past twenty-seven years his reputation has grown as a middlebrow writer who has mastered the basics of his craft. Few writers today have a firmer sense of milieu. His ear for dialogue is accurate, and his grasp of narrative technique is impressive. With his talent, his tolerance of human foibles, and his total commitment to writing, Braine is a significant figure in modern British fiction, an honest and perceptive observer of the social scene.

Major publications other than long fiction
NONFICTION: *Writing a Novel*, 1974; *J. B. Priestly*, 1978.

Bibliography
Alayrac, Claude. "Inside John Braine's Outsider," in *Caliban*. VIII (August, 1971), pp. 113-138.
Allsop, Kenneth. *The Angry Decade: A Survey of the Cultural Revolt of the Nineteen-Fifties*, 1958.
Blehl, Vincent F. "Look Back at Anger," in *America*. CIII (April 16, 1960), p. 65.
Burgess, Anthony. *The Novel Now: A Guide to Contemporary Fiction*, 1967.
Corke, Hilary. "Getting to the Bottom of the Top," in *The New Republic*. CXLVII (November 3, 1962), pp. 23-24.
Fixx, James F. "The Author," in *Saturday Review*. XLV (October 6, 1962), p. 20.
Fraser, G. S. *The Modern Writer and His World*, 1964.
Harkness, Bruce. "The Lucky Crowd—Contemporary British Fiction," in *English Journal*. XLVIII (October, 1958), pp. 395-396.
Harvey, W. T. "Have You Anything to Declare? Or, Angry Young Men: Facts and Fiction," in *International Literary Annual*, 1958.
Hilton, Frank. "Britain's New Class," in *Encounter*. X (February, 1958), pp. 62-63.
Hurrell, John D. "Class and Conscience in John Braine and Kingsley Amis," in *Critique*. II (Spring-Summer, 1958), pp. 40-42.
Karl, Frederick R. *The Contemporary English Novel*, 1962.
Meckier, Jerome. "Looking Back at Anger: The Success of a Collapsing Stance," in *Dalhousie Review*. LII (Spring, 1972), pp. 53-57.
Salwak, Dale. *John Braine and John Wain: A Reference Guide*, 1980.
_____ . *Literary Voices No. 2: Britain's Angry Young Men*, 1982.
Whannel, Paddy. "Room at the Top," in *Universities and Left Review*. VI (Spring, 1959), pp. 21-24.
Wilson, Colin. "The Writer and Publicity: A Reply to Critics," in *Encounter*. XIII (November, 1959), pp. 10-11.

Dale Salwak

RICHARD BRAUTIGAN

Born: Tacoma, Washington; January 30, 1935

Principal long fiction

A Confederate General from Big Sur, 1965; *The Abortion: An Historical Romance*, 1966; *Trout Fishing in America*, 1967; *In Watermelon Sugar*, 1968; *The Hawkline Monster: A Gothic Western*, 1974; *Willard and His Bowling Trophies: A Perverse Mystery*, 1975; *Sombrero Fallout: A Japanese Novel*, 1976; *Dreaming of Babylon: A Private Eye Novel 1942*, 1977; *The Tokyo-Montana Express*, 1980; *So the Wind Won't Blow It All Away*, 1982.

Other literary forms

Richard Brautigan began his literary career as a poet. "I wrote poetry for seven years," he noted, "to learn how to write a sentence." Though a poet for many years, Brautigan maintained that his ambition was to write novels: "I figured I couldn't write a novel until I could write a sentence." Although most of Brautigan's recent work has been in the novel form, he has also published several books of poetry and a collection of short stories (*Revenge of the Lawn*, 1971).

Achievements

Short-story writer, novelist, and poet, Brautigan has created a stream of works which resist simple categories—in fact, defy categorization altogether. Much of his popularity can be attributed to his peculiar style, his unconventional plots, simple language, and marvelous humor which together provide a melancholy vision of American life and the elusive American dream.

Brautigan's novels are generally characterized by the appearance of a first-person narrator (sometimes identified in the third person as Brautigan himself) who presents an autobiographical, oftentimes whimsical story. Brautigan's work employs simple, direct, short, and usually repetitive sentences. In his best work, he has an uncanny ability to create vibrant and compelling scenes from apparently banal subject matter. It is the voice of the "I," however, that carries the Brautigan novel, a voice that often unifies virtually plotless and quite heterogeneous materials.

Much of Brautigan's work involves the search for simplicity—an expansion of the Emersonian search for pastoral America. Yet, the complacent rural life is no longer available in Brautigan's world: all the trout streams have been sold to the highest bidder, all the campgrounds are already filled, in fact overflowing; yet, the search must go on for new places where the imagination can still roam free—to a pastoral America where the individual can escape the suffocating din of technocracy.

Brautigan's work has evolved into a new, unorthodox version of the American novel. His experimentation with language, structure, characterization, plot, and motif breaks new ground. Because of this, many critics have been unable to characterize his work with ease. Unable to pinpoint his exact standing, they have dismissed him as a counterculture phenomenon, a faddish nonentity. Although Brautigan's oeuvre is indeed very uneven, his best work is genuinely original and insures him a lasting place in American literature.

Biography

Richard Brautigan was born and reared in the Pacific Northwest. The son of Bernard F. Brautigan and Lula Mary Keho Brautigan, he spent his early years in Washington and Oregon. His literary career took hold when, in 1958, he moved to San Francisco, California, and began writing poetry in the company of Lawrence Ferlinghetti, Robert Duncan, Philip Whalen, and Michael McClure. The company he kept led to his initial identification as a Beat poet, but Brautigan's unique and now well-known style resisted the classification.

Resisting crass commercialism and the profits linked with corporate America, Brautigan's first books were published primarily for the benefit of his friends and acquaintances. Success finally forced him to allow a New York publication of his work in the 1960's, however, and Grove Press published his *A Confederate General from Big Sur*. Shortly after his change of allegiance from Four Seasons Foundation in San Francisco to Grove Press in New York, Brautigan was invited to become poet-in-residence at Pasadena's California Institute of Technology. Although he had never attended college, he accepted the invitation, and spent the 1967 academic year at the prestigious school.

In 1957, Brautigan married Virginia Diorine Adler. They had one daughter, Ianthe, and later were divorced. Brautigan now divides his time among three places: Tokyo, San Francisco, and, when in retreat or fishing, a small town in Montana.

Analysis

Richard Brautigan's first published novel, *A Confederate General from Big Sur*, is perhaps his funniest. A burlesque of American society long after the Civil War, the story is told by Jesse, a gentle, shy, withdrawn narrator (not unlike Brautigan himself) who meets Lee Mellon, a rebel, dropout, and activist living in San Francisco. Lee soon moves to Oakland, where he lives, rent-free, at the home of a committed mental patient. The story then moves to Big Sur, where Lee and Jesse live in a cabin, again owned by a mental patient. As Jesse and Lee figure out how to cope with life and no money, they find a fortune of six dollars and some loose change, get rip-roaring drunk in Monterey, and discover Elaine and a great deal of money. Johnston Wade, a crazed insurance man, arrives on the scene, informing everyone that he is fleeing from his wife and daughter (they want to commit him to a mental institution). He leaves as abruptly as he arrived, remembering an important business appointment he must keep. The book ends, as it must, without ending.

In *A Confederate General from Big Sur*, Brautigan is facing the question of how to cope with civilization. The flight from technology toward wilderness holds risks of its own. Brautigan offers no answers. Human life is not unlike that of the bugs sitting on the log Jesse has thrown into the fire. They sit there on the log, staring out at him as the flames leap around them.

The theme of the novel is the ambition to control one's life and destiny. The ownership of the Big Sur log cabin by a mental patient, and Johnston Wade's own mental aberrations, only serve to illustrate the fleeting control all people have over their lives. Brautigan introduces Wade to burlesque the myth of American destiny. He is a parody, a ridiculous image of American business and technocracy: the self-made man running away from his wife and child who suddenly remembers an important business engagement.

Although not published until 1968, *In Watermelon Sugar* was written in 1964, during Brautigan's evolution from poet to novelist. The book reflects this evolutionary change, for in many ways it is more poetic than novelistic in its form. The story is that of a young man who lives in a small commmunity after an unspecified cataclysm. In the first of the three parts of the book, the shy and gentle narrator tells the reader about himself and his friends. Their gentle life was not always so, he explains, and he tells about iDEATH, a central gathering place which is more a state of mind than an actual physical location. In the second part of the novel, the narrator has a terrible dream of carnage and self-mutilation. The third part of the book begins with the narrator's awakening, strangely refreshed after the terrible dream. The gentle, leisurely pace of the first part then restores itself.

In Watermelon Sugar is like Aldous Huxley's *Brave New World* (1932): a Utopian novel of the Garden of Eden, springing forth out of the chaos of today's world. It is his vision of the rustic good life in postindustrial society. From watermelons come the juice that is made into sugar that is the stuff of the lives and dreams of the people of iDEATH. By controlling their own lives, by creating their own order, the people of iDEATH recover society from chaos. The sense of order and recurrence is set in the very first line of the book, which both begins and ends "in watermelon sugar." That phrase is also used as the title of the first part of the book, as well as the title of the first chapter. Like a refrain, it sets a pattern and order in a world in which people live in harmony with nature and with their own lives.

Like several of Brautigan's books, *The Abortion: An Historical Romance* spent some time in the library of unpublished books which it describes, where dreams go (and can be found). The world of *The Abortion* is that of a public library in California; not an ordinary library, but one where losers bring their unpublishable books. Again Brautigan's narrator is a shy, introverted recluse—the librarian, unnamed because he is ordinary, like the people who bring their books to the library to have them shelved. Brautigan himself visits the library at one point in the novel, to bring in *Moose*; he is tall and blond, with an anachronistic appearance, looking like he would be more comfortable in another era. That circumstance is certainly the case with the narrator as well.

There is less action in *The Abortion* than in most of Brautigan's novels; the book plods along slowly, mimicking its central theme, which is that a series of short, tentative steps can lead one out of a personal and social labyrinth and toward the promise of a new life. Before the reader knows it, however, the librarian is out in the rain with a girl; she gets pregnant; and they journey to Tijuana to have an abortion. The girl is called Vida, and she represents life in the twentieth century. The librarian struggles with his inner self, afraid to move from the old ways, afraid to let go of his innocence. Brautigan contrasts him with his partner, Foster, a wild caveman who takes care of the books that have been moved from the library to dead storage in a cave. Foster is loud and outgoing—the opposite of the timid librarian— and he thinks of the library as an asylum.

With Vida, the librarian becomes embroiled in a quest for survival. Vida brings him out of the library into the world of change and conflict. He is frightened by it, but, step by tentative step, he confronts it.

The Abortion is a commentary on American culture. Brautigan draws a loose parallel between the library and American history; the librarian-narrator is the thirty-sixth caretaker of the library; at the time the book was written, there had been thirty-six presidents of the United States. The origins of the mysterious library go back into the American past as well, just as Brautigan himself appears as an anachronism from an earlier, easier time.

While Brautigan laments the times gone by and yearns for the "good old days," the leisurely pace of the library, he also holds out hope for a fresh alternative. American culture has nearly been destroyed—the playboy beauty queen named Vida hates herself, and bombs and industrial technocracy threaten lives and deaden spirits. Strangely enough, by destroying life—by the abortion—one can begin anew, start a new life. The narrator and Vida share this hopefulness, which was widespread in the counterculture when *The Abortion* was published.

With *The Hawkline Monster: A Gothic Western*, Brautigan began a series of novels which adapt the conventions of genre fiction in a quirky, unpredictable manner. Not strictly parodies, these hybrids sometimes achieve wonderful effects—odd, unsettling, comical—and sometimes fall flat. Combining the Gothic novel, the Western, and a dash of romance, *The Hawkline Monster* is set in eastern Oregon during 1902 and centers on a magical Victorian house occupied by two equally baffling Victorian maidens with curious habits. The unreality of the situation does not affect the two unruffled Western heroes of the book, however, who methodically go about their task of killing the Hawkline Monster. The problem is not only to find the monster but also to discover what it is; the ice caves under the house complete the unreality of the situation. Brautigan moves lyrically from the mundane to the magical in this fusion of the real and the surreal.

Trout Fishing in America, Brautigan's most famous novel and still his best, is a short, visionary inscape on the American nightmare. Brautigan has created a tragic symbol of what has happened to America: the trout streams are all gone, the campgrounds are full; escape to the American pastoral is no longer possible. Yet Brautigan assures his readers that all is not lost—there is still a place where they can find freedom. If all the land is being used and one cannot physically escape the city, then one must escape to the pastoral realm of one's imagination. Trout fishing, Brautigan insists, is thus a way of recapturing the simple while remaining aware of the complex.

Trout Fishing in America, like much of Brautigan's work (including his latest novel, *So the Wind Won't Blow It All Away*), is autobiographical. The gentle, withdrawn narrator uses trout fishing as a central metaphor. A victim of the technological world, the narrator creates his own watery realm, complete with its own boundaries—a place where he can find solace from the technological stranglehold. His vision implies that all people have a fundamental right to the abundant richness and good life that America can provide, but that are denied to many because the bankrupt ideas of the past still hold sway. Aware of the complexities of American life, Brautigan seems to be exhorting his readers to recapture the simple life, to escape the confinement of the city for the freedom of the wilderness. If that wilderness in the actual sense is cut off and no longer accessible; if all the trout streams have been developed, disassembled, and sold; if the horizon is now not new but old and despoiled; if the parks are already overcrowded; if there is no other way, then one must escape through the imagination.

In *So the Wind Won't Blow It All Away*, Brautigan gives readers a glimpse of what post-Trout-Fishing-in-America life has become. Billed as an American Tragedy, *So the Wind Won't Blow It All Away* instead focuses on the tragedy that America and American life has become: "dust . . . American . . . dust."

Written, as are most of his novels, in the first person, Brautigan's novel is the memoir of an anonymous boy reared in welfare-state poverty somewhere in the Pacific Northwest. Unloved but tolerated by his mother, the boy and his family go from town to town, meeting an odd assortment of minor characters. Although undeveloped, these characters serve to carry the novel's theme and serve as victims of the technocracy America has become. There is an old pensioner who lives in a packing-crate shack; adept at carpentry, the old man built a beautiful dock and boat and knows all the best fishing spots on the pond near his home, but he does not use his knowledge or equipment. A gas-station attendant who cares nothing about selling gas but likes to sell worms to fishermen also appears on the scene. There is a thirty-five-year-old alcoholic who traded ambition for beer; charged with the safety of the sawmill, the man dresses in finery (although readers are told that his appearances are not true-to-life), cares nothing about his job, and passes his life by, continually encircled by boys who swoop like vultures to take the empty bottles back to the store for credit. Like America herself, the guard had brittle bones resembling dried-out weeds. Finally, Brautigan introduces a husband and wife who, each night, carry their living-room furniture to the pond, set it up, and fish all night.

Like the end of a late summer afternoon, Brautigan presents America as having come to the end of its greatness. The technological success that spurred the country to greatness has resulted in its downfall. The husband and wife have changed all their electrical lamps to kerosene and await the cool evening with its refreshing possibilities, but as they patiently fish in the wrong spot, America goes on, killing its imagination with the technology of mindless television.

So the Wind Won't Blow It All Away ends with the horrible climax of the death of a boy, shot by mistake in an orchard that has been left to die. With that end, however, is the beginning of a new life, for, like the orchard left alone to die, new fruit will grow. The novel recalls the message of *The Abortion*: the confinement of the city for the freedom of the wilderness, television for imagination are choices people have; with this novel, Brautigan returns to the successful themes of his earliest novels, warning that to go on will result only in dust, American dust.

Major publications other than long fiction
SHORT FICTION: *Revenge of the Lawn: Stories 1962-1970*, 1971.
POETRY: *The Return of the Rivers*, 1957; *The Galilee Hitch-Hiker*, 1958; *Lay the Marble Tea: Twenty-four Poems*, 1959; *The Octopus Frontier*, 1960; *All Watched over by Madness of Loving Grace*, 1967; *The Pill Versus the Springhill Mine Disaster*, 1968; *Please Plant This Book*, 1968; *Rommel Drives on Deep into Egypt*, 1970; *Loading Mercury with a Pitchfork*, 1976; *June 30th, June 30th*, 1978.

Bibliography
Clayton, John. "Richard Brautigan: The Politics of Woodstock," in *New American Review*. XI (1971), pp. 56-68.
Malley, Terence. *Richard Brautigan*, 1972.

David Mike Hamilton

CHARLOTTE BRONTË

Born: Thornton, England; April 21, 1816
Died: Haworth, England; March 31, 1855

Principal long fiction
Jane Eyre, 1847; *Shirley*, 1849; *Villette*, 1853; *The Professor*, 1857.

Other literary forms
The nineteen poems which Charlotte Brontë selected to print with her sister Anne's work in *Poems by Currer, Ellis, and Acton Bell* (1846) were her only other works published during her lifetime. The juvenilia produced by the four Brontë children—Charlotte, Emily, Anne, and Branwell—between 1824 and 1839 are scattered in libraries and private collections. Some of Charlotte's contributions have been published in *The Twelve Adventurers and Other Stories* (1925), *Legends of Angria* (1933), *The Search After Hapiness* (1969), *Five Novelettes* (1971), and *The Secret and Lily Hart* (1979). A fragment of a novel written during the last year of Brontë's life was published as *Emma* in *Cornhill Magazine* in 1860 and is often reprinted in editions of *The Professor*. *The Complete Poems of Charlotte Brontë* appeared in 1924. Other brief selections, fragments, and ephemera have been printed in *Transactions and Other Publications of the Brontë Society*. The nineteen-volume *Shakespeare Head Brontë* (1931-1938), edited by T. J. Wise and J. A. Symington, contains all of the novels, four volumes of life and letters, two volumes of miscellaneous writings, and two volumes of poems.

Achievements
Brontë brought to English fiction an intensely personal voice. Her books show the moral and emotional growth of a protagonist almost entirely by self-revelation. Her novels focus on individual self-fulfillment; they express the subjective interior world not only in thoughts, dreams, visions, and symbols but also by projecting inner states through external objects, secondary characters, places, events, and weather. Brontë's own experiences and emotions inform the narrative presence. "Perhaps no other writer of her time," wrote Margaret Oliphant in 1855, "has impressed her mark so clearly on contemporary literature, or drawn so many followers into her own peculiar path."

The personal voice, which blurs the distance between novelist, protagonist, and reader, accounts for much of the critical ambivalence toward Brontë's work. Generations of unsophisticated readers have identified with Jane Eyre; thousands of romances and modern gothics have used Brontë's situations and invited readers to step into the fantasy. Brontë's novels, however, are much more than simply the common reader's daydreams. They are rich enough to allow a variety of critical approaches. They have been studied in relation to traditions (Gothic, provincial, realistic, romantic); read for psychological, linguistic, Christian, social, economic, and personal interpretations; analyzed in terms of symbolism, imagery, metaphor, viewpoint, narrative distance, and prose style. Because the novels are so clearly wrought from the materials of their author's life, recent psychoanalytic and feminist criticism has proved rewarding. In Brontë's work, a woman author makes significant statements about issues central to women's lives. Most of her heroines are working women; each feels the pull of individual self-development against the wish for emotional fulfillment, the tension between sexual energies and social realities, the almost unresolvable conflict between love and independence.

Biography

Charlotte Brontë was the third of six children born within seven years to the Reverend Patrick Brontë and his wife Maria Branwell. Patrick Brontë was perpetual curate of Haworth, a bleak manufacturing town in Yorkshire. In 1821, when Charlotte Brontë was five years old, her mother died of cancer. Three years later, the four elder girls were sent to the Clergy Daughter's School at Cowan Bridge—the school which appears as Lowood in *Jane Eyre*. In the summer of 1825, the eldest two daughters, Maria and Elizabeth, died of tuberculosis. Charlotte and Emily were removed from the school and brought home. There were no educated middle-class families in Haworth to supply friends and companions. The Brontë children lived with a noncommunicative aunt, an elderly servant, and a father much preoccupied by his intellectual interests and his own griefs.

In their home and with only one another for company, the children had material for both educational and imaginative development. Patrick Brontë expected his children to read and to carry on adult conversations about politics. He subscribed to *Blackwood's Edinburgh Magazine*, where his children had access to political and economic essays, art criticism, and literary reviews. They had annuals with engravings of fine art; they taught themselves to draw by copying the pictures in minute detail. They were free to do reading that would not have been permitted by any school of the time—by the age of thirteen Charlotte Brontë was fully acquainted not only with John Milton and Sir Walter Scott but also with Robert Southey, William Cowper and (most important) Lord Byron.

In 1826, Branwell was given a set of wooden soldiers which the four children used for characters in creative play. These soldiers gradually took on personal characteristics and acquired countries to rule. The countries needed cities, governments, ruling families, political intrigues, legends, and citizens with private lives, all of which the children happily invented. In 1829, when Charlotte Brontë was thirteen, she and the others began to write down materials from these fantasies, producing a collection of juvenilia that extended ultimately to hundreds of items: magazines, histories, maps, essays, tales, dramas, poems, newspapers, wills, speeches, scrapbooks. This enormous creative production in adolescence gave concrete form to motifs that were later transformed into situations, characters, and concerns of Charlotte Brontë's mature work. It was also a workshop for literary technique; the young author explored prose style, experimented with viewpoint, and discovered how to control narrative voice. A single event, she learned, could be the basis for both a newspaper story and a romance, and the romance could be told by one of the protagonists or by a detached observer.

Because Patrick Brontë had no income beyond his salary, his daughters had to prepare to support themselves. In 1831, when she was almost fifteen, Charlotte Brontë went to Miss Wooler's School at Roe Head. After returning home for a time to tutor her sisters, she went back to Miss Wooler's as a teacher. Over the next several years, all three sisters held positions as governesses in private families. None, however, was happy as a governess; aside from the predictable difficulties caused by burdensome work and undisciplined children, they all suffered when separated from their shared emotional and creative life. A possible solution would have been to open their own school, but they needed some special qualification to attract pupils. Charlotte conceived a plan for going abroad to study languages. In 1842, she and Emily went to Brussels to the Pensionnat Heger. They returned in November because of their aunt's death, but in the following year Charlotte went back to Brussels alone to work as a pupil-teacher. An additional reason for her return to Brussels was that she desired to be near Professor Constantine Heger, but at the end of the year she left in misery after Heger's wife had realized (perhaps more clearly than did Charlotte herself) the romantic nature of the attraction.

In 1844, at the age of twenty-eight, Charlotte Brontë established herself permanently at Haworth. The prospectus for "The Misses Brontë's Establishment" was published, but no pupils applied. Branwell, dismissed in disgrace from his post as tutor, came home to drink, take opium, and disintegrate. Charlotte spent nearly two years in deep depression: her yearning for love was unsatisfied and she had repressed her creative impulse because she was afraid her fantasies were self-indulgent. Then, with the discovery that all three had written poetry, the sisters found a new aim in life. A joint volume of poems was published in May, 1846, though it sold only two copies. Each wrote a short novel; they offered the three together to publishers. Emily Brontë's *Wuthering Heights* (1847) and Anne Brontë's *Agnes Grey* (1847) were accepted. Charlotte Brontë's *The Professor* was refused, but one editor, George Smith, said he would like to see a three-volume novel written by its author. *Jane Eyre* was by that time almost finished; it was sent to Smith on August 24, 1847, and impressed him so much that he had it in print by the middle of October.

Jane Eyre was immediately successful, but there was barely any time for its author to enjoy her fame and accomplishment. Within a single year, her three companions in creation died: Branwell on September 24, 1848; Emily on December 19; Anne on May 28, 1849. When Charlotte Brontë began work on *Shirley*, she met with her sisters in the evenings to exchange ideas, read aloud, and offer criticism. By the time she finished the manuscript she was alone.

Charlotte Brontë's sense that she was plain, "undeveloped," and unlikely to be loved seems to have been partly the product of her own psychological condition. She had refused more than one proposal in her early twenties. In 1852 there was another, from Arthur Bell Nicholls, curate at Haworth. Patrick Brontë objected violently and dismissed his curate. Gradually, however, the objections were worn away. On June 29, 1854, Charlotte Brontë and the Reverend Nicholls were married and, after a brief honeymoon tour, took up residence in Haworth parsonage. After a few months of apparent content— which did not prevent her from beginning work on another novel—Charlotte Brontë died on March 31, 1855, at the age of thirty-eight; a severe cold made her too weak to survive the complications of early pregnancy.

Analysis

The individualism and richness of Charlotte Brontë's work arises from the multiple ways in which her writing is personal: observation and introspection, rational analysis and spontaneous emotion, accurate mimesis and private symbolism. Tension and ambiguity grow from the intersections and conflicts among these levels of writing and, indeed, among the layers of the self.

Few writers of English prose have so successfully communicated the emotional texture of inner life while still constructing fictions with enough verisimilitude to appear realistic. Brontë startled the Victorians because her work was so little influenced by the books of her own era. Its literary forebears were the written corporate daydreams of her childhood and the Romantic poets she read during the period when the fantasies took shape. Certain characters and situations which crystallized the emotional conflicts of early adolescence became necessary components of emotional satisfaction. The source of these fantasies was, to a degree, beyond control, occurring in the region the twentieth century has termed "the unconscious"; by writing them down from childhood on, Brontë learned to preserve and draw on relatively undisguised desires and ego conflicts in a way lost to most adults.

The power and reality of the inner life disturbed Brontë after she had passed through adolescence; she compared her creative urge to the action of opium and was afraid that she might become lost in her "infernal world." When she began to think of publication, she deliberately used material from her own experience and reported scenes and characters in verifiable detail. In this way, she hoped to subdue the exaggerated romanticism—and the overwrought writing—of the fantasy-fictions. "Details, situations which I do not understand and cannot personally inspect," she wrote to her publisher, "I would not for the world meddle with." Her drawing from life was so accurate that the curates and the Yorkes in *Shirley* were recognized at once by people who knew them, and Brontë lost the protection that her pseudonym had provided.

The years of practice in writing fiction that satisfied her own emotional needs gave Brontë the means to produce powerful psychological effects. She uses a variety of resources to make readers share the protagonist's subjective state. The truth of the outside world is only that truth which reflects the narrator's feelings and perceptions. All characters are aspects of the consciousness which creates them: Brontë uses splitting, doubling, and other fairy-tale devices; she replicates key situations; she carefully controls the narrative distance and the amount of information readers have at their disposal.

The unquietness which Brontë's readers often feel grows from the tension between direct emotional satisfactions (often apparently immature) on the one hand, and, on the other, mature and realistic conflicts in motive, reason, and sense of self. Read as a sequence, the four completed novels demonstrate both Brontë's development and the story of woman's relationship to the world. Brontë's heroines find identity outside the enclosed family popularly supposed to circumscribe nineteenth century women. Isolation allows the heroines' self-development, but it impedes their romantic yearning to be lost in love.

At the beginning of *The Professor*, William Crimsworth is working as a clerk in a mill owned by his proud elder brother. He breaks away, goes to Brussels to teach English, survives a brief attraction to a seductive older woman, and then comes to love Frances Henri, an orphaned Anglo-Swiss lace-mender who had been his pupil.

Brontë's narrative devices supply shifting masks that both expose and evade the self. The epistolary opening keeps readers from identifying directly with Crimsworth but draws them into the novel as recipients of his revelations. The masculine persona, which Brontë used frequently in the juvenilia, gives her access to the literary mainstream and creates possibilities for action, attitude, and initiative that did not exist in models for female stories. The juvenile fantasies supply the feud between two brothers; the Belgian scenes and characters come from Brontë's own experiences. Although nominally male, Crimsworth is in an essentially female situation; disinherited, passive, timid. He has, furthermore, an exaggerated awareness and fear of the sexual overtones in human behavior.

Biographical details also go into the making of Frances Henri, the friendless older student working to pay for her lessons in the Belgian school. The poem that Frances writes is one Brontë had created out of her own yearning for Professor Heger. In *The Professor*, the dream can come true; the poem awakens the teacher's response.

Like the central figures on all Brontë novels, both Crimsworth and Frances enact a Cinderella plot. Each begins as an oppressed outcast and ends successful, confident, and satisfactorily placed in society. The details of Crimsworth's story work both symbolically and functionally. The imprisoning situations in the factory and the school reflect his perception of the world. At the same time, these situations are created by his own inner barriers. His bondage as a despised clerk is self-induced; he is an educated adult male who could move on at any time. In Belgium, he plods a treadmill of guilt because of Zoraïde Reuter's sexual manipulativeness—for which he is not responsible. His self-suppression is also seen through Yorke Hunsden, who appears whenever Crimsworth must express strong emotion. Hunsden voices anger and rebellion not permitted to the male/female narrator, and becomes a voyeur alter ego to appreciate Frances and love.

The novel is weakest when it fails to integrate the biography, the emotion, and the ideas. True moral dilemmas are not developed. The heroine, seen through sympathetic male eyes, wins love for her writing, her pride, and her self-possession, and she continues to work even after she has a child. Brontë solves her chronic romantic dilemma (how can a strong woman love if woman's love is defined as willing subordination?) by letting Frances vibrate between two roles: she is the stately directress of the school by day, the little lace-mender by night.

In *Jane Eyre*, Brontë created a story that has the authority of myth. Everything which had deeply affected her was present in the book's emotional content. The traumatic experiences of maternal deprivation, the Clergy Daughters' School, and Maria's death create the events of Jane's early life. The book also taps universal feelings of rejection, victimization, and loneliness, making them permissible by displacement: the hateful children are cousins, not siblings; the bad adult an aunt, not a mother. Rochester's compelling power as a lover derives from neither literal nor literary sources—Rochester is the man Brontë had loved for twenty years, the Duke of Zamorna who dominates the adolescent fantasies, exerting a power on both Jane and the reader that can hardly be explained by reason. Jane defied literary convention because she was poor, plain, and a heroine; she defied social convention by refusing to accept any external authority. Placed repeatedly in situations that exemplify male power, Jane resists and survives. At the end of the narrative, she is transformed from Cinderella to Prince Charming, becoming the heroine who cuts through the brambles to rescue the imprisoned sleeper. Identification is so immediate and so close that readers often fail to notice Brontë's control of distance, in particular the points of detachment when an older Jane comments on her younger self and the direct addresses from Jane to the reader that break the spell when emotions become too strong.

Place controls the book's structure. Events at Gateshead, Lowood, Thornfield, and Moor House determine Jane's development; a brief coda at Fearndean provides the resolution. Each of the four major sections contains a figure representing the sources of male power over women: John Reed (physical force and the patriarchal family), Reverend Brocklehurst (the social structures of class, education, and religion), Rochester (sexual attraction), and St. John Rivers (moral and spiritual authority). Jane protects herself at first by devious and indirect means—fainting, illness, flight—and then ultimately, in rejecting St. John Rivers, by direct confrontation. Compelled by circumstances to fend for herself, she comes—at first instinctively, later rationally—to rely on herself.

The book's emotional power grows from its total absorption in Jane's view of the world and from the images, symbols, and structures that convey multiple interwoven reverberations. The red room—which suggests violence, irrationality, enclosure, rebellion, rebirth, the bloody chamber of emerging womanhood—echoes throughout the book. The Bridewell charade, Jane's paintings, the buildings and terrain, and a multitude of other details have both meaning and function. Characters double and split: Helen Burns (mind) and Bertha Mason (body) are aspects of Jane as well as actors in the plot. Recurring images of ice and fire suggest fatal coldness without and consuming fire within. Rochester's sexuality is the most threatening and ambiguous aspect of masculine power because of Jane's own complicity and her need for love. Her terrors and dreams accumulate as the marriage approaches; there are drowning images, abyss images, loss of consciousness. She refuses to become Rochester's mistress, finally, not because of the practical and moral dangers (which she does recognize) but because she fears her own willingness to make a god of him. She will not become dependent; she escapes to preserve her self.

As Jane takes her life into her own hands, she becomes less needy. After she has achieved independence by discovering a family and inheriting money, she is free to seek out Rochester. At the same time, he has become less omnipotent, perhaps a code for the destruction of patriarchal power. Thus, the marriage not only ends the romance and resolves the moral, emotional, and sexual conflicts, but also supplies a satisfactory woman's fantasy of independence coupled with love.

For the book that would follow *Jane Eyre*, Brontë deliberately sought a new style and subject matter. *Shirley*, set in 1812, concerns two public issues still relevant in 1848—working-class riots and the condition of women. Brontë did historical research in newspaper files. She used a panoramic scene, included a variety of characters observed from life, and added touches of comedy. *Shirley* is told in the third person; the interest is divided between two heroines, neither of whom is a persona. Nevertheless, Brontë is strongly present in the narrative voice, which remains objective only in scenes of action. The authorial commentary, more strongly even than the events themselves, creates a tone of anger, rebellion, suffering, and doubt.

The novel is clearly plotted, although the mechanics are at times apparent.

Brontë shifts focus among characters and uses reported conversations to violate the time sequence so that she can arrange events in the most effective dramatic order. Robert Moore, owner of a cloth mill, arouses the workers' wrath by introducing machinery. Caroline Helstone loves Robert but her affection is not reciprocated. Although Caroline has a comfortable home with her uncle the rector, she is almost fatally depressed by lack of love and occupation. Property-owner Shirley Keeldar discovers that having a man's name, position, and forthrightness gives her some power but fails to make her man's equal; she is simply more valuable as a matrimonial prize. Louis Moore, Shirley's former tutor, loves her silently because he lacks wealth and social position. Eventually Robert, humbled by Shirley's contempt and weakened by a workman's bullet, declares his love for Caroline, who has in the meantime discovered her mother and grown much stronger. Shirley's union with Louis is more ambivalent; she loves him because he is a master she can look up to, but she is seen on her wedding day as a pantheress pining for virgin freedom.

The primary source of women's tribulation is dependency. Caroline Helstone craves occupation to fill her time, make her financially independent, and give her life purpose. Women become psychologically dependent on men because they have so little else to think about. Brontë examines the lives of several old maids; they are individuals, not stereotypes, but they are all lonely. Shirley and Caroline dissect John Milton, search for female roots, and talk cozily about men's inadequacies. They cannot, however, speak honestly to each other about their romantic feelings. Caroline must hold to herself the deep pain of unrequited love.

Although *Shirley* deliberately moves beyond the isolated mythic world of *Jane Eyre* to put women's oppression in the context of a society rent by other power struggles (workers against employers, England against France, Church against Nonconformity), the individualistic ending only partially resolves the divisions. Brontë's narrative tone in the final passage is bleak and bitter. She reminds readers that *Shirley*'s events are history. Fieldhead Hollow is covered by mills and mill housing; magic is gone from the world.

Villette is Brontë's most disciplined novel. Because *The Professor* had not been published, she was able to rework the Brussels experience without masks, as a story of loneliness and female deprivation, deliberately subduing the wish-fulfillment and making her uncompromising self-examination control form as well as feeling. Lucy Snowe is a woman without money, family, friends, or health. She is not, however, a sympathetic friendly narrator like Jane Eyre. Her personality has the unattractiveness that realistically grows from deprivation; she has no social ease, no warmth, no mental quickness. Furthermore, her personality creates her pain, loneliness, and disengagement.

In the book's early sections, Lucy is not even the center of her narrative. She watches and judges instead of taking part; she tells other people's stories instead of her own. She is so self-disciplined that she appears to have neither feelings nor imagination, so restrained that she never reveals the facts about her family or the incidents of her youth that might explain to readers how and why she learned to suppress emotion, hope, and the desire for human contact. Despite—or perhaps because of—her anesthetized feeling and desperate shyness, Lucy Snowe drives herself to actions that might have been inconceivable for a woman more thoroughly socialized. Thrust into the world by the death of the elderly woman whose companion she had been, she goes alone to London, takes a ship for the Continent, gets a job as nursemaid, rises through her own efforts to teach in Madame Beck's school, and begins laying plans to open a school of her own.

The coincidental and melodramatic elements of the story gain authenticity because they grow from Lucy's inner life. When she is left alone in the school during vacation, her repressed need to be heard by someone drives her to enter the confessional of a Catholic church. Once the internal barrier is breached, she immediately meets the Bretton family. Realistically, she must have known they were in Villette; she knew that "Dr. John" was Graham Bretton, but she withheld that information from the reader both because of her habitual secretiveness and also because she did not really "know" the Brettons were accessible to her until she was able to admit her need to reach out for human sympathy. The characterization of Paul Emanuel gains richness and detail in such a manner that readers realize—before Lucy herself dares admit it—that she is interested in him. The phantom nun, at first a night terror of pure emotion, is revealed as a prankish disguise when Lucy is free to express feelings directly.

The novel's ending, however, is deliberately ambiguous, though not in event. (Only the most naïve readers dare accept Brontë's invitation to imagine that Paul Emanuel escapes drowning and to "picture union and a happy succeeding life.") The ambiguity grows from Lucy's earlier statement: "M. Emanuel was away for three years. Reader, they were the three happiest years of my life." In those years, Lucy Snowe prospered, became respected, expanded her school. Her happiness depends not on the presence of her beloved but rather on the knowledge that she is loved. With that knowledge, she becomes whole and independent. No longer telling others' stories, she speaks directly to the reader about her most private concerns. Only when her lover is absent, perhaps, can a woman treasure love and emotional satisfaction while yet retaining the freedom to be her own person.

Major publications other than long fiction

POETRY: *Poems by Currer, Ellis, and Acton Bell*, 1846; *The Complete Poems of Charlotte Brontë*, 1924.

CHILDREN'S LITERATURE: *The Twelve Adventurers and Other Stories*, 1925 (C. K. Shorter and C. W. Hatfield, editors); *Legends of Angria*, 1933 (Fannie

E. Ratchford, compiler); *The Search After Hapiness*, 1969; *Five Novelettes*, 1971 (Winifred Gérin, editor); *The Secret and Lily Hart*, 1979 (William Holtz, editor).

MISCELLANEOUS: *Shakespeare Head Brontë*, 1931-1938 (T. J. Wise and J. A. Symington, editors, 19 volumes).

Bibliography
Allott, Miriam, ed. *The Brontës: The Critical Heritage*, 1974.
Craik, W. A. *The Brontë Novels*, 1968.
Gaskell, Elizabeth. *The Life of Charlotte Brontë*, 1857.
Gérin, Winifred. *Charlotte Brontë: The Evolution of Genius*, 1967.
Gilbert, Sandra M., and Susan Gubar. *The Madwoman in the Attic*, 1979.
Moglen, Helene. *Charlotte Brontë: The Self Conceived*, 1978.
Ratchford, Fannie Elizabeth. *The Brontës' Web of Childhood*, 1941.

Sally Mitchell

EMILY BRONTË

Born: Thornton, England; July 30, 1818
Died: Haworth, England; December 19, 1848

Principal long fiction
Wuthering Heights, 1847.

Other literary forms
Poems by Currer, Ellis, and Acton Bell (1846) contains poems by Charlotte, Emily, and Anne Brontë. Juvenalia and early prose works on the imaginary world of Gondal have all been lost.

Achievements
Brontë occupies a unique place in the annals of literature. Her reputation as a major novelist stands on the merits of one relatively short novel which was misunderstood and intensely disliked upon publication, yet no study of British fiction is complete without a discussion of *Wuthering Heights*. The names of its settings and characters, particularly Heathcliff, have become part of the heritage of Western culture familiar even to those who have neither read the novel nor know anything about its author's life and career. Several film versions, the two most popular in 1939 and 1970, have helped perpetuate this familiarity.

The literary achievement of *Wuthering Heights* lies in its realistic portrayal of a specific place and time and in its examination of universal patterns of human behavior. Set in Yorkshire in the closing years of the eighteenth century, the novel delineates the quality of life in the remote moors of northern England, and also reminds the reader of the growing pains of industrialization throughout the nation. In addition, more than any other novel of the period, *Wuthering Heights* presents in clear dialectic form the conflict between two opposing psychic forces, embodied in the settings of the Grange and the Heights and the people who inhabit them. Although modern readers often apply the theories of Sigmund Freud and C. G. Jung to give names to these forces, Brontë illustrated their conflict long before psychologists pigeonholed them. *Wuthering Heights* is so true in its portrayal of human nature that it fits easily into many theoretical and critical molds, from the historical to the psychological. The novel may be most fully appreciated, however, as a study of the nature of human perception and its ultimate failure in understanding human behavior. This underlying theme, presented through the dialectic structure of human perception, unites many of the elements that are sometimes singled out or overemphasized in particular critical approaches to the novel.

Brontë's skill is not confined to representing the world and the human forces at work within her characters, great as that skill is. She has also created a complex narrative structure built upon a series of interlocking memories and perceptions, spanning three generations and moving across several social classes. Told primarily from two often unreliable and sometimes ambiguous first-person points of view, the structure of the novel itself illustrates the limitations of human intelligence and imagination. Faced with choosing between Lockwood or Nelly Dean's interpretation of Heathcliff's life, the reader can only ponder that human perception never allows a full understanding of another soul.

Biography

Emily Jane Brontë was born at Thornton, in Bradford Parish, Yorkshire, on July 30, 1818, the fifth child of the Reverend Patrick and Maria Brontë. Patrick Brontë had been born in County Down, Ireland, one of ten children, on March 17, 1777. He was a schoolteacher and tutor before obtaining his B.A. from Cambridge in 1806, from where he was ordained to curacies, first in Essex and then in Hartshead, Yorkshire. He married Maria Branwell, of Penzance, in Hartshead on December 19, 1812, and in 1817, they moved to Thornton. The other children at the time of Emily's birth were Maria, Elizabeth, Charlotte, and Patrick Branwell; another daughter, Anne, was born two years later. Charlotte and Anne also became writers.

In early 1820, the family moved to Haworth, four miles from the village of Keighley, where the Reverend Brontë was perpetual curate until his death in 1861. Maria Brontë died on September 15, 1821, and about a year later, an elder sister, Elizabeth Branwell, moved in to take care of the children and household. She remained with them until her own death in 1842.

Life at Haworth was spartan but not unpleasant. There was a close and devoted relationship among the children, especially between Charlotte and Emily. Reading was a favorite pastime, and a wide range of books, including the novels of Sir Walter Scott and the poetry of William Wordsworth and Robert Southey, as well as the more predictable classics, were available to the children. Outdoor activities included many hours of wandering through the moors and woods. Their father wanted the children to be hardy and independent, intellectually and physically, indifferent to the passing fashions of the world.

Maria, Elizabeth, and Charlotte had already been sent away to a school for clergymen's daughters, at Cowan's Bridge, when Emily joined them in November, 1824. Emily was not happy in this confined and rigid environment and longed for home. Two of the sisters, Elizabeth and Maria, became ill and were taken home to die during 1825; in June, Charlotte and Emily returned home as well.

From 1825 to 1830, the remaining Brontë children lived at Haworth with their father and Miss Branwell. In June, 1826, their father gave them a set of wooden soldiers, a seemingly insignificant gift that stimulated their imaginative and literary talents. The children devoted endless energy to creating an imaginary world for these soldiers. During these years, Charlotte and [brother] Branwell created in their minds and on paper the land of "Angria," while Emily and Anne were at work on "Gondal." Although all of these early prose works have been lost, some of Emily's poetry contains references to aspects of the Gondal-Angria creations.

In July, 1835, Emily again joined Charlotte, already a teacher, at the Roe Head School. She remained only three months, returning home in October. Three years later, she accepted a position as governess in a school in Halifax for about six months, but returned to Haworth in December; Charlotte joined her there early in the following year. During 1839 and 1840, the sisters were planning to establish their own school at Haworth, but the plan was never carried through.

Charlotte left home again to serve as a governess in 1841, and in February, 1842, she and Emily went to Mme. Héger's school in Brussels to study languages. They returned to Haworth in November because of Miss Branwell's death. Charlotte went back to Brussels to teach in 1843, but Emily never left Yorkshire again.

From August, 1845, the Brontë children were again united at Haworth. They did not have much contact with neighbors, whose educational level and intellectual interests were much inferior to theirs. They kept busy reading and writing, both fiction and poetry. *Wuthering Heights* was probably begun in October, 1845, and completed sometime in 1846, although it was not published until December, 1847, after the success of *Jane Eyre* (1847).

Meanwhile, the sisters published *Poems by Currer, Ellis, and Acton Bell* in May, 1846. Finding a press was very difficult and the pseudonyms were chosen to avoid personal publicity and to create the fiction of male authorship, more readily acceptable to the general public. The reaction was predictable, as Charlotte reports: "Neither we nor our poems were at all wanted." The sisters were not discouraged, however, and they continued to seek publishers for their novels.

The first edition of *Wuthering Heights* was published in 1847 by T. C. Newby, with Anne's *Agnes Grey* as the third volume. It was a sloppy edition and contained many errors. The second edition, published in 1850, after the author's death, was "corrected" by Charlotte. The public reaction to *Wuthering Heights* was decidedly negative; readers were disturbed by the "wickedness" of the characters and the "implausibility" of the action. Until Charlotte herself corrected the misconception, readers assumed that *Wuthering Heights* was an inferior production by the author of *Jane Eyre*.

In October, 1848, Emily became seriously ill with a cough and cold. She suffered quietly and patiently, even refusing to see the doctor who had been called. She died of tuberculosis at Haworth on December 19, 1848. She was buried in the church alongside her mother, her sisters Maria and Elizabeth, and her brother Branwell.

These facts about Emily Brontë's life and death are known, but her character will always remain a mystery. Her early prose works have been lost, only three personal letters survive, and her poems give little insight to her own life. Most information about the Brontë family life and background comes from Mrs. Elizabeth Gaskell's biography of Charlotte and the autobiographical comments on which she based her work. Charlotte comments that Emily was "not a person of demonstrative character" and that she was "stronger than a man, simpler than a child." She had a nature that "stood alone." The person behind this mystery is revealed only in a reading of *Wuthering Heights*.

Analysis

Wuthering Heights is constructed around a series of dialectic motifs which interconnect and unify the elements of setting, character, and plot. An examination of these motifs will give the reader the clearest insight to the central meaning of the novel. Although *Wuthering Heights* is a "classic," as Frank Kermode points out in a recent essay, precisely because it is open to many different critical methods and conducive to many levels of interpretation, the novel grows from a coherent imaginative vision that underlies all the motifs. That vision demonstrates that all human perception is limited and failed. The fullest approach to Emily Brontë's novel is through the basic patterns that support this vision.

Wuthering Heights concerns the interactions of two families, the Earnshaws and Lintons, over three generations. The novel is set in the desolate moors of Yorkshire and covers the years from 1771 to 1803. The Earnshaws and Lintons are in harmony with their environment, but their lives are disrupted by an outsider and catalyst of change, the orphan Heathcliff. Heathcliff is, first of all, an emblem of the social problems of a nation entering the age of industrial expansion and urban growth. Although Brontë sets the action of the novel entirely within the locale familiar to her, she reminds the reader continually of the contrast between that world and the larger world outside.

Besides Heathcliff's background as a child of the streets and the description of urban Liverpool from which he is brought, there are other reminders that Yorkshire, long insulated from change and susceptible only to the forces of nature, is no longer as remote as it once was. The servant Joseph's religious cant, the class distinctions obvious in the treatment of Nelly Dean as well as of Heathcliff, and Lockwood's pseudosophisticated urban values, are all reminders that Wuthering Heights cannot remain as it has been, that religious, social, and economic change is rampant. Brontë clearly signifies in the courtship and marriage of young Cathy and Hareton that progress and enlightenment *will* come and the wilderness *will* be tamed. Heathcliff is both an embodiment of the force of this change and its victim. He brings about a change but cannot change himself. What he leaves behind, as Lockwood attests and the relationship of Cathy and Hareton verifies, is a new society, at peace with itself and its environment.

It is not necessary, however, to examine in depth the Victorian context of *Wuthering Heights* to sense the dialectic contrast of environments. Within the limited setting that the novel itself describes, society is divided between two opposing worlds, Wuthering Heights, ancestral home of the Earnshaws, and Thrushcross Grange, the Linton estate. Wuthering Heights is rustic and wild; it is open to the elements of nature and takes its name from "atmospheric tumult." The house is strong, built with narrow windows and jutting cornerstones, fortified to withstand the battering of external forces. It is identified with the outdoors and nature, and with strong, "masculine" values. Its appearance, both inside and out, is wild, untamed, disordered, and hard. The Grange expresses a more civilized, controlled atmosphere. The house is neat and orderly and there is always an abundance of light—to Brontë's mind, "feminine" values. It is not surprising that Lockwood is more comfortable at the Grange, since he takes pleasure in "feminine" behavior (gossip, vanity of appearance, adherence to social decorum, romantic self-delusion), while Heatchliff, entirely "masculine," is always out of place there.

Indeed, all of the characters reflect, to greater or lesser degrees, the masculine and feminine values of the places they inhabit. Hindley and Catherine Earnshaw are as wild and uncontrollable as the Heights: Catherine claims even to prefer her home to the pleasures of heaven. Edgar and Isabella Linton are as refined and civilized as the Grange. The marriage of Edgar and Catherine (as well as the marriage of Isabella and Heathcliff) is ill-fated from the start, not only because she does not love him, as her answers to Nelly Dean's catechism reveal, but also because each is so strongly associated with the values of his (or her) home that he lacks the opposing and necessary personality components. Catherine is too willful, wild, and strong; she expresses too much of the "masculine" side of her personality (the animus of Jungian psychology), while Edgar is weak and effeminate (the anima). They are unable to interact fully with each other because they are not complete individuals themselves. This lack leads to their failures to perceive each other's true needs.

Even Cathy's passionate cry for Heathcliff, "Nelly, I *am* Heathcliff," is less love for him as an individual than the deepest form of self-love. Cathy cannot exist without him, but a meaningful relationship is not possible, because Cathy sees Heathcliff only as a reflection of her self. Heathcliff, too, has denied an important aspect of his personality. Archetypally masculine, Heathcliff acts out only the agressive, violent part of himself.

The settings and the characters are patterned against each other, and explosions are the only possible results. Only Hareton and young Cathy, each of whom embodies the psychological characteristics of both Heights and Grange, can successfully sustain a mutual relationship.

This dialectic structure extends into the roles of the narrators as well. The story is reflected through the words of Nelly Dean—an inmate of both houses, a participant in the events of the narrative, and a confidante of the major characters—and Lockwood, an outsider who witnesses only the results of the characters' interactions. Nelly is a companion and servant in the Earnshaw and Linton households, and she shares many of the values and perceptions of the families. Lockwood, an urban sophisticate on retreat, misunderstands his own character as well as others'. His brief romantic "adventure" in Bath and his awkwardness when he arrives at the Heights (he thinks Cathy will fall in love with him; he mistakes the dead rabbits for puppies) exemplify his obtuseness. His perceptions are always to be questioned. Occasionally, however, even a denizen of the conventional world may gain a glimpse of the forces at work beneath the surface of reality. Lockwood's dream of the dead Cathy, which sets off his curiosity and Heathcliff's final plans, is a reminder that even the placid, normal world may be disrupted by the psychic violence of a willful personality.

The presentation of two family units and parallel brother-sister, husband-wife relationships in each also emphasizes the dialectic. That two such opposing modes of behavior could arise in the same environment prevents the reader from easy condemnation of either pair. The use of flashback for the major part of the narration—it begins *in medias res*—reminds the reader that he or she is seeing events out of their natural order, recounted by two individuals whose reliability must be questioned. The working out of the plot over three generations further suggests that no one group, much less one individual, can perceive the complexity of the human personality.

Taken together, the setting, plot, characters, and structure combine into a whole when they are seen as parts of the dialectic nature of existence. In a world where opposing forces are continually arrayed against each other in the environment, in society, in families, and in relationships, as well as within the individual, there can be no easy route to perception of another human soul. *Wuthering Heights* convincingly demonstrates the complexity of this dialectic and portrays the limitations of human perception.

Major publications other than long fiction
POETRY: *Poems by Currer, Ellis, and Acton Bell*, 1846 (with Charlotte Brontë and Anne Brontë); *The Complete Poems of Emily Jane Brontë*, 1941 (C. W. Hatfield, editor).

Bibliography
Gaskell, Mrs. Elizabeth. *The Life of Charlotte Brontë*, 1908.
Hewish, John. *Emily Brontë: A Critical and Biographical Study*, 1969.
Kermode, John Frank. *The Classic*, 1975.

Lawrence F. Laban

CHARLES BROCKDEN BROWN

Born: Philadelphia, Pennsylvania; January 17, 1771
Died: Philadelphia, Pennsylvania; February 22, 1810

Principal long fiction

Wieland: Or, The Transformation, 1798; *Ormond: Or, The Secret Witness*, 1799; *Arthur Mervyn: Or, Memoirs of the Year 1793, Part I*, 1799; *Edgar Huntly: Or, Memoirs of a Sleep-Walker*, 1799; *Arthur Mervyn: Or, Memoirs of the Year 1793, Part II*, 1800; *Clara Howard: In a Series of Letters*, 1801; *Jane Talbot: A Novel*, 1801.

Other literary forms

Charles Brockden Brown published two parts of a dialogue on the rights of women, *Alcuin*, in 1798; the last two sections appeared in William Dunlap's 1815 biography of Brown. Brown's later political and historical essays have not been collected but remain in their original magazine and pamphlet publications. Several fictional fragments appear in *Carwin, the Biloquist, and Other American Tales and Pieces* (1822) and in the Dunlap biography, notably the Carwin story and "Memoirs of Stephen Calvert." Several collected editions of his novels were published in the nineteenth century. Harry Warfel's edition of *The Rhapsodist and Other Uncollected Writings* (1943) completes the publication of most of Brown's literary works. Letters have appeared in scattered books and essays, but they are not yet collected. *Wieland and Memoirs of Carwin*, the first volume in the definitive edition of Brown's fiction underway at Kent State University Press, appeared in 1977.

Achievements

The significant portion of Brown's literary career lasted little more than a year, from 1798 to 1800, during which he published the four novels for which he is best known: *Wieland*, *Ormond*, *Arthur Mervyn*, and *Edgar Huntly*. Though his career began with the essays comprising "The Rhapsodist" in 1789 and continued until his death, most of his other fiction, poetry, and prose is thought to be of minor importance.

Brown's literary reputation rests heavily on his historical position as one of the first significant American novelists. An English reviewer, quoted by Bernard Rosenthal in *Critical Essays on Charles Brockden Brown* (1981), wrote in 1824 that Brown "was the first writer of prose fiction of which America could boast." Brown's contemporaries recognized his abilities and he received praise from William Godwin, John Keats, and Percy Bysshe Shelley. Though his American reputation remained unsteady, he was read by nineteenth century novelists such as James Fenimore Cooper, Edgar Allan Poe, and Herman Melville. In the twentieth century, scholars and advanced students of American culture are his most frequent readers; they have redis-covered him in part because his concerns with identity and choice in a dis-ordered world prefigure or initiate some of the major themes of American fiction.

Brown's four best-known novels begin the peculiarly American mutation of the Gothic romance. There are similarities between his novels and the political Gothic of Godwin and the sentimental Gothic of Ann Radcliffe, but Brown's adaptations of Gothic conventions for the exploration of human psychology, the analysis of the mind choosing under stress, and the repre-sentation of a truly incomprehensible world suggest that he may be an impor-tant bridge between the popular Gothic tradition of eighteenth century England and the American Gothic strain which is traceable through Poe, Melville, and Nathaniel Hawthorne to Henry James, William Faulkner, and such late twentieth century novelists as Joyce Carol Oates.

Biography

Born on January 17, 1771, Charles Brockden Brown was the fifth son of Elijah Brown and Mary Armitt Brown. Named after a relative who was a well-known Philadelphia official, Brown grew up in an intellectual Quaker family where the works of contemporary radicals such as Godwin and Mary Wollstonecraft were read, even though they were unacceptable by society's norms. Brown's health was never good; his parents tended to protect him from an active boy's life and to encourage his reading. When he was eleven, he began his formal education at the Friends' Latin School in Philadelphia under Robert Proud, a renowned teacher and scholar who later wrote *The History of Pennsylvania* (1797). Proud encouraged Brown to strengthen his constitution by taking walks in the country similar to those Edgar Huntly takes with Sarsefield in *Edgar Huntly*. After five or six years in Latin School, Brown began the study of law under Alexander Willcocks (variously spelled), a prominent Philadelphia lawyer. Though he studied law for five or six years until 1792 or 1793, he never practiced. During Brown's years studying law, he taught himself French and increasingly leaned toward literary work. He became a member of the Belles Lettres Club, which met to discuss current literary and intellectual topics. In 1789, he published his first work, "The Rhapsodist," in the *Columbian Magazine*. In 1790, he met and became friends with Elihu Hubbard Smith of Litchfield, Connecticut, a medical student with literary interests. Smith encouraged Brown's literary aspirations, helping to draw him away from law. Brown's acquaintance with Smith brought him to New York City in 1794 where he came to know the members of the Friendly Club, a group of young New York intellectuals, one of whom was to be his first biographer, William Dunlap.

During this period, Brown wrote poetry, and by 1795 he had begun a novel. He began active publishing in 1798 in the Philadelphia *Weekly Magazine*. In the summer of 1798, when he was visiting Smith in New York, he published *Wieland*. Smith died at his work during the yellow fever outbreak of that summer; Brown also became ill, but recovered. In 1799, Brown suddenly became an extremely busy writer. He published two novels and part of a third and also began *The Monthly Magazine and American Review*. In 1800, he published the second half of *Arthur Mervyn*, abandoned his magazine, and joined his brothers in business. After publishing his last two novels in 1801, he turned to political and historical writing. His 1803 pamphlet on the Louisiana Territory was widely read and provoked debate in Congress. In 1803, he began another magazine, *The Literary Magazine and American Register*, which lasted until 1806. His final magazine venture was *The American Register: Or, General Repository of History, Politics, and Science* (1807-1810). He was working on a geography publication when he died on February 22, 1810, of tuberculosis, a disease which had pursued him most of his life.

Brown's personal and intellectual life are known primarily through his writings. He married Elizabeth Linn on November 19, 1804, and his family eventually included three sons and a daughter. There is evidence that Brown entertained the liberal Quaker ideas of his parents, the Deism of Smith, and the ideas of the English radicals at various times. His dialogue on the rights of women, *Alcuin*, advocates sound education and political equality for women and, in the two posthumously published parts, even suggests a utopian state of absolute social equality between the sexes in which there would be no marriage. Though he entertained such radical ideas in his youth, Brown seems to have become more conservative with maturity, affirming in his later works the importance of reason and religion in living a good life.

Analysis

Charles Brockden Brown's aims in writing, aside from attempting to earn a living, are a matter of debate among critics. In his Preface to *Edgar Huntly*, he makes the conventional claim of novelists of the time, that writing is "amusement to the fancy and instruction to the heart," but he also argues the importance as well as the richness of American materials:

> One merit the writer may at least claim:—that of calling forth the passions and engaging the sympathy of the reader by means hitherto unemployed by preceding authors. Puerile superstition and exploded manners, Gothic castles and chimeras, are the material usually employed for this end. The incidents of Indian hostility, the perils of the Western wilderness, are far more suitable; and for a native of America to overlook these would admit of no apology.

This statement suggests several elements of Brown's primary achievement, the development of Gothic conventions for the purposes of exploring the human mind in moments of ethically significant decision. Such an achievement was important for its example to later American novelists.

Brown's novels are like William Godwin's in their use of radical contemporary thought; they are like Ann Radcliffe's in that they continue the tradition of the rationalized Gothic. Brown, however, proves in some ways to be less radical than Godwin, and his fictional worlds differ greatly from Radcliffe's. Brown brings into his novels current intellectual debates about education, psychology and reason, epistemology, ethics and religion. Characters who hold typical attitudes find themselves in situations which thoroughly test their beliefs. The novels do not seem especially didactic; they are rather more like Radcliffe's romances in form. A central character or group undergoes a crisis which tests education and belief. Brown's novels tend to be developmental, but the world he presents is so ambiguous and disorderly that the reader is rarely certain that a character's growth really fits him better for living.

This ambiguity is only one of the differences which makes Brown appear, in retrospect at least, to be an Americanizer of the Gothic. In one sense, his American settings are of little significance, since they are rather simple equivalents of the castle grounds and wildernesses of an Otranto or Udolpho; on the other hand, these settings are recognizable and much more familiar to an American reader. Rather than emphasizing the exoticism of the Gothic, Brown increases the immediacy of his tales by using an American setting. He also increases immediacy and the intensity of his stories by setting them close to his readers in time. Even though his novels are usually told in retrospect by the kinds of first-person narrators who would come to dominate great American fiction, the narratives frequently lapse into the present tense at crises, the narrators becoming transfixed by the renewed contemplation of past terrors. Brown avoids the supernatural; even though his novels are filled with the inexplicable, they do not feature the physical acts of supernatural beings. For example, Clara Wieland dreams prophetic dreams which prove accurate, but the apparently supernatural voices which waking people hear are hallucinatory or are merely the work of Carwin, the ventriloquist. All of these devices for reducing the distance between reader and text contribute to the success of his fast-paced if sometimes over-complicated plots, but they also reveal Brown's movement away from Radcliffe's rationalized Gothic toward the kind of realism that would come to dominate American fiction in the next century.

Perhaps Brown's most significant contribution to the Americanization of the Gothic romance is his representation of the human mind as inadequate to its world. Even the best minds in his works fall victim to internal and external assaults, and people avoid or fall into disaster seemingly by chance. In Radcliffe's fictional world, Providence actively promotes poetic justice; if the hero or heroine persists in rational Christian virtue and holds to his or her faith that the world is ultimately orderly, then weaknesses and error, villains and accidents will be overcome and justice will prevail. In Brown, there are no such guarantees. At the end of *Wieland*, Clara, the narrator, reflects: "If Wieland had framed juster notions of moral duty, and of the divine attributes; or if I had been gifted with ordinary equanimity or foresight, the double-tongued deceiver would have been baffled and repelled." Clara's moralizing is, in fact, useless, even to herself. She was not so "gifted"; therefore, she could never have escaped the catastrophes which befell her. Furthermore, she persists in seeing Carwin, the double-tongued deceiver, as a devil who ruined her brother, even though Carwin is no more than a peculiarly gifted and not very moral human being. Clara is able to moralize in this way only because, for the time being, disasters do not threaten her. Placed once again in the situation in which she completed the first portion of her narrative, she would again reject all human comfort and wish for death. Brown's fictional worlds defy human comprehension and make ethical actions excessively problematic.

This apparent irony in *Wieland* illustrates a final significant development in Brown's adaptation of the Gothic romance. Though it is difficult, given his sometimes clumsy work, to be certain of what he intends, Brown seems to have experimented with point of view in ways which foreshadow later works. *Arthur Mervyn*, written in two parts, seems a deliberate experiment in multiple points of view. Donald Ringe points out that while the first part, told primarily from Mervyn's point of view, emphasizes Mervyn's naïve victimization by a sophisticated villain, the second part, told from a more objective point of view, suggests that Mervyn may unconsciously be a moral chameleon and confidence man. This shifting of point of view to capture complexity or create irony reappears in the works of many major American novelists, notably in Herman Melville's "Benito Cereno" and in William Faulkner.

By focusing on the mind dealing with crises in an ambiguous world, making his stories more immediate, and manipulating point of view for ironic effect, Brown helps to transform popular Gothic conventions into tools for the more deeply psychological American Gothic fiction which would follow.

Clara Wieland, the heroine of *Wieland*, is a bridge between the Gothic heroine of Radcliffe and a line of American Gothic victims stretching from Edgar Allan Poe's narrators in his tales of terror through Henry James's governess in *The Turn of the Screw* (1898) to Faulkner's Temple Drake and beyond. Most of her life is idyllic until she reaches her early twenties, when she encounters a series of catastrophes which, it appears, will greatly alter her benign view of life. When her disasters are three years behind her and she has married the man she loves, Clara returns to her view that the world is reasonably orderly and that careful virtue will pull one through all difficulties.

The novel opens with an account of the Wieland family curse on the father's side. Clara's father, an orphaned child of a German nobelman cast off by his family because of a rebellious marriage, grows up apprenticed to an English merchant. Deprived of family love and feeling an emptiness in his spiritual isolation, he finds meaning when he chances upon a book of a radical Protestant sect. In consequence, he develops an asocial and paranoid personal faith which converts his emptiness into an obligation. He takes upon himself certain duties which will make him worthy of the god he has created. These attitudes dominate his life and lead eventually to his "spontaneous combustion" in his private temple on the estate he has developed in America. The spiritual and psychological causes of this disaster arise in part from his guilt at failing to carry out some command of his personal deity, perhaps the successful conversion of American Indians to Christianity, the project which brought him to America. Clara's uncle presents this "scientific" explanation of her father's death and, much later in the novel, tells a story indicating that such religious madness has also occurred on her mother's side of the family. Religious madness is the familial curse which falls upon Clara's immediate family: Theodore Wieland, her brother; his wife, Catharine; their children and a ward; and Catharine's brother, Pleyel, whom Clara comes to love.

The madness strikes Theodore Wieland; he believes he hears the voice of God commanding him to sacrifice his family if he is to be granted a vision of God. He succeeds in killing all except Pleyel and Clara. The first half of the novel leads up to his crimes and the second half deals primarily with Clara's discoveries about herself and the world as she learns more details about the murders. Clara's ability to deal with this catastrophe is greatly complicated by events that prove to be essentially unrelated to it, but which coincide with it. In these events, the central agent is Carwin.

Carwin is a ventriloquist whose background is explained in a separate short fragment, "Memoirs of Carwin the Biloquist." Because ventriloquism is an art virtually unknown in Clara's world, Carwin seems monstrous to her. As he explains to Clara near the end of the novel, he has been lurking about the Wieland estate and his life has touched on theirs in several ways. He has used his art to avoid being detected in his solitary night explorations of the grounds. The apparently supernatural voices he has created may have contributed to the unsettling of Theodore Wieland, but Wieland's own account during his trial indicates other more powerful causes of his madness. Much more dangerous to Clara has been Carwin's affair with her housekeeper, Judith, for by this means he has come to see Clara as a flower of human virtue and intellect. He is tempted to test her by creating the illusion that murderers are killing Judith in Clara's bedroom closet. This experiment miscarries, leading Clara to think she is the proposed victim. He later uses a "supernatural" voice which accidentally coincides with one of her prophetic dreams; though his purpose is to frighten her away from the place of his meetings with Judith, Carwin confirms Clara's fears and superstitions. He pries into her private diary and concocts an elaborate lie about his intention to rape her when he is caught. Out of envy and spite and because he is able, Carwin deceives

Pleyel into thinking that Clara has surrendered her honor to him.

Throughout these deceptions, Carwin also fosters in Clara the superstition that a supernatural being is watching over and protecting her by warning her of dangers. Carwin's acts are essentially pranks; he never intends as much harm as actually occurs when his actions become threads in a complex net of causality. The worst consequence of his pranks is that Pleyel is convinced that Clara has become depraved just at the moment when she hopes that he will propose marriage, and this consequence occurs because Carwin over-estimates Pleyel's intelligence. Pleyel's accusation of Clara is quite serious for her because it culminates the series of dark events which Clara perceives as engulfing her happy life. Carwin's scattered acts have convinced her that rapists and murderers lurk in every dark corner and that she is the center of some impersonal struggle between forces of good and evil. Pleyel's accusation also immediately precedes her brother's murders. These two crises nearly destroy Clara's reason and deprive her of the will to live.

The attack on Clara's mind is, in fact, the central action of the novel. All the Gothic shocks come to focus on her perception of herself. They strip her of layers of identity until she is reduced to a mere consciousness of her own integrity, a consciousness which is then challenged when she comes to understand the nature of her brother's insanity. When all the props of her identity have been shaken, she wishes for death. Tracing her progress toward the wish for death reveals the central thematic elements of the novel.

The attack on Clara's mind is generated from poles represented by her brother and Pleyel. Wieland crumbles from within and Pleyel is deceived by external appearances. Each falls prey to the weakness to which he is most susceptible. Clara's more stable mind is caught in the midst of these extremes. Theodore Wieland has the family temperament, the tendency to brood in isolation over his spiritual state and over "last things." Pleyel is the gay and optimistic rationalist, skeptical of all religious ideas, especially any belief in modern supernatural agencies. While Wieland trusts his inner voice above all, Pleyel places absolute faith in his senses. Both are certain of their powers to interpret their experience accurately and both are wrong on all counts. Wieland sees what he wants to see and Pleyel's senses are easily deceived, especially by the skillful Carwin. Wieland interprets his visions as divine revelations even though they command murder, and Pleyel believes Clara is polluted even though such a belief is inconsistent with his lifelong knowledge of her.

Clara's sense of identity first suffers when her idyllic world begins to slip away. Her world becomes a place of unseen and unaccountable danger. As her anxiety increases, she finds herself unable to reason about her situation. Brown shows this disintegration in one of his more famous scenes, when Clara comes to believe there is someone in her closet, yet persists in trying to enter it even though she has heard the murderers there and even after her protecting voice has warned her away. Critics take various attitudes toward this scene, which prolongs the reader's wait to learn who is in the closet in order to follow minutely Clara's thoughts and reactions. Brown creates suspense which some critics have judged overwrought, but his main purpose is clearly the close analysis of a strong mind coming apart under great pressure. Even though Pleyel's mistakes emphasize the inadequacy of individual rationality to the complexity of the world, that faculty remains the isolated person's only means of active defense. As Clara's rationality disintegrates, her helplessness increases.

Seeing her world divide into a war between good and evil in which her reason fails to help her, Clara's anxiety develops into paranoia. After Carwin tells how he intended to rape her, she begins to see him as a supernatural agent of Satan. When Pleyel accuses her of self-transforming wickedness with Carwin, Clara loses her social identity. Unable to change Pleyel's mind, she can only see recent events as a devilish plot against her happiness. Just when she thinks she is about to complete her identity in marriage, she is denied the opportunity. When she loses the rest of her family as a result of Wieland's insanity, she loses the last supporting prop of her identity, leaving only her faith in herself, her consciousness of her own innocence, and her belief that the satanic Carwin has caused all of her catastrophes.

Two more events deprive Clara of these remaining certainties. She learns that Wieland rather than Carwin, whom she has suspected, was the murderer, and when she understands Wieland's motives, she loses confidence in her perceptions of herself, for should she be similarly transformed, she would be unable to resist. In fact, she sees herself, prostrate and wishing for death, as already transformed: "Was I not likewise transformed from rational and human into a creature of nameless and fearful attributes?" In this state, she understands her brother's certainty of his own rectitude. She cannot know herself. When she finally meets Carwin and hears how trivial and without malice his acts have been, she is unable to believe him, unable to give up her belief that she is the victim of a supernatural agency. Like Wieland, whom she meets for the last time on the same evening she talks with Carwin, she insists that divinity stands behind her disasters; the paranoid Wielands stand at the head of the line of American monomaniacs of whom Melville's Ahab is the greatest example. Deprived of her ordered world, Clara asserts against it an order which gives her reason, at least, to die. Wieland himself commits suicide when Carwin convinces him he has listened to the wrong voice.

Criticism has been rightly skeptical of the apparent clumsiness of the last chapter, Clara's continuation of the narration three years after Wieland's suicide. That chapter tidies up what had appeared earlier to be a subplot involving the Wielands' ward, Louisa Conway, and it also puts together a conventional happy ending. The recovered Clara marries Pleyel after he resolves several complications, including learning the truth about Clara and losing his first wife. Though it remains difficult to determine what Brown intended, it is unlikely that a writer of Brown's intelligence, deeply interested in the twistings of human thought, could be unaware that Clara's final statement is a manifest tissue of illusion. No attainable human virtue could have saved her or Wieland from the web of events in which they become enmeshed. That she persists in magnifying Carwin's responsibility shows that she fails to appreciate the complexity of human events even as Carwin himself has failed. That the Conway/Stuart family disasters of the last chapter recapitulate her own, emphasizes Clara's failure to appreciate fully the incomprehensibility of her world.

Brown apparently intended in the final chapter to underline the illusory quality of social normality. When life moves as it usually does, it appears to be orderly, and one's ideas of order, because they are not seriously challenged, seem to prevail and become a source of comfort and security. That these ideas of order all break down when seriously challenged, leads Clara to the wisdom of despair: "The most perfect being must owe his exemption from vice to the absence of temptation. No human virtue is secure from degeneracy." Such wisdom is not, however, of much use under normal conditions and is of no use at all in a crisis. Perhaps more useful is Clara's reflection as she looks back from the perspective of three years, her idea that one's perceptions and interpretations, because of their imperfection, must be tested over time and compared with those of other observers. The Wieland family curse and Pleyel's errors might be moderated if each character relied less on his unaided perceptions and interpretations. In the midst of chaos, however, this maxim may be no more helpful than any other; Clara, for example, violently resists the sympathy of friends who might help to restore the order of her mind.

Though not a great novel, *Wieland* is both intrinsically interesting and worthy of study for the degree to which it foreshadows developments of considerable importance in the American novel. By subjecting Clara to a completely disordered world and by taking her through a loss of identity, Brown prepares the way for greater American Gothic protagonists from Captain Ahab to Thomas Sutpen.

Edgar Huntly appears at first to be a clumsily episodic adventure novel, but the more closely one looks at it, the more interesting and troubling it becomes. The protagonist-narrator, Edgar Huntly, writes a long letter to his betrothed, Mary Waldegrave, recounting a series of adventures in which he has participated. This letter is followed by two short ones from Huntly to his benefactor, Sarsefield, and one final short letter from Sarsefield to Huntly. The last letter suggests some of the ways in which the apparent clumsiness becomes troubling. Midway through the novel, Edgar learns that he will probably be unable to marry his fiancée, for her inheritance from her recently murdered brother seems not really to belong to her. Later, it appears that the return of Edgar's recently well-married friend, Sarsefield, once again puts him in a position to marry, but Sarsefield's last letter raises doubts about this event which remain unresolved. The reader never learns whether Edgar and Mary are united. The purpose of Sarsefield's letter is to chastise Edgar.

Edgar's main project in the novel becomes to cure the mad Clithero, who mistakenly believes he has been responsible for the death of Sarsefield's wife, formerly Mrs. Lorimer. By the end of his adventures, Edgar understands the degree to which Clithero is mistaken about events, and believes that when Clithero learns the truth, he will be cured. To Edgar's surprise, when Clithero learns the truth, he apparently sets out to really kill his benefactress, Mrs. Sarsefield. Edgar writes his two letters to Sarsefield to warn of Clithero's impending appearance and sends them directly to Sarsefield, knowing that his wife may well see them first. She does see the second letter, and collapses and miscarries as a result. Sarsefield chastises Edgar for misdirecting the letters, even though Sarsefield knew full well from the first letter that the second was on its way to the same address. While, on the one hand, Edgar's error seems comically trivial, especially in comparison with the misguided benevolence which drives him to meddle with Clithero, on the other hand, the consequences are quite serious, serious enough to make one question why Edgar *and* Sarsefield are so stupid about their handling of the letters. The reader is left wondering what to make of Edgar and Sarsefield; does either of them know what he is doing?

The novel seems intended in part as a demonstration that one is rarely if ever aware of what he or she is doing. Paul Witherington, in *Narrative Techniques in the Novels of Charles Brockden Brown* (1967), notes that the novel takes the form of a quest which never quite succeeds, a story of initiation in which repeated initiations fail to take place. Edgar returns to his home shortly after the murder of his closest friend, Waldegrave, in order to solve the crime and bring the murderer to justice. When he sees Clithero, the mysterious servant of a neighbor, sleepwalking at the murder scene, he suspects Clithero of the murder. When he confronts Clithero, Edgar learns the story of his past. In Ireland, Clithero rose out of obscurity to become the favorite servant of Mrs. Lorimer. His virtue eventually led to Mrs. Lorimer's allowing an engagement between Clithero and her beloved niece. This story of virtue rewarded turned sour when, in self-defense, Clithero killed Mrs. Lorimer's blackguard twin brother. Mrs. Lorimer believed her life to be mysteriously entwined with her brother's and was convinced that she would die when he did. Clithero believed her and was convinced that by killing the father of his bride-to-be he had also killed his benefactress. In a mad refinement of benevolence, he determined to stab her in order to spare her the pain of dying from the news of her brother's death. Failing with the sword, he resorted to the word, telling her what had happened. Upon her collapse, he took flight, ignorant of the actual consequences of his act. Mrs. Lorimer did not die; she married Sarsefield and they went to America. Though Clithero's guilt seems unconnected with the murder of Waldegrave, except that the event has renewed Clithero's anguish over what he believes to be his crime, Edgar still suspects him. Furthermore, Clithero's story has stimulated Edgar's benevolence.

Edgar becomes determined to help Clithero, for even if he is Waldegrave's murderer, he has suffered enough. Clithero retires to the wilderness of Norwalk to die after telling his story to Edgar, but Edgar pursues him there to save him. After three trips filled with wilderness adventures, Edgar receives a series of shocks. He meets the man who is probably the real owner of Mary's inheritance and loses his hope for a speedy marriage. Fatigued from his adventures in the wilderness and frustrated in his efforts to benefit Clithero, perhaps guilty about prying into Clithero's life and certainly guilty about his handling of Waldegrave's letters, he begins to sleepwalk. His sleepwalking mirrors Clithero's in several ways, most notably in that he also hides a treasure, Waldegrave's letters, without being aware of what he is doing. After a second episode of sleepwalking, he finds himself at the bottom of a pit in a cave with no memory of how he arrived there; this is the second apparent diversion from his quest for Waldegrave's murderer.

Edgar takes three days to return to civilization, moving through a fairly clear death and rebirth pattern which parallels the movement from savagery to civilization. His adventures—drinking panther blood, rescuing a maiden, fighting Indians, losing and finding himself in rough terrain, nearly killing his friends, and successfully evading his own rescue while narrowly escaping death several times—are filled with weird mistakes and rather abstract humor. For example, he is amazed at his physical endurance. When he finds himself within a half-day's walk of home, he determines, despite his three days of privation, to make the walk in six hours. Six hours later, he has not yet even gained the necessary road, and, though he knows where he is, he is effectively no closer to home than when he started out. Though he has endured the physical trials, he has not progressed.

Of his earlier explorations of the wilderness, Edgar says, "My rambles were productive of incessant novelty, though they always terminated in the prospects of limits that could not be overleaped." This physical nature of the wilderness is indicative of the moral nature of human life, which proves so complex that while one believes he can see to the next step of his actions, he finds continually that he has seen incorrectly. Edgar repeatedly finds himself doing what he never thought he could do and failing at what he believes he can easily accomplish. The complexities of his wilderness experience are beyond the reach of this brief essay, but they seem to lead toward the deeper consideration of questions Edgar raises after hearing Clithero's story:

If consequences arise that cannot be foreseen, shall we find no refuge in the persuasion of our rectitude and of human frailty? Shall we deem ourselves criminal because we do not enjoy the attributes of Deity? Because our power and our knowledge are confined by impassable boundaries?

In order for Edgar to be initiated and to achieve his quest, he needs to come to a just appreciation of his own limits. Although he can see Clithero's limitations quite clearly, Edgar fails to see his own, even after he learns that he has been sleepwalking, that he has been largely mistaken about the events surrounding the Indian raid, that he has mistaken his friends for enemies, and that he has made many other errors which might have caused his own death. Even after he learns that an Indian killed Waldegrave and that his efforts with Clithero have been largely irrelevant, he persists in his ignorant attempt to cure the madman, only to precipitate new disasters. Edgar does not know himself and cannot measure the consequences of his simplest actions, yet he persists in meddling with another equally complex soul which he understands even less. Before Clithero tells Edgar his story, he says, "You boast of the beneficence of your intentions. You set yourself to do me benefit. What are the effects of your misguided zeal and random efforts? They have brought my life to a miserable close." This statement proves prophetic, for prior to each confrontation with Edgar, Clithero has determined to try to live out his life as best he can; each of Edgar's attempts to help drives Clithero toward the suicide which he finally commits.

Insofar as Edgar's quest is to avenge his friend's murder, he succeeds quite by accident. Insofar as his quest is for ethical maturity, he fails miserably, but no one else in the novel succeeds, either. If a measure of moral maturity is the ability to moderate one's passions to the benefit of others, no one is mature. The virtuous Mrs. Lorimer cannot behave rationally toward her villainous brother, and her suffering derives ultimately from that failure. Clithero will murder out of misguided benevolence. Sarsefield, a physician, will let Clithero die of wounds received from Indians because he believes that to Clithero, "Consciousness itself is the malady, the pest, of which he only is cured who ceases to think." Even though Edgar must assent to this statement, concluding that "Disastrous and humiliating is the state of man! By his own hands is constructed the mass of misery and error in which his steps are forever involved," he still wishes to correct some of Clithero's mistakes. In doing so, he provokes Clithero's suicide. No character understands himself, his limitations, or his actions thoroughly; in the case of each of these characters, benevolence issues in murder, direct or indirect. One of the novel's many ironies is that among Edgar, Sarsefield, and Clithero, only Clithero is never morally responsible for a death other than his own.

In *Edgar Huntly* as in *Wieland*, the stage of human action is beyond human comprehension. In *Wieland*, although there is no sanctuary for the virtuous, virtue remains valuable at least as a source of illusions of order, but in *Edgar Huntly* positive virtue becomes criminal because of inevitable human error.

The phenomenon of sleepwalking and the motif of ignorance of self encourage the reader to consider those darker motives which may be hidden from the consciousness of the characters. Edgar must indeed affirm that men are criminal because they have not the attributes of Deity.

Wieland and *Edgar Huntly* are good examples of Brown's interests and complexity of fiction. His wedding of serious philosophical issues with forms of the popular Gothic novel accounts for his distinctive role in the development of the American novel and his continuing interest for students of American culture.

Major publications other than long fiction
SHORT FICTION: *Carwin, the Biloquist, and Other American Tales and Pieces*, 1822; *The Rhapsodist and Other Uncollected Writings*, 1943.
NONFICTION: *Alcuin: A Dialogue*, 1798.

Bibliography
Berthoff, W. B. "'A Lesson on Concealment': Brockden Brown's Method in Fiction," in *Philological Quarterly*. XXXVII (1958), pp. 45-57.
Clark, D. L. *Charles Brockden Brown: Pioneer Voice of America*, 1952.
Dunlap, William. *The Life of Charles Brockden Brown*, 1815.
Ringe, Donald A. *Charles Brockden Brown*, 1966.
Rosenthal, Bernard, ed. *Critical Essays on Charles Brockden Brown*, 1981.
Warfel, Harry R. *Charles Brockden Brown: American Gothic Novelist*, 1949.

Terry Heller

JOHN BUCHAN

Born: Perth, Scotland; August 26, 1875
Died: Montreal, Canada; February 11, 1940

Principal long fiction

Sir Quixote of the Moors, Being Some Account of an Episode in the Life of the Sieur de Rohaine, 1895; *John Burnet of Barns*, 1898; *A Lost Lady of Old Years*, 1899; *The Half-Hearted*, 1900; *Prester John*, 1910 (published in the United States as *The Great Diamond Pipe*); *Salute to Adventurers*, 1915; *The Thirty-Nine Steps*, 1915; *The Power-House*, 1916; *Greenmantle*, 1916; *Mr. Standfast*, 1919; *Huntingtower*, 1922; *Midwinter: Certain Travellers in Old England*, 1923; *The Three Hostages*, 1924; *John Macnab*, 1925; *The Dancing Floor*, 1926; *Witch Wood*, 1927; *The Courts of the Morning*, 1929; *Castle Gay*, 1930; *The Blanket of the Dark*, 1931; *A Prince of the Captivity*, 1933; *The Free Fishers*, 1934; *The House of the Four Winds*, 1935; *The Island of Sheep*, 1936 (published in the United States as *The Man from the Norlands*); *Sick Heart River*, 1941 (published in the United States as *Mountain Meadow*).

Other literary forms

Although John Buchan is remembered chiefly for his novels, more than half of his published work is in the form of nonfiction prose. He wrote numerous biographies and works of history, and he published speeches and lectures, educational books for children, and countless articles, essays, pamphlets, notes, and reviews. Late in his life, he produced an autobiographical work, and after his death his widow edited and published two collections of selections from his works.

Buchan's fictional works include not only novels, but also a story for children, *The Magic Walking-Stick* (1932), and several collections of short stories. Some of the settings and situations in these stories later appeared in slightly altered form in Buchan's novels, and several of the stories in the later collections make use of characters from the novels, including Richard Hannay, Sandy Arbuthnot, and Sir Edward Leithen. Two of Buchan's volumes of short stories, *The Path of the King* (1921) and *The Gap in the Curtain* (1932), connect independent episodes and are bound together by a narrative frame; as a result, these works are sometimes listed as novels, although the individual episodes are actually quite distinct from one another.

In addition to his prose works, Buchan published a number of poems and edited three volumes of verse. He also edited several works of nonfiction, including Francis Bacon's *Essays and Apothegms of Francis Lord Bacon* (1597, edited in 1894) and Izaak Walton's *The Compleat Angler: Or, The Contemplative Man's Recreation* (1653, edited in 1901).

Achievements

While he was still an undergraduate at Oxford, Buchan received two major prizes for writing: the Stanhope Historical Essay Prize for an essay on Sir Walter Raleigh (1897) and the Newdigate Prize for Poetry for *The Pilgrim Fathers* (1898). He was graduated in 1899 with a first-class honors degree, and shortly thereafter he was appointed private secretary to the High Commissioner for South Africa (1901-1903). This was the first of many prestigious posts that Buchan filled: he was a conservative member of Parliament for the Scottish universities (1927-1935), president of the Scottish History Society (1929-1933), Lord High Commissioner to the general assembly of the Church of Scotland (1933, 1934), chancellor of the University of Edinburgh (1937-1940), and Governor-General of Canada (1935-1940). In 1935, in recognition of his accomplishments and of his new post as governor-general, he was created Baron Tweedsmuir of Elsfield.

In part because of his political prominence and his reputation as a historian, and in part because of his achievements as a novelist, Buchan received honorary doctorates from Oxford, Harvard, Yale, Columbia, McGill, and McMaster Universities, and from the Universities of Glasgow, St. Andrews, Edinburgh, Toronto, Manitoba, and British Columbia. He also became an honorary fellow of Brasenose College, Oxford.

Although Buchan was clearly not a full-time writer of fiction, his achievements as a novelist include some degree of critical success and a great deal of commercial popularity, particularly during the period between World War I and the 1960's. His novels appealed to a wide and varied audience, including schoolboys, laborers, clergymen, academics, members of various professions, and such celebrities as A. J. Balfour, Stanley Baldwin, Clement Atlee, Ezra Pound, C. S. Lewis, J. B. Priestly, King George V, and Czar Nicholas II. Although they have declined in popularity in the United States since the early 1960's, Buchan's novels continue to sell moderately well in Great Britain, and they have been translated into a number of foreign languages, including French, German, Spanish, Dutch, Danish, Czech, Swedish, and Arabic.

Biography

John Buchan was born in Perth, Scotland, on August 26, 1875. He spent his early childhood near the Firth of Forth, an area to which he often returned for holidays and which served as the setting for a great deal of his fiction. His father was a minister of the Free Church of Scotland; his mother was the daughter of a sheep-farmer. From both of his parents, but particularly from his strong-minded mother, Buchan learned to value endurance, hard work, and, above all, perseverance, and he placed such emphasis on these qualities in his novels that many readers have come to regard this emphasis as the hallmark of his work.

When Buchan was thirteen, his father was called to the John Knox Free

Church in Glasgow. There Buchan attended Hutchesons' Grammar School and, later, the University of Glasgow, whose faculty then included such scholars as Lord Kelvin, A. C. Bradley, George Ramsay, and Gilbert Murray; the latter became one of Buchan's closest friends. At the end of his third year at the University of Glasgow, Buchan won a Junior Hulme Scholarship to Oxford University, and in the autumn of 1895, he began his studies at Brasenose College.

Because his scholarship was not sufficient to meet all of his expenses, Buchan earned extra money by reading manuscripts for the publishing firm of John Lane; among the manuscripts that he recommended for publication was Arnold Bennett's first novel, *A Man from the North* (1898). Buchan also became a regular reviewer for several publications and continued to work steadily on his own novels and nonfiction prose. In 1898, he had the distinction of being listed in *Who's Who*: he had at that time six books in print, two in press, and three in progress, and he had published innumerable articles, essays, and reviews. He was also an active member of several prestigious Oxford and London clubs and organizations, notably the Oxford Union, of which he was librarian and later president. In 1899, he sat for his final examinations and earned a first-class honors degree; one year later, having "eaten his dinners" and passed the examination, he was called to the bar.

During the two years following his graduation, Buchan wrote leading articles for *The Spectator*, worked as a barrister, and continued to write both fiction and nonfiction. In 1901, he accepted the post of political private secretary to Lord Milner, who was then High Commissioner for South Africa. During the two years that he spent in that country, Buchan became familiar with the practical administrative aspects of political situations which he had discussed on a more theoretical level in *The Spectator* essays. He also acquired background material for several of his novels, notably *Prester John*.

When he returned to London in 1903, Buchan resumed his legal work at the bar and his literary work on *The Spectator*. In 1906, he became second assistant editor of *The Spectator*, and, in 1907, he accepted the position of chief literary adviser to the publishing firm of Thomas Nelson. He also continued to extend the circle of acquaintances that he had begun to form at Oxford, and he became one of the best-known and most promising young men in London society and politics.

Buchan was greatly attracted to a young lady whom he met at a London dinner party, and on July 15, 1907, he and Susan Grosvenor were married at St. George's, Hanover Square. Their first child, Alice, was born one year later, followed by John (1911), William (1916), and Alastair (1918). Until the outbreak of World War I, the Buchans lived comfortably in London while John Buchan continued to write fiction, legal opinions, and essays and articles for such publications as *The Spectator* and *The Times Literary Supplement*.

Shortly after World War I began, Buchan, who had been asked to write a continuing history of the war for Nelson's and who also acted as correspondent for *The Times*, visited a number of French battlefields as a noncombatant. In 1916, he returned to France as a temporary lieutenant-colonel, acting as press officer and propagandist for the foreign office and working for Field Marshal Lord Douglas Haig as official historian. In February, 1917, he was appointed director of information, in charge of publicity and propaganda. In the midst of all of his war-related activities, between 1914 and 1918, he wrote three of his most popular novels: *The Thirty-Nine Steps*, *Greenmantle*, and *Mr. Standfast*.

When World War I ended, Buchan purchased Elsfield, a country house near Oxford, and settled down to a routine of writing, working at Nelson's, and entertaining his numerous friends, including T. E. Lawrence, Robert Graves, W. P. Ker, Gilbert Murray, and A. L. Rowse. In 1919, he became a director of Reuters news agency, and four years later he became deputy chairman. Buchan's peaceful routine at Elsfield, however, ended in the spring of 1927, when he was elected to parliament as the member for the Scottish Universities, a position he held until 1935. He became as active a member of London society during his term in parliament as he had been as a younger man, and he became increasingly well known and influential in political circles. He was appointed Lord High Commissioner to the general assembly of the Church of Scotland in 1933 and again in 1934, and in 1935 he was appointed to a much more important post: Governor-General of the Dominion of Canada. In recognition of his accomplishments and of his new position, he was created a baron; he chose as his title Lord Tweedsmuir of Elsfield.

Buchan's tenure of office as governor-general (1935-1940) coincided with the growing tension in Europe which eventually led to World War II, and, because his post was largely a ceremonial one, he had to be extremely cautious in his statements and in his behavior. Among the delicate diplomatic situations that he handled well were the visits of President Franklin Delano Roosevelt and of King George VI and Queen Elizabeth to Canada; his greatest error in diplomacy occurred when he made a speech in which he suggested that Canada's defense policy was inadequate. Despite occasional lapses of this type, however, Buchan was a successful governor-general, in part because he made a point of visiting not only such cultural centers as Montreal and Quebec, but also more remote places such as Medicine Hat, Regina, Saskatoon, and Edmonton. In addition to enhancing his popularity as governor-general, these trips provided background material for his last novel, *Sick Heart River*.

As the end of his five-year term of office approached, Buchan was asked to allow himself to be nominated for another term. He refused because of his steadily declining health and he had planned to leave Canada at the end of 1940. On February 6, 1940, however, he suffered a cerebral hemorrhage and, falling, struck his head; five days later he died. He left an autobiographical work, a novel, a children's history of Canada, a volume of essays, and a volume of lectures, all of which were published posthumously, as well as an unfinished novel and two chapters of a nonfiction work; these chapters appear at the end of the autobiography.

Analysis

Despite his manifold activities, John Buchan is remembered primarily as a writer of implausible but exciting adventure fiction with overtones of the nineteenth century romance. Most of his novels fall into the general category of thrillers, but a few, such as *Salute to Adventurers*, *Midwinter*, *Witch Wood*, and *The Blanket of the Dark*, are more accurately classified as historical romances. Despite some variations in form and emphasis, however, all of Buchan's novels share certain features which contribute to the characteristic flavor of his fiction; these include melodramatic sequences, unusually effective descriptions of landscape and atmosphere, frequent references to such qualities as endurance and perseverance, and exciting but comparatively nonviolent action.

The melodramatic quality of Buchan's fiction arises from a number of sources, including his admiration for the highly melodramatic thrillers of E. Phillips Oppenheim and his own overdeveloped sense of the theatrical. Although Buchan was seldom original in his choice of melodramatic elements, he made good use of them in enhancing the suspense and excitement of his novels. For example, *Prester John*, *Greenmantle*, *The Three Hostages*, *The Dancing Floor*, and *Witch Wood* owe a great deal of their atmosphere and effect to indistinctly defined and therefore singularly mysterious antique rituals and ceremonies, including pagan sacrifice and devil worship. Other novels, including *Huntingtower*, *Midwinter*, and *The House of the Four Winds*, feature royalty in distress and simple but noble-hearted adventurers who risk their lives for "the cause." Buchan also made frequent use of such staple elements of melodramatic fiction as secret societies, talismans and tokens, fairylike heroines (milky-skinned and graceful), exotic villainesses (brunette and slinky), and characters who bear a Burden of Secret Sorrow.

As these examples suggest, Buchan did not hesitate to employ many of the clichés of the thriller and romance genres. Moreover, his work is not only derivative, but also repetitive, containing numerous examples of devices which he found successful and therefore used repeatedly. For example, in addition to the novels that make use of some form of magic and those that deal with royalty and adventurers, he wrote five novels in which foiling the villain depends upon decoding a cipher, six in which one of the villains tries to mesmerize the protagonist, and eleven in which one of the villains passes for a time as an irreproachable member of society. In addition to reusing successful plot devices, Buchan had the irritating habit of repeating certain favorite words, including "eldritch," "dislimn," "totem," and "frowst."

Buchan's tendency to repeat himself is not surprising in view of the speed with which he wrote. In the period between 1915 and 1936, he produced twenty-one volumes of fiction and almost thirty volumes of nonfiction. Despite his hasty writing, his repetitiveness, and his overuse of clichés, however, Buchan was by no means a mere hack. He wrote disciplined, polished, occasionally elegant prose, seldom stooping to sensationalism and describing even the most exciting or dramatic scenes in a clear and narrative style that was seldom equaled in the thriller fiction of that period. More important, like Sir Walter Scott and Robert Louis Stevenson, whose work Buchan greatly admired, he was not only acutely sensitive to local color and atmosphere but also gifted in expressing that sensitivity in his fiction. He was particularly adept at making use of settings with which he was familiar: many of his novels, including *The Thirty-Nine Steps*, *John Macnab*, and *Witch Wood*, are set in the Scottish countryside where Buchan grew up and to which he often returned; *Prester John* is set in South Africa, where Buchan served as Lord Milner's secretary; several novels, including *The Power House* and *The Three Hostages*, contain scenes in the parts of London that he frequented during the years before World War I and during his term in parliament; and most of the action in *Sick Heart River* takes place in the far north of Canada, which he visited during his term as governor-general.

Buchan's depiction of these familiar settings and of the atmospheres associated with them is both denotative and connotative, and this combination, which is responsible for a great deal of the power and charm of his books, does much to raise his work above the level of run-of-the-mill adventure fiction. The denotative quality of Buchan's descriptions stems from his talent in selecting the salient features of a landscape and producing vividly lifelike verbal pictures of them in disciplined and concise prose. The connotative quality results from his ability to imbue the landscape with an atmosphere that is so vivid that it might almost be called a personality, and to derive from the landscape a mood or even a moral valence that complements the action of the novel. In *Witch Wood*, for example, the open and innocent Scottish countryside is marred by a black wood, which is not only an appropriate setting for the devilish rites that take place in it, but also, the novel implies the cause of them in some obscure manner.

In a number of Buchan's novels, the complementary relationship between the setting and the action reaches the level of allegory when the protagonist and, in some cases, other characters, undertake a long and arduous journey through a landscape that includes steep hills, swamps or difficult waters, natural pitfalls, and traps designed by enemies who often pose as friends. The difficulties that arise in the course of this journey provide opportunities for the exciting chase scenes and the suspenseful action that are essential to adventure literature, but they also do more: as a character overcomes each of the obstacles presented by the landscape through which he moves, he acquires or displays appropriate qualities of soul that redeem him or confirm him in his moral character and status. This allegorical use of landscape, which is clearly based on one of Buchan's favorite books, John Bunyan's *The Pilgrim's Progress* (1678), serves as the central plot device in almost all of his best-known novels, including *The Thirty-Nine Steps*, *The Power-House*, *Greenmantle*, *Mr. Standfast*, *Midwinter*, and *Sick Heart River*.

The most important effect of Buchan's repeated use of landscape as an allegory is the stress that this technique enables him to place upon the redeeming quality of certain types of behavior. In order to overcome the obstacles that beset them, the characters in his novels must display courage, endurance, and, above all, perseverance in hard work despite fatigue, setbacks, and apparently hopeless delays. These qualities are so central to his novels that all of his major characters are defined and evaluated in terms of them. Some characters already possess these attributes before the action begins and are finally triumphant because they successfully apply to a particular set of circumstances the qualities they had already developed and, in some cases, displayed in earlier adventures; other characters develop these attributes as the action progresses.

The protagonist with predeveloped virtues is a character type common to almost all adventure literature, and, in most cases, Buchan's treatment of it is not particularly memorable. In the novels that center around Sir Edward Leithen, however, Buchan handles the theme quite effectively, showing that even someone who spends a great deal of time at a desk can possess the courage, endurance, and perseverance of a true hero. Further, in addition to these basic qualities, Buchan endows Leithen with a degree of sensitivity that allows him to absorb and to respond to the influences of various landscapes, thus deriving from his adventures not only the satisfaction of accomplishing his external objective, but also increased insight, depth of soul, and spiritual regeneration. This theme is consistent and progressive in the Leithen novels, so that in the last one, *Sick Heart River*, Leithen's renewal of soul, resulting from his responsiveness to the influences of the environment, is carried almost to the point of apotheosis.

In addition to characters such as Leithen, who clearly possess the qualities necessary for success, Buchan's novels include a number of lesser characters who, as the action progresses, display or attain unexpected greatness of soul through unaccustomed exertion and suffering. Buchan was generally successful in dealing with such characters, in part because of the surprising liberality of his attitude toward character types who would, in most of the other adventure literature of that period, have no redeeming—or even redeemable— qualities whatsoever. Because his initial description of these characters is unusually balanced, their conversion in the course of participating in the adventure is far more convincing than it otherwise would have been.

One such character, found in Buchan's thriller, *Mr. Standfast*, is a World War I conscientious objector named Launcelot Wake who first appears as a hot-eyed, sallow young man ridiculing everything that is held sacred by the protagonist, Brigadier-General Richard Hannay. Nevertheless, Hannay, and through him the reader, finds it impossible to dislike Wake, who is strong-willed, intelligent, and sincere in his beliefs. As he willingly accompanies Hannay on a difficult and dangerous climb through an Alpine pass, voluntarily exposing himself to enemy fire on the front lines, and finally receiving his death wound, Wake gradually achieves dignity, self-respect, and spiritual regeneration—yet he remains, to the end of the novel, a staunch pacifist who resolutely refuses to take up arms. No other major thriller-writer of Buchan's generation would have had the tolerance or the breadth of mind to make a demi-hero of a recusant conscientious objector, particularly in a novel written in the middle of World War I while its author was on active service as a lieutenant-colonel in the British army.

As Buchan's sympathetic depiction of Launcelot Wake suggests, his overall point of view was far from the bellicose and sometimes Fascist attitude associated with writers such as "Sapper," Edgar Wallace, and Gerard Fairlie, whose protagonists unhesitatingly inflict physical injury and even death upon villains whom they encounter. Buchan's protagonists seldom administer any form of punishment, and if the villains die at all it is usually the result of an accident or, more rarely, at the hands of a minor character in the story. In *Greenmantle*, for example, the exotically beautiful villainess is accidentally killed by artillery fire; in *Mr. Standfast*, a German spy is killed by German fire in the trenches; in *The Three Hostages*, the arch-villain falls to his death despite Hannay's efforts to save him; in *Midwinter*, one traitor is placed on parole in consideration of his wife's feelings and another is sent into exile; in *Witch Wood*, the principal warlock is beset by his own demons and dies in his madness. Buchan never dwelt upon or glorified any form of bloodshed, and some of his novels involve no violence at all, stressing instead imaginative if occasionally melodramatic situations, suspenseful action, and seemingly insurmountable challenges to the strength and determination of the characters.

Although all of his novels share certain common features, in some cases Buchan made use of one of his three major series protagonists, each of whom imbues the novels in which he appears with his distinctive flavor. By far the most popular of these is Richard Hannay, who is the central figure in *The Thirty-Nine Steps*, *Greenmantle*, *Mr. Standfast*, and *The Three Hostages*, and appears in *The Courts of the Morning* and *The Island of Sheep*. Hannay is by far the most typical thriller hero whom Buchan created: physically strong and morally intrepid, he is always ready for a bracing climb in the Scottish hills or a brisk run across the moors, usually dodging at least two sets of pursuers and an occasional dog. Becomingly modest regarding his own accomplishments and courage, Hannay generously admires the greatness—albeit perverted greatness—of his foes. Although several villains, including the old man with the hooded eyes in *The Thirty-Nine Steps*, Hilda von Einem in *Green-*

mantle, and most notably, Dominic Medina in *The Three Hostages*, try to hypnotize Hannay, he is protected by his solid common sense and by a strong will fortified by frequent cold baths. He is also more sportsmanlike than practical; for example, when he finally gets a clear shot at the highly elusive and dangerous villain of *Mr. Standfast*, he allows him to escape yet again because firing at him under those conditions seems "like potting at a sitting rabbit." On the other hand, Hannay is far from being one of the mindless anti-intellectuals who infest early twentieth century thriller literature. In *Mr. Standfast*, for example, he willingly undertakes a course of reading in the English classics, and throughout the series most of his attitudes and reflections are, if not profound, at least reasonably intelligent.

Although Hannay is by no means a mere beefy dolt, many of the opinions expressed in the course of his first-person narration reflect the prejudices common to his generation and social class, and these include racial and ethnic attitudes which many readers find offensive. Since most of the slighting references to blacks, Germans, Italians, Russians, and Jews that appear in Buchan's work are concentrated in the Hannay stories, it is possible to argue, as several of Buchan's supporters have done, that Hannay's attitudes and language arise from his characterization rather than from the kind of prejudice on Buchan's part that is associated with such writers as "Sapper," Gerald Fairlie, and Dornford Yates. Buchan's partisans also point out that there are comparatively few such references even in the Hannay books, and that these are not nearly so virulent as similar references in the works of many of Buchan's contemporaries. Further, Buchan is known to have supported a number of Jewish causes; for example, in 1932 he succeeded Josiah Wedgwood as chairman of a pro-Zionist parliamentary committee, and in 1934 he spoke at a demonstration organized by the Jewish National Fund.

Buchan's detractors, on the other hand, point to passages in his personal correspondence that are critical of various ethnic groups. They also maintain that his attitude toward blacks, formed in part during his experience in South Africa, was paternalistic and patronizing, and it is certainly true that even when he meant to express admiration for members of the black race, as he did in *Prester John*, his attitude and his choice of language were often unconsciously—and therefore all the more offensively—condescending. Perhaps the fairest conclusion that can be drawn from this controversy is that, although some of Buchan's racial and ethnic prejudices would be considered offensive today, the prejudices that he attributed to the fictional character of Richard Hannay are probably more extreme than his own. Further, by the standards of his age and class he was commendably moderate in his use of racial and ethnic stereotypes.

Buchan's second series protagonist was Dickson McCunn. The three McCunn novels are the most overtly, yet humorously, romantic of Buchan's thrillers: *Huntingtower* features an exiled Russian princess who is loved by a left-wing poet and rescued with the help of a group of Glasgow street urchins, and *Castle Gay* and *The House of the Four Winds* deal with the restoration of the rightful Prince of Evallonia with the help of the same urchins (now grown), a reluctant newspaper magnate, and a circus elephant. McCunn himself is a middle-aged, recently retired grocer who looks forward to "Seeing Life" and "Doing Noble Deeds." He dreams of becoming involved in pure Sir Walter Scott adventures, and, because of his dreams, he tends to view real-life people and situations through a rosy, romantic haze; for example, he reverences the rather weak and worldly Prince of Evallonia as the embodiment of all the qualities associated with the Bonnie Prince Charlie of legend. Nevertheless, McCunn is saved from being ridiculous by his solid common sense and essential decency and by Buchan's implication that, if what McCunn sees is not precisely what *is*, it is at least what *should be*.

The dramatic, in some respects melodramatic, quality of the McCunn novels is blessedly undercut by the verbal and situational humor that is their hallmark. In *Huntingtower*, for example, Wee Jaikie, the street boy who later bcomes the true protagonist of *Castle Gay* and *The House of the Four Winds*, helps to rescue a Romanov princess while singing garbled versions of Bolshevik hymns that he learned at a socialist Sunday School. Similarly, at one point in *The House of the Four Winds*, a friend of Jaikie who assists him in a series of swashbuckling episodes appears outside his second-story window mounted on an elephant named Aurunculeia and asks in German for a match. Through his handling of these humorously improbable situations, Buchan gently ridiculed the more preposterous aspects of an excessively romantic view of life, while retaining and even enhancing those qualities which he never ceased to admire, such as constancy, devotion, and faith.

Buchan's last series protagonist, Sir Edward Leithen, is featured in four novels: *The Power-House, John Macnab, The Dancing Floor*, and *Sick Heart River*. These are somewhat atypical adventure stories, largely because they are "about" not only a series of suspenseful activities, but also a group of central themes, including the thinness of civilization and the ethic of success. These themes are expressed through the first-person narration of Leithen, who is a far more sophisticated and reflective character than Richard Hannay, Buchan's other first-person series narrator.

In view of the legal and political background with which Buchan endowed Leithen, it is not surprising that he demonstrates an intense awareness of the thinness of the shell of civilization within which he and his contemporaries desire to believe themselves safe. This concept is explored from a number of perspectives within the series: for example, in *The Power-House*, which is the earliest Leithen novel and the closest to the traditional thriller mode, the expression of this theme centers around the imminence of violence and the vulnerability of ordinary individuals, while in the more recondite novel *The Dancing Floor*, the thinness of civilization is associated with the terrifying attractiveness of obscurely fearsome pre-Christian religious rites to whose power Leithen himself, in many respects the quintessential civilized man, nearly succumbs.

Buchan provided a balance for the sensibility that Leithen displays in his reflections upon the thinness of civilization by attributing to him not only a shrewd and practical legal mind, but also a respect for worldly success which is so marked that it borders upon careerism. Although this emphasis upon competitive success is by no means confined to the Leithen novels, it is most evident in them. Leithen himself is greatly in demand as a solicitor, is elected to parliament, and eventually becomes solicitor-general, and more important, the novels which he narrates contain numerous approving references to persons who are not merely successful but unsurpassed in their fields. Nevertheless, a close reading of the Leithen novels shows that although worldly success is spoken of with respect, it is treated not as an end in itself, but as a testimony to the stamina, hard work, and perseverence of the individual who has attained it. If the Leithen novels abound in references to success, they also abound in references to exhaustion, and both types of references apply to the same individuals. Success in competition with others in one's field is, in the Leithen's novels, simply an extension of the Bunyanesque ethic of hard work and perseverance which, in all of Buchan's fiction, leads to success in competition with villains and with natural forces. Further, in all of Buchan's novels worldly success is second in importance to more basic values, such as courage, honor, and compassion. To Leithen and to Buchan's other major characters, success is admirable but it is emphatically not enough.

As the preceding discussion indicates, Buchan's novels are written in polished prose and include sensitive descriptions of settings which are incorporated into both the plots of the novels and the development of the characters. Further, his liberal attitudes not only redeem his work from jingoism, egregious racism, and gratuitous violence, but also contribute to the development of less stereotyped, more varied, and more complex characters than are usually found in adventure fiction. Buchan was not, however, a serious literary figure and never claimed to be. He wrote his novels quickly and in the midst of numerous distractions, seldom revised, and often made use of clichéd situations and of devices which he himself had used, in many cases repeatedly, in earlier stories. Further, although he did create some unusually good characters, he also created a large number of cardboard ones. His villains, in particular, are with few exceptions unsubstantial figures whose machinations are overshadowed to the point of eclipse by the journey and chase scenes that dominate and, in this respect, upset the balance of several of his novels. The structure of the novels is further weakened by the fact that, although the emphasis which Buchan places upon the moral order seldom becomes overtly didactic, it does provide an excuse for the use of a profusion of providential occurrences which are virtually indistinguishable from mere blatant coincidences. Despite their flaws, however, Buchan's novels are well-written and sensitive tales of adventure whose *raison d'être* is to provide salutary entertainment; that they usually succeed in doing so is no minor accomplishment.

Major publications other than long fiction

SHORT FICTION: *Grey Weather: Moorland Tales of My Own People*, 1899; *The Watcher by the Threshold and Other Tales*, 1902; *The Moon Endureth: Tales and Fancies*, 1912; *The Path of the King*, 1921; *Modern Short Stories*, 1926 (edited); *The Runagates Club*, 1928; *The Gap in the Curtain*, 1932.

POETRY: *Musa Piscatrix*, 1896 (edited); *The Pilgrim Fathers, 1898*, 1898; *Ordeal by Marriage: An Eclogue*, 1915; *Poems, Scots and English, 1917*, 1936; *The Northern Muse*, 1924; *The Poetry of Neil Munro*, 1931.

NONFICTION: *Essays and Apothegms of Francis Lord Bacon*, 1894 (edited); *Scholar Gipsies*, 1986; *Sir Walter Raleigh, 1897*, 1897; *Brasenose College*, 1898; *The Compleat Angler: Or, The Contemplative Man's Recreation*, 1901 (edited); *The African Colony: Studies in the Reconstruction*, 1903; *The Law Relating to the Taxation of Foreign Income*, 1905; *Some Eighteenth Century Byways and Other Essays*, 1908; *The Marquis of Montrose*, 1913; *Andrew Jameson, Lord Ardwall*, 1913; *Britain's War by Land*, 1915; *The Achievements of France*, 1915; *Nelson's History of the War*, 1915-1919 (24 volumes); *The Battle of Jutland*, 1916; *The Battle of Somme, First Phase*, 1916; *The Battle of Somme, Second Phase*, 1917; *These for Remembrance*, 1919; *The Battle-Honours of Scotland, 1914-1918*, 1919; *The History of South African Forces in France*, 1920; *Francis and Riversdale Grenfell: A Memoir*, 1920; *Great Hours in Sport*, 1921 (edited); *Miscellanies, Literary and Historical*, 1921 (2 volumes); *A History of the Great War*, 1921-1922 (4 volumes); *A Book of Escapes and Hurried Journeys*, 1922; *The Last Secrets: The Final Mysteries of Exploration*, 1923; *Days to Remember: The British Empire in the Great War*, 1923 (with Henry Newbolt); *A History of English Literature*, 1923 (edited); *The Nations of Today: A New History of the World*, 1923-1924 (edited); *Lord Minto: A Memoir*, 1924; *The History of the Royal Scots Fusiliers, 1678-1918*, 1925; *The Man and the Book: Sir Walter Scott*, 1925; *Homilies and Recreations*, 1926; *The Fifteenth Scottish Division, 1924-1919*, 1926 (with John Stewart); *Montrose*, 1928; *The Teaching of History*, 1928-1930 (edited, 11 volumes); *What the Union of the Churches Means to Scotland*, 1929; *The Kirk in Scotland, 1560-1929*, 1930 (with George Adam Smith); *Lord Rosebery, 1847-1930*, 1930; *The Novel and the Fairy Tale*, 1931; *Sir Walter Scott*, 1932; *Julius Caesar*, 1932; *The Massacre of Glencoe*, 1933; *Gordon at Khartoum*, 1934; *Oliver Cromwell*, 1934; *The King's Grace, 1910-1935*, 1935 (published in the United States as *The People's King: George V*); *Augustus*, 1937; *Presbyterianism Yesterday, Today, and Tomorrow*, 1938; *Comments and Characters*, 1940 (W. Forbes Gray, editor); *Memory Hold-the-Door*, 1940 (published in the United States as *Pilgrim's Way: An Essay in Recollection*); *The Clearing House: A*

Survey of One Man's Mind, 1946 (Lady Tweedsmuir, editor).

CHILDREN'S LITERATURE: *Sir Walter Raleigh*, 1911; *The Magic Walking-Stick*, 1932; *The Long Traverse*, 1941 (published in the United States as *Lake of Gold*).

MISCELLANEOUS: *A Lodge in the Wilderness*, 1906; *What the Home Bill Means*, 1912; *The Future of the War*, 1916; *The Purpose of the War*, 1916; *The Island of Sheep*, 1919 (with Susan Buchan); *The Memory of Sir Walter Scott*, 1923; *Some Notes on Sir Walter Scott*, 1924; *Two Ordeals of Democracy*, 1925; *To the Electors of the Scottish Universities*, 1927; *The Causal and the Casual in History*, 1929; *Montrose and Leadership*, 1930; *The Revision of Dogmas*, 1930; *Andrew Lang and the Border*, 1933; *The Margins of Life*, 1933; *The University, the Library, and the Common Weal*, 1934; *The Scottish Church and the Empire*, 1934; *The Principles of Social Service*, 1934; *The Western Mind, An Address*, 1935; *A University's Bequest to Youth, An Address*, 1936; *The Interpreter's House*, 1938; *Canadian Occasions: Addresses by Lord Tweedsmuir*, 1940.

Bibliography
Blanchard, Robert G. *The First Editions of John Buchan*, 1981.
Buchan, Susan. *John Buchan, by His Wife and Friends*, 1947.
Daniell, David. *The Interpreter's House: A Critical Assessment of John Buchan*, 1975.
Hanna, Archibald. *John Buchan, 1875-1940: A Bibliography*, 1953.
Smith, Janet Adam. *John Buchan: A Biography*, 1965.
_____ . *John Buchan and His World*, 1979.

Joan DelFattore

PEARL S. BUCK

Born: Hillsboro, West Virginia; June 26, 1892
Died: Danby, Vermont; March 6, 1973

Principal long fiction
East Wind: West Wind, 1930; *The Good Earth*, 1931; *Sons*, 1932; *The Mother*, 1934; *A House Divided*, 1935; *House of Earth*, 1935; *This Proud Heart*, 1938; *The Patriot*, 1939; *Other Gods: An American Legend*, 1940; *Dragon Seed*, 1942; *China Sky*, 1942; *The Promise*, 1943; *China Flight*, 1945; *Portrait of a Marriage*, 1945; *The Townsman*, 1945 (as John Sedges); *Pavilion of Women*, 1946; *The Angry Wife*, 1947 (as John Sedges); *Peony*, 1948; *Kinfolk*, 1949; *The Long Love*, 1949 (as John Sedges); *God's Men*, 1951; *The Hidden Flower*, 1952; *Bright Procession*, 1952 (as John Sedges); *Come, My Beloved*, 1953; *Voices in the House*, 1953 (as John Sedges); *Imperial Woman*, 1956; *Letter from Peking*, 1957; *Command the Morning*, 1959; *Satan Never Sleeps*, 1962; *The Living Reed*, 1963; *Death in the Castle*, 1965; *The Time Is Noon*, 1967; *The New Year*, 1968; *The Three Daughters of Madame Liang*, 1969; *Mandala*, 1970; *The Goddess Abides*, 1972; *All Under Heaven*, 1973; *The Rainbow*, 1974.

Other literary forms
An overwhelmingly prolific writer, Pearl S. Buck wrote short stories; juvenile fiction and nonfiction; pamphlets; magazine articles; literary history; biographies; plays (including a musical); educational works; an Oriental cookbook; and a variety of books on America, democracy, Hitler and Germany, Japan, China, Russia, the mentally retarded, the sexes, and the Kennedy women. In addition, she translated *Shui Hu Chuan* (1933, *All Men Are Brothers*) and edited a book of Oriental fairy tales, several Christmas books, and a book of Chinese woodcuts. Besides *The Good Earth*, her finest works are her biographies of her parents, *The Exile* (1936) and *Fighting Angel: Portrait of a Soul* (1936). *The Exile* portrays the unhappy and frustrating life of her mother, a missionary wife. *Fighting Angel*, a better biography because of its greater objectivity, shows the ruthless missionary zeal of Buck's father. Of her early articles, "Is There a Case for Foreign Missions?," printed in *Christian Century* in 1933, created a furor in its charges that missionaries, and churches themselves, lacked sympathy for the people, worrying more about the numbers of converts than the needs of the flock. Buck also delivered several important addresses which reveal much about her own literary philosophy, including her Nobel Prize lecture on the Chinese novel. *Of Men and Women* (first issued in 1941; reissued in 1971 with a new epilogue) is one of Buck's most important nonfictional works because it gives her views of Chinese and

American family life and her warnings about "gunpowder" American women who are educated for work yet lead idle and meaningless lives at home.

During World War II, Buck delivered many speeches and published articles, letters, and pamphlets on the Asian view of the war, particularly on colonial rule and imperialism. Her most famous war essay is probably "Tinder for Tomorrow." Buck's canon further includes personal works, such as the autobiographical *My Several Worlds: A Personal Record* (1954) and *A Bridge for Passing* (1962). Several of her plays were produced off Broadway or in summer stock. As of 1980, her publishers had twenty-six more short stories and one novella of Buck's yet to be released.

Achievements

Buck has been enormously successful with popular audiences, more so than with the literati. She is the most widely translated author in all of American literary history. In Denmark, for example, her popularity exceeded that of Ernest Hemingway and John Steinbeck in the 1930's, and in Sweden, ten of her books were translated between 1932 and 1940, more than those of any other American author. *The Good Earth*, her most famous work, has been translated into more than thirty languages (seven different translations into Chinese alone) and made into a play and a motion picture.

Buck's early novels received much acclaim. *The Good Earth* was awarded the Pulitzer Prize; in 1935, she was awarded the William Dean Howells medal by the American Academy of Arts and Letters for the finest work in American fiction from 1930 to 1935, and in 1936, she was elected to membership in the National Institute of Arts and Letters. In 1938, she was awarded the Nobel Prize, the third American to receive it and the first woman, for her "rich and generous epic description of Chinese peasant life and masterpieces of biography." *The Good Earth*, a staple of high school and undergraduate reading, is undoubtedly a masterpiece; and her missionary biographies, *The Exile* and *Fighting Angel*, though currently neglected, have merit in the depth of their analysis. Three other books of the 1930's—*Sons*, *The Mother*, and *The Patriot*—have effective passages. In all her works, Buck evinces a deep humanity, and she did much to further American understanding of Asian culture.

Buck has not fared so well with the literary establishment. Critics of the 1930's disdained her work because she was a woman, because her subjects were not "American," and because they thought she did not deserve the Nobel Prize. Her success in writing best-seller after best-seller and her optimistic faith in progress and humanity have irked later critics. She did, however, achieve success by her own standards. Her books have reached and touched middle-class American women, an enormous body of readers largely ignored by serious writers. Her innate storytelling ability does "please," "amuse," and "entertain" (her three criteria for good writing) but even the kindest of her admirers wish that she had written less, spending more time exploring the minds of her characters and polishing her work.

Biography

Pearl S. Buck was born Pearl Comfort Sydenstricker on June 26, 1892, in the family home at Hillsboro, West Virginia, to Absalom and Caroline (Stulting) Sydenstricker. Her parents were missionaries in China, home on a furlough. After five months she was taken to China. Her parents' marriage was not a particularly happy one because of their disparate natures. Her mother, fun-loving and witty, was torn by her devotion to God; her father, single-minded and zealous, had success with his mission but not with his family. Buck grew up in Chinkiang, an inland city on the Yangtze River. In 1900, during the Boxer Rebellion, her family was forced to flee and she experienced the horrors of racism. Her education included one year at boarding school in Shanghai and four years at Randolph-Macon Women's College in Virginia.

In 1917, she married John Lossing Buck, an agricultural specialist. They lived in Nanhsuchon in Anhwei province (the setting of *The Good Earth*). Buck learned much about farming from her husband and from her own observations. After five years, they moved southward to Nanking, where her husband taught agriculture and she taught English at the university. She published her first article in *The Atlantic* (January, 1923); "In China, Too" described the growing Western influence in China, particularly on Chinese youth.

Tragedy struck Buck's life with the birth of Carol, her only natural child, who was mentally retarded (she later adopted eight children). She took Carol to the United States for medical treatment in 1925. When her husband took a year's leave of absence, Buck studied English at Cornell University and received her master's degree. Her first published novel, *East Wind: West Wind*, combined two short stories, one of which was originally published in 1925 in *Asia* magazine. She had written a novel before *East Wind: West Wind*, but the novel was destroyed by soldiers entering her home in the 1926-1927 Nationalist Communist uprising. (During the takeover of Nanking, Buck and her family barely escaped, hiding in a mud hut until relief came.) On March 2, 1931, *The Good Earth* appeared, creating a literary sensation.

Buck's early literary influences included her parents and her old Chinese nurse. Her parents, of course, encouraged her to read the Bible and told her tales of their American homeland, while her nurse told her fantastic Buddhist and Taoist legends of warriors, devils, fairies, and dragons. She learned to speak Chinese before English, but she learned to read and write in English sooner than in Chinese. She read incessantly, Charles Dickens as a child and later Theodore Dreiser. Émile Zola and Sinclair Lewis were also important in her adult life. She paid particular tribute to Dickens: "He opened my eyes to people, he taught me to love all sorts of people." Even as a child, she decided to write: "One longs to make what one loves, and above all I loved to hear stories about people. I was a nuisance of a child, I fear, always curious to know about people and why they were as I found them." Her first writing appeared in the children's section of the Shanghai *Mercury*; in college, she contributed stories to the campus monthly and helped write the class play.

The Bucks were divorced in 1932, and that same year Pearl married her publisher, Richard J. Walsh, president of John Day and editor of *Asia* magazine. Their marriage lasted until his death in 1960. Buck loved both the United States and China throughout her life, serving as an intermediary between the two. In her last years, she was bitterly disappointed when the Chinese Communists would not grant her a visa, despite the *rapprochement* between the United States and China.

Buck's parents instilled into their daughter principles of charity and tolerance. Her love for the needy was also awakened by Miss Jewell, the mistress of her boarding school. Jewell took Buck along as an interpreter on errands of mercy—to visit institutions for slave girls who had fled from their masters and institutions where prostitutes went for help. Buck's own humanitarian efforts began in 1941 with the founding of the East and West Association, which endeavored to increase understanding between diverse cultures. During World War II, Buck actively spoke against racism, against the internment of Japanese-Americans, and against the yielding of democratic privileges during wartime.

Her sympathy extended to all, but especially to children and the helpless. In 1949, she and her husband founded Welcome House, an adoption agency for Amerasian children. In 1954, her letter of protest to *The New York Times* led to the changing of a policy which put immigrants in federal prisons with criminals. In 1964, she founded the Pearl S. Buck Foundation to care for Amerasian children who remain overseas. She also worked for the Training School, a school for the retarded in Vineland, New Jersey. For her many humanitarian efforts, she received the Brotherhood Award of the National Conference of Christians and Jews, the Wesley Award for Distinguished Service to Humanity and more than a dozen honorary degrees from American colleges and universities.

Along with her extensive humanitarian activities, Buck continued to write. Because her American novels *This Proud Heart* and *Other Gods* were not well received, Buck assumed the pen name "John Sedges" to write with freedom on American subjects. Between 1945 and 1953, five novels were published under this name while she wrote Asian stories under her own name. Unfortunately, as Buck's humanitarian efforts increased, the quality of her fiction declined. Its strident and moralistic tone reflected her growing concern with social issues rather than artistic technique. She continued writing, however, and by the time of her death in 1973 had written more than eighty novels and novellas.

Analysis

Pearl S. Buck's reputation for excellence as a writer of fiction rests solely on *The Good Earth* and segments of a few of her other novels of the 1930's. The appeal of *The Good Earth* is undeniable and easy to explain: its universal themes are cloaked in the garments of an unfamiliar and fascinating Chinese culture. Echoing many elements of life, the book speaks of animosity between town and country, love of land, decadent rich and honest poor, marital conflicts, interfering relatives, misunderstandings between generations, the joys of birth and sorrows of old age and death, and the strong bonds of friendship. Added to these universal themes is the cyclical movement of the growth and decay of the crops, the decline of the House of Hwand and the ascent of the House of Wang, the changes of the years, and the birth and death of the people.

Buck fittingly chose to tell her story in language reminiscent of the Bible with its families and peoples who rise and fall. Her style also owes something to that of the Chinese storytellers, to whom she paid tribute in her Nobel Prize lecture, a style which flows along in short words "with no other technique than occasional bits of description, only enough to give vividness to place or person, and never enough to delay the story." Most of Buck's sentences are long and serpentine, relying on balance, parallelism, and repetition for strength. While the sentences are long, the diction is simple and concrete. She chooses her details carefully: her descriptions grow out of close observation and are always concise. The simplicity of the diction and the steady, determined flow of the prose fit the sagalike plot. In Chinese folk literature, the self-effacing author, like a clear vessel, transmits but does not color with his personality the life which "flows through him." So, also, Buck presents her story objectively. Her authorial presence never intrudes, though her warm feeling for the characters and her own ethical beliefs are always evident.

The strength of the novel also lies in its characterization, particularly that of the two main characters, O-lan and her husband Wang Lung. Whereas characters in Buck's later novels too easily divide into good and bad, the characters of *The Good Earth*, like real people, mix elements of both. Ching, Wang Lung's faithful, doglike friend and later overseer, early in the novel joins a starving mob who ransack Wang Lung's home for food; Ching takes Wang Lung's last handful of beans. The eldest son is a pompous wastrel, but he does make the House of Hwang beautiful with flowering trees and fish ponds and he does settle into the traditional married life his father has planned for him. Even O-lan, the almost saintly earth mother, seethes with jealousy when Wang Lung takes a second wife, and she feels contempt and bitterness for the House of Hwang in which she was a slave. Her major flaw is her ugliness. Wang Lung delights the reader with his simple wonder at the world and with his perseverance to care for his family and his land, but he, too, has failings. In middle age, he lusts for Lotus, neglecting the much-deserving

O-lan, and in old age, he steals Pear Blossom from his youngest son. Rather than confusing the morality of the novel, the intermingling of good and bad increase its reality. Buck acknowledged literary indebtedness to Émile Zola, and the influence of naturalism is evident in *The Good Earth* in its objective, documentary presentation and its emphasis on the influence of environment and heredity. Unlike the naturalists, however, Buck also credits the force of free will.

The Good Earth aroused much fury in some Chinese scholars, who insisted that the novel portrays a China that never was. Younghill Kang criticized the character of Wang Lung. Professor Kiang Kang-Hu said that Buck's details and her knowledge of Chinese history were inaccurate. Buck defended herself by granting that customs differed in the many regions of China. In later novels, she retaliated by harshly portraying Chinese scholars such as Kang and Kiang, who, she believed, distorted the picture of the real China either because of their ignorance of peasant life or because of their desire to aid propagandistic efforts of the Chinese government. Other native Chinese, including Phio Lin Yutang, sprang to Buck's defense, insisting on the accuracy of her portrayal.

Like *The Good Earth*, *The Mother* follows the cyclical flow of time: the protagonist, who begins the novel in vigorous work, caring for an elderly parent, ends the novel as an elderly parent himself, cared for by the new generation. *The Mother* is also written in the simple, concrete, and sometimes poetic style of *The Good Earth*. The old mother-in-law, for example, in her early morning hunger, "belched up the evil winds from her inner emptiness." *The Mother*, however, portrays a different side of Chinese peasant life from that seen in *The Good Earth*—a more brutal one. The main character, named only "the mother," is carefully drawn; the other characters are flat and undeveloped, serving only as objects for her attention.

Deserted by her irresponsible, gambling husband, the mother lies about her spouse's absence to protect her family and cover her shame. She proves easy prey for her landlord's agent, by whom she becomes pregnant, later aborting the baby by taking medicine. Her eldest son eventually supports her, but his unfeeling wife will not tolerate having his blind sister underfoot. A husband is found for the blind girl, but when the mother travels to visit her daughter after a year, she discovers that the husband is witless and her daughter, after much mistreatment, has died. Even more sorrow darkens the mother's life. Her younger and most beloved son joins the Communists, is used as their dupe, and finally is arrested and beheaded.

This is not the honest-work-brings-rewards world of Wang Lung, but a world of victims, deformity, hatred, and cruelty. It is a portrait of the life of a woman in China, where girl babies routinely were killed and young girls of poor families were sold as slaves. Only new life—the excitement of birth and spring—balances the misery of the mother's life.

In *The Good Earth* and *The Mother*, Buck provides compelling visions of old age. Her children are mostly silent and inconsequential, her adolescents merely lusty and willful, but her elderly are individuals. The old father in *The Good Earth* cackles with life, drawing strength from his grandchildren-bed-fellows. Wang Lung drowses off into a peaceful dream with his Pear Blossom. The mother-in-law basks in the sun and prides herself on wearing out her burial shrouds. The elderly mother in *The Mother* is frustrated because she no longer has the strength to work the land but remains as active as possible, trying to save her blind daughter and her Communist son, finally turning her affections to a new grandchild.

The main flaw in *The Mother* is that the mother seems too distant, too self-contained, for the reader to identify with her, to accept her as the universal mother that Buck intends her to be. The mother's story is interesting, but the reader does not feel her shame or her misery as he does O-lan's, nor does he feel her delight or her pride as he does Wang Lung's. Also, Buck's feelings about Communism are blatantly evident in the simplistic and oft-repeated phrase that the Communists are a "new kind of robber."

As Buck became more interested in social and political issues and in the media—magazines, film, and radio—her fiction began to deteriorate. She claimed, "The truth is I never write with a sense of mission or to accomplish any purpose whatever except the revelation of human character through a life situation." Her fiction, however, did not demonstrate this belief: more and more it became a forum for her own social and political ideas rather than an exploration of human character and life. Further, Hollywood and women's magazines began to influence her stories: they became drippingly romantic.

Dragon Seed is one of Buck's most popular post-1930's works, with the first half of the novel containing many of the strengths of her earlier work. Her characters are not as fully realized as the mother or Wang Lung, but the story is intriguing. A peasant farming family work the land, much as their ancestors have done for centuries, until the coming of war—flying airships and enemy troops—thrusts them into a world of violence and deprivation. As long as Buck keeps her eye sharp for details, describing the atrocities the people must endure and their struggles to understand what is happening to them, the novel remains interesting.

In the second half of the novel, however, Buck's purposes split. Rather than concentrating on the war story—the people and their experiences—she uses the novel to argue that the Western world is blind and uncaring about the troubles of the Chinese in World War II. In contrast to this didacticism are the Hollywood-style love-stories of Lao-Er and Jade and Lao San and Mayli. The dialogue between the happily married Lao-Er and Jade seems straight from a "B"-movie, and the overly coincidental coming together of Lao San and Mayli is a women's magazine romance of the self-made man and the rich, beautiful woman. Buck tries to portray the strong new woman of

China (and the Western world) in Jade and Mayli, but they are *too* strong, *too* clever, almost always posturing with a defiant chin against the sunset. At one point in the novel, Buck even writes that Jade is so skillful in disguising herself that she should have been a film actress. O-lan, in her stoic silence—grudging, jealous, yet loving—is a believable woman; Jade and Mayli are creatures of fantasy.

Buck's power as a novelist derived from her intelligence, her humanity, her interesting stories, and her ability to make Chinese culture real to readers from all over the world. Her weaknesses as a novelist include didacticism, sentimentalism, and an inability to control her energy long enough to explore deeply, revise, and improve. In her later novels, she lost control of her point of view, her language, and her characterization. Her legacy is an enduring masterpiece, *The Good Earth*, and an inestimable contribution to cultural exchange between China and the West.

Major publications other than long fiction

SHORT FICTION: *The First Wife and Other Stories*, 1933; *Today and Forever*, 1941; *Twenty-Seven Stories*, 1943; *Far and Near, Stories of Japan, China and America*, 1947; *American Triptych*, 1958; *Hearts Come Home and Other Stories*, 1962; *The Good Deed and Other Stories*, 1969; *Once Upon a Christmas*, 1972; *East and West*, 1975; *Secrets of the Heart*, 1976; *The Lovers and Other Stories*, 1977; *The Woman Who Was Changed and Other Stories*, 1979.

NONFICTION: *East and West and the Novel*, 1932; *All Men Are Brothers*, 1933 (translation); *The Exile*, 1936; *Fighting Angel: Portrait of a Soul*, 1936; *The Chinese Novel*, 1939; *Of Men and Women*, 1941, 1971; *American Unity and Asia*, 1942; *What America Means to Me*, 1943; *China in Black and White*, 1945; *Talk About Russia: With Masha Scott*, 1945; *Tell the People: Talks with James Yen About the Mass Education Movement*, 1945; *How It Happens: Talk About the German People, 1914-1933, with Erna von Pustau*, 1947; *American Argument: With Eslanda Goods*, 1949; *The Child Who Never Grew*, 1950; *My Several Worlds: A Personal Record*, 1954; *Friend to Friend: A Candid Exchange Between Pearl Buck and Carlos F. Romulo*, 1958; *A Bridge for Passing*, 1962; *The Joy of Children*, 1964; *Children for Adoption*, 1965; *The Gifts They Bring: Our Debt to the Mentally Retarded*, 1965; *The People of Japan*, 1966; *To My Daughters with Love*, 1967; *China As I See It*, 1970; *The Kennedy Women: A Personal Appraisal*, 1970; *The Story Bible*, 1971; *Pearl S. Buck's America*, 1971; *China Past and Present*, 1972.

CHILDREN'S LITERATURE: *The Young Revolutionist*, 1932; *Stories for Little Children*, 1940; *One Bright Day and Other Stories for Children*, 1952; *Johnny Jack and His Beginnings*, 1954; *The Man Who Changed China: The Story of Sun Yat-Sen*, 1953; *Fourteen Stories*, 1961; *The Chinese Story Teller*, 1971.

Bibliography
Doyle, Paul A. *Pearl S. Buck*, 1980.
Spencer, Cornelia. *Revealing the Human Heart: Pearl S. Buck*, 1964.
Thompson, Dody Weston. "Pearl Buck," in *American Winners of the Nobel Literary Prize*, 1968. Edited by Warren G. French and Walter E. Kidd.

Ann Willardson Engar

FREDERICK BUECHNER

Born: New York, New York; July 11, 1926

Principal long fiction

A Long Day's Dying, 1950; *The Season's Difference*, 1952; *The Return of Ansel Gibbs*, 1958; *The Final Beast*, 1965; *The Entrance to Porlock*, 1970; *Lion Country*, 1971; *Open Heart*, 1972; *Love Feast*, 1974; *Treasure Hunt*, 1977; *The Book of Bebb*, 1979; *Godric*, 1980.

Other literary forms

Frederick Buechner has published an autobiography in two slim volumes: *The Sacred Journey* (1982) and *Now and Then* (1983). He has also published a number of theological and homiletical volumes—idiosyncratic and often humorous works which illuminate his fiction and his novelistic techniques: *The Magnificent Defeat* (1966); *The Hungering Dark* (1969); *The Alphabet of Grace* (1970); *Wishful Thinking: A Theological ABC* (1973); *Telling the Truth* (1977); and *Peculiar Treasures* (1979). Finally, Buechner contributed commentary for the art book, *The Faces of Jesus* (1974).

Achievements

Buechner's major achievement as a novelist is his ability to "sanctify the profane," to depict in his novels the essentially religious nature of all human endeavor, to communicate the meaning of Christian faith in a time in which the Christian vocabulary and world view are considered defunct and impotent. An ordained Presbyterian minister, Buechner demonstrates in his later works a Christian theological viewpoint and an essential optimism about the human condition in an earthy, disarmingly comic narrative style. His craft and his vision of the world are comparable to those of two contemporary Christian fiction-writers, Walker Percy and Flannery O'Connor.

While several of his volumes of nonfiction have achieved a very wide circulation, Buechner's readership as a novelist has been relatively small since his appearance on the literary scene with his 1950 novel, *A Long Day's Dying*, a book conceived and substantially written while he was an undergraduate student at Princeton. This first work was highly praised by leading critics, who noted its labored, "Jamesian" narrative voice—a fact which amuses and bewilders Buechner, who claimed to have read little of James at the time of its writing. His following two novels, *The Season's Difference* and *The Return of Ansel Gibbs*, were much less successful, and between 1958 and 1965, Buechner's narrative style and his subject matter radically changed. *The Final Beast* in 1965 signaled Buechner's evolution from a "modernist storyteller" into a comic novelist possessing a keen sense of life's ambiguities and contradictions—all tempered by his Christian vision. *The Final Beast*, coupled with his later "Bebb" novels and his recent *Godric*, represent a revitalization of religious fiction: a rejection of proselytizing and an acceptance of proclamation as a mode of narration. Buechner's prose reveals new metaphors by which faith can be experienced and communicated, a transformation of the secular into the sacred—demonstrating the presence of the Divine in all living things. By his own account, Buechner is an apologist to "the cultured despisers" of religion:

> My novels are not Sunday School stories with detachable morals at the end. They are my attempt to describe the world as richly and truly as perhaps only fiction can describe it, together with the truth that God is mysteriously with us in the world. That is in essence what I am saying to Christians and to anybody else who will listen. ("Interview," in *Christianity and Literature*, XXXII, Fall, 1982.)

Biography

Carl Frederick Buechner was born in New York City on July 11, 1926, one of two sons of Carl Frederick and Katherine Buechner. The family moved a great deal during his childhood, until he reached the tenth grade. After he was graduated from the Lawrenceville School in New Jersey in 1943, Buechner attended Princeton University. He completed his B.A. in English in 1948, after serving in the military from 1944 to 1946. It was during his later undergraduate years at Princeton that he conceived and wrote his first novel, *A Long Day's Dying*, "a study of the relationships of a small, sophisticated and highly articulate group of people" including a college student, his widowed mother and grandmother, and his mother's several lovers—characters and situations emblematic of Buechner's early baroque style and content. "Maroo," the grandmother in *A Long Day's Dying*, is clearly based on Buechner's grandmother, Naya, whom he lovingly commemorates as a witty and worldly-wise influence and inspiration for his fiction in his memoir *The Sacred Journey*. Buechner returned to his alma mater, the Lawrenceville School, in 1948 to teach English; during that time, he also conducted summer creative writing sessions at New York University.

Buechner's second book, *The Season's Difference*, appeared in 1952; it is a prophetic work in that, though it still bears the mannered style of his first novel, it deals with a strongly religious theme: the effect of a religious experience upon the lives of a sophisticated coterie of people in an academic setting. Two years later, Buechner himself would undergo a religious conversion which would lead him to Union Theological Seminary in New York. During his seminary training, he conducted an employment clinic in an East Harlem Protestant parish. Paul Tillich, one of his professors at Union Theological Seminary, had a profound influence on his view of culture and theology; Tillich taught Buechner that the presence of the Divine permeates human society, and thereby sparked a dramatic change in Buechner's narrative strategies. Buechner was ordained a Presbyterian minister in 1958, just after his third novel, *The Return of Ansel Gibbs*, was published. This novel marked a transition from his two earlier works in its transcendence of his earlier baroque style and its topical subject matter.

From 1958 to 1967, Buechner served as school minister and chair of the Department of Religion at Phillips Exeter Academy, and during this time completed his fourth novel, *The Final Beast*, and two homiletical volumes, *The Magnificent Defeat* and *The Hungering Dark*. Since 1967, Buechner has become a full-time writer and lecturer, living with his wife, Judith, and his family in Vermont. During the 1970's, Buechner completed five novels: *The Entrance to Porlock* and the celebrated Bebb tetralogy, *Lion Country, Open Heart, Love Feast*, and *Treasure Hunt*. In 1980, Buechner published *Godric*, a piece of fiction set in the middle ages—a departure in time and place, but a story framed in the same theological and comic terms as those of the Bebb tetralogy.

Analysis

In a 1971 issue of *Publisher's Weekly*, Frederick Buechner told his interviewer:

> Writing *is* a kind of ministry. I do not feel I am doing much different in my preaching and in my writing. . . . The process of telling a story is something like religion if only in the sense of having a plot leading to a conclusion that makes some kind of sense.

Buechner's view of narrative, exemplified in his novels after *The Season's Difference*, is that storytelling reveals the form of human life, its direction and its meaning. Each human life contains a hidden agenda, a pattern of events that bears close attention and a listening ear; since most people are deaf and blind to this agenda, it is up to the storyteller, the writer of novels, the creator of metaphors, to reveal that agenda. When he or she is successful, the novelist not only lays bare the meaning of human events but also reveals— sometimes in spite of himself—the presence of the Divine in human affairs. Since Buechner believes God works "behind the scenes" and almost never explicitly in history (the grand exception being the "magnificent defeat," the crucified Christ and his resurrection), he finds the novel an appropriate medium for conveying theological truth.

Given his view of narrative, one is not surprised to find Buechner's novels populated by characters whose lives contain a central ambiguity, a tension between faith and doubt, which Buechner the storyteller does not attempt to resolve. His task is to present the ambivalence of human life as faithfully as possible in the hope that, as the reader sees his own ironies and incongruities, he will be led to a consideration of their source and their potential resolution. While some of Buechner's characters come to a faith with which they can face life, others reject supernatural notions out of hand. Others fall in between, reflecting Buechner's own sentiments that he himself is only a "part-time Christian" because, as he writes in *The Alphabet of Grace*, "part of the time seems to be the most I can live out my faith."

Buechner's fiction is best studied chronologically, since his work falls into three fairly distinct periods and modes. The early Buechner novels, *A Long Day's Dying* and *The Season's Difference*, form one unit for analysis; two transitional novels, *The Return of Ansel Gibbs* and *The Final Beast*, prepare the reader for Buechner's later ribald and boisterous novels; the remainder of the Buechner canon, which includes the Bebb tetralogy and *Godric*, represents the mature Buechner, a writer whose narrative powers are fully developed and whose themes are compelling and provocative. All of his works are introspective, even contemplative in texture, despite his sometimes comic stance; as such, they form a rich complement to Buechner's memoirs and meditations. Buechner's oeuvre is thus strikingly symmetrical and consistent, with the chief demarcations reflected in the evolution of his narrative technique.

A Long Day's Dying and *The Season's Difference* form a novelistic couplet of rarefied and intellectualized treatments of modern life, its tensions and its ethical malaise. Their style, referred to by critics of the time as "mandarin" and intentionally "mythic," overshadows characterization and plot; one critic asserted that *A Long Day's Dying* in particular was an example of "writing for a teacher"—reflecting the dominance at that time of the New Criticism, which emphasized and prized such features as "ambiguity" and "ambivalence." The estrangement of the modern age from its genteel and cultured roots is a primary theme in both works: *A Long Day's Dying* documents the fragility of relationships in postwar America and the absence of a moral center: *The Season's Difference* confronts the same scenario while exploring in particular the callousness of its characters toward the mystical and the supernatural. While neither of these novels is as explicitly "religious" as Buechner's later works, their thematic concerns foreshadow dilemmas voiced in *The Final Beast* and the Bebb novels, whose resolutions are intertwined with faith and acceptance of Divine providence.

Modern life as depicted in these two novels has no place for innocence. Paul Steitler, the cynical English professor in *A Long Day's Dying*, says that his mission is to corrupt young innocents who, in their naïveté, fail to realize that "they're never going to have it so good again." "In a few years," he laments, "they're going to break their legs and need the crutches I'm offering now, but they don't believe it . . . at moments like these, I really don't myself." The "crutches" he can offer them—a stoical resignation and a weak antidote for their felt loss of religious convictions—recall Matthew Arnold's prophecy that poetry would replace religion in the future's brave new world. Steitler, Buechner's prototypal "clear-eyed realist," is a foil for the more trusting, priest-like character of Tristram Bone. Bone, nevertheless, is a failed "priest"; he is no mediator of the Divine, no consoler of the downtrodden. Empty of spiritual substance, he can recognize "sin" but can offer no redemption, either for himself or for his beloved Elizabeth and her son, Leander. The one potential center of moral conviction and action in the novel is Maroo, Leander's grandmother. Her death signals the spiritual demise of those whom she might have influenced and reflects the fate of all those who confront the secular world with merely secular weapons. The novel's title comes from Book 10 of John Milton's *Paradise Lost* (1667), an ironic counterpoint that juxtaposes the eventual reconciliation of Adam and Eve with the painful alienation of the novel's characters from one another.

The Season's Difference continues several of the themes Buechner articulated in *A Long Day's Dying* while emphasizing more strongly the skepticism of the modern age toward the experience of the supernatural. Though Buechner treats this theme with great earnestness and includes several passages of crisp, refreshingly direct prose, the merits of this work are blunted by its extraordinarily verbose and philosophical mode of narration. Despite these weaknesses, however, Buechner's second novel clearly anticipates the apologetics of later works, his defense of God's ways to secularized man.

The Return of Ansel Gibbs and *The Final Beast*, Buechner's first two post-seminary novels, reflect a dramatic shift in narrative technique; his emerging understanding of theology-as-story seems to have transformed his novelistic sensibilities. Gone for the most part are "drawing-room" characters and situations; in their place are social issues, direct, unpretentious dialogue, and, for the first time, a sense of humor. It is in *The Return of Ansel Gibbs* that Buechner first broaches explicitly the possibility of Christian faith as a viable option in the modern world, something placed in the mouth of Dr. Kuykendall. Kuykendall is loosely based on one of Buechner's seminary professors, and it is he who serves as Gibbs's mentor and counselor as Gibbs vacillates about accepting a cabinet post. Buechner has Kuykendall address a seminary audience, articulating both the risk of faith and its problematic nature:

> If you tell me Christian commitment is a thing that has happened once and for all like some kind of spiritual plastic surgery . . . you're either pulling the wool over your own eyes or trying to pull it over mine. Every morning you should wake up in your beds and ask yourself: "Can I believe it all again today?"

The exigencies of modern life make faith—along with hope, love, courage, commitment—a daily affirmation, not a once-and-for-all declaration, not the faith in "cheap grace" which Dietrich Bonhoeffer railed against. The "return" of Ansel Gibbs is a rediscovery of life's center, its core; fearful that he is aloof and detached, Gibbs fights his way out of his own ambivalence to confront a world made not of words but of people and relationships. Still, Gibbs cannot quite embrace a "holy cause," one which is reflected in Kuykendall's implicit call for prophetic responsibility on Gibbs's part; this is

Buechner's way of presenting the tension of faith, of making room for the agnostic who can bring himself only to say that "you can cross your fingers and hold your tongue and do what you can in the time that's left."

Buechner's transition from a mannered stylist into a colloquial and whimsical storyteller was complete in *The Final Beast*, his fourth novel. Appearing seven years after *The Return of Ansel Gibbs*, *The Final Beast* reflects Buechner's years of preaching and pastoral work, which tempered and softened his narrative technique. In his most autobiographical work of fiction, Buechner is at ease, conversational and delightfully humorous. While *The Final Beast* takes up themes introduced earlier in Buechner's writing, there is a discernible boldness and joyousness in this novel previously submerged or excluded in his work. Its protagonist, Theodore Nicolet, is a recently widowed young minister whose religious experience is analogous to Buechner's own. Searching for a sign of God's presence, Nicolet retreats to the countryside, composing a Sunday sermon on the grass near his father's barn. Here there is no dramatic "Damascus road" encounter; instead, in this tranquil, pastoral setting, Nicolet hears the "click-clack" of two apple branches brushing against each other. In *The Alphabet of Grace*, Buechner explains Nicolet's experience and, implicitly, his own as "the occasional, obscure glimmering through of grace. The muffled presence of the holy. The images, always broken, partial, ambiguous of Christ." Man can ultimately only bear "the click-clack"; any more of the Divine presence would be overwhelming, devastating. God must not intrude; He must imply. Despite these glimmers of grace, the novel is not all sweetness and light; the "beast" of the novel's title refers, evidently, to the "mark of the beast" discussed in the Book of Revelation; it is the undeniable presence of evil in a world created by a gracious God. Nicolet's joyful affirmation of life and of God's care is counterbalanced by the character of Irma Reinwasser, a German native and concentration-camp victim who has suffered much. Irma cannot bring herself to put confidence in "Harold," the name by which Nicolet's children refer to God (a garbling of the Lord's Prayer: "Harold be thy name"). Though she cannot express faith, her vicarious sacrifice on behalf of Nicolet after the young minister's integrity is compromised demonstrates her implicit understanding of redemptive love. While some critics complained that *The Final Beast* was the predictable effort of a "minister-novelist," the novel in fact inaugurated a revitalization of religious fiction; it is an achievement matched in the last three decades only by such writers as Graham Greene, Flannery O'Connor, and Walker Percy.

Buechner's next novel, *The Entrance to Porlock* was in some ways an experiment: a whimsical treatment of serious themes in which he used L. Frank Baum's Oz stories for mythical resonance. This was a 180-degree turn from *A Long Day's Dying*, in which Buechner employed an elaborate—and somewhat stultifying—Greek mythology to convey his thematic concerns. *The Entrance to Porlock* is the story of Peter Ringkoping and his family, a household of dreamers, each on a quest to discover self and therefore to come to grips with the reality of his life. Along the way, Peter, looking for a "heart," discovers it in his recognition that he loves the land of which he is about to divest himself; Tip is a Dorothy-like character, seeking a home, which he finds toward the end of the novel; Tommy, eventually facing himself as he is, is the scarecrow finding a brain; Nels is a lion seeking courage, which is mustered up in confronting a problematic situation with a student; finally, Hans Strasser plays the Wizard's role, inspiring each of the Ringkopings to introspection and a renewal of self.

The Entrance to Porlock, whose title is derived from Samuel Taylor Coleridge's famous account of the composition of "Kubla Khan," was in Buechner's estimation the most difficult book he has ever attempted to write. Written in the aftermath of the political assassinations of the late 1960's, *The Entrance to Porlock* is a dreamy, lyrical book that exhorts the reader to press on in the face of ugliness and brutality, an affirmation of the human spirit's resiliency. Despite its highly symbolic texture, the book is eminently readable and, in its own way, exuberant. A reader could not have been prepared, however, for the rollicking and ribald novels that would follow it and that would represent Buechner's greatest creation.

In the 1970's, Buechner published four novels centered around his most animated and most fully realized character, Leo Bebb: *Lion Country*, *Open Heart*, *Love Feast*, and *Treasure Hunt*. These four novels form a tetralogy which was reissued as one volume entitled *The Book of Bebb* in 1979 (it is upon this 1979 format that the following analysis will be based). Buechner took advantage of the reissuing of the four novels to make some slight revisions, none of which materially altered the structure, characterization, or tone of his raucously comic creations. The Bebb novels well illustrate the wry comment of one critic who suggested that Buechner's art is too religious for the secular reader and too secular for the religious reader. Buechner creates Leo Bebb as the supreme example of grace operating through the least likely channel; Bebb is profane, earthy, sometimes blasphemous in the way he chooses to "preach the gospel." Nevertheless, he is but one more reminder that all men have feet of clay, that God loves his creatures in spite of their shortcomings, and that the evidence of grace is all around for people to see; what people lack, Buechner intimates, are "eyes to see and ears to hear." In Leo Bebb, Buechner is—in Flannery O'Connor's terms—"shouting to the hard of hearing and drawing large figures for the almost blind." Bebb is perhaps the most memorable fictional character of the 1970's; his stories take their place alongside John Updike's Rabbit series, and Bebb is sacred counterpart to Updike's Rabbit Angstrom. In *The Book of Bebb*, one sees most clearly the fruition of Buechner's narrative strategies and the fulfillment of his writing "ministry" in the sanctification of the profane.

Leo Bebb is a "rogue preacher," founder of Church of Holy Love, and later, the Church of the Open Heart. His story is told by his son-in-law, Antonio Parr—who originally intends to expose Bebb as a charlatan, an operator of a shameless religious diploma mill. While Bebb is the fulcrum upon which the tetralogy balances—even after his death in the third novel, *Love Feast*, one is quite done with Bebb, since he is "reincarnated" as Jimmy Bob in *Treasure Hunt*—in many ways the tetralogy is the private journey of Antonio Parr, a tracing of one man's "sacred journey." Parr's narration is the best witness to Buechner's dictum, advanced in his memoir *The Sacred Journey*, that God "speaks to us not just through the sounds we hear . . . but through events in all their complexity and variety, through the harmonies and disharmonies and counterpoint of all that happens." While faith is Leo Bebb's "business," Parr is not so easily won; his encounter with Bebb and the trail of sorrows, joys, paradoxes, and incongruities that follow it serve to illustrate the winding path a man's life takes. Faith, as Buechner wants to underscore, is difficult: "Hard as hell," in Bebb's words.

Reading *The Book of Bebb*, one has the sense of following a single continuous narrative—a remarkable achievement, given the fact that the four novels were written over a six-year period without an initial design for a tetralogy. Buechner accounts for the unity of the four works by reference to the ease with which the characters and situations came to him; whereas he regards *The Entrance to Porlock* as the first "Caesarian birth" of his writing career, the Bebb novels flowed freely from his imagination. Speaking of *Lion Country*, Buechner declares "I could hardly wait to get to it in the morning, and I hated to leave it when I had to go home in the afternoon . . . the whole thing was finished in about six to eight weeks." In regard to its expansion into a tetralogy, Buechner explains that when he wrote the last sentence of *Lion Country*, "I thought I had finished with them all for good but soon found that they were not finished with me."

The Book of Bebb is Buechner's "loveletter" to that "beloved stranger," his reader, who might for a moment entertain the reality of the author's characters. Bebb and Parr, their intermingled families, the colorful cast of characters surrounding them—the profane Indian chief who wants to restore his sexual potency, the "octogenarian dottiness" of a UFO museum director—all of these richly crafted creations awaken the reader to the oddness of life, which is incarnated in its very ordinariness, in the mundane world through which life's meaning is mediated and God's presence is confirmed.

Leafing through a dictionary of saints, Buechner happened upon the story of the twelfth century churchman Godric, which immediately captured the novelist's imagination and provoked another fictional experiment. Using a narrative style that might be characterized as "colloquial Anglo-Saxon," *Godric* emerges as a narrative trek into the past to discover an earlier incarnation of Leo Bebb. Godric is no rogue preacher, but neither is he a conventional saint. From the first sentence of the novel, "Five friends had I and two of them snakes," the reader is taken on a lively journey into a historical epoch strangely like the present one. Here, one discovers that the Middle Ages were no less troubled than the twentieth century; more important, one discovers that the faith of medieval Christians was achieved no more easily than it is among modern man. Mirrored in the experience of Godric—a man desperately trying to avoid celebrity and sainthood—are the same ambiguities and tensions that confront contemporary believers and agnostics. Turning the clock back is no guarantee of simplicity or of easy answers. The earthiness of Godric's time is reassuring, however—Buechner's way of saying that the human condition is unaltered by time and space. Men and women, in Buechner's view, have always had the same needs, hopes, dreams, and sorrows they have today.

Godric is a chronicle whose narrator is Godric himself. Here, Buechner has created a credible voice, flavored with archaic cadences and intonations, which evokes the past and the present simultaneously, thus engaging the reader on two levels. The novel ends with a tremendous irony; Reginald, Godric's faithful companion and servant, is left to write the epilogue to Godric's eloquent autobiography. In so doing—filling his prose with Latinate locutions and fatuous exaggerations—he unwittingly provides a dramatic counterpoint to Godric's spiritual pilgrimage. Reginald's elegy presents faith, Godric's in particular, in an idealized manner, conveying the opposite of his master's actual experience. Godric's life was characterized not by constant victory and miracle but by daily struggle. By making Godric "larger than life," Reginald condemns him to being less than a man, merely a cartoon.

In many ways, *Godric* encompasses the best features of Buechner's work: a wry, sometimes bawdy humor; a serious reflection on mankind's limitations and need for spiritual vision; and a refusal to paint a simplistic picture of the spiritual dimensions of existence that lie just beyond the horizon of man's consciousness.

Buechner is a literary jack-of-all-trades, impressive in his control of diverse fictional and nonfictional modes of discourse. He is at once a leading Christian apologist, a writer of meditations, a homiletician, a novelist, and an autobiographer. The common strain through all of these roles is Buechner's conviction that life is, in the end, a story: a story to be celebrated, a story to be endured, but above all, a story to be told. No one who has read a bit of Buechner's prose can come away from it knowing less of himself; his readers are, finally, the parish of this novelist-turned-minister-turned-storyteller.

Major publications other than long fiction

NONFICTION: *The Magnificent Defeat*, 1966; *The Hungering Dark*, 1969; *The Alphabet of Grace*, 1970; *Wishful Thinking: A Theological ABC*, 1973; *The Faces of Jesus*, 1974; *Telling the Truth*, 1977; *Peculiar Treasures*, 1979; *The Sacred Journey*, 1982; *Now and Then*, 1983.

Bibliography

Aldwridge, John W. *After the Lost Generation*, 1951.

Davies, Horton, "Frederick Buechner and the Strange Work of Grace," in *Theology Today*. July, 1979.

Riley, Carolyn, ed. *Contemporary Literary Criticism*, 1974, 1975 (Vols. III, IV).

Bruce L. Edwards, Jr.

JOHN BUNYAN

Born: Elstow, England; November, 1628
Died: London, England; August 31, 1688

Principal long fiction

Grace Abounding to the Chief of Sinners, 1666; *The Pilgrim's Progress from This World to That Which Is to Come*, Part I, 1678; *The Life and Death of Mr. Badman*, 1680; *The Holy War*, 1682; *The Pilgrim's Progress from This World to That Which Is to Come the Second Part*, 1684.

Other literary forms

Between 1656 and 1688, John Bunyan published forty-four separate works, including prose narratives and tracts, sermons, and verse; ten posthumous publications appeared in a folio edition of 1692, which the author himself had prepared for the press. A nearly complete edition, in two volumes, was printed between 1736 and 1737, another in 1767 by George Whitefield, and a six-volume Edinburgh edition in 1784. The best of Bunyan's verse can be found in a small collection (c. 1664) containing "The Four Last Things," "Ebal and Gerizim," and "Prison Meditations." In addition, he wrote *A Caution to Stir Up to Watch Against Sin* (1664), a half-sheet broadside poem in sixteen stanzas; *A Book for Boys and Girls: Or, Country Rhymes for Children* (1686); *Discourse of the Building, Nature, Excellency, and Government of the House of God* (1688), a poem in twelve parts.

Achievements

The spirit of seventeenth century Protestant dissent burst into flame within the heart and mind of Bunyan. He attended only grammar school, served in the parliamentary army at age sixteen, and returned to Bedfordshire to undergo religious crisis and conversion. Imprisoned after the Restoration of Charles II for refusing to obey the laws against religious dissent, he turned to his pen as the only available means of performing his divinely ordained stewardship. He wrote his most significant work, the vision of *The Pilgrim's Progress*, while in jail, and the piece became a companion to the Scriptures among lower-class English Dissenters. His limited education came from two sources: the *Actes and Monuments* (1563) of John Foxe, containing the accounts of the martyrdom of sixteenth century English Protestants; and the Authorized Version of the Bible, the content and style of which he skillfully applied to his own prose.

Bunyan's art grew out of his natural abilities of observation and analysis. He was a Puritan and a product of the Puritan movement yet, as can be seen clearly from the autobiographical *Grace Abounding to the Chief of Sinners*, he was chiefly interested in actual human experience, not in religious doctrine for its own sake. His allegorical characters—Mr. Timorous, Mr. Talkative, Mrs. Diffidence, Mr. By-ends, Lord Turn-about, Mr. Smooth-man, Mr. Facing-bothways—originated in everyday life. Similarly, the Valley of Humiliation, the Slough of Despond, Vanity Fair, and Fair-speech can be found by all people everywhere, no matter what their culture or religion. In *The Pilgrim's Progress*, Bunyan universalized his Puritanism, depicting every earnest Christian's search for salvation, every upright person's attempt to achieve some degree of faith. He wrote to awaken conscience, to strenghten faith, and to win souls—the last being the true object of his evangelical mission. At the same time, he managed to write tracts and narratives worthy of recognition as *literature*—even, in certain instances, as masterpieces.

Biography

John Bunyan was born at the village of Elstow, in Bedfordshire (one mile south of Bedford) in November, 1628. The parish register of Elstow records his baptism on November 30. His father, Thomas Bunyan, a native of Elstow, married three times between January, 1623, and August, 1644; John Bunyan was the first child of his father's second marriage—on May 23, 1627, to Margaret Bentley, also of Elstow. The boy's father was a "whitesmith," a maker and mender of pots and kettles, although by the time the son adopted the same vocation, the job reference had changed to "tinker." Young Bunyan attended a nearby grammar school (either the one at Bedford or another at Elstow), where he learned to read and write—but little else. In fact, what he did learn he promptly forgot after his father removed him from school to help in the family forge and workshop. When, in 1644, his mother died and the elder Bunyan promptly remarried, Bunyan lost all interest in his family; he entered the parliamentary army in November, at age sixteen, and remained until the disbanding of that force in 1646. He then returned to Elstow and the family trade.

At the end of 1648 or the beginning of 1649, Bunyan married a pious but otherwise unidentified woman who bore him four children—one of whom, Mary, was born blind. He spent some four years wrestling with his finances and his soul, and in 1653 joined a dissenting sect that met at St. John's Church, Bedford. Shortly after his removal to that city in 1655, his wife died, and two years later he was called upon to preach by the Baptist sect whose church he had joined. In 1659, he married again, to a woman named Elizabeth, who spent considerable time rearing his children, bearing him two more, and trying to secure her husband's release from a series of prison terms.

Bunyan's career as a writer cannot be separated from his difficulties immediately preceding and during the Restoration of Charles II. The period of Cromwell's Commonwealth produced a number of dissenting preachers, both male and female, who achieved their offices through inspiration rather than ordination; they professed to be filled with inner light and the gifts of the Holy Spirit rather than with learning. Charles II had promised to tolerate these preachers, but the established Church, in November, 1660, set about to persecute and to silence them. Thus, Bunyan, who chose imprisonment rather than silence, spent all but a few weeks of the next eleven years in jail in Bedford, where he preached to his fellow prisoners, made tagged laces, and wrote religious books—the most noteworthy being his spiritual auto-biography, *Grace Abounding to the Chief of Sinners*. He was freed in Sep-tember, 1672, when Charles II, through his Declaration of Indulgence, suspended all penal statutes against Nonconformists and papists.

Upon his release from prison, Bunyan returned to his ministerial duties at St. John's Church in Bedford, this time with a license (given to him by royal authority) to preach. By 1675, however, he was again imprisoned in Bedford, the result of refusing to declare formal allegiance to Charles II (against whom he had no real objection) and the Church of England. While serving this particular sentence, Bunyan produced his most significant piece of prose, *The Pilgrim's Progress*. Bunyan's major prose works were written within the last ten years of his life, the period during which he both suffered from intolerance and received honors from the intolerant. In the last year of his life, he served as the unofficial chaplain to Sir John Shorter, the Lord Mayor of London. Indeed, Bunyan endured the entire tide of religious and political trauma of the middle and late seventeenth century: parliamentary acts, ministerial changes, popish plots, the rebellious factions. His work bears testimony to that endurance, to the patience of a nonpolitical yet deeply pious man who lost much of his freedom to the impatience of a supposedly pious but terribly political religious establishment.

Bunyan died on August 31, 1688, at the London house of his friend, John Strudwick, a grocer and chandler. Supposedly, in order to settle a dispute between a father and his son, he rode through heavy rain and caught a severe cold that led to his death. He was buried in Bunhill Fields, the burial ground of London Dissenters.

Analysis

John Bunyan viewed his life as a commitment to Christian stewardship, to be carried on by gospel preaching and instructive writing. Although practically everything that he wrote reflects that commitment, he possessed the ability to create interesting variations on similar themes, keeping in mind the needs of his lower-class audience. Thus, *The Pilgrim's Progress* is an allegory of human life and universal religious experience. In *The Life and Death of Mr. Badman*, Bunyan abandoned allegory and developed a dialogue betweeen Mr. Wiseman and Mr. Attentive through which he publicized the aims and methods of the late seventeenth century bourgeois scoundrel, whose lack of principle and honesty was well known among Bunyan's readers (the victims of Mr. Badman). Finally, his first major work, *Grace Abounding to the Chief*

of Sinners, is a "spiritual autobiography" which presents adventures and ex-
preiences not unlike those undergone by any human being at any moment in
history who must wrestle with the fundamental questions of life. The function
of Bunyan's prose in every case was to spread the Word of God and to establish
a holy community of mankind in which that Word could be practiced. Once
the Word took hold, Bunyan believed, the world would become a veritable
garden of peace and order.

Published in 1666, *Grace Abounding to the Chief of Sinners* remains one
of the most significant spiritual autobiographies by an English writer. Bunyan's
style is perhaps more formal in this piece than in *The Pilgrim's Progress*,
although he did well to balance the heavy phrasing of Scripture (as it appeared
in the Authorized Version) with picturesque, colloquial English. A richly
emotional work in which such highly charged experiences as the Last Judgment and the tortures of Hell become as clear as the mundane experiences
of daily existence, Bunyan's autobiography is a narrative of spiritual adventure
set against the backdrop of a real village in Britain. Although he omitted
specific names and dates, obviously to universalize the piece, he did not forget
to describe what he had seen after his return from the army: the popular
game of "cat," with its participants and spectators; the bellringers at the parish
church; the poor women sitting, in sunlight, before the door of a village
house; the puddles in the road. Woven into this fabric of reality are the
experiences of the dreamer; the people of Bedford appear as though in a
vision on the sunny side of a high mountain, as the dreamer, shut out by an
encompassing wall, shivers in the cold storm. Such interweaving of reality
and fantasy was to take place again, with greater force and allegorical complexity, in the first part of *The Pilgrim's Progress*.

Bunyan's intention in *Grace Abounding to the Chief of Sinners* was to point
the way by which average Christians, convinced of their own sins, can be led
by God's grace to endure the pain of spiritual crisis. He determined to record
how, as an obscure Bedfordshire tinker, he had changed his course from sloth
and sin to become an eloquent and fearless man of God. Of course, when
he wrote the work, he had been in prison for ten years, and (as stated in the
Preface) he set about to enlighten and assist those from whom he had, for
so lóng a period, been separated.

From the confinement of his prison cell, Bunyan felt the desire to survey
his entire life—to grasp his soul in his hands and take account of himself.
Thus, *Grace Abounding to the Chief of Sinners* emerged from the heart and
the spirit of a man isolated from mankind to become not merely one more
testimonial for the instruction of the faithful, but a serious, psychological self-
study—one so truthful and so sincere (and also so spontaneous) that it may
be the first work of its kind. Bunyan's language is simple and direct, and his
constant references to Scripture emphasize the typicality of his experiences
as a struggling Christian. His fears, doubts, and moments of comfort are

filtered through the encounter between David and Goliath and God's deliv-
erance of the young shepherd, while his lively imagination gathers images
from the Psalms and the Proverbs and reshapes them to fit the context of his
spiritual experiences.

Bunyan's ability to universalize his experience is supremely evident in *The
Pilgrim's Progress*, perhaps the most successful allegory in British literature.
The Pilgrim's Progress has as its basic metaphor the familiar idea of life as
a journey. Bunyan confronts his pilgrim, Christian, with homely and commonplace sights: a quagmire, the bypaths and shortcuts through pleasant
country meadows, the inn, the steep hill, the town fair on market day, the
river to be forded. Such places belong to the everyday experience of every
man, woman, and child; on another level, they recall the holy but homely
parables of Christ's earthly ministry, and thus assume spiritual significance.
Those familiar details serve as an effective background for Bunyan's narrative,
a story of adventure intended to hold the reader in suspense. Bunyan grew
up among the very people who constituted his audience, and he knew how
to balance the romantic and the strange with the familiar. Thus, Christian
travels the King's Highway at the same time that he traverses a perilous path
to encounter giants, wild beasts, hobgoblins, and the terrible Apollyon, the
angel of the bottomless pit with whom the central character must fight. Other
travelers are worthy of humorous characterization as they represent a variety
of intellectual and moral attitudes, while Christian himself runs the gamut of
universal experience, from the moment he learns of his sins until the account
of his meeting with Hopeful in the river.

As always, Bunyan molds his style from the Authorized Version of the
Bible. By relying upon concrete, common language, he enables even the
simplest of his readers to share experiences with the characters of *The Pilgrim's
Progress*. Even the conversations relating to complex and tedious theological
issues do not detract from the human and dramatic aspects of the allegory:
Evangelist pointing the way; Christian running from his home with his fingers
stuck in his ears; the starkness of the place of the Cross in contrast to the
activity of Vanity Fair: the humorous but terribly circumstantial trial. It is
this homely but vivid realism which accounts for the timeless appeal of Bunyan's allegory. *The Pilgrim's Progress* reveals the truth about mankind—its
weakness, its imperfection, its baseness, but also its search for goodness and
order.

The Life and Death of Mr. Badman represents Bunyan's major attempt at
a dialogue, a confrontation between the Christian and the atheist, between
the road to Paradise and the route to Hell. Mr. Wiseman, a Christian, tells
the story of Mr. Badman to Mr. Attentive, who in turn comments upon it.
Badman is an example of the reprobate, one whose sins become evident
during childhood. In fact, he is so addicted to lying that his parents cannot
distinguish when he is speaking the truth. Bunyan does not place much blame

upon the parents, for they indeed bear the burden of their son's actions; they even attempt to counsel him and to redirect his ways. The situation becomes worse, however, as Badman's lying turns to pilfering and then to outright stealing. All of this, naturally, leads to a hatred of Sunday, to the Puritan demands of that day: reading Scripture, attending conferences, repeating sermons, praying to God. Wiseman, the defender of the Puritan Sabbath, maintains that little boys, as a matter of course, must learn to appreciate the Sabbath; those who do not are victims of their own wickedness. Hatred of the Sabbath leads to swearing and cursing, which become as natural to young Badman as eating, drinking, and sleeping.

Badman's adult life is painstakingly drawn out through realistic descriptions, anecdotes, and dialogue. He cheats and steals his way through the world of debauchery and commerce and creates misery for his wife and seven children. Growing in importance, he forms a league with the devil and becomes a wealthy man by taking advantage of others' misfortunes. When the time comes for his end, he cannot be saved—nor does Bunyan try to fabricate an excuse for his redemption and salvation. As Mr. Wiseman states, "As his life was full of sin, so his death was without repentance." Throughout a long sickness, Badman fails to acknowledge his sins, remaining firm in his self-satisfaction. He dies without struggle, "like a chrisom child, quietly and without fear."

The strength of *The Life and Death of Mr. Badman* derives in large part from Bunyan's ability to depict common English life of the mid- and late seventeenth century. The details are so accurate, so minute, that the reader can gain as much history from the piece as morality or practical theology. Bunyan places no demands upon the reader's credulity by providential interpositions, nor does he alter his wicked character's ways for the sake of a happy ending. In portraying Badman's ways, Bunyan concedes nothing, nor does he exaggerate. Badman succeeds, gains wealth and power, and dies at peace with himself. Bunyan creates a monstrous product of sin and places him squarely in the center of English provincial life. The one consolation, the principal lesson, is that Badman travels the direct route to everlasting hell-fire. On his way, he partakes of life's pleasures, is gratified by them as only an unrepentant sinner could be. For Bunyan, the harsh specificity of Badman's life is a sufficient lesson through which to promote his version of positive Christianity.

Beneath the veil of seventeenth century British Puritanism, for all its seeming narrowness and sectarian strife, there was something for all persons of all eras—the struggle to know God, to do His will, to find peace. If Bunyan's first major prose work was a spiritual autobiography, then it is fair to state that the principal efforts that followed—*The Pilgrim's Progress* and *The Life and Death of Mr. Badman*—constituted one of the earliest spiritual histories of all mankind.

Major publications other than long fiction

POETRY: *A Caution to Stir Up to Watch Against Sin*, 1664; *A Book for Boys and Girls: Or, Country Rhymes for Children*, 1686; *Discourse of the Building, Nature, Excellency, and Government of the House of God*, 1688.

RELIGIOUS WRITINGS: *Some Gospel Truths Opened*, 1656; *A Vindication . . . of Some Gospel Truths Opened*, 1657; *A Few Signs from Hell*, 1658; *The Doctrine of the Law and Grace Unfolded*, 1659; *Profitable Meditations Fitted to Man's Different Condition*, 1661; *I Will Pray with the Spirit*, 1663; *A Mapp Shewing the Order and Causes of Salvation and Damnation*, 1664; *One Thing Is Needful*, 1665; *The Holy City: Or, The New Jersalem*, 1666; *A Confession of My Faith and a Reason for My Practice*, 1671; *A New and Useful Concordance to the Holy Bible*, 1672; *A Defence of the Doctrine of Justification By Faith*, 1672; *The Strait Gate: Or, The Great Difficulty of Going to Heaven*, 1676; *Saved by Grace*, 1676; *A Treatise of the Fear of God*, 1679; *A Holy Life, the Beauty of Christianity*, 1684; *Solomon's Temple Spiritualized: Or, Gospel Light Fecht Out of the Temple at Jerusalem*, 1688; *The Jerusalem Sinner Saved*, 1688.

Bibliography

Baird, Charles W. *John Bunyan: A Study in Narrative Technique*, 1977.

Brittain, Vera. *In the Steps of John Bunyan: An Excursion into Puritan England*, 1950.

Froude, James Anthony. *John Bunyan*, 1880.

Furlong, Monica. *Puritan's Progress: A Study of John Bunyan*, 1975.

Greaves, Richard Lee. *John Bunyan*, 1969.

Harrison, G. B. *John Bunyan: A Study in Personality*, 1928.

Knox, Edmund Arbuthnott. *John Bunyan in Relation to His Time*, 1928.

Lindsay, Jack. *John Bunyan, Maker of Myths*, 1937.

Newey, Vincent, ed. *The Pilgrim's Progress: Critical and Historical Views*, 1980.

Saddler, Lynn Veach. *John Bunyan*, 1979.

Sharrock, Roger. *John Bunyan*, 1954.

Talon, Henri Antoine. *John Bunyan: The Man and His Works*, 1951.

Winslow, Ola Elizabeth. *John Bunyan*, 1961.

Samuel J. Rogal

ANTHONY BURGESS

Born: Manchester, England; February 25, 1917

Principal long fiction
Time for a Tiger, 1956; *The Enemy in the Blanket*, 1958; *Beds in the East*, 1959; *The Doctor Is Sick*, 1960; *The Right to an Answer*, 1960; *Devil of a State*, 1961; *One Hand Clapping*, 1961 (as Joseph Kell); *The Worm and the Ring*, 1961; *A Clockwork Orange*, 1962; *The Wanting Seed*, 1962; *Honey for the Bears*, 1963; *Inside Mr. Enderby*, 1963 (as Joseph Kell); *The Eve of Saint Venus*, 1964; *Nothing Like the Sun: A Story of Shakespeare's Love-Life*, 1964; *The Long Day Wanes*, 1965 (includes *Time for a Tiger*, *The Enemy in the Blanket*, *Beds in the East*); *A Vision of Battlements*, 1965; *Tremor of Intent*, 1966; *Enderby*, 1968 (includes *Mr. Enderby*, *Enderby Outside*); *Enderby Outside*, 1968; *MF*, 1971; *The Clockwork Testament: Or, Enderby's End*, 1974; *Napoleon Symphony*, 1974; *Beard's Roman Woman*, 1976; *Moses: A Narrative*, 1976; *Abba, Abba*, 1977; *1985*, 1978; *Man of Nazareth*, 1979; *Earthly Powers*, 1980; *The End of the World News*, 1983.

Other literary forms
In addition to his novels, Anthony Burgess has published eight works of literary criticism. He has paid tribute to his self-confessed literary mentor, James Joyce, in such works as *Re Joyce* (1965) and *Joysprick* (1973). His book reviews and essays have been collected in *The Novel Now* (1967) and *Urgent Copy* (1968). His fascination with language and with the lives of writers has led to such works as *Language Made Plain* (1964), *Here Comes Everybody* (1965), *Shakespeare* (1970), and *Ernest Hemingway and His World* (1978).

Achievements
In his twenty-seven novels, Burgess has extended the boundaries of English fiction. His love of language, his use of symphonic forms and motifs, his rewriting of myths and legends, his examination of cultural clashes between the Third World and the West, and his pursuit of various ways to tell a story have established him as one of the chief exemplars of postmodernism. His novels are studied in contemporary fiction courses, and he has also achieved popular success with such works as *A Clockwork Orange* and *Earthly Powers*. Stanley Kubrick's controversial film *A Clockwork Orange* (1971) further established Burgess' popular reputation.

Biography
John Anthony Burgess Wilson was born in Manchester, England, on February 25, 1917. His mother and sister died in the influenza epidemic of 1918.

Of Irish background, his mother had performed in the music halls of the period and was known as "the Beautiful Belle Burgess." His father performed as a silent-film pianist and when he remarried, played piano in a pub called "The Golden Eagle," owned by his new wife; Burgess himself began to compose music when he was fourteen. Burgess was graduated from the Bishop Bilsborrow School and from Xaverian College in Manchester; in 1940, he wrote his senior honors thesis on Christopher Marlowe, while Nazi bombs fell overhead.

In October, 1940, Burgess joined the army and was placed in the Army Medical Corps. He was later shifted to the Army Educational Corps—a prophetic move, since he became a teacher for nearly twenty years afterwards. In 1942, Burgess married Llewela Isherwood Jones, a Welsh fellow student. He spent three years, from 1943 to 1946, with the British Army on Gibraltar, during which time he wrote his first novel, *A Vision of Battlements* (which was not published until 1965).

Burgess left the army as a sergeant major and as a training college lecturer in speech and drama in 1946 to become a member of the Central Advisory Council for Adult Education in the armed forces. He lectured at Birmingham University until 1948, when he served as a lecturer in phonetics for the Ministry of Education in Preston, Lancashire. From 1950 until 1954, he taught English literature, phonetics, Spanish, and music at the Banbury grammar school in Oxfordshire.

Throughout these years, Burgess was painfully aware of his Irish heritage and Catholic religion. Though he had renounced Catholicism early, the Irish-Catholic stigma remained with him in rigorously Protestant England. His decision to apply for the job of education officer for the Colonial Service may have had something to do with his desire to leave England and his need to exile himself physically from a homeland that had already exiled him in spirit. From 1954 to 1957, he was the Senior Lecturer in English at the Malayan Teachers Training College in Kahta Baru, Malaya. There, he had more leisure time to write, and he published his first novel, *Time for a Tiger*, in 1956 under his middle names, "Anthony Burgess." Members of the Colonial Service were not allowed to publish fiction under their own names.

Burgess continued working for the Colonial Service as an English language specialist in Brunei, Borneo, from 1957 to 1959 and published two more novels, which, with his first, eventually constituted his Malayan trilogy, *The Long Day Wanes*. The clash between the manners and morals of East and West became the major focus of his early novels.

Apparent tragedy struck in 1959, when Burgess fainted in the classroom and was rushed to a neurological institute in London. There, he was given a year to live, after excruciating medical tests; the diagnosis was a possible brain tumor. Unable to teach, virtually penniless, Burgess set himself to writing as much as he could in order to provide for his wife. Not only had she already shown signs of the cirrhosis of the liver that was eventually to kill her, but also she had attempted suicide. In the next three years, Burgess wrote and published nine novels, including *A Clockwork Orange* and *Inside Mr. Enderby*.

On the first day of spring, March 20, 1968, Llewela Burgess finally died. That October, Burgess married Liliana Macellari, a member of the linguistics department at Cambridge; they had had a son, Andrew, in 1964. The personal guilt involved with his first wife's death has always haunted Burgess and provides one of the major underlying themes of his fiction. "Guilt's a good thing," Burgess once said, "because the morals are just ticking away very nicely." In fact, persistent guilt shadows all of his characters and consistently threatens to overwhelm them completely.

Burgess, Liliana, and Andrew left England in October, 1968; they have never returned. They moved to Malta, to Bracciano in Italy, and eventually settled in Monaco. Burgess is still a prolific writer. In 1980, he published *Earthly Powers*, a long and ambitious novel on which he had been working for more than ten years; his novel *The End of the World News* was published in 1983. He continues to compose symphonies, write film scripts and television scripts, review at great length in major newspapers and periodicals, and write fiction.

Analysis

Anthony Burgess shares with many postmodernist writers an almost obsessive awareness of his great modernist predecessors—particularly James Joyce. The vision which Burgess inherited from modernism is informed by the anguish of a sensitive soul lost in a fragmented, shattered world. Each of Burgess' novels reveals one central character virtually "at sea" in a landscape of battered, broken figures and events. Burgess conveys this fragmented world-view by means of many of the literary devices of his modernist predecessors. Often he employs a stream-of-consciousness narration, in which his main character tells his own story; he also has used what T. S. Eliot, reviewing Joyce's *Ulysses* (1922), called the "mythic method," in which contemporary chaos is compared with and contrasted to heroic myths, legends, religious ceremonies, and rituals of the past. As Eliot remarked, the mythic method "is simply a way of controlling, of ordering, of giving a shape and significance to the intense panorama of futility and anarchy which is contemporary history."

Like many postmodernists, convinced that most literary forms are serious games devised to stave off approaching chaos and collapse, Burgess delights in the play of language for its own sake. Here again, Joyce is a prime source of inspiration: surprising images, poetic revelations, linguistic twists and turns, and strange evocative words nearly overwhelm the narrative shape of *Ulysses* and certainly overwhelm it in *Finnegans Wake* (1939). Burgess' best novels are those in which language for its own sake plays an important role, as in *Enderby*, *Nothing Like the Sun*, *A Clockwork Orange*, and *Napoleon Symphony*.

At the heart of his vision of the world lies Burgess' Manichaean sensibility, his belief that there is "a duality that is fixed almost from the beginning of the world and the outcome is in doubt." God and the Devil reign over a supremely divided universe; they are equal in power, and they will battle to the end of the world. In the Manichaean tradition—most notably, that of the Gnostics—Burgess sees the world as a materialistic trap, a prison of the spirit and a place devised by the Devil to incarcerate man until his death. Only art can break through the battlelines; only art can save him. The recasting of a religious commitment in aesthetic terms also belongs to the legacy of modernism. Burgess' Manichaean vision produces such clashes of opposites as that between East and West, between the self and the state, and between a single character and an alien social environment. These recurring polarities structure Burgess' fiction.

This principle of polarity or opposition is evident in the early novel *The Right to an Answer*, in which J. W. Denham, businessman and exile, returns to his father's house in the suburban British Midlands and finds a provincial, self-satisfied community engaged in wife-swapping, television-viewing, and pub-crawling. He remains a detached observer, longing for a kind of communion he cannot find, and in his telling his own tale, he reveals himself as friendless, disillusioned, and homeless.

The wife-swapping quartet at the Black Swan pub is disturbed by the entrance of Mr. Raj, a Ceylonese gentleman, interested in English sociology and in satisfying his lust for white women. He plays by no rules but his own and espouses a kind of deadly Eastern realism that threatens the suburban sport. Moving in with Denham's father, he unfortunately kills the old man by "currying" him to death with his hot dishes. The upshot of this clash of cultural and social values is that Raj kills Winterbottom, the most innocent member of the *ménage à quatre*, and then kills himself.

Throughout the novel, Burgess explores both Denham's point of view and Raj's within the seedy suburban landscape. Their viewpoints reflect the irreconcilable differences between East and West, between black and white, between sex and love, and between true religion and dead ritual. Denham's stream-of-consciousness narration eventually reveals his own spirit of exile, which he cannot overcome. He remains disconnected from both worlds, from England and the East, and epitomizes the state of lovelessness and isolation that has permeated modern culture. This early novel clearly explores Burgess' main themes and narrative forms.

In the guise of a thriller *à la* James Bond, *Tremor of Intent* explores a world of "God" and "Not-God," a profoundly Manichaean universe. Soviet spies battle English spies, while the real villains of the novel, the "neutralists," play one camp off against the other purely for personal gain. Burgess derides the whole notion of the spy's realm, but he insists that taking sides is essential in such a world, whether ultimate good or evil is ever really confronted.

Denis Hillier, aging technician and spy, writes his confessional memoirs in the light of his possible redemption. His Catholic sense of original sin never falters for an instant, and he is constantly in need of some higher truth, some ultimate communion and revelation. In the course of the novel, he fights every Manichaean division, drinks "Old Mortality," sees himself as a "fallen Adam," and works his way toward some vision of hope. Finally, he abandons the spy game and becomes a priest, exiling himself to Ireland. From this new perspective, he believes that he can approach the real mysteries of good and evil, of free will and predestination, beyond the limiting and limited categories of the Cold War.

Hillier's opposite in the novel is Edwin Roper, a rationalist who has jettisoned any religious belief and who hungers for an ultimately unified universe based on scientific truth and explanation. Such rationalism leads him to the Marxist logic of Soviet ideology, and he defects to the Russian side. Hillier has been set to rescue him. One section of the novel consists of Roper's autobiographical explanation of his actions; its flat, logical prose reflects his methodical and disbelieving mind, in contrast to Hillier's more religious sensibility.

Within the complicated plot of the novel, self-serving scoundrels such as Mr. Theodorescu and Richard Wriste set out to destroy both Hillier and Roper and gather information to sell to the highest bidder. They fail, owing largely to the actions of Alan and Clara Walters, two children on board the ship that is taking Hillier to meet Roper. The children become initiated into the world of double agents and sexual intrigue, and Theodorescu and Wriste are assassinated.

Burgess displays his love of language for its own sake in exotic descriptions of sex, food, and life abroad a cruise ship. Such language intensifies the Manichaean divisions in the book, the constant battle between the things of this world and the imagined horrors of the next. The very language that Hillier and Roper use to tell their own stories reveals their own distinctly different personalities and visions.

Tremor of Intent insists on the mystery of human will. To choose is to be human; that is good. Thus, to choose evil is both a good and a bad thing, a Manichaean complication that Burgess leaves with the reader. In allegorical terms the novel presents the problems of free will and its consequences which underlie all of Burgess' fiction.

Nothing Like the Sun, Burgess' fanciful novel based on the life of Shakespeare, showcases every facet of his vision and technique as a novelist. Shakespeare finds himself caught between his love for a golden man and a black woman. Sex feeds the fires of love and possession, and from these fires grows his art, the passion of language. From these fires also comes syphilis, the dread disease that eventually kills him, the source of the dark vision that surfaces in his apocalyptic tragedies. Shakespeare as a writer and Shakespeare as man battle it out, and from that dualistic confrontation emerges the perilous equilibrium of his greatest plays.

In part, Burgess' fiction is based on the theories about Shakespeare's life which Stephen Dedalus expounds in *Ulysses*. Dedalus suggests that Shakespeare was cuckolded by his brother Richard, that Shakespeare's vision of a treacherous and tragic world was based on his own intimate experience. To this conjecture, Burgess adds the notion that the Dark Lady of the sonnets was a non-Caucasian and that Shakespeare himself was a victim of syphilis. All of these "myths" concerning Shakespeare serve Burgess' Manichaean vision: sex and disease, art and personality are ultimately at war with one another and can only be resolved in the actual plays that Shakespeare wrote.

Nothing Like the Sun is written in an exuberant, bawdy, pseudo-Elizabethan style. It is clear that Burgess relished the creation of lists of epithets, curses, and prophecies, filled as they are with puns and his own outrageous coinings. Burgess audaciously attempts to mime the development of Shakespeare's art as he slowly awakens to the possibilities of poetry, trying different styles, moving from the sweet rhymes of "Venus and Adonis" to the "sharp knives and brutal hammers" of the later tragedies.

The book is constructed in the form of a lecture by Burgess himself to his Malayan students. He drinks as he talks and explains his paradoxical theories as he goes along. His passing out from too much drink at the novel's end parallels Shakespeare's death. He puns also with his real last name, Wilson, regarding himself as in fact "Will's son," a poet and author in his own right.

Earthly Powers, Burgess's longest novel, features perhaps his most arresting first sentence: "It was the afternoon of my 81st birthday, and I was in bed with my catamite when Ali announced that the archbishop had come to see me." Thus begin the memoirs of Kenneth Toomey, cynical agnostic and homosexual writer, a character based loosely on Somerset Maugham.

Toomey's memoirs span the twentieth century—its literary intrigues, cultural fashions, and political horrors. Toomey is seduced on June 16, 1904, that Dublin day immortalized by Joyce in *Ulysses*, revels in the Paris of the 1920's, the Hollywood of the 1930's, and the stylish New York of the 1940's and 1950's; his old age is spent in exotic exile in Tangiers and Malta in the 1970's. During his long life he writes plays and movie scenarios, carries on with a host of male secretary-lovers, and experiences the traumas of Nazism and Communism. He abhors the state-controlled collective soul which he sees as the ultimate product of the twentieth century.

Burgess' huge, sprawling novel displays a plot crowded with coincidence and bursting with stylistic parodies and re-creations. A priest on his way to becoming pope saves a dying child, only to see him grow up to be the leader of a fanatical religious cult akin to that of Jim Jones in Guyana. An American anthropologist and his wife are butchered during a Catholic mass in Africa: the natives there take the commands of the ceremony all too literally and swallow their visitors.

Toomey believes that evil lies firmly within man and that his experiences of this century prove that the world is a murderous place. His Manichaean opposite in faith is his brother-in-law, Carlo Campanati, the gambler-gourmet priest who becomes Pope Gregory XVII. Evil remains external to man, the Pope maintains; man is essentially good. In Burgess' jaundiced view of things, such misconceived idealism produces only further evils. Any similarities between Gregory and John XXIII are strictly intentional.

The world of *Earthly Powers* is Toomey's world, a bright place with clipped, swift glimpses of fads and fashion. Librettos, snippets of plays, even a re-creation of the Garden of Eden story from a homosexual point of view appear in this modernist memoir. The style itself reflects Burgess' conception of the "brittle yet excruciatingly precise" manner of the homosexual.

Earthly Powers wobbles. More than six hundred pages of bright wit can cloy. Verbal surfaces congeal and trail off into trivial documentation. The Pope's spiritual observations impede the novel's progress, encased as they are in lectures, sermons, and tracts. Indeed, Gregory's is as thin a character as Toomey's is an interesting one.

The book proves that Toomey is right: things are rotten. No amount of linguistic fun, modernist maneuverings, or Manichaean machinations can change the fact that this is the worst of all possible worlds. Chunks of smart conversation cannot hide that fact; they become stupefying and evasive in the end. The nature of man's free will, however, and its legacy of unquestionable evil in the twentieth century pervade Burgess' fat book and linger on to undermine any "safe" position the reader may hope to find.

Burgess' Manichaean nightmare in *A Clockwork Orange* occupies the center of his most accomplished book. The language of *nadsat* in its harsh, Russian-accented diction, the ongoing battle between the State and Alex the *droog*, the vision of an urban landscape wracked with violence and decay, the mysterious interpenetration of Beethoven and lust, and the unresolved issues of good and evil reflect and parallel one another so completely that the novel emerges as Burgess' masterpiece.

The issue raised is an increasingly timely one: can the state program the individual to be good? Can it eradicate the individual's right to freedom of choice, especially if in choosing, he chooses to commit violent and evil acts? Burgess replies in the negative. No matter how awful Alex's actions become, he should be allowed to choose them.

Since the novel is written from Alex's point of view, the reader sympathizes with him, despite his acts of rape and mayhem. Alex loves Beethoven; he "shines artistic"; he is brighter than his ghoulish friends; he is rejected by his parents. He is in all ways superior to the foul futuristic landscape that surrounds him. When the state brainwashes him, the reader experiences his pain in a personal, forthright manner. The violence in the rest of the book falls upon outsiders and remains distanced by the very language Alex uses to describe his actions.

Burgess' slang creates a strange and distant world. The reader approaches the novel as an outsider to that world and must try diligently to decode it to understand it. Never has Burgess used language so effectively to create the very atmosphere of his fiction. The Russian-influenced slang of the novel is a *tour de force* of the highest order and yet functions perfectly as a reflection of Alex's state of mind and of the society of which he is a rebellious member.

The world of *A Clockwork Orange* recognizes only power and political force. All talk of free will dissolves before such a harrowing place of behaviorist psychologists and social controllers. Individual freedom in such a world remains a myth, not a reality, a matter of faith, not an ultimate truth. Everyone is in some sense a clockwork orange, a victim of his or her society, compelled to act in a social order that celebrates only power, manipulation, and control.

Even the cyclical form of *A Clockwork Orange* reveals a world trapped within its own inevitable patterns. At first, Alex victimizes those around him. He in turn is victimized by the state. In the third and final part of the novel, he returns to victimize other people once again: "I was cured all right." Victimization remains the only reality here. There are no loopholes, no escape hatches from the vicious pattern. The frightening cityscape at night, the harsh language, the paradoxical personality of Alex, the collaborationist or revolutionary tactics of Alex's "friends," and the very shape of the novel reinforce this recognition of utter entrapment and human decay. "Oh, my brothers," Alex addresses his readers, as Eliot in *The Waste Land* (1922) quoted Charles Baudelaire: "*Hypocrite lecteur, mon semblable, mon frère.*"

Despite Burgess' pessimistic vision of contemporary life and the creative soul's place in it, the best of his novels still reveal a commitment to literature as a serious ceremony, as a game which the reader and the writer must continue to play, if only to transcend momentarily the horrors of Western civilization in the twentieth century.

Major publications other than long fiction
NONFICTION: *English Literature: A Survey for Students*, 1958 (as John Burgess Wilson); *The Novel Today*, 1963; *Language Made Plain* 1964; *Here Comes Everybody: An Introduction to James Joyce for the Ordinary Reader*, 1965 (published in the United States as *Re Joyce*, 1965); *The Novel Now*, 1967, 1971; *Urgent Copy: Literary Studies*, 1968; *Shakespeare*, 1970; *Joysprick: An Introduction to the Language of James Joyce*, 1972; *Ernest Hemingway and His World*, 1978.

Bibliography
De Vitis, A. A. *Anthony Burgess*, 1972.
Le Clair, Thomas. "Essential Opposition: The Novels of Anthony Burgess," in *Critique: Studies in Modern Fiction*. XII (1971), pp. 77-94.
Morris, Robert K. *Consolations of Ambiguity*, 1971.
Pritchard, William H. "The Novels of Anthony Burgess," in *Massachusetts Review*. VII (1966), pp. 525-539.

Samuel Coale

FANNY BURNEY

Born: King's Lynn, England; June 13, 1752
Died: London, England; January 6, 1840

Principal long fiction
Evelina: Or, The History of a Young Lady's Entrance into the World, 1778;
Cecilia; Or, Memoirs of an Heiress, 1782; *Camilla: Or, A Picture of Youth*,
1796; *The Wanderer: Or, Female Difficulties*, 1814.

Other literary forms
In addition to editing the memoirs of her father—the noted organist, composer, and music historian, Dr. Charles Burney (1726-1814)—Fanny Burney
wrote an *Early Diary, 1768-1778* (1889) and then a later *Diary and Letters,
1778-1840* (1842-1846). The first work, not published until 1889, contains
pleasant sketches of Samuel Johnson, James Boswell, David Garrick, and
Richard Brinsley Sheridan. Notable figures from government and the arts
march across the pages of the early diary, which scholars have claimed surpasses her fiction in literary quality. The latter diary and correspondence
appeared between 1842 and 1846; the seven volumes are notable for the record
of the writer's meeting in her garden with the insane George III of England,
the account of her glimpse of Napoleon I, and the recollections of her chat
with the weary Louis XVIII of France.
Of her eight dramatic productions, three are worthy of mention: *The
Witlings* (never published); *Edwy and Elgiva; A Tragedy*, written in 1790,
performed at Drury Lane on March 21, 1795, and withdrawn after the first
night; and *Love and Fashion*, written in 1800, accepted by the manager at
Covent Garden, but never performed. Finally, Burney published, in 1793, a
political essay entitled *Brief Reflections Relative to the French Clergy*, an
address to the women of Great Britain in behalf of the French emigrant
priests.

Achievements
Most critics tend to place the reputation of Burney within the shadow of her
most immediate successor, Jane Austen. Reasons for this assessment are not
immediately clear, especially in the light of responses to the novels from
contemporary readers. Burney's problem during the past two centuries, however, has not concerned popularity, subject matter, or even literary style;
rather, certain personal circumstances under which she wrote seriously
reduced her artistic effectiveness and considerably dulled her reputation.
Essentially, Burney produced fiction at a time in history when a lady of means
and social standing could not easily write fiction and still be considered a lady.
Adding to that inhibition was the aura of her noted and influential father and

his circle of even more influential friends: Samuel Johnson, Mrs. Hester Lynch Thrale Piozzi, Oliver Goldsmith, and Sir Joshua Reynolds. Both her father and his friends held literary standards not always easy for a self-educated young woman to attain. She burned her early manuscript efforts, wrote secretly at night, and published anonymously; she labored under the artistic domination of her father and the advice of his friends; she remained cautious, intimidated by and dependent on elderly people who served as guardians of her intellect.

Nevertheless, Burney succeeded as a novelist and achieved significance as a contributor to the history and development of the English novel. She brought to that genre an ability to observe the natural activities and reactions of those about her and to weave those observations through narrative structures and character delineations similar to those employed by her predecessors: Samuel Johnson, Henry Fielding, Samuel Richardson, Tobias Smollett, Aphra Behn, Mary De La Riviere Manley, Eliza Heywood, and Clara Reeve. In her Preface to *Evelina*, she set forth the criteria that, throughout her fiction, she would develop and maintain. For Burney, the novel would be the means by which to portray realistic persons and to represent the times in which they functioned. In her own concept of the form, those characters had to be real but not necessarily true; they had to be drawn "from nature, though not from life." Further, those same fictional characters had to confront and, hopefully, solve complex human problems—problems that they might avoid for a time but eventually would be forced to encounter.

Although Burney's four novels were published anonymously, the sophisticated readers of the day recognized the woman's point of view and immediately set the works apart from those of their contemporaries. The female readership, especially, both appreciated and praised the woman's view of the contemporary world; on the other hand, the young dandies of the late-eighteenth century and the pre-Victorian age scoffed at the novels' heroines as comic sentimentalists, products of blatant amateurism, and characteristic examples of a sex that would continue to be dominated by men.

The real basis on which to place Burney's popularity, however, rests with the ability of the novelist to develop fully the effects of female intelligence upon and within a society dominated by men and to convince her audience that coexistence between the sexes was far more beneficial than the dominance of one over the other. The essential differences between Fanny Burney and her female predecessors (Aphra Behn is the most obvious example) is the extent to which the issue of feminism was developed and then thrust forward as a major consideration.

As a woman writing about women, Burney could not cling too long to the models that the past century had provided for her. Despite the mild increase in the numbers of female novelists during the last quarter of the eighteenth century, Burney had little guidance in developing the woman's point of view.

She had, essentially, to find her own way within the confines of a limited world and even more limited experience. Thus, she determined early to purge her fictional environment of masculine influence. In its place, she would establish the importance of her titled characters as working parts in the machinery of eighteenth century British society. Burney's heroines do not convey appearances of being rebels, radicals, or social freaks; rather, their creator has drawn each one of them with a fine and firm hand. As a group, they are indeed meant to be carbon copies of one another; individually, each portrays a young lady in pursuit of traditional goals: marriage, money, and the discovery of the self.

Biography

Fanny (Frances) Burney, later Madame D'Arblay, the third of six children of Charles Burney and Esther Sleepe Burney, was born on June 13, 1752, at King's Lynn, Norfolk, where her father served as church organist while recuperating from consumption. In 1760, his health completely restored, Burney moved his family to London, where he resumed his professional involvements in teaching, composition, and music history. Upon the death of Esther Burney on September 28, 1761, two of the children (Esther and Susannah) went to school in Paris, while Frances remained at home. Apparently, Dr. Burney feared that his middle daughter's devotion to her grandmother (then living in France) would bring about the child's conversion to Catholicism. He seemed prepared to change that point of view and send Frances to join her sisters, when, in 1766, he married Mrs. Stephen Allen: thus, the fourteen-year-old girl remained at home in London, left to her own educational aims and directions, since her father had no time to supervise her learning. She had, at about age ten, begun to write drama, poetry, and fiction; on her fifteenth birthday, she supposedly burned her manuscripts because she felt guilty about wasting her time with such trifles.

Still, she could not purge her imagination, and the story of Evelina and her adventures did not die in the flames of her fireplace. Her brother, Charles, offered the first two volumes of *Evelina* to James Dodsley, who declined to consider an anonymous work for publication; Thomas Lowndes, however, asked to see the completed manuscript. After finishing *Evelina* and then securing her father's permission, Burney gave the work to the London publisher, who issued it in January, 1778, and paid the writer thirty pounds and ten bound copies. Its success and popularity owed some debt to Dr. Burney, who passed the novel on to Mrs. Thrale, a prominent figure in London's literary society. From there, it made its way to the select seat of London's intellectual empire, presided over by Dr. Johnson, Joshua Reynolds, and Edmund Burke. Shortly afterward, Fanny Burney met Mrs. Thrale, who took the new novelist into her home at Streatham (south of London) and introduced her to Johnson, Reynolds, Sheridan, and Arthur Murphy—all of whom pressed her to write drama. The result took the form of *The Whitlings*, a dramatic piece that, principally because of her father's displeasure over the quality of the work, she never published.

Returning to the form that produced her initial success, Burney published *Cecilia* in the summer of 1782, further advancing her literary reputation and social standing. She met Mary Delany, an intimate of the royal family, who helped secure for her an appointment in July, 1786, as second keeper of the Queen's robes, a position worth two hundred pounds per year. Her tenure at court proved to be more of a confinement than a social or political advantage because of the menial tasks, the rigid schedule, and the stiffness of the Queen and her attendants.

The activities and events at court, however, did contribute to the value of Burney's diaries, though her health suffered from the extreme physical demands of her labors. She continued in service until July, 1791, at which time she sought and gained permission to retire on a pension of one hundred pounds per annum. Then followed a period of domestic travel aimed at improving her health, followed by her marriage, on July 31, 1793, to General Alexandre D'Arblay, a comrade of the Marquis de Lafayette and a member of the small French community living at Juniper Hall, near Mickleham (north of Dorking, in Surrey). The couple's entire income rested with Madame D'Arblay's pension, and thus she sought to increase the family's fortunes through her writing. A tragedy, *Edwy and Elgiva*, lasted but a single night at Drury Lane, but a third novel, *Camilla*, generated more than three thousand pounds from subscriptions and additional sales, although the piece failed to achieve the literary merit of *Evelina* or *Cecilia*.

In 1801, General D'Arblay returned to France to seek employment but managed only a pension of fifteen hundred francs. His wife and son, Alexander, joined him the next year, and the family spent the succeeding ten years at Passy, in a state of quasi-exile that lasted throughout the Napoleonic wars. Madame D'Arblay and her son returned to England in 1812, and there, the novelist attended her aged father until his death in April, 1814. Her last novel, begun in France in 1802 and entitled *The Wanderer*, appeared early in 1814. Again, the financial returns far exceeded the literary quality of the piece; there were considerable buyers and subscribers but extremely few readers. After Napoleon's exile, the novelist returned to her husband in Paris; she then went to Brussels after the Emperor's return from Elba. General D'Arblay, meanwhile, had been seriously injured by the kick of a horse, which brought about an immediate end to his military career. The family returned to England to spend the remainder of their years: General D'Arblay died on May 3, 1818, and Alexander died on January 19, 1837—less than a year after having been nominated minister of Ely chapel. In November, 1839, Madame D'Arblay suffered a severe illness and died on January 6, 1840, in her eighty-seventh year.

Analysis

Despite the relative brevity of her canon, Fanny Burney's fiction cannot be dismissed with the usual generalizations from literary history: specifically that the author shared the interests of her youthful heroines in good manners. She possessed a quick sense for the comic in character and situation, and those talents distinctly advanced the art of the English novel in the direction of Jane Austen. From one viewpoint, she indeed exists as an important transitional figure between the satiric allegories of the earlier eighteenth century and the instruments that portrayed middle-class manners in full flourish during the first quarter of the nineteenth century.

Burney's contemporaries understood both her method and her purpose. Samuel Johnson thought her a "real wonder," one worth being singled out for her honest sense of modesty and her ability to apply it to fiction; while Edmund Burke seemed amazed by her knowledge of human nature. Three years after her death, Thomas Babington Macaulay proclaimed that the author of *Evelina* and *Cecilia* had done for the English novel what Jeremy Collier, at the end of the seventeenth century, did for the drama: maintain rigid morality and virgin delicacy. Macaulay proclaimed that Fanny Burney had indeed vindicated the right of woman "to an equal share in a fair and noble promise of letters" and had accomplished her task in clear, natural, and lively "woman's English."

Nevertheless, Fanny Burney contributed more to the English novel than simply the advancement of her sex's cause. Her heroines are mentally tormented and yet emerge as wiser and stronger human beings. The fictional contexts into which she placed her principal characters are those that readers of every time and place could recognize: situations in which the proponents of negative values seem to prosper and the defenders of virtue cling tenaciously to their ground. Burney's women must learn the ways of a difficult world, a society composed of countless snares and endless rules; they must quickly don the accoutrements for survival: modesty, reserve, submission, and (above all else) manners. What makes Burney's depiction of women in society particularly poignant is the knowledge that the author herself had to endure trials of survival. An awareness of the author's accounts of actual struggles for social survival, then, becomes a necessity for understanding and appreciating the problems confronted by her fictional characters.

In Burney's first novel, *Evelina*, the titled character brings with her to London and Bristol two qualities most difficult for a young provincial girl to defend: her sense of propriety and her pure innocence—the latter quality not to be confused with ignorance. In London, Evelina stumbles into false, insecure situations because she does not comprehend the rules of the social game. During the course of eighty-five epistles, however, she learns. The learning process is of utmost importance to Burney, for it serves as both plot for her fiction and instruction for her largely female readership. Once in London, life unfolds new meanings for Evelina Anville, as she samples the wares of urbanity: assemblies, amusements, parks and gardens, drawing rooms, operas, and theaters. Accompanying the activities is a corps of sophisitcates by whose rules Evelina must play: Lord Orville, the well-bred young man and the jealous lover; Sir Clement Willoughby, the obnoxious admirer of Evelina who tries (through forged letters) to breach the relationship between Orville and Evelina; Macartney, the young poet whom Evelina saves from suicide and against whom Orville exercises his jealous streak; Captain Mirvan, the practical joker who smiles only at the expense of others; Mrs. Beaumont, who would have the heroine believe that good qualities originate from pride rather than from principles; Lady Louisa Larpent, the sullen and distraught (but always arrogant) sister of Lord Orville who tries to separate her brother from Evelina; Mr. Lovel, a demeaning fop who constantly refers to Evelina's simple background; the Watkins sisters, who chide Evelina because they envy her attractiveness to young men.

Despite these obstacles of situation and character, however, Evelina does not lack some protection. The Reverend Arthur Villars, her devoted guardian since the death of her mother, guides and counsels the seventeen-year-old girl from his home in Dorsetshire. Villars receives the major portion of Evelina's letters; in fact, he initally advises her to be wary of Lord Orville, but then relents when he learns of his ward's extreme happiness. Since Evelina cannot count on immediate assistance from Villars, she does rely on several people in London. Mrs. Mirvan, the amiable and well-bred wife of the captain, introduces Evelina to a variety of social affairs, while their daughter, Maria, becomes the heroine's only real confidante, sharing mutual happiness and disappointment. Finally, there is the Reverend Villars' neighbor, Mrs. Selwyn, who accompanies Evelina on a visit to Bristol Hot Wells. Unfortunately, the one person closest to Evelina during her London tenure, her maternal grandmother, Madame Duval, proves of little use and even less assistance. A blunt, indelicate, and severe woman, she is bothered by her granddaughter's display of independence and vows that the young lady will not share in her inheritance.

Villars emerges as the supporting character with the most depth, principally because he is ever present in the letters. From the novel's beginning, the heroine reaches out to him for guidance and support, scarcely prepared "to form a wish that has not [his] sanction." The local clergyman, Villars serves as parent for a motherless and socially fatherless young lady who, for the first time, is about to see something of the world. Thus, Villars' caution and anxiety appear natural, for he knows the bitter effects of socially unequal marriages, as in the cases of Evelina's own parents and grandparents. He naturally mistrusts Lord Orville and fears the weakness of the young girl's imagination. Everyone knows that as long as Evelina remains obedient to Villars' will, no union between her and Orville can occur. Once the girl's father, Sir John Belmont, repents for his many years of unkindness to his daughter and then bequeaths her thirty thousand pounds, however, the guardian cleric no longer remains the dominant influence. Lord Orville proceeds to put his own moral house in order and supplants his rivals; the reserve felt by Evelina because of the Reverend Villars' fears and anxieties gradually disintegrates, and the romance proceeds towards its inevitable conclusion.

The process may be inevitable, but it is sufficiently hampered by a series of struggles and conflicts, as is typical of the late eighteenth century novel of manners. Both her grandmother and Mrs. Mirvan provide Evelina with fairly easy access to fashionable society, but the socialites in that society involve the girl in a number of uncomfortable and burdensome situations. For example, Biddy and Polly Branghton and Madam Duval use Evelina's name in requesting the use of Lord Orville's coach. Evelina realizes the impropriety of the request and knows that Orville's benevolence would never permit him to refuse it. Furthermore, Tom Branghton, an admirer of Evelina, solicits business from Orville also by relying on Evelina's name; he does so after damaging the borrowed vehicle. Evelina's innocence forces her to bear the responsibility for her relatives' actions and schemes, although she opposes all that they attempt. Fortunately, the fierce determination with which she advances her innocence and honesty enables her to endure such problems until rescued, in this case, by Lord Orville and Mrs. Selwyn. Vulgarity (Madam Duval), ill breeding (the Branghtons), and impertinence (Sir Clement Willoughby) eventually fall before the steadfastness and the force of Evelina's emerging wisdom and strength. Burney here demonstrates the specific means by which an eighteenth century woman could surmount the perplexities of that era.

If Evelina Anville must defend her innocence and honesty against the social vultures of London and Bristol, Cecilia Beverley, the heroine of *Cecilia*, carries the added burden of retaining a fortune left to her by an eccentric uncle. She must withstand assaults upon her coffers from a variety of attackers. One of her guardians, Mr. Harrel, draws heavily upon Cecilia's funds to repay the moneylenders who underwrite his fashionable existence. At the other extreme, Mr. Briggs, the third legally appointed guardian, manages Cecilia's money during her minority. Although wealthy in his own right, Briggs evidences obvious eccentricity and uncouthness; he is a miser who wants the heroine to live with him to conserve money. In the middle stands another guardian, Compton Delvile, who has priorities other than money; however, he can hardly be recommended as an asset to the development of his ward. Simply, Delvile cares only to preserve the family name, and beneath his pride lie hard layers of meanness. Against such onslaughts upon her morality and her fortune, Cecilia must rebel; she is both angry and bewildered at what Burney terms as "acts so detrimental to her own interest."

Unlike Evelina, who has many opportunities to address and receive concerns from a surrogate parent, Cecilia has few people and even less guidance upon which to rely. *Cecilia* revealed to the world not only a trio of impotent guardians, but also a number of irritating male characters who devote considerable time to tormenting her. Obviously bent upon revealing the grotesqueness and instability of London life, Burney created a variety of grotesque and unstable supporting players: Harrel, Dr. Lyster, Mrs. Wyers, and Mrs. Hill are some examples. Clearly, Burney's characters in *Cecilia* were total strangers to the mainstream of the late-eighteenth century fictional world, even though they truly belonged to reality. While at times creating humorous scenes and incidents, these ugly characters nevertheless produced a disturbing effect upon the novelist's reading audience. Unfortunately, from a social or historical perspective, that audience was not yet ready for significant action to affect social change, which meant that much of the novel's force was lost amid the apathy of its audience.

The publication of *Camilla*, eighteen years after *Evelina* and fourteen following *Cecilia*, marked the reappearance of a young lady entering society and enduring shameful experiences. Like her immediate predecessor, Cecilia Beverley, Camilla Tyrold has money problems, only hers involve involuntary indebtedness. Also like Cecilia, the novel contains several grotesque minor characters, whose manners and actions play psychological havoc with Camilla's attempts to overcome her distress. Particularly vulgar are Mr. Dubster and the mercenary Mrs. Mittin, aided by the over-scholarly Dr. Orkborne and the foppish Sir Sedley Clarendel. A major problem, however, is that these characters are pulled from the earlier novels. On the surface, *Camilla* gives evidence that Burney has matured as a writer and as a commentator on the affairs of women, but that maturity did not broaden her literary experience. If anything, there are signs of regression, for Camilla definitely lacks Evelina's common sense and her instinct toward feminine resourcefulness.

Camilla further suffers from its length; Burney barely holds the plot together through countless episodes, intrigues, misunderstandings, all in front of a backdrop of drollery and absurdity. Stripped of its comic elements, the novel is no more than an overstrained romance. Burney's motive, however, was to draw the exact conditions that brought about Camilla's collection of debts and thus contributed to her highly anxious state of mind. Burney rises to her usual level of excellence in detailing the plight of a woman distracted and deprived by misfortune not of her own doing. For late-eighteenth century woman, especially, such misfortune carried with it an underlying sense of shame. Thus, Burney gave to English prose fiction a sense of psychological depth not always apparent in the works of her female counterparts or in those fictional efforts written by men but concerned with women.

Burney's last novel, *The Wanderer*, appeared in 1814 and became lost in the new sensibility of Jane Austen and Maria Edgeworth. The work, however, reveals Burney's determination that the nineteenth century should not forget its women. Her heroine—known variously as L. S. (or Ellis), Incognita, Miss

Ellis, and Juliet—determines that the cause of her suffering points directly
to the fact that she was born a woman, which automatically places her on
the lowest rung of the social order. The woman's lot contains little beyond
the usual taboos, disqualifications, discomforts, and inconveniences; and the
novelist, through the various predicaments of Juliet Granville, rarely allows
her readers to forget the degree to which her heroine must suffer because of
society's insensitivity and stupidity. *The Wanderer*, as in Burney's previous
novels, has a number of supporting characters; some of those, while they do
not always understand Juliet's plight, at least try to help her through her
difficulties. Others, such as Mrs. Ireton and Miss Arbe, represent the tyranny,
frivolity, and insensitivity of the times and thus merely compound Juliet's
problems.

The strength of *The Wanderer*, however, lies in its thematic relationship to
the three earlier novels. Although Burney tends to repeat herself, particularly
through her minor characters—and again the plot hardly deserves the length
of the narrative—her ability to depict the misgivings of those who are driven
by external circumstances to earn a livelihood through unaccustomed means
is powerful. In coming to grips with an obvious and serious problem of her
time she demonstrated how her major ficitonal characters and herself, as a
character from the real world, could indeed rely successfully upon the
resources endowed upon all individuals, female as well as male. If nothing
else, the novelist showed her society and the generations that followed not
only how well women could function in the real world, but also how much
they could contribute and take advantage of opportunities offered them. In
a sense, Burney's compositions belong to social history as much as to literature, and they serve as some of the earliest examples of a struggle that has
yet to be won.

Major publications other than long fiction
PLAYS: *Edwy and Elgiva*, 1790; *Love and Fashion*, 1800.
NONFICTION: *Brief Reflections Relative to the French Emigrant Clergy*, 1793;
Memoirs of Dr. Charles Burney, 1832 (edited); *Early Diary, 1768-1778*, 1889;
Diary and Letters, 1778-1840, 1842-1846 (7 volumes).

Bibliography
Adelstein, Michael E. *Fanny Burney*, 1968.
Bloom, Lillian D., and Edward Bloom. "Fanny Burney's Novels: The Retreat
from Wonder," in *Novel*, XII (1979), pp. 215-235.
Copeland, Edward W. "Money in the Novels of Fanny Burney," in *Studies
in the Novel*, VIII (1976), pp. 24-37.
Cutting, Rose Marie. "Defiant Women: The Growth of Feminism in Fanny
Burney's Novels," in *Studies in English Literature* XVII (1977), pp. 519-
530.

Hemlow, Joyce. *The History of Fanny Burney*, 1958.
Spacks, Patricia M. "'Ev'ry Woman Is at Heart a Rake,'" in *Eighteenth-Century Studies*. VIII (1974), pp. 27-46.
Tinker, Chauncey Brewster. *Dr. Johnson and Fanny Burney*, 1911.
Voss-Clesly, Patricia. *Tendencies of Character Depiction in the Domestic Novels of Burney, Edgeworth, and Austen: A Consideration of Subjective and Objective Worlds*, 1977.

Samuel J. Rogal

WILLIAM BURROUGHS

Born: St. Louis, Missouri; February 5, 1914

Principal long fiction

Junkie, 1953; *The Naked Lunch*, 1959 (republished as *Naked Lunch*, 1962); *The Soft Machine*, 1961; *The Ticket That Exploded*, 1962; *Dead Fingers Talk*, 1963; *Nova Express*, 1964; *The Wild Boys: A Book of the Dead*, 1971; *Cities of the Red Night*, 1981.

Other literary forms

Because of their experimental techniques, William Burroughs' works are especially difficult to classify within established literary forms. *Exterminator!* (1973), for example, although published as a "novel," is actually a collection of previously published poems, short stories, and essays. Other unclassifiable works are book-length experiments, often written in collaboration and in the "cut-up, fold-in" technique pioneered by Burroughs, which might be considered novels by some. Examples of such works are *Minutes to Go* (1960), written in collaboration with Sinclair Beiles, Gregory Corso, and Brion Gysin; *The Exterminator* (1960), written with Gysin; *Time* (1965), which contains drawings by Gysin; and *Oeuvre Croisee* (1976), written in collaboration with Gysin and reissued as *The Third Mind* in 1978. *White Subway* (1965), *Apomorphine* (1969), and *The Job: Interviews with William S. Burroughs* (1970), written in collaboration with Daniel Odier, are additional short-story and essay collections. *The Dead Star* (1969) is a journalistic essay that contains photocollage inserts; *APO-33 Bulletin: A Metabolic Regulator* (1966) is a pamphlet; and *Electronic Revolution 1970-71* (1971) is an essay that fantasizes bizarre political and business uses for the cut-up, fold-in technique. Burroughs has also published scores of essays, stories, and articles in numerous journals, periodicals, and short-lived magazines. One of Burroughs' most revealing publications, *The Yage Letters* (1963), collects his correspondence with Allen Ginsberg concerning Burroughs' 1952 expedition to South America in search of yage, a legendary hallucinogen. In these letters, Burroughs is Govinda, the master, to Ginsberg's Siddhartha, the disciple.

Achievements

Although his novel, *Naked Lunch*, was made notorious by American censorship attempts and consequently became a best-seller, Burroughs writes primarily for a cult audience. He is essentially a fantasist and satirist, is often misread, and in these respects has accurately been compared to Jonathan Swift. Both writers focus on the faults and evils of man and society, employ fantastic satire to ridicule these shortcomings, and hope through this vehicle to effect some positive change in the human condition. Burroughs' works are exceptionally vicious satires, however, "necessarily brutal, obscene and disgusting"—his own description of them—because they must mime the situations from which their recurring images and metaphors (of drug addiction, aberrant sexual practices, and senseless violence) are drawn.

Superficially, Burroughs' satiric attacks are aimed at mankind's "addictions" to pleasure or power in any of the many forms either craving might take. Men who, obeying the dictates of "the algebra of need," will stop at nothing to fulfill their desires have, in the terms of the moral allegory Burroughs creates, "lost their human citizenship" and become nonhuman parasites feeding on the life essences of others. They shamelessly lie, cheat, and manipulate to attain what Burroughs' associative imagery repeatedly equates with perversion, excrement, and death. Burroughs' satire, however, cuts deeper than this. It attacks not only man and his addictions, but also the structures of the cultures that enable these addictions to flourish and proliferate. It attacks the myths and linguistic formulas that imprison man, the stone walls of patriotism and religion. It demands that men first free themselves from these "word and image addictions" before they kick their more obvious habits and regain their humanity, and thus calls for nothing less than a revolution of consciousness.

The Grove Press edition of *Naked Lunch* became a national best-seller and was cleared of obscenity charges in Los Angeles in 1965 and in Massachusetts in 1966. Ginsberg and Norman Mailer, who asserted that Burroughs is "the only American novelist living today who may conceivably be possessed by genius," were among those who testified in the book's defense. While it does detail with exceptional brutality the ugly, revolting, and perverse, *Naked Lunch* is at bottom a strikingly moral but darkly comic work that employs irony and allegory, as well as more unconventional techniques, to satirize much that is false and defective in modern American life in particular and human nature in general. Especially effective as a subliminal argument against heroin abuse, the book's successful publication in America elevated its heretofore practically unknown author to membership in the literary elite.

Many reviewers, however, some seemingly oblivious to the irony of Burroughs' works, have not been responsive or sympathetic to his themes and techniques, and none of his novels since *Naked Lunch*, with the exception of *The Wild Boys: A Book of the Dead*, has received comparable critical acclaim. While *Naked Lunch* was lauded by Terry Southern, Mary McCarthy, Karl Shapiro, and Marshall McLuhan, as well as by Ginsberg and Mailer, the less successfully realized subsequent novels were considered by some critics, not totally inaccurately, as "language without content" and "the world's greatest put-on." Burroughs himself admits that "*Naked Lunch* demands silence from the reader. Otherwise he is taking his own pulse." He warns that his novels do not present their "content" in the manner the reader ordinarily anticipates. One of the triumphs of Burroughs' unique style is that he has created a low-content form, a narrative near vacuum, upon which the unwary reader is tempted to project his own psyche, personal myths, or forgotten dreams. While they do have their own message to convey, his works also encourage the reader to develop or invent his private fictions and to append them to the skeletal narrative structure provided by the author. The reader is thus invited to create the work as he reads it. In place of relying on the easily perceived, clearly coherent story the reader might have expected, Burroughs's best work keeps one reading through the hypnotic fascination of the author's flow of images and incantatory prose.

Biography

William Seward Burroughs was born on February 5, 1914, in St. Louis, Missouri, to Perry Mortimer Burroughs, son of the industrialist who invented the cylinder that made the modern adding machine possible, and Laura Lee, a direct descendant of Robert E. Lee, Civil War general and commander in chief of the Confederate army. Dominated by his mother's obsessive Victorian prudery and haunted by vivid nightmares and hallucinations, Burroughs led a restless childhood. He was educated in private schools in St. Louis and Los Alamos, New Mexico, where he developed seemingly disparate fascinations with literature and crime, and later studied ethnology and archaeology at Harvard University, where he encountered a set of wealthy homosexuals. He was graduated with an A.B. in 1936.

Subsequently, Burroughs traveled to Europe, briefly studied medicine at the University of Vienna, and returned to the United States and Harvard to resume his anthropological studies, which he soon abandoned because of his conviction that academic life is little more than a series of intrigues broken by teas. Although he attempted to use family connections to obtain a position with the Office of Strategic Services, Burroughs was rejected after he deliberately cut off the first joint of one finger in a Vincent Van Gogh-like attempt to impress a friend. Moving to New York City, he worked as a bartender and in an advertising agency for a year and underwent psychoanalysis. Burroughs entered the army in 1942 as a glider pilot trainee, engineered his discharge for psychological reasons six months later, and then moved to Chicago, where he easily found work as an exterminator and a private detective, among other odd jobs.

In 1943, Burroughs returned to New York City and met Joan Vollmer, a student at Columbia University whom he married on Jaunary 17, 1945. She introduced Burroughs to Jack Kerouac, who in turn introduced him to Ginsberg. The Beat generation was born in Burroughs' 115th Street apartment after Burroughs acquainted Kerouac and Ginsberg with the writings of William Blake, Arthur Rimbaud, and others; the three friends soon emerged as leaders of the movement. Late in 1944, Herbert Huncke, a Times Square hustler involved in criminal activity to support his drug habit, introduced

Burroughs to the use of morphine and its derivatives. Burroughs was for most of the next thirteen years a heroin addict who frequently altered his place of residence to evade the police.

He moved to Waverly, Texas, where he tried farming, in 1946; had a son, William, Jr., in 1947; and voluntarily entered a drug rehabilitation center at Lexington, Kentucky, in 1948. Returning to Waverly and already back on drugs, Burroughs was hounded by the police until he moved to Algiers, Louisiana, later that same year. To avoid prosecution for illegal possession of drugs and firearms after a 1949 raid on his Algiers farm, Burroughs relocated to Mexico City in 1950, where he began writing *Junkie*. He continued his archaeological studies at Mexico City University, pursuing an interest in the Mayan codices. On September 7, 1951, Burroughs accidentally killed his wife while allegedly attempting to shoot a champagne glass off her head while playing "William Tell." Although Mexican authorities let the matter drop, Burroughs soon left Mexico for the jungles of Colombia and his search for yage.

He returned again to New York City in 1953, the year *Junkie* was published, lived for a while with Ginsberg, and then settled in Tangier, Morocco, where from 1955 to 1958 he was frequently visited by other Beat writers and worked on the manuscript that would develop into his quartet of science-fiction-like novels: *Naked Lunch*, *The Soft Machine*, *Nova Express*, and *The Ticket That Exploded*. In 1957, Burroughs again sought treatment for his heroin addiction. This time he placed himself in the care of John Yerby Dent, an English physician who treated drug addicts with apomorphine—a crystalline alkaloid derivative of morphine—a drug Burroughs praises and mythologizes in his writings. The following year, cured of his addiction, Burroughs moved to Paris, where *The Naked Lunch* was published in 1959.

In 1960, Gysin, who had helped Burroughs select the Paris edition of *The Naked Lunch* from a suitcase full of manuscript pages, introduced his experimental "cut-up" technique to Burroughs and collaborated with him on *The Exterminator* and *Minutes to Go*. Burroughs' literary reputation was firmly established with the American publication of *Naked Lunch* in 1962, and by the mid-1960's Burroughs had settled in London. He returned to St. Louis for a visit in 1965, covered the Democratic National Convention for *Esquire* in 1968, and moved again to New York to teach writing at City College of New York in 1974. In 1975, he embarked on a reading tour of the United States and conducted a writers' workshop in Denver, Colorado. He has since returned to London, where he is still an active writer.

Analysis

William Burroughs did not begin writing seriously until 1950, although he had unsuccessfully submitted a story entitled "Twilight's Last Gleaming" to *Esquire* in 1938. His first novelistic effort, *Queer*, which deals with homosexuality, also remains unpublished. Allen Ginsberg finally persuaded Ace Books to publish Burroughs' first novel, *Junkie*, which originally appeared with pseudonym William Lee, as half of an Ace double paperback. It was bound with Maurice Helbront's *Narcotic Agent*. While strictly conventional in style, *Junkie* is a luridly hyperbolic, quasi-autobiographical first-person account of the horrors of drug addiction. Of little literary merit in itself, this first novel is interesting in that it introduces not only the main character, Lee, but also several of the major motifs that appear in Burroughs' subsequent works: the central metaphor of drug addiction, the related image of man reduced to a subhuman (usually an insectlike creature) by his drug and other lusts, and the suggestion of concomitant and pervasive sexual aberration.

In *Naked Lunch* and its three less celebrated sequels, *The Soft Machine*, *Nova Express*, and *The Ticket That Exploded*, Burroughs weaves an intricate and horrible allegory of human greed, corruption, and debasement. Like Aldous Huxley's *Brave New World* (1932) and George Orwell's *Nineteen Eighty-Four* (1949), these four works seize on the evils or tendencies toward a certain type of evil—that the author sees as particularly malignant in the contemporary world—and project them into a dystopian future, where, magnified, they grow monstrous and take on an exaggerated and fantastic shape. While progressively clarifying and developing Burrough's thought, these novels share themes, metaphorical images, characters, and stylistic mannerisms. In them, Burroughs utilizes the "cut-up, fold-in" technique which has its closest analog in the cinematic technique of montage. He juxtaposes one scene with another without regard to plot, character, or, in the short view, theme to promote an association of the reader's negative emotional reaction to the content of certain scenes (sexual perversion, drug abuse, senseless violence) with the implied allegorical content of others (examples of "addictions" to drugs, money, sex, power). The theory is that if such juxtapositions recur often enough, the feeling of revulsion strategically created by the first set of images will form the reader's negative attitude toward the second set of examples.

In these novels, Burroughs develops a science-fiction-like, paranoid fantasy wherein, on a literal level, the Earth and its human inhabitants have been taken over by the Nova Mob, an assortment of extraterrestrial, non-three-dimensional entities who live parasitically on the reality of other organisms. Exploitation of the Earth has reached such proportions that the intergalactic Nova Police have been alerted. The Nova Police are attempting to thwart the Nova Mob without so alarming them that they will detonate the planet in an attempt to destroy the evidence (and thus escape prosecution in the biologic courts) while trying to make what escape they can. The most direct form of Nova control, control that enables the Nova Mob to carry on its viruslike metaphysical vampirism with impunity, is thought control of the human population through control of the mass communication media. Nova Mob concepts and perspectives attach themselves to and are replicated by the terrestrial host media much as a virus invades and reproduces through a host organism, a thought-control process analogous to the "cut-up, fold-in" technique itself. By the middle of *Nova Express*, the reader is caught up in a war of images in which the weapons are cameras and tape recorders. The Nova Police and the inhabitants of Earth have discovered how to combat the Nova Mob with their own techniques (of which these novels are examples) and are engaged in a guerrilla war with the Nova Criminals, who are desperately trying to cut and run. The ending of *The Ticket That Exploded* is optimistic for Earth but inconclusive, leaving the reader to wonder if the Earth will be rid of the Nova Mob or destroyed by it.

A vividly and relentlessly tasteless fantasy-satire that portrays man's innate greed and lack of compassion in general and contemporary American institutions and values in particular, *Naked Lunch* immerses the reader in the impressions and sensations of William Lee (Burroughs' pseudonym in *Junkie*). Lee is an agent of the Nova Police who has assumed the cover of a homosexual heroin addict because with such a cover he is most likely to encounter Nova Criminals, who are all addicts of one sort or another and thus prefer to operate through human addict collaborators. Nothing of importance seems to occur in the novel, and little of what does happen is explained. Only toward the conclusion does the reader even suspect that Lee is some sort of agent "clawing at a not-yet of Telepathic Bureaucracies, Time Monopolies, Control Drugs, Heavy Fluid Addicts." The "naked lunch" of the title is that reality seen by Lee, that "frozen moment when everyone sees what is on the end of every fork." The random scenes of mutilation and depravity, bleak homosexual encounters, and desperate scrambles for drug connections into which the book plunges yield its two key concepts: the idea of addiction, the central conceit that men become hooked on power, pleasure, illusions, and so on much as a junkie does on heroin, and that of "the algebra of need," which states simply that when an addict is faced with absolute need (as a junkie is) he will do anything to satisfy it.

The Nova Criminals are nonhuman personifications of various addictions. The Uranians, addicted to Heavy Metal Fluid, are types of drug addicts. Dr. Benway, Mr. Bradley Mr. Martin (a single character), and the insect people of Minraud—all control addicts—are types of the human addiction to power. The green boy-girls of Venus, addicted to Venusian sexual practices, are types of the human addiction to sensual pleasure. The Death Dwarf, addicted to concentrated words and images, is the analog of the human addiction to various cultural myths and beliefs; he is perhaps the most pathetic of these depraved creatures. Burroughs explains that "Junk yields a basic formula of 'evil' virus: the face of evil is always the face of total need. A dope fiend is a man in total need of dope. Beyond a certain frequency need knows absolutely no limit or control." As John Ciardi noted,

Only after the first shock does one realize that what Burroughs is writing ᵢ
only the destruction of depraved men by their drug lust, but the destructionᵗ
by their consuming addictions, whether the addiction be drugs or over-righteou
or sixteen-year-old-girls.

Burroughs sees *The Soft Machine* as "a sequel to *Naked Luncł*
ematical extension of the Algebra of Need beyond the Junk viru¯
the consuming addiction, displayed again in juxtaposition with sceneᵉ
abuse and sexual perversion, and through a number of shifting nar
the addiction to power over others. The central episode is the destru
a time-traveling agent of the control apparatus of the ancient Mayan th
(Burroughs' primary archaeological interest), which exercises its
through the manipulation of myths; this is a clear analog of the prese
struggle between the Nova Police and the Nova Mob that breaks in
open in the subsequent two novels.

The time traveler uses the same technique to prepare himself for time
as Burroughs does in writing his novels, a type of "cut-up, fold-in" mon
"I started my trip in the morgue with old newspapers, folding in today
yesterday and typing out composites." Since words tie men to time, the
traveler character is given apomorphine (used to cure Burroughs of his heɪ
addiction) to break this connection.

The "soft machine" is both the "wounded galaxy," the Milky Way seen
a biological organism diseased by the viruslike Nova Mob, and the humₐ
body, riddled with parasites and addictions and programmed with the "ticket,
obsolete myths and dreams, written on the "soft typewriter" of culture anɪ
civilization. Burroughs contends that any addiction dehumanizes its victims.
The Mayan priests, for example, tend to become half-men, half-crab creatures
who eventually metamorphosize into giant centipedes and exude an erogenous
green slime. Such hideous transformations also strike Lee, a heroin addict,
and other homosexuals. Bradley the Buyer, who reappears as Mr. Bradley
Mr. Martin, Mr. and Mrs. D., and the Ugly Spirit, has a farcical habit of
turning into a bloblike creature who is addicted to and absorbs drug addicts.

Instances of metamorphosis are almost innumerable in *Nova Express* and
The Ticket That Exploded. These novels most clearly reveal the quartet's plot
and explore the Nova Mob's exploitation of media. Here addiction to language
is investigated. As Stephen Koch argues, here

> Burroughs's ideology . . . is based on an image of consciousness in bondage to the organ-
> ism: better, of consciousness as an organism, gripped by the tropisms of need. Conscious-
> ness is addicted—it is here the drug metaphor enters—to what sustains it and gives it
> definition: in particular, it is addicted to the word, the structures of language that define
> meaning and thus reality itself.

Thus, while in *The Soft Machine* the time traveler is sent to Trak News Agency

motto is "We don't report the news—we write it") to learn how to
he Mayan theocracy by first learning "how this writing the news before
ens is done," in *The Ticket That Exploded* it is axiomatic that "you
n a government without police if your conditioning program is tight
h but you can't run a government without bullshit."
ntemporary existence is seen ultimately as a film that is rerun again and
, trapping the human soul like an insect imprisoned in amber, negating
possibility of choice or freedom. In these last two novels, Burroughs
es a call for revolt against man's imprisoning addiction to language. In
a Express*, he notes that "their garden of delights is a terminal sewer"
demands that everyone heed the last words of Hassan I Sabbah (cribbed
of context from Fyodor Dostoevski's Ivan Karamazov): "Nothing is
ue—Everything is Permitted." In *The Ticket That Exploded*, he rages,
3etter than the "real thing?'—There is no real thing—Maya—Maya—It's
ll show business."

Burroughs' other notably science-fiction-like novel, *The Wild Boys*, is also
composed of scenes linked more by associated images than by any clearly
linear narrative framework. Here, the author posits a bizarre alternative to
the problematical apocalypse-in-progress depicted in his earlier quartet. In
a world wrecked by famine and controlled by police, the wild boys, a homosexual tribe of hashish smokers, have withdrawn themselves from space and
time through indifference and have developed into a counterculture complete
with its own language, rituals, and economy. The existence of this counterculture, of course, poses a threat to those who create the false images upon
which the larger, repressive, external society is based; but the wild boys cannot
be tamed because their cold indifference to the mass culture entails a savagery
that refuses to submit to control. Although Burroughs' thinking clearly
becomes more political in *The Wild Boys* and in the book that followed it,
Exterminator!, a collection of short stories and poems that revolve around
the common theme of death through sinister forces, his primary concern for
freedom from the controllers and manipulators—chemical, political, sexual,
or cultural—has remained constant from the beginning of his literary career.

Major publications other than long fiction

NONFICTION: *The Yage Letters*, 1963 (with Allen Ginsberg); *APO-33 Bulletin: A Metabolic Regulator*, 1966; *The Job: Interviews with William S. Burroughs*, 1970 (with Daniel Odier); *Electronic Revolution 1970-71*, 1971.

MISCELLANEOUS: *The Exterminator*, 1960 (with Brion Gysin); *Minutes to Go*, 1960 (with Sinclair Beiles, Gregory Corso, and Brion Gysin); *Time*, 1965; *White Subway*, 1965; *The Dead Star*, 1969; *Apomorphine*, 1969; *The Last Words of Dutch Schultz*, 1970; *Exterminator!*, 1973; *The Book of Breeething*, 1974; *Oeuvre Croisee*, 1976 (with Brion Gysin, also known as *The Third Man*, 1978); *Blade Runner: A Movie*, 1979.

Bibliography

Beml, Maxy. "William Burroughs and the Invisible Generation," in *Telos*. XIII (Fall, 1972), pp. 125-131.

Bryant, Jerry H. *The Open Decision: The Contemporary American Novel and Its Intellectual Background*, 1970.

Cook, Bruce. *The Beat Generation*, 1971.

Cordesse, Gerard. "The Science Fiction of William Burroughs," in *Caliban*. XII (1975), pp. 33-34.

Fiedler, Leslie A. "The New Mutants," in *Partisan Review*. XXXII (Fall, 1965), pp. 505-525.

Hassan, Ihab. "The Subtracting Machine: The Work of William Burroughs," in *Critique*. VI (Spring, 1963), pp. 4-23.

Knickerbocker, Conrad. "William Burroughs," in *Paris Review*. XXXV (Fall, 1965), pp. 13-49.

Lee, A. Robert. "William Burroughs and the Sexuality of Power," in *Twentieth Century Studies*. II (November, 1969), pp. 74-88.

Manganotti, Donatella. "William Burroughs," in *Studi Americani*. VIII (1962), pp. 245-291.

Michelson, Peter. "Beardsley, Burroughs, Decadence and the Poetics of Obscenity," in *Tri-Quarterly*. XII (1968), pp. 139-155.

Mottram, Eric. *William Burroughs: The Algebra of Need*, 1971.

Oxenhandler, Neal. "Listening to Burroughs' Voice," in *Surfiction: Fiction Now . . . and Tomorrow*, 1981.

Palumbo, Donald. "William Burroughs' Quartet of Science Fiction Novels as Dystopian Social Satire," in *Extrapolation*. XX (Winter, 1979), pp. 321-329.

Stull, William L. "The Quest and the Question: Cosmology and Myth in the Work of William S. Burroughs, 1953-1960," in *Twentieth Century Literature*. XXIV (1978), pp. 225-242.

Tanner, Tony. *City of Words: American Fiction, 1950-1970*, 1971.

_____ . "The New Demonology," in *Partisan Review*. XXX (Fall, 1966), pp. 547-572.

Vernon, John. *The Garden and the Map: Schizophrenia in Twentieth Century Literature and Culture*, 1973.

Donald Palumbo

SAMUEL BUTLER

Born: Langar Rectory, England; December 4, 1835
Died: London, England; June 18, 1902

Principal long fiction
Erewhon, 1872; *The Fair Haven*, 1873; *Erewhon Revisited*, 1901; *The Way of All Flesh*, 1903.

Other literary forms
The Shrewsbury editions of Samuel Butler's works, published between 1923 and 1926, reveals the breadth of his interests. Butler's fiction was perhaps less important to him than his work in other fields, notably his theorizing on religion and evolution. He was also an art critic (*Ex Voto*, 1888; *Alps and Sanctuaries of Piedmont and the Ticino*, 1881); a literary critic (*The Authoress of the "Odyssey,"* 1897; *Shakespeare's Sonnets Reconsidered*, 1899); the biographer of his famous grandfather, Dr. Samuel Butler; a letter-writer; and a poet. An age which produces "specialists" may find Butler to be a talented dabbler or dilettante, but his unifying philosophy gives a center to all his work.

Achievements
Butler was a figure of controversy during his lifetime, and perhaps his greatest achievement resides in his ability to challenge: he contended with Charles Darwin and Darwinism; he took on the established scholars of William Shakespeare, classical literature, and art; and he was part of the nineteenth century revolt against traditional religion. He approached all of these areas in such a way that his opponents could not ignore him; whether he was right or wrong, any subject benefitted by his treatment, which opened it up to new and candid thought.

Of his four works which may be labeled as fiction, by far the greatest is *The Way of All Flesh*. Virginia Woolf, in *Contemporary Writers* (1965), described this novel as a seed from which many others developed—a biological image which would have pleased Butler. In earlier novels, indifferent or cruel families had been portrayed as agents of the hero's youthful unhappiness— witness Charles Dickens' *David Copperfield* (1849-1850)—but only in *The Way of All Flesh* did the oppressiveness and cruelty of family life become a theme in itself, worthy of generation-by-generation treatment.

Biography
Samuel Butler was born in 1835, the son of a clergyman who wished him to go into the Church. After a successful career at Cambridge, Butler prepared for a career in the Church but found himself unable to face the prospect of

that life. Letters between Butler and his father show the young man to be considering a half-dozen plans at once: art, the army, cotton-growing, and bookselling among them. Finally, father and son agreed that the young man should emigrate to New Zealand and try his fortune there, with Butler's father providing capital. Both father and son hoped that the experience would "settle" Butler and build his character.

Butler arrived in New Zealand in January of 1860, remaining there for four years. It was a useful time: he made money which freed him of his family, at least financially, and he saw an unusual country which gave him a subject and setting for his later writings. New Zealand, however, was too rough a land to be his permanent home. His "hut" there was an island of comfort and civilization, where Butler devoted himself to music and study. His optimistic letters home became the basis of *A First Year in Canterbury Settlement* (1863), a book assembled and published by Butler's father.

Returning to England in 1864, Butler settled at Clifford's Inn in London, which would be his home for the rest of his life. He began to study art; his paintings had some success. He wished to do something greater, however, something which would express his developing ideas. Out of this desire grew *Erewhon*, a satire which was published anonymously in 1872 at the author's own expense. By that time, Butler was already at work on *The Fair Haven*. This book may or may not be considered fiction; it is a dispute over the validity of Christianity, but the dispute is conducted in a fictional frame.

The following year, 1873, was an important one for Butler. *The Fair Haven* was published, his mother died, he made a risky financial investment, and he began *The Way of All Flesh*. All of these events shaped his later years. *The Fair Haven*, following on the heels of *Erewhon*, marked him as a belligerent enemy of traditional religion. His mother's death caused him some grief, but it spurred him to begin *The Way of All Flesh*, the work for which he is most remembered. That work was slowed, though, by financial troubles. Butler invested his New Zealand fortune in a Canadian venture which soon failed. He salvaged less than a quarter of his investment and had to seek help from his father. Not until 1886, when his father died, was Butler wholly free of financial pressures.

The next several years were occupied by work on evolution and religion. In 1882, Butler returned to *The Way of All Flesh*, completing it the following year. He felt, however, that the book should not be published while anyone who could be hurt by it was still alive; therefore it did not appear until a year after his own death.

In 1883, Butler began to write music. Music and music criticism were to occupy him intermittently for several years, interspersed with art criticism. The last decade of his life was filled with the study of literature, culminating in his publications on Shakespeare's sonnets and his translations of the *Iliad* (1898) and the *Odyssey* (1900). These works were characterized by the combativeness that to some degree sums up Butler's life. He was always the rebellious, contradictory son.

Butler's life was shaped by a number of intense relationships. His relationship with his family was unresolved; the work (*The Way of All Flesh*) which might have laid the ghosts to rest was haunted by another ghost, Butler's lifelong friend Eliza Mary Ann Savage. A fellow art student, she gave the writer friendship, friendly criticism, advice, and approval. Her own understanding of the relationship can never be known, but Butler feared she wished to marry him. His implicit rejection disturbed him deeply after her death. Other friendships were equally ambiguous. Charles Paine Pauli consumed much of Butler's attentions and resources from their first meeting in New Zealand until Pauli's death in 1897, when Butler discovered that Pauli had been supported by two other men. The perhaps sexual ambiguities of this relationship were repeated in Butler's affection for a young Swiss, Hans Faesch, and to a lesser degree in his long-lasting bonds with Henry Festing Jones and Alfred Emery Cathie. Butler's emotional make-up seems similar to that of Henry James. Both men formed passionate attachments to other men; both appreciated women more as memories than as living beings.

Analysis

On his deathbed, Samuel Butler spoke of the "pretty roundness" of his career, his beginning with *Erewhon* and ending, thirty years later, with *Erewhon Revisited*.

Erewhon must be understood first of all as a satire rather than as a novel. It is in the tradition of Jonathan Swift's *Gulliver's Travels* (1726-1727) and Samuel Johnson's *The History of Rasselas, Prince of Abyssinia* (1759), works which sacrifice unity and development to a vision of the writer's society, in the guise of an imaginary foreign land. Like Rasselas and Gulliver, Higgs of *Erewhon* is a young man, ready for adventure, out to learn about the world. He quickly reveals his image of himself as sharp, cunning, and bold. Before he tells his story, he lets the reader know the things he will hold back so that no reader will be able to find Erewhon and thus profit financially from Higgs's exploration.

His story begins as he is working on a sheep farm in a colony, the name of which he will not reveal. Intending to find precious metals or at least good sheep-grazing land, he journeys alone inland, over a mountain range. On the other side, he finds a kingdom called Erewhon (Nowhere), which looks very much like England. Higgs's point of reference is England; all aspects of Erewhonian life he measures by that standard.

Many such satires work through the narrator's quick judgment that his new land is either much better or much worse than his native country: the narrator's rather simple view plays against the author's more complex perspective. In *Erewhon*, however, the narrator is not quite so naïve. His own failings, rather than his naïveté, become part of the satire, which thus has a dual focus, much like Book IV of *Gulliver's Travels*. Higgs, like many good Victorian heroes, is out to make money. It is this prospect which motivates him most strongly. Coexisting with his desire for fortune is his religiosity. Here, Butler's satire upon his character is most pronounced and simplistic. Higgs observes the Sabbath, but he seduces Yram (Mary) with no regret. He plans to make his fortune by selling the Erewhonians into slavery, arguing that they would be converted to Christianity in the process; the slaveholders would be lining their pockets and doing good simultaneously. Thus, Butler exposes, to no one's great surprise, the mingled piety and avarice of British colonialists.

Butler satirizes European culture through the Erewhonians more often than through his hero, Higgs, gradually unfolding their lives for the reader to observe. Their lives are, on the surface, peaceful and pleasant; they are a strikingly attractive race. Only through personal experience does Higgs learn the underpinnings of the society: when he is ill, he learns that illness is a crime in Erewhon, while moral lapses are regarded in the same way as illnesses are in England. When his pocket watch is discovered, he learns that all "machines" have been banned from Erewhon. Erewhonian morality is based on reversals: the morally corrupt receive sympathy, while the ill are imprisoned; a child duped by his guardian is punished for having been ignorant, while the guardian is rewarded; children are responsible for their own birth, while their parents are consoled for having been "wronged" by the unborn. This pattern of reversals is of necessity incomplete, a problem noted by reviewers of *Erewhon* in 1872.

"The Book of the Machines" is the section of the satire which has drawn the most attention, because of its relationship to Darwinian thought. It may well be, as it has often been considered, a *reductio ad absurdum* of Darwinism, but the chapter also takes on reasoning by analogy as a less complex target of satire. "The Book of the Machines" is Higgs's translation of the Erewhonian book which led to the banning of all mechanical devices. Its author claimed that machines had developed—evolved—more rapidly than humankind and thus would soon dominate, leaving humans mere slaves or parasites. He argued that machines were capable of reproduction, using humans in the process as flowers use bees. The arguments proved so convincing that all machines in Erewhon were soon destroyed, leaving the country in the rather primitive state in which Higgs found it.

The purpose of "The Book of the Machines" becomes clearer in the following two chapters, which detail Erewhonian debates on the rights of animals and the rights of vegetables. At one point in the past, insistence on the rights of animals had turned Erewhon into a land of vegetarians, but the philosophers went a step further and decreed that vegetables, too, had rights, based upon their evolving consciousness. Again, Butler plays with argument by analogy, as the philosophers compare the vegetables' intelligence to that of a human embryo.

The Erewhonians who believed in the rights of vegetables were led nearly to starvation by their extremism, and it is this same extremism which causes Higgs to leave Erewhon. Fearful that disfavor is growing against his foreign presence, he plans to escape by balloon, taking with him his beloved Arowhena. The perilous escape takes place, and the hero, married to Arowhena and restored to England, becomes a fairly successful hack writer. His account of Erewhon, he says at the end, constitutes an appeal for subscriptions to finance his scheme to return to Erewhon.

The broad, traditional satire of *Erewhon* is abandoned in its sequel. Written years later, *Erewhon Revisited* reflects the maturity of its author, then in his sixties. In the later work, Butler treats Erewhon as a habitation of human beings, not satiric simplifications. *Erewhon Revisited* is thus a novel, not a satire; its focus is on human relationships. Butler had already written (though not published) *The Way of All Flesh*, and the preoccupations of that work are also evident in *Erewhon Revisited*. Both works grew out of Butler's fascination with family relationships, especially those between father and son.

The narrator of *Erewhon Revisited* is John Higgs, the son of George Higgs and Arowhena. He tells of his mother's early death and of his father's desire to return to Erewhon. This time, though, Higgs's desire is sentimental; he has grown past his earlier wish to profit from the Erewhonians. He goes to Erewhon, returns in ill-health, tells the story of his adventure to John, and dies. The book in this way becomes John's tribute to his father.

Although *Erewhon Revisited* may be identified as a novel rather than as a satire, it does have a satiric subject as part of its plot. Upon reentering Erewhon, Higgs discovers that his ascent by balloon has become the source of a new religion. The Erewhonians revere his memory and worship him as the "Sun Child." Higgs is horrified to find that there are theologians of Sunchildism fighting heretics. Unfortunately, Sunchildism has not made the Erewhonians a better or kinder people. Here is the heart of Butler's satire: that a religion based upon a supernatural event will divide people, place power in the wrong hands, and humiliate reason.

In *Erewhon*, Higgs was a pious and hypocritical prig, a target of satire himself. In the sequel, he is a genial, loving humanist, appalled by the "evolution" of his frantic escape into the ascent of a god. Much of *Erewhon Revisited* develops his plans to deflate Sunchildism, to reveal himself as the "Sun Child" and tell the truth about his "ascent."

Higgs has a special motive which transcends his disgust with Sunchildism. Upon arriving in Erewhon, he meets a young man whom he soon recognizes as his own son, a son he did not know he had. The young man is the product of Higgs's brief romance with Yram, the jailer's daughter. Higgs keeps his identity from his son (also named George) for a while, but eventually the two are revealed to each other in a touching and intense scene. To earn his newfound son's respect, Higgs determines to deflate Sunchildism. Thus, the process of satire in *Erewhon Revisited* is rooted in its human relationships.

Higgs's son John, the narrator of the novel, feels no jealousy toward his half brother. Instead, he shares the elder Higgs's enthusiasm for young George. Following his father's death, John goes to Erewhon himself to meet George and to deliver a large gift of gold to him. This legacy exemplified one of Butler's tenets about parent-child relations: that the best parents are kind, mostly absent, and very free with money. This theme is repeated throughout *The Way of All Flesh*. In *Erewhon Revisited*, however, it has a simpler expression. The relationship of Higgs and his two sons forms the emotional center of the novel and creates the impetus for some of its plot, but it is distinct from the satire on religion which makes up much of the book.

It is fitting that Butler's last work, *Erewhon Revisited*, should have presented a genial hero determined to strip away what he saw as ridiculous supernatural beliefs. Much of "Sunchildism" is a response to the religious foment of the nineteenth century with which Butler had begun contending early in his career. *The Fair Haven* was his first satire concerned with Christian belief. This work is "fiction" only in a very limited sense: Butler creates a persona, John Pickard Owen, whose arguments in favor of Christianity are in fact the vehicle for Butler's satire against it. *The Fair Haven* begins with a fictional memoir of John Pickard Owen by his brother. The memoir reveals that Owen moved from faith to disbelief to faith, and that his efforts to prove the validity of his religion pushed him to mental exhaustion and, eventually, death.

The characters of *The Fair Haven* are forerunners of the Pontifex family in *The Way of All Flesh*, Butler's fullest and most characteristic work. *The Way of All Flesh* encompasses all of Butler's concerns: family life, money, sexual attitudes, class structure, religion, and art. This novel too is a satire, but in it, Butler does not portray an Erewhon; much more disturbingly, he keeps the reader at home.

The Way of All Flesh is Ernest Pontifex's story, but it does not begin with Ernest. Butler the evolutionist shows Ernest as the product of several generations of social changes and personal tensions. The genealogical background, as well as the title and biblical epigraph, "We know that all things work together for good to them that love God," helps to create the ironic treatment of religion which will permeate the novel. What is the way of all flesh? The biblical echo suggests sin and decay; Butler's fiction, however, reminds the reader that the way of all flesh is change, for better or worse.

Ernest is the product of three generations of upward mobility. His great-grandfather is a simple, kind craftsman who sends his only son into the city. The son, George Pontifex, becomes successful as a publisher and even more successful as a bully. He chooses the Church as a career for his second son, Theobald, who revolts briefly, then acquiesces and evolves into the image of his father. Butler is careful to show personalities as products of environment.

George's bullying is only that of an egotistical, self-made man; Theobald's is more harsh, the product of his own fear and suppressed anger. The unfortunate object of this anger is Theobald's first born son, Ernest Pontifex.

Ernest's childhood is dominated by fear of his father. His mother, Christina, is of little help; Butler portrays her as the product of her own family life and the larger social system, both of which make marriage a necessity for her. Like Theobald, Christina becomes a hypocrite pressed into the service of "what is done." Much later in life, Ernest reflects that the family is a painful anachronism, confined in nature to the lower species. His opinion is shared by Overton, the narrator of the novel, an old family friend who takes an interest in young Ernest and becomes his lifelong friend and adviser. The two of them, in fact, eventually come to constitute a kind of family, an evolved, freely chosen family, not one formed by mere biological ties.

This outcome occurs only after long agony on Ernest's part. As a child, he believes all that is told: that he is, for example, a wicked, ungrateful boy who deserves Theobald's frequent beatings. His young life is lightened, however, by the interest taken in him by his aunt Alethea and by Overton, who has known all of the Pontifexes well and who tells their story with compassion.

Ernest is still an innocent and unformed young man when he goes to Cambridge to prepare for a career in the Church. Near the end of his peaceful, happy years there, he comes under the influence of an Evangelical group which alters his perceptions of what his life as a clergyman ought to be. Instead of stepping into a pleasant rural parish, Ernest becomes a missionary in the slums of London. He falls under the spell of the oily clergyman Nicholas Pryor, who "invests" Ernest's money and eventually absconds with it. Pryor, the Cambridge enthusiasts, and Theobald Pontifex all represent the clerical life; they are radically different kinds of people, and they are all portrayed negatively. Butler took no prisoners in his war on the clergy; his use of the genial Overton as a narrator partially masks this characteristic.

Sexual ignorance, imposed (and shared) by Theobald and his kind, provides Butler with his next target for satire. In despair over his religious life, Ernest seeks a prostitute and approaches the wrong woman, the eponymous Miss Snow. Ernest's ignorance lands him in prison and cuts him off forever from mere gentility. It redeems him, however, from a life circumscribed by his father: ironically, Theobald's strict control over Ernest liberates Ernest at last. In prison, stripped of all his former identity, Ernest begins to come to terms with what his life has been and may be. A long illness serves to clarify his mind; he rejects traditional religion, society, and his family's condescending offers of help. Overton alone stands by Ernest, and it is at this point in Ernest's development that they become fast friends. Overton takes on the role of the ideal father—fond, genteel, and moneyed.

It is in this last area that Overton's role is most important to the events of the book: he keeps Alethea's substantial bequest in trust for Ernest, allowing him knowledge of it and access to it, according to Alethea's wish, only when he judges that Ernest is prepared to use it wisely. Ernest's ill-advised marriage and his decision to work as a tailor cause Overton to hold the money back. Eventually, Ernest's maturity evolves to a level acceptable to Overton, and the two of them lead a pleasant life of wealth and, on Ernest's side at least, accomplishment: he has become a writer who, like Butler, writes thoughtful, theoretical books.

In his role as a father, Ernest also has evolved. The children of his marriage to Ellen are reared by simple country people and grow up free of the pressures of Ernest's childhood. After four generations, the Pontifexes have returned to the peaceful and happy life of Ernest's great-grandfather.

Liberal amounts of money, however, keep Ernest's son and daughter from any want that ordinary country folk might experience. Ernest's son wants to be a riverboat captain: Ernest buys him riverboats. This scenario is nearly as idealized a version of country life as was Marie Antoinette's. What makes this vision disconcerting is that Ernest's attitudes are clearly shared by Butler. Early in the novel, Ernest the bullied child is the object of the reader's pity. As a student and young cleric, his life creates a sense of pity but also humor. The more fully Ernest evolves, however, the less appealing the reader is likely to find him. The Ernest who finally comes into his aunt's fortune is a rather dull prig, who, upon learning of his wealth, considers how his emotion might be rendered in music. He tells Overton that he regrets nothing—not his parents' brutality, not prison—because everything has contributed to his evolution away from the "swindle" of middle-class expectations. Unfortunately, this self-satisfied view makes his character seem shallow, consisting only of words and affectations.

In spite of this problem, Butler's achievement is considerable. *The Way of All Flesh* is an immensely ambitious book, and much of it succeeds. Butler articulated fully and convincingly the varied stresses of family life, and that aspect alone would make the novel worthwhile. *Erewhon* and *Erewhon Revisited* share some of that evocative power. They also express Butler's optimism. For all his satirical vision and contentiousness, Butler does offer happy endings: Higgs's successful escape from Erewhon with his beloved, the reunion of the brothers in *Erewhon Revisited*, and the pleasant life of Ernest and Overton in *The Way of All Flesh*. Though societies may often be in the wrong, Butler seems to tell the reader, there is hope in freely chosen human relationships.

Major publications other than long fiction
POETRY: *Iliad*, 1898 (translation); *Odyssey*, 1900 (translation).
NONFICTION: *A First Year in Canterbury Settlement*, 1863; *Life and Habit*, 1877; *Evolution Old and New*, 1879; *God the Known and God the Unknown*, 1879; *Unconscious Memory*, 1880; *Alps and Sanctuaries of Piedmont and the*

Ticino, 1881; *A Psalm of Montreal*, 1884; *Luck or Cunning*, 1887; *Ex Voto*, 1888; *The Life and Letters of Dr. Samuel Butler*, 1896; *The Authoress of the "Odyssey,"* 1897; *Shakespeare's Sonnets Reconsidered*, 1899; *The Note-books*, 1912 (H. Festing Jones, editor).

Bibliography

Harkness, Stanley B. *The Career of Samuel Butler, 1835-1902: A Bibliography*, 1956.

Henderson, Philip. *Samuel Butler, the Incarnate Bachelor*, 1953.

Holt, Lee Elbert. *Samuel Butler*, 1964.

Jeffers, Thomas L. *Samuel Butler Revalued*, 1981.

Jones, Joseph Jay. *The Cradle of Erewhon: Samuel Butler in New Zealand*, 1959.

Stillman, Clara G. *Samuel Butler, a Mid-Victorian Modern*, 1932.

Deborah Core

JAMES BRANCH CABELL

Born: Richmond, Virginia; April 14, 1879
Died: Richmond, Virginia; May 5, 1958

Principal long fiction
The Eagle's Shadow, 1904; *The Cords of Vanity*, 1909; *The Soul of Melicent*, 1913 (republished as *Domnei*, 1920); *The Rivet in Grandfather's Neck*, 1915; *The Cream of the Jest*, 1917; *Jurgen*, 1919; *Figures of Earth: A Comedy of Appearances*, 1921; *The High Place*, 1923; *The Silver Stallion*, 1926; *Something About Eve*, 1927; *The White Robe*, 1928; *The Way of Ecben*, 1929; *Smirt*, 1934; *Smith*, 1935; *Smire*, 1937; *The King Was in His Counting House*, 1938; *Hamlet Had an Uncle*, 1940; *The First Gentleman of America*, 1942; *There Were Two Pirates*, 1946; *The Devil's Own Dear Son*, 1949.

Other literary forms
James Branch Cabell was both prolific and versatile. In addition to his many novels, he produced a volume of poetry entitled *From the Hidden Way* (1916) and a play, *The Jewel Merchants* (1921). His short stories are collected in *The Line of Love* (1905), *Gallantry* (1907), *Chivalry* (1909), and *The Certain Hour* (1916). Included among his writings are critical volumes on his contemporaries Joseph Hergesheimer and Ellen Glasgow; *Taboo* (1921), a satire dedicated to Cabell's nemesis, John S. Sumner, who initiated obscenity charges against his novel *Jurgen*; *Some of Us* (1930), a defense of the individualism of such writers as Elinor Wylie, Sinclair Lewis, and H. L. Mencken; and *The St. Johns* (1943), a history of a Florida river, written with A. J. Hanna, for Stephen Vicent Benét's series entitled "The Rivers of America."

Perhaps Cabell's most interesting volumes are those that illuminate his life and literary development. He wrote two epistolary volumes: *Special Delivery* (1933), which presents both his conventional responses to letters he received and the nonconventional replies he would have preferred to send, and *Ladies and Gentlemen* (1934), a collection of addresses to dead historical figures—from Solomon to George Washington, from Pocahontas to Madame de Pompadour—who have inspired myths and legends. He explores the past of his native region and its impact upon his writings in his trilogy "Virginians Are Various," consisting of *Let Me Lie* (1947), *Quiet, Please* (1952), and *As I Remember It* (1955). Providing readers with insight into Cabell's art are *Beyond Life* (1919), which clarifies his values, literary precedents, and thematic concerns: *These Restless Heads* (1932), a discussion of creativity based upon the four seasons of the year; and *Straws and Prayer-Books* (1924), an explanation of his reasons for writing *The Biography of the Life of Manuel* (1927-1930). Two volumes of Cabell's letters have been published: *Between Friends: Letters of James Branch Cabell and Others* (1962), edited by his second wife, Margaret Freeman Cabell, and Padraic Colum; the other, *The Letters of James Branch Cabell* (1975), edited by Edward Wagenknecht. His manuscripts and memorabilia are in the James Branch Cabell Collections at the University of Virginia in Charlottesville.

Achievements

Cabell's aesthetic individualism—as expressed in his highly artificial style, his loose, episodic structure, and his peculiar synthesis of romance and comedy, idealism and cynicism, mythology and personal experience—has limited both his popular and critical appeal. As Arvin R. Wells observes in *Jesting Moses: A Study in Cabellian Comedy* (1962), "It seems fair to say that rarely has a serious literary artist had so little luck in finding a responsive, judicious, and articulate audience." The essays, short stories, and books that Cabell published from 1901 to 1919 received only a small readership along with generally negative reviews, although both Mark Twain and Theodore Roosevelt praised his collection of chivalric tales, *The Line of Love*. Most readers, advocates of realism, found his works too romantic, whereas those with a taste for romance complained that Cabell was too abstruse.

In 1920, when obscenity charges were brought against *Jurgen*, Cabell found himself in the public eye, perceived as a valiant iconoclast battling the forces of puritanical repression. Sales of *Jurgen* skyrocketed, and Cabell enjoyed praise from such respected literary figures as Vernon Louis Parrington, Carl Van Doren, H. L. Mencken, and Sinclair Lewis, who in his Nobel Prize address of 1930, acknowledged Cabell's achievement. Suddenly, in critical studies, literary histories, and anthologies, Cabell was elevated to, as the critic Joe Lee Davis explains, "the rank of a 'classic' and an 'exotic' in the movement of spiritual liberation led by H. L. Mencken, Theodore Dreiser, Eugene O'Neill, and Sinclair Lewis." The public fanfare of the 1920's, however, inspired primarily by the eroticism in Cabell's works, proved to be short-lived—not to the surprise of Cabell, who, in *These Restless Heads*, predicted the decline of his literary generation. In the 1930's and 1940's, Cabell was viewed as a trifling talent, rooted to the 1920's and to his native Virginia. His aestheticism displeased the ethical neohumanists; his escapism annoyed the Marxists. The New Critics and mythic critics paid him scant attention. In the 1950's, three major literary historians—Edward Wagenknecht, Edd Winfield Parks, and Edmund Wilson—called for a reevaluation of Cabell's career, but they did little to change public opinion. Virtually all of Cabell's books are out of print, although the recent surge of interest in fantasy literature has brought some attention to his work, and he is appreciated primarily by a coterie of scholars and graduate students.

Biography

Born on April 14, 1879, in Richmond, Virginia, James Branch Cabell grew up there as a Southern gentleman. His parents—Robert Gamble Cabell II, a physician, and Anne Branch—were both from distinguished Southern families. Cabell's paternal great-grandfather was a governor of Virginia; his paternal grandfather held two claims to fame, having been a schoolmate of Edgar Allan Poe at the English and Classical School in Richmond and later a neighbor and the personal physician of General Robert E. Lee. On his mother's side of the family, Cabell was related through marriage to a number of prominent Virginia families and was cousin to a governor of Maryland. Fostering Cabell's aristocratic pride still further was his "mammy," Mrs. Louisa Nelson, who, in her several decades of service in the Cabell household, doted upon James and encouraged him to consider himself a privileged member of society.

Cabell's outstanding intellect asserted itself early. He performed brilliantly at the College of William and Mary in Williamsburg, which he attended from 1894 to 1898. His professors suggested that he revise a sophomore paper entitled "The Comedies of William Congreve" for publication, and later asked him to teach courses in French and Greek at the college. The only blemish upon Cabell's academic career was a scandal during his senior year. One of his professors was accused of having homosexual relations with his students; Cabell, because he had been friends with the man, was briefly implicated. The unpleasant episode had positive repercussions, however, for in wandering about Williamsburg alone and troubled, Cabell met Ellen Glasgow, who had come to town to research the background for a novel. She offered him sympathy, and thus began a lifelong friendship. Soon, the charges against Cabell were dropped for lack of evidence, and he was graduated with highest honors.

After his graduation, Cabell pursued writing both as a vocation and an avocation. He served as a copyholder on the *Richmond Times* in 1898, then spent two years working for the *New York Herald*, and in 1901, he worked for the *Richmond News*. For the next decade, he worked as a genealogist, traveling about America, England, Ireland, and France to examine archives. Not only did this occupation result in two volumes of the Branch family history—*Branchiana* (1907), a record of the Branch family in Virginia, and *Branch of Abingdon* (1911), a record of the Branch family in England, but it also prepared Cabell for his future literary endeavors in tracing the lineage of a character through twenty-two subsequent generations. During that same time, Cabell wrote several novels and steadily produced short stories, which he contributed to such periodicals as *The Smart Set*, *Collier's Weekly*, *Red Book*, *Lippincott's*, and *Harper's Monthly*. In 1911, Cabell, disappointed by his lack of acclaim as a writer, took a position in coal-mining operations in West Virginia; in 1913, he abandoned the experiment and returned to Richmond to resume work as a genealogist.

On November 8, 1913, at the age of thirty-four, Cabell gave up what had been a carefree bachelorhood, filled with romantic intrigues, to marry

Rebecca Priscilla Bradley Shepard, a widow with five children. Marriage proved mutually satisfying to Cabell and Priscilla. He enjoyed the domesticity of his new life-style, including the rearing of their son Ballard Hartwell; she delighted in performing the literary and social duties that came with being his wife. Their thirty-five-year union was marked by undying affection and loyalty.

Literary prominence, or perhaps one should say notoriety, came to Cabell in 1920 when John S. Sumner, the executive secretary of the New York Society for the Suppression of Vice, seized the plates and copies of his novel *Jurgen* and accused the publishing company, McBride, of violating the anti-obscenity statutes of the New York State penal code. Sumner's action proved ill-advised, for it only increased the public's interest in Cabell's writings during the two and a half years before the obscenity trial was finally held. On October 19, 1922, after a three-day trial, the jury acquitted McBride, and Cabell emerged as a celebrity.

During the 1920's, Cabell took a more active role as a literary leader and was instrumental, along with Ellen Glasgow, in making the nation aware of Richmond as a literary center. While writing books with great regularity (during the 1920's, he published seven novels, one play, and several works of short fiction and nonfiction), Cabell also entertained and corresponded with a number of important literary figures, including Sinclair Lewis, Hugh Walpole, and Carl Van Vechten. In addition, he served as a writer and guest editor for *The Reviewer*, Richmond's impressive contribution to the vogue of little magazines. As active as Cabell was on the literary scene, he was still able to continue his career as a genealogist, working for the Virginia Chapter of the Sons of the Revolution and other historical societies, as well as serving as editor of the Virginia War History Commission.

The last decades of Cabell's life were anticlimactic, fraught with physical ailments and an increasing disillusionment with the American reading public. With the advent of the Great Depression, his literary fame seemed to weaken and then die. From 1932 to 1935, Cabell—like Sherwood Anderson, George Jean Nathan, Eugene O'Neill, and Theodore Dreiser—attempted to rekindle the vital skepticism of the 1920's, serving as editor of the *American Spectator*; he soon realized, however, that his efforts to enlighten the public were useless. In the mid-1930's, Cabell suffered from repeated attacks of pneumonia, and Priscilla developed severe arthritis; thus, they frequently sought relief in the warm climate of St. Augustine, Florida. There, Priscilla died of heart failure on March 29, 1949. Her death left Cabell feeling bitter, lost, and angry, but he continued to write steadily. In 1950, he regained some of his former zest for life when he decided to wed Margaret Waller Freeman, a member of the Richmond literati whose acquaintance he had made years earlier while writing for *The Reviewer*. Cabell died of a cerebral hemorrhage on May 15, 1958, in Richmond.

Analysis

James Branch Cabell's art rests upon a paradox. On the one hand, he contends that man is idealistic and must therefore create dreams to sustain himself. On the other, he mocks man's tendency "to play the ape to his dreams"—that is, to seek the unattainable foolishly. Manipulating the polarities of romance and comedy, Cabell responded to the predominant intellectual trend of the early twentieth century—naturalism. From a cosmic perspective, he had no difficulty accepting the premise that man is like a bit of flotsam in a deterministic universe, subject to environmental forces, but unable to control or understand them. From a humanistic point of view, however, he could not tolerate the limitations that naturalism imposed upon man's mind. For Cabell, man does not survive because he adapts to biological, social, or economic forces, but rather because he persists in believing in the products of his own imagination—what he terms "dynamic illusions." These illusions, according to Cabell, emanate from the demiurge, or psyche, yet they are rooted in man's primitive, animal instincts. Their source of energy is the libido. Thus, Cabell's protagonists move between two realms of experience. They are romantic questers after ideal beauty, perfection, and salvation; they are also comic bumblers whose lusts, vanities, and misconceptions entangle them in a web of complexities. Cabell's narratives follow a Hegelian pattern. His thesis is that man desires to escape from the dull, routine world of actuality. His antithesis is that such a desire can never be attained; disillusionment is inevitable. Yet in the synthesis, man achieves a degree of satisfaction. He learns that his ideals are illusions, but also that they should be cherished, for in the realm of the imagination, dreams themselves have a reality.

Cabell's background explains his propensity for blending the romantic and the comic. Quite early, he developed a love for myth and legend. As a child, he delighted in such books as *Old Greek Stories Simply Told*, *Stories of Old Rome*, *Book of Bible Stories*, and *Stories of the Days of King Arthur*. Cabell gained a strong sense of aristocratic pride—an appreciation of the southern characteristics of chivalry and gallantry—yet he was no dreamy-eyed romantic. He saw the ironic underside of life. In growing up, he heard frank gossip, as well as heroic tales, from his elders. In college, Cabell became interested in the Restoration comedy of manners, which heightened his awareness of the hypocrisies and absurdities of human behavior. Such weaknesses became more immediately apparent when, as a bachelor in his twenties and early thirties, he vacationed at the Virginia resort of Rockbridge Alum. There, he witnessed and participated in affairs that assumed the facade of chaste, genteel encounters, but were actually indulgences in lust. From his various experiences, Cabell developed a dichotomous concept of the artist, appropriate to his blending of romance and comedy. The artist assumes an exalted status, painting beautiful visions of life as it ought to be. Ironically, however, because of this detached, godlike perspective, skepticism intrudes. The world that the artist portrays becomes a caricature; it mocks and contradicts his idealistic presentation. For Cabell, the ideal and the real coexist.

Cabell's major literary achievement is his eighteen-volume *The Biography of the Life of Manuel*, which he wished readers to regard as a single book. In 1915, Cabell conceived the idea of bringing together his writings into one vast architectural construct, and for the next fifteen years, he strove to achieve his plan: revising published works, deciding upon a logical arrangement, and writing new tales and romances to clarify his design. The result was the Storisende Edition of *The Works of James Branch Cabell*, bound in green and gold. Cabell's magnum opus represents an ingenious application of his genealogical talents to the realm of fiction. Spanning seven centuries and moving from the imaginary medieval realm of Poictesme to modern Virginia, it celebrates the life force passed on by Manuel to his descendants.

The design of *The Biography of the Life of Manuel* is best viewed in musical terms. Whether one considers it to be a fugue, as does Louis Untermyer in *James Branch Cabell: The Man and the Masks* (1970), or a sonata, which is the thesis of Warren McNeil in *Cabellian Harmonics* (1928), it revolves upon three themes and their variations. These themes are three philosophies of life: the chivalrous, the gallant, and the poetic. The chivalrous attitude views life as a testing; dominated by the will, it represents an ideal tradition in which men revere first God and then noble women. Quite the opposite, the gallant attitude views life as a toy; its social principle is hedonism. This attitude emphasizes the intelligence and is thus skeptical. Celebrating both chivalry and gallantry, the final attitude, the poetic, views life as raw material out of which it creates something that transcends life. It is controlled by the imagination.

These attitudes of the chivalrous, the gallant, and the poetic determine the structure of Cabell's work. In *Beyond Life*, the Prologue to *The Biography of the Life of Manuel*, he defines them. Then, in *Figures of Earth*, Cabell presents the life of Manuel of Poictesme, who at various times is affected by all three codes; and follows it with *The Silver Stallion*, which traces the development of the legend of Manuel the Redeemer. The fourth volume—composed of *Domnei* and *The Music from Behind the Moon*—treats one aspect of the chivalric code: woman-worship. Cabell then elaborates upon the subject in his short-story collection entitled *Chivalry*. He next examines the gallant attitude in *Jurgen*; inserts *The Line of Love*, which treats all three attitudes; then returns to gallantry in *The High Place* and the short-story collection *The Certain Hour*. The next four volumes move to the modern world: *The Cords of Vanity* presents Robert Townsend, a gallant; *From the Hidden Way* offers Townsend's verses; *The Rivet in Grandfather's Neck* portrays a chivalrous character; and *The Eagle's Shadow* examines the poet. Finally, *The Biography of the Life of Manuel* circles back upon itself, as the soul of Felix Kennaston, the protagonist of *The Cream of the Jest*, journeys back to Poictesme through his dreams. Cabell's vast design concludes with an epilogue, *Straws and Prayer-Books*, and *Townsend of Lichfield*, containing notes and addenda.

Figures of Earth, one of Cabell's finest novels, follows its author's typical tripartite pattern of quest, ensuing disillusionment, and final transcendence, as it traces the career of the swineherd Manuel. Subtitled *A Comedy of Appearances*, it is a complex allegorical work peopled with supernatural and preternatural beings who reside in the imaginary medieval land of Poictesme. The tale begins when Miramon Lluagor, the master of dreams, appears to Manuel at the pool of Haranton. There, he convinces Manuel to abandon his job as a swineherd—that is, to rebel against the elemental forces of life— and to pursue knight-errantry in seeking the beautiful yet unattainable Lady Gisele. Eager to make a fine figure in the world, Manuel repudiates his lover Suskind, a mysterious creature who represents the unconscious desires of the libido, and sets forth, unaware that he is being victimized by Horvendile, the diabolical spirit of romance. On his journey, he has a series of encounters with allegorical women. He first meets Niafer, a rather plain kitchen servant, who symbolizes worldly wisdom and domesticity. Dressed as a boy, she accompanies Manuel on his quest until, when faced with his own death unless he gives up Niafer, Manuel decides to sacrifice her to Grandfather Death. His next encounter is with the Princess Alianora, who represents political power, worldly position, and the undercurrent of sexual excitement that accompanies them. Manuel surrenders to lust, but eventually rejects Alianora, discovering the limitations of self-seeking gallantry. His third important encounter is with the supernal Queen Freydis, who symbolizes creative inspiration. Using magic, Manuel persuades her to leave her realm of Audela and enter the ordinary world. She does so out of love for him and animates a set of clay figures that he sculpted as a swineherd. These eventually enter history as major writers.

Manuel soon discovers that Freydis cannot give him fulfillment; only Niafer can, so he submits to thirty years of slavery to The Head of Misery to bring Niafer back from the dead. Then he settles down to a comfortable existence as a husband, father, and the Count of Poictesme. One day, however, while watching his wife and daughter through the window of Ageus (Usage) in his palace study, he discovers to his horror that their figures are only scratched upon the glass—that beyond the window is a chaos containing the images of preexistence, including the disturbing Suskind. Manuel must then choose whether to die himself or to allow his child Melicent to die in his place, while he resumes his relationship with Suskind. Acting decisively, he murders Suskind, bricks up the study window, and departs with Grandfather Death. In the last chapter, Grandfather Death accompanies him to the River Lethe, where he watches the images of his life as they sweep by him. Then the scene blurs, as Cabell moves his readers back to the pool of Haranton where Manuel began his quest. He repeats the dialogue of the first chapter, in which Miramon refers to Count Manuel, who has just died. Thus, Cabell ends with an appropriate reminder of his view of life as a cycle in which one life passes into other lives through heredity.

Manuel is Cabell's man of action, driven by dreams of a better life than that of a swineherd, yet the pursuit of dreams proves frustrating. Even in the mythical realm of Poictesme, Cabell constantly emphasizes through allegory the realities of death, misery, and madness. Life, Manuel learns, is full of obligations: to Alianora, Melicent, and especially to Niafer. Indeed, Cabell underscores this lesson by structuring his episodes into five books entitled "Credit," "Spending," "Cash Accounts," "Surcharge," and "Settlement." Yet it is in confronting his obligations that Manuel finds fulfillment. The romantic quest results in a comic exposure of man's limitations, but the final picture is of human dignity in accepting those limitations. Manuel can never completely obliterate discontent, but he decides that the human possessions of a kingdom, a wife, and a family, even if they are illusions, are better than a return to the primitive unconsciousness. Thus, although he never achieves the object of his initial quest, he does transcend experience through belief in his destined role as the Redeemer of Poictesme and his ultimate rejection of lust for love.

Figures of Earth, because of its confusing cast of characters—some of whom are figures of earth; some, unearthly—and the artificialities of Cabell's prose, makes difficult reading. The effort is rewarding, however, for Cabell offers some intriguing insights into man's values: that the demands of the family and the aspirations of the individual often conflict; that the world is duplicitous; and that the search for perfection involves paradoxically the self-realization of imperfection. The work is thought-provoking and timely.

Jurgen follows the same movement as *Figures of Earth*: the pursuit of perfection, the discovery that it does not exist, and then the satisfaction achieved through accepting actuality; it merely views these ideas from a different perspective. The controlling concept is justice, which to Cabell's title character, a poetry-producing pawnbroker, means that in the universe, every idealistic desire should have a means of being fulfilled. Jurgen's problem, however, is that existence is unjust; since man's intellect increases as his physical prowess diminishes, he can never completely realize his potential. Granting Jurgen a temporary respite from his dilemma, Cabell allows his middle-aged poet to retain his youthful body and then lets his reader see the subsequent effects upon his protagonist's values.

Jurgen began as a tale entitled "Some Ladies and Jurgen," which Cabell published in *The Smart Set* in 1918. His novel simply expands upon the narrative of that story. The hero meets a monk, who curses the devil for causing him to trip over a stone. Jurgen, playing the devil's advocate, defends evil. Shortly thereafter, he meets a black gentleman who thanks him for the defense and expresses the hope that his life will be carefree. When Jurgen replies that such a life is impossible, since he is married, the stranger promises to reward him. The reward turns out to be the disappearance of Jurgen's wife, Dame Lisa. When he returns home, she is gone; he later learns that she has been seen near a cave outside town. Feeling an obligation, he goes there, only to encounter the black gentleman—who, he learns, is Koshchei the Deathless, the controller of the universe. Koshchei tempts Jurgen by evoking three women that he feels would be more suitable for a poet: Queen Guenevere, Queen Anaïtis, and Queen Helen—standing respectively for faith, desire, and vision. Jurgen rejects each, however, and asks for Dame Lisa back. She appears, lectures him, and then leaves for home. In response, Jurgen praises her as a source of poetic inspiration more valuable than faith, desire, and vision, and then follows her home.

Expanding his narrative for the novel, Cabell added two fantasy sequences that would explain Jurgen's ultimate attraction to Lisa. In the first, Jurgen visits the Garden between Dawn and Sunrise, where he relives falling in love with Dorothy la Désirée, one of the daughters of Manuel. She destroys his romantic bliss when she marries the wealthy Heitman Michael and then engages in adulterous affairs. Because of Dorothy's behavior, Jurgen marries Lisa. In the second episode, Jurgen, having been granted by Mother Sereda the recovery of a bygone Wednesday, fantasizes about how his relationship with Dorothy might have developed. He imagines himself killing Heitman Michael and claiming her, but as the Wednesday ends, he finds himself embracing the Dorothy of reality, an aged femme fatale.

Cabell also expanded his original tale by depicting Jurgen's adventures in five realms: Glathion, Cocaigne, Leukê, Hell, and Heaven. Throughout these episodes, Jurgen assumes the roles of charlatan and womanizer, as he tests historical systems of values. In Glathion, he examines the medieval tradition of Christian chivalry, but rejects it as being irrational. In Cocaigne, he becomes equally dissatisfied with hedonistic paganism. Leukê, a stronghold of the Helenic tradition, teaches him the danger of the realm of utilitarian Philistia. In Hell, Jurgen learns of the sin of pride, and in Heaven encounters selfless love. Feeling the shadow of worldly wisdom trailing him, Jurgen finally decides to give up his youthful body and return to the domestic comforts that Dame Lisa can provide. He trades the ideal for the actual, yet in so doing bestows romantic value upon his ordinary existence and his ordinary wife.

Although entertaining, *Jurgen* lacks clarity of design. The reader who is steeped in mythology may enjoy Cabell's manipulation of the legends of Faust, Don Juan, King Arthur, Troilus and Cressida, and Ulysses and Penelope, but somehow, the integration of the hero's adventures with the narrative line exploring the feelings between husband and wife is incomplete. The episodic looseness of the novel is distracting. Thus, modern readers, like those titillated readers of the 1920's, may be absorbed by Jurgen's amorous exploits without fully considering Cabell's analysis of the values that make life worth living.

Cabell's great achievement is that he celebrated the illusion-making capacity of the mind while simultaneously exposing man's follies in pursuing dreams. He merged the traditions of humanism and skepticism. Reacting against naturalism, Cabell had the courage to present a transcendent view of life—one that acknowledged not man's impotency, but his potential. A meticulous craftsman, a daring iconoclast, an imaginative thinker, Cabell deserves recognition as a major writer of the twentieth century.

Major publications other than long fiction

SHORT FICTION: *The Line of Love*, 1905; *Gallantry*, 1907; *Chivalry*, 1909; *The Certain Hour*, 1916; *The Music from Behind the Moon*, 1926; *The White Robe*, 1928.

PLAY: *The Jewel Merchants*, 1921.

POETRY: *From the Hidden Way*, 1916.

NONFICTION: *Branchiana*, 1907; *Branch of Abingdon*, 1911; *Beyond Life*, 1919; *The Judging of Jurgen*, 1920; *Taboo*, 1921; *Joseph Hergesheimer*, 1921; *Straws and Prayer-Books*, 1924; *Some of Us*, 1930; *These Restless Heads*, 1932 (contains two short stories and personal reminiscences); *Special Delivery*, 1933; *Ladies and Gentlemen*, 1934; *Of Ellen Glasgow*, 1938; *The St. Johns*, 1943 (with A. J. Hanna); *Let Me Lie*, 1947; *Quiet, Please*, 1952; *As I Remember It*, 1955; *Between Friends: Letters of James Branch Cabell and Others*, 1962 (Margaret Freeman Cabell and Padraic Colum, editors); *The Letters of James Branch Cabell*, 1975 (Edward Wagenknecht, editor).

MISCELLANEOUS: *The Biography of the Life of Manuel: The Works of James Branch Cabell*, 1927-1930 (18 volumes).

Bibliography

Canary, Robert H. "Whatever Happened to the Cabell Revival?," in *Kalki*. VI (1974), pp. 55-60.

Davis, Joe Lee. *James Branch Cabell*, 1962.

Flora, Joseph M. "Cabell as Precursor: Reflections on Cabell and Vonnegut," in *Kalki*. VI (1975), pp. 118-137.

Godshalk, William Leigh. *In Quest of Cabell: Five Exploratory Essays*, 1976.

Himelick, Raymond. "Figures of Cabell," in *Modern Fiction Studies*. II (Winter, 1956-1957).

Rubin, Louis D., and Robert D. Jacobs, eds. "Two in Richmond: Ellen Glasgow and James Branch Cabell," in *The South: Modern Southern Literature and Its Cultural Setting*, 1961.

Tarrant, Desmond. *James Branch Cabell: The Dream and the Reality*, 1967.

Untermeyer, Louis. *James Branch Cabell: The Man and His Masks*, 1970.

Wells, Arvin. *Jesting Moses: A Study in Cabellian Comedy*, 1962.

Lynne P. Shackelford

GEORGE WASHINGTON CABLE

Born: New Orleans, Louisiana; October 12, 1844
Died: St. Petersburg, Florida; January 31, 1925

Principal long fiction

The Grandissimes, 1880; *Dr. Sevier*, 1884; *Bonaventure*, 1888; *John March, Southerner*, 1894; *The Cavalier*, 1901; *Bylow Hill*, 1902; *Kincaid's Battery*, 1908; *Gideon's Band*, 1914; *Lovers of Louisiana*, 1918.

Other literary forms

In addition to nine novels, George Washington Cable published a novella, *Madame Delphine* (1881), and four collections of short stories: *Old Creole Days* (1879); *Strong Hearts* (1899); *Posson Jone' and Père Raphaël* (1909); and *The Flower of the Chapdelaines* (1918). He also wrote a dramatized version of one of his novels, *The Cavalier*. His eight books of nonfiction cover miscellaneous subjects. *The Creoles of Louisiana* (1884) is a collection of history articles, and *Strange True Stories of Louisiana* (1889) is a collection of factual stories; both collections are set in Cable's native state. *The Silent South* (1885) and *The Negro Question* (1890) are collections of essays on Southern problems. *The Busy Man's Bible* (1891) and *The Amateur Garden* (1914) grew out of Cable's hobbies of Bible-teaching and gardening. *A Memory of Roswell Smith* (1892) is a memorial tribute to a friend. *The Cable Story Book: Selections for School Reading* (1899) is a book of factual and fictional material for children. Cable also wrote magazine articles and a newspaper column.

Achievements

In his study *George W. Cable* (1962), Philip Butcher shows the high position that Cable held in American literature in the last years of the nineteenth century. In 1884, the *Critic* ranked him ahead of fourteenth-place Mark Twain in its list of "Forty Immortals." A cartoon in *Life* (May 27, 1897) depicted Cable among the ten most popular authors of the day. In the American edition of *Literature* in 1899, he was tenth on the list of greatest living American writers.

Popular both with critics and with the reading public in his own time, Cable is little known today. His reputation as a writer of fiction rests on three works: the novel *The Grandissimes*, the novella *Madame Delphine*, and the collection of short stories *Old Creole Days*, later editions of which include *Madame Delphine* as the lead story. Although *Dr. Sevier* and *John March, Southerner* contain serious commentary, the three novels which followed in the first decade of the new century are trivial romances. His last two novels, *Gideon's Band* and *Lovers of Louisiana*, signal only an incomplete return to the artistic level and social worth of his first three books. Because much of his energy went into provocative social essays on Southern racial problems, into humanitarian reforms in such areas as prisons and insane asylums, into cultural projects, and, as a major source of income, into platform tours, Cable found insufficient time for the fiction he might otherwise have created. Nevertheless, as late as 1918 he published a collection of short stories and a novel, and up to his death in 1925 he was working on still another novel.

Cable was much admired by his contemporaries. William Dean Howells praised him privately and in print. Twain took him as a partner on a reading tour, and for four months (1884-1885) the two shared the stage as they read from their respective works. Cable also read on programs that included Hamlin Garland, James Whitcomb Riley, Eugene Field, and other popular writers of the day.

Popular in Britain as well, he was invited to England by James S. Barrie for the first of two trips abroad (1898, 1905). For nearly three months in 1898, he traveled and visited in the homes of Barrie, Sir Arthur Conan Doyle, Rudyard Kipling, Henry James, and other well-known figures. He was an interesting conversationalist, an effective speaker, and an entertaining performer. His British friends arranged for him to read his fiction, play a guitar, and sing Creole-Negro songs in their homes and in public halls. Andrew Carnegie, his host at Skibo Castle, was so impressed with Cable's personality and writing that he later bestowed a lifetime pension on him. Among his honorary degrees was the Doctorate of Letters given by Yale University in 1901 to Cable, Twain, Howells, Theodore Roosevelt, Woodrow Wilson, and other contemporary notables.

Cable's reputation began to decline before his death and has never recovered. In the 1980's he is considered too important a writer to be omitted from Southern literature anthologies and American literature textbooks, but he has not yet been deemed worthy of widespread revival.

Biography

George Washington Cable was born in New Orleans, Louisiana, on October 12, 1844. Ancestors of his mother, Rebecca Boardman Cable, had lived in New England since the seventeenth century and had moved to Indiana in 1807. The background of his father, the elder George Washington Cable, dates back to pre-Revolutionary times in Virginia. The elder Cable lived in Virginia and Pennsylvania with his parents before moving to Indiana, where he married Rebecca in 1834. The Cable family migrated to New Orleans in 1837, where young George became their fifth child.

In the 1840's, the Cables lived a comfortable existence, owning several household slaves until the father's business failed. Through the 1850's, the elder Cable worked at a series of jobs until, weakened in health, he died on February 28, 1859. Because young George's older brother, along with an older sister, had died of scarlet fever, his father's death required him, not yet fourteen, to leave school to support the family. Until the third year of the Civil War, he held his father's former position as a clerk at the customhouse.

Slight in size—with a height of five feet five inches and a weight of one hundred pounds—and deceptively youthful in features, Cable enlisted in the Confederate Army on October 9, 1863, three days before his nineteenth birthday. Incurring two slight wounds during his service, he was discharged in 1865.

After the war, Cable worked as errand boy, store clerk, and, until malaria stopped him, as a rodsman with a surveying party on the Red River. In 1868, he became a bookkeeper for two cotton firms in New Orleans. He married Louise Stewart Bartlett on December 7, 1869, and soon fathered the first of a large family of children. At one time, he worked simultaneously for the cotton house of William C. Black and Company, the New Orleans Cotton Exchange, and the National Cotton Exchange.

Newspaper work provided Cable's first opportunity to see his writing in print. While continuing as an accountant, he worked for newspapers as a free-lance contributor and then as a full-time reporter. For eighteen months, beginning February 27, 1870, he wrote "Drop Shot," a column, weekly and then daily, for the New Orleans *Picayune*. While working for the *Picayune*, his research into Louisiana history at city hall, the cathedral, and the Cabildo, former seat of colonial government, led him to factual stories later to be shaped into fiction. In addition, his newspaper reports on contemporary local affairs interested him in reform on civic, regional, and national levels.

Appearing in *Scribner's Monthly*, Cable's stories were based on his knowledge of the people and activities of New Orleans and of events in Louisiana history. Six of the stories appearing in *Scribner's Monthly* and a seventh story, "Posson Jone'," which was published in *Appleton's Journal*, were later collected as *Old Creole Days*, published by Scribner's. His first novel, *The Grandissimes*, also based on the people and history of Louisiana, was serialized in *Scribner's Monthly* over a twelve-month period and then published in book form in 1880. Next came the novella *Madame Delphine*, first printed in *Scribner's Monthly* as a three-part serial, and then published in book form in 1881.

In 1881, Cable gave up his position as an accountant, depending for the rest of his life on lectures and public readings of his fiction to supplement his income as a writer. One of his successes was a series of six lectures at Johns Hopkins University in 1883, and he continued to find himself in demand on platforms in many cities. In 1884, his regional history *The Creoles of Louisiana* appeared, and in the same year his second novel, *Dr. Sevier*, was published. In 1884-1885 he went on a successful reading tour with Mark Twain.

Cable, son of a slaveholding family, was a loyal Confederate soldier during the Civil War and apparently remained unchanged in political stance for some time thereafter. Later, however, he began to express feeling against racial injustice. Although criticism of discrimination is present in his fiction, it was only through the direct statements of his magazine articles and public lectures that fellow Southerners became fully aware of his radical stance. The publication of a volume of his essays, *The Silent South* (1885), made his stand clear. Newspaper editorialists who had acclaimed his fiction now began to attack his social and political views.

Cable had two households to support—one including his wife and children, the other his mother, his sisters, and the children of his widowed sister. His wife, who traced her ancestry back to the Mayflower, was born and reared in New England. Cable believed that a return to the climate of New England would be beneficial for his wife's frail health. In addition, the attraction that a location near his publishers in New York held for him, and a sensitivity to the criticism aimed at him in the South, influenced his decision to leave New Orleans after forty years of residence there. Having previously visited Northampton, Massachusetts, he moved his wife and children to a home there in 1885, and his mother, sisters, and cousins followed soon thereafter.

Despite his desire to write fiction, Cable allowed other interests to take much of his time. In 1885, he championed black rights in an essay read nationwide, "The Freedman's Case in Equity." In 1886, he founded the first of the Home Culture Clubs, in which he would be involved for the next thirty-five years. Through his Open Letter Club (1888-1890), in whose name he lectured, wrote, and published, Cable completed the period identified as his greatest effort for reform in the South. From 1887 to 1889, he undertook an extensive program of religious writing and teaching; he conducted a large Bible class in Northampton each Sunday, traveling to Boston on Saturdays to hold a similar class.

For five years, Cable published a book annually; *Bonaventure, Strange True Stories of Louisiana, The Negro Question, The Busy Man's Bible,* and *A Memory of Roswell Smith* were all published during this period. At the same time, he was giving readings and lectures from coast to coast. A popular speaker, he was frequently invited to deliver commencement addresses and to give talks on literary subjects, Southern problems, and Creole history. Despite his endeavors, however, he remained constantly in debt—receiving advances on royalties from his publishers, obtaining loans, repaying old debts, and incurring new ones.

By this time, Cable had ceased actively campaigning for civil rights, and his writing developed a noncontroversial tone. His third novel, *John March, Southerner,* although concerned with Reconstruction problems, avoided racial issues, as did his collection of short stories *Strong Hearts. The Cable Story Book,* needless to say, offended no one. The following novels, *The Cavalier* and *Bylow Hill,* veered even more sharply from controversy to entertainment, their artistic value diminishing proportionately.

Meanwhile, in 1898, Cable had made a triumphal reading tour in Britain.

Philanthropist Andrew Carnegie, with whom Cable became friends while in Scotland, donated money to one of Cable's long-enduring projects. In 1903, Carnegie agreed to give fifty thousand dollars for a building for the Home Culture Clubs on the condition that five thousand dollars a year be guaranteed locally for five years.

Dimming Cable's good fortune, his beloved wife died on February 27, 1904, ending a devoted marriage of nearly thirty-five years. Cable continued to write, although without immediately readying a book for publication. Two years and nine months after Louise's death, he married Eva C. Stevenson. In 1908, he published the novel *Kincaid's Battery*, and in 1909 he put two of his short stories (one of them selected from the *Old Creole Days* collection) into book form, *Posson Jone' and Père Raphaël*. In 1911, Carnegie began sending Cable one thousand dollars a year to support his writing. Three years later, *Gideon's Band* and *The Amateur Garden* were published.

Despite his debts, Cable managed to travel outside the United States even before Carnegie began to subsidize him. When traveling, he often carried with him an unfinished manuscript, working on it when he had time. In later years, no longer dependent on the platform circuit, he began staying in Northampton in the summer, spending the winter in New Orleans, Florida, and Bermuda. In 1918, at the age of seventy-four, he published two books—*The Flower of the Chapdelaines*, a collection of short stories, and *Lovers of Louisiana*.

When Carnegie died in 1919, his will provided Cable with five thousand dollars a year for life, the annuity to be transferred to Eva if she survived her husband. Eva, however, died on June 7, 1923. Six months after her death, Cable married his third wife, Hanna Cowing. A little more than a year later, on January 31, 1925, he died. Among his literary papers was an unfinished novel on which he had been working.

Analysis

Although George Washington Cable's reputation rests primarily on one collection of short stories and two pieces of longer fiction, his total output includes twenty-two books. For an understanding of Cable as a writer of fiction, one should first consider his nonfiction and his reasons for writing it. Cable's interest in history is shown in two books centered on Creole culture, *The Creoles of Louisiana*, a collection of history articles, and *Strange True Stories of Louisiana*, a collection of factual stories about the Creoles. On a juvenile level, *The Cable Story Book* is a combination of factual and fictional material that emphasizes the same Creole subjects as his fiction. *The Silent South* and *The Negro Question*, his best-known works of nonfiction, are collections of essays on controversial Southern problems, notably the problem of racial discrimination. Characteristic of Cable's prose is a moral posture and a humanitarian zeal, openly stated in his nonfiction and imaginatively expressed in the most important of his fiction. He worked for the reform of men and institutions and for a reversal in racial attitudes.

Cable's first novel, *The Grandissimes*, is his unqualified masterpiece. Louis D. Rubin, Jr. has called it the first "modern" Southern novel, dealing realistically as it does with the role of the black in American society. Added to the rich portrayal of aristocratic Creole settings and family problems, a panoramic array of characters of Indian, black, and mixed bloods vivify problems of social castes and racial discrimination in Louisiana in 1803, the year of the Louisiana Purchase. Using the historical actuality of racially tangled bloodlines as the theme for dramatic episodes, Cable emphasizes the ramifications of black-white relationships. The free quadroon caste, for example, had its special role in Southern society, as shown historically in the New Orleans "quadroon balls." Beautiful young women of one-quarter black blood (quadroons) or, perhaps, one-eighth (octoroons) danced at these balls with white men, were chosen by them as mistresses, and were set up in separate households in the city.

Two principal quadroons interact in *The Grandissimes*. A male quadroon is the identically named half-brother of the aristocratic Creole, Honoré Grandissime. The darker Honoré Grandissime flouts the law by refusing to inscribe the letters "f.m.c." (free man of color) after his name. Educated in Paris along with his half-brother and heir to most of their deceased father's wealth, the quadroon nevertheless remains unrecognized as a legitimate member of the Grandissime family. The Creoles' acceptance of an Indian chieftain as ancestor is introduced to point up their unwonted prejudice against the taint of black blood. The main female quadroon is Palmyre Philosophe, a freed slave who bears a hopeless love for the all-white Honoré Grandissime and, in turn, is loved by his quadroon half-brother. To illustrate the injustices perpetrated against blacks, Cable inserts the episode of the black Bras-Coupé, a historical figure used earlier in Cable's unpublished short story "Bibi." Palmyre hates Agricola Fuselier, her former owner and uncle to Honoré Grandissime, who forced her unconsummated marriage to Bras-Coupé.

The character who serves throughout the novel as spokesman for Cable is Joseph Frowenfeld, a German-American newcomer to New Orleans, who observes, participates in, and comments critically on the action. Honoré Grandissime, the leading male character, is a Creole who recognizes the faults of his society and works with moderation to correct them. He provides a liberal Creole viewpoint, supplementary to the rigid moral judgment of Frowenfeld. Agricola Fuselier, in direct contrast to Frowenfeld, represents the proud old Creoles who insist on purity of race.

Action antecedent to the year-long events of the novel goes back to 1673, the year of the birth of the Indian girl whose choice of a De Grapion suitor began a feud between two Creole families, the De Grapions and the Grandissimes. Preceding the main plot by eight years comes the tale of Bras-

Coupé. Otherwise, the action takes place between September, 1803, and September, 1804.

The leading female character, Aurora Nancanou, daughter of a De Grapion, is the young widow of a man killed by Agricola Fuselier in a duel over a card game. Agricola took Nancanou's estate in payment for the gambling debt, passing the estate on to his nephew, the white Honoré, and leaving Aurora and her daughter Clotilde without land or money. The novel opens at a masked ball in New Orleans where Aurora and Honoré meet, unaware of each other's identity, thus beginning a romantic complication. Paralleling the love triangle of Palmyre and the Grandissime half-brothers, Joseph Frowenfeld falls in love with Clotilde, who, at the same time, is desired by Frowenfeld's friend Dr. Charlie Keene.

Honoré Grandissime, as leader of the Grandissime family and as Cable's symbol of right-thinking Creoles, upsets his relatives on several occasions: endangering the Grandissime finances, he returns Aurora Nancanou's property to her; in an act socially degrading to the family, he becomes a partner with the quadroon Honoré, under the business title "The Grandissime Brothers"; on an uneasy political level, he cooperates with Claiborne, the newly appointed territorial governor.

Romance, realism, and melodrama are mingled in *The Grandissimes*. In a romantic resolution, the De Grapion-Grandissime feud is ended, and marriage is imminent for two sets of lovers—Aurora and the white Honoré Grandissime, Clotilde and Frowenfeld. On the realistic side—with an admixture of melodramatic incidents—the two leading quadroons of the story are defeated. After Palmyre's several attempts to get revenge on the object of her hate, Agricola Fuselier, and after he is stabbed by the quadroon Honoré, she is forced to flee for safety to Paris. She is accompanied by her fellow refugee, Honoré Grandissime (f.m.c.), who commits suicide by drowning because of her final rejection of him.

Intentional obscurity is a characteristic of Cable's style in *The Grandissimes*. Lack of direct statement and slow revelation of relationships mark the progress of the plot. Facts are given through hints and implication; full information is withheld in a dense accumulation of incidents. This technique, typical of his early and best works, has been praised for its artistry and criticized for its lack of clarity.

Cable's portrayal of slaveholders, slaves, and the stubbornly held traditions of French Louisiana added a new dimension to Southern literature. Succeeding in his aim as a novelist, Cable found that fame brought a painful backlash. His radical views caused this native son to be identified as a traitor to New Orleans and the South.

In 1881, Cable published the novella *Madame Delphine*, the third in the three-year sequence of Cable's finest literary works (after the short-story collection *Old Creole Days* and the novel *The Grandissimes*). First published as a three-part novelette in *Scribner's Monthly* from May to July, 1881, *Madame Delphine* was published by Scribner's in book form later that year. In editions of *Old Creole Days* succeeding its initial publication, *Madame Delphine* is included and given lead position in the book.

The story begins with beautiful Olive Delphine returning from France on a ship that is boarded by the Creole pirate Ursin Lemaitre. Confronted by Olive's piety and charm, Lemaitre is struck with repentance for his sinful life and with love for the unidentified stranger. Settling in New Orleans, the reformed Lemaitre changes his name to Vignevielle and turns from piracy to banking. When not in his banker's office, he wanders through the streets, searching for the mysterious young woman.

Eventually, the lovelorn banker and Olive develop a friendship and marriage becomes their intention. Olive, however, is not legally able to become Lemaitre's wife, for she has black ancestry. Her mother, Madame Delphine, is a quadroon, the mistress to a white man, Olive's father. Madame Delphine, despite the laws against miscegenation, approves of the marriage. Indeed, she has made it clear that she is seeking a white husband for her daughter.

Vignevielle's relatives and friends, knowing that Madame Delphine is a quadroon, attempt to stop the illegal marriage, going so far as to threaten to turn him over to government agents who are searching for him. Madame Delphine meanwhile puts forth the ultimate effort to make the union possible. Producing fabricated evidence, she perjures herself by swearing that she is not the girl's blood mother. After Vignevielle and Olive are married, Madame Delphine goes for confession to the priest Père Jerome, admits her lie, and dies. Père Jerome speaks the closing line: "Lord, lay not this sin to her charge!"

The style of *Madame Delphine* is leisurely. Little mysteries cling to characters and actions, with revelation coming in glimpses, suggestions, and half-expressed statements. Early reviewers compared Cable to Nathaniel Hawthorne in achievement of mood, atmosphere, and ambiguity. Adverse criticism of *Madame Delphine*, however, finds the work excessively obscure; most troubling to critics is the needlessly complicated unfolding of the plot.

Furthermore, the characterization of the lovers is weak. Vignevielle's switch from dashing pirate to banker is inadequately motivated. Olive is a shadowy figure without distinguishable traits. Madame Delphine, despite her maneuvers, approaches the stereotype of the helpless mother. The only strong character, is Père Jerome, a compassionate observer and spokesman for Cable. Père Jerome sees that society deserves blame, both for its actions and for its failure to act. Society acquiesces in evil—from its unprotesting profit in Lemaitre's smuggled goods to its deliberate manipulation of the lives of mulattoes.

More significant than the style of *Madame Delphine* is its portrayal of the Southern attitude toward miscegenation. Although romanticism embellishes the outwardly happy ending of the story, Cable's recognition of the female mulatto's untenable position is clear. Looking beyond the temporary bliss of the wedding day, the reader realizes that prospects for Olive in New Orleans are not favorable. Madame Delphine's perjury has made the marriage legally permissible, but in the eyes of Lemaitre's friends, Olive is not and will never be an acceptable member of their aristocratic society.

The developing social consciousness revealed by Cable in *Madame Delphine* gives the work a lasting value. After this novella, though, he confined the most telling of his indictments to essays, disappointing readers who waited for his familiar critical tone in future novels. He was never able to duplicate the blend of artistic craftsmanship, authentic local color, and social commentary which distinguishes *Madame Delphine*, *The Grandissimes*, and *Old Creole Days*.

Major publications other than long fiction
SHORT FICTION: *Old Creole Days*, 1879; *Madame Delphine*, 1881; *Strong Hearts*, 1899; *Posson Jone' and Père Raphaël*, 1909; *The Flower of the Chapdelaines*, 1918.

NONFICTION: *The Creoles of Louisiana*, 1884; *The Silent South*, 1885; *Strange True Stories of Louisiana*, 1889; *The Negro Question*, 1890; *The Busy Man's Bible*, 1891; *A Memory of Roswell Smith*, 1892; *The Amateur Garden*, 1914.

MISCELLANEOUS: *The Cable Story Book: Selections for School Reading*, 1899.

Bibliography
Biklé, Lucy Leffingwell Cable. *George W. Cable: His Life and Letters*, 1928.
Butcher, Philip. *George W. Cable*, 1962.
——————. *George W. Cable: The Northampton Years*, 1959.
Ekström, Kjell. *George Washington Cable*, 1969.
Rubin, Louis D., Jr. *George W. Cable: The Life and Times of a Southern Heretic*, 1969.
Turner, Arlin. *George W. Cable: A Biography*, 1957.
——————. "George Washington Cable's Literary Apprenticeship," in *The Louisiana Historical Quarterly*. XXIV, no. 1 (January, 1941).
——————. *Mark Twain and George W. Cable: The Record of a Literary Friendship*, 1960.

Bernice Larson Webb

ERSKINE CALDWELL

Born: White Oak, Georgia; December 17, 1903

Principal long fiction

The Bastard, 1929; *Poor Fool*, 1930; *Tobacco Road*, 1932; *God's Little Acre*, 1933; *Journeyman*, 1935; *Trouble in July*, 1940; *All Night Long: A Novel of Guerrilla Warfare in Russia*, 1942; *Tragic Ground*, 1944; *A House in the Uplands*, 1946; *The Sure Hand of God*, 1947; *This Very Earth*, 1948; *Place Called Estherville*, 1949; *Episode in Palmetto*, 1950; *A Swell-Looking Girl*, 1951 (originally published as *American Earth*, 1931); *A Lamp for Nightfall*, 1952; *Love and Money*, 1954; *Gretta*, 1955; *Claudelle Inglish*, 1958; *Jenny by Nature*; 1961; *Close to Home*, 1962; *The Last Night of Summer*, 1963; *Miss Mamma Aimee*, 1967; *Summertime Island*, 1968; *The Weather Shelter*, 1969; *The Earnshaw Neighborhood*, 1972; *Annette*, 1974.

Other literary forms

Erskine Caldwell's first published work was "The Georgia Cracker," a 1926 article. Other pieces were printed in "little" magazines, and then in *Scribner's Magazine*. For several decades, he regularly wrote articles for magazines and newspapers. He has produced several nonfiction books, some in collaboration with photojournalist Margaret Bourke-White (at one time his wife): *You Have Seen Their Faces* (1937), *North of the Danube* (1939), *All-Out on the Road to Smolensk* (1942), and *Russia at War* (1942). His collections of short stories include *American Earth* (1931), *We Are the Living: Brief Stories* (1933), *Kneel to the Rising Sun and Other Stories* (1935), *Southways: Stories* (1938), and *Jackpot: The Short Stories of Erskine Caldwell* (1940), which contains all the stories of the first four books in addition to nine new ones.

Achievements

More than sixty-four million copies of Caldwell's books have been published in thirty-four countries, with 320 editions released in such languages as Croatian, Chinese, Slovene, Turkmenian, Arabic, Danish, Hebrew, Icelandic, Russian, and Turkish. He has been called the best-selling writer in America.

In 1933, Caldwell received the *Yale Review* award for fiction for his short story "Country Full of Swedes." Between 1940 and 1955, he was editor of twenty-five volumes of a regional series, *American Folkways*. His novel *Tobacco Road* was adapted for the stage in 1934 by Jack Kirkland and ran seven and a half years on Broadway, a record run. It was made into a motion picture in 1941. *Claudelle Inglish* became a film in 1961. *God's Little Acre*, possibly his best-known novel, sold more than eight million copies in paperback in the United States alone and became a film in 1959.

Biography

Erskine Caldwell is the son of a preacher, Ira Sylvester Caldwell. His mother was Caroline "Carrie" Preston (Bell) Caldwell of Staunton, Virginia. At the time Erskine was born, on December 17, 1903, the Reverend Caldwell was minister in Newman, Georgia, Coweta County, forty miles from Atlanta. His wife, active in helping her husband in his ministry, also ran a small school. She taught Caldwell through much of his elementary and secondary education, both in her school and at home. He actually spent only one year in public school and one in high school.

Between 1906 and 1919, the Caldwells moved several times as the ministry dictated. This not-quite-nomadic existence and the straitened circumstances under which the family lived were probably influential in molding Caldwell into early self-reliance and in fostering a wanderlust that persisted throughout his youth and adult life. Caldwell left home at fourteen, roaming about the Deep South, Mexico, and Central America. He did return home, however, to complete his high school education.

In 1920, Caldwell enrolled in Erskine College in Due West, South Carolina. From 1923 to 1924, he attended the University of Virginia on a scholarship; in 1924, he studied for two terms at the University of Pennsylvania. In 1925, he returned to the University of Virginia for an additional term, but he was never graduated.

While attending the University of Virginia, he married Helen Lannegan, and it was at this time that he decided to write for a living. With his wife and growing family of three children (Erskine Preston, Dabney Withers, and Janet), he lived in Maine between 1925 and 1932 while he wrote and earned a living at odd jobs; seven years of writing elapsed before any of his work was published. In his lifetime, Caldwell has been a mill laborer, cook, cabdriver, farmhand, stonemason's helper, soda jerk, professional football player, bodyguard, stagehand at a burlesque theater, and once even a hand on a boat running guns to a Central American country in revolt.

He published his first piece in 1926 (an article, "The Georgia Cracker"). Maxwell Perkins, the legendary editor at Charles Scribner's Sons, discovered some of his works and was enthusiastic and encouraging about his talent. Subsequently, Perkins published *American Earth* and *Tobacco Road*, which brought Caldwell his first real recognition. When Caldwell and Perkins had a serious disagreement, Caldwell switched his publishing allegiance to The Viking Press.

Divorced from his first wife in 1938, Caldwell married the photojournalist Margaret Bourke-White. They collaborated on several successful books, but the marriage ended in divorce in 1942. The same year, he married June Johnson, with whom he had one son, Jay Erskine. In 1957, after divorcing his third wife, he married Virginia Moffett Fletcher.

During the 1940's, Caldwell traveled to China, Mongolia, Turkestan, and

Russia. Because of the powerful, enthusiastic way in which he wrote about Russia and in turn indicted certain aspects of American capitalism, some accused him of being a Communist, a charge he emphatically denies.

Caldwell is a member of the National Institute of Arts and Letters, Authors League of America, the Phoenix Press Club, and the San Francisco Press Club. Active as a writer and lecturer, Caldwell toured Europe in the 1960's under the auspices of the United States State Department. In the 1970's, he made a series of speeches in Georgia, promoting the paperback reprint of his 1937 book *You Have Seen Their Faces*. He used this opportunity to decry the remaining extent of poverty in the South despite its industrialization.

In 1974, Caldwell underwent surgery for the removal of a growth on his lung; he submitted to similar surgery the following year. He is presently living in Scottsdale, Arizona.

Analysis

Erskine Caldwell is the chronicler of the poor white. He has told the story of the diversions and disasters of the poor Southerner with more detail and sympathetic attention than any other American writer of his time. In doing so, he has created memorable characters and unforgettable episodes and has provoked scandalized eyebrow-raising at his language, his imagery and his view of life.

Obscenity charges have been filed against an inordinate number of Caldwell's books, only to be fought down in court, one man's obscenity is another man's earthy realism. The attendant publicity generated more curiosity about his books, and sales soared. The self-appointed censors who attacked his books in court were only slightly more antagonistic than the reviewers who labeled his works "orgiastic litanies" and "particularly ugly stories" to be read with disgust and "a slight retching."

Charges of obscenity barraged the publication of *God's Little Acre* from New York to Denver. *Tobacco Road* had an arduous struggle to stay on the booksellers' shelves. *Tragic Ground* ran into trouble with Canadian censors. But how obscene are these books? By today's standards even *God's Little Acre* seems only mildly lewd. Under the layer of animalistic sexual behavior and uncouth, uncultured dialogue, qualities of literary merit are readily discernible.

The most prominent and lasting quality of Caldwell's fiction—the one which has made *Tobacco Road* a minor classic and several other of his earlier novels important literary pieces—is comic grotesquerie. Caldwell conveys a kind of ludicrous horror that becomes more horrible when the reader realizes that hyperbole does not negate the truth behind the most ridiculous episodes: the poor people of the South were deprived to the point of depravity. Writing in a naturalisitc style, Caldwell allows the reader to observe the day-to-day activities of poor white families whose impoverished condition has created tragicomic eccentricities.

Those impoverished conditions are the key to understanding Caldwell's main thrust in nearly all of his earlier novels. Living in hopeless hunger, illiterate, and essentially cut off from the world of progress, ambition, and culture, Caldwell's characters seem not quite human. The veneer of civilized attitudes and activities has been ground away by the endless struggle to satisfy the daily hunger and to find some hope, in a vast vista of barren prospects, of a better day tomorrow.

Caldwell is deeply concerned that this segment of society he has chosen to depict in his work has been repressed by ignorance and poverty as an almost direct result of society's indifference. In more recent works such as *The Weather Shelter* or even *Claudelle Inglish*, he has shifted his attention from the thoroughly downtrodden to the merely browbeaten, but he is still making a statement about society's indifference to the poor and about the survival instinct of the poor that makes them persevere.

Caldwell's earlier books are generally considered his better efforts; his themes and characters were fresh, and he had not yet begun to rework them with regularity. Still, there is a kind of plot formula in his first important novels: the main characters are introduced with a recounting of their day-to-day activities wherein their basic problem is presented; a new character is introduced bringing what seems to be an opportunity for some degree of betterment; then tragedy strikes, usually resulting in the death of a sympathetic character. There are seldom any "bad guys" in Caldwell's novels, no dastardly villains. The villain is society, which allows abject poverty, ignorance, hunger, and hopelessness to exist without trying to correct the circumstances that caused them. His characters, victims of society, flounder into tragic situations without knowing how to save themselves.

In the case of *Tobacco Road*, tragedy strikes as unpredictably as lightning and the characters accept their lot as though it is a natural, unalterable phenomenon. This book, perhaps his best-known work, is the story of a family of ignorant poor white Georgians who at the outset are already at the depths of degradation. They have no food, no prospects, and no apparent opportunity to get either. They have settled into a bleak routine, planning to plant a crop in the vague future and hoping for something to happen to change their lot. Jeeter Lester, the patriarch, has the last trace of a noble love of the land and a strong inherent need to farm his land and produce a crop, yet he cannot or will not do any of the practical things that must be done for serious, lifesaving farming. He has no money and no credit, and he will not leave his farm to find work in the town to get the money for seed and fertilizer. Thus, he drifts from day to day with good intentions but takes no positive action. Survival for him and his family has reached an "every man for himself" level. His old mother is treated with less consideration than a dog: when any food is acquired, as when Jeeter steals a bag of turnips from his son-in-law, the old mother is not given any. The others in the family—Jeeter's wife Ada and the two remaining children, Ellie Mae and Dude—are equally unfeeling.

These people seem to be as far down the scale of humanity as anyone can get, yet the story relates a series of episodes that carries them progressively further to degeneracy and death. The casual attitude toward sex, as shown in the scenes with Dude and his "new" wife Bessie, brings to mind the blasé attitude that farmers show toward the breeding of their farm animals. There is no particularly lewd interest in the family's attempts to spy on the "honeymooning" couple. Rather, their curiosity seems born of boredom or the simple need for distraction. Because Caldwell has narrated these episodes in blunt, realistic language, a puritanical mind might see a moral looseness in them which could be (and was) attributed to an immoral intent on the part of the author. Viewed from the perspective of fifty years, however, the actions of the characters appear not obscene but merely uncivilized.

Another scene involves the accidental killing of a black in a wagon. Rammed and overturned by the new car acquired by Bessie (as a not-very-subtle enticement to persuade Dude to marry her), the black is crushed by the wagon. The Lesters, having caused the accident, go blithely on their way. Their only concern is the wrecked fender of the car. They philosophize that "niggers will get killed." The killing of another human being is as casually natural to them as the killing of a dog on a highway.

The most inhuman and inhumane episode involves the death of Mother Lester, who is hit by the car in the Lester yard. She is knocked down and run over, "her face mashed on the hard white sand." She lies there, unaided by any of the family, hardly even referred to beyond Ada's comment that "I don't reckon she could stay alive with her face all mashed like that." The old woman struggles a bit, every part of her body in agonizing pain, and manages to turn over. Then she is still. When Jeeter at last decides something must be done with his old mother, he looks down and moves one of her arms with his foot, and says "She aint stiff yet, but I don't reckon she'll live. You help me tote her out in the field and I'll dig a ditch to put her in."

When Caldwell depicts the indifference of the family members to Mother Lester's slow, painful death, he is really depicting the degeneracy of people whom society has deprived of all "human" feeling. Thus, when in the last chapter the old Lester house catches fire and burns up the sleeping occupants without their ever waking, the reader may well feel that poetic justice has been served: the Lesters have lived a subhuman existence, and their end is fittingly subhuman. Yet, one does not entirely blame the Lesters for their lack of humanity; Caldwell moves his readers to wonder that a rich, progressive country such as the United States could still harbor such primitive conditions.

The comic quality that is so much a part of Caldwell's work saves *Tobacco Road* from utter grimness. Some of the episodes with the car, Jeeter's maneuverings to get money from his new daughter-in-law, the turnip filching—all create a climate that lightens the pervading ugliness. The sexual adventures are irreverent and bawdy; the dialogue is the ridiculous, repetitive gibberish of single-minded illiterates engrossed in their own narrow concerns. There is a particularly comic quality in Jeeter's serious pronouncements that bespeak a completely unrealistic creature out of touch with himself and his true condition. The enduring ridiculousness of Jeeter and his family is undercoated with a pathos that is obvious to the thoughtful reader. The condition and ultimate end of Jeeter and Ada are perhaps atypical but are still symptomatic of the condition and ultimate end of the many others like them living in the destitute areas of the South.

Caldwell's *God's Little Acre* was considered by some critics his best work up to that time. A *Forum* review said it was "the first thing [Caldwell] has done which seems . . . to justify in any way the praise the critics have heaped upon him." There are flaws, as some reviewers were quick to point out, including repetitiousness and a too sudden and unexpected transition from a comic atmosphere to violent tragedy, yet it is second in quality only to *Tobacco Road* among Caldwell's novels.

God's Little Acre tells the story of Ty Ty Walden, a Georgia dirt farmer who for fifteen years has been digging enormous holes in his land looking for gold. Ty Ty, who is in most other respects a man with considerable mother wit, has a curious tunnel vision where this quest for gold is concerned. Because of it, he neglects his farming to the point of endangering his livelihood and that of his family. Worse yet, he fails to see the peril in the growing tension among the members of his family living on the farm with him. The inevitable tragedy results from the fact that he has two beautiful daughters and an even more beautiful daughter-in-law, Griselda. Ty Ty himself praises Griselda so much to anyone who will listen that he is largely instrumental in encouraging the fatal allurement she has for the other men in the family. When these men—a son, Jim Leslie, and a son-in-law, Will Thompson— make advances toward Griselda, her husband Buck understandably becomes enraged. He is thwarted in his revenge against Will Thompson by another calamity— Will, a mill worker, is killed during a strike action—but Jim Leslie does not escape his brother Buck's wrath, nor does the tragedy stop there, for Buck's action is harshly punished.

The opening episodes of the novel are comic: Pluto Swint, the fat, lazy suitor of the younger daughter, Darling Jill, is clearly a comic character in the mold of the sad clown. The enthusiastic search for the albino Dave, who according to black lore can divine gold lodes, is humorous: the process of finding him, roping him, dragging him away from his home and wife, and keeping him under guard like a prized animal is handled with a matter-of-fact detachment that makes these actions acceptable, predictable, and ridiculous, all at once. Darling Jill's sexual promiscuity and amoral attitude is refreshingly animalistic, even though some readers might disapprove of her untouched conscience.

When Darling Jill steals Pluto's car to go joyriding, when Ty Ty along with the rest goes to town to ask the well-off son Jim Leslie for money to help him through the winter because of inadequate crops, when Rosamond finds Will Thompson, her husband, in bed with her sister Darling Jill and chases him, buck-naked, out of the house—these richly comic scenes create a humorously cockeyed view of the Georgia poor white.

The deaths which occur later in the novel, however, are not funny, nor are their reasons; the comic existence Caldwell has depicted turns somber. This shift in tone has been described as a flaw, but such a judgment assumes that *God's Little Acre* is a comic novel gone astray. In fact, it is a serious story about people who in their daily lives do things that seem comic to those who observe them from a distance. Caldwell begins with a feckless existence that gradually becomes tragic; the comical infighting and escapades of Ty Ty's clan assume a grim inevitability.

Ty Ty has set aside one acre of his land for God. His intent is to farm the land, raise a crop, and give the proceeds to God through the church. Ty Ty has been digging for gold all over his farm, however, and there is very little land left that can still be farmed. Because he needs to raise a crop to feed his family and the two black families who tenant-farm for him, Ty Ty must constantly shift the acre for God from place to place. He readily admits that he will not dig for gold on God's little acre because then he would be honorbound to give the gold to the church. He has no compunctions about doing God out of what he has declared is God's due. Later in the story, however, when he learns of Will Thompson's death, he has a sudden need to bring the acre closer to the homestead:

> He felt guilty of something—maybe it was sacrilege or desecration—whatever it was, he knew he had not played fair with God. Now he wished to bring God's little acre back to its rightful place beside the house where he could see it all the time. . . . He promised himself to keep it there until he died.

After this decision, however, blood is shed on God's little acre: Buck kills his own brother, Jim Leslie. The blood letting on God's ground is almost a ceremonial sacrifice wherein Ty Ty, albeit involuntarily, atones for a life spent giving only lip-service to God. This ironic justice has the tragicomic grotesquerie characteristic of Caldwell's best work. The fall of his protagonists is both inevitable and absurd, utterly lacking in dignity.

Beginning in 1936, Caldwell produced different work. Perhaps he was aware that he had gone to the well often enough and needed to find new or different subjects. At any rate, traveling about the United States and Europe, with the drama of Adolf Hitler's Germany taking form, he wrote other books on uncustomary subjects: *North of the Danube, You Have Seen Their Faces, Some American People* (1935), *Southways, Jackpot, Say! Is This the U.S.A.?* (1941, with Margaret Bourke-White), *All-Out on the Road to Smolensk, Russia at War*, and more.

The novels that poured from Caldwell's pen on into the 1940's, 1950's, 1960's, and 1970's more or less followed the pattern of his early work. Reviewers observed that Caldwell seemed to have grown lackadaisical, content with repeating himself. He no longer seemed to instruct the reader subtly about the social and economic problems of the South; his work had begun to take on the dullness that results from the same joke and the same protestations repeated too often in the same way. He continued to use the same old formula without the zest and the imagination that made *Tobacco Road* and *God's Little Acre* so memorable.

Of the more than thirty novels Caldwell has written over more than forty years, it is disappointing to find that two written in the 1930's—*Tobacco Road* and *God's Little Acre*—are the only ones likely to endure. Still, Caldwell is considered to be among the significant contemporary writers produced by the South. His major contribution has been his naturalistic comedic approach to his subjects. His best work depicts, with admirable craftmanship, the harsh life of the sharecropper and tenant farmer through painful explicitness and comic vigor, juxtaposing social issues with the grotesque.

Major publications other than long fiction

SHORT FICTION: *American Earth*, 1931; *Mama's Little Girl*, 1932; *Message for Genevieve*, 1933; *We are the Living: Brief Stories*, 1933; *Kneel to the Rising Sun and Other Stories*, 1935; *Southways: Stories*, 1938; *Jackpot: The Short Stories of Erskine Caldwell*, 1940; *Georgia Boy*, 1943; *Stories by Erskine Caldwell: 24 Representative Stories*, 1944; *The Caldwell Caravan: Novels and Stories*, 1946; *Jackpot: Collected Short Stories*, 1950; *The Courting of Susie Brown*, 1952; *Complete Stories*, 1953; *Gulf Coast Stories*, 1956; *Certain Women*, 1957; *When You Think of Me*, 1959; *Men and Women: 22 Stories*, 1961.

NONFICTION: *Tenant Farmer*, 1935; *Some American People*, 1935; *You Have Seen Their Faces*, 1937 (with Margaret Bourke-White); *North of the Danube*, 1939 (with Margaret Bourke-White); *Say! Is This the U.S.A.?*, 1941 (with Margaret Bourke-White); *All-Out on the Road to Smolensk*, 1942 (with Margaret Bourke-White, also known as *Moscow Under Fire: A Wartime Diary, 1941*); *Russia at War*, 1942 (with Margaret Bourke-White); *The Humorous Side of Erskine Caldwell*, 1951; *Call it Experience: The Years of Learning How to Write*, 1951; *Around About America*, 1964; *In Search of Bisco*, 1965; *In the Shadow of the Steeple*, 1967; *Deep South-Memory and Observation*, 1968; *Writing in America*, 1968; *Afternoon in Mid-America*, 1976.

CHILDREN'S LITERATURE: *Molly Cottontail*, 1958; *The Deer at Our House*, 1966.

Bibliography

Beach, Joseph Warren. "Erskine Caldwell," in *American Fiction 1920-1940*, 1941.

Cook, Sylvia J. "Caldwell's Politics of the Grotesque," in *From Tobacco Road to Route 66*, 1976.

Devlin, James E. *The Fiction of Erskine Caldwell*, 1976 (thesis).

Korges, James. *Erskine Caldwell*, 1969.

Warfel, Harry R. "Erskine Caldwell," in *American Novelists of Today*, 1951.

White, William. "About Erskine Caldwell: A Checklist, 1933-1980," in *Bulletin of Bibliography* (March, 1982).

Woodress, James. "Erskine Caldwell," in *American Fiction 1900-1950*, 1974.

Jane L. Ball